Physical — wires + modems 1 to sender + receiver electrical Open Systems Interconnect

Data link — packages messages for Transmission

Network — routes info from source node

Transport — makes + maintains the connection

Session — establishes + controls communication.

Presentation — format is okay

Application — receives on other end.

Information Systems for Managers

Third Edition

Information Systems for Managers

Third Edition

George W. Reynolds
University of Cincinnati

West
Publishing
Company

Minneapolis/
St. Paul
New York
Los Angeles
San Francisco

**West's
Commitment
to the
Environment**

In 1906, West Publishing Company began recycling materials left over from the production of books. This began a tradition of efficient and responsible use of resources. Today, up to 95 percent of our legal books and 70 percent of our college and school texts are printed on recycled, acid-free stock. West also recycles nearly 22 million pounds of scrap paper annually—the equivalent of 181,717 trees. Since the 1960s, West has devised ways to capture and recycle waste inks, solvents, oils, and vapors created in the printing process. We also recycle plastics of all kinds, wood, glass, corrugated cardboard, and batteries, and have eliminated the use of Styrofoam book packaging. We at West are proud of the longevity and the scope of our commitment to the environment.

**Production
Credits**

Interior Design: David Farr, Imagesmythe
Copyediting: Michele Scheid
Composition: Parkwood Composition
Proofreading: Lynn Reichel
Illustration: Weist Publications International
Cover Design: John Rokusek

Production, Prepress, Printing and Binding by West Publishing Company.

 TEXT IS PRINTED ON 10% POST CONSUMER RECYCLED PAPER   Printed with **Printwise**
Environmentally Advanced Water Washable Ink

COPYRIGHT ©1988, 1992   By WEST PUBLISHING COMPANY
COPYRIGHT ©1995   By WEST PUBLISHING COMPANY
610 Opperman Drive
P.O. Box 64526
St. Paul, MN 55164-0526

Library of Congress Cataloging in Publication Data

Reynolds, George Walter, 1944–
   Information systems for managers / George W. Reynolds. —3rd ed.
      p. cm.
   Includes index.
   ISBN: 0-314-04597-X (Hard)
   1. Management information systems. I. Title.
T58.6.R48 1994
658.4'038–dc20
                                                94-37682
                                                CIP

To Ginnie

About the Author

George Reynolds has a B.S. in Engineering from the University of Cincinnati and an M.S. in Systems Engineering from West Coast University.

In the early stages of the space program, he worked as a Mission Analyst with NASA at the Johnson Space Center in Houston, Texas and at the Jet Propulsion Laboratory in Pasadena, California. He left the aerospace industry to work as a Systems Analyst at the University of Cincinnati. For the last 20 years he has held a number of assignments of increasing responsibility within the Management Systems Division at the Procter & Gamble Company.

Mr. Reynolds served as an Adjunct Professor at Xavier University in Cincinnati from 1973 to 1983 where he helped develop their initial courses in systems analysis and design and telecommunications. He has been an Adjunct Professor at the University of Cincinnati since 1981 teaching the basics of information technology to non-MIS majors at both the graduate and undergraduate levels.

His previous textbooks include: *Systems Analysis and Design: A Case Study Approach* and *Effective Information Systems Management.* Both texts were co-authored with Dr. Robert Thierauf. He has also written *Introduction to Business Telecommunications* with Donald Riecks. This is the third edition of *Information Systems for Managers,* originally published in 1988.

Contents in Brief

Contents

Chapter 6   **Transaction Processing and Management Reporting Systems   186**

Chapter 7   **Decision Support and Expert Systems   212**

Chapter 10

Information Technology Planning   324

Chapter 11

Design, Construction, and Maintenance   364

Preface

The ability to use information systems technology effectively is essential to the successful operation of many organizations. While some companies may greatly benefit from the innovative use of information systems technology, other companies competing in the same industry may make no progress whatsoever. The key to capturing real business benefits is the role that managers take in accepting responsibility for the management of the information systems resource.

The most basic of decisions regarding information systems involve when, where, and how to apply them. These fundamental questions must be addressed by business managers, who often lack both a detailed understanding of computer technology and a clear perspective of its capabilities and limitations. *Information Systems for Managers,* Third Edition, will help business managers identify and assess potential applications. It will also outline basic principles to help managers make the fundamental decisions involving the use of information systems in their own area.

Managers allocate people, money, and equipment to the development and operation of information systems. Increasingly, managers are held accountable for the use and results of information systems in their particular area of the business. Managers are even called on to lead information systems projects and to be a direct user of systems to support their business decisions. This text will help managers take an active role in the complete information systems development process and, where appropriate, in the "selling" of information systems proposals to upper management.

Thus, the purpose of *Information Systems for Managers,* Third Edition, is to help prepare managers and future managers to provide leadership in managing the use of information systems technology. The focus of this book is on defining the fundamental management issues, recognizing and evaluating the trade-offs, and outlining approaches for resolving them using current technology.

Changes from the First Edition

At the time this revision was prepared, the first and second editions had been in use at more than one hundred and fifty universities for over six years. I am indebted to the many students, adoptors, and reviewers of both editions whose helpful suggestions provided valuable input to the revision process. Specific areas of improvement in this third edition include the following:

■ The most commonly suggested area of improvement for the second edition was to expand the breadth and depth of coverage of the various information system applications—transaction processing, management reporting, decision support, and expert systems. In this edition, the discussion of these topics has been expanded from one chapter to three.

■ The second most commonly mentioned opportunity for improvement was to address office automation systems more directly and completely. A new chapter has been added to cover this important topic.

■ The single chapter Computer Hardware and Software has been divided into two chapters. This expanded coverage provides an excellent foundation for the non-MIS undergraduate student who has little or no previous MIS course work or experience. This change was strongly recommended by those adoptors who used the text in an undergraduate program for non-MIS majors.

■ The second edition used a modified structured analysis and design methodology for the development of information systems. This edition adopts the Information Engineering methodology for the planning, defining, and building of information systems. This methodology is much more broadly accepted and used in the industry.

■ There is greatly expanded coverage of business process reengineering.

■ Learning objectives have been added at the beginning of each chapter to help the student focus on the key issues.

■ The text has been updated to address the many new topics that have arisen since the second edition was published in 1992.

Principles on Which This Text is Based

The process of developing managerial competence in information technology can be aided by the setting of basic goals and objectives. The setting of objectives must be grounded on principles regarding management's use of technology. There are two basic principles upon which this text is founded. First, managers manage people, organizations, and processes. Computers cannot be a substitute for sound management but can only assist managers. Second, managers are the people who can make the most informed decisions about the development and operation of computer systems, since they know the most about the business. Therefore, it is critical that managers become competent partners with members of the information technology organization in the evaluation of potential information system applications and their development.

Based on these two basic principles, *Information Systems for Managers,* Third Edition, is structured around ten key learning objectives:

Part I—Appreciating the Role of Management in Information Systems Technology

1. Appreciate the increasing importance of information systems technology and how it is changing the role of the business manager.

Part II—Understanding the Technology Architecture

2. Understand the evolving role played by the microcomputer, workstation, midrange, mainframe, and supercomputer in the business organizations of today.

3. Recognize how networks are being used to reduce costs and delays associated with traditional means of communications, provide improved customer service, and build strong links with customers and suppliers.

4. Appreciate the need for data management and understand management's key role in establishing and maintaining an effective data management environment.

5. Identify the fundamental types of information systems used to provide real business benefits.

Part III—Developing Information Systems

6. State the need for an effective information system development process, and describe the tools needed to support it.

7. Appreciate the need for an information technology plan, identify its key elements, and outline a process to develop one.

8. Define the term business process reengineering and explain how it can lead to dramatic changes in the business.

Part IV—Managing Information Technology Resources

9. Define management's key role in ensuring the successful development and acquisition of information technology resources.

10. Appreciate the need for management to make certain that the organization has a sound plan for ensuring computer security and disaster recovery.

Unique Features of This Text

This text has a number of unique features that distinguish it from other texts. First, it is aimed squarely at helping today's manager obtain real business results from information systems. This is done by keeping a strong focus on basic principles and on identification of key issues and associated trade-offs.

Second, the text is based on the assumption that it is business managers who can make the most informed decisions about which information systems to develop, because they know the most about the business those systems are intended to support. Thus the text clearly emphasizes the role of the business manager in the management of information system resources.

Third, the text covers a number of increasingly important topics not addressed in other texts:

- The use of information systems technology to meet the challenge of globalization
- The key role of the business manager in reengineering the business
- Current and future hardware, network, and software developments that will create major new business improvement opportunities
- Creating networks to build strategic alliances with customers and suppliers
- Developing a business information systems plan consistent with the organization's business strategy
- Performing a business area analysis to determine what business processes and data are most critical for the firm.
- Steering the application development effort to ensure that business needs are met with a quality system
- Creating strategies for effective management of end-user computing
- Ensuring computer security and disaster recovery

Learning Aids

This text has been carefully designed to maintain reader interest and to ensure that important concepts are easily understood through the inclusion of these special features in each chapter.

Preview A preview appearing at the start of each chapter helps to orient the reader by presenting a brief overview of the main topics to follow. The preview also includes:

Learning Objectives Specific behavioral learning objectives are stated.

Management Issues The issues to be discussed are explicitly stated at the beginning of each chapter.

Trade-offs The choices that face management in dealing with the specific issues to be addressed in each chapter are highlighted.

A Manager Struggles with the Issues A true-to-life vignette involving the issues to be addressed in the chapter is presented in the preview section of each chapter.

Real World Perspective Many examples from actual organizations illustrate the principles and issues that are the theme of each chapter.

Summary A summary appears at the end of each chapter as a valuable aid for quickly reviewing key points.

A Manager's Checklist A brief checklist summarizes the key questions that management must answer when working the issues presented in the chapter.

Key Terms A list of the key terms introduced in the chapter is provided. The glossary provides definitions for these terms.

Review Questions The review questions at the end of each chapter can be used for self-evaluation or student testing. The answers to these questions can be found through careful reading of the text.

Discussion Questions The discussion questions are designed to stimulate class discussion or to serve as essay questions for student testing. While the text provides students with the basic concepts and understanding to address these questions, considerable thought and insight are required to answer them. In many cases, there is no one correct answer. The questions encourage students to develop and express their opinions.

Recommended Readings Each chapter includes a short list of readings that reinforce the ideas presented in the chapter. Many classic as well as current references are included.

A Manager's Dilemma Several case studies are presented at the end of each chapter to reinforce the material just covered. There are over fifty case studies throughout the text.

Glossary The glossary provides concise definitions of over seven hundred commonly used information technology terms. The glossary is a useful reference for other MIS courses or future on-the-job needs.

The Ancillaries

The Instructor's Manual With Test Bank, by the text author, comes complete with lecture notes to support each chapter, and includes answers to the end-of-chapter review and discussion questions, and solutions to the case studies. A comprehensive test bank of over 600 questions is included, and the test bank is available on WESTEST™, a computerized test generation program for IBM PCs and compatibles and Macintosh computers.

Transparency Masters with Lecture Outlines are available to instructors. These include figures and tables from the text, along with Lecture Outlines prepared by Fred S. Patterson, St. Edward's University. They may be copied for student use, and will allow students to focus their attention on the lecturer, rather than on excessive note-taking.

The *Casebook to Accompany Information Systems for Managers,* by Carl R. Ruthstrom and Charlene A. Dykman, University of Houston—Downton, continues to be available for use with this text. It contains 23 cases which range from managerial to technically-oriented topics.

Videos also accompany *Information Systems for Managers,* Third Edition, and contain segments on the information systems of companies such as Frito-Lay, Federal Express, and Boeing.

Using This Text in Your Curriculum

Information Systems for Managers, Third Edition, is highly modular and flexible enough to support either a quarter- or semester-length course. (See exhibits A and B.) The text has been used primarily at the undergraduate (junior and senior) and MBA levels in courses aimed at providing a manager's perspective on information systems. Its intent is not to turn the business major or MBA into a computer scientist. Changes made to the second edition should increase its appeal for support of MBA courses as well as its attractiveness for use in undergraduate courses.

Unlike introduction to computing books, which emphasize detailed how-to directions for the popular spreadsheet, word processing, data base, personal productivity, and other types of software packages, the focus of this textbook is on fundamental management issues and information system principles that do not change as rapidly over time as the software which is currently in vogue. The book provides a valuable perspective on how these tools can be employed by the manager to meet business needs.

Exhibit A
Proposed Schedule
for Quarter Course

Non-MIS Major Undergraduates	Week	Undergraduate MIS Majors or MBA Students
Part I Chapter 1	1	Part I Chapter 1
Part II Chapters 2–8	2	Part II (Selected Chapters)
	3	
	4	
	5	Part III Chapters 9–11
Part III Chapters 9–11	6	
	7	Part IV Chapters 12–14
	8	
Part IV Chapters 12–14	9	
	10	
Final	11	Final
Use fewer case studies or less involved case studies.		Use more case studies or more involved case studies.

Exhibit B
Proposed Schedule
for Semester Course

Non-MIS Major Undergraduates		Week	Undergraduate MIS Majors or MBA Students	
Part I	Chapter 1	1	Part I	Chapter 1
Part II	Chapters 2–8	2		
		3	Part III	Chapters 9–11
		4		Plus midterm
		5		
Part III	Chapters 9–11	6		
	Plus midterm	7		
		8		
		9	Part IV	Chapters 12–14
		10		
Part IV	Chapters 12–14	11		
		12		
		13		
		14		
Final		15	Final	
Use fewer case studies or less involved case studies.			Use more case studies or more involved case studies.	

Acknowledgments

I wish to express my deep appreciation to: Al Bruckner, my editor, who provided guidance and encouragement throughout this project; Susan Smart, my developmental editor, who coordinated the input from reviewers and offered many positive suggestions during the development and production stages of this book; and Cliff Kallemeyn, my production editor, who directed the creation of the new design and handled the many details that resulted in the final, physical text. I also wish to thank the following reviewers for their careful reading of the manuscript and for their constructive criticism, which greatly improved the quality of the final work.

Shawn Bird
Seattle University

Normal D. Brammer
Emporia State University

James Buffington
Indiana State University

Karen L. Cooper
Pennsylvania State University-
The Behrend College

Charles K. Davis
University of Houston-Downtown

Sasa Dekleva
DePaul University

Ali Emdad
Morgan State University

Eugenia Fernandez
Butler University

Dale Foster
Memorial University of Newfoundland

Kevin L. Fox

Albert L. Harris
Appalachian State University

William K. Jackson
Southern Oregon State University

Marius Janson
University of Missouri-St. Louis

Tor J. Larsen
Norwegian School of Management

Diane L. Lockwood
Seattle University

David B. Meinert
Southwest Missouri State University

Fred S. Patterson
St. Edwards University

John V. Quigley
East Tennessee State University

Thomas E. Sandman
California State University

Jerry D. Sawyer
Kennesaw College

Stanley Schenkerman
University of Bridgeport

Jennifer L. Wagner
Roosevelt University

George H. Walther
University of Mary Hardin-Baylor

Fons Wijnhoven
University of Twente, The Netherlands

Appreciating the Role of Management in Information Systems Technology

The ability to use information systems technology effectively is essential to the successful operation of most organizations. While some companies may greatly benefit from the innovative use of the technology, other companies competing in the same industry may make no progress whatsoever.

When new information systems technology was first introduced, managers tended to adopt the technology first and then tried to figure out what to do with the new information and cope with the business and organizational implications. Such an approach is now recognized as woefully inadequate. The new technology is more powerful, more diverse, and increasingly entwined with the organization's critical business processes. Continuing to merely react to new technology and the changes it triggers will likely cause major business disruptions. Companies successful at adopting new technology recognize that the key to capturing real business benefits is the role that business managers take in leading the introduction of information systems.

This section addresses the role of the general manager and end-user manager in leading the effective use of information systems technology. Upon completion of this section, you will be able to discuss the increasing importance of information systems technology and how it is changing the role of the business manager.

Chapter 1

Management and Information Technology

Upon completion of this chapter, you will be able to:

1. Provide a dozen examples of the use of information technology (IT) to meet key business needs.

2. Define the terms globalization, business reengineering, and strategic information system, and give an example of each.

3. Discuss four reasons why business managers must understand information technology.

4. Describe the four core activities of the IT organization.

5. Explain the difference between a centralized and decentralized IT organization.

Preview

The ability to use information technology effectively is essential to the successful operation of most organizations. While some companies may greatly benefit from the innovative use of the technology, other companies competing in the same industry may make no progress whatsoever.

When new information technology was first introduced, managers tended to adopt the technology first and then tried to figure out what to do with the new information and cope with the business and organizational implications. Such an approach is now recognized as woefully inadequate. The new technology is more powerful, more diverse, and increasingly entwined with the organization's critical business processes. Continuing to merely react to new technology and the changes it triggers will likely cause major business disruptions. Companies successful at adopting new technology recognize that the key to capturing real business benefits is the role that business managers take in leading the introduction of information systems.

This chapter addresses the role of the general manager and end-user manager in leading the effective use of information technology. Upon completion of this chapter, you will be able to discuss the increasing importance of information technology and how it is changing the role of the business manager.

Issues

1. Why is it that for many companies, there has been little improvement in profits and productivity growth to show for their investment in information technology?

2. Why must business managers understand information technology?

3. What is meant by the terms globalization and reengineering? Why do they represent both a major challenge to business managers and a tremendous opportunity for applying information technology?

Trade-offs

1. In addition to their other, more traditional responsibilities, how much time should managers invest in providing leadership in the deployment of information technology?

2. Should information technology be considered strategic in nature and fundamental to achieving the goals of the organization or simply as a means to improve efficiency?

3. What is the difference between a centralized and decentralized information technology organization?

A Manager Struggles with the Issues

John had just returned from a visit to one of the more advanced mass merchandisers that carries the firm's line of industrial cleaning products. He had been amazed with what he saw. One of the firm's competitors had installed an adviser system that helped the buyer decide which combination and quantities of the competitor's product would best fit the company's needs. There had actually been a line of buyers waiting to try the new system! Another competitor had installed an interactive video display system that showed different ways the product could be used to solve various industrial cleaning problems. Again, the display had been very impressive and generated lots of interest. Unfortunately, John's firm had no such plans to enhance their traditional sales presentations to industrial buyers. John wondered whom he should speak with about what he had seen and if he should make some recommendations to modernize the firm's sales presentations.

■ THE INFORMATION SOCIETY

In his book *Megatrends* (reference 7), John Naisbitt points to the year 1956 as the beginning of the **information society.** In this year for the first time in American history, white-collar workers in technical, managerial, and clerical positions outnumbered blue-collar workers. Industrial America has given way to a new society, where most of us work with information rather than produce goods. These people who spend most of their working day creating, using, and distributing information are called **knowledge workers.** Managers including executives, department heads, and supervisors; professionals such as engineers, teachers, and bankers; and staff personnel such as secretaries and clerical office personnel are involved. Knowledge workers represent over 60 percent of the U.S. work force and the percentage is increasing.

The information society of the 1990s requires that organizations not only continue to use IT wherever they can to reduce costs, but also to package technology into the products and services they offer customers. American Airlines, American Hospital Supply, and Kraft Foodservice were among the earliest companies to follow this strategy, and many are following their lead. Companies increasingly differentiate themselves through superior information systems that enable them to deliver better customer service. The managers and executives of these companies consider investment in IT an integral and essential part of their business strategy—no longer a corporate expenditure, but a vital corporate asset, an important element of staying competitive.

Peter Drucker (author, consultant, and management theorist—reference 1) argues that the single greatest challenge facing managers today is to raise the productivity of knowledge workers. Productivity will dominate management thinking for decades. Information technology has great potential for making the substantial and on-going productivity gains that will shape the leaders (individuals, companies, institutions, and countries) of the twenty-first century.

However, during the 1980s, U.S. businesses invested a whopping $1 trillion in IT. For a long time, there was little return to show for this

Real World Perspective

American Airlines Sabre System—Gaining Competitive Advantage

When completed in the early 1960s at a cost of over $250 million, the Sabre system, a sophisticated on-line computer reservation system (CRS), gave American Airlines a competitive advantage. Prior to the Sabre system, reservation clerks had to rely on telex messages and phone calls to track seat availability—data that were several hours or even a day old. Without current seating information, booking space for flights was pretty much a gamble.

With the Sabre CRS, each time a seat is sold, a transaction is generated to update a data base of seating data for all flights. Reservation clerks and travel agents access this data/information base of up-to-the-minute data for booking seats. Sabre enabled American Airlines to reduce the number of staff required to handle reservations, increase the number of passengers on a flight without fear of overbooking, and guarantee passengers a seat.

Strategic competitive advantage is often short lived. Competition must react or go out of business. Thus those airlines that could afford the investment soon developed their own CRS. These airlines earned additional revenue from selling or renting their CRS to other airlines and travel agencies to handle their bookings.

Many people think that CRSs have benefited the consumer because they improved competition around the globe and created a perfect marketplace in the airline industry. Others are criti-

cal of the CRSs. They claim that there is a bias in the two most popular reservation systems (American's Sabre and United's Apollo) favoring the airline that owns the CRS. When a reservation clerk requests the system to display flights between two cities, the flights of the airline that created the CRS are displayed first. It takes additional time and effort to display other airlines' flights.

In addition, the Justice Department filed suit against American Airlines, Continental Airlines, Delta Air Lines, Midway Airlines, Northwest Airline, Pan American World Airways, Trans World Airlines, United Airlines, and US Air because the airlines used their CRS to signal price changes and enforce discipline. For example, carrier A floats a new lower fare: $350 to San Francisco. Carrier B responds—at 1 AM Sunday morning—with a suicidally low $100 fare, that expires Sunday at noon. Each CRS continuously tracks and monitors all rates so that all airlines are aware of price changes at approximately the same time. All airlines also get carrier B's message to carrier A. If carrier A increases its fare to match the other airlines, carrier B will drop its cutthroat offer at noon on Sunday. Otherwise Carrier B will extend its cutthroat offer indefinitely—and A will go bankrupt before B does! In other words, airlines could change fares on the weekend and if others don't match them, the change could be rolled back by Monday before much revenue is lost.

---

investment—profits were flat and productivity growth averaged a puny 1% per year. Clearly the benefits of IT were elusive for many firms. What managers are learning is that the emphasis must be placed on what IT is used for and not how IT is used. In other words, a business perspective must be taken in solving business problems, not a technology perspective. In addition, some form of organizational restructuring is often necessary before the full benefits of IT can be obtained. Work processes, procedures, people's roles and responsibilities, and the very nature of the work itself may need to change.

The marketplace—customers, suppliers, competitors, the environment—in which goods and services are sold is rapidly changing. New U.S. companies are being formed at the rate of over 500,000 per year, versus less than 100,000 per year in 1950. We are moving from a national economy to a worldwide economy—one where all the countries of the world are increasingly interdependent. Eastern Europe, China, the former Soviet Union, and the Far East are opening up as major new markets. The European Common Market and the North American Free Trade Agreement have greatly reduced trade barriers and impediments to the free flow of goods and services. The formal hierarchical organizational structure is giving way to informal networks that support people talking with one another—sharing ideas, information, and resources. Suppliers and customers are moving to form **strategic alliances** with one another and working more closely than ever before considered.

IT is needed to keep up with the rapid pace of this change. More and more solutions are becoming feasible. These solutions are getting easier to use, provide increased data processing and data communications capacity, and are available with a wide range of options. Portable, laptop computers as powerful as the large, mainframe computers of a decade ago are being used to support salespeople in the field. Standard telephone lines and advanced cellular radio technology provide access to high-speed networks that can whisk data, text, graphics, voice, and video information from one part of the world to another instantly. Optical storage media, similar to the compact-disk technology used to store music, can hold prodigious amounts of data and are being used to store and retrieve full-motion video images. Expert systems are used to help people perform tasks that require judgment, experience, and expert knowledge. Information systems with easy-to-use interfaces are able to extract, aggregate, analyze, and present data in a variety of formats including graphical.

Exhibit 1.1 illustrates a dozen common examples of the use of IT.

■ NEW CHALLENGES FOR THE MANAGER

Each decade presents its major challenges. During the 1990s, the issues of **globalization** and **business reengineering** loom important. To be successful, organizations and managers will need to deal with these issues.

Globalization

All companies that sell their goods or services (or both) on an international basis face a dilemma: to what extent should they give up the economies of scale achieved in their home market to achieve economies of scope in the foreign markets to which they must adapt their products and services?

Some companies choose to design and produce their products at home and treat foreign countries as sales and service colonies. As a result, they gain economies of scale in the centralized production of standard products. The major weakness of this approach is that their products and services are not customized to meet the needs of local markets.

Exhibit 1.1 A Dozen Examples of the Use of Information Technology

Business Process Reengineering

The Fundamental Analysis and redesign of everything associated with a business area to achieve dramatic performance improvement.

Step 1
Step 2
Step 3

Globalization

Use telecommunications networks to enable the organization to operate and compete on a global basis.

Form Strategic Alliances With Suppliers

Adopt standard work processes, procedures, formats, and computer communications for order entry, inventory control, invoicing and payment.

Locking in Customers

Create exclusive computer communications with customers for order entry and exchange of product and service data. This can thwart the competition.

Customer Service

Let customers tap into your data base to track their orders and shipments. This builds loyalty and good relations.

Expert Systems

Provide novices with knowledge and inference procedures to enable them to perform at the level of an expert.

Sales Force Automation

Give sales people portable computers. They can recieve messages quickly and enter orders directly. This adds up to faster deliveries, better cash flow, and less paperwork.

Executive Information System

Accumulate data from a variety of internal and external sources to delivery times and pertinent information to managers.

Training

Train and retain workers using multimedia which allows them to learn at their own speed—and allows you to cut training costs.

Electronic Meeting Systems

The use of audio and video communications to enable meetings to occur without the participants having to meet together physically.

Transaction Processing System

Process the detail data necessary to update records about the fundamental business operations of the organization.

Input
Process
Output

Strategic Information Systems

Information technologies make new operations possible. Federal Express revolutionized overnight delivery with computer equipped trucks and facilities.

Other companies realize that products and services have to be tailored to meet local and regional needs. Thus they choose to locate research and development, manufacturing, engineering, and other functions in foreign countries. Over time, these foreign operations become self-sufficient business units leading to a massive duplication of effort and spending.

The new strategy is globalization, taking a worldwide perspective to the firm's business. Following this approach, work is organized on a worldwide basis to produce products and services for a worldwide market. The business and its products and services continue to be managed regionally and locally. But increasingly, these become world products and services, sharing global technology and common positioning but with appropriate regional tailoring of product aesthetics and form, packing materials, advertising, and promotion executions—whatever it takes to satisfy local consumer demand for quality and value.

To compete in this arena, the global company develops and exploits its strengths on a world scale, whether they are in research and development, marketing, manufacturing, distribution, or some other area. A global company operates like its international predecessors never could: coordinating the actions of people, production facilities, and other resources to respond quickly to customers and competitors anywhere. New products can be launched at multiple locations around the world simultaneously. Several technical centers collaborate on research and development. Manufacturing schedules are coordinated worldwide. Customer needs—and not geography—drive the decision on which plant will fill an order.

Information technology has assisted many companies in meeting the need to convert from an international organization into a global organization. For example, telecommunications networks that support electronic mail provide speedy and low-cost communications across continents. Today, the expertise that is three thousand miles and several time zones away can be summoned easily, quickly, and cost effectively. Such effective communications enable people around the world to work as a cohesive team to design new products, conduct joint research and development, plot new business strategies, and do any work that traditionally required face-to-face meetings.

Corporate data bases attached to telecommunications networks allow employees around the world to access data on customers, products, and services. Data can be treated as a worldwide asset that is easily accessible rather than being stashed away in file drawers in remote locations. Thus people involved in any aspect of customer service (e.g., order processing, customer credit, shipment scheduling, processing customer payments, handling consumer comments) can draw on a common source of data to operate as a single entity around the world.

Elaborate computer systems and flexible manufacturing processes enable plants to alter products without losing economies of scale. Coupled with telecommunications systems to coordinate orders and inventory worldwide, plants can serve global—not just local—markets with custom products.

Business Reengineering

In the past, companies used information technology to mechanize the way they do their business. They kept the existing processes intact and used computers to speed them up. But simply automating ineffective processes cannot remove their fundamental performance deficiencies. Many of today's job designs, work flows, control mechanisms, and organizational structures were developed in the 1950s, a time of a much different competitive environment and before the advent of the computer. These processes are geared toward efficiency and control. Yet the watchwords of the 1990s are cost, innovation, speed, service, and quality.

Most companies are coming to realize that business as usual is a path to disaster. The old ways of processing orders, developing new products, dealing with suppliers, and managing assets are obsolete. The world in general and business in particular have grown more complex and competitors more aggressive. Firms recognize the need to achieve order-of-magnitude improvements in their key performance measures: cost, innovation, speed, service, and quality.

There is a strong shift in the focus of productivity programs from the traditional cost-cutting efforts to sweeping changes aimed at improving organizational performance and effectiveness. This trend is occurring for two reasons. First, most cost restructuring programs failed to eliminate the root cause of a company's problems—ineffectiveness in meeting customer needs. The result was often a weakening of the company in its market, thus compromising its chances for survival. Second, the enabling effect of IT is leading to completely new high-performance work-system models. Human energy is reinvested in new and better ways of doing things as opposed to being eliminated through head-count reduction. Increasingly, business leaders are working to blend new work processes and advanced IT with changed corporate structures to achieve real productivity gains.

Michael Hammer (reengineering guru of the 90s—references 3 and 4) defines business reengineering as the fundamental analysis and redesign of everything associated with a business to achieve dramatic performance improvement and the management of associated business changes. Thus reengineering is a way to achieve the major improvements that are needed.

To be successful in reengineering, managers must revamp the business's most critical processes in a way that capitalizes on the power of information technology. This starts with creating a vision of how things will work. To develop the vision, people must put aside their old ways of doing things. As a result, they will be able to set a course to make the dramatic changes and improvements necessary for the future.

Real World Perspective

Information Technology Supports Globalization at Ford Motor Company

The building of an automobile has been one of the most complex manufacturing challenges of the twentieth century. For each new model, designers and engineers must meticulously sketch out thousands of parts. Factories must be retooled to machine and assemble them. Coordinating the work of designers, engineers, and manufacturing people is a gargantuan task as changes in one stage ripple through the rest of the process.

Pressure from Japanese competitors to cut time and costs out of the design-to-development process grows every year. And that's why Ford Motor Company has embarked on an ambitious journey to redefine the way it produces cars for the global market.

As Ford evolved as an international powerhouse over the century, it found that cars the Germans liked were different from the cars the British liked, which were different from the American versions. Building cars to meet local tastes required hiring designers who were close to those markets, then supporting them with engineers and manufacturing plants as sales volumes (or country trade requirements) warranted.

The design-to-engineering-to-manufacturing process requires daily and close coordination between these professionals. Having them thousands of miles away was unwieldy. They had to be close geographically. The decision on locating the various phases of the design to the manufacturing process, therefore, was not based on economics but rather on the logistical problems of coordinating work across great distances.

The result: unique cars demanding their own designs, engineers, and manufacturing facilities. For example, in Europe alone, Ford has eight factories that are fed by another twenty-five plants producing components. The United States has an even larger infrastructure in place. One design, one engineering, and one manufacturing organization could not serve the world.

Of course, that was before information technology changed the rules of how work could be accomplished. Today, computers linked via vast telecommunications networks enable a designer in Detroit to gaze at the same blueprints that an engineer in Brussels and a manufacturing professional in Spain are examining. People no longer have to be physically together to work together.

That leads us to the next logical argument: If IT allows us to disperse business functions like R&D, design, engineering, and manufacturing, do we still need designers, engineers, and manufacturing professionals clustered around every product?

The answer is no. While those parts of the business closest to the customer (notably sales, marketing, and research and development) should remain local, other parts (engineering and manufacturing, in Ford's case) can be located anywhere. Rather than the next office or town, they should reside where the best talent exists, anywhere on the globe.

Essentially, this is Ford's vision for building the "world car"—a car to be marketed and produced globally. Former Chairman Donald Petersen envisioned the production of a small car (called the Tempo and Topaz in the United States, and Sierra in Europe) that would use identical parts save for some exterior differences. The job of designing, engineering, and building the car would be parceled out around the world to "centers of responsibility." In other words, one design team, one engineering team, one set of parts. Overhead would be greatly reduced.

The glue holding together functions that are oceans apart would be computer and communications technology. Videoconferencing would let designers in Detroit hold intensive discussions with engineers in England. Computer-aided design systems electronically connected on both sides of the Atlantic would allow car designers in Europe to update their plans and notify engineers in the United States instantly.

A major step in that direction is a computer system that makes changes on parts specifications immediately available to manufacturing personnel, so they can rapidly adjust their tools and techniques. In the auto business, the delays and snafus from last-second parts changes are a major factor in the long development time of new car models.

"Through on-line access, the system provides the necessary data on new parts to everyone throughout the company who needs to know,"

Continued

says S. I. Gilman, executive director of information systems and Ford's top information technology executive. "In a company the size of Ford, disseminating those parts specifications could take weeks. On a computer system, nearly instantaneously."

All together, some twelve thousand engineers and manufacturing personnel can tap into the data base, which operates on a mainframe computer at Ford headquarters. If a part doesn't fit a new model, the designers can change it, and the change is communicated to Ford operations throughout the world.

Known as the "worldwide engineering release system," because it releases elaborate engineering documentation from the parts designers to people who will manufacture the parts, the computer application was an enormous undertaking. The biggest difficulty was getting design engineers from around the world to standardize their business practices, such as who has the authority to change a part and how to do it.

The system is part of a larger effort at Ford to push common design in cars and parts, while still allowing for regional and local differences. It has turned out to be a challenging though rewarding step toward a global auto industry.

SOURCE: Robert S. Buday, ed., "How Ford Is Reinventing the Wheel on a Global Basis," CSC Insights 2, no. 2 (Summer 1990). Published by CSC Index, Inc., Five Cambridge Center, Cambridge, MA 02142. □

With a clear vision of how things should work in the future, it is now possible to take a hard look at the current business process and radically change how it's done. Everything is challenged: work flow, job definitions, management procedures, control processes, organizational structures, and even corporate values and culture. For example, every company operates according to a great many rules—most of them undocumented, many of them decades old, and some of them no longer valid. Reengineering requires finding and vigorously challenging the rules blocking major business process changes. These rules are like anchors weighing the firm down and keep it from competing effectively. Some examples of these rules are:

Small orders must be held until full truckload shipments can be assembled.

No order can be accepted until the customer credit is checked and approved.

Local inventory is needed to provide good customer service.

Merchandising decisions are made at headquarters.

Managers need to find imaginative new processes to accomplish work that leads to real breakthroughs in performance. One approach is to reengineer the business process around the outcomes to be achieved, not the tasks to be performed. This often leads to having one person perform all the steps in a process. That person's job is designed to achieve an objective or outcome instead of designed to complete a single task. For example, in some companies, a customer order is processed by several different people in multiple organizations. The customer order moves systematically from one step to the next with many handoffs responsible for numerous errors and misunderstandings. Some companies are moving to a customer service representative who oversees the entire process: taking the order, entering order processing data, and scheduling product delivery and setup. The customer service rep expedites and coordinates the process, and the customer has just one contact who always knows the status of the order.

This simple example illustrates that reengineering causes fundamental changes in the way things are done with an impact across multiple departments. Asking people to work differently often meets with stiff resistance. Senior line managers with the authority to approve changes in the existing rules must get involved and rationalize the conflicting goals and beliefs of the various groups affected. They must change the beliefs, understandings, culture, structure, and behavior of the organization to capture the benefits of reengineering.

Most important, the new employee skills required to carry out the new processes must be articulated. New work flows and new job descriptions are developed. Employees have to gain new skills to meet the demands of the redesigned business.

IT plays a key role in reengineering. Managers need information systems that deliver critical operating information enabling them to redirect, accelerate, and sharpen their planning, decision making, and control. IT can reduce the complexity of communicating effectively across organizations. Thus, information systems that facilitate new ways of working must be designed. Often, not just information systems but a whole new technology infrastructure—computers, communications equipment, software, and data—must be constructed.

■ WHY BUSINESS MANAGERS MUST UNDERSTAND INFORMATION TECHNOLOGY

Significant improvements in information technology continue to occur at an ever-increasing pace. The speed, size, cost, and capabilities associated with computers, office automation, and telecommunications provide a wealth of highly attractive opportunities for using this technology to solve business problems or enhance current ways of doing business (or both). Indeed, the ability of most organizations to assimilate and apply IT lags far behind the recognition of its use.

Business managers must understand IT for four reasons: 1) they must ensure that the use of IT supports corporate strategy, 2) they are in the best position to identify opportunities to apply IT to achieve strategic competitive advantage, 3) they must ensure that there are strong linkages between the business and IT, and 4) they must use IT to be efficient and effective in their jobs.

Ensure Information Technology Supports Corporate Strategy

The value attached to IT varies widely from company to company and even among different organizations within the same company. For some, IT is perceived as a tool to improve organizational effectiveness and profitability. For others, however, such technology is viewed as merely an administrative convenience or, worse, a necessary evil. Sen-

Real World Perspective

Ford Motor Company Reengineers Accounts Payable

In the early 1980s, when the American automotive industry was in a depression, Ford's top management put accounts payable—along with many other departments—under the microscope in search of ways to cut costs. Accounts payable in North America alone employed more than five hundred people. Management thought that by rationalizing processes and installing new computer systems, it could reduce the head count by some 20 percent.

Ford was enthusiastic about its plan to tighten accounts payable—until it looked at Mazda. While Ford was aspiring to a four-hundred-person department, Mazda's accounts payable organization consisted of a total of five people. The difference in absolute numbers was astounding, and even after adjusting for Mazda's smaller size, Ford figures that its accounts payable organization was five times the size it should be. . . .

Ford managers ratcheted up their goal: accounts payable would perform with not just one hundred fewer but many hundred fewer clerks. [They] then set out to achieve this [goal]. . . .

Ford instituted "invoiceless processing." Now when the purchasing department initiates an order, it enters the information into an on-line data base. It doesn't send a copy of the purchase order to anyone. When goods arrive at the receiving dock, the receiving clerk checks the data base to see if they correspond to an outstanding purchase order. If so, he or she accepts them and enters the transaction into the computer system. If receiving can't find a data base entry for the received goods, it simply returns the order.

Under the old procedures, the accounting department had to match fourteen data items between the receipt record, the purchase order, and the invoice before it could issue payment to the vendor. The new approach requires matching only three items—part number, unit of measure, and supplier code—between the purchase order and the receipt record. The matching is done automatically, and the computer prepares the check, which accounts payable sends to the vendor. There are no invoices to worry about since Ford has asked its vendors not to send them. . . .

Ford didn't settle for the modest increases it first envisioned. Management opted for a radical change—and achieved dramatic improvement. Where it has instituted this new process, Ford has achieved a 75 percent reduction in head count, not the 20 percent it would have gotten with a conventional program. *Reprinted by permission of* **Harvard Business Review.** *An excerpt from "Reengineering Work: Don't Automate, Obliterate," by Michael Hammer, 90, no. 4 (July–August, 1990). Copyright © 1990 by the President and Fellows of Harvard College; all rights reserved.* □

ior managers often feel that the company should receive greater benefits from its investment in IT. To increase the return on investment, IT must be tied into the business strategy of the organization.

Successful companies within a given industry attempt to position themselves relative to their competition by adopting one of the following three basic strategies:

■ Become the lowest-cost producer or service provider within the industry.

■ Develop specialized services or products that set the company apart from others in the industry.

■ Concentrate on selling to a particular market or occupying a specific product niche.

The strategy that is selected supplies a general framework to guide the activities of the organization. Furthermore, the success of the organization will depend on the extent to which it successfully implements its chosen strategy. The primary purpose of IT should be to support the basic business strategy. This must be clearly understood by the information systems organization and used as the basis for setting system project priorities.

Companies that adopt the lowest-cost-producer strategy can use IT to reduce costs. System projects that lead to increased productivity of people and other resources, such as machinery or inventory, should be given the highest priority. Exhibit 1.2 outlines several computer applications of high interest to a firm that adopts this strategy.

A company that adopts a strategy for providing specialized goods or services to differentiate itself from the competition can use IT to add unique features to its product or its service. System projects that can improve product quality or enhance the uniqueness of customer services should be given the highest priority. Exhibit 1.2 also lists several computer applications of special interest to such a firm.

The company that adopts a strategy for offering a product or service to a niche of selected customers can use IT to better serve these customers. This can be accomplished by following either the lowest-cost or product differentiation strategy for the selected group of customers.

Exhibit 1.2 Information Systems Applications Supporting Lowest-Cost or Product Differentiation Strategies

Information System Applications that Support a Low-Cost-Producer Strategy *Computer Application*	*Business Area*	Information System Applications that Support a Product Differentiation Strategy *Computer Application*
Planning and budgeting systems Cost control systems	Finance	Office automation that supports the integration of functions performed by various business areas
Systems that maximize the return on dollars spent on advertising and promotions Systems that establish sales-call priorities to ensure that accounts with the highest-profit potential are given the most attention	Sales	Differential pricing systems Systems that improve sales support of customers Systems that simplify and speed up the order-entry and product-distribution processes
Process control systems Inventory planning and control systems	Manufacturing	Quality assurance/monitoring systems Systems that track the delivery of raw materials or semifinished products from suppliers
Project control systems Computer-aided design systems	Product research and development	Systems that support access to public data bases for gathering research information Electronic mail that supports the informal sharing of results among people who are geographically dispersed

Exhibit 1.3
Possible Outcomes
of Management
Trying to Match
Technology Strategy
to Business Strategy

Quality of Implementation	Technology Strategy Consistent with the Business Strategy	Technology Strategy Inconsistent with the Business Strategy
Technology Implemented Well	Success is likely	Success is possible
Technology Implemented Poorly	Problems are likely	Failure is expected

The information system applications that support a lowest-cost-producer strategy are not the same as those needed to support a product differentiation strategy. Thus, understanding the firm's basic strategy is an essential first step toward appropriate computer applications selection.

The need to align projects with corporate strategy means that project identification and prioritization, once considered the sole province of technologists, are now recognized as needing business manager input and direction. This creates yet another major challenge for management: building an effective working partnership between business strategists and information technologists. Thus companies are experimenting with coordinating roles, creating new senior positions such as Chief Information Officer (CIO), linking strategic planning and IT planning, and reengineering their operations to ensure improved coordination and communication among the various critical organizational units. Exhibit 1.3 summarizes the possible outcomes of management trying to match technology and business strategies.

Identify Strategic Competitive Advantage Opportunities

As well as ensuring IT supports corporate strategy, managers must be able to identify opportunities to seize a competitive advantage. Michael Porter (reference 8) states that the fundamental basis for achieving and maintaining above-average profitability over the long run is sustainable competitive advantage. He offers these basic strategies for achieving this competitive advantage: cost leadership (become the low-cost producer in all market segments), differentiation (distinguish your products and services from others in all market segments), and focus (concentrate on a particular market segment and then either become the low-cost producer or differentiate) (see Exhibit 1.4).

Exhibit 1.4
Basic Strategies for
Achieving
Competitive
Advantage

MARKET SEGMENT	LOW-COST-PRODUCER	DIFFERENTIATION
All Market Segments		
Focused Market Segment		

Real World Perspectives

Information Systems Help Achieve Low-Cost-Producer Status at Deere & Company

Deere & Company is the leading manufacturer of farming tractors. It employs information systems to help achieve the position of low-cost producer. One such system is a parts inventory system. The dimensions and characteristics of the more than 250,000 different parts used in manufacturing have been cataloged and entered into the systems' data base—everything from large hydraulic pumps to tiny screws. Engineers search the data base to find an existing part with similar characteristics to what is needed in a new part. In many cases, the engineer ends up not having to design the new part or buy equipment and raw materials to manufacture it. Using this system, Deere & Company has saved over $9 million in two years.

Strategy of Selling to a Selected Niche of Customers at Sears

Sears, Roebuck & Company has been able to create a powerful marketing tool that is helping to boost income as well as improve customer goodwill. Sears keeps track of the appliance purchases of each of its customers and the associated service contracts and maintenance calls on those appliances. The giant retailer sends out reminder postcards to customers when it comes time to renew their maintenance contracts. Without the yearly reminder, most customers would forget to renew.

Information Systems Help Support Product Differentiation Strategy at Owens-Corning Fiberglas Corporation

Owens-Corning is a leader in the home insulation market. The company has conducted considerable research on the energy efficiency of a wide variety of house designs. It has developed a computer program that uses the data to develop energy efficiency ratings for new designs. To boost sales of its home-insulation products, Owens-Corning offers builders free evaluations of their designs if they will buy all their insulation from the company and agree to a minimum energy efficiency standard. Owens-Corning is also creating more demand for insulation by educating consumers about energy ratings, which are similar to the mile-per-gallon ratings used on cars, and promoting their use.

Rackoff, Wiseman, and Ullrich (reference 11) developed a planning process for the implementation of information systems for competitive advantage. Their model is based on the identification of five strategic thrust areas where the company can make a major offensive or defensive competitive move. These five thrust areas are:

1. **Differentiation** Achieve an advantage by distinguishing your products and services from those of your competitors.

2. **Cost** Achieve an advantage by reducing your firm's costs, suppliers' costs, or customers' costs, or raising the costs your competitors must pay to match the quality and service your firm provides.

3. **Innovation** Achieve an advantage by introducing a product or process change that results in a fundamental transformation in the way business is conducted in the industry.

4. **Growth** Achieve an advantage by volume or geographic expansion, backward or forward integration, or product line or entry diversification.

Exhibit 1.5
A Framework for
Identifying
Competitive
Advantage
Opportunities

	STRATEGIC TARGET		
STRATEGIC THRUST	Supplier	Customer	Competitor
Differentiation			
Cost			
Innovation			
Growth			
Alliance			

5. **Alliance** Achieve an advantage by forging marketing agreements, forming joint ventures, or making acquisitions related to
the thrusts of differentiation, cost, innovation, or growth.

The theory of strategic thrusts is further developed in Wiseman's
Strategy and Computers: Information Systems as Competitive Weapons
(reference 12). Wiseman points out that these thrusts can be aimed at
three strategic targets: suppliers, customers, and competitors. The concept of strategic targets and strategic thrusts can be put together to
form a matrix of opportunities for gaining competitive advantage (Exhibit 1.5).

A **Strategic Information System** (SIS) is a system that supports the
firm's fundamental plan for gaining or sustaining a competitive advantage. A strategic information system supports the firm's initiatives in
one or more of the five key thrust areas and is directed at suppliers,
customers, or competitors. Such a system can shift the balance of competitive power in the company's favor.

Four real-life examples of strategic systems are discussed on the
following page. Exhibit 1.6 clarifies where these systems fit into the
strategic thrust/strategic target matrix.

Ensure Linkages Between Business and Information Technology

Information technology projects frequently fail in spite of the information system itself being well designed and executed. The root prob-

Exhibit 1.6
Classification of
Several Strategic
Information
Systems

	STRATEGIC TARGET		
STRATEGIC THRUST	Supplier	Customer	Competitor
Differentiation			Owens-Corning
Cost	Shop 'n Save		Deere & Co
Innovation		American Hospital	
Growth		United Airlines	
Alliance	Sears		Department Stores

Real World Perspectives

Use of SIS at United Airlines: Growth Strategy Aimed at Customers

In an attempt to increase its number of customers, United Airlines is enhancing its aging Apollo reservation system. While American Airlines' Sabre system is usually given credit as being the first on-line reservation system and initially provided that company with a competitive advantage, United Airlines is trying to catch up. American's system is used by over eleven thousand travel agents worldwide; nearly eight thousand U.S. travel agents use United's.

The Enterprise system is a key enhancement to United's Apollo Service that represents one United attempt to improve its relations with travel agencies, which account for 80 percent of their business. Enterprise integrates a travel agent's front-office client operations (reservations, ticketing, and so on) with the back-office accounting and management functions. Such a system will enable travel agencies to improve their own internal efficiency and profitability, thus providing a strong incentive to attract new customers to Apollo Service.

Use of SIS by New York City Department Stores: Alliance Strategy Aimed at Competitors

Large retailers suffer significant losses due to fraudulent returns of customer purchases:

1. Employees with discount privileges who buy merchandise at special employee discounts and then have friends return the items for cash at the full price
2. Shoplifters who remove sales tags and then try to obtain refunds at the service counter
3. Models who purchase clothes, use them for a shooting session, and then return the used items for a refund

A group of New York City department stores banded together to prevent refund abusers from continuing their activities. All refunds for the participating stores were processed through a strategic information system. The system helped identify abusers by producing frequency-of-return reports. The stores were then able to issue warning letters and take other actions to help cut refund abuse.

Use of SIS by American Hospital Supply: Innovation Strategy Aimed at Customers

By connecting hospitals directly to an on-line order-entry system, American Hospital Supply eliminated the effort required to order supplies and differentiated itself from its competitors. The system allows purchase orders to be placed by less-skilled, lower-paid clerks instead of purchase agents, reduces customer-service problems, cuts order-entry costs, and provides more flexibility to customers in the time and process of order submission. The system provided a large competitive advantage by adding value for customers, with a resulting substantial rise in sales. It was also a strong force in driving a division of a major Fortune 500 competitor (the Paper Products Division of Procter & Gamble) out of the market.

Use of SIS at Shop 'n Save: Low-Cost Strategy Aimed at Suppliers

Over half of the nation's supermarkets are equipped with scanners, those computerized checkout machines that read the bar code on each item purchased. Data also flow in from stores and warehouses to allow calculation of virtually every cost in getting goods from manufacturer to consumer—including shipping expenses, warehouse handling requirements, bulkiness of display, energy needs at the store, and the time the product spends on the shelf before it is purchased. This wealth of detailed data is captured and processed for more than seventeen thousand products at sixty-five Shop 'n Save stores. The data flow into a collection of systems that provide strategic information system (SIS) information. By using computers in all phases of its business, Shop 'n Save has boosted its profit margin from a respectable 1 percent in 1980 (then the industry average) to 1.8 percent in the first quarter of 1986, a quarter in which the industry average was 1.2 percent.

Direct Product Profitability (DPP) is a SIS for Shop 'n Save. The wealth of detailed data compiled for DPP helps the retailer streamline its operations in many ways. The output of DPP is

Continued

translated into Plan-A-Grams—printouts that show store managers, shelf by shelf, exactly where to place their stock to maximize profit. DPP helps to decide whether to place two or three rows of a product. DPP has also helped Shop 'n Save to identify those 20 percent of the items in the store that actually lose money.

DPP also helps the retailer provide input to manufacturers on how to design more efficient containers and shipping methods. For example, DPP studies have shown that stocking lighter-weight packages of detergents is more cost efficient. These findings were shared with manufacturers, which have set out to limit the air and water content in their packages. As such changes are made, the profitability of the retailer is improved and the sales of the cooperating manufacturers are also increased.

lem is that insufficient attention has been paid to the information systems linkages with the business with which it must interface. The new IT is more powerful, more diverse, and increasingly entwined with the organization's critical business processes.

Operating or business managers expect that when an information system is delivered to them, they will be able to use it in the context of their current decision processes. On the other hand, system designers expect that the need they are to satisfy is to distill large amounts of data into useful information. These perspectives are both correct, but there is a gap between them (Exhibit 1.7). This gap is in addressing the changes in behavior the new information system will trigger: What decision process currently in place will be affected by the new information? Exactly how will the information generated be applied by those contributing to those decision processes? Unless the way the new information is to be used is thought through in advance, merely dumping new and differently organized data onto the desk of a busy manager will add only to its clutter and create an "information overload" situation.

Continuing to merely react to new technology and the changes it triggers can throw a business into a tailspin. As a result, business managers are called on to lead IT projects and are held accountable for the use and results of IT in their area. The risks are great, but so too are the rewards.

Provide Leadership for IT Projects

A **runaway project** is one that greatly exceeds budget, perhaps by millions of dollars, and is months, sometimes years, behind schedule. A

Exhibit 1.7
The Operating/
Business Manager
System Designer
Gap

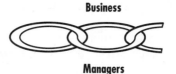

Business

Managers

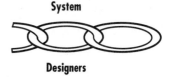

System

Designers

Real World Perspective

Procter & Gamble Managers Ensure Link Between Business and IT Projects

Procter & Gamble (P&G) is establishing cooperative efforts with major customers like Kroger, Wal-Mart, and K-Mart to provide increased responsiveness in meeting their needs. Long considered a technology leader, P&G—in its effort to be more responsive to customers—ironically has begun taking a more cautious approach. P&G decided to move away from being a technology innovator and move toward being a business innovator. Management recognizes that P&G is a consumer products company, not a computer company. Rather than be the first to use technology, P&G's goal is to employ proven technologies in unique and creative ways.

Through technologies such as in-store scanning of purchases, retailers have access to a wealth of data regarding customer buying patterns. P&G marketing managers understand that they will get more support and sales if they work with the retailers to use this data to make decisions, rather than try to dictate to retailers how to run their business. As a result, they led an effort to have technology people from P&G working on-site at customer locations. Their role is to help manage and develop applications that help P&G product managers and customer buyers track buying trends. Managers have access to marketing information and data bases from their desktop computers and terminals.

P&G is also working with customers to implement Electronic Data Interchange (EDI). With EDI, customers send all inventory data and purchase orders directly to a P&G computer, which uses the information to determine shipping and production schedules. This means that P&G can get orders, generate inventory, and get products to customers faster. *SOURCE: © 1990 by CMP Publications, Inc., 600 Community Drive, Manhasset, NY 11030. Reprinted from* InformationWeek *with permission.* □

recent KPMG Peat Marwick survey shows that about 35 percent of all major information systems projects become runaways. Other surveys say that every Fortune 200 company has at least one runaway project. Clearly with that sort of track record, managers must recognize the need to take an active role in systems development when a key business initiative depends on it. Experience has shown that Murphy's law prevails—indeed, everything will go wrong unless management forces it to go right. Managers need to find ways to better control the outcome of critical projects. Yet many managers feel unsure about how to achieve this control. At what level should they get involved and how often? Who should own such systems, and what role must they play? How can managers best effect a partnership between information technology and the business? These issues will be addressed in this text.

Use of Information Technology

Managers at all levels, in all kinds of firms, and in all industries are personally using information technology to improve their own effectiveness.

VisiCalc, the first financial spreadsheet package, was introduced in 1980. This package ran on a personal computer and permitted anyone

Real World Perspective

Blue Cross and Blue Shield Learns the Need for Management Leadership in IT Projects

The need for a major change in its computer systems drove Blue Cross and Blue Shield of Wisconsin to launch an ambitious information systems project. While the project turned into a runaway and cost the company millions in lost business, a valiant rescue effort was the catalyst for positive changes in everything from interpersonal communications and corporate structure to project management. Today managers at Blue Cross and Blue Shield believe that the company is much better equipped to manage projects and implement change in the business.

The company signed a contract for facilities management of its computer center. Part of the contract called for the development of an integrated computer system to handle all functions of the business claims processing, enrollment processing, cost containment—the works. Several incompatible computer systems had to be merged. It was estimated to cost $200 million and take eighteen months to build.

The project was completed on time, but there was one major problem: It didn't work. At one point the system sent out hundreds of checks to a nonexistent town in Wisconsin. The company says $60 million in overpayments or dupli-

cate checks were sent out in the system's first year. The debacle cost Blue Cross and Blue Shield 35,000 members.

Executives say both the contractor and Blue Cross and Blue Shield are to blame. The contractor underestimated how long it would take and how complex the project was. Blue Cross and Blue Shield also erred in its failure to involve the new system's users in its development. There was a need for commitment from all levels of the organization during the transition period. The chief sponsors of the project were technical staffers who knew the information systems requirements for the job but were not in tune with the business requirements.

In the end, the company president stepped in and made sweeping changes, removing three levels of management, giving senior VPs more authority, and halving the chain of command to twelve managers. The result was a better flow of communication between all departments. Blue Cross and Blue Shield came to know what they were trying to achieve with the system. It took a whole new discipline to force that change.

SOURCE: © 1989 by CMP Publications, Inc., 600 Community Drive, Manhasset, NY 11030. Reprinted from InformationWeek *with permission.* □

who dealt with figures to manipulate large, sophisticated financial spreadsheets and tables. The successor to VisiCalc, Lotus 1-2-3, became the largest-selling software in history by the end of the 1980s. Word processing software also appeared in the early 1980s and, together with spreadsheet software, made it possible for nonprogrammers to use computer power to increase their productivity. This breakthrough led to a phenomenal growth in both the number of personal computers and the number of personal computer users. In fact, today personal computers are ubiquitous, with over 60 million already installed in offices and at least 3 million additional acquired for use in the office each year. There are few managers who today do not come into contact with a personal computer on at least a weekly, if not daily, basis to hook up to information networks, create presentation graphics, prepare a memo, or develop a spreadsheet for analysis.

■ THE ROLE OF THE INFORMATION TECHNOLOGY ORGANIZATION

The Typical IT Organization

The size and organizational form of the Information Technology organization vary greatly from company to company. Some small companies have no or very few permanent full-time people in their IT organization. At the other extreme, Fortune 500 companies may have hundreds or even thousands of people in their IT department. However, once the IT department has more than a dozen or so people, it is usually subdivided into four parts, as shown in Exhibit 1.8.

Operations Group

The operations group plays a critical role in running and supporting the computer hardware and software systems and telecommunications networks that support the business. They also implement technical changes by providing more cost-effective services, implementing communications networks, and managing the installation and use of new technologies. They provide service to both the employees of the company and customers who use the network and computing services in their everyday jobs.

Applications Development Group

The applications development group is responsible for developing new business applications to meet business needs. They also make enhancements and modifications to existing systems to enable the system to meet changing business needs or changes in the computing or tele-

---

Exhibit 1.8
Typical Information
Systems
Organization

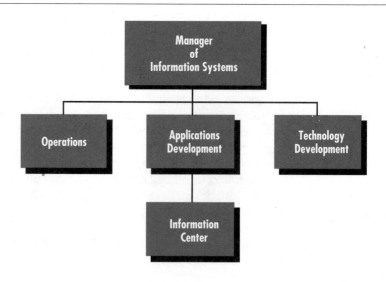

communications environment (e.g., installation of a new release of the operating system).

In a small company, there may be just one applications development group. The members of this group work on whatever projects are currently the most important for the company. In larger companies, there may be many different applications development groups. For example, there may be an applications development group for each major division and staff organization (human resources, finance, purchasing, and so on) of a multidivision company. This approach enables each major division or staff organization to set its own system development priorities. The organization must also justify its own budget and staffing for information system development.

The applications development group includes different kinds of information system specialists, such as systems analysts, programmers, and project managers.

Information Center

The idea of establishing an information center is not to replace traditional systems development but to help people to use information processing to meet their demand for data and decision-making support. Thus many organizations have their information center report to a manager in the applications development organization.

The **information center** helps end users become comfortable with information processing so that they can use it in their day-to-day operations for increased efficiency and enhanced decision-making ability. The key strategy necessary to accomplish this goal is to promote, support, and encourage end-user application development. A side benefit of this approach is that by increasing end users' ability to develop their own solutions, the IT department has more time to address the more complex applications that are beyond the capabilities of end users.

Members of the Information Center provide troubleshooting, perform maintenance, offer consulting, deliver training, enable access to data bases, acquire hardware and software, and investigate new products and services of interest to end users.

Technology Development Group

Those organizations that recognize that information technology can make a great impact on the products and services they offer often form a technology development group. This group is responsible for finding matches between unmet business needs and new IT.

Ideally the technology development group is kept as a separate and distinct organizational entity. This reduces the likelihood of diverting development people and resources to work on system development or perform maintenance and support work. Without this separation, the development effort will be frequently interrupted and not yield new ideas and applications for the organization.

Centralization and Decentralization

Centralization of information services creates a single functional unit with responsibility for providing information processing services to all operating units in the organization. The information systems organization members report directly to technology managers and ultimately to the top information systems executive.

In the fifties through the early seventies, companies centralized their operations for the purpose of reducing information systems costs based on economy of scale and improved efficiency of systems development. Centralization allowed the acquisition and running of large, expensive mainframe computers for the benefit of the entire company. Centralization also enabled the development of corporate standards and guidelines. Standardization led to economies of scale with many users all using the same hardware, software, and vendors. Centralization also aided the design and use of common corporate data bases as well as common system development approaches.

Starting in the mid-seventies, the availability of cost-effective minicomputers stimulated an interest in decentralizing some information processing services. **Decentralization** creates a functional unit within each operating unit with responsibility for servicing the information processing needs of that unit. The information systems people report to managers within the operating unit, who ultimately report to line managers (Exhibit 1.9). These line managers are able to direct and control information resources to meet their business unit needs with solutions most appropriate for them, without the burden of trying to develop solutions that are "best" for the company as a whole.

The basic difference between centralization and decentralization, then, is the degree to which information processing decision making, authority, and responsibility are disseminated throughout the organization. For the 1990s, most organizations will have a mix of centralization and decentralization. Central information services will establish certain guidelines and directions for hardware and software selections.

Exhibit 1.9   Organization Chart for a Decentralized Information Systems Organization

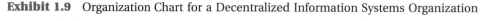

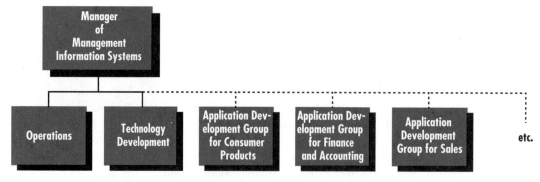

Central information services will also develop key infrastructure applications for use by the entire organization (e.g., corporate telecommunications networks, corporate data bases). Decentralized information services organizations in business units follow these guidelines and use infrastructure components to develop efficient and effective solutions to meet their business unit's needs.

The role of the information systems professional varies depending on whether the person is working in a centralized or a decentralized organization. In the centralized organization, the emphasis is more on technology and large projects to implement the infrastructure (computer hardware, telecommunications networks, corporate data bases) for the rest of the company. In the decentralized organization, the emphasis is more on understanding business needs and developing timely solutions to meet those needs.

Few people can operate effectively in both a large, centralized information systems organization and a small, decentralized group in a business unit. Quite different skills and interests are required. The decentralized information specialists are expected to expand their business skills; rather than make solely technical decisions, these specialists must make business decisions that ensure that their business unit makes the most cost-effective use of IT to support the unit's business plan. They must make a shift in their allegiance and in skills. The need

Real World Perspective

Decentralized Information Systems at Met Life

New York City–based insurer Metropolitan Life and Affiliated Companies has distributed information systems into its lines of businesses. The information systems specialists report to managers in the business groups. They are considered to be full-fledged members of the business group. There is also a corporate information systems staff, which maintains four large computer centers.

The most frequently mentioned benefit of decentralization is time savings in implementing new business applications. For example, at Met Life, workers used to have to prepare written requests for information systems services and equipment. These requests were then sent to central information systems managers to be further evaluated and have a priority assigned. Now when a business organization identifies a need, they can assign their own specialists to complete the work. Thus, the elapsed time from business

articulation to completed system is greatly reduced by eliminating the need to go through committees to get things done. To a certain degree, when the information specialists are working in a business area they understand, they can better anticipate what is needed.

To meet business needs effectively requires that the information systems specialists understand both their users and the business they are trying to support. This takes time. Being included in meetings with workers sounds simple, but it is a vital and initially difficult feat. Where your office is located is also important. Communications improve when the specialists are located and work among the people whom they serve. Information specialists must eliminate the technical jargon and speak in plain business English. Being a member of the business unit also helps.

SOURCE: Susan Kerr, "The New IS Force," Datamation 35, no. 15 (1 August 1989). Reprinted with permission from Datamation. Copyright 1991 by Cahners Publishing Company. ☐

to develop or even conform to corporate information system strategies is low on their list of concerns. Instead the business-unit information systems culture requires information systems specialists to identify and understand the needs of the users who depend upon them and become their advocates. Often this may put people in decentralized organizations at odds with the centralized information systems organization.

Summary

Globalization involves taking a worldwide perspective of the firm's business—its challenges and opportunities, markets, customers, suppliers, competitors, and employees.

Reengineering is the fundamental analysis and redesign of everything associated with a business area to achieve dramatic performance improvement.

Successful companies follow one of three strategies to position themselves relative to the competition: become a low-cost producer, provide specialized products or services, or concentrate on selling to a particular market.

Managers have a key role in identifying strategic competitive advantage opportunities that provide above-average profitability over the long run.

A strategic information system supports the firm's fundamental plan to gain or sustain a competitive advantage.

Business managers must ensure that the changes in behavior required to gain business benefit from the implementation of new systems are identified and made.

Managers must provide strong leadership to ensure that IT efforts do not turn into runaway projects.

Managers at all levels are increasingly using IT.

The typical information systems organization is divided into four groups: Operations, Applications Development, Information Center, and Technology Development.

Centralization of IT creates a single functional unit with responsibility for providing information services to all units in the organization.

Decentralization creates a functional unit within each operating unit with responsibility for servicing the information processing needs of that unit.

A Manager's Checklist

✔ Does your company face global competition?

✔ Are you participating in a business reengineering project?

✔ Can you state your company's basic strategy for positioning itself versus competitors?

✔ Do you review information technology projects for their "fit" with corporate strategy?

✔ Do you encourage identification of strategic competitive advantage opportunities?

✔ Have you been involved in any projects where there was a missing link between the information technology and the business?

✔ Could you recognize a runaway project if you saw one?

✔ Are you a user of information technology?

Key Terms

business reengineering
centralization
decentralization
globalization
information society

information technology
knowledge workers
runaway project
strategic alliance
strategic information system

Review Questions

1. What does the term information society imply?

2. Define the term information technology.

3. What is meant by globalization? Why does it present both a challenge and an opportunity?

4. What is business reengineering? Why are so many companies going through this?

5. State three key business objectives for applying information technology.

6. What role must managers play to ensure the successful application of information technology? p. 12

7. What are the four core activities of the information technology group within the company?

8. What is the difference between a centralized and a decentralized information technology organization?

Discussion Questions

1. What do you need to get out of this course for it to be considered of high value to you?

2. Do business managers really need to understand information technology? Why or why not?

3. Provide examples that show investments in information technology have paid off. Provide examples where there has been no payoff. Why do you think the results have been mixed?

4. How much time should managers spend addressing information technology?

5. Should information technology be considered strategic in nature or is it simply a means to improve efficiency?

6. Make a list of the key management issues for the 21st century. Which of these will be the most important? Can you identify any way that information technology can help managers deal with these issues?

7. Which of the four groups in the typical information technology organization is most important to the firm? Why?

8. Do you think that the use of information technology can create new opportunities for conspiracy and/or unethical behavior on the part of individuals and companies? Why?

Recommended Readings

1. Drucker, Peter F. "The New Productivity Challenge." *Harvard Business Review,* (Nov–Dec 1991).

2. Gleckman, Howard. "The Technology Payoff." *Business Week.* June 14, 1993.

3. Hammer, Michael. "Reengineering Work: Don't Automate, Obliterate." *Harvard Business Review* 90, No. 4 (July–August 1990).

4. Hammer, Michael and James Champy. "Reengineering the Corporation: A Manifesto for Business Revolution." *HarperBusiness,* 1993.

5. Kindel, Sharon. "World Without End: Learning at Last How to Harvest the Huge Investment in Computer Systems." *Financial World,* Vol 162. Nov. 9, 1993.

6. Mangurian, Glenn and Allen Cohen. "Reengineering Stress Points: Dealing with the Inevitable." *Insights Quarterly,* Vol. 5, No. 3 (Winter 1993).

7. Naisbitt, John. *Megatrends.* New York: Warner Books, 1982.

8. Porter, Michael. "Michael Porter on the New Global Strategy." *Insights Quarterly,* Vol. 5, No. 3 (Winter 1993).

9. Sirkin, Harold and George Stalk, Jr. "Fix the Process, Not the Problem." *Harvard Business Review* 90, No. 4 (July–August 1990).

10. Von Simson, Erbest M. "The Centrally Decentralized IS Organization." *Harvard Business Review* 90, No. 4 (July–August 1990).

11. Rackoff, Nick, Charles Wiseman, and Walter Ulrich. "Information Systems for Competitive Advantage: Implementation of a Planning Process." *MIS Quarterly* (December 1985).

12. Wiseman, Charles. *Strategy and Computers: Information Systems as Competitive Weapons.* Homewood, Ill.: Dow-Jones-Irwin, 1985.

A Manager's Dilemma

Disappointing Results Applying Information Technology

It is year-end review meeting time again. As you sit listening to the Vice-president of Information Systems, you can't help but wonder if the company is getting real value for its investment in information technology. So many projects seem to be simple patches to existing systems to enable them to continue functioning. Sometimes the need to change a system was because of some new release of the hardware or operating system—whatever that was. Other times, the changes were in response to changes in the way the company was managing the business. For example, the recent sales restructure necessitated a number of changes in information systems.

You feel disappointed about the impact that IT is making on the firm. You are sure your competitors are more aggressive in using the technology in ways to achieve competitive advantage. You decide to spend a few days over the next couple weeks seeking some more impactful ways for IT to be applied in your firm. How would you conduct your search? Who might you speak with—both inside and outside the firm—to gain some ideas for potential projects?

Heading Off Runaway Projects

Blue Cross and Blue Shield of Wisconsin experienced a major disaster trying to develop an integrated computer system to handle all functions of the business including claims processing, enrollment processing, and cost containment. Although completed on time, the system did not function properly and generated over $60 million in overpayments or duplicate checks in its first year.

The company president and surviving senior managers are determined never to have such a disaster again. They also wish to safeguard against future projects being completed months late or millions of dollars over budget (or both).

You have been commissioned by the president to develop a set of criteria to identify runaway projects. Outline a process that includes participation by both senior managers and project managers to develop a set of criteria. Identify two or three criteria likely to be included.

Training Program for Senior Management

The Vice-president of Information Systems has come to you for help. She has asked you, as head of Corporate Training, to help prepare senior management to deal with the explosion in the use of IT. She feels a strong need to educate them in the way the technology is being used by competitors within the industry. She wants them to appreciate the potential benefits that can be achieved through the use of technology. She wants them to feel comfortable in investing dollars and people in the many technical projects the Information Systems organization will propose in the next few months. How would you go about meeting these training needs?

Case Study 1.4

Reengineering Challenge

The Director of Purchasing has assigned you the task of straightening out several problems associated with the purchasing of and payment for raw materials. The current operation works as follows:

1. Inventory Control monitors stock levels of raw material by comparing stock on hand to the stock required to meet the weekly production schedule. The weekly production schedule is always available seven working days before the start of the planning cycle.

2. Inventory Control sends a requisition to Purchasing specifying the specific raw materials and quantities needed.

3. Purchasing prepares a purchase order and sends it to the appropriate supplier. A copy of the purchase order is also sent to Accounts Payable.

4. The supplier ships the raw material to Inventory Control, where a receiving report is prepared and a copy is sent to Accounts Payable. The lead time from receipt of the requisition to receipt of the raw materials from the supplier is eight to twelve days.

5. The supplier fills the order and mails the invoice to Accounts Payable. The invoice is matched to the copy of the receiving report and purchase order. If everything agrees, a check is prepared and mailed to the supplier.

Unfortunately, this seemingly simple system has a number of problems. The biggest problem is a frequent shortage of certain raw materials and an overabundance of others. The production schedule must be changed frequently to wait for the raw materials to arrive. The delays in the schedule have been as long as five days. Another serious problem is that suppliers complain of slow payment, and the company is unable to take advantage of the 2 percent discount for payment within ten days. The loss is estimated to be in excess of $100,000 per year.

Inventory Control blames the problem on internal paperwork delays in processing the requisitions within Purchasing. Accounts Payable complains that they never get a copy of the purchase order, so that when the receiving report and the invoice arrive, there is no record of what was ordered.

How would you approach solving this problem? Who all needs to be involved in its solution? Develop a description of the work flow for a solution based on reengineering the whole process.

Understanding the Technology Architecture

Managers need a framework for using information technology in the firm and for ensuring that systems and data can be shared across organizational units. Technology architecture is the term used for such a framework. The technology architecture provides principles, standards, and models that guide decisions on investments in information technology.

Although this section is not intended to turn managers into computer scientists, it will provide them with an understanding of key concepts, terminology, and principles. The goal is to prepare managers to work effectively with their counterparts in the IT organization to make sound decisions about information technology—when, where, and how to apply it.

Chapter 2

Computer Hardware—
Trends and Issues

Upon completion of this chapter, you will be able to:

1. Name the five basic hardware components found in every computer and state their purpose.

2. Define the evolving role played by the microcomputer, workstation, midrange, mainframe, and supercomputer in the business organizations of today.

3. Identify the major types and capabilities of computer input, output, and secondary storage devices.

4. Define the term downsizing, state its goal, and discuss three advantages and three disadvantages of this approach to meeting computing needs.

Preview

This chapter will cover key concepts and terminology to help you understand computer hardware, including the various classes of computers, their capabilities, how they are used, and future trends. You will learn that the continuing evolution of the microprocessor and fierce competition among hardware vendors are fueling a steady improvement in the price/performance of hardware, which means lower prices for the same or more computer performance. Evolution and competition have also led to a wide range of computing power and capability available to match most business needs. Increases in computer power and capacity can be expected to continue at an accelerating rate thus providing tremendous new capabilities to end users.

Issues

1. What increases in speed and capacity of computer hardware can be expected? What are the implications of this?

2. Why do organizations continue to run out of computing capacity?

3. Why do business managers need to understand computer hardware?

Trade-offs

1. Where should the cost of computer hardware appear—in the budget of the organization using the equipment or the information technology organization?

2. Who should have final approval of expenditures for computer hardware?

3. What are the pros and cons of computer hardware downsizing?

A Manager Struggles with the Issues

The $6 million mainframe computer the company had purchased just two years ago was out of capacity. Finance had decided on a five-year depreciation schedule so the machine was not even half depreciated. Fortunately, the Manager of Information Systems was not recommending that the system be scrapped. Instead, the Manager's strategy was to purchase minicomputers and move several business applications off the mainframe, which would free up capacity on the mainframe, making it useful again. It would also put in place three new minicomputers, each of which have the computing capacity of the original mainframe. The computing power of the firm would quadruple at a cost of less than $2 million! Before approving this strategy, the controller has requested that you review the capacity plan to ensure that investment in additional computing power is sound. What has led to the increase in demand for computing power? Is the strategy of downsizing to minicomputers sound? When will the next increment of computing power be required and how much will be needed?

■ WHY MANAGERS NEED TO UNDERSTAND COMPUTER HARDWARE

The demand for more and more computing power continues as firms increasingly rely on information technology to help run their business and build products and services. Because it is not uncommon for such projects to require an investment of millions of dollars in hardware, senior managers hold business managers accountable for the success of these business building projects. Often a key success criterion is that the hardware purchased meets the business needs while being cost effective. Thus business managers must have a basic understanding of computer hardware before the investment is made. This understanding includes making sure that business needs are identified and clearly expressed in a manner that helps determine hardware requirements. Effective business managers will also dig in and understand the business impact of the various options developed by the IT managers and specialists. Such a business manager may well influence the final choice of hardware.

In addition to the major business building projects, much of the routine, ongoing spending on information technology goes on outside the IT organization's budget. In many companies, the final approval for the purchase of microcomputers, minicomputers, printers, and other hardware comes from a business organization, not the IT organization. Furthermore, the cost of this hardware appears in the business organization's budget—not the IT budget. The line manager in charge of the budget needs to understand hardware well enough to determine whether or not what is being purchased really makes good business sense. Is it required to meet a real business need? Will it be cost effective? What is the expected useful life? How does it integrate to already existing equipment?

■ COMPUTER SYSTEM COMPONENTS

There are five fundamental hardware components that make up every computer: the central processing unit (CPU), main memory, secondary storage, input devices, and output devices (Exhibit 2.1). These five components are defined below and will be discussed more fully later in the chapter.

Exhibit 2.1
Five Basic Hardware Components of Every Computer

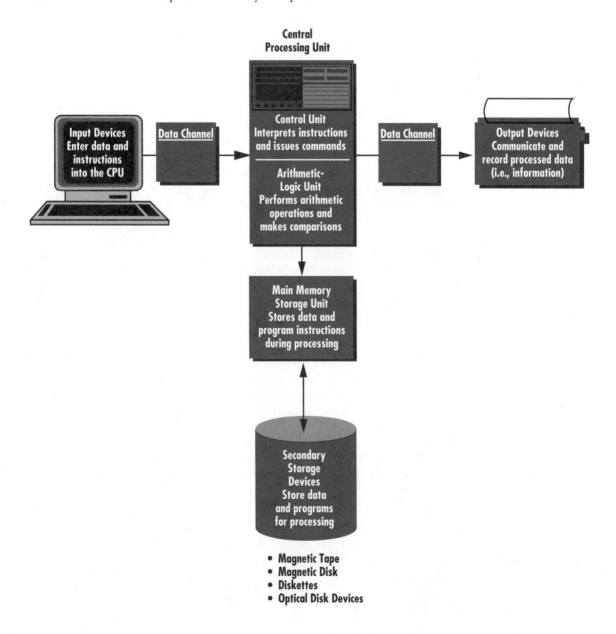

Central Processing Unit

The **CPU** is a highly complex, extensive set of electronic circuitry that executes program instructions stored in main memory. The CPU consists of a control unit that fetches instructions from main memory, interprets them, and issues commands to other computer components to carry out the requested operations. The Arithmetic and Logic Unit **(ALU)** actually executes the instructions by performing basic operations such as add, divide, multiply, and compare. The time it takes to fetch, decode, and execute an instruction varies widely depending upon the power of the CPU. An **internal clock** governs the rate at which these operations occur. Clock speed is measured in megahertz **(MHz)** or millions of cycles per second. Thus a computer with a 66 MHz CPU is one whose clock drives internal operations at the rate of 66 million cycles per second. CPU speed is measured in units of millions of instructions per second **(MIPS).** MIPS is a function of clock speed (cycles/second) times the number of instructions executed per cycle. The trend is toward faster and faster CPUs capable of executing hundreds of MIPS.

Main Memory

The **main memory** of the computer holds data and program instructions. The **bit,** a simple 0 or 1, is the basic unit of data stored by the computer. Bits are formed into groups called **bytes** to represent a letter, digit, or special character (e.g., $, #, @, etc.). The location in memory for each program instruction and piece of data is assigned an address. The computer refers to this address to retrieve the contents of that storage address. The size of memory is measured in **megabytes** (2 to the 10th power) or 1,024,000 bytes. The trend is for larger and larger amounts of main memory with size measured in hundreds of megabytes.

Secondary Storage

Secondary storage includes devices used to store data and program instructions that are inactive. Data and program instructions must be loaded from secondary storage into the main memory of the computer to be executed. Secondary storage devices provide an economical means of storing large amounts of data with minimal risk of loss or destruction. The trend is for secondary storage to be able to transfer data into main memory faster and faster with speed measured in tens of megabytes per second. Another trend is for secondary storage devices to increase in capacity with size measured in **gigabytes** (billions of bytes).

Input Devices

Input devices are used to provide data and instructions to the computer. The trend is to make computers easier to use through the use

Exhibit 2.2
Basic Trends in
Computer
Hardware
Components

Component	Trend	Measure
CPU	Increase in speed	MIPS
Main Memory	Increase in size	Megabytes
Secondary Storage	Increase in data transfer rate	Megabytes/sec
	Increase in size	Gigabytes
Input Devices	Become more natural to use	Ease of use
Output Devices	Multimedia	Quality of output

of input devices that provide a natural user interface such as pen-based systems, which recognize human handwriting, and voice recognition.

Output Devices

Output devices convert electronic bits of data stored in the computer into a form understandable by humans or computer-controlled devices. The trend is to be able to display output to the user in a number of different media, including graphics, audio, video, and text.

Exhibit 2.2 summarizes the basic trends in computer hardware components.

■ CLASSES OF COMPUTERS AND THEIR ROLES

There has never been a commonly accepted definition of the various classes of computers. Indeed, the functions and capabilities of the various classes keep expanding so that even the number of classes is debatable. Instead, there is now a broad spectrum of computing hardware from the supercomputer to the microprocessor, with no sharp line dividing the classes. In general, the computers decrease in size and cost as you go from supercomputer to microcomputer. The raw computing power in terms of MIPS very much overlap among the classes. The supercomputer, mainframe, midrange, workstation, and microcomputer are discussed below. Exhibit 2.3 summarizes characteristics of the various classes of computers.

Exhibit 2.3   A Summary of Basic Characteristics of the Five Computer Types

Characteristics of Typical System	Supercomputer	Mainframe	Minicomputer	Workstation	Microcomputer
Cost	> $5 million	> $1 million	> $25,000	> $5,000	> $1,000
Physical Size	Automobile	Refrigerator	Filing cabinet	Desktop	Desktop
CPU Speed	> 6 Gigaflops	> 100 MIPS	> 50 MIPS	> 40 MIPS	> 10 MIPS
Main Memory	> 4 Gigabytes	> 1 Gigabyte	> 1 Gigabyte	> 256 Megabytes	> 16 Megabytes

Supercomputer

Supercomputers are the largest, fastest, and most expensive systems available. They are extremely powerful computers especially designed for high-speed numeric computation needed in complex applications such as weather forecasting, engineering, and other instances where it is necessary to crunch lots of data quickly. Supercomputers can perform arithmetic calculations at a speed of billions of floating-point operations per second **(gigaflops).** Cray Research, NEC, and Fujitsu are the leading manufacturers of supercomputers. Only a few dozen are purchased each year for use in government agencies, military defense systems, and major corporations. These machines are extremely expensive—starting at $5 million and going up to over $50 million.

Mainframe

The traditional role of the **mainframe** computer was as the large, central (and in many cases, the only) computer resource for the firm (Exhibit 2.4). Mainframes have been the cornerstone of the computing infrastructure in large corporations for many years. From the early 1950s until the late 1960s, virtually all commercial computer processing was mainframe based. Computers were brought into many companies to automate accounting and financial processes such as payroll, general ledger, accounts receivable, and accounts payable. Order processing, billing, and inventory control were other early computer applications.

Today the role of the mainframe is undergoing some remarkable changes as lower-cost midrange and microcomputers become increas-

Exhibit 2.4
Mainframe
Computer

Courtesy of International Business Machines Corporation.

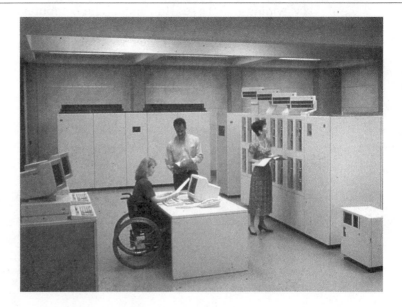

ingly more powerful. The mainframe with its strong security, connectivity, and data management capabilities can provide these services:

Security The mainframe controls corporate security and user authentication services. It monitors and permits users to access resources on the corporate network.

Network Management The mainframe provides central services for monitoring and controlling the corporate network.

Enterprise-wide Backup The mainframe provides prodigious amounts of storage capacity for use in backing up files and data bases created on other combinations of hardware and software.

Data Management The corporate repository (a directory of what data is stored where, data definitions and standards, and various data and system models) resides on the mainframe.

Tool Repository Mainframes are a computer version of the tool crib in the machine shop. Application developers throughout a firm can share tools and development procedures stored on the mainframe.

Batch Processing Systems that require large amounts of data and processing, such as corporate payroll, process on the mainframe.

As of 1994, mainframe computers can crunch numbers at a rate of over forty MIPS and cost over $1 million for a fully configured system.

The mainframe itself must reside in a specially controlled environment—a computer room or data center with special heating, venting, and air-conditioning (HVAC) equipment to control the temperature, humidity, and dust level around the computer. Most mainframes are kept in a secured data center with limited access to the room through some type of security system.

IBM has been the dominant world manufacturer of mainframe computers since the mid-1950s. Unisys (a company formed from the merger of Burroughs Corporation and Sperry Corporation in 1986) is a distant second to IBM. Amdahl, National Advanced Systems, Hitachi, and Fujitsu are manufacturers who sell what are called **plug-compatible** systems to IBM. Their hardware can run the IBM software including the operating system. The plug-compatible manufacturers (PCMs) attempt to deliver better price, performance, or service than IBM. For the PCMs to succeed, they must be able to react quickly to IBM's lead in new product and development changes.

Midrange Computers

The **midrange** computer was formerly called the minicomputer and was confined to a relatively narrow range between the mainframe and the still-embryonic **microcomputer.** Computer hardware manufacturers saw the minicomputer as the ideal way to provide their customers with a low-cost entry system with a large growth capacity. As a result, this class of computer expanded rapidly through the 1970s and 1980s.

Minicomputers were originally designed to handle a limited set of jobs and peripheral devices. As a result, they are physically smaller and less costly than mainframe computers. The earliest applications of minicomputers were in the late 1960s in engineering and scientific areas. Minicomputers (or their bigger brothers and sisters, the super-minicomputers) are still common in those areas. Later, minicomputers were brought to bear against the problems of small businesses. The use of minicomputers grew rapidly because of their relatively low cost, ease of operation and support, and the ready availability of software to solve business problems. Soon business managers were acquiring minicomputers to support the operations of their business unit. Thus began a significant trend: moving away from the large, central mainframe and distributing computer power into the hands of the end users.

Minicomputers gained their greatest popularity as **departmental computers** or work group systems. In this role, the business functions of an organizational unit are supported by the minicomputer. For example, a minicomputer could be used to support the credit and accounts receivable organization. They also serve in manufacturing environments as process control computers and plant computers.

High-end minicomputers are more powerful than some mainframes. Midrange computers cost from $10,000 to over $1 million fully configured. The IBM AS/400, Digital Equipment Corporation VAX family, and the Hewlett Packard 3000 and 9000 series are the most widely used midrange computers.

Most important, minicomputers can function in ordinary office environments; they do not need to be in an environmentally controlled computer room. They are also relatively easy to operate, certainly compared with mainframe computers. In many cases, office workers can be trained to run them and provide basic support in just a few days.

Workstations

Workstations are computers used to support individual users performing heavy mathematical computing or computer-aided design (CAD). Such users need very powerful CPUs, large amounts of main memory, and extremely high-resolution graphic displays to meet their needs. The difference in computing power between low-end workstations and high-end microcomputers is shrinking fast; some high-end workstations are more powerful than some minicomputers.

Microcomputer

Microcomputers are used to support the more than 60 percent of the work force known as **knowledge workers**—people who spend most of their workday creating, using, and distributing information. They include managers such as executives, department heads, and supervisors; professionals such as engineers, teachers, and bankers; and staff personnel such as secretaries and clerical office personnel. Use of microcomputers is so widespread that it is quite common for knowledge workers to use them for hours each day. It is a rare worker that does not make use of a microcomputer during the course of a work week.

Knowledge workers use the microcomputer and associated software to improve their ability to communicate (word processing and electronic mail), manage their time (time management and calendaring), in project management (estimating and scheduling), and in decision support processes (spreadsheets and statistical analysis).

During the past decade, people have tried to define a microcomputer based on attributes such as cost, processing speed, and physical dimensions, but none of these definitions has proved useful. A microcomputer is also called a personal computer or PC. The label **personal computer** was associated with microcomputers because they were designed for use by one person at a time.

The microcomputer is not to be confused with the **microprocessor,** which is literally a computer on a chip. In a microcomputer, the microprocessor, electronic circuitry for handling input/output signals from the peripheral devices, and memory chips are mounted on a single circuit board called a **motherboard.** It is the motherboard that distinguishes one microcomputer from another.

The processing components of most microcomputers have several empty expansion slots so that you can purchase and plug in optional capabilities in the form of add-on boards. For example, you can purchase more memory, a board that permits graphics output, or a **modem** (a device that permits data communications between computers).

■ COMPUTER HARDWARE COMPONENTS—TECHNICAL TOPICS

Alternative Computer Architectures

Initially computers were serial machines that executed instructions sequentially. This meant that they could perform only one operation at a time. Each operation involved retrieving an instruction from memory, decoding it, fetching data from memory, making a calculation, sending the results to memory, and then starting the process over again. This is called **serial processing.** Serial processing limits the processing speed of the computer and restricts its ability to solve certain kinds of problems. As a result, several other designs are now in vogue.

Parallel Processing

A **parallel processing** design uses multiple ALUs (actually instruction processors) that allow a computer to simultaneously execute multiple instructions (Exhibit 2.5). Parallel processing obviously can be much faster than serial processing since the computer is capable of executing multiple instructions in the same amount of time that it takes a serial processing computer to execute a single instruction. There are two forms of parallel processing: parallel data computers, which simultaneously perform the same operation on many different data items; and

Exhibit 2.5
Comparison of Serial, Parallel, and Coupled Processors

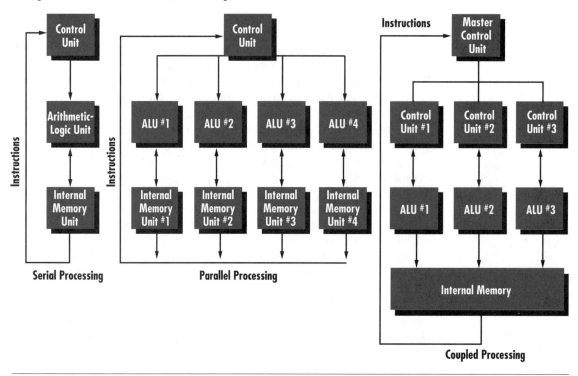

parallel process computers, which divide a problem into many small parts that are each solved by a separate computer. Some massive parallel designs contain thousands of processors and are based on simple models of the human brain's meshlike network of interconnected processing elements called neurons. Such computers are called neural networks.

Coupled Processors

With a **coupled processor** design, the computer actually has more than one complete CPU which allows it to perform multiprocessing, i.e., to execute more than one instruction at the same time (Exhibit 2.5). This provides for more work to get done at the same time. There are two types of coupled processors: asymmetric and symmetric. In **asymmetric multiprocessing** systems, each processor handles a different task. One processor may handle general processing while the other handles input/output operations. In **symmetric multiprocessing,** any processor can handle any task. Special operating systems (discussed in the next chapter) are required to distribute processing tasks to any processor that is available. In addition to providing a high level of processing speed, coupled processors are used by some manufacturers to provide a high-reliability or fault tolerant design. In the event that one CPU fails, the other can replace it.

Moore's Law

In the 1960s, shortly after patenting the integrated circuit, Gordon Moore, chairman of the board of Intel, formulated what is now known as Moore's Law. This hypothesis states that transistor (the microscopic on/off switches or the microprocessor's brain cells) densities on a single chip will double every 18 months. Moore's Law has held up amazingly well over the years as can be seen from Exhibit 2.6. If this trend continues, the amount of computing capacity available in the year 2000 will be measured in billions of instructions executed per second! A brief chronology of the evolution of Intel microprocessors is presented below.

In 1981, IBM tapped Intel to provide the microprocessor for the original IBM PC. This processor was called the Intel 8088 microprocessor and ran at 4.77 MHz. The 8088 communicated with other peripherals—disk, video—along a bus that is 8 bits wide and handled internal calculations 8 bits at a time.

In 1983, IBM announced the IBM-PC AT computer using the Intel 80286 processor. The 80286 communicates using a 16-bit bus and performs internal calculations 16 bits at a time.

The 80386DX chip performs internal calculations 32 bits at a time and talks to RAM along a 32-bit bus, but communicates with peripherals along a 16-bit path to maintain compatibility with existing devices. Originally shipped as a 16 MHz processor, versions were also built to run at 20, 25, and 33 MHz.

Exhibit 2.6
Moore's Law

Reprinted by permission of Intel Corporation, Copyright/Intel Corporation 1993.

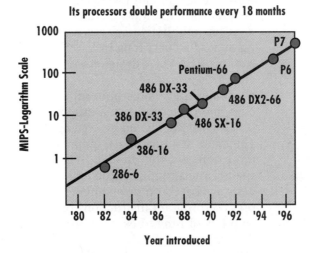

Keeping Up With The Intels

Its processors double performance every 18 months

The 80386SX chip was introduced in 1988 as a low-cost alternative to the full 32-bit implementation of the 80386DX. Instead of using a 32-bit bus to communicate with RAM, the SX uses the same 16-bit bus used by the AT class computers, while performing internal calculations 32 bits at a time.

The 80486, also called the i486, operates at 16, 33, and 66 MHz, thus offering even greater speed than the 80386DX.

Intel's latest generation processor, the Pentium, a marketing name for the 80586, is an engineering marvel. Pentium incorporates more than 3 million transistors on a single silicon chip. And, with a performance rating of 100 MIPS, it computes as fast as a mainframe.

Alternative Microprocessor Designs

The **control unit** of the CPU contains a block of circuits that enables this device to fetch data and instructions from main memory, interpret the instructions, and issue commands to other computer components to carry out the required operations. The control unit contains a built-in set of permanent instructions, called **microcode** or instruction sets. You can think of microcode as predefined, elementary circuits and logical operations that the processor performs when it executes an instruction. The microcode determines which transistor switches are open and which are closed to perform a specific operation.

Most CPUs for personal computers and mainframes in the early 1990s were built using the complex instruction set computer (**CISC**) design. CISC chips contain a large amount of microcode. Chip manufacturers have been moving toward RISC designs, which provide less built-in microcodes. RISC chips generally enable faster execution of instructions than CISC chips because each operation requires fewer microcode steps prior to execution. They are also easier and cheaper to make. Exhibit 2.7 illustrates that some overlap exists in the capabilities of these two designs, but that eventually the CISC design will fail to keep pace with computers built with the RISC design. Today, most workstations and an increasing number of minicomputer manufacturers are using the RISC architecture.

Chip manufacturers are beginning to look at another design approach called very long instruction word (**VLIW**) to use in future workstations. The VLIW design may begin to replace the RISC design by the end of the decade.

When RISC chips perform multiple instructions per cycle, an on-chip interpreter must first examine every instruction before executing it to see whether it can be executed in parallel with another instruction. The more instructions a chip executes in one cycle, the bigger and more complex the on-chip interpreter must be and the more time it spends interpreting instructions rather than executing them. The VLIW design is based on development of a software compiler that will interpret the program instructions only once, off-line, which will leave the chip lots of time to execute instructions.

While the CISC design approach may be reaching its limit in terms of processing speed, both the RISC and VLIW designs have plenty of

Exhibit 2.7
Forecasted
Capabilities of
Various Chip
Designs—Years
Approximate

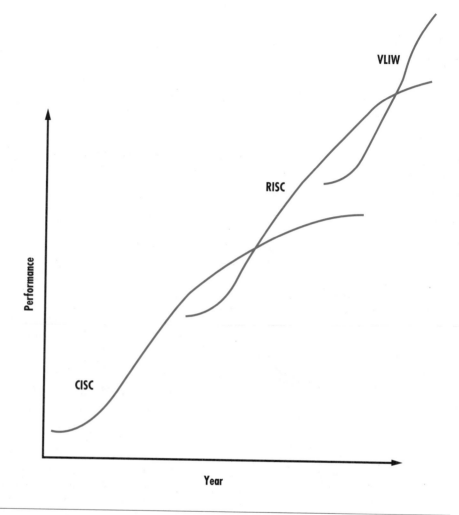

room for improvement. These design approaches indicate that micro-processors will continue to double in power every 18 months on into the 21st century! As a result, the functionality and capability of computers will continue to grow.

Competing Against Intel

In 1992, Intel earned a net profit of $1.1 billion on revenue of $5.8 billion while selling 32 million microprocessors worldwide. Intel has a huge installed base of more than 100 million personal computers and 50,000 software applications written for the 80286, 80386, and 80486 (this combination is often called **80X86**).

However, there is competition. Advanced Micro Devices took over the 386 market with its clone chips and is set to deliver an advanced 486 chip of its own design. Cyrix sold 800,000 of its 486 chips in 1993

Real World Perspective

Infighting Among the Chip Makers

Intel is the major microprocessor chip maker with a market share in excess of 80% of annual sales of chips used for IBM and IBM compatible personal computers. Cyrix and Advanced Micro Devices, Inc. are much smaller companies who compete against Intel. The paragraphs below chronicle the ongoing legal battles among these competitors.

July 1991

The U.S. Federal Trade Commission investigates Intel's business practices within the math coprocessor market in response to antitrust lawsuits filed by Cyrix and Tokyo Cobra Corp. Cyrix charges that Intel took measures to maintain its monopoly in the market. Intel consequently filed a cross-complaint for patent infringement. Tokyo Cobra Corp. sued Intel for breach of contract when Intel cut off its supply of math coprocessors after it began carrying a competing product from Cyrix. Later testimony revealed an Intel policy of punishing distributors who carry products that compete with Intel's.

April 1992

Cyrix claims that it is isolated from Intel's patent claims because SGS-Thomson, who supplies math coprocessors to Cyrix, has a cross-licensing contract with Intel.

June 1992

Texas Instruments (TI) petitions the court to allow it to join the Cyrix suit against Intel involving patents, licenses, and control of the 80X86 microprocessor market. TI claims that a cross-licensing agreement with Intel gives it the right to make and sell chips based on the Intel architecture.

December 1992

Cyrix files for a preliminary injunction against Intel for allegedly harassing and intimidating Cyrix customers. Intel sent letters to Cyrix clients indicating that a royalty of $25 is due Intel for each 80486-based machine purchased. Cyrix purchases its processors from SGS-Thompson, which is licensed by Intel. Intel claims that the processors violate its memory management patent for a microprocessor.

May 1993

Intel asks the International Trade Commission (ITC) to bar from the United States the Slimnote notebook computer made by Twinhead Inc. of Taiwan. The computer uses microprocessors from AMD and Cyrix. Intel asks the ITC to determine whether the Taiwan machines infringe the Crawford patent (the Crawford patent covers the interaction of the 80X86 microprocessor series with external memory and paging software). Cyrix claims that Intel is trying to pressure a foreign customer to submit to a licensing agreement.

June 1993

Cyrix appeals Intel's Crawford patent to the U.S. Patent Office claiming there is substantial evidence of prior art and seeks to have the patent overturned.

August 1993

Cyrix CEO Jerry Rogers states that his firm is not guilty of infringing on Intel's copyrights in Cyrix's efforts to build Intel-compatible microprocessors and math coprocessors. Rogers contends that Intel brought suit to slow competition. Intel has been successful in this strategy, Rogers believes, because it has made venture capital firms reluctant to invest in firms that might compete with Intel. Cyrix has spent well over $4 million on litigation.

August 1993

Intel and Cyrix agree to settle the lawsuit over alleged math coprocessor patent infringement, but the terms will depend on the resolution of another case involving Cyrix's right to manufacture 80X86-based microprocessors. Cyrix claims that it is protected from patent infringement claims because its primary foundry, SGS-Thomson Microelectronics, is licensed to manufacture Intel circuits. Cyrix will pay Intel $2 million for a math coprocessor license if it loses the current court battle; Intel will pay Cyrix $500,000 if the courts find in Cyrix's favor. Intel plans another lawsuit against Cyrix's customers that are using

Continued

the 80X86 architecture. The company claims manufacturers must purchase Intel board-level patent rights. A trial on this issue is scheduled for January 1994.

November 1993

Intel sues Cyrix for trademark infringement in its advertising spoof of Intel's ad "Intel Inside." At the center of the trademark dispute is Intel's $100 million advertising campaign with the trademark of an oblong surrounding the words "Intel Inside." In Cyrix's advertisements the company uses the same oblong surrounding the word "ditto."

December 1993

Lawsuits filed end the partnership between Cyrix and TI, in which Cyrix provided TI with designs for clones of Intel microprocessing chips. Cyrix has now spent over $12 million for various legal disputes with Intel. The $8 billion TI is suing for Cyrix's latest Intel 80486 clone designs. The $73 million Cyrix, which does not have produc-

tion facilities, contends that it terminated partnership in July because TI delivered less than 40% of the chips it agreed to make. Cyrix's countersuit calls for an injunction that will stop production of chips designed by Cyrix. Cyrix's chips account for about 1% of TI's sales.

January 1994

Intel charges that Cyrix is making Intel-compatible devices in an unnamed nonlicensed foundry. Cyrix normally uses TI and SGS-Thomson foundries but has admitted to using the nonlicensed foundry.

January 1994

Cyrix wins a court decision that keeps Intel from charging Cyrix customers a licensing fee for using Cyrix chips. Cyrix also wins $500,000 from Intel in settlement of the math coprocessor dispute. Cyrix agrees to dismiss its antitrust and patent misuse claims against Intel in exchange for Intel's dismissal of its patent infringement claims against Cyrix regarding the Crawford patent.

and is preparing a challenge to Intel's Pentium chip. Both these competitors have been tied up in legal battles with Intel for years over patent infringements and monopolistic behavior.

The PowerPC chip is a new reduced instruction set computing **RISC** processor created by Motorola under an agreement with IBM and Apple Computer. By almost any benchmark, RISC processors run faster than Intel's Pentium processor. And because RISC chips are a simpler design and require less silicon, they're cheaper to produce. The PowerPC chip is designed to provide portable and desktop personal computers the processing power normally associated with much more expensive workstations. For example, the PowerPC has the power to make functions such as voice activation, dictation, pen input, and touch screens practical. Another hoped-for result of the joint design of the PowerPC chip is that it will enable IBM and Apple to create a product line that can run one another's applications. In other words, IBM systems will be able to run Macintosh software and Macintosh systems will be able to run IBM software.

Main Memory Types

There are two basic forms of memory chips, ROM and RAM, and each form has a couple variations as shown in Exhibit 2.8.

In **ROM,** data and instructions are stored in binary form with a permanent set of switches in the chip. Even if power is lost, the con-

Exhibit 2.8
Memory Types

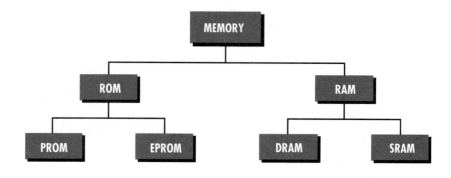

tents of the ROM chip are maintained. ROM can be read but not erased or overwritten. Thus the instructions to be executed during the start-up of a personal computer are stored in ROM memory. As soon as the computer is turned on, instructions are read from ROM to boot up the system. Because the instructions on the ROM chip are permanent, they are often called firmware to differentiate them from the programmable, volatile instructions that the user places in RAM. Programmable Read Only Memory (**PROM**) and Erasable Programmable Read Only Memory (**EPROM**) are variations of ROM memory.

In **RAM,** storage is accomplished by the use of "flip-flops," mini-ature transistors on a chip that act as switches to store the information in binary form. Each bit of information corresponds to one transistor (switch), which is turned on if the bit equals 1, or left off if the bit equals 0. The miniaturized transistors on the memory chip must be maintained in an "on" or "off" state by a constant electric current. Once the current is removed by turning the computer off, the transistors lose the stored information. RAM is thus called volatile memory. Each bit of RAM memory can be both read and updated. Thus RAM memory is also called read/write memory.

RAM chips come in two basic forms: DRAM and SRAM. Dynamic RAM (**DRAM**) chips use one transistor switch and a tiny storage device called a capacitor to store one bit of data. The capacitors must be energized hundreds of times each second to continue to hold the bit of information. Static RAM (**SRAM**) chips use transistors that do not require constant energizing but that are more expensive than DRAM. Data can be accessed from SRAM chips about twice as fast as it can be from the DRAM chips. Thus SRAM chips are often used in very fast memory called cache memory.

Memory chips are typically installed on a plug-in board called a single inline memory module (**SIMM**).

Secondary Storage Devices

There are many different types of secondary storage devices as listed in Exhibit 2.9 and briefly summarized below.

Exhibit 2.9
Secondary Storage
Devices

Magnetic Tape
DAT Tape
Diskettes
Magnetic Disk
    Hard Drive
    Disk Pack
    RAID
Optical Disk Storage
    Laser Disks
    Compact Disk—Read Only Memory
    Write Once, Read Many Disks
    Erasable Optical Disks

Magnetic Tape

Magnetic tape is a common form of low-cost, high-volume, sequential data storage. The magnetic tape is coated with ferrous oxide on which bits of data can be stored by selectively magnetizing spots on the tape. The old-style magnetic reel-to-reel tapes (Exhibit 2.10) are being replaced by cartridge tapes (Exhibit 2.11). The old reel-to-reel tapes were 16 inches in diameter, had a capacity of 100 million bytes of data, could transfer data at the rate of 1.8 million bytes per second, and cost about $20 per tape.

DAT Tape

The newer cartridge tapes, called **DAT tapes,** (Exhibit 2.11) are only 5 inches square, can store more than 600 million bytes of data, are able to transfer data at the rate of 9 million bytes per second, and cost less than $5.

Diskettes

Diskettes are the most common form of storage for personal computers. Diskettes come in two sizes: 5 1/4 inches and 3 1/2 inches in di-

Exhibit 2.10
Reel-to-Reel
Magnetic Tape

*Courtesy of International
Business Machines
Corporation.*

Exhibit 2.11
Cartridge Tape

ameter (Exhibit 2.12). The head window is the area of the diskette that comes in contact with the read/write head of the disk drive as it rubs against the diskette to read/write data. For data recording purposes, the diskette is divided into sectors with the number and sizes of sectors depending upon the type of diskette and the operating system. The process by which the operating system creates sectors and records codes on the diskette to identify each track and sector is called formatting. During the formatting process, a content list for the diskette, called the file allocation table (FAT), is recorded on a specific sector and track. The disk controller and operating system use the FAT to locate programs and data so that the read/write head can move directly to the proper position on the disk.

Magnetic Hard Disk

The **magnetic disk** (Exhibit 2.13) is a metal disk coated with ferrous oxide. As with the magnetic tape, a bit pattern is magnetically encoded onto the ferrous oxide to represent bits of data. The disk spins like a CD in the disk drive and read/write heads move over the disk to reach any data directly rather than searching sequentially as in the case for magnetic tapes. Compared with diskettes, the data and programs stored on the hard disk can be accessed much faster. Furthermore, diskettes hold 1.44 million bytes while hard disks have a capacity of 1 gigabyte or more. The hard disk must be stored in a protected environment to keep dust, smoke, and hair out of the drive. Thus, the hard

Exhibit 2.12
Diskettes

*Courtesy of Verbatim
Corporation.*

disk and its drive are usually built into the personal computer with an air filtration and movement system.

MAGNETIC DISK PACK Although microcomputers and workstations use a single hard disk, several magnetic disks can be grouped together as shown in Exhibit 2.14 to form a **magnetic disk pack.** Disk packs are a common form of direct access storage for minicomputers, mainframes, and supercomputers.

Exhibit 2.13
Personal Computer
Magnetic Hard
Drive

*Courtesy of International
Business Machines
Corporation.*

Exhibit 2.14
Magnetic Disk Pack

RAID   Redundant arrays of independent disks (**RAID**) are an option for the traditional magnetic disk packs. RAID disks are configured to work in parallel, reading or writing data simultaneously. They are designed to provide highly reliable data backup and recovery features. If an individual disk in the disk pack is unreadable, the RAID system can still recover all data from the other disks in the array. All RAID disks are managed by the computer's I/O system. The RAID array of disks appears to the CPU as a single disk. The RAID subsystem receives I/O requests from the CPU, calculates redundancy information, and writes both the original I/O request and redundancy information to the individual disks. All operations and calculations are performed by the subsystem, with no involvement from the host CPU. RAID systems are generally more expensive than traditional large disk drive systems, but they offer benefits, including **fault tolerance,** high availability, and improved I/O performance.

Optical Disk Storage

With **optical storage** media, a laser burns bits of information onto the surface of a shiny disk. Another laser, in the optical disk drive reads the information from the disk. This form of storage enables prodigious amounts of information to be stored on a single disk. There are four types of optical disks summarized below.

LASER DISK   **Laser disks** have been in use since the mid-1980s for storing text, audio, and video information (Exhibit 2.15). A laser disk

Exhibit 2.15
Laser Disks

Photo Courtesy of 3M Corporation.

has storage capacity in excess of 1 gigabyte (1 billion bytes), which is roughly equivalent to 500,000 pages of text. One side of a laser disk can store 30 minutes of motion video or 54,000 individual video scenes with a much higher resolution than a videocassette recorder.

COMPACT DISK—READ ONLY MEMORY   **CD-ROM** is the data storage equivalent of the popular CD audio medium. A single CD-ROM can store more than 650 megabytes of data—equivalent to 450 1.44 megabyte diskettes, or 200,000 typed pages or 1,000 books! CD-ROM is an ideal medium for economical distribution of software and databases. There are over 3 million CD-ROM players in American homes and offices, and CD-ROM players will soon be standard issue with every new desktop personal computer. Hundreds of CD-ROM titles are currently available with hundreds more being developed each year (Exhibit 2.16).

WRITE ONCE, READ MANY DISKS   **WORM** disks can be written to once, and then only read. Typical uses of WORM involve combining the use of a scanner device with laser technology. For example, all purchase orders for several years could be scanned and the digitized images stored on a WORM disk. This saves paper storage space requirements and enables rapid searching of documents.

ERASABLE OPTICAL DISKS   The other forms of optical disk storage mentioned here all have the shortcoming that they are read only. **Erasable optical disks** enable the user to write, read, and erase data and/or instructions.

Exhibit 2.16
A Brief List of Some of the More Popular CD-ROM Titles

The Concise Columbia Encyclopedia
The American Heritage Dictionary
Roget's Thesaurus
Bartlett's Familiar Quotations
Hammond Atlas
The World Almanac and Book of Facts
Business Periodical Indices
DeLorme Street Atlas (contains street maps to any place in the United States)
Dow Jones Stock Prices
World Atlas (includes 1,000 color photos and 300 detailed topics)
Grolier's Encyclopedia (21 volumes and 33,000 articles on one disk)
Library of the Future (complete text of 950 historical and classical titles)
Monarch Notes (Monarch notes for over 700 historical and classical titles)
U.S. History (contains every word of over 107 U.S. history books)
The National Yellow Pages (4 CD-ROMs, millions of entries)
Thomas's Register (25 volume directory of American manufacturers)
Time Magazine (5,000 articles from *Time*'s inception in 1923 to 1989)
PhoneDisc USA (72 million residential and 9 million business telephone listings)
Accumail (the nation's Zip Codes and mailing information)

Input Devices

While there are many input device types, two of the more interesting are voice recognition and pen-based systems, which are discussed below. These input devices illustrate the trend toward providing a natural user interface.

Pen-Based Systems

Many users are uncomfortable with keyboarding. Perhaps they have never learned to type or they feel typing is an activity inappropriate for them (some executives still feel this way). Other users are in a situation where keyboarding is impractical (police writing a report or ticket, food service workers taking food and beverage orders) or could disrupt others around them (students taking notes in a lecture hall or participants trying to capture key points during the meeting). A **pen-based system** offers what many users have long wanted, a system that allows them to input information by writing, much as they would on a sheet of paper.

Notebook sized personal computers are available that contain software to recognize and digitize handwriting and drawings. These devices have a pressure sensitive layer like a graphics pad under their slatelike liquid crystal display screen. Instead of writing on a paper form fastened to a clipboard and then later keying this information into the computer, a special pen or stylus is used to enter handwritten data directly into the computer. The stylus emits a faint signal from its tip digitizing the screen and turning it dark wherever the stylus touches. Pattern recognition software then recognizes the letters, numbers, punctuation marks, and other symbols and stores them in memory for processing. The software can be taught to recognize the user's handwriting, so that any handwritten symbols, including shorthand and scientific notation, can be coverted to text within the computer.

Voice Recognition Input

Voice recognition input of data has become technically and economically feasible for a number of applications where operators need to perform data entry without using their hands to key in data or instructions. Practical applications include support of people who perform inspection activities, inventory and quality control of products, and airline and parcel delivery workers for voice-directed sorting of baggage and parcels.

Voice recognition systems analyze and classify speech patterns and convert them into digital codes. Most voice recognition systems require "training" the computer to recognize a limited vocabulary of standard words for each user. Operators train the system to recognize their voices by repeating each word to be added to the vocabulary several times. Trained systems can achieve a 99 percent plus word recognition rate.

Speaker-independent voice recognition systems allow a computer to understand a voice it has never heard. Such systems do not have as high an accuracy rate as a trained system. In this case, the computer must be able to recognize more than one pronunciation of the same word—imagine trying to understand the same word or phrase spoken by someone from Louisville, New Orleans, Chicago, or Los Angeles! Throw in English-speaking people from other countries and you can begin to appreciate the challenge.

Voice input will have truly arrived when it is fast and accurate enough to support dictation and automatic capture of words into a document for further editing by word processing software. This will require extremely intelligent systems that can understand continuous speech from multiple users. Such a breakthrough will enable many more people to use computers in a variety of interesting new applications.

Printers

Printed material is one of the most common forms of computer output. Printers are generally divided into two types—impact and nonimpact. **Impact printers** form characters and other images on paper through the impact of a printing mechanism against a sheet of paper. The printing mechanism may be a print wheel, cylinder, chain, an inked ribbon, or a roller. Multiple copies can be produced at once if the printing mechanism strikes the paper with sufficient force to transmit the image onto multiple pages. The dot matrix printer uses short print wires that form a character as a grouping or matrix of dots.

Nonimpact printers are quieter than impact printers, since the sound of a printing mechanism striking the paper is eliminated. However, they are unable to produce multiple concurrent copies. Laser printers and ink jet printers are two common forms of printers used to produce high-speed, high-quality prints. The laser printer uses a laser light to write dots on a drum coated with toner similar to that used in a copier. These printers produce a very high-quality print since they use 600 or more dots to the inch to form characters. Because they print an entire page at a time, laser printers are often called page printers. The ink jet printer forms dots on paper by spraying ink from a row of tiny nozzles.

Printers are often compared on quality of print (measure = dots per inch or **dpi**) and speed (measure = pages per minute).

Monitors

The **monitor** is a TV screenlike device on which output from the computer is displayed. Because the monitor uses a cathode ray tube to display images it is sometimes called a **CRT** (Exhibit 2.17). It is also called a video display tube (**VDT**).

The monitor works in much the same manner as a TV screen—one or more electron beams are generated from cathode ray tubes. As the beams strike a phosphorescent compound (phosphor) coated on the inside of the screen, a dot on the screen called a pixel lights up. The electron beam sweeps back and forth across the screen so that as the phosphor starts to fade, it is struck again by the beam and lights up again.

Monitors are available in monochrome or color versions. Monochrome monitors use one color for the background and a different color for the foreground text; color monitors are able to display multiple colors.

Exhibit 2.17
Operation of a
Cathode Ray Tube

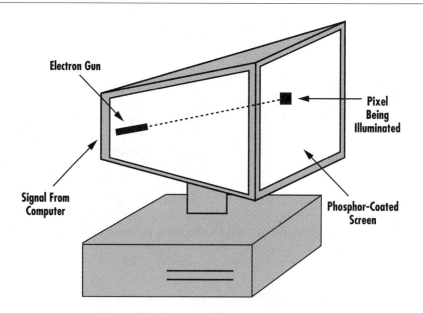

Electron Gun

Pixel
Being
Illuminated

Signal From
Computer

Phosphor-Coated
Screen

Exhibit 2.18   Comparison of Various Monitors and Adapters—Capabilities as of Spring 1994

Type Monitor	Year Introduced	Resolution	Number of Colors
Text-only Monochrome Monitor	1981	560 × 225	1
Text-only Monochrome with Hercules Graphics Card	1982	720 × 348	1
Color/Graphics Adapter with Red Green Blue (RGB) Color Monitor	1983	320 × 200	4
Enhanced Graphics Adapter with Enhanced Color Display Monitor	1984	640 × 350	16 with bright and soft shades
Video Graphics Array with VGA Analog Monitor	1987	540 × 480	8 colors with 32 shades
Super VGA/XGA	1989	1,280 × 1,024	16 million colors from which to choose to display 256 colors on screen

One way to measure the quality of the monitor is by its pixel density and dot pitch. Pixel density is the number of horizontal pixels by the number of vertical pixels (e.g. 1024 × 768). For two monitors of the same screen size, the monitor with the higher number of pixels has the higher resolution and a sharper picture. The distance between one phosphor dot on the screen and the next nearest dot of the same color is known as **dot pitch.** Pitch of .28 mm or less is considered good. Greater pixel densities and smaller dot pitches yield sharper images of higher resolution.

The original IBM PC introduced in 1981 came with a text-only monochrome monitor. The capabilities of monitors have continually improved as summarized in Exhibit 2.18.

Because CRT monitors use an electron gun, there must be a distance of over one foot between the gun and the screen, causing them to be fairly large and bulky. Thus a different technology, **flat screen display,** is used for portable personal computers and laptops. One common technology for flat screen displays is the same liquid crystal display technology used for pocket calculators and digital watches. **LCD** technology uses a thin layer of liquid crystal molecules placed between two sheets of glass and separated into sections. An individual liquid crystal molecule is made opaque when voltage is applied to it, resulting in a dark spot on a light background, equivalent to a pixel in a CRT monitor. Flatscreen displays using LCD have a low-power requirement so they can be used in the laptop portables, and new technology is constantly improving the quality of this type of display.

Another flat screen technology is the **plasma display** device. Plasma displays are generated by electrically charged particles of gas (plasma) trapped between glass plates. Plasma display units are significantly more expensive than CRT and LCD units. However, they use less power, provide a faster display speed, and produce clearer displays that are easier to see from any angle and in any lighting conditions.

■ DOWNSIZING

A recent trend has been **downsizing**—migrating applications off the mainframe onto smaller, less expensive computers such as workstations or midrange computers. Firms that have downsized do so primarily to save costs of the IT staff required to run and maintain the mainframe. They also find they are able to develop applications more quickly by acquiring software packages readily available for the midrange computers. Downsizing also makes computing more responsive to the users. By shifting applications to business units, the user has much more control over development priorities and processing. Firms also achieve more flexibility to implement new technologies by leaving the proprietary mainframe world. In addition, downsizing allows firms to respond more quickly to new business conditions.

Downsizing has its disadvantages. Network issues (see Chapter 4) are the top trouble spot. One key issue is the need to secure the network against unauthorized access. Another set of issues arises because users are not familiar with the traditional IT disciplines of backup, disaster planning, and documentation. Downsizing also creates friction with old-line data processing professionals and their management. These people are reluctant to believe that there are advantages to migrating applications off the mainframe.

Summary

Management has a key role in overseeing the definition and implementation of information technology that meets the needs of the business.

There are five hardware components that make up every computer: the Central Processing Unit (CPU), main memory, secondary storage, input devices, and output devices.

The CPU is increasing in speed, main memory is increasing in capacity, secondary storage devices are increasing in speed and capacity, input devices are becoming more natural to use, and output devices are moving to multimedia.

Supercomputers are the largest, fastest, and most expensive systems available and are used by large organizations to meet their need for high-speed computations.

The role of the mainframe computer is changing from the single, large, central data processing resource to that of overall systems manager, data manager, communications manager, and computer-intensive server.

The role of the midrange computer is as a department computer supporting the business needs of an organizational unit.

Workstations support individual users performing heavy mathematical computing or CAD.

Microcomputers support the more than 60% of the workforce known as the knowledge worker.

Initially computers were serial machines that executed instructions sequentially; however, other designs are now in vogue including parallel processing and coupled processors.

Moore's Law states that transistor densities on a single chip will double every 18 months—thus continuing to bring us increasingly powerful computers.

CISC, RISC, and VLIW are alternative microprocessor designs with overlapping performance capabilities.

Main memory of the computer is made from semiconductor storage devices that hold data and program instructions. The two primary forms of memory are RAM and ROM.

Secondary storage devices provide an economical means of storing large amounts of data with minimal risk of loss or destruction.

Input devices are used to communicate with the computer—to get data and instructions into the computer. Pen-based systems and voice recognition systems are two examples of how the computer input process is becoming more natural.

Printers are usually classified as either impact or nonimpact.

A wide variety of computer monitors with varying characteristics are available.

Downsizing is the movement of applications off the mainframe onto smaller, less expensive hardware such as workstations or midrange computers in an attempt to reduce costs.

A Manager's Checklist

✔ Are business managers involved in overseeing the investments made in computer hardware?

✔ What classes of computers are in use within your organization?

✔ Do you know if your organization is involved in downsizing of computing hardware?

✔ Do you know who your firm's key hardware vendors are?

✔ Are you using input devices that make the computer–human interface natural?

✔ Are your systems capable of using multimedia output devices?

Key Terms

ALU
asymmetric multiprocessing
bit
byte
CAD
CD-ROM
CISC
control unit
coupled processors
CPU
CRT
DAT tape
departmental computers
diskettes
dot pitch
downsizing
dpi
DRAM
EPROM
erasable optical disks
fault tolerant
flat screen display
gigabytes
gigaflops
impact printer
internal clock
knowledge workers
laser disk
LCD
magnetic disk pack
magnetic hard disk
magnetic tape
mainframe
main memory
megabytes

MH_z
microcode
microcomputer
microprocessor
midrange
MIPS
modem
monitor
Moore's Law
motherboard
nonimpact printer
optical storage disks
parallel processing
pen-based system
pixel
plasma display
plug-compatible
PROM
RAID
RAM
RISC
ROM
secondary storage
serial processing
SIMM
speaker-independent
SRAM
supercomputer
symmetric multiprocessing
VDT
VLIW
voice recognition input
workstation
WORM
80X86 microprocessor

Review Questions

1. Name the five basic hardware components found in every computer and state their purpose.

2. What is the trend for each of the five basic hardware components of a computer?

3. Name the five classes of computers.

4. What is the difference between parallel processors and coupled processors?

5. What is the difference between CISC, RISC, and VLIW? What are the implications of these alternative chip designs?

6. Define the term downsizing and state one advantage and one disadvantage of this approach to meeting computing needs.

7. Sketch a simple diagram showing the various forms of main memory.

8. Name 11 different forms of secondary storage devices. Why are secondary storage devices needed?

9. How is the speed and quality of printers measured?

10. What are the key characteristics for evaluating various computer monitors?

Discussion Questions

1. Why is it important for business managers to understand computer hardware?

2. How would you summarize what business managers must know about computer hardware?

3. Discuss the evolving roles of the microcomputer, workstation, midrange, mainframe, and supercomputer.

4. State Moore's Law. Is it an absolute law of physics? What are its implications?

5. In what ways has Intel made it difficult for its competition? Do you think Intel has operated fairly? Why or why not?

6. What do you think are the implications of developing highly accurate pen-based and/or voice recognition systems?

Recommended Readings

1. Arinze, Bay. *Microcomputers for Managers.* Belmont, CA: Wadsworth, Inc. 1994.

2. Bates, Ken. "RAIDing Your Host." DEC professional, February 1993.

3. Burrows, Peter and Ira Sager. "Servers: A PC Money Machine." *Business Week,* March 28, 1994.

4. Corcoran, Cate. "PC Makers Look Beyond RISC to Faster VLIW Systems." *Infoworld,* January 17, 1994.

5. Holzberg, Carol S. "Chips Off the Old Block: Intel's 486 Family." *PC Novice,* April 1994.

6. Hsu, Jeffrey. "Making Sense of Monitors." *PC Novice,* February 1994.

7. Kidder, Tracy. *The Soul of a New Machine.* Boston: Atlantic-Little, Brown, 1981.

8. McKeown, Patrick G. *Living with Computers,* 4th Edition. Orlando, FL: The Dryden Press, Harcourt Brace Jovanovich College Publishers, 1993.

9. Soat, John and Anthony Vecchione. "Leap of Faith." *InformationWeek,* Issue 439, August 23, 1993.

A Manager's Dilemma

Time to Upgrade the Mainframe

ACME Manufacturing and Distributing is a privately held company that makes and sells fastener devices (screws, bolts, clamps, and so on). Sales have varied between $25 to $35 million per year for the past six years. The company earns a profit of roughly 10 percent of sales before taxes.

ACME has been an all-IBM shop ever since it was formed twenty-five years ago. Not just the mainframe computer and microprocessors, but all the peripheral devices—input/output devices and secondary storage—are IBM products. One of the original ACME founders had a lifelong friend who was an IBM salesperson, and there never seemed to be a good enough reason to migrate from IBM. That founder and his friend retired two years ago.

When you were hired six months ago to replace the retiring data center manager, he had passed along to you his advice: "Nobody has ever lost their job recommending IBM." Those words are still ringing in your ears as you ponder the choices for upgrading ACME's main-frame computer. An upgrade is necessary because the current machine is running out of capacity to provide adequate service to the current and indicated future users.

There are a number of midrange computers and peripheral devices that can provide the needed capacity. A quick analysis of several alternatives showed that ACME could save over $50,000 per year by converting to a non-IBM midrange computer.

What are some additional benefits that might be achieved by moving to non-IBM midrange computers? What are all the possible risks and issues that might be raised in making such a move? How would you proceed to make the choice and present your recommendation to the senior executives of the firm?

Moving to Standard Computer Platforms

You are the Controller for a $5 billion retailer with operations throughout the southwestern United States. You have just received a proposal from the Director of Information Technology to spend $10 million for hardware over the next three years to implement standard computer platforms throughout all your retail stores, warehouses, and headquarters. The proposal comes as no surprise, for you have been involved in several discussions leading up to this formal recommendation. While you are generally in agreement with the principle of converting to standard equipment, you still have several questions. Timing is also an issue: the organization is trying to expand nationally over the same time period and will need its cash flow to help pay for the expansion.

Case Study 2.3

Capital Forecasting and Capacity Planning

Kelly looked at the purchase order from the IT Department in disbelief! This was the second time since she had become controller that the IT Department had tried to sneak through a major capital expenditure. This time they planned to spend $3.5 million for a new mainframe computer. Last year it had been $2 million for additional direct access storage devices for the computer.

The frustrating part was that neither time had they followed company procedures for capital forecasting. Thus there was no money set aside for the expenditures. Senior management would have to get involved, and lots of embarrassing questions would be asked. Eventually, the money would be found somewhere, but only after a delay of several months.

Kelly had talked with the IT Manager last time about the need to include anticipated major expenditures in the capital forecast. The manager had just shrugged his shoulders and said, "Yes, I understand you would like us to input to the capital forecast, but it is just impossible for us to forecast the growth in computer usage and hence the additional equipment we will need."

Do you think that it is impossible to estimate the growth of computer usage within the firm? If not, what approach might you use to get a handle on growth? Do you think that it is useless to try to include IT Department input into the capital forecast? Can you identify any way to avoid this problem in the future?

Chapter 3

Computer Software—Trends and Issues

Upon completion of this chapter, you will be able to:

1. Explain the difference between systems software, system development software, and application software and give several examples of each.

2. Discuss the basic functions performed by the operating system and compare the capabilities of the most significant microcomputer operating systems.

3. Discuss the trend in programming languages.

4. Identify the factors that go into the build-versus-buy decision for computer software.

5. State the goal of the open-systems movement and discuss its potential impact on business and the information processing industry.

Preview

Software is a set of instructions that is executed by a computer to accomplish some task. There are three fundamental types of software: systems management software, system development software, and application software. One of the key management decisions with regard to application software is build versus buy—in other words, develop the applications from scratch or purchase a standard software package off the shelf. There is a strong movement toward so-called open systems—systems that will allow computer programs to run on any manufacturer's hardware.

Issues

1. What are the differences between the operating system for a microcomputer and other classes of computers?
2. What are the important trends in programming languages?
3. Why is there increasing use of off-the-shelf software packages?
4. What are open systems and why should you care?

Trade-offs

1. Buy a standard software package off-the-shelf or build software from scratch—how can you decide?
2. Which operating system best meets your needs?
3. How can one evaluate which operating system is superior for a given use?

A Manager Struggles with the Issues

This was the third request this year to purchase a major software package to support one of the firm's fundamental business processes. As the assistant controller of the firm, you understand, and in fact, support the firm's downsizing strategy. This involves moving business applications from the mainframe to powerful, but less expensive minicomputers. However, you had not been told that this strategy would also entail conver-

sion to new software at a cost now exceeding $300,000! You are just now learning that the software on the mainframe will not run on the operating system of the minicomputers. Why hadn't this been discussed? What other software packages must be purchased? Why aren't the in-house programmers developing these applications rather than spending so much money for packages?

■ WHY MANAGERS NEED TO UNDERSTAND COMPUTER SOFTWARE

Software is a set of instructions that is executed by a computer to accomplish some task. There are three fundamental types of software: system management software, system development software, and application software, as shown in Exhibit 3.1. **System management software** controls and coordinates the operation of the various components and peripheral devices of a computer system. **System development software** enables programmers and end users to develop programs and complete systems to meet their needs. **Application software** runs on top of systems software and enables users to perform specific tasks with the computer.

Software gives your hardware a personality and defines how users will interact with the computer. Without software, computer hardware would be useless. Indeed, it was the introduction of VisiCalc, an early spreadsheet software package, that clearly demonstrated that the computer could make work easier. Over 200,000 copies of VisiCalc were sold the first two years it was on the market. This software dramatically stimulated sales for the Apple II and IBM-PC microcomputers.

Business managers increasingly find themselves in a position of approving major software expenditures. It may be software to support a new corporate initiative to create new products and services based on information technology. Or it may be for new personal productivity software to support members of the manager's department. Business managers must understand the various kinds of software and how the pieces interoperate to make computers useful. They cannot afford to make a mistake such as purchasing application software that cannot run with the existing systems software. They are well advised to use resources from the IT organization in making their purchasing decision, however, they must know enough to be able to communicate their needs and to ask intelligent questions to explore various options.

Exhibit 3.1
Classes of Software

System Management Software	System Development Software	Application Software

Operating Systems	**Programming Languages**	**General Purpose**
Database Management	**Language Translators**	**Application Specific**
Teleprocessing Monitors		
Performance Monitors		
Security Monitors		

■ SYSTEM MANAGEMENT SOFTWARE

System management software includes programs that manage and control the resources and operations of the computer system as it performs various information processing tasks. Systems management software includes the operating system, database management system, teleprocessing monitors, performance monitors, and security monitors as outlined in Exhibit 3.1.

The Operating System

The most important component of system management software is the **operating system,** an integrated set of programs that manages the user interface to the computer, governs the execution of tasks, manages input/output and storage resources, performs file management, and provides various support services as the computer executes the application programs of users. The operating system can be thought of as establishing the personality of the hardware by providing users and their program access to the physical resources of the computer (Exhibit 3.2).

The primary differences between the operating systems for microcomputers and other classes of computers are the number of users and the complexity of the peripheral devices to be managed. The other classes of computers are usually multiuser machines with users numbering in the hundreds or even thousands, while most microcomputers are single-user machines, although multiuser systems are becoming available. Mainframe operating systems are extremely large, complex programs that require a staff of specially trained system programmers to maintain them. Personal computer operating systems are less complex and must be able to operate without any day-to-day maintenance.

Operating Systems Functions

Manages the User Interface

The user interface allows the user to communicate with the computer to accomplish tasks such as load programs, read files, and create di-

Exhibit 3.2
The Role of the Operating System

Operating System:
  Manages User Interface
  Governs Execution of Tasks
  Manages Input/Output and Secondary Storage Devices
  Performs File Management
  Provides Support Services

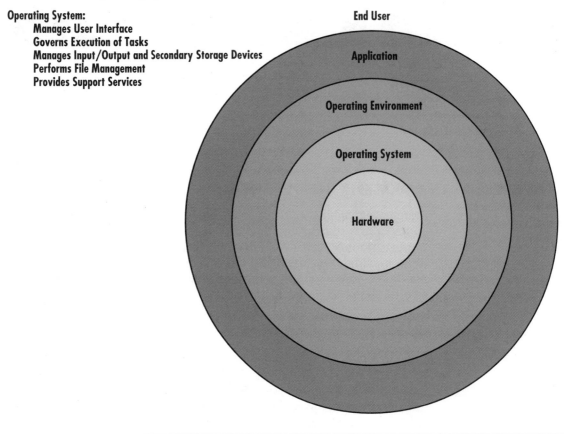

rectories to store data. Early operating systems were command driven systems that required users to enter brief, arcane commands (e.g., copy *.* b:, to copy the contents of a file to a diskette). Later operating systems were menu driven where users selected choices from menus of options. The most popular approach today is a graphical user interface (**GUI**) where a mouse is used to point and click on icons that represent the desired action. If the user knows the meaning of the icon, then it is not necessary to learn any operating system commands (e.g., a user can erase a file by pointing to a file folder icon and then dragging it to a trash can icon). Clicking on an icon sets off actions within the computer that includes toolboxes to paint the screen, coprocessors to perform intense computations, device drivers for reading disks and printing, and communications between applications. The GUI operating system approach was pioneered by the Xerox Palo Alto Research Center in the 1970s.

The user interface of command driven or menu driven operating systems can be enhanced by the use of operating environments such as Microsoft Windows or Desqview to add a graphical user interface. These packages serve as a shell to provide icon displays and support the use of a mouse. They also can interconnect several separate application packages so that they can communicate and work together to share data files. They also allow the output of several programs to be displayed at the same time in multiple windows.

Governs the Execution of Tasks

The task management routines of an operating system manage the operation of the CPU by interleaving periods of CPU activity among tasks and programs.

Multiprogramming is the ability to execute multiple programs concurrently through a sharing of the computer's resources. The CPU can execute only one program instruction at a time, however, it is much faster than the other components of the computer. Thus the CPU would be idle if it did nothing while waiting for data to be transferred from secondary storage to main memory or to an output device. A multiprogramming operating system takes advantage of this fact by allowing another program to use the CPU when it would otherwise be idle. By switching back and forth between different programs and tasks, the operating system is able to give users the impression that they are the only one using the system.

Multitasking provides multiprogramming capabilities to single-user operating systems. Multitasking allows the user to run two or more programs at the same time. Thus a user may be updating a spreadsheet at the same time that a long text document is being spell checked using a word processor. Multitasking is becoming an important feature of advanced microcomputer operating systems such as Windows NT and OS/2, which are discussed later.

Manages Input/Output and Secondary Storage Devices

The operating system supervises input and output to and from the computer. It specifies how devices such as keyboards, printers, scanners, and monitors are used. For example, for keyboards, this would include specifying where the keyboard storage locations buffers are located in RAM, how data are routed from RAM to actual physical output channels, and the protocols or standards for coding and transmitting the data.

Manages Internal Memory

Memory management programs keep track of where programs and data are stored. Reliable memory management becomes especially important when more than one program can run on the computer at the same time. **Virtual memory** is one approach to memory management pioneered on mainframe computers in the early 1970s. With virtual memory, main memory is subdivided into a number of pages or sections that match equal-size sections of memory on secondary storage. The sections of memory stored on secondary storage are referred to as virtual memory. Pieces of main memory are exchanged, or swapped, with the virtual memory when needed. Processing proceeds as normal as long as the data and instructions currently in main memory are all that is needed. However, when the needed data or instructions are on secondary storage, a page is swapped into main memory from virtual memory. The CPU tries to anticipate which pages from virtual memory will be needed next. As a result, the apparent main memory is greater than the actual main memory with minimal loss of processing speed. In this manner, a computer with virtual memory can process larger programs and greater amounts of data than the capacity its main memory circuits would normally allow. Virtual memory is used in mainframes today and greatly increases the ability of these machines to run multiple jobs at high speeds. Virtual memory can also be used with the 80386 and later personal computers to expand their memory capacity.

Performs File Management

The operating system contains file management routines to control the creation of, access to, and deletion of files of data and programs. File management also involves keeping track of the physical location of files on secondary storage devices, so the operating system maintains a directory of information about the location and characteristics of stored files.

Provides Support Services

The operating system includes many utility programs that provide disk and file management functions to perform such functions as formatting disks; creating, deleting, and selecting directories and subdirectories; listing files; creating, copying, naming, and deleting files; and displaying and printing file contents.

Additional System Management Software

In addition to the operating system, there are several other system management software programs including data base management systems, telecommunications monitors, security monitors, and performance monitors. These programs are discussed briefly below.

Data Base Management System

A data base is a well-defined and managed collection of data that serves as a common source of information for many users in many different organizations within the company. It contains facts of significant value to many people. For example, consider a large consumer goods company that sells its products through retail stores. Its customers are the retail stores (the people who visit the store to purchase products are consumers). Each retailer may have many different store locations and a different headquarters location for corporate offices. Many different groups within the consumer products company need different facts about customers. Sales is interested in customer name, store locations, and the salesperson assigned to the account. Credit needs to know the customer credit rating and outstanding accounts receivable balance. Accounts receivable needs to know amount owed and billing address. Shipping needs to know the ship-to address. The customer data base contains basic information about customers useful to all these people. It is a shared data resource that is the definitive source of customer data.

A **data base management system** is a software program that provides an interface between applications programs and the data base. It manages the access and storage of data and prohibits access to data by unauthorized users. The role of the data base management system is to facilitate the creation, maintenance, access, backup, and security of the data base. There are three main components to a data base management system, which will be discussed further in Chapter 5.

Telecommunications Monitor

The **telecommunications monitor** is a program used in a network where a mainframe computer serves as the host computer to support dozens or even hundreds of concurrent users. This program runs in the mainframe computer or possibly in a hardware device called a front end processor (Chapter 4). The monitor controls and supports the data communications related activities occurring in a telecommunications environment as described in Chapter 4. Specific functions performed by the monitor include: executes the introductory "handshaking" required to initiate communications between a device and the host, polls devices asking them one at a time if they wish to transmit to the host, edits incoming and outgoing messages, queues messages to a direct access storage device or main memory, intercepts messages containing errors and initiates corrective action, passes messages to application programs, places messages from application programs into a message queue for transmission, and logs a copy of each message onto secondary storage in the event of a system failure.

Security Monitors

A **security monitor** is software that monitors and controls access to the computer system. The system administrator uses the facilities of the security monitor to create a login name and password combination for each authorized user. The security monitor then checks each user as they attempt to access the computer for their login name and password. Should the user not enter a valid combination of login name and password, they are not granted access to any of the resources of the computer. The security monitor provides warning messages to users when their attempt to sign onto the computer is unsuccessful. It also records evidence of unsuccessful attempts to sign onto the system or any unauthorized use of computer resources.

Performance Monitor

The **performance monitor** captures and summarizes data about the utilization of key computer resources such as CPU (% utilized), secondary storage (disk accesses per second), and memory (% utilized). This data can be used to predict system performance, perform capacity planning, establish production schedules, and plan for hardware/software acquisitions. The data gathered on use of computer resources can also be used as input to chargeback systems, which allocate costs to users based on the information resources used. All resources usage is measured and costs are determined by multiplying by a usage rate. In this manner, costs incurred for each job run on the computer are recorded, allocated, and charged back to specific end users and their departments. Under this arrangement, the computer center is like a service center whose costs are charged directly to computer users. The alternative is that these costs are lumped in with other administrative service costs and treated as an overhead cost. A chargeback system provides users with a much clearer picture of what the costs are so that they can make cost-based decisions regarding the use of computer-based resources.

■ SYSTEM DEVELOPMENT SOFTWARE

Programming Languages

A **programming language** allows a programmer or end user to develop a set of instructions that constitute a computer program. The computer program when executed by the computer accomplishes useful work. Several sets of programming languages are briefly discussed below.

Machine Language

Machine language represents the first generation and the most basic form of programming. Instructions are written in binary code unique to the computer on which the program will run. Programmers must have a detailed understanding of the internal operations of the specific type of CPU to be used. They write long strings of detailed instructions to accomplish even the most simple of processing tasks. For example, the programmer must specify the precise storage locations for every item of data and instruction used. Machine language programming is extremely tedious, error prone, and time-consuming (even for the most simple of programs). Also, programs must be completely rewritten if they are transferred to another hardware platform (not portable).

Assembler Languages

Assembler language represents the second generation of programming languages. The use of assembler language requires a **language-translator** program called an assembler to convert the assembler code into machine-language instructions. Convenient alphabetic abbreviations called mnemonics (memory aids) and other symbols are used to represent operation codes, storage locations, and data elements. With assembler language, the programmer controls how the program will execute, and well-written programs coded in assembler language can execute faster than equivalent programs written in high-level languages (see next section). However, the assembler language used on one computer is different than that on another. Thus an assembler program is not portable—it cannot be easily converted to run on a different model machine from that on which it was initially developed.

High-Level Languages

High-level languages are programming languages that are English-like languages; the programmers use English words combined with a specific grammar to form instructions. These languages are standardized so that a program written in a high-level language on one machine may require only slight revision to run on another machine. The most commonly used high-level languages are BASIC, COBOL, FORTRAN, C, and Pascal. These languages are also called third-generation languages or 3GL.

The program written in the 3GL used by the programmer is called the **source code.** The source code must be translated into machine language before the computer can execute it. This translation process is performed by another program that reads the programmer's source code, analyzes the vocabulary, checks the syntax of each statement, relates names used by the programmer for various quantities to storage locations in the computer, finds operations that are called for in a library of such operations, and generates the appropriate machine code.

Fourth-Generation Languages

Fourth-generation languages are much less procedure oriented than the third-generation languages, which means that it is not necessary to specify all the procedural details of how the computer must accomplish a desired result; it is only necessary to specify what is to be done. This eliminates the need for users of a fourth-generation language (4GL) to develop detailed specifications to define the precise sequence of instructions the computer must execute to achieve the desired result. It also eliminates the need to write detailed instructions to specify exactly where and how to format reports. As a result, users of a fourth generation language are much more productive than users of lower-level languages. If a program can be written to accomplish the result using either a 3GL or 4GL, the 4GL program will be done much sooner than the 3GL program.

4GLs are also referred to as nonprocedural languages. With 4GLs, the programmer is often not a professional programmer, but an end user or a manager who perhaps has had only a few hours training on how to use the language. Thus the advent of 4GLs has made the com-

Exhibit 3.3
Fourth Generation
Programming
Languages

Category/Product	Vendor
Query Language/Report Writers	
Datatrieve	DEC
RPG III	IBM
Intellect	Artificial Intelligence
Natural Language	Natural Language,Inc.
QBE	IBM
QMF	IBM
SQL/DS	IBM
Graphics Languages	
Harvard Graphics	Software Publishing Company
Tell-A-Graf	Isso
Business Graphics	Business Professional Graphics
Statistical Analysis	
Express	Management Decision Systems
SAS	SAS, Inc.
Decision Support/Financial Modeling	
LOTUS 1-2-3	Lotus Development
Excel	Microsoft
Products with Modules That Address	
More Than One of the Above Categories	
FOCUS	Information Builders, Inc.
System W	Comshare, Inc.
IFPS PLUS	Execucom Systems Corp.

puter a much more accessible tool. There are many, many 4GLs as shown in Exhibit 3.3.

The ease of use of 4GLs is gained at the expense of some loss of flexibility and performance. It is difficult for the user to override the defaults, prespecified formats, and procedures embedded in the language. Also, the machine code generated from translating a 4GL is often slower to execute and requires more storage capacity to hold than if the program had been written using a lower-level language. As a result, if the business requirement is that the output report be formatted in a manner counter to the defaults of the 4GL or it is necessary to provide extremely fast response time for a large number of concurrent users, at least portions of the system may need to be developed in more flexible and more efficient lower-level languages.

Object-Oriented Language

Object-oriented programming systems (OOPS) are based on the use of objects (self-contained items that combine data and processes that cooperate by passing strictly defined messages to one another to form working programs). An object is any thing about which we store data and those methods that manipulate the data. OOPS software developers use objects as the basis to create information systems. For example, a system for customer order processing would have objects called orders. The order objects would have data about each order and the procedures to perform such tasks as calculate the total order amount; add, change, and delete items from the order; and deduct the items ordered from available inventory. Because objects have "intelligence" (they know what they are and what they can and cannot do), object oriented programs are said to be "event driven." This means that an object responds to various events to automatically carry out tasks. For example, when the new order handling object processes a new order, it calls another object (which may reside on another computer) to update inventory and yet another object to update accounts/receivable when an order is shipped. Simula 67, Smalltalk, C++, Eiffel, and Turbo Pascal are examples of commonly used OOPS languages.

One of the most significant benefits of OOPS is the reuse of already existing objects. The object-oriented approach uses inheritance to facilitate reuse: a newly created object can be defined as a "subclass" of an existing object and automatically inherit the attributes and processes of its parent. After programmers build routines and data sources into objects, they can retrieve and insert them at will without having to reinvent the wheel every time they sit down to write software. Programmers can combine the objects with relative ease to create new systems and extend existing ones and thus greatly reduce the time required for these activities.

Moreover, when the system is complete, object-oriented programming is easier to update and maintain; there's a trail of tools, in the form of objects used to write the original program, that can be reused (with slight modifications) to alter the program or repair it. According to a recent "Trends in Information Technology" report from Andersen Consulting, about 80% of the typical organization's IT budget goes toward maintaining existing systems. Thus the ability to reuse existing objects represents a major productivity and quality improvement opportunity. OOPS makes software far easier to create, simpler to use, and far more reliable.

OOPS technology lends itself particularly well to the GUI environment. Once companies move to the GUI environment, they rethink the way they program. People are compelled by the fact that they need to deliver very complex applications that are highly reliable. OOPS provides a fast way to meet these needs. As more and more complex applications are demanded by end users, there is no other language that seems to combine the deftness at managing complexity, development speed, and reusability that OOPS offers.

Some people believe that OOPS will do for software what the microchip has done for hardware. Instead of microchips, the software revolution will be driven by objects—simple, self-contained, reliable software components. Like the microprocessor, OOPS has the potential to radically change the data processing industry.

Visual Languages

Visual programming **languages** use the object orientation of OOPS languages to enable software developers to create working applications by connecting various objects. Programmers draw, point, and click instead of write code. Thus the developer does not need to learn a programming language and its associated rules and syntax. Visual programming is best used to develop the user interface of the application, such as the GUI for the end user. ObjectVision from Borland is an example of one of the more popular visual programming languages.

Natural Languages

To use a computer properly, you must first learn special commands, languages, and key words. This takes considerable time and effort and much trial and error. It is one of the main reasons computers are considered unfriendly by many managers. Menus and a GUI interface can help, but these provide less than a natural interface.

The goal of **natural languages** is to allow an end user to access stored data and interact with the computer using natural or ordinary words so that the computer is extremely easy to use. One approach is to use a natural language "front end" interface to simplify and improve the communications between an application program and an end user. Such an interface allows the user to type in directions or requests for information. The user types ordinary English words and an interpreter translates what is entered into commands meaningful to the computer. When words or phrases are not clear to the interpreter, it requests that the end user provide clarification. An even more exciting approach is to "teach" the computer to respond to the spoken word! Unfortunately, natural languages suffer from ambiguity in the ways key words are used. Strict syntax and vocabulary limitations reduce this ambiguity. Natural language is also sometimes called fifth-generation language.

Language Translators

For source code to be executed by a computer, it must be translated into fundamental machine instructions. There are two methods for translating high-level source code.

Interpreter

An interpreted language is one in which the instructions are translated one at a time as they are executed. A program that reads high level language source code and follows this process to convert it to machine language is called an **interpreter.**

Compiler

In a compiled language the high-level source code is translated as a unit to form a complete machine language program that can be executed. The program that performs this process is called a **compiler,** and the machine language version of the program is called the object code.

Exhibit 3.4 illustrates the difference between the interpretation and compilation process. Note that with a program written in an inter-

Exhibit 3.4
The Interpretation and Compilation Process

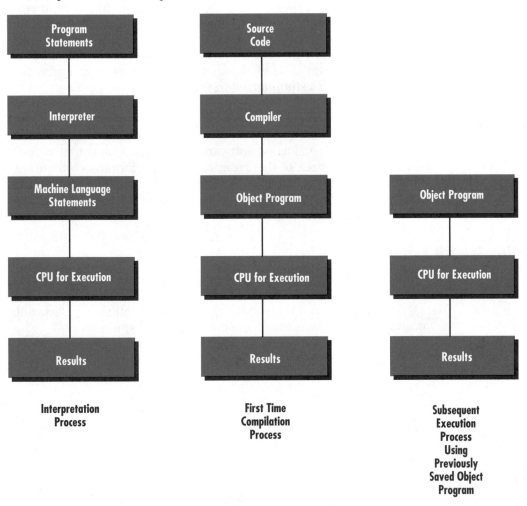

preted language, no object code is produced. Thus each time an interpreted language program is executed, each instruction must be interpreted prior to its execution. This can mean slower execution time compared to a program that has been compiled into an executable object-code version.

It is sometimes advantageous to provide users with the object code of a program and not the source code; it makes it extremely difficult for anyone to change the program code. Software package vendors typically provide object code and not source code so that they can guarantee the user does not modify the code. Vendors often cannot support modified code.

■ APPLICATION SOFTWARE

Application software consists of programs that direct the computer to perform the processing required for a particular use, or application, that end users want accomplished. While the applications for which software has been written cover nearly any topic that you can imagine, application software is divided into general purpose and application specific software, as summarized in Exhibit 3.5.

General Purpose Software

General purpose application **software** includes programs that support end users in any area of the organization in performing common information processing activities. Such applications include spreadsheet, word processing, and graphics packages. These applications are discussed in Chapter 8.

Application Specific Software

Application specific software meets specific business needs of specific users. Such software includes payroll accounting, human resource management, sales forecasting, order entry, inventory control, and accounts receivable. These applications are discussed in Chapters 6 and 7.

Exhibit 3.5
Common
Application
Software

General Purpose Software
   Support End User Personal Productivity
      Spreadsheets
      Word Processing
      Telecommunications
      Data Base Management Software
      Query and Report Writing
      Graphics
      Personal Budgeting
   Support Group Productivity
      Electronic Mail
      Calendaring/Scheduling

Application Specific Software
   Accounting Packages
      Payroll
      General Ledger
      Accounts Receivable
      Accounts Payable
   Order Processing
   Inventory Control

■ MANAGEMENT ISSUES

Features Important in Operating Systems

The capabilities of a computer depend, to a large extent, upon the capabilities of the operating system. Unfortunately, the computer industry sells operating systems based on their technical features, for example, "Windows NT is a 32-bit operating system offering true multitasking, pre-emptive multithreading, and a hardware abstraction layer." As a result, corporate customers are forced to learn the complicated features of operating systems and determine the benefits for themselves. However, there are a set of key operating system features useful for comparison purposes. These features are defined below.

Ease of Use

How easy is it to learn to use the features and power of the operating system?

Programs Available

Regardless of their source, application software is always written to run on a specific operating system. Thus an important feature of any operating system is the number and quality of application programs that have been written for it. The set of application programs written for any one operating system is referred to as the library for that operating system. A common end-user headache is that a mission critical application program is not available for the chosen operating system.

Many commercial software firms develop different versions of the same application software program to run on many different operating systems. For example, WordPerfect is one of the most popular word processing packages. Versions of WordPerfect run under DOS, Windows, UNIX, OS/2, and other operating systems. Software that is available for many operating systems allows you to use what appears to be the same application regardless of which computer system you use. (Unfortunately, in the real world, subtle differences often confuse the user familiar with running the application under one operating system who tries to run it under another.) By developing their software to run under different operating systems, commercial software vendors expand the number of potential users of their package. Targeting for only one class of user (e.g., users of DOS personal computers) can prove to be nearsighted and disastrous in the marketplace if another operating system suddenly becomes popular.

An operating system can run programs designed for other operating systems using a process called emulation. Calls for the underlying microprocessor's functions are intercepted by the emulation software and translated into appropriate instructions for the native processor. This two-stage process is inefficient and can greatly reduce the processing power of the computer when running in native mode. Through software emulation, the Macintosh computer, with its Motorola 68000 microcomputer chip and System 7 operating system, can run software written to run on IBM-PC compatible microcomputers and the MS-DOS operating system using Insigna Solutions' Soft-PC program as an Intel/MS-DOS emulator. Emulation capability can also be built into the operating system to eliminate the need for special emulation software.

Reliability

The operating system must be highly reliable. End users cannot tolerate system crashes due to bugs or system overload.

Portability

How easy is it to get the operating system to run on more than one manufacturer's hardware?

Networking Capability

How easy is it to connect a computer using this operating system into a network of similar computers? Dissimilar computers?

Security

Computers handle sensitive data and can be accessed over networks (Chapter 4). The operating system needs to provide some level of security against unauthorized access.

Task Management

Does the operating system support multiprogramming, multitasking, or virtual memory management?

Which features are the most important depend on who is using the operating system and what functions are to be performed. Operating systems can be used for server devices or workstations or microcomputers used by end users or programmers.

Server computers provide services such as file server, print server, or telecommunications server for network users. **Server** computers are usually microcomputers or workstations, but can be minicomputers, mainframes, and even supercomputers. Servers require an operating system that provides high performance, high reliability, and high security. They also must have good networking capability and be portable to other computers.

End users demand ease of use and low cost. End users do not want an operating system that demands a powerful computer and prodigious amounts of main memory to run efficiently. Most end users run just a few applications, so high performance and enhanced reliability are not critical.

Exhibit 3.6
Desirable Operating
System
Characteristics

Desirable Characteristics for Servers
   Reliability
   Networking capability
   Multitasking
   Portability
   Security
Desirable Characteristics for End Users
   Ease of use
   Availability of end-user applications
   Minimal hardware
   Networking capability
   Multitasking
Desirable Characteristics for Programmers
   Availability of development utilities
   Reliability
   Portability
   Networking capability
   Multitasking

Software developers need an operating system that is reliable, portable, has good networking capabilities and that offers an extensive library of development utilities.

Exhibit 3.6 summarizes the features important to computers being used as servers and by end users and programmers.

Common Microcomputer Operating Systems

The five most significant microcomputer operating systems are MS-DOS from Microsoft; System 7 from Macintosh; OS/2 originally developed by Microsoft and IBM and now sold and enhanced by IBM; Unix originally developed by AT&T; and Windows NT from Microsoft. These operating systems are discussed below, and a summary of their comparison factors is shown in Exhibit 3.7.

MS-DOS

In the past, IBM always developed and supplied its own operating system software for its computers. In 1980, however, IBM contracted with Microsoft Corporation (then a small software company near Seattle, Washington) to develop an operating system for its new IBM-PC. Microsoft developed PC-DOS for the IBM-PC and **MS-DOS,** its generic equivalent for IBM-compatible PCs. This operating system today is the most widely used operating system in the world. IBM's choice of MS-DOS led to the emergence of Microsoft Corporation as one of the world's leading software companies.

Since the original IBM-PC was based on the 8088 microprocessor, MS-DOS has had to evolve to match the capabilities of five more generations of microprocessors—the 8086, 80286, 80386, 80486, and Pen-

Exhibit 3.7 Comparison of Personal Computing Operating Systems

Systems	MS-DOS	DOS/Windows 3.1	Windows/NT	OS/2	Unix
Company	Microsoft	Microsoft	Microsoft	IBM	AT&T/SCO
Hardware	Intel 80X86	Intel 80X86	Intel 80X86 DEC Alpha MIPS 4000	Intel 80X86 Motorola 680X0 Others	Intel 80X86
Programs Available (Native Mode)	> 25,000	> 25,000	hundreds	hundreds	thousands
User Interface	CLI*	GUI	GUI	GUI	CLI
Support Task Switching	Yes	Yes	Yes	Yes	Yes
Support Multitasking	No	Yes	Yes	Yes	Yes
Support Multiprocessing	No	No	Yes	No	No
Support Virtual Memory	No	Yes	Yes	Yes	Yes
Minimum Hardware Required for Efficient Operation	80286 CPU 640K RAM 80 Meg HD	80386 CPU 4 Meg RAM 80 Meg HD	80486 CPU	80386 CPU 8 Meg RAM 80 Meg HD	80386 CPU

*CLI = Command Language Interface   GUI = Graphical User Interface

tium (80586). Each subsequent version of MS-DOS added new features and power. Versions 4 and 5 departed from the earlier, strictly command-driven form to offer either a menu-driven or command-driven structure. DOS 5.0 also added a full screen editor and the capability to swap data and text between programs.

MS-DOS is a single-user, single-task operating system. This was acceptable to PC users as long as they worked with relatively slow PCs and floppy-disk systems. Now, with the heavy use of high-volume hard disks and faster processors, PC users need to be able to run multiple programs and work on multiple tasks concurrently. They want to be able to do spell checking of a long word processing document while accessing a mainframe to retrieve E-mail messages. The need for multitasking is one reason for interest in more advanced operating systems.

DOS with Windows

Windows is not technically an operating system, but a shell that sits on top of the DOS operating system to form an additional layer between the operating system and the end user (Exhibit 3.8). Windows was developed in response to the highly popular, easy-to-use, icon-driven operating system of the Apple Macintosh. Windows provides an intuitive graphical user interface where users choose on-screen icons and pull down menus rather than enter commands by typing them at the keyboard.

Exhibit 3.8
Windows Forms an
Extra Layer
Between User and
Operating System

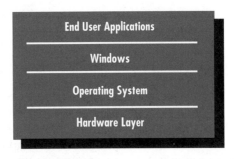

Windows also adds some multitasking capabilities and makes it easier to move data from one application to another. A window is a portion of a display screen dedicated to a specific purpose (e.g., word processing). The computer screen can be divided into multiple windows thus allowing the user to treat the computer screen like a desktop where several programs can remain open simultaneously (Exhibit 3.9). The user can open multiple programs at the same time and can move between them without having to shut a program down as is required with DOS. The user can also transfer information or visuals from one window (program) to another. Thus a spreadsheet can be moved from a spreadsheet program into a document being created in a word processing program.

Exhibit 3.9
Typical Windows
Screen

*Screen shot reprinted with
permission from Microsoft
Corporation.*

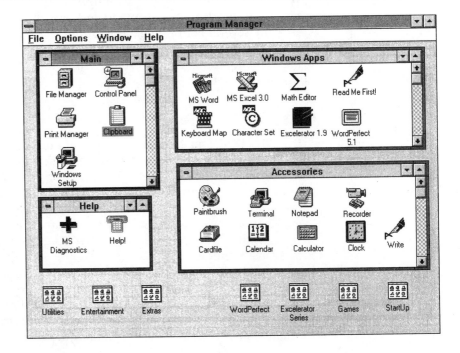

Windows requires at least an 80386 microprocessor, 4 megabytes of RAM, and an 80 megabyte hard drive to operate effectively.

System 7

System 7 is the operating system for the Apple Macintosh microcomputers. The Macintosh icon-oriented operating system set a standard for ease of use that other operating systems try to emulate. It is designed to make use of the capabilities of a 32-bit microprocessor and works best on computers with 4 megabytes or more of RAM. It also supports multitasking and virtual memory. The operating system provides multimedia capabilities that allow its users to integrate sound, video, and animation with conventional text and graphics. It also supports powerful graphics capabilities with a greatly expanded use of color. System 7 supports interapplication communication so that when data in one file is changed, changes are automatically made to all other documents into which you previously copied that data.

Windows NT

Windows NT (New Technology) is the successor to both DOS and DOS with Windows. It is designed to take advantage of the newer 32-bit processors and features multitasking and networking capabilities. Unlike MS-DOS, NT is designed to run on multiple hardware platforms, not only Intel-based machines. For example, NT can run on DEC's Alpha and MIPS's R4000 RISC microprocessors. Using emulation software, NT can run MS-DOS, Windows, and OS/2 programs. NT supports symmetric multiprocessing, with the ability to make simultaneous use of 2, 4, 8, or 16 microprocessors. NT also has built-in networking to support several communications protocols. NT supports RAID for increased storage reliability. The many features and capabilities of NT make it very attractive for use on computers that are servers in a network of computers.

OS/2

In 1987, IBM and Microsoft jointly announced the development of **OS/2,** the operating system planned and designed to replace MS-DOS. At the same time, Microsoft was developing Microsoft Windows as an interim graphical user interface shell for DOS. The popularity of Windows far exceeded expectations while OS/2 initial sales were lagging expectations. Microsoft and IBM terminated the joint development of OS/2, with IBM continuing to evolve OS/2 and Microsoft continuing to evolve Windows.

OS/2 includes a shell program called the Workplace Shell that provides end users with a graphical user interface similar to that of Microsoft Windows. This is not surprising, considering its heritage. OS/2 is a multitasking operating system that can run multiple programs simultaneously, whether the programs were written for Windows, OS/2, or DOS. OS/2 comes in a standard edition and an extended edition, which offers built-in data base and networking features.

OS/2 is designed to take full advantage of the memory capacities of the Intel 80386 and i486 chips, so it can address up to 4 gigabytes of main memory. Other sophisticated functions include virtual storage; protection between applications so that applications and data cannot write over other applications and data; error logging; trace utilities to isolate and report software problems; multimedia capabilities; enhanced graphics; and pen-computing compatibility. OS/2 does require a 80486 or above microprocessor, at least 8 megabytes of RAM, and at least 80 megabytes of disk storage to operate efficiently.

Unix

Originally developed by AT&T's Bell Labs in 1969, **Unix** is a multi-user, multitasking operating system that also supports networking. Unix can run on all classes of computer from microcomputer to super-computers. Unix can even run on different manufacturer's computers. This high degree of portability is one reason for the popularity of this operating system. A user can select a software application that runs under Unix and have a high degree of flexibility in choosing the computer hardware manufacturer. The use of Unix also makes it much easier to move programs and data among computers or to connect mainframes and microcomputers together to share resources.

Unix is often considered to have a complex user interface with strange and arcane commands. GUIs, such as Open System Founda-

Real World Perspective

Implementing UNIX and Downsizing at Wal-Mart

Wal-Mart Stores is the nation's largest retailer with 1992 sales of $52 billion. Wal-Mart has consistently been able to do more with technology while spending a lower percentage of sales for information technology than other major retailers. For example, Wal-Mart was one of the first retailers to give store clerks hand-held scanners to update inventory, to establish satellite links to remote stores, and to automate regional distribution warehouses.

Freedom is the main reason behind the company's decision to adopt UNIX workstations for a new 1,600-unit in-store system. Wal-Mart went to UNIX to make code portable across different hardware and software. Portability allows users to develop applications for one type of UNIX hardware platform and run it on another as long as the suppliers of each adhere to the same set of operating system standards.

Wal-Mart wants a store computing hardware and software combination that will span successive generations of technology and grow in capacity as more and more applications are added. UNIX offers this flexibility. It is portable between vendors, spans a variety of technology architectures, and is stable from very small to very large systems.

The new software will track inventory, reorder depleted stock automatically while tipping management off to sales trends, and control cash registers. Private satellite links will allow the workstations to update mainframes at headquarters. The company plans to roll the systems out to its stores by mid-1990.

tions Motif and Sun Microsystems' Open Look, are available that help users avoid the complexity of Unix.

Early variations of Unix lacked many of the systems management tools for performance monitoring, tuning, storage management, tape management, capacity planning, and system security against unauthorized access—essential features commonly found in operating systems for minicomputers and mainframes. As a result, organizations were slow to adopt Unix for running traditional business applications such as accounting, order entry, and inventory control.

Today there are many variants of Unix including HP/UX from Hewlett Packard, AIX from IBM, Ultrix from DEC, UNIX System V from UNIX Systems Lab, Solaris from Microsystems, and SCO from Santa Cruz Operations, which have addressed many of the original Unix shortcomings. These variants have created a lack of common standards, although most organizations do not find this to be an insurmountable problem.

Build versus Buy

Many of the application specific programs used by organizations that have mainframe or midrange computers were written and developed by the application programmers employed in the company's IT organization. In other cases, the application program was custom written by consultants or programmers external to the company. Such custom-written software is often very expensive. Increasingly, application specific programs are produced by professional software development companies. These commercially developed application programs can be purchased off-the-shelf by users to meet their specific business needs. Such applications are called canned software or software packages. They include a copy of the object code of the program, a written technical description of the program, and a user's manual that provides detailed instructions on how to use the package.

Which approach to take to acquire software to meet an organization's business needs is often debatable: in-house developed programs, custom-written packages, or off-the-shelf software.

The advantage of using an in-house or **custom-written** application is that the software is designed and tailor-made to exactly meet the specific needs of your firm. However, there are several disadvantages. It can take months or years to develop the software, so end-user needs must be anticipated well in advance to avoid a negative impact on the business. Furthermore, the nature of the application development process leads to uncertainty over when the application will be fit for use and what the total development cost will be.

The advantage of using a commercially developed application is that it can be bought **off-the-shelf** today for a known price. The disadvantage of this approach is that it may be necessary to make changes to the business processes addressed by the package if the software is not 100% compatible with your current way of doing things. However, if your firm performs a specific business process (e.g., accounts payable) so different from the process automated to meet the needs of other firms in your industry, you should really ask yourself why your firm is so different! Is there really any advantage to doing things differently? Have complexity and time-consuming exceptions creeped into your internal business process?

There are two other sources of application software. **Shareware** is relatively inexpensive software that is produced by individuals or very small firms and distributed on the honor system through electronic bulletin boards. Prices for shareware software are typically under $50. Thousands of shareware programs are available that can be of value. If you use this software, however, be careful in downloading the shareware from the bulletin board to your computer as this is a common source of computer viruses. Also, be sure to pay the small fee to the developers. The other source is **freeware,** or public domain software. It is similar to shareware except that the programs are completely free.

Open Systems

It used to be that because the operating system interfaces with the hardware, computer manufacturers designed and built their own operating system to take advantage of the unique characteristics of the hardware used in their computer. As a result, computer manufacturers developed proprietary operating systems that worked only on their computer. In addition, application software was developed to run on one manufacturer's computer under a proprietary operating system. This meant that the application would not run on another manufacturer's computer with a different proprietary operating system. Thus users often found themselves in a "chicken or the egg" situation. Which do they choose first—the computer platform (hardware and operating system) or the application software? Once they chose a particular platform, they were limited in their choice of application software. Conversely, if they elected to use certain application software, they were limited in their choices of computer platforms.

The term **open systems** refers to a vision of how computing and communications products will work together. The goal is to create software that can run on any machine, anywhere, anytime, thus providing people with access to information when, how, and where they require it. This provides users with the freedom not only to choose the best information tools and products, but also to orchestrate and adapt these components into a whole that best suits the way their company wants to work. With open systems, you can choose a suite of general purpose application programs from different vendors, say A, B, C, and D, that will integrate with an application specific package from vendor E that runs on a computer made by vendor F with an operating system from vendor G. At some future date, you may switch to a different computer vendor altogether and everything continues to work!

Completely open systems are still years in the future. Instead, today we strive for interoperable systems. This means linking together mul-

Real World Perspective

How Vendors Are Addressing the Open-Systems Issue

Digital Equipment Corporation (DEC) is an example of one approach vendors have taken to address the need for open systems. DEC is a major computer manufacturer and software development company. DEC developed a RISC microprocessor for its Alpha line of processors with a new proprietary operating system called Open VMS. DEC designed the chip to support not only the DEC proprietary VMS operating system, but also OSF/1, DEC's variant of Unix and Microsoft's Windows NT operating system. This strategy provides the over 10 million DEC customers worldwide with a bridge to the Alpha processors while they decide between Unix and NT. However, the DEC strategy does not provide unlimited flexibility to choose an operating system and associated application software.

Brock Control Systems is an example of another approach to open systems. Brock is a $100 million vendor of application specific software to support telemarketing and sales activities. Their software is designed to run on over a dozen different computer manufacturer's hardware using any combination of operating system and data base management system that exists for that hardware. Such a strategy provides the users of their software with ultimate flexibility. Thus a user could select to run the software on an HP-9000 computer under the Unix operating system using an Oracle data base management system or IBM RS6000 computer using the AIX operating system and the Sybase data base management system or a DEC VAX computer running the Open VMS operating system and Informix as the data base management system.

tiple computer platforms to run specific software packages. Thus an application running on a computer somewhere in the firm can share processes and data or exchange information with applications running on other computer platforms.

The above example makes it clear that the advent of open systems will inject a great deal of competition into both the hardware and software industries. Open systems enable users to purchase the best software package for the job without the constraint of worrying if it will run on the hardware. There is also increased flexibility to select the manufacturer's hardware whose service, reliability, performance, and cost best fit the business needs without worry that the software will run on that vendor's hardware. Clearly business managers should be keenly interested in seeing the organization's IT group make strong efforts to achieve an open-systems environment.

Exhibit 3.10
Advantages of Open Systems

Provides flexibility to choose the best software solution

Provides flexibility to choose the best hardware solution

Enables applications to share processes and information

Hardware can be upgraded without affecting the way the software is run

Lowers total cost of software and computer platform through increased competition among both hardware and software vendors

Summary

Management has a key role in overseeing the definition and implementation of software that meets the needs of the business.

Managers are well advised to use resources from the IT organization in making their purchasing decision, however, they must know enough to be able to communicate their needs and to ask intelligent questions to explore various options.

System management software includes programs that manage and control the resources and operations of the computer system as it performs various information processing tasks.

The operating system is an integrated set of programs that manages the user interface to the computer, governs the execution of tasks, manages input/output and storage resources, performs file management, and provides various support services as the computer executes the application programs of users.

The most popular user interface today is the GUI approach.

There are a number of key characteristics upon which to evaluate an operating system including ease of use, number of end-user applications available, reliability, security, and task management. The relative importance of these characteristics depends on who will use the computer and for what purpose.

The most significant microcomputer operating systems are MS-DOS, DOS with Windows, System 7, Windows NT, OS/2, and Unix.

Utility programs, security monitors, performance monitors, telecommunications monitors, and data base management systems are examples of system management software.

There are four generations of programming languages—machine, assembler, high level, and fourth generation. In addition, object-oriented, visual, and natural languages are being used.

The use of object-oriented languages holds the potential to enable programmers to combine objects with relative ease to create new systems and extend an existing one thus reducing development time.

Visual languages use the object orientation of OOPS languages to enable software developers to create working applications by connecting various objects and drawing, pointing, and clicking instead of writing code.

Natural languages allow an end user to access stored data and interact with the computer using natural or ordinary words, making the computer extremely easy to use.

Language translators convert the programmer's source code into fundamental machine instructions that can be executed by the computer.

An interpreter translates instructions one at a time as they are executed.

A compiler translates the source code as a unit to form a complete machine language program that can be executed.

There is application software available to meet a very wide range of needs. Application software is divided into general purpose and application specific software.

There are three common approaches to acquiring software—in-house developed programs, custom-written packages, and off-the-shelf software.

Downsizing involves migrating applications off the mainframe onto smaller, less expensive workstations or midrange computers.

The term open systems refers to a vision of how computing and communications products will work together. The goal is to create software that can run on any machine, anywhere, anytime, thus providing people with access to information when, how, and where they require it.

A Manager's Checklist

✔ What approach is followed to acquire application software? Does it include clear guidelines on what sort of hardware or operating system the software must be able to execute on?

✔ Does your organization have a clear set of guidelines to help make the build-versus-buy software decision?

✔ Do you know who your firm's key hardware and software vendors are? Do you know their position on open systems?

✔ Is your IT organization moving to an open-systems environment? If not, are you doing anything to encourage this approach?

Key Terms

application software	off-the-shelf software
assembler language	OOPS
build versus buy	open systems
compiler	operating system
custom-written software	OS/2
data base management system	performance monitors
fourth-generation language	portability
freeware	programming language
general purpose software	reliability
GUI	security monitors
high-level languages	server
interpreter	shareware
language translator	software
MS-DOS	source code
multiprogramming	System 7
multitasking	system development software
natural languages	system management software
network capability	telecommunications monitor
object-oriented language	Unix

virtual memory   Windows
visual languages   Windows NT

**Review
Questions**

1. Explain the difference between system management software, system development software, and application software and give several examples of each.

2. List and briefly describe the five basic functions of the operating system.

3. Explain the difference between multiprogramming and multitasking.

4. List four types of system management software besides the operating system.

5. Define the term emulation and explain how software emulation enables software to be run on different computers and operating systems.

6. List the features important to evaluate various operating systems.

7. Name five operating systems and identify the software vendor associated with each.

8. Identify four common approaches for obtaining software.

9. Define the term open systems and state its goal.

**Discussion
Questions**

1. Why is it important for business managers to understand computer software?

2. Why are there so many different types of programming languages? Is there one that is clearly the best?

3. How would you summarize what business managers must know about computer software?

4. Should a business manager know how to program using a 4GL? Why or why not?

5. Why are there so many operating systems? Is there one operating system that is clearly the best?

6. Is Windows an operating system? Why or why not?

7. What is meant by the build-versus-buy decision in considering software? What guidelines would you use to help make this decision?

8. State the goal of the open-systems movement and discuss its potential impact on business and the information technology industry.

**Recommended
Readings**

1. Appleby, Doris. "BASIC." *BYTE*, March 1992.

2. Bermant, Charles. "ObjectVision Eases Data Gathering, Present Information Graphically." *ComputerWorld*, April 6, 1992.

3. Henning, Jeffry. "The Operating Systems Soup." *Chief Information Officer Journal*, September/October 1993.

4. Parker, John. "A Reusable Revolution." *InformationWeek*, January 6, 1992.

5. Pepper, Jon. "OOPS, Promised Too Much." *InformationWeek*, January 4, 1993.

6. Verity, John W. and Evan I. Schwartz. "Software Made Simple." *Business Week*, September 30, 1991.

A Manager's Dilemma

Meeker Insurance

Billy Joe Meeker left a major insurance company to form his own company five years ago. He had outstanding success and now has over two hundred independent agents throughout the United States selling his products. As independent agents, they could sell the insurance products of any one of several companies. Billy has been successful by being able to keep the paperwork and processing details to a minimum. This, coupled with high commissions earned on each policy sold, has made Meeker Insurance one of the most popular policies for independents to sell.

Now Meeker Insurance is facing a stiff challenge. Due to the increase in regulations and reporting requirements, the paperwork required when an agent sells a policy is becoming burdensome. In addition, Billy has ideas for a wider variety of products and services. Billy desperately needs a way to simplify the paperwork and enable the agents to demonstrate details of the new products and services.

One approach, recommended by his brother-in-law, is to provide all the agents with a standard portable microcomputer loaded with software to support the selling of Meeker Insurance policies and simplify claims processing. Billy worries about the $10 million required just to purchase the hardware and software. One option might be to charge each agent $1,000 to $2,000 per year to recover the expense. Billy believes there are other expenses that must be covered. He is also worried about picking a standard microcomputer and set of software that all agents can use and will agree to use.

How should Billy proceed? What next steps can he take to further evaluate this idea without making a major commitment?

Problems with Software Packages

You are the Assistant Finance Director with responsibility for reviewing all computer hardware and software purchases. The IT organization has been following a strategy of buying off-the-shelf application specific software to meet the needs to automate various business processes. The software is implemented as is, with no customization. The strategy seemed sound when first presented, however, you are beginning to have doubts.

Recently an accounts payable software package was installed in your area of responsibility. You have heard nothing but complaints. The new system requires people to do things differently than they have in the past. All standard codes used to identify products, vendors, and departments had to be modified. The new system doesn't produce reports that the old system did. End users from the lowest clerk to the manager of accounts payable have had to undergo tremendous changes to get their work processes to conform to the new system. They long for the old system with its familiar ways.

You are concerned for two reasons. First, these people report to you. If their needs are not being met through the new purchased software, you want to correct the situation. Second, you routinely approve the purchase of packages for use in all areas of the company. What if others of the company using these packages are having similar problems?

What advantages are there to using purchased software? What are some reasons why purchased software may not match current business processes and practices? Does a mismatch necessarily mean that the package is not right to use? How can you assess if the company's policy of always using off-the-shelf software packages with no customization is correct? Should some customization be allowed? If so, how could guidelines be developed to determine how much customization to allow? If not, what should be done when there is a mismatch?

Case Study 3.3

Influencing Vendors to Move to Open Systems

The Manager of Information Technology has come to you for help. She is determined to move to an open-computing environment. There are many advantages for your firm. However, a small, but important set of the total hardware and software vendors with which your firm does business have not yet made a commitment to support her in this effort. She complains that they keep proposing "closed solutions" based on their own proprietary hardware and software. As a result, it takes a lot of custom programming to interface their hardware and software with the rest of the computing architecture.

She has asked you to use your influence as the Vice President of Purchases of a Fortune Top 10 company to persuade these vendors to "get with the program." Your company's total IT budget is in excess of $300 million per year. Spending with these three small, but key vendors is about $3 million per year. Unfortunately, the products they provide are unique; the vendors could not easily be replaced.

What approach might you take with these vendors to convince them to provide more open solutions? What additional data might you request of the Manager of Information Technology to determine a plan of attack? Are there ethical or legal issues that must be avoided?

Chapter 4

Data Communications and Networks

Upon completion of this chapter, you will be able to:

1. Identify three key business benefits that networks can deliver.

2. Describe the function of each of the five basic components of a network and give an example of each.

3. Describe the business purpose and two business applications supported through the use of a LAN.

4. Describe the business purpose and three business applications supported through the use of a WAN.

5. Define the term telecommuting and discuss its pros and cons.

6. Identify the five functions of network management and discuss why these functions are important.

7. Identify five critical issues associated with setting up and operating a global network.

Preview

Every organization is filled with people who need to identify opportunities and solve business problems. Good information may be one of the most valuable tools in meeting these needs. Large, geographically dispersed organizations especially need networks to share information to coordinate the activities of many people in diverse locations. Networks can be used by organizations to reduce costs and delays associated with traditional means of communication and increase sales through better customer service. Progressive companies are increasingly using networks to build strong links with both customers and suppliers.

Issues

1. Why is improved business communications of increasing importance?

2. How is the development of standards helping organizations to build more effective networks?

3. How are organizations using networks to forge strategic alliances with their customers and suppliers?

Trade-offs

1. What are some of the fundamental tradeoffs between the various communications transmission media?

2. What are some of the fundamental tradeoffs between using vendor proprietary communications protocols versus the emerging standards?

A Manager Struggles with the Issues

You are shocked as you learn that your single most important customer has issued an ultimatum: "All suppliers have six months to eliminate paper-based orders and invoices and convert to a paperless EDI system conforming to industry standards. Any supplier who fails to comply will be removed from the list of approved suppliers!"

Many thoughts go racing through your mind: Why? What are the advantages of converting to such a system? What will this mean for your company? Should you fall into line or try to resist the ultimatum? Can the IT organization rise to the occasion and meet this challenge? What will be required of you to help them meet the challenge? What will happen if you fail to comply? What if this action causes other customers to respond similarly?

■ WHY COMPANIES ARE USING NETWORKS

What separates good management from poor management is the ability to identify problems and solve them with available resources. **Networks** may be one of the most valuable of these resources, because they enable a company to keep in touch with its operating divisions, customers, suppliers, and stockholders. For example, intercompany networks support the movement of key operating data (purchase orders, invoices, and payments) between customers and suppliers providing improved service and quicker response at lower cost. Such uses of networks can provide the participants with a competitive advantage. Networks also enable an organization to plan and control its various activities. As companies become larger, more widely dispersed, and more broadly diversified, their communications problems become more complex. Networks provide good solutions to communications problems that arise as companies try to render better customer service.

Networks can provide three fundamental business benefits: improve decision-making response time, support organizational decision-making processes, and enable the formation of strategic alliances.

Improve Response Time

The use of a well-designed network allows an organization to capture basic information about business transactions from remote locations and relay this data to another remote location within a relatively short time after it is requested. This reduction in communication time effectively shrinks distances between distant locations. This effect is sometimes called time compression (Hammer and Mangurian, reference 4) or reduction of information float (Naisbitt, reference 8). Reduced response time enables a company to provide improved customer service, speed up decision making and the execution of those decisions, and get more work done over a given time period.

Support Organizational Decision-Making Processes

Networks can support either centralized or decentralized decision-making processes. For a firm that implements centralized decision making, all important decisions are made by managers at a central headquarters. Networks enable the easy flow of information back and forth to support this mode of management: decisions can be communicated quickly to the remote locations, and headquarters can receive data to measure and control the implementation of decisions. For a firm that uses decentralized decision making, management delegates authority for making decisions to local managers. Furthermore, the remote locations have the resources (people, capital, raw materials) to implement these decisions. The local managers use networks to access data and resources to support their decision-making process. Networks are used to communicate the decision and the resulting consequences back to headquarters.

Enable the Formation of Strategic Alliances

Many companies are forming superior working relationships with customers and suppliers by linking to them via networks. Such intercompany networks enable all the participants to improve response time, reduce costs, and eliminate distance barriers, which provides many tangible benefits. For example, allowing the supplier to access the inventory data base of a customer, coupled with faster delivery time, enables the two companies to maintain less aggregate inventory. A supplier that is able to build such a network among many customers gains a strong advantage over its competitors. The cost to change to a different supplier may be so great that the customers are, in effect, locked in to that supplier and other competitors are locked out.

■ NETWORK FUNDAMENTALS

Basic Communications Model

Communication is any process that permits information to pass from a sender to one or more receivers. The information is also called data or a message. To communicate, a source first generates a message. Then an **encoder** converts the message into a form that can be sent over the transmission media to a receiving **decoder,** which, in turn, converts the message into a form useful to the receiver (Exhibit 4.1). The source and receiver must follow a common communication **protocol** or set of rules to "talk with" one another. This protocol defines the format of the message, certain message initiation and termination procedures, and what should be done in the event that the message is not understood by the receiver. In the real world, messages are corrupted by **noise** or unwanted signals that interfere with the communications. Noise can be caused by many sources, but primarily by

Exhibit 4.1
Basic
Communications
Model

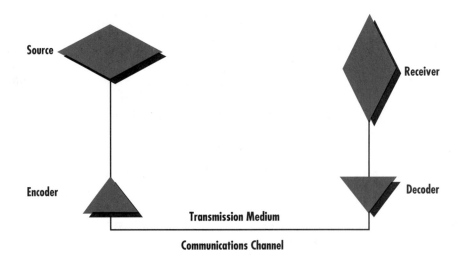

imperfections in the components of the network or by interference generated within the environment in which the network operates (e.g., the operation of electrical equipment can generate noise that disrupts the message sent over a network).

An example of this basic communications model is a network used to connect a personal computer to a mainframe computer. The personal computer (sender) sends its message through a **modem** (encoder) that converts the signal into a form suitable for transmission over the transmission media, perhaps simple telephone wires. At the other end, the message goes through a second modem that decodes the message into a form that can be understood by the mainframe computer (receiver). Along the way, the message may be corrupted by noise in the network or surrounding environment. The network devices are connected in a simple point-to-point arrangement.

Network Design Parameters

In the design, installation, and operation of networks, some fundamental parameters are used to define how the network must perform to meet the needs of its users. These terms are defined below.

Availability

The **availability** parameter defines the hours the network is operational. The maximum, of course, is 24 hours/day × 7 days per week. Practice has shown that such high availability is difficult to achieve. Components of the system need to be brought down from time to time to allow for scheduled maintenance or replacement. Thus most network managers schedule some downtime during hours that cause minimal inconvenience to its users (e.g., 2 hours/month between 1 AM and 3 AM the third Sunday of the month) to allow for scheduled repairs.

Reliability

The **reliability** parameter measures how well the network meets its availability goal. It is the percent of the scheduled available time that the network is actually useful and fully operational. Thus, if during one month, the network was scheduled to be available 718 hours, but it could only be used 711 of those scheduled hours, then the reliability is 99 percent (711/718 $\times$ 100%). Notice that 99 percent reliability means that the network was actually down for 7 hours when it was needed. This amount of downtime could well cause a major disruption of the business. Network users have come to expect very high reliability.

Security

A network manager's worst nightmare is access of the network by unauthorized users. One measure of the **security** of a network is the number of detected security incidents over a time period, such as a month, quarter, or year. Obviously, management wants this to be an extremely small number or zero. Unfortunately, it is very costly to guarantee zero incidents. Chapter 13 will provide some guidelines on security.

Response Time

The elapsed time from when the user hits the "enter" or "send" key to send a message until the response to that message begins to appear on the sender's screen is a measure of the total "network" **response time.** This elapsed time also includes the computer time required to process the message. If the message involves extensive calculations or the accessing of hundreds of records in a data base, the computer processing time may well be longer than the time required for the message and its response to travel through the network. This parameter is important to interactive users.

Throughput

Throughput is a measure of the number of characters that can be sent correctly through the network over a period of time. In some transmissions, if there is an error, the data must be resent. Thus if there is a high error rate, the effective throughput may be much lower than expected. This parameter is important for users who wish to send large amounts of data through the network, such as for uploading or downloading data or the sending of long report files.

Robustness

Robustness is a measure of the network's ability to continue operating through, or to recover after, the failure of one or more of its devices. Some networks have redundant components that kick in if the primary component fails so there is literally no disruption. A high degree of robustness is consistent with high reliability.

Cost

The key costs to be controlled and managed include the cost to design, build, install, operate, upgrade, and maintain the network. Cost is obviously a function of the other design parameters. A highly reliable, fast response time, extremely secure, robust, high throughput network is much more expensive than one with lower standards.

Networks are designed by making a trade-off among the various parameters. For example, if the network is not going to be used for data and file transfers, throughput may be of less importance than fast response time and reliability.

Topology

Topology is the manner in which devices on the network are physically arranged relative to one another. Several options are shown in Exhibit 4.2 and briefly summarized below.

Point-to-Point

When **point-to-point** topology is used, each pair of devices is connected by a single communications line. All of the communications capacity of that line is dedicated to support communications between the two devices. Such a connection provides high capacity and, should the communications line fail, only the two devices connected to that line would be unable to communicate. Point-to-point is used when there is a high volume of traffic between two devices or when there is a desire to keep the communications network simple at the expense of higher operating costs.

Multi-drop

When **multi-drop** lines are used, special communications devices such as multiplexers help many devices share a single data communications line. This approach reduces the number of communications lines and thus reduces the costs for a network with a large number of devices. As long as no one device on the multi-drop line is "too talkative," this arrangement can provide excellent response time and throughput at low costs. However, should the multi-drop line fail, none of the devices on it can communicate.

Star

A **star** network has a central node that connects to each device by a single point-to-point link. Any communication between one device and

Exhibit 4.2
Network Topology
Options

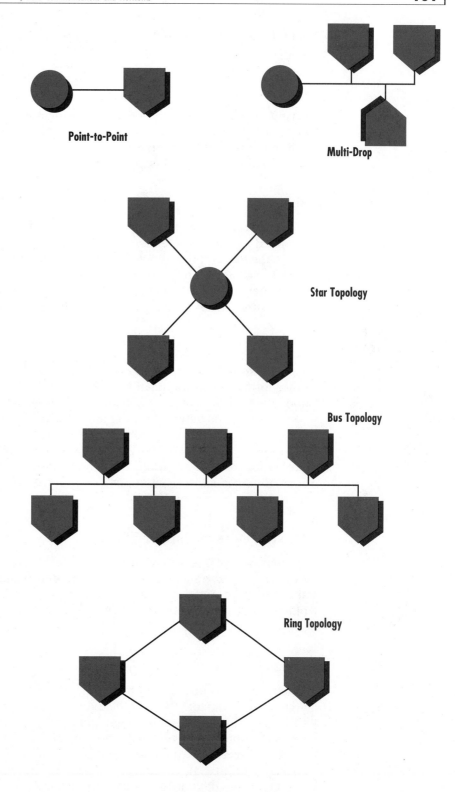

Point-to-Point

Multi-Drop

Star Topology

Bus Topology

Ring Topology

another must pass through the central node. If the central node should fail, communications among the devices is impossible.

Ring

A **ring** network has all the devices tied together on a single communications path so that a signal passes through one device at a time before returning to the originating device. The devices are arranged to form a complete, closed circle.

Bus

All devices are arranged along a single communication line that can be extended at one of the ends.

In the **bus** and ring topologies, all transmissions are broadcast. This means that any signal transmitted on the network passes all devices on the network. The receiving intelligence in each device recognizes its address on a given signal and copies only signals addressed to it.

Transmission Media

The **transmission medium** is the physical path over which data and other forms of communications are transmitted between the sending and receiving devices on a network. A **channel** is a path that supports communications between sender and receiver. A **circuit** is a transmission facility that provides one or more channels of communication. For example, a standard telephone line can be subdivided to provide twenty-four channels. When the circuit must span a great distance, such as across a state, nation, or ocean, it may be provided by one or more common carriers.

Twisted Pairs of Copper Wire

Ordinary telephone wires, consisting of a pair of copper wires, are a frequently used transmission media. **Twisted copper wire** is inexpensive and many offices already have telephone wire running to their offices to provide telephone service. These same wires can be used to support data communications as well as voice communications.

Coaxial Cable

Coaxial cable comes in several forms, but all forms are composed of a central conductor, the part of the cable carrying the signal that is surrounded by a dielectric, or nonconducting insulator; a solid or woven metal shielding layer; and finally, a protective plastic outer coating. All these layers are concentric around a common axis, thus the term coaxial (Exhibit 4.3). Coaxial cable is largely immune to electric noise and can carry data at higher rates over longer distances than twisted copper wire.

Exhibit 4.3
Coaxial Cable

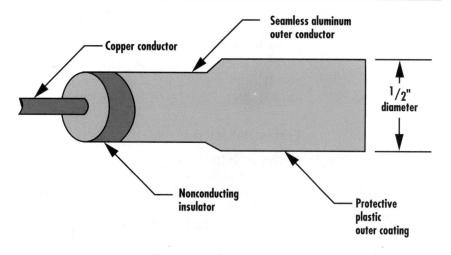

Optical Fiber

Optical fiber uses laser technology to produce an intense narrow beam of light that can be modulated or changed in frequency to convey prodigious amounts of data. The light is transmitted through nearly flawless tubes of glass less than half the diameter of a human hair. The glass fibers are flexible and can be bent in any direction without breaking. Thousands of glass fibers can be combined into an optical fiber cable (Exhibit 4.4). As such, optical fiber cables are direct replacements

Exhibit 4.4
Optical Fiber

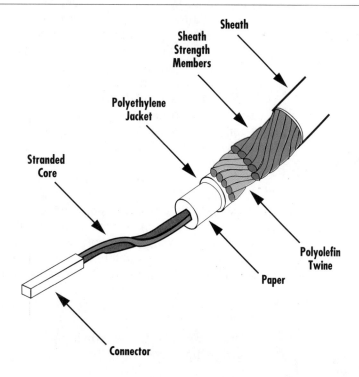

for coaxial cables and wire pairs. They occupy much less space for an equivalent transmission capacity, which is a major advantage in crowded ducts. Optical fibers can transmit data faster than other technology, and signals are impervious to electromagnetic interference from lightning, nearby electric motors, or other sources.

Terrestrial Microwave

At very high frequencies, a radio signal has the ability to carry a large amount of information. Beyond the television spectrum, in the super high frequency range, microwave radios focus narrow beams of concentrated energy that can be transmitted in a line of sight for up to 30 miles. In inaccessible areas, such as mountainous terrain, the signal can be sent from mountaintop to mountaintop, eliminating miles of path clearing and wiring. One problem encountered by microwave transmission is absorption and scattering of energy as it travels through the atmosphere; some atmospheric conditions may cause fading and loss of signal. The ability to space microwave stations up to 30 miles apart was such a significant breakthrough that in a very short time, microwave transmission became the primary intercity transmission medium.

Communications Satellites

Another approach to establishing a microwave link is through the use of **communications satellites** placed into geosynchronous orbit 22,500 miles above the equator. A satellite at this distance from the Earth takes the same time to orbit the Earth as it takes the Earth to rotate around its axis—one day. Thus the satellite remains stationary relative to a specific location on Earth (Exhibit 4.5). This simplifies the design and operation of an Earth station since the Earth station transmitter and receiver need not move to track the satellite. At microwave frequency, radio waves are relatively unaffected by the ionosphere (an ionized layer of air 25 to 250 miles above the Earth) and pass through it in a straight line out into space. Thus the communications satellite serves as a relay station in space. The satellite transponder receives a weak signal from the Earth station (approximately 22,500 miles away), amplifies it, changes its frequency, and retransmits it back to Earth where it is received by another Earth station near the final destination of the message. The retransmission frequency must be changed to avoid interference between the weak incoming signal and the powerful outgoing signal. Many large corporations and other users have developed networks of small satellite dish antennae known as VSAT (very small aperture terminal) to connect various locations.

Cellular Radio

Cellular radio is based on dividing a geographical area (typically a large metropolitan area) into a honeycomb of communications cells. Rather

Exhibit 4.5
Illustration of Satellite Communications

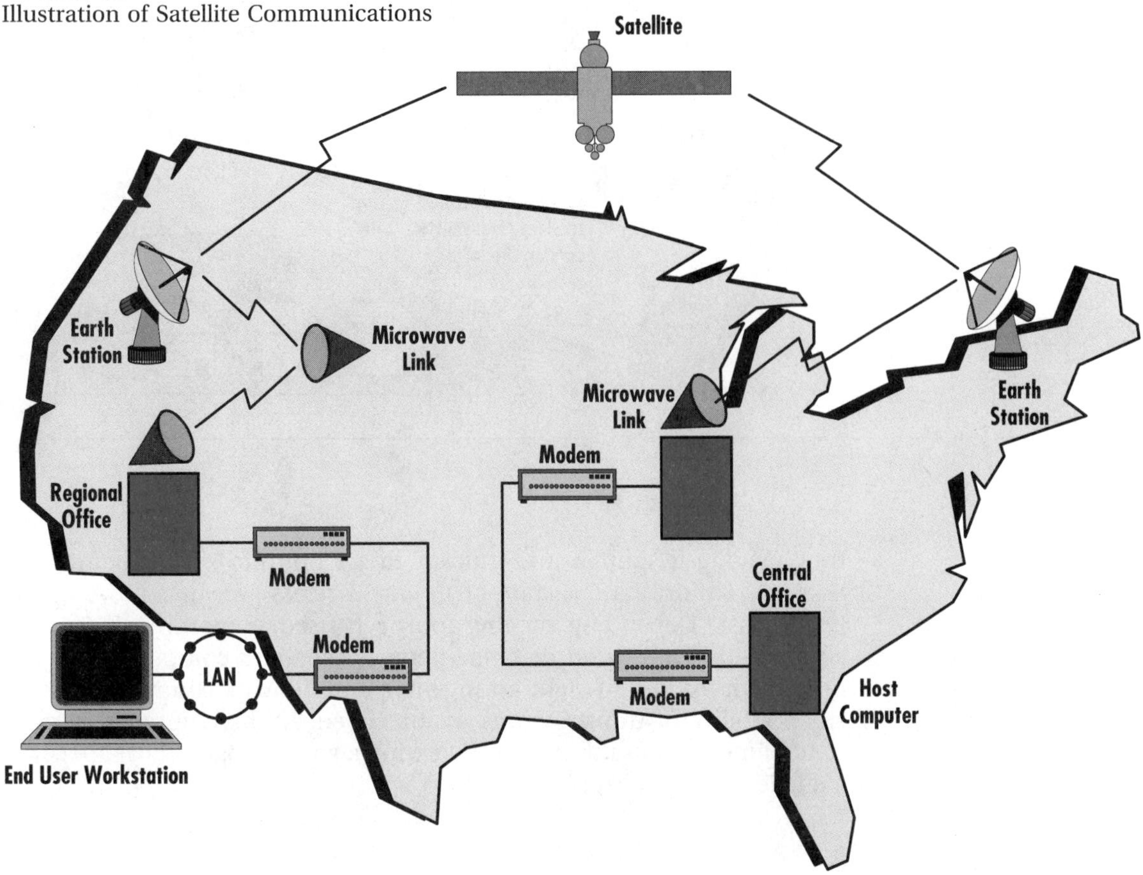

than one high-powered radio transmitter to serve the entire area, each cell has its own low-power transmitter. However, a central computer is required to coordinate and control the transmissions of thousands of mobile phone users as they move from one cell to another (Exhibit 4.6). Cellular radio has become an important communications medium for mobile voice and data communications.

Wireless

Wireless is based on one of several different approaches. One approach uses infrared light to establish communication links among network components. Another approach uses high-frequency radio transmissions to interconnect network components in a fashion similar to cellular radio. Yet another approach involves low-frequency radio transmissions employing a technique called spread spectrum. Wireless is an exciting solution since it eliminates the need for wires and cables,

Exhibit 4.6
Cellular
Communications

Source: "How a Cellular Call Works." USA Today August 17, 1993, p. 28. Copyright 1993, USA Today. Reprinted with permission.

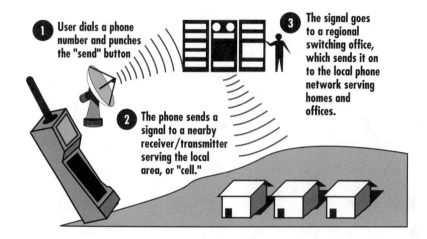

1 User dials a phone number and punches the "send" button

2 The phone sends a signal to a nearby receiver/transmitter serving the local area, or "cell."

3 The signal goes to a regional switching office, which sends it on to the local phone network serving homes and offices.

thus making it simpler and quicker to set up, move, and maintain a network. Unfortunately, state-of-the-art wireless networks have a high initial cost. Depending on the approach used, there are other constraints—limitations on distance between network components, a requirement for line-of-sight arrangements of network components, and susceptibility of transmissions to interference. This approach is currently limited to use in networks serving a small geographical area, say a single floor in a building.

Access Control

Access control is the means by which traffic is controlled on the network. It is a critical factor in determining response time and throughput on the network. There are two general classes of access control: **random** (also called contention) and **deterministic.** With a random access method, any device on the network can initiate a transmission at any time. With a deterministic method, each device must wait its turn.

Carrier Sense Multiple Access (**CSMA**) is a common random access method. In a CSMA network, all devices can sense traffic on the network. When a device wishes to transmit, it listens for what it recognizes as traffic. If the device senses traffic, it delays its transmission for a random time interval and then resumes listening. When the station senses no traffic, it transmits. Carrier Sense Multiple Access with Collision Detection (**CSMA/CD**) is a refinement of this approach in which the devices continue to "listen" after they transmit to ensure that no other device interrupts its transmission as it travels to its destination.

Token passing is a widely used deterministic access method. A token is a data packet used to transmit information. With this approach, devices give up the right to transmit to whichever device has the token. A device with something to transmit waits until it receives

Real World Perspective

Satellite Communications at Kmart

Kmart, one of the world's largest retailers, implemented a satellite network with very small aperture terminals (VSAT) at each of its more than 2,200 stores to support on-line credit authorization. The satellite network puts Kmart on-line with its credit card providers, who can then look at a customer's live credit record and check up-to-date balances and payment history to make a credit authorization decision.

When a retailer does $1,000 worth of credit sales and turns their credit vouchers over to the credit card companies (MasterCard, Visa, etc.), it gets paid something less than $1,000. The difference is called the discount. Implementing an improved credit authorization process based on satellite communications earned Kmart a lower discount rate. The savings are significant, enough to recover the costs of the satellite network. Thus other uses and the resulting business benefits derived from the network essentially "ride free."

Not only does on-line credit authorization lead to savings from a lower discount rate, but it also provides improved customer service. Credit authorizations are now completed in three seconds versus the half minute or minute that it takes at other retailers not employing this approach.

Customers notice the difference, especially at peak holiday buying seasons. The faster credit authorization provides a competitive edge.

The network includes a $3 million central hub at the Troy, Michigan, headquarters and satellite transceivers at nearly 2,200 Kmart stores throughout the United States. Kmart leases satellite transponder services from GTE Spacenet to provide seven-day-a-week service over the Kmart Information Network (KIN). The network employs 56 kilobytes per second (Kbps) communications channels to connect each store's IBM series 1 minicomputer to headquarters via the satellite link.

Every night, Kmart collects sales data for the previous day from each store. The network also collects detailed data on all credit card purchases. While the on-line credit process speeds up credit authorization, it isn't until the charge is processed that the credit card companies reimburse Kmart. Each store runs its own payroll system locally and sends data to headquarters to update employee records. Information on new drugs and new programs is sent to and from each store's pharmacy system. Any purchasing, store-to-store transfers, or returns are also sent over the network to headquarters. *SOURCE: Scott Wallace, "Satellites Dish Up Service Edge." Datamation, Aug. 15, 1990.* □

the token from the previous device in the token-passing order. When the device receives the token, it transmits its data, then passes the token to the next station.

Polling is another common deterministic access method. A central controlling device "polls" each possible sending device on the network asking if it has anything to send. If it does, the device is allowed to send its message, if not, the polling continues to the next device in the polling order.

Random access networks such as CSMA perform better with bursty traffic patterns in which some devices transmit a great deal of data at one time (burst) or transmit very often, while others transmit a smaller amount of data less frequently. Deterministic access methods perform better under conditions of uniform, heavy traffic than do random access networks. Under any loading conditions, performance is more predictable for deterministic access methods than for random access methods.

Hardware

Many different hardware devices are used in building a network. These devices are summarized below.

Dumb Terminals

Dumb terminals are low-speed devices that transmit in asynchronous mode in which characters travel individually down the line as they are keyed in by the operator. A dumb terminal usually does not have the capability to be addressable. Without an address, it cannot tell when the computer is selecting it from among other terminals to either transmit or receive data (polling). This means that it cannot be connected with other dumb terminals to the same line.

Intelligent Terminals

An **intelligent terminal** can be programmed by the end user to perform useful tasks and can process data with no help from the host computer. The intelligent terminal is quite independent and "talks with" the host computer to access or update data in a data base or to send messages to other devices on the network. A personal computer is the most common example of an intelligent terminal.

Modem

This device converts the message from the sending device into a form that can be sent over the transmission media. This process is called **modulation.** At the receiving end, the modem translates the message taken off the transmission media into a form that can be understood by the receiver. This process is called **demodulation** and is shown in Exhibit 4.7 and described below. An important network design parameter is the number of bits/second (expressed as **bps**) that can be transmitted through the network. Most modems on the market today perform additional functions to facilitate the control and monitoring of the communications process. For example, built-in diagnostic capabilities permit the modem to continuously monitor the entire com-

Exhibit 4.7
Modulation and Demodulation

Modems perform a modulation-demodulation process that converts digital signals to analog and back.

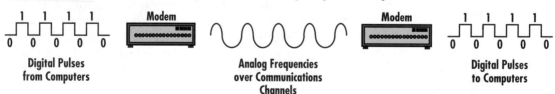

Digital Pulses from Computers   Analog Frequencies over Communications Channels   Digital Pulses to Computers

munications circuit simultaneously with message transmission. The modem can communicate circuit status to a network control center.

Multiplexer

A **multiplexer** is a device that allows a single communications channel to carry data transmissions from many devices. Adding multiplexers to a communications network reduces the number of communications lines needed to support a given number of devices. In many situations, the use of multiplexers can greatly reduce network operating costs. A multiplexer has equal input and output rates. For example, as shown in Exhibit 4.8, four input devices operating at 2400 bps can be multiplexed onto a single 9600 bps line to eliminate the need for three additional lines, thus reducing data transmission costs.

Concentrator

A **concentrator** is a device similar in purpose to the multiplexer, but it allows a large number of input channels to share a smaller number of output channels on a demand basis. The assumption is that not all devices need to transmit at the same time, thus the potential maximum input rate can exceed the output rate as shown in Exhibit 4.9. The ratio of aggregate input rate to maximum output rate is called apparent ef-

Exhibit 4.8
Multiplexer

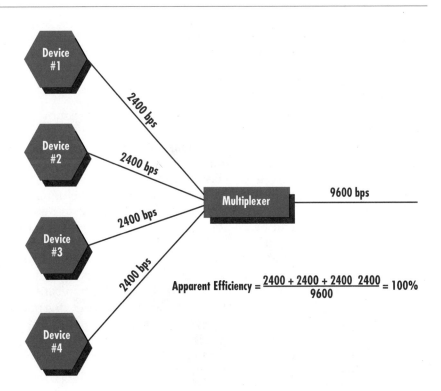

$$\text{Apparent Efficiency} = \frac{2400 + 2400 + 2400\ 2400}{9600} = 100\%$$

Exhibit 4.9
Concentrator

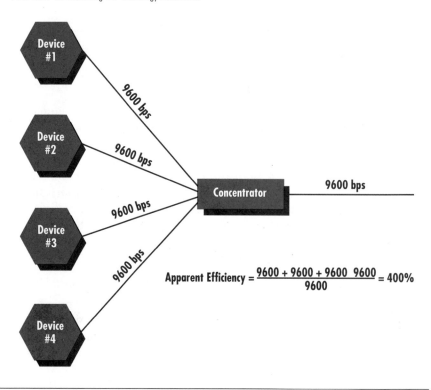

$$\text{Apparent Efficiency} = \frac{9600 + 9600 + 9600 \ 9600}{9600} = 400\%$$

ficiency. The concentrator must have the capacity to store (buffer) data during those brief periods when input rates exceed output rate.

Front-end Processor

The **front-end processor** is a programmable computer that is positioned between the network and the mainframe computer(s). It executes telecommunciations control programs to interpret incoming bit streams and assemble them into characters and messages to be processed, collects messages and data directed to the host and holds them until the host is ready to process them, performs error detection and recovery functions, and polls remote terminals and devices. The front-end processor can also be programmed to provide network management functions such as checking all user logons and passwords for validity prior to granting access to the network, logging all communications activity, gathering statistics on network activity, and routing messages along alternate telecommunications paths in the event of a failure or congestion in the network. By performing these tasks, the front-end processor reduces the amount of telecommunications overhead that must be performed by the host. This saves processing power of the host and enables it to perform more basic data processing for more users more effectively.

PBX

The **PBX** is essentially a specialized minicomputer that uses automatic switching and stored computer programs to act as an automatic switchboard within your company (Exhibit 4.10). With a PBX, you can set up conference calls, transfer calls, instruct the PBX to redial if a call does not go through, and perform many other functions. Calls that originate and terminate within that location are handled completely by the PBX. Other calls are routed to the local telephone company's end office. There are typically several lines, called trunks, between a PBX and end office. For example, an organization with two hundred telephone extensions connected through a PBX may have about a dozen trunks. When a call comes into the organization, the PBX determines the extension of the called party, makes the correct connection, and rings the extension.

In addition to supporting voice communications, the PBX is capable of switching digital information among computers and office equipment. For example, you can compose a letter using word processing on your microcomputer in the office, dial up the local copying machine, and direct your memo to that machine to be copied. The great advantage of using the PBX as a central hub in a star network (Exhibit 4.10) is the ease of connecting devices to it. There are phone wires and a phone jack in every office of a modern office building. Data communications equipment can therefore be installed or moved whenever necessary with little worry about the need to install additional transmission media.

■ LAN APPLICATIONS

A local area network (**LAN**) is a communications network used by a single organization over a limited distance that enables users to share information and resources. It is privately owned, rather than a public utility, with use limited to the members of a single firm or organization. A LAN supports intraoffice, intrabuilding, or intrafacility communications over distances up to a few miles. It provides interconnections for electronic equipment such as computers, terminals, printers, and data storage devices. Some 60 to 90 percent of business communications take place within the few square miles of geographic area that might be served by a LAN. Well over 50 percent of PCs are connected to a LAN.

VLAN

A Very Local Area Network is a LAN that supports a work group within a very small area—say all the workers in the northeast corner of the seventh floor of an office building.

Campus LAN

A campus area is a LAN that supports a work group spread out over several acres perhaps in many different buildings. An example would

Exhibit 4.10
The PBX Connecting Various Devices

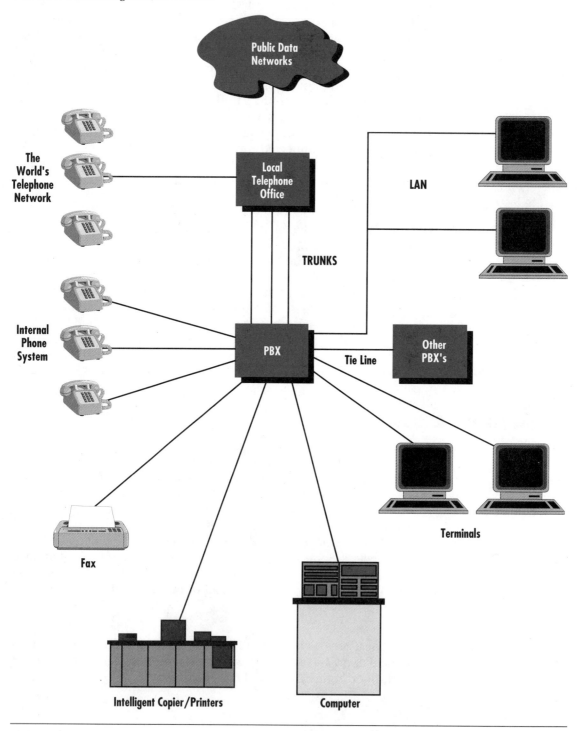

be a LAN serving a university campus or a company with operations in several buildings in a downtown area or industrial park.

Enterprise LAN

An **enterprise LAN** is a corporate LAN that provides people with the ability to connect to host computers, servers, personal computers, and terminals across the company. The enterprise LAN permeates the company so that it is possible to connect to the LAN in any office, lab, or manufacturing area at any company location worldwide. The word LAN implies that the network exhibits the characteristics of a LAN—very high transmission speed, high reliability, device and information sharing, and cooperative processing between clients and servers. Having an enterprise LAN does not imply that this one LAN carries all the data traffic for the company regardless of its destination. Local traffic remains local and only data destined for other locations and/or other LANs travels to those locations over the enterprise LAN.

LAN Operating System Software

The network operating system runs on the **file server,** a workstation or microcomputer that manages the operation of the LAN. The network operating system has many of the same features of a stand-alone personal computer operating system. It must manage disk accesses, file storage, and memory for the file server. In addition, the network operating system controls access to the server by determining who can log onto the server and use its files. The network operating system also manages the interactions among the various personal computers, the file server, and other devices on the network. It provides basic network management, security, file transfer, and connectivity functions to members of a work group served by a LAN. Individual users can specify the type of access they wish for various documents, spreadsheets, and data bases that they create and put on the network. In addition, network services such as electronic messaging, mail, and print spooling functions may also be available as either part of the basic network software or add-on modules. The most important consideration in choosing network software is how it interacts with the personal computer operating system software and with the applications software running on the computers attached to the network. Exhibit 4.11 lists the most common LAN operating systems.

Work Group Computing

A work group is a collection of people acting together to accomplish a common goal or business objective. The work group may represent a formal group on the organizational chart of the company (e.g., the field sales support group), but increasingly work is getting done by small, informal, ad hoc groups thrown together quickly to meet an important business need. Once the goal is met, the work group may quickly dis-

Exhibit 4.11
Popular Local Area
Network Operating
System Vendors

Vendor	Product	1993 Share of Network Operating System Market
Novell	NetWare	64%
Banyan	Vines	8%
IBM	LAN Server	6%
Microsoft	LAN Manager	5%
Apple Computer	Apple Talk	3%
Microsoft	Windows NT	1%

solve with the members going on to other work groups. Thus people find themselves formally positioned in a large organizational group but often doing their real work as members of small work groups. The IT support needed by small work groups includes the ability to create, share, and update business documents and models; the sending and receiving of messages; quick access to information in shared data bases; and the ability to share personal and project calendars to schedule meetings and set deadlines for work activities. Word processing, spreadsheets, data base, and graphics are the most common applications run on personal computer LANs. These needs can be met through use of a properly designed LAN.

The personal computer user was traditionally a stand-alone user. Moving into a work group computing environment by becoming a member of a LAN requires some sort of agreement regarding access to the data files each user creates and maintains. For example, a manager may elect to make some department information, such as employee work schedules, meeting schedules, and memos available to the entire work group. Other information such as a department budget in spreadsheet form might be necessarily shared with only a select subset of the work group. A third type of information might be private and for the individual manager's review and edit only.

Resource Sharing

A LAN supports the sharing of data, software, and peripheral devices. Such sharing not only reduces expenses, but also improves the productivity and effectiveness of the work group.

Data Sharing

Data, documents, and spreadsheets can be stored on the LAN file server where they can be accessed by others. Users can retrieve this information onto their machine, load it into RAM, and view it. If the user has the necessary authorization, they may update the information and place a revised version back on the file server. In this manner, all members of the work group can be working off the same page in terms of the latest information.

Software Sharing

LANs enable organizations to save money on software licenses. Most software vendors now offer multi-user LAN-based software licenses. A multi-user license is purchased to support the maximum anticipated number of concurrent users of the package. LAN users who need to use the package simply request the file server to download a copy to their personal computer. This eliminates the need to purchase a personal copy of the software for each individual user. The savings can be considerable. For example, assume that a department has 140 people who need to use a word processing package from time to time, however, at any one moment, no more than 50 people will be doing word processing. The department can buy a 50-user LAN-based version of the package rather than 140 individual copies. For a word processing package costing $300, the software savings is $27,000.

Peripheral Device Sharing

Peripheral devices connected to the LAN can be accessed and used by the LAN users thus reducing the need for each user to have their own high-speed, letter quality printer. Users simply route their output to the network printer and wait a few moments for their job to be printed. Not only printers can be shared, but other peripheral devices as well, such as an expensive flat-bed, color plotter. Few users have frequent enough need to justify such a device for themselves, but putting the device on the network for all users to share can be very cost effective.

■ WAN APPLICATIONS

Telecommunications networks covering a large geographic area are called wide area networks (**WANs**). Such large networks are becoming

---

Real World Perspective

LANs at Canadian Imperial Bank of Commerce

The Toronto-based Canadian Imperial Bank of Commerce is Canada's second largest bank with assets of $131 billion. The bank upgraded the PC LANs at all of its 1,600 branches to improve customer service and become more competitive. This was done by speeding up its token-ring LANs from 4-Mbps transmission to 16 Mbps and installing IBM's new LAN Server 3.0 network operating system. Users were running 8088 and 286-based PCs with the DOS operating system. They were upgraded to 486 PCs running the OS/2 operating system. Users were then provided both shrink-wrapped business applications and internally developed software to support them in their work.

High reliability is needed so that the LANs can operate unattended, thus allowing the branch banking people to serve customers and not manage complex technology. The bank does not want to be forced to place a LAN Administrator at each branch location. The bank's solution is to manage the LANs remotely via a central location. This is a challenge since there are 1,600 LANs dispersed across thousands of miles and six time zones. SOURCE: John McMullen, "LANs Get the Royal Treatment." InformationWeek, Nov. 16, 1992. □

a necessity for carrying out the day-to-day activities of many businesses and government organizations and their end users. Two key functions provided by WANs are to provide support for corporate information services and for access to the information highway. These are briefly described below.

Support for Corporate Information Services

There is a strong business need for fast, reliable WANs to support such business needs to access up-to-date corporate data. Many types of users need to be able to quickly retrieve and update information in a centralized corporate data base. These include users in accounting, order processing, shipment planning, sales, marketing, inventory control, human resources, or production scheduling. An order entry clerk at a district sales office must access the corporate customer data base to check credit prior to accepting an order. A plant cost accountant needs to check unit production cost data in the manufacturing cost data base to prepare a spreadsheet for analysis of plant costs. A branch personnel manager must search the corporate human resources data base for individuals qualified to fill an open position.

Electronic Data Interchange

Electronic data interchange (**EDI**) is the electronic exchange of routine business transactions (e.g., orders, invoices, shipment notices, etc.) between different organizations using a standardized format that is read

---

Real World Perspective

Using Networks for Transaction Processing at Midland Bank, Plc.

The use of telephone banking to replace traditional branch banking is meeting with success in the United States and Europe. Telephone banking saves time for customers and reduces costs for the banks. It also demands high-quality, high-performance voice and data networks.

The United Kingdom telephone banking service Firstdirect was created by the British bank Midland Bank, Plc. Firstdirect has no branches, all customer transactions are conducted by phone. The service is drawing new customers at a rate of over 10,000 per month and currently supports over a quarter of a million customers who can call anytime day or night to check balances and conduct transactions.

The customer service representatives who handle customer calls use terminals connected to a data network to access a variety of on-line applications such as customer accounting and electronic payment. These applications run on mainframe computers operated by the parent company, Midland. The representatives can also access customer data over the network, including instructions about automatic bill payments that are stored on two other fault-tolerant computers linked to the network. Firstdirect customer service representatives also complete application forms for prospective customers during an initial phone conversation; people need not fill them out themselves. The completed application form is printed out and mailed to the customer for signing and mailing back. This process simplification is responsible for boosting new customers by 40 percent. SOURCE: H. Eugene Lockhart, "First Direct: A Case Study." Bank Management, Vol. 70, Jan.–Feb. 1994. □

directly by a computer application with no manual effort. EDI was originally conceived as a means to help companies minimize paperwork, reduce data entry staffs, and eliminate data input error handling and correction. Managers are just beginning to realize what EDI really is— a powerful facilitator for change in companies whose leadership is sharply focused on profitability, competitiveness, and survival.

EDI works as follows. Two companies agree to use standard EDI transactions for communication. The basic transaction data to be sent originates on the sender's computer. The sender's computer uses the network to call the receiver's computer and confirm that the receiver's computer is an authorized recipient of the data. Software in the sender's computer then composes a message in strict conformance with EDI standards. This message is transmitted over the network to the receiver. Software in the receiver's computer receives the message and processes the data it contains. All transmissions are carefully checked, and the communications protocol includes procedures for error detection and correction. See Exhibit 4.12.

Exhibit 4.12
Electronic Data
Interchange

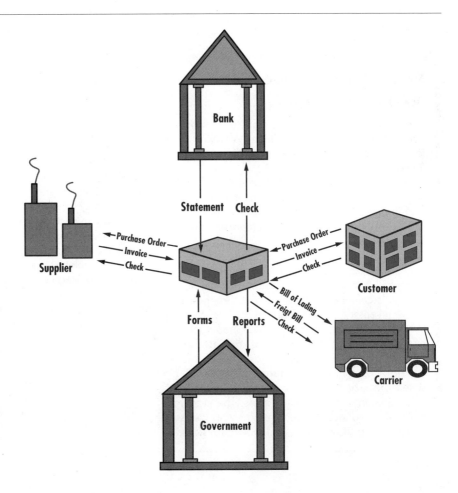

EDI eliminates the printing, mailing, checking, and handling by employees of numerous multiple-copy forms of business documents thus reducing postage, stationery, and labor expenses. It also cuts the time delays that accompany traditional intercompany communications, resulting in significant cost savings and improved cash flow. For example, a customer who places an order through the mail must anticipate several days' delay before the order is received and transcribed into a form compatible with the supplier's internal order processing system. The delay may be on the order of three to five days, requiring the customer to carry additional inventory to ensure that stock is on hand. EDI transmission of the purchase order eliminates this delay and thus reduces the amount of inventory that must be carried. From the purchaser's standpoint, EDI produces significant savings in lowering inventory holding costs. From the supplier's viewpoint, EDI improves customer service and can provide an edge over competitors. EDI transmission of invoices and customer statements also improves the cash flow of the creditor.

The move to EDI accelerated when Chrysler, Ford, and General Motors informed suppliers that as of mid-1990, EDI would be the only acceptable method for doing business. Wal-Mart, K-mart, and Sears also jumped on the bandwagon. Today some 30 industries and

Real World Perspective

Use of EDI at Wal-Mart

Wal-Mart is the nation's leading retailer with annual sales exceeding $35 billion. Wal-Mart also leads the retail industry in the use of EDI technology.

Wal-Mart has implemented an automated replenishment system to increase inventory turnover and improve cash flow. Under this system, Wal-Mart stores capture customer purchases using bar codes and scanners at the checkout locations. Sales data for each manufacturer's products are transmitted daily to that manufacturer using EDI formats. This data is fed into the manufacturer's computer programs, which keep track of the inventory of their products for Wal-Mart. When stock begins to run low, the manufacturer's information system generates an electronic purchase order for Wal-Mart's approval.

Prior to automatic replenishment, Wal-Mart ordered products from manufacturers in quantities equivalent to three months of sales. The manufacturers shipped their product to Wal-Mart warehouses where it was held until individual stores needed it to restock store shelves. Over $5 billion was tied up in inventory, representing a serious drain on cash flow.

Automatic replenishment puts Wal-Mart into the retail equivalent of "just-in-time" manufacturing with costly warehousing all but eliminated. It is the manufacturer's responsibility to manage the inventory and ensure that out-of-stock and overstocking is avoided. Product is shipped in much smaller quantities equivalent to two to four weeks of sales and is sent directly to the Wal-Mart store requiring replenishment. In addition to eliminating warehousing costs and reducing inventory holding costs, Wal-Mart is in a position, due to the fast inventory turnover, where they can sell the product before they have to pay for it.

A controversial side effect of the automatic replenishment system is that it eliminates the role of the independent sales representative and merchandise broker since the giant retailer now does business directly with the manufacturers.

SOURCE: Bruce Caldwell, "Wal-Mart to Middlemen: Bye, Bye, Thanks to EDI." InformationWeek, Dec. 9, 1991. □

thousands of companies worldwide are heavily involved in implementing EDI to facilitate data transfer processes.

Access to the Information Highway

Innovative entrepreneurs, exciting new technology, and imaginative users have combined to create the information highway. By gaining access to this highway, users can access on-line services, subscribe to bulletin boards, and send electronic mail.

On-Line Services

Many people need to access data about things happening outside their company. A number of data base vendors are available who provide data from government and industry sources. Other vendors are available who provide access to full-text data bases of articles from newspapers, magazines, trade publications, government publications, and technical journals. Some of the more popular services include America Online, CompuServ, Delphi, GEnie, Lexis, and Prodigy. These vendors operate a wide area network that allows users to gain access to the data stored on their computers. A user pays a subscription fee and usually an hourly usage fee to use an on-line service.

Bulletin Boards

Bulletin board services are electronic meeting places used to share information and to communicate. Bulletin boards are often sponsored by government agencies, community service organizations, and computer user groups. Computer hardware and software companies provide bulletin boards so that users can ask questions and receive information about their products. Such bulletin boards include files that can be downloaded for use with the product (e.g., to provide fixes to bugs in the software). A large number of bulletin boards are available that cover a wide range of topics such as books, videos, sports, job-hunting, games, the environment, politics, automobiles, and favorite travel locations. After users access the bulletin board, they can browse through it to read messages, news, and articles or they can elect to send a message of their own. Other users may then respond. Users can obtain descriptions of files that are available to download from the bulletin board to the user's own personal computer. Users may also send files to upload to the bulletin board. All bulletin boards have some sort of house rules that set the tone for the bulletin board. Users agree to abide by these rules when they subscribe to the service. The rules may cover such things as what language is unacceptable in messages and what kinds of files may not be uploaded to the system. They may even set a minimum age requirement for members. The rules of the service are set and monitored by the board's sysops. The sysops monitor messages and may "bounce" any user who fails to abide by the rules.

Real World Perspective

Accessing the Information Highway Via Internet

In the early 1970s, the United States Department of Defense developed an experimental computer network called ARPAnet. Its goal was to support military research by linking computers and researchers at various companies, universities, and federal agencies. This network has grown and expanded over time to become the mammoth source of information known as the Internet—a vast collection of networks and computers with access to a whole world of data.

Services available on the Internet include electronic mail and bulletin board services. There are over one thousand separate bulletin board topics including skiing, the Koran, gay and lesbian discussion groups, artificial intelligence, economics, woodcutting, and architecture.

When a user accesses Internet, the computer sends out a packet "wrapped" in an envelope that provides an "address" to which it is to be sent. Special computers called routers read the address and determine the path that moves the packet quickly and reliably to its destination. Thus the Internet is like a busy highway in which envelopes act like vehicles merging with one another.

An incredible amount of information is stored in public files and all you need to do to get that information is to log on, use your Internet electronic mail address as a password, search for the files you want, and then download them to your computer. However, figuring out how to use the Internet can be overwhelming for the beginner. Given the huge amount of data accessible through the Internet, new users initially experience information overload. To overcome this, users need to determine what information they wish to access and where it is located. They then must obtain the address of the computer they wish to access and determine how to use the particular service. This requires some knowledge of UNIX conventions such as how servers and files are named. The Internet offers several indexes of information and their location, such as Gopher Jewels, Global Network Navigator, and InterNIC Directory and Database services. Once you know where to go, you can use a search-and-retrieve system such as Gopher, Archie, or Mosaic, or WWW to locate the files you want.

Electronic Mail

For users of corporate electronic mail systems (e-mail), access to the information highway is eye opening. Suddenly the community of people with whom you may communicate is expanded from the employees of your company to 40 million people worldwide, including heads of state, leading scientists, heads of major corporations, authors, and movie stars.

■ COMPUTER/NETWORK ARCHITECTURES

Architecture Types

There are several approaches for connecting computers together using data communications networks.

Terminal-to-Host Architecture

With **terminal-to-host** architecture, the application and the data base reside on the same host computer. The user interacts with the application and data using a "dumb" terminal. Since the dumb terminal has no data processing capability, all computations, data accessing and formatting, as well as data display, are done by an application that runs on the host computer (Exhibit 4.13).

File Server

In this type of architecture, the application and the data base reside on the same host computer, called the **file server.** The data base management system runs on the end user's personal computer or workstation. If the user needs even a small subset of the data that resides on the file server, the file server sends the user the entire file that contains the data requested, including a lot of data the user does not want or need. The downloaded data can then be analyzed, manipulated, formatted, and displayed by a program that runs on the user's personal computer (Exhibit 4.14).

Distributed Data Processing

Distributed data processing provides computer capability on multiple computers that can process independently and that also interact regularly by exchanging data over a network. This architecture works well in organizations where microcomputers, minicomputers, and mainframe computers are placed in plants, sales offices, warehouses, and other locations geographically remote from central headquarters (Exhibit 4.15). These distributed processors are used to support business functions (e.g., order entry, production planning, shipment scheduling, inventory control, and so on) at these remote locations. Summary information or even data transactions are communicated from the remote processors to the central headquarters for management review, planning, and control.

Client/Server Architecture

In **client/server** architecture, multiple computer platforms are dedicated to special functions such as data base management, printing, communications, and program execution. These platforms are called servers. Each server is accessible by all computers on the network. A client is any computer (often an end user's personal computer) that sends messages requesting services from the servers on the network. A client can converse with many servers concurrently. A user at a personal computer initiates a request to extract data that resides in a data base somewhere on the network. A data request server intercepts the request and determines on which data server the data resides. The server then formats the user's request into a message that the data base server will understand. Upon receipt of the message, the data base server extracts and formats the requested data and sends the results to the user's personal computer. Only the data needed to satisfy a specific query is sent—not the entire file (Exhibit 4.16). As with the file server

Exhibit 4.13
Terminal-to-Host Architecture

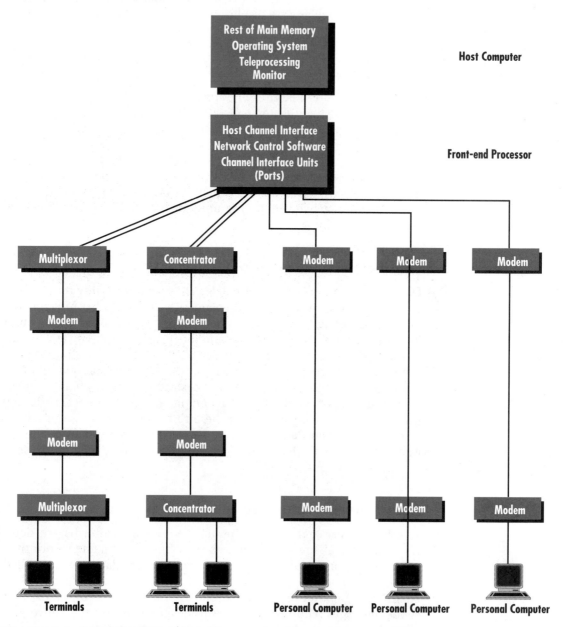

Exhibit 4.14
File Server Architecture

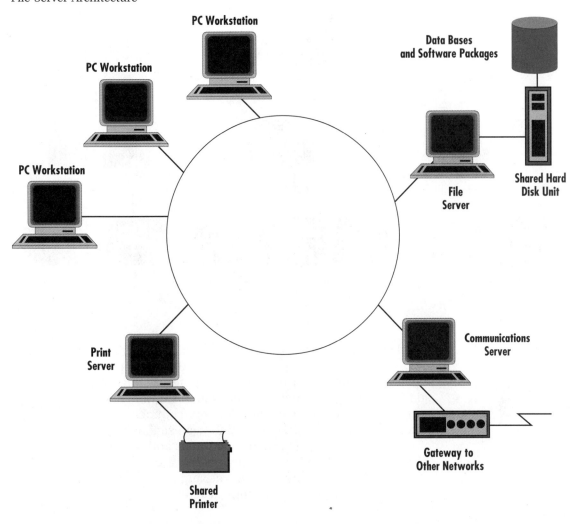

approach, once the downloaded data is on the user's machine it can then be analyzed, manipulated, formatted, and displayed by a program that runs on the user's personal computer.

Advantages/Disadvantages of Client/Server

There are several advantages of the client/server approach over the file server.

Reduced Cost

The functionality achieved with client/server computing can exceed that provided by a traditional minicomputer or even a mainframe

Exhibit 4.15
Distributed Data Processing Architecture

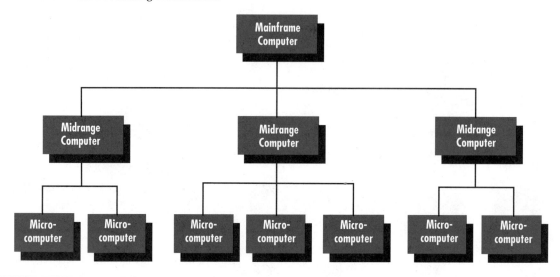

based computer system at a lower total cost. With client/server, a powerful workstation costing less than $25,000 may replace much of the function provided by a midrange computer costing over $100,000. In addition, vendor contracts for workstation software and hardware support are cheaper than vendor support contracts for midrange and mainframe computers. Thus, many organizations view the migration of applications from mainframe computers and terminal-to-host architecture to file servers and the client/server architecture as a significant cost savings opportunity. This downsizing, or as some call it "rightsizing," can yield significant savings in reduced hardware and software support costs.

Exhibit 4.16
Client/Server
Architecture

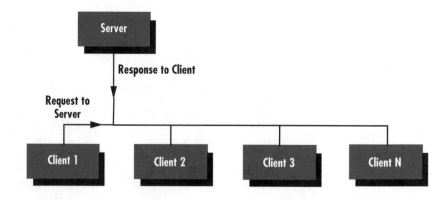

Improved Performance

The most important difference between the file server architecture and client/server is that the latter much more efficiently minimizes traffic on the network. With client/server, only the data needed to satisfy a user query is moved from the data base to the client device, whereas the entire file is sent in file server. The smaller amount of data being sent over the network greatly reduces the time delay for the user to receive a response.

Increased Security

Security mechanisms can be implemented directly on the data base server through the use of stored procedures. These procedures execute faster than the password protection and data validation rules attached to individual applications on a file server. They can also be shared across multiple applications.

The type of application most appropriate for a client/server architecture is one that uses large data files, requires fast response time, and needs strong security and recovery options. All these factors point to the kind of applications that are central to the operation and management of the business. On-line transaction processing or decision-support applications are particularly good candidates for client/server computing.

While client/server systems have much to offer in terms of practical benefits, it should be noted that there are some problems.

If all costs associated with client/server are accounted for, expected savings may fail to materialize. Moving to a client/server architecture is a major two-to-five year conversion process. Over that time period, considerable costs will be incurred for hardware, software, communications equipment and links, data conversion, and training. Costs will be even higher for multiple-site companies converting to client/server. These expenses are hard for the IT organization to track because they are often paid by the end users directly. Thus the move to client/server may be much more expensive than the IT organization realizes.

Implementation of the client/server architecture leads to operating in a multivendor environment with, in many cases, relatively new and immature products. Situations such as these make it likely that problems will arise. Often such problems are difficult to identify and to route to the appropriate vendor.

Mainframe computers have been around a long time, PC networks have not. Consequently, many IT organizations are not staffed with people who have all the skills required to install and support LANs, deal with data base architecture issues, develop applications using graphical user interfaces, and administer multiple data bases spread across multiple computers. This may cause start-up problems in system support and operation as well as some initial delays in bringing up early applications.

Nevertheless, the dominance of single-vendor environments and terminal-to-host architecture is fading fast as corporations move into

Real World Perspective

Use of Client/Server at Brewers Retail, Inc.

Brewer's Retail, Inc. is a Mississauga, Ontario, company who once held a legal monopoly for beer distribution in Ontario. The company is changing to the client/server architecture to meet business needs resulting from the loss of their monopoly and increased global competition.

Approval of the General Agreement on Trade and Tariff (GATT) in 1993 generated an onslaught of foreign imports, many of them less expensive American beers. The increased competition has completely upset the traditional Canadian beer market, which is estimated to be a 17 million-barrel market, about one-tenth the size of the U.S. market. Currently sixteen brewers based in Ontario distribute their products through Brewers Retail, a cooperative owned by Labatt's Ontario Breweries, The Molson Cos. Ltd., and Northern Breweries Ltd. The number of brewers selling to the Ontario market will likely more than double as beer makers worldwide gain access to Brewer Retail's 450-plus stores.

In anticipation of the increased competition, Brewers Retail decided to accelerate key elements of its five-year IT plan. Plans to upgrade to new ordering and point-of-sale systems were deferred, and focus was placed on completing a new stock-management system as soon as possible. The more open market resulting from GATT meant heavier sales volume and a wider variety of brands to manage (already brewers are launching nonalcoholic, dry, and ice brewed versions of their products). Brewer's Retail recognized that a more responsive stock management system was essential to their survival.

Brewers old inventory-balancing application ran on workstations that processed daily point-of-sale data from in-store systems and communicated with a mainframe computer for order and distribution processing. Under this arrangement, the company could update inventory only on a weekly or monthly basis. With the new client/server system, the entire ordering function, as well as truck routing and statistical reporting, has moved from the mainframe to workstations connected to a LAN network. Now inventory can be updated daily. The move to client/server computing also reduced data processing costs by eliminating costs associated with the maintenance of mainframe hardware and software.

the much more complex client/server environment with multiple vendors for networks, hardware, and software. Open systems are essential to implementing a client/server architecture so that managers are free to choose clients and servers and be assured that their combinations will be able to communicate with one another.

■ MANAGEMENT ISSUES

Telecommuting

Work places are changing with more and more work being done away from the traditional office (Exhibit 4.17). Many businesses are adopting policies that allow workers to remain at home and use a microcomputer to communicate via electronic mail to other workers and to pick up and deliver results. The technology exists to make this practical. Managers of the 90s increasingly will need to consider alternative work situations, such as telecommuting, both for themselves and their people.

There are several reasons why telecommuting is popular among workers. Single parents find it helps in balancing family and work re-

Exhibit 4.17
U.S. Telecommuter
Forecast

*Source: Link Resources
Inc., New York, NY.*

Working from Home

U.S. telecommuter forecast

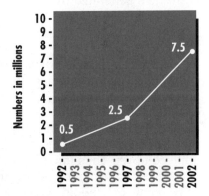

Note: Telecommuter defined as part-time at home, part-time at company office

sponsibilities. Telecommuting eliminates the daily work commute. It enables qualified workers who are unable to participate in the normal workforce (i.e., those who are physically challenged or who live in rural areas too far from a city office to commute on a regular basis) to become productive workers.

The acceptance of telecommuting is increasing among employers, especially large employers. Several studies have shown telecommuting can increase worker productivity, improve communications, heighten employee retention, and improve employee morale. Most important, extensive use of telecommuting can lead to decreased need for office space, potentially saving a large company millions of dollars. Corporations are also being encouraged by public policy to try telecommuting as a means to reduce traffic congestion and pollution. Some companies have been forced to try telecommuting as a result of natural disasters (e.g., extensive flooding in the midwest in 1993 and the Los Angeles earthquake in 1994) and have discovered it really can work.

Some types of jobs are better suited for telecommuting than others. These include salespeople, secretaries, real estate agents, computer programmers, and legal assistants, to name a few. It also takes a special personality type to be effective while telecommuting. Telecommuters need to be strongly self-motivated, organized, able to stay on track with minimal supervision, and have a low need for social interaction. Jobs not good for telecommuting include those that require frequent face-to-face interaction, lots of supervision, and have lots of short-term deadlines.

On the downside, telecommuters often feel isolated as a result of infrequent interaction with fellow employees. Managers of telecommuters recommend that employees work at home no more than four consecutive days and come into the office at least one day per week to socialize with coworkers and experience the creativity and cohesiveness generated by being with fellow coworkers.

Network Management

As organizations have become increasingly dependent on electronic communications to support the business, they have learned the importance of managing their network to ensure that it continues to operate reliably and efficiently. When networks support hundreds or even thousands of users, the sheer number and variety of components and the dependencies among components makes network management quite complex. Thus the quality of an organization's network manager and staff is a vital concern. Acquiring, training, and retaining good network managers should be a top business priority. Network management addresses the following functions.

Fault and Error Detection

For many organizations, the loss of their network for even an hour can wreak havoc on operations and cause great loss of revenue. For such organizations, monitoring the network status and overall operation is essential. Network managers detect, isolate, and correct problems that can lead to or result from system downtime. Some helpful network management features include automatic network alert messages ("Server Down," "Excessive Noise on Line 101"), self-healing hardware devices that switch to backup components in the event of an internal component failure, and network error logs to trace problem history. Communication errors are usually caused by distortions in the communications channel, such as line noise and power surges. Self-correcting modems can adjust for some level of distortion. Other modems can be programmed to measure the noise level and to send messages when the level exceeds a preset tolerance limit. The message from the modem then alerts the network manager to a problem.

Performance Analysis

Network managers need tools that determine the origin of bottlenecks that slow system response time or throughput. The source of the problem must be isolated from any one of dozens of potential causes, such as insufficient capacity in the network communication channels, an overloaded processor, improper configuration of the network operating system, or a workstation that is improperly configured for the network. Performance analysis is also essential for capacity planning. Will a bottleneck be introduced if twenty new users are added to the network? Some system management features that help with performance analysis are the automatic generation of network alert messages ("Server Disk Almost Full" or "CPU Utilization Exceeds 90 percent") and intelligent self-adjusting network hardware capable of easing periodic congestion on the fly (for instance, routing network communications over an alternate path to equalize loads). Software determines the transmission priorities, routes (switches) messages, polls terminals in the network, and forms waiting lines (queues) of transmission requests. It also logs statistics of network activity and the use of network resources by end users.

Installation and Remote Configuration

Network managers spend much of their time installing and configuring network components, especially user software. Network administrators need the tools to look into a user's system from across the network to see how it is configured and what operations the user is attempting. They also need tools to assign software to users, distribute and install software over the network, and monitor software usage.

Security and Audit

Protecting system data, software, and other components from unauthorized modification or access is an essential responsibility of the network manager. Access control usually involves network logon procedures that limit access to parts of the network by various categories of users, as determined by the network manager. Network security is often implemented through use of a logon code and user password assigned to individual users. A network user must enter the correct logon and its associated password to access that portion of the network to which the individual user has been granted permission. In addition, when the user tries to access a particular application on a host computer attached to the network, a second logon and password pair associated with that application must be correctly entered. Another area of concern is the interception of messages routed over the network by unauthorized individuals. Data transmissions can be protected by coding techniques called encryption in which the data is scrambled into a coded form before transmission and decoded upon arrival. Network managers require tools that allow them to allocate appropriate access permissions and that notify them of attempted security violations via alert messages and log entries.

Inventory and Accounting

An accurate and up-to-the-minute inventory of all devices and software on the network is an essential prerequisite for planning purposes and cost accounting. For instance, a company might need to know how many of its workstation personal computers have under 4 megabytes of memory so as to accurately estimate the total cost of a Windows application rollout.

As networks continue to grow in size and complexity, automated network management systems become even more essential to the operation and maintenance of these networks. This type of control is gen-

Exhibit 4.18
Network Management Ensures Meeting Network Design Goals

	Fault and Error Detection	Performance Analysis	Installation and Remote Configuration	Security and Audit	Inventory and Accounting
Availability	X	X	X		
Reliability	X	X	X		
Security				X	
Response Time	X	X	X		
Throughput	X	X	X		
Robustness	X	X	X		
Cost		X			X

erally software based and resident in a network processor. Simple Network Management Protocol (SNMP) has emerged as a de facto network management standard. SNMP gained rapid and widespread acceptance because it is easy to implement and provides useful though rudimentary network management support. SNMP provides standards for the network management data that is to be stored by network devices and mechanisms to retrieve this data.

Network management is a key management tool in helping ensure that the network meets the business needs for which it was developed. Exhibit 4.18 illustrates the relationship between network management functions and the design parameters used to define how the network must perform to meet the needs of its users.

Real World Perspective

FAA Designs Network for High Reliability

The Federal Aviation Administration (FAA) takes network reliability very seriously. For the FAA, network downtime means passenger delays or, worse yet, potential air disasters!

The FAA's network, the Leased Interfacility National Aerospace Communications Systems (LINCS), had very limited network management capabilities—network operations staff would find out about network outages after the fact, usually by phone calls from the affected parties. Furthermore, there was no monitoring system to detect degradation of the circuits, thus corrective action could not be initiated in time to prevent problems. As a result, the air-traffic control network had serious problems. Over a one-year period ending September 1991, there were 114 network outages, an average of nine per month. The outages lasted an average of six hours. The FAA was especially hard hit by two AT&T network outages that shut down New York area airports backing up air traffic around the country. An accidental cut of an AT&T fiber optic cable in January grounded 262 flights. Electrical power outages in September shut down the New York airports for six hours, delaying over 80,000 passengers.

In early 1992, the FAA began a major overhaul of LINCS. The primary network design consideration was to ensure a high degree of network reliability—the network must be available 99.999 percent of the time. This translates to five minutes of downtime per year. The goal is achieved by redundant transmission paths and round-the-clock, end-to-end network management of both the local and long-distance portions of the voice and data network. SOURCE: Mary E. Thyfault, "FAA Targets the Five Nines." InformationWeek, March 23, 1992. □

Global Networks

As companies are forced to operate and compete on an international basis, global networks become essential. Several issues are involved in establishing a global network.

Costs

In establishing a global network, a company may elect to use facilities available to the general public that are provided by common carriers or public services. These facilities are essentially long distance communications links and network management services. Another option is to build a private network by purchasing, renting, or building communications links for exclusive use by that firm. Many costs must be considered, but usually, establishing a private network requires a high initial investment but results in lower ongoing operating costs. Often a network that is a combination public and private network is an excellent low-cost solution. Basic, high-usage services required by most network users may be most economically provided through the private network. Special services required only by a few users may be more cost effective when obtained through the public network.

Network Access

A key design factor in establishing a global network is who will be allowed to access the network and for what purposes. Will the network connect only employees of your company or will strategic business partners, such as customers, suppliers, distributors, and sales representatives, be encouraged to use it? If other companies use the network, will their base of equipment and communications protocols need to be considered? Furthermore, opening up network access to people outside the firm increases network security concerns. A well-designed private network designed for use by only company employees provides the tightest control over network access, but such a network may be too restrictive to meet the true business needs for open communication with the broad business community. When public facilities are used, there are few restrictions on communications; however, since the network can be accessed by the general public, security becomes a major concern.

Transborder Data Flow

Many countries place restrictions on the kinds of data that can be sent across its borders. For example, many European countries do not allow names to be associated with personnel data (salary, education, experience) that crosses it borders. It will be necessary to identify all such restrictions to avoid violation of various national laws.

Software Licensing

Vendors often sell software on the basis of a site license. For example, all employees located at a single given site have unlimited use of the

Real World Perspective

Elf Aquitaine's Global Network

Elf Aquitaine Production (EAP), a major division of Elf (one of the world's largest petrochemical companies), has built a global network that enables it to keep track of operations at remote sites—from the jungles of Colombia to offshore drilling rigs in Antarctica—and encourages the growth of its revenues in today's complex market. EAP, headquartered in La Defense, France, has 20 subsidiaries, mostly in Europe and Africa, and more than 15,000 employees worldwide involved in the drilling, production, refining, and distribution of petroleum products.

In recent years, EAP's business has become more closely linked to the rate of the dollar and the price of a barrel of oil, both of which can fluctuate rapidly. Consequently, it's critical that information moves rapidly between EAP facilities. This not only gives management a way to react more quickly to operational activity, but it also encourages the rapid dissemination of data that could affect the company's response to market fluctuations.

EAP began to build a network to improve the transfer of voice information and data between different French sites in 1988. By 1990, its network included links into England, The Netherlands, Norway, and Italy. However, in 1991, EAP's management saw a vital need to expand the network even further because of the growing amount of information transmitted between facilities.

Built in a double star configuration, EAP's network is decentralized, with workstations at one end and common services such as e-mail and centralized data bases at the other. The network supports multiple protocols and connects personal computers and workstations. Information comes from scientific, technical, financial, and accounting applications. The network also serves to interconnect local area networks at the different sites. The network is designed to fully utilize leased lines to minimize costs, with each link adapted to serve the functional needs of the node to which it is connected and to support the flow of applications from that node.

At the international level, all information needed on a daily basis from outlying sites is transmitted through the Inmarsat communications systems (a satellite system). By connecting to the Inmarsat system, with its suitcase-sized parabolic antenna, workers at drilling sites can transfer files to operational bases that have similar equipment. Then the operational bases forward the reports to Pau, France.

To manage the network, EAP relies on a Motorola Codex Network Management System, which automatically gathers error rates. Motorola Codex services Elf's network from 8 AM to 6 PM Monday through Friday. EAP is working to achieve its goal of near 100 percent network reliability. *SOURCE: Multipoint, The Networking Newsletter for Motorola Codex Customers, Spring 1993. Reprinted by permission of Motorola Information Systems Group. © 1994 Motorola Inc.* □

---

software for a certain total cost. However, what is the definition of a site if the software is stored on a file server and accessed by employees from several countries? There may be vendor licensing issues if software is moved across borders, even if it is done electronically. Many organizations avoid such problems by negotiating worldwide license agreements.

Network Management

Should the network be managed from a single location or multiple locations? A single site provides the greatest degree of control, but the latter also has its advantages. For example, Hewlett Packard, the computer manufacturer, has a global network that operates continuously in eight-hour shifts by network managers in Europe, North America, and Asia. This solution provides continuous, focused management attention in those locations where network utilization is highest.

■ ADDITIONAL TECHNICAL TOPICS

Communications Protocols

A communications protocol is a set of ground rules that devices on the network follow to send and receive data. Think of a protocol as defining the procedures and data formats required to initiate and maintain communications. If all devices on the network use the same protocol, they will be able to communicate with one another. Insisting on using only equipment that adheres to a common industry standard protocol ensures freedom to choose from among a large set of vendors based on factors such as cost, support, service, and performance. Thus a network manager could choose modems from vendor A, multiplexers from vendor B, and terminals from vendor C, and be assured that they could communicate with one another.

On the other hand, a **proprietary communication protocol** supports communications among equipment that adheres to a set of communications procedures and data formats defined and used by a single or very limited number of equipment manufacturers. Choosing to use such equipment greatly restricts the choice of equipment manufacturers for the various components of the network. Furthermore, the use of proprietary communications standards guarantees complications if it becomes desirable to interconnect this network to another network—either another network within the same company or in trying to link up with a customer's or supplier's network.

In response to the need for data communications standards, the International Standards Organization (**ISO**) developed a model for network architecture, called the Open Systems Interconnection (**OSI) reference model** (Exhibit 4.19). The model divides data communications functions and services into seven layers. Each layer is designed to be largely independent of the others and to perform only specific functions. Together the seven layers provide the total set of capabilities and services needed in data communications.

Detailed standards define the services provided by each layer and the protocol by which each layer communicates with adjacent and peer layers. Using the OSI model, two computer or data communications manufacturers can build open systems that can interchange information, provided both define the standards the same way. The transport and session layers are the easiest to define. The application, presentation, and physical layers can be implemented using a great many standards. For example, the application layer standards may be particular to specific industries, such as banking, manufacturing, retailing, and so on. There are many different standards with a bewildering array of acronyms. Some of the more common standards are summarized below.

Exhibit 4.19
The ISO OSI Model

Application Layer	Controls user input from the terminal and executes the user's application program in the host computer.
Presentation Layer	Formats the data so that it can be presented to the user or the host. For example, data to be displayed on the user's screen is formatted into the correct number of lines per screen and characters per line.
Session Layer	Initiates, maintains, and ends each session. A session consists of all the frames that make up a particular activity plus the signals that identify the beginning and end.
Transport Layer	Enables the use and host nodes to communicate with each other. It also synchronizes fast- and slow-speed devices and avoids overburdening a device with too much output.
Network Layer	Causes the physical layer to transfer the frames from node to node.
Data Link Layer	Formats the data into a record called a *frame* and performs error detection.
Physical Layer	Transmits the data from one node to another.

ISDN

Integrated Services Digital Network (ISDN) is a communications protocol that provides functions and services associated with the first two levels of the ISO OSI model—the physical and data link levels (Exhibit 4.20). For geographic areas with access to this service, a single ISDN phone line provides each user with simultaneous phone and medium-speed (64 Kbps) communications. For years, providers of local telephone services have tried to sell ISDN to major corporations as a way of extending data communications to the desktop of any employee who already has a telephone. But it has been a hard sell since most organizations have already installed local area networks that run at 10 Mbps or higher—a 64 Kbps channel does not impress them. However, ISDN is viewed as ideal for home offices, small businesses, or at-home workers who can use a single ISDN line for voice, facsimile, and data communications. ISDN is not currently available in all areas of the United States and costs for the service and necessary equipment are highly variable, depending on where services are needed.

FDDI

Fiber Distributed Data Interface (FDDI) is a communications protocol that provides the functions and services of the physical layer and some of the data link layer of the ISO OSI model. As the name implies, FDDI is associated with transmission over optical fiber networks, although work is under way to standardize FDDI over simple copper wires for

Exhibit 4.20
Internetwork Connections

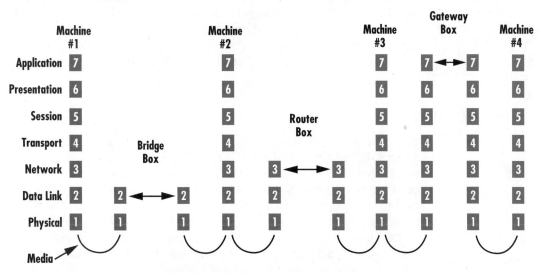

Device costs are approximations to show degree of cost difference.

short distances (CDDI). FDDI is an extremely fast (at least 100 Mbps) and reliable network medium. Since contention-based networks degrade under heavy load, FDDI is based on a modified token-passing (deterministic) scheme that ensures that each device receives fair and frequent access to the medium. FDDI is used as the backbone segment of networks where there is extremely heavy traffic. There is built-in redundancy of the transmission media. If a fault occurs on the primary communications path, a secondary ring can be used.

ATM

Asynchronous Transfer Mode (ATM) is yet a third communications protocol that provides the functions and services of the physical layer and some of the data link layer of the ISO OSI model. ATM supports extremely fast communications (at least 155 Mbps). At the local level, the hub provides each user with their own dedicated channel operating at 155 Mbps. The link between the hubs, the only place users must share a common communications channel, operates at the Gbps rate to avoid any potential network congestion.

TCP/IP

Transmission Control Protocol/Internetwork Protocol (TCP/IP) evolved from a 1970s research project to find a way to link a few computers around the United States. The project was funded by the Defense Advanced Research Project Agency (DARPA) and led to the development of APRANET, a wide area network linking hundreds of computers at various research facilities. In 1980, DARPA began changing APRANET over to a newly developed communications protocol: TCP/IP. TCP/IP is actually a collection of network protocols that together support host-to-host communications for host computers connected via a number of various methods including land-based, long-haul networks, satellite networks, mobile packet radio networks, and high-speed local area networks. TCP provides services at the transport layer and IP provides services at the network layer of the ISO OSI model.

Complications with EDI

There are some problems associated with EDI. For one, changing from a paper-based system to an EDI system requires that a new set of internal controls be developed. The lack of a paper audit trail with copies of all transactions is a difficult concept for many managers and auditors to accept. In an EDI system, the focus of control changes from ensuring that paper documents exist to ensuring security over access to the data received, stored, and generated in the EDI system; tight control of the access and approval necessary to change the computer programs; and limiting access to the system.

Real World Perspective

Data Communications Standards for the Utility Industry

Electric utility companies must interact quickly with adjacent utilities to buy or sell power as the need arises. Complications can arise, however, in trying to automate this function because each utility uses different computers and/or communications devices with a resulting Tower of Babble of communications protocols.

The Electric Power Research Institute, a trade group representing over 700 power companies, set out to solve the communications problem by defining the Utility Communications Architecture (UCA), a set of common communications protocols to be used across the industry. UCA sets guidelines for establishing data communications networks and provides a framework to make it easier for utilities to select compatible equipment that will support intercompany communications. Rather than define a whole new set of protocols,

the UCA standard is based on a subset of already existing protocols that meet utilities' needs for local and wide area networking.

Equipment manufacturers must conform to the standards to be certified as UCA-compliant. Participating utilities will be strongly encouraged to purchase and install only equipment that is UCA-compliant. Digital Equipment Corporation (DEC) was one of the equipment manufacturers quickest to support the new standard. DEC announced incorporation of the UCA specifications into its product line shortly after the standard was defined.

Initially two dozen utilities elected to evaluate the new standard through participation in a set of pilot programs to be conducted over a year.

SOURCE: Henry Stein, "EPRI starts UCAEXCHange, DEC Supplies Networking." Electric Light & Power, Jan. 1993. ☐

Once EDI standards develop for a particular industry, all companies in that industry will need to have an EDI system because their customers will demand it. As the business environment becomes more and more information intensive, companies failing to adopt EDI simply will not last. Companies who wait until industry standards are completely defined run the risk of being left behind by those who have already adopted some form of EDI. The company that acts to put in place some form of EDI system will have the advantage of familiarity with the EDI technology and will be able to contribute to developing industry standards. Should the final industry standards differ from their proprietary format, they will only have to adapt to new standards instead of new technology.

Because an open exchange of data is inherent to the concept of EDI, each industry mandates that EDI standards not be dependent on a specific type of computer platform. Since the inception of EDI in the late 1960s, organizations have developed hundreds of standards, although most are proprietary to an industry, company, or specific business activity. In 1979, the American National Standards Institute (ANSI) approved an official X.12 standard for broadscale EDI access and use. Because X.12 is an approved national standard, it is generally the easiest for businesses to adopt, accounting for X.12's wide acceptance.

EDIFACT

The International Standards Organization (ISO) approved the worldwide EDI standard called EDI for Administration, Commerce, and Transport (**EDIFACT**) in 1987 and, in 1988, the United Nations accepted EDIFACT. The EDIFACT standard is intended to replace both the ANSI X.12 (current U.S. EDI standard) and the Article Numbering Association's Tradacoms, which are widely used in Europe. While EDIFACT is the most comprehensive standard available for EDI, most U.S. companies are taking a "wait-and-see" attitude. Many U.S. companies have already begun using the X.12 standard and are reluctant to become involved in another massive change effort. Companies with foreign trading partners may elect to use the ANSI X.12 domestically and EDIFACT with their overseas partners. Another option is to use a third-party to convert between the two EDI standards. As acceptance of the EDIFACT standard increases, the majority of U.S. corporations will eventually be affected in one form or another. However, until EDIFACT grows significantly in the United States, many companies simply won't make the conversions necessary to establish trading relationships with the smaller circle of EDIFACT trading partners. The U.S. Customs Service has endorsed the use of EDIFACT for import and export. Obtaining invoice detail in advance of the shipment's arrival at the port of entry should reduce the amount of time it takes to clear a ship through customs.

Value Added Networks

A value added network (**VAN**) is a public network that is available on a subscription basis to provide users with communications facilities and services. The VAN operator manages the network to provide a specified level of availability, reliability, response time, throughput, and security, at a published rate. The VAN provides connections or ports to subscribers by giving them a local phone number, logon, and password. By using communications channels that are shared by many users, these public data networks take advantage of economies of scale to provide services at an acceptable cost to their customers. One of the services that can be provided by VANs is to convert one company's business transactions into a form acceptable to another company's EDI system. In this manner, the VAN operates as a clearinghouse for EDI transactions between two companies. This is especially true if one or the other company is following a commonly accepted EDI standard.

Internetwork Communications

Many networks were built outside the control of the IT organization or acquired through mergers or acquisitions. As a result, most companies now have a number of disparate networks to tie together. As the number of separate, different types of networks in an organization grows, interest in linking them increases. An April 1993 survey by Dataquest, Inc. (a market research firm in San Jose, California) estimates that the number of LANs in use at the end of 1992 was 20 million and that the number will grow to 48 million by 1996, thus the situation is likely to worsen. Bridges, routers, and gateways are devices that help link networks, with each operating at a different level in the network (Exhibit 4.20).

Bridges connect two or more networks at the media access control portion of the data link layer, where differences in the high-level protocols used in the two networks are not a factor. A bridge will pass data packets of any protocol, but the device receiving the data packet must employ that protocol to read the packet. Bridges, therefore, generally connect networks with common architectures and protocols.

Routers operate at the network level of the OSI model and feature more sophisticated addressing software than bridges. Where bridges simply pass along everything that comes to them, routers can determine preferred paths to a final destination. They can be programmed to select the cheapest or fastest route, depending on the needs of the network and its users. In addition, a particular router works with only one protocol. In **internetwork communications** with segments that operate under different protocols, a separate router is necessary for each protocol, but several router devices may reside in one equipment chassis.

Gateways operate at the OSI transport layer or above and link LANs to networks that employ different high-level protocols. Packets of data received by a gateway must be restructured into a format understandable by the destination network. This restructuring results in delays in the transmission.

Users on one LAN share data, software, and peripheral devices with other users on the same LAN, but through gateways and bridges they can access other LANs. A gateway allows a LAN user to access a mainframe network or to send electronic mail from the LAN to a wide area network. A bridge connects two similar networks. If two LANs are connected by a bridge, the users of each LAN can access the other's file server and network devices.

Yet another approach to providing interconnection is via the network operating system. Some vendors are developing add-on software modules that allow LANs following different communications protocols to communicate.

Summary

The intelligent use of networks can improve decision-making response time, support organizational decision-making processes, and enable the formation of strategic alliances.

Availability, reliability, security, response time, throughput, robustness, and cost are key design and measurement parameters.

Topology is the manner in which devices are physically arranged relative to one another. Primary options include point-to-point, multidrop, star, ring, and bus.

Transmission media is the path over which data and other forms of communications are transmitted. Alternatives include twisted pairs of copper wire, coaxial cable, optical fiber, terrestrial microwave, communications satellites, cellular radio, and wireless.

Access control is the means by which traffic is controlled on the network. Control may be random or deterministic.

Networks require special software to perform their functions and to provide network management capabilities.

Terminals, modems, multiplexers, concentrators, and front-end processors are hardware types frequently found in a network.

A PBX is a specialized minicomputer that acts as a switchboard and can also route data among the devices attached to it.

A communications protocol is a set of ground rules that devices on the network follow to send and receive data.

The International Standards Organization is active in setting a wide range of communications standards.

A LAN is a privately owned communications network used by a single organization over a limited distance that enables its users to share information and resources.

A WAN is a network serving a large geographical area.

EDI is the electronic interchange of routine business transactions between different organizations using a standardized format that is directly readable by computers.

EDIFACT is a worldwide EDI standard proposed by the ISO.

Computer/network architectures include terminal-to-host, file server, distributed, and client/server.

Internetwork communications require bridges, routers, or gateways.

Network management includes a number of activities that ensure that a network continues to operate in a reliable and efficient manner.

Costs, network access, transborder data flow, software licensing, and network management are just some of the issues that face companies trying to establish a global network.

A Manager's Checklist

✔ Is your firm using networks to achieve the kinds of benefits mentioned in this chapter?

✔ Are you aware of the kinds of network access available to your firm's employees, customers, and suppliers?

✔ Have you been involved in the definition or evaluation of the operation of your firm's networks?

✔ Do you know if there are outside data services of use to you in your role? Do you know how to access these services?

Key Terms

access control	LAN operating system
availability	modem
bps	modulation/demodulation
bridge	multi-drop
bus	multiplexer
cellular radio	network management
channel	noise
circuit	optical fiber
client/server	PBX
coaxial cable	point-to-point
communications satellites	polling
computer/network architecture	proprietary communications protocol
concentrator	random access
CSMA	reliability
CSMA/CD	response time
decoder	ring
deterministic access	robustness
distributed	router
downtime	security
dumb terminals	star
EDI	terminal-to-host architecture
EDIFACT	terrestrial microwave
encoder	throughput
enterprise LAN	token passing
file server	topology
front-end processor	transmission media
gateway	twisted pair of copper wire
intelligent terminals	VAN
internetwork communications	WAN telecommunications software
ISO	wireless
ISO OSI reference model	

Review Questions

1. State three fundamental business benefits companies can achieve through the intelligent use of data communications networks.

2. What are the key parameters used to design and measure the performance of a network?

3. Describe the function of each of the six basic components of a network and give an example of each component.

4. What kinds of resource sharing are supported by a LAN?

5. Define the term work group. What IT services are critical to the work group?

6. Define the term computer/network architecture and identify four approaches.

7. Identify five key functions of network management.

Discussion Questions

1. How are organizations using networks to forge strategic alliances with their customers and suppliers? Discuss a specific example.

2. What role should business managers play in developing the requirements for their company's communications network?

3. What is meant by an industry standard and how is it helpful in setting up a network?

4. Should a company follow industry standards if they can gain a competitive advantage using proprietary standards to "lock in" their customers and suppliers?

5. Discuss three key management issues associated with building and operating a global network.

6. What business benefits can be achieved through use of the client/server architecture? Are there any drawbacks to this approach?

Recommended Readings

1. Drummond, Rik. "EDI: Taking Strategic Steps Toward a Paperless Office." *Network Computing*, Vol. 4, Issue 10, October 1, 1993.

2. Hahn, Harley, and Rick Stout. *The Internet Complete Reference.* Berkely, CA: Mc-Graw-Hill. 1994.

3. Hall, Eric. "State of the Client—Plugging the Desktop into the Enterprise." *Network Computing*, Vol. 4, Issue 6, June 1993.

4. Hammer, Michael, and Glenn E. Mangurian. "The Changing Value of Communication Technology." *Sloan Management Review*, Winter 1987.

5. Inmon, W. H. *Developing Client/Server Applications.* Wellesley, MA: QED Information Services, Inc., 1991.

6. Locke, Chris, "The Internet Gold Rush." *Network Computing*, Vol. 5, No. 1, January 15, 1994.

7. Mamis, Robert A. "Telecommuting on the Increase." *INC.* Vol. 15, November 1993.

8. Naisbitt, John. *Megatrends.* New York: Warner Books, 1982.

9. Orrange, Kate. "Telecommuters Gain Ground." *InfoWorld*, February 14, 1994.

10. Quiat, Barry. "V.Fast, ISDN, or Switched 56—Which Remote Solution is the Right One?" *Network Computing*, Vol. 5, No. 3, March 1, 1994.

11. Robertson, Bruce, and Timothy Haight. "The NOS Report Card." *Network Computing*, Vol. 4, Issue 10, October 1, 1993.

12. Shiplet, Chris. *How to Connect, Driver's Ed for the Information Highway.* Emeryville, CA: Ziff-Davis Press, 1993.

13. Spiegel, Leo. "Removing Barriers to Global Integration Projects." *InfoWorld*, March 21, 1994.

14. Strom, David. "It's Not Easy to SLIP into the Internet; It's a Long, Rocky Road." *InfoWorld*, January 17, 1994.

15. Symonds, William C. "Servers: A PC Money Machine." *Business Week*, March 28, 1994.

A Manager's Dilemma

Infrastructure for a Retail Department Store Chain

Target Stores was founded in 1965 and had 1989 sales of $8 billion. In 1989, its parent, Dayton-Hudson Corporation in Minneapolis, decided to spend more than $1.5 billion over the next two years expanding the number of Target stores from 452 to over 750. Among the 300 new Target stores to be opened will be several "superstores"—enlarged versions of Target stores with expanded inventory.

Management at Target and its parent have been very supportive of the move toward network computing. Imagine that you are the Manager of Store Operations for Target and have been invited to a management briefing of the planned computing and communications infrastructure—briefly presented next.

> All Target stores (scattered throughout the West, Midwest, and South) will communicate via a Hughes Network Systems satellite system, with two IBM 3090 mainframe computers and a fault-tolerant Tandem Computers system at headquarters.

> Each prototype superstore will have an IBM Token Ring LAN with twenty-five IBM PS/2 microcomputers running OS/2. Regular stores will have only ten IBM PS/2s.

> There will not be a designated network manager at each store location. Instead, remote network management tools will monitor and fix network problems. A special network alert system has been developed in-house that works. The only network expertise is centralized at headquarters. This should provide adequate support capability at greatly reduced cost.

First, do you understand the basic infrastructure planned for Target Stores? If not, what questions would you ask to gain a better understanding? As the Manager of Store Operations, can you develop a set of questions to get answers to any concerns you may have?

Forming a Global EDI Network

Your firm, a large U.S.-based manufacturer of consumer products, just acquired a European subsidiary that was a former competitor. The strategy is to create a global organization of the two firms with common customers, suppliers, and products worldwide. Over time, production planning, scheduling, and order processing will be done worldwide from a single location in the United States. There will be a need for sharing data and rapid communications to implement operational decisions. Senior management wants the two companies to blend into one as quickly as possible. The merged company should "present one face" to customers, suppliers, and stakeholders.

143

Your company has long been a proponent of EDI standards and communications with suppliers and customers. In early discussions with the newly acquired subsidiary, the U.S. IT people have learned that the European subsidiary is also a strong advocate of EDI. Unfortunately, they follow a different set of standards called EDIFACT (EDI for Administration, Commerce, and Transport) set by the United Nations and in common use in Europe.

Explain fully why the use of two different standards for communicating via EDI is disturbing to senior management and a conflict with the globalization strategy of presenting one face to the world. How might this problem be resolved? What are some of the sensitive issues that might come up in trying to deal with this problem?

Case Study 4.3

Problems Implementing EDI at Sears

At Sears, Roebuck & Company, any cost savings will be welcome. Now number two behind Wal-Mart, Sears has seen sluggish growth and decreased market share in the past few years. Sales are increasing at a mere 3 percent per year. The Sears Merchandise Group—the company's centerpiece and principal revenue generator—reported essentially no sales growth from 1990 to 1991 (both years roughly $332 billion). Net income in the same period fell from $647 million to $257 million.

Like many retailers looking to cut costs, Sears, Roebuck & Company began implementing EDI in the late 1980s. In the summer of 1989, Sears announced a three-year plan to convert 100 percent of its suppliers to EDI by the end of 1992. The first phase of that program involved moving approximately 350 Sears catalog suppliers onto EDI. The second phase, which began December 1990, involved convincing the remaining 5,000-plus suppliers to do electronic ordering and invoicing. The company plans to invest over $5 million into the program and expects to fully recover the cost of implementation within three years of the project start-up.

To ease the transition, Sears has implemented a formal, five-step process. Since December 1990, Sears has sent letters to approximately 1,000 suppliers and plans to move 200 of them per month to ANSI X.12 EDI. If the supplier is not EDI compatible, Sears is offering extra incentives, such as free software and monthly training seminars.

It is now May 1991, several months into the second phase of an aggressive plan to move all 6,000 of its suppliers to standards-based EDI. The program has hit a snag. Some suppliers are dragging their feet, while others appear unwilling to go to EDI at all. Sears is encountering resistance from suppliers in the form of unanswered letters and calls of disbelief.

The EDI program, seen by some as the largest ever mounted, is highly ambitious, but the company remains confident of its approach. The Sears Director of EDI implementation says, "We're trying to make sure the suppliers understand that they may be jeopardizing their business relationship with Sears if they don't adopt EDI." The Director is also quoted as saying, "We tell our suppliers, 'We're going to stick a sharp stick in your ear, but here's how you're gonna like it.'"

Because the program is just taking off—the first ninety-day deadline came due at the end of March—Sears hasn't yet gotten to the point where it is severing business ties with suppliers on this account. However, the EDI Director warns, "Where support doesn't work, I'll use pressure," adding that the ninety-day deadline is not likely to be extended more than once.

Observers outside Sears do not share this optimism and feel that any firm that expects to have 100 percent of their trading partners convert to EDI is setting unrealistic goals. For example, for the small partner, who probably doesn't even have a PC, Sears is its lifeblood, and embarking on EDI is a very frightening endeavor.

Furthermore, convincing someone to convert to EDI is not easy; many of the presumed benefits—such as reduction in staff and errors—aren't easy to prove because of a lack of studies in the area. Indeed, the results are mixed in this regard. Preliminary results of one set of studies show that EDI can be 50 percent more effective than manual transactions in reducing inventory. Others argue that much of the time savings is eaten up by correcting orders transmitted in error. Sears may end up saving time and paper, but their vendors probably won't.

The EDI Director hopes his suppliers believe that they're making the right choice in supporting Sears. "My goal in life is not to reduce our vendor base. It worries me that we would impose a technology that may screw up the relationship. But if we weren't getting a payback, we wouldn't be doing it."

It is now May 1991 and you are preparing for your weekly meeting with the Director of EDI implementation. What questions might you ask to assess the status of the program and to determine the likelihood of achieving 100 percent conversion by December 1992? How would you evaluate if Sears should continue the strategy of taking a strong position with vendors and forcing them to convert to EDI? If you are not comfortable that this strategy is correct, what alternative strategy or goals (or both) might be considered?

Case Study 4.4

Determining Network Costs

OKKO Company must connect four order processing workstations at each of its five sales office locations to its mainframe computer in Tulsa, Oklahoma. Determine the cost for two alternative networks: (1) each workstation at each sales office connected to Tulsa using a point-to-point line, and (2) all data entry terminals at each sales office connected to a multiplexer and sharing a single communications line to Tulsa from each sales office location. Use the cost data and worksheet on page 146 to cost out each option. Are there other factors to consider in evaluating these two network options?

Cost Data and Worksheet for Case Study 4.4

Equipment	Number Required	Purchase Price (each)	Monthly Cost (each)	First Year's Cost	Second Year's Cost
Workstation		$3,500	$ 35		
Modems		800	8		
Multiplexer		2,500	25		
Communications Line					
Los Angeles to Tulsa		500	750		
Denver to Tulsa		500	600		
New York to Tulsa		500	1,200		
Atlanta to Tulsa		500	750		
Chicago to Tulsa		500	750		

Chapter 5

Data Management

Upon completion of this chapter, you will be able to:

1. Identify three sources of data critical to a business organization and explain how this data is organized into a data base.

2. Discuss what it means to manage data as a resource of the company and tell why managers should be interested in good data management.

3. Discuss the key role that business managers must take to ensure good data management.

4. State three advantages of building systems using relational data bases and normalized data.

5. Identify the type of business applications for which an object-oriented data base is used.

6. Define the term text management system and describe the type of business applications for which it is used.

Preview

Data management (also called Information Resource Management) is a philosophy of managing data as a company resource. Treating data as an important, sharable resource and implementing a data management philosophy can provide an organization with a competitive edge delivering information to decision makers. Business managers have a key role in establishing and maintaining an effective data management environment.

Issues

1. What does it mean to manage data as an asset of the company? What are the benefits of doing so?

2. What is the concept of a shared data resource?

3. What automated and human resources are needed to manage the data resource?

Trade-Offs

1. What are the tradeoffs of operating in a file-oriented environment versus a data-base-oriented environment?

2. Are there organizations where data should not be treated as a resource?

A Manager Struggles with the Issues

Your company is a multidivision organization that is highly decentralized. Each division is so autonomous that salespeople from each of its four divisions call on the same customer to sell products that are unique to that division.

You have asked the IT organization to prepare a simple list of the top twenty-five customers by total sales volume. You are shocked when you are told that it will take several weeks to prepare the report! It seems each highly autono-

mous division assigns its own customer identification number to its customers. A customer who is called on by more than one division has more than one customer identification number. Thus, there is no simple way to aggregate a single customer's business.

Although the IT organization promises to have your report in two weeks, you are left wondering what other data booby traps are lurking out there!

■ DATA AND INFORMATION: BASIC INGREDIENTS FOR DECISION MAKING

The Quality of Data and Information

Data have many basic characteristics that determine their quality. Five key characteristics are *accuracy, completeness, relevance, timeliness,* and *auditability.*

Accuracy means freedom from error. Hopefully, the data capture and data edit processes will detect and reject inaccurate data. It is possible, however, that inaccurate data may go undetected, as if, for example, $10.00 is entered rather than $100.00.

Completeness of data is needed to ensure that valid information is derived from the data. Each piece of data received may be completely accurate, but if only half the data are received, then any information derived from the data may be invalid. For example, the final score of the game was Cincinnati 4. With this incomplete data, it is not possible to tell who won the game.

Relevance means that the data must pertain to the decision at hand to be useful. A common complaint of managers today is that they receive too much data instead of just the information they need to make decisions.

Timeliness of data is important for decisions that involve rapidly changing conditions. Operational decisions about what must be done today to keep the business running require timely data.

Auditability of data refers to the ability to verify the accuracy and completeness of the data. For example, in accounting systems that help people manage the assets of the company, auditability is an important characteristic. The term **audit trail** refers to the step-by-step process by which each item of data can be traced back to its original source.

Because information is derived from data, these same five characteristics apply to it. Useful information can vary widely in the value of each of these quality attributes. For example, with market-intelligence data, some inaccuracy and incompleteness is acceptable,

Real World Perspective

Poor Data Quality Leads to Poor Decision

Super Valu temporarily discontinued self-service cigarette sales—a major source of profits—because of faulty data. The chain believed that its shrink/pilferage rate was 18 percent and thus decided to sell cigarettes only from its service counters. This decision raised labor costs, caused Super Valu to lose tobacco display allowances, and most important, caused cigarette sales to drop by 23 percent.

The company's shrink statistics were later found to be faulty. Many cigarette sales had failed to be captured because of a variety of problems. Some cigarette brands were not in the computer price and item data files used to run the scanner system. Some self-service counters had no scanners. Transmission of scanner data from the stores to the central processing facility was often garbled and unreadable. Because so many sales were unaccounted for, the chain thought its shrink/pilferage rate was much higher than it actually was.

Fortunately, the error was detected before self-service of cigarette sales were discontinued at all the stores in the chain. Otherwise, the error would have cost Super Valu over $9 million in lost revenue and $1 million in profit per year!

but timeliness is essential. Market-intelligence may alert us that our competitors are about to make a major price cut. The exact details and timing of the price cut may not be as important as being warned far enough in advance to plan how to react. On the other hand, accuracy and completeness are critical for data used in accounting for the use of company assets such as cash, inventory, and fixed assets.

Data Critical to the Success of the Organization

Successful organizations must gather data, analyze it to create information, disseminate that information to the appropriate people, and act on their interpretation of this information. Indeed, the ability of an organization to gather data, interpret it, and act on it quickly is a trait that can distinguish the winners from the losers in a highly competitive marketplace.

An organization usually begins by gathering data about its own internal operations, activities, and plans. If the proper transaction processing systems and corporate data bases have been put into place, this data should be readily available to support planning and control activities.

For example, the order-entry transaction processing system captures data that can support both the planning and operating functions of the organization. Examining the open orders and shipped orders over different time frames allows Sales to forecast future sales and plan the suitable size and proper deployment of the sales force. Open and shipped orders can also help Manufacturing prepare short- and long-range production schedules. The open-order data are used by people in the distribution function to schedule warehouse crews and transport carriers. People in the customer-service organization can query the order data base to check the status of specific orders. Financial managers can use the order data to project future cash flow from sales.

Internal data are also used to compare actual results to plans and, through this monitoring, allow managers to initiate appropriate action. How do actual sales compare to the sales forecast? How does actual production compare to the schedule?

A second major set of data that must be processed is the data that describe the business transactions that flow into the firm from external sources—invoices from suppliers, orders from customers, and statements from banks, to name a few. Likewise, the organization sends out orders to suppliers, invoices to customers, and checks to creditors. U.S. businesses participate in billions of such transactions each year. Most of this intercompany data are exchanged in paper form. Some companies engage in *electronic data interchange* (EDI), a process by which the output of one company's information system (e.g., Purchasing) is transmitted electronically for direct input to another company's transaction processing system (e.g., Order Entry) without the delay associated with regular mail or the need for data-entry processes by humans in both companies. EDI is discussed in depth in Chapter 4.

Most of these data are numeric and are expressed in fairly standard forms such as invoices, purchase orders, receiving reports, and bank statements. These data become input to the transaction processing systems and may be used to update corporate data bases.

A third, very significant set of data that a firm must gather is data that provide insight about the industry, market, and other elements of the environment in which the firm competes. This may include market measurement data from data vendors such as A. C. Nielsen and SAMI. Data about competitors and potential competitors, suppliers, customers, and products or services that can substitute for the products and services of the firm are also gathered. These data are needed to provide the firm with a competitive edge. Many times these data are best expressed in text or graphic, not numeric, form. Sometimes the data do not really represent hard facts, but are a collection of rumors, assumptions, suppositions, and just plain "street news" that is needed to keep a jump or two ahead of the competition.

All three types of data are frequently stored in corporate data bases: (1) data about the internal operations of an organization, (2) data that describe the business transactions that flow into the firm, and (3) data that provide insight about the industry, market, and other elements of the environment. A **corporate data base,** then, is a collection of computer-accessible data that is carefully planned and managed to support the data needs of multiple users. Exhibit 5.1 summarizes the data critical to the organization's success.

Not all computer-accessible data are stored in a single, monolithic data base. Instead, an organization is likely to have several data bases. Each data base contains data on a different subject. Thus, an organization may have a customer data base separate and distinct from its vendor data base. The same organization may also have employee,

Exhibit 5.1
Data Critical to
Organization

Data About	Data Source	Primary Data Users	Purpose
Internal operations of the company	Internal	First-line up to middle managers	Operations and control
Routine interactions with customers, suppliers, and creditors	Internal	First-line up to middle managers	Operations and control
Industry, customers, competitors, substitute products, and services	External	Upper and middle managers	Planning

finished-product inventory, and market-measurements (shipments, consumption, price) data bases.

The Data Hierarchy

To understand the concepts of data management, we need to understand the levels in the **hierarchy of data:**

Bits Data to be processed or stored in a computer are represented as binary numbers (0 or 1) called **bits.**

Character (Byte) Eight bits are needed to form a **character** letter, digit, or special character (e.g., $, #, @, and so on).

Data Element A single fact or piece of data that describes an entity (person, place, or thing) is a **data element** also called a data field or an attribute. Examples include: name, warehouse code, product identification number, and so on.

Record Related data elements describing the same person, place, or thing are grouped to form a record. Examples include: the employee record, the warehouse **record,** the product record, and so on.

File A **file** is a collection of related records. Each record on the file has the same data elements, but the values are different. For example, each record on the customer file has the same data elements, but because each record is for a different customer, the values are different. To access a specific record in the file, one data element in the record is used to uniquely identify that record. The data element that uniquely identifies the record from any other record is called the *primary key.* For example, a customer account number may be the key for the accounts receivable file, and social security number the key for the payroll file. Records in some files may require more than one data element for a key. For example, in an airline reservation system file, the key might be a combination of flight number, date, and seat number.

Data Base A **data base** is a well-defined and managed collection of data that serves as a common source of information for many users in many different organizations. It contains facts of significant value to many people.

Content and Types of Data Bases

Consider a consumer goods company that sells its products through retail stores. Its customers are the retail stores (the individuals who visit the store to purchase the products are consumers). Each retailer may have many different store locations and a separate headquarters location for corporate offices. Many different groups within the consumer products company need different facts about the customer. Sales is interested in customer name, store locations, and salesperson assigned to the account. Credit needs to know the customer credit rating. Shipping needs the customer ship-to address. Accounts receivable needs to know the billing address. The customer data base for the consumer products company contains the basic information about customers useful to all these people. It is a shared data resource that is the definitive source of customer data.

In some cases, the data base may contain a massive amount of detail (e.g., three years of customer order data for a Fortune 500 company may represent millions of records). Typically the data are stored at a low level of detail to permit aggregation in unanticipated ways in the future. Clearly the data base represents a vast storehouse of facts of significant value to the entire organization and is often referred to as a *corporate data base.*

One useful way to classify data bases is by the extent to which the data base is a true shared data resource. At one extreme is what is called the **subject data base.** A subject data base contains data about a subject of broad interest to many people throughout the company (e.g., customers, shipments). It is intended that multiple organizations will access and use the data found in the subject data base. At the other extreme is the functional data intended to be used and accessed in a more limited manner. A **functional data base** serves the needs of a particular organizational unit (e.g., Accounts Payable, Human Resources) or the needs of people performing certain activities where there is a need for cross-functional information sharing (e.g., sales planning and forecasting). Exhibit 5.2 lists a number of subject and functional data bases that might be found in an organization.

■ DATA ENVIRONMENT

Traditional File-Oriented Approach

The traditional file-oriented approach to designing an information system takes the view that the primary purpose of a computer system is to maintain a master file of the data required to produce management information. The system and its associated files are designed to meet the specific needs of a single, particular business unit such as payroll

Exhibit 5.2
Examples of Subject
and Functional
Data Bases

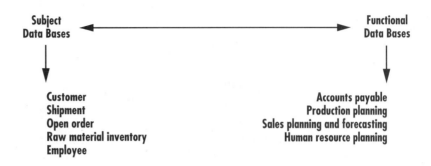

or personnel. The system is designed and built to maintain its own master file and have its own files of maintenance transactions to add new records and change or delete existing records (Exhibit 5.3). This one-master-file-per-system approach results in the creation of very similar, but different, files. For example, two similar but different master files are created to support the payroll and personnel functions. Furthermore, custom-designed files do not support the sharing of data among different systems or organizations (or both).

Now imagine that you are the Vice-president of Sales of a company and that you are told that some basic customer information you need is too difficult and too costly to obtain. Suppose the Vice-president of Information Systems gave you the following explanation: "There is no one source for the information you need. We must extract the data to fulfill your request from several different files. This will require developing a series of programs to extract the data, sort it, and then combine the data according to a common key. Unfortunately, because the data are coming from several different sources, we cannot guarantee the accuracy, completeness, and consistency of the results."

Does such a scenario seem impossible? Well, it is not. Such situations are common when an organization relies on file processing systems in which data are organized, stored, and processed in independent files of data records. This is the major problem of the traditional **file-oriented approach** to developing information systems.

Exhibit 5.3
Traditional File-
Oriented Approach

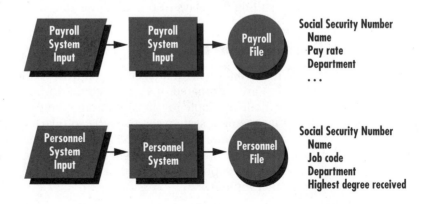

Some of the disadvantages of the file-oriented approach are listed below.

Data Redundancy

Often identical data are stored on two or more master files (Exhibit 5.3). For example, the employee social security number, name, and department are stored in records associated with both payroll and personnel master files. Such **data redundancy** increases data editing, maintenance, and storage costs. In addition, data stored on two master files (which, in theory, should be identical) are often different, and such differences inevitably cause confusion.

Program/Data Dependence

Under the file-oriented approach, any change in the physical format of the master file, such as the addition of a data attribute, requires a change in all programs that access that master file. This undesirable condition is called **program/data dependence.** One of the most extreme impacts of program/data dependence occurred when the U.S. Postal Service changed from a five-digit to a nine-digit zip code. Thousands of computer programs at companies around the world had to be modified at great expense to accommodate the change.

Lack of Data Integration

Management often wants data that exist on different files to be integrated to produce a report of useful information. For example, management may want a report displaying employee name, department, pay rate, job title, and highest degree received. However, the file-oriented approach does not easily support accessing these data to make them useful for management's needs. It will be necessary to design and build another system that matches records from the two files and merges records with the same social security number to create yet another file with the necessary data attributes (Exhibit 5.4). This lack of **data integration** leads to additional design and programming effort, resulting in delays in providing needed management information.

Data Base Environment Approach

In the data base management approach, the many individual master files are eliminated. Instead, a common pool of data—the data base—is made available to many different systems. In addition, the data base management system serves as the software interface between end users and the data base. The DBMS helps end users more easily access the records in the data base. There are many advantages associated with building applications within a data base management system environment.

Exhibit 5.4
Systems Design Required to Create Management Reports in a File-Oriented Environment

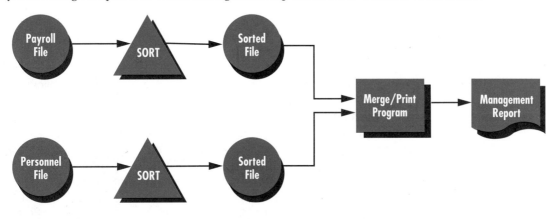

Enables Sharing of Integrated Data

The ability to integrate data is made possible by use of common keys for each data type to be integrated. The key, as already discussed, is an attribute that uniquely identifies a data entity. To enable data of different kinds from different sources to be integrated, the data must have common keys. For example, to integrate manufacturing data (e.g., raw material costs for each job) with payroll data (e.g., hours worked and rate per hour by employee for each job) to calculate total costs, the manufacturing data and payroll data must have a common key. In this case, it would be job identification number.

Minimizes Data Redundancy

Data that are stored on two or more files in a file-oriented environment (e.g., social security number, name, department, and so on, stored in both payroll and personnel files) are stored once in a data base management system environment. This both reduces storage costs and eliminates the confusion that occurs when data from one file do not match with data from another file. Furthermore, by minimizing data redundancy, data collection and update procedures are simplified. Unlike in a file-oriented environment, there need be only one update for each data attribute when something changes; if a customer moves, for example, the street address is updated in only one place: the data base. It is not necessary to update the customer address on multiple files.

Increases Data Integrity

Data integrity is a measure of the accuracy, completeness, and currency of data. Data integrity is enhanced because there is one version of the data that is kept accurate and complete.

Improves Programmer Productivity

The existence of a data base enables new computer applications to be developed more quickly. Much of the effort associated with writing a new computer program is spent on creating the data source that will provide input data. Given that the data base already exists, this portion of the development effort may be eliminated. A standard interface is used to define how the data are physically stored and accessed. The programmer need understand only the interface and not the details of the physical storage and file system dependencies. **Programmer productivity** improves since programmers can concentrate on developing functions to be performed by the computer application rather than designing data file formats, file access procedures, or other details associated with the physical storage and access process. The separation of the physical workings of the data base management system and the physical storage of data from the logical functions that the programmer needs to perform is called **program and data independence.**

Improves Data Security

Data contained in a data base are likely to be more secure from unauthorized access than data in traditional files for two basic reasons. First, the data base management system has a data base administrator, whose primary function is to ensure the **security** of the data. Second, the data base management system itself provides increased security. When data are stored in standard data files, a user can typically be given access to either all the data or none of it. A data base management system contains control mechanisms that can allow access rights to be regulated down to the data attribute level. That is, a user may be allowed to read one part of the data base but be denied access to another part. So it is possible to allow a personnel clerk to retrieve the name of an employee's manager but not to see the employee's salary. Some users may be authorized to access the data base to read the contents only, some to update the data base only, and some to do both.

■ DATA MANAGEMENT

What Is Data Management?

The primary tenet of data management is that data are a vital resource of the enterprise and thus must be managed as an important asset. **Data management** is an abstract concept that serves to group a number of related activities directed at managing data as a resource. The objective of data management is to ensure that the data needed to solve business problems or exploit business opportunities are made available to the right people at the right time and in the proper form to be of use. These activities are summarized in Exhibit 5.5 and discussed next.

Real World Perspective

Pacific Gas & Electric Converts from the Traditional File-Oriented Approach to the Data Base Environment

Pacific Gas & Electric Co. (PG&E) with headquarters in San Francisco, is the largest investor-owned utility in the United States. PG&E is developing a new customer information system (CIS) to replace a 20-year-old traditional file-oriented system containing PG&E's nearly terrabyte-sized (trillion bytes) customer database.

Work on the CIS, which would help the utility serve its entire customer base of 7.5 million, started in 1990. Officials decided to focus the initial effort on a CIS that would serve a relatively small but extremely important subset of its customers: large industrial customers who can get their power elsewhere because of changes in federal and state utility regulations. That group includes about 10,000 PG&E customers or about 30,000 accounts. Utilities call these customers "at-risk" because they can get their electricity from other sources, including on-site generation using excess heat from their manufacturing processes. Eventually, the CIS will add the remainder

of PG&E's customers, starting with other commercial customers and later adding residential customers.

PG&E wants to convert to the data base environment as soon as possible. The current CIS is starting to show its age. While most of PG&E's large customers already use PC-based billing systems, it is difficult to give them timely and accurate bills. Fixing that is the number one goal. In addition, PG&E wants a new system that is much more flexible and that can aggregate various accounts to reflect the customer's view of the world.

The first pieces of the new system will focus only on billing, the heart of any CIS. Once billing is working properly, future system changes will address customer service, workflow management, and managing resources.

First tests on the system are scheduled for August 1994. The goal is to have the initial, basic billing system running by April 1995. PG&E plans to start its rollout for additional functions and accounts in January 1996, staging by types of customer and types of accounts. *SOURCE: Richard A. Danca, "PG&E Levels the Load on Its Customer Information System." Client/Server Computing, July 1994.* □

Why Data Management Is Important

The increasingly competitive global market and the availability of more powerful personal computers coupled with increasingly computer literate employees has created an unquenchable thirst for more and better data. In response, the more progressive organizations are working toward a goal of enabling their people to access high-quality data from multiple sources, integrate the data in a manner that is consistent and

Exhibit 5.5
The Broad Scope of
Data Management

Goal: Make data available to the right people at the right time and in the proper form to be of use
- Develop a data resource strategy and plan
- Obtain management commitment to shared data resources
- Get business managers involved in data-related decisions
- Build an organization to support data management
- Build and share an enterprise data model
- Establish data standards
- Select tools and processes to implement the data resource plan
- Train people to use data, data models, tools, and processes

Exhibit 5.6
Why Data
Management Is
Important

- Demand for more and better data
- Need to access high-quality data from multiple sources
- High value placed on integrated data that is consistent and meaningful
- Need to form useful aggregations of data

meaningful, and form useful aggregations of the data at whatever level of detail is needed (Exhibit 5.6).

In organizations where data management is not being addressed or has been poorly implemented, decision-making processes are bogged down and people are buried under an avalanche of data. Often the data that are available are inconsistent and conflicting. Such a situation makes it impossible to make decisions based on the facts of the matter. Instead, managers must resort to hunches and intuition based on their view of the situation. In today's rapidly changing world, such an approach can be extremely dangerous.

Managers have a key role to play in achieving effective data management. They must recognize whether their information needs are being met. If not, they must define their unmet needs and communicate them. They need to develop linkages to the right people and work with them to put in place the elements necessary for effective data management. Along the way, many tradeoffs will need to be considered and organizational issues will need to be resolved. Managers must take a leadership role in ensuring that needs are met effectively through a sound data management program.

■ COMPONENTS NEEDED FOR EFFECTIVE DATA MANAGEMENT

Data Resource Strategy

Develop a Data Resource Strategy

The **data resource strategy** establishes a basic position and provides a set of consistent principles to guide decision making in regard to data-related issues. Exhibit 5.7 provides an example of a data resource strategy and the principles associated with that strategy.

Data Resource Plan

Develop a Data Resource Plan

The **data resource plan** identifies the data most important to the enterprise and outlines the projects necessary to develop a shared data resource of this data. For example, a consumer goods company might identify that data about customers, consumer comments, and promotional activity are key sets of data.

Exhibit 5.7
A Possible Data
Resource Strategy

Strategy #1   Manage data on a common basis across business processes, functional organizations, and applications.

Principle #1   Data are to be shared among organizations throughout the enterprise.

Rationale: Data become more valuable the more widely they are used. **Sharable data** allows multiple business functions to add value to each other's data investment rather than developing data for local use only. Also changes in data in one area are then readily reflected in other areas as well.

Implication: All organizations must understand and adhere to corporate data standards.

Principle #2   Data are to be standardized according to name, definition, format, and use.

Rationale: Data standards reduce data redundancy, confusion, and misuse.

Implication: Data standards must be developed and documented and made available to users.

Top Management Support

Obtain Management Commitment to Shared Data Resources

The concept of **shared data resources** means that data are accessible by multiple users and computer programs. This implies a single source for data that allows the reuse of the valuable data asset rather than each user and computer program creating its own version of the data. Management support is a key to the success of this approach.

Management Involvement

Get Business Managers Involved in Data-related Decisions

The business manager is the real consumer of the information resource and uses this resource to make business decisions. The consumer needs to be involved in decisions regarding the product, including its costs, accessibility, and so on.

Data Models

A data model identifies things of importance to an organization (**entities**), the properties of those entities (attributes), and how the entities are related to one another (**relationships**). The data model provides an accurate picture of the information needs of the organization. Business managers and IT specialists are finding that understanding what corporate information is needed is a necessary prerequisite for building high-quality, well-integrated information systems.

Actually several different data models at increasing levels of detail are developed when an information system is formed. A high-level corporate data model is developed as part of the strategic planning process. A more detailed business area data model is developed covering the scope of each area of the business undergoing further analysis (e.g., a data model to cover the sales function or product supply function). An even more detailed data model is developed prior to beginning any major information systems project.

While there are several ways to present a data model, the most useful ones are in a graphical form rather than a narrative form. Likewise, there are several ways to develop a data model, but one of the most frequently used techniques is the **Entity Relationship Diagram (ERD).** The ERD technique is supported by rigorous standards and conventions to remove ambiguity and aid communication. It is a data modeling technique that is applicable to the information needs of any organization or industry. Examples of ERD diagrams and an effective process on how to construct an ERD are described later in this chapter.

Data Standards

Corporate data standards are rules and practices used to ensure that data are understood and processed uniformly with predictable results. **Data standards** are recommended strategies, procedures, and requirements for storing, managing, and using data. Data standards include the naming conventions to be used for each data entity and attribute.

Data Dictionary

The **data dictionary** is really a data base in its own right—a data base that contains data about data. The data base administrator uses the data dictionary to capture and maintain data that are invaluable in managing the use of the data base. For example, the high-level logical view of the data base is stored in the dictionary.

The data dictionary contains a definition of each data entity and data attribute stored in the data base. Since data are shared by many users, each of the stored items must have a clear and commonly agreed upon meaning. The definition also includes the agreed-to logical name to be used by all application programs that wish to use a particular data element. The definition may also describe data entry validation checks (e.g., must be numeric and less than $100).

A comprehensive data dictionary also contains cross-reference information, showing, for example, which programs use which data elements, which department requires which reports, and so on. This enables the impact of any proposed change in the system to be quickly determined by means of a query to the dictionary.

A **data directory** is a tool that identifies where data may be found. In a large organization with several computers and many hundreds of magnetic tapes and magnetic disks, such a tool can be extremely valuable. The person or program needing specific data can consult the data directory to quickly identify the physical storage location of the desired data.

Data Management Specialists

Data Administrator

The **data administrator** leads the process to develop a data resource strategy and data resource plan to make corporate data available to all users in a shared and controlled manner. This requires working with top management to gain their support for the concept of shared data resources. It also requires working with business managers throughout the organization to ensure that they are aware of the data assets of the firm and keep involved in decisions regarding data.

The data administrator is responsible for the coordination and consistency of data across many data bases. To meet this objective, the data administrator creates processes for developing data standards that apply across the firm. The data administrator also creates data models to show the relationships among the data elements of the various data bases. The implementation of data standards and useful data models enables users to pull data from several different data bases and blend it to meet the organization's needs.

Data administration is primarily a nontechnical job. The data administrator must be able to communicate with middle- and top-level managers as well as with many data base administrators. The ability to communicate clearly and to anticipate business needs for data are more important than a data processing background.

Data Base Administrator

A **data base administrator** is a highly skilled and trained systems professional who works with end users and programmers in order to design, build, maintain, and manage the data base. In effect, the data base administrator is the liaison between the data base and its users. Serving in this role, the data base administrator must have an understanding of the business of the organization, the data base management system, and the process of designing and building information systems. Data base administration is becoming an attractive career option to individuals with a combined systems, programming, and business background.

The data base administrator's role is to work with the users to decide the content of the data base—in other words, exactly what entities are of interest and what attributes are to be recorded about those entities. Information about the number of occurrences of the various data entities, attributes, and their interrelationships is needed to create a model that presents the logical view of the data base that satisfies the needs of its users.

The data base administrator then works with the users to learn the specifics of how the data base will be used. It is necessary to determine the number and frequency of different kinds of requests for information from the data base. The frequency of updating or changing the data base, including the deletion of inactive records, must also be determined. The users' desire for response time to various queries must also be determined (e.g., less than a three-second response time for an inquiry to check customer credit). These needs are then used to convert the high-level logical model into lower-level logical models that represent the view of the data base necessary to satisfy each demand that will be placed on it.

The data base administrator also works with the users to define the data edits and controls regarding changes and additions to the data base. For example, some people may need both update and read access to particular data entities or attributes (or both) in the data base, while others may be restricted to access only. Importantly, the need for security and disaster recovery procedures is defined.

The data base administrator then takes all this into account along with the features of the specific data base management system to create a definition of the physical structure of the data base that will satisfy the users' needs in as cost-effective and as efficient a manner as possible. Having done this, the data base administrator uses the data definition language to define the data base schema and subschemas needed to support the various views of the data base. These will be used by the data base management system to respond to access requests. This process will be discussed further in the next section.

The data base administrator works with the programmers as they build applications to ensure that their programs are written in compliance with data base management system standards and conventions. They will particularly enforce adherence to definition and naming standards by centrally defining all data base entities and attributes so that all application programs share a common model of data resources.

Once the data base is built and operational, the data base administrator monitors operations logs for data base security violations. Data base performance is also monitored to ensure that users' response time needs are being met and that the system operates efficiently. If there is a problem, the data base administrator attempts to correct it before it gets too serious.

■ DATA BASE MANAGEMENT SYSTEM SOFTWARE

A data base management system (**DBMS**) is software that provides an interface between computer applications and the set of coordinated and integrated physical files contained in the data base (Exhibit 5.8). These physical files may be on several disks or other storage media. The role of the DBMS is to facilitate the creation, maintenance, access, backup, and security of the data base. At least 85 percent of all medium- to large-scale computer installations use some form of DBMS.

The DBMS may be thought of as consisting of the following components: the data definition language, the data manipulation language, the access method, and the query language described below.

Exhibit 5.8
The Components of
a DBMS

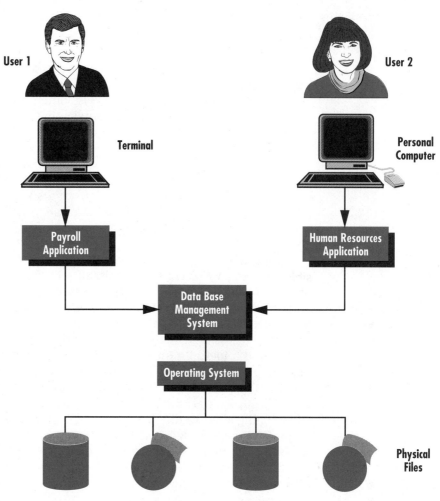

Data Definition Language

Programmers designing and building systems using the traditional file-oriented approach face several data-related problems. First, because the data they need to access may reside on one or more of many different storage devices, they need to understand the technical characteristics of these devices. These devices include magnetic tape, disks, drums, and other devices—each with a number of different manufacturers and models with varying characteristics. Second, programmers need to know the physical layout of the data records to know in what position on the record to find a particular data element, its length, and other characteristics. Third, the programmer may have to use data files designed by another programmer. Often a lot of time is wasted just trying to figure out what a particular data field is supposed to represent.

In the data base environment, the data definition language of the DBMS helps the programmer avoid these problems. The **data definition language** describes how the data are stored and provides two views of the data: logical and physical. The data definition language forms the link between the logical and physical views of the data base.

The logical view of the data base is sometimes called a **schema.** A **subschema** is the way a particular application views the data from the data base. This view is likely to be a simplified one that does not include all the data elements, entities, and relationships in the data base. Because there may be many different applications that access the data base, there may be many different subschemas. A set of data definition language statements is used to construct a subschema that includes only the data elements that are of interest to each application. In a sense, the subschema for each application defines a master file for that application.

The physical view describes how the data are actually stored. It describes the physical characteristics of each data element in each record type of the data base. These characteristics include: data type (e.g., alphabetic or numeric), starting position of the data element in the actual data base record (e.g., employee last name begins in byte 10), the length of the data element (e.g., 22 bytes are reserved for employee name), and a logical name to which the data element can be referred (e.g., employee last name is called *lastname*).

The physical views of the data are created by the data base administrator with special training on the technical details of the particular DBMS being employed. The data base administrator uses the data definition language to define how the data are physically stored and to establish the data base schema. Once this is done, application programmers do not have to worry about these details and can use the data manipulation language to create business applications.

Data Manipulation Language

The **data manipulation language** is used by the application programmer to access, retrieve, and update the data in the data base. This language allows one to add, delete, or change records in the data base as well as retrieve data using the value of the key data element that uniquely identifies a record (e.g., social security number uniquely identifies records in an employee data base). The data manipulation language refers to the data elements by their logical name without requiring knowledge of the details of how they are stored. This is possible because the data description language has already been used to define how the data are physically stored and to assign a logical name to each data element.

Usually the data manipulation language is used with a traditional programming language such as COBOL, FORTRAN, or PL/1 to create application programs. Use of the programming language enables a programmer to perform processing on the data that the DBMS data manipulation language cannot perform. Thus the data base management facilities would be used to retrieve employee data for a payroll application, but the calculation of gross and net pay would be made using the contents of that record and the processing routines written in a programming language.

Access Method

In a data base management environment, the actual data might be physically segregated and stored on multiple storage devices and accessible only through a complex addressing mechanism. The data base management system uses an **access method** to handle the details of physical access to the data base.

The access mechanism retrieves and aggregates the data into the simple, logical format needed for the application program. The access method conceals all storage-device-dependent details from the data base management system and presents the data base management system with a simple stored record interface. This frees the applications programmers from having to worry about the tracks and cylinders, and lets them concentrate on the business aspects of the problem to be solved.

The stored record interface permits the data base management system to view the storage structure as a collection of simple master files, each one consisting of all the occurrences of one type of stored record. When a new stored record occurrence is first created and entered into the data base, the access method assigns it a unique address.

Query Language

Most data base management systems also provide a **query language** that enables nonprogrammers to prepare report requests using simple English phrases. The query language can be used to specify which records are to be extracted from the data base, define necessary calculations, and tell in what order and format the results are to be shown. The query language uses powerful key words and verbs to enable the user to communicate even a fairly complex request. Reports may be created by the user sitting at a video display device and in an interactive mode. Once the program development and testing are complete, the checked-out version of the program may be stored in a library for future use. A similar request will then retrieve the program from the library, thus saving the user the unnecessary reentry of the program instructions.

Nonprogrammers can learn to write a simple program using the query language with less than a day of training and practice. Acquiring this skill enables them to access the data base and generate their own reports without the assistance of a professional programmer. Even professional programmers often use the query language to generate reports for users quickly.

■ THE RELATIONAL DATA MODEL

The principles of the relational data model were originally documented by Dr. E. F. Codd in 1968. Codd, a mathematician, first realized that the discipline of mathematics could be used to interject some solid principles and rigor into a field (data base management) that, prior to that time, was sorely lacking these qualities. Codd's ideas were first published in a now classic paper, "A Relational Model of Data for Large Shared Data Banks" (reference 2).

Characteristics of a Relational DBMS

A **relational data base system** has two primary characteristics. First, the data are perceived by the user as consisting of simple two-dimensional tables. Second, the data base operators at the user's disposal are operators that generate new tables from old. In mathematical terms, a table is very similar to an unordered set or relation. Relational data base systems are based on what is called the relational model of data, which, in turn, is an abstract theory of data that is based in part on the mathematical theory of relations. Relation is just a mathematical term for table or a collection of data. Tables and table operations are well defined because relational theory is based on set theory, relational algebra, and relational calculus. All this means that there is a respectable body of theoretical results that can be applied to practical problems of data base usage and design.

The key components of the relational data model are described below.

Table

A **table** is the data structure that holds data in a relational data base. A table is comprised of columns and rows. A table can represent a single entity (person, place, or thing) that you wish to track or to keep information about, such as employees or departments (Exhibits 5.9 and 5.10).

Exhibit 5.9
Employee Table

EMP#	Name	Job	Emp. Date	Rate	Dept. No.
4321	King	Welder	120389	15.25	30
4412	Arnold	Polisher	030191	10.45	30
2276	Samuels	Foreman	060779	18.55	30
1432	Fox	Mill Operator	102491	10.25	50
5005	Green	President	010179	75.00	00
2004	Long	Foreman	081281	18.55	40
3009	Carson	Supervisor	031279	25.45	30
3214	Brown	Painter	021489	36.25	20
6073	Wallinger	Foreman	031591	19.25	50
6523	Stone	Supervisor	020190	27.50	50

Exhibit 5.10
Sample Department
Table

Dept. No.	Dept. Name	Location
00	Accounting	Cincinnati
10	Sales	Cincinnati
20	Human Resources	Cincinnati
30	Welding	Harrison
40	Assembly	Harrison
50	Machining	Harrison
60	Painting	Harrison
70	Maintenance	Harrison

Column

Each **column** of a table represents one attribute of the entity. For example, the employee table contains EMP#, NAME, JOB, EMPDATE, RATE, and DEPTNO, which represent an employee's identification number, last name, job title, employment date, hourly pay rate, and department number.

Row

Each **row** of a table represents one occurrence of an entity or relationship represented by the table. In the employee table, each row represents data about one employee. Rows should not be duplicated within a table. Primary keys are assigned to prevent this duplication.

Primary Key

A **primary key** is an attribute (or set of attributes) that uniquely identifies one record from another. In the employee table, the EMP# attribute is the primary key.

View

A **view** is a logical representation of another table or combination of tables. Views do not actually contain data; rather they derive their data from the tables on which the view is based. Views are extremely powerful as they allow one to tailor the presentation of data to different types of users. One important application of views is to provide an additional level of security by restricting access to a predetermined set of rows and/or columns of a table. As an example of row restriction, separate views could be created for each department manager so that they could only see data for the employees in their department (e.g., display only employee data for employees in department 30 for the manager of department 30, Exhibit 5.11). As an example of column restriction, separate views could be created of the employee table so that the user of this view cannot see the pay rate field (Exhibit 5.12).

Exhibit 5.11
A View of the
Employee Table—
Employees in
Department 30

Emp. #	Name	Job	Emp. Date	Rate	Dept. No.
4321	King	Welder	120389	15.25	30
4412	Arnold	Polisher	030191	10.45	30
2276	Samuels	Foreman	060779	18.55	30
3009	Carson	Supervisor	031279	25.45	30

Indexes

Indexes are used to provide quick access to rows within a table and to enforce uniqueness of rows within a table. Generally, one creates a unique index based on the primary key of every table.

Normalized Data

When data in a table are **normalized,** the attributes in the table depend on the primary key, the full primary key, and nothing else but the primary key according to Dr. E. F. Codd.

Exhibit 5.13 is a sample employee file. The file is designed to hold up to five skills for each employee. While the file may seem to be well designed, asking a few basic questions will uncover some of the problems with this design.

What if an employee gains more than five skills?

What if the name of one skill was changed; how many records in the file would need to be updated?

What if management asks which department has taught the most skills to its employees; which one the least? What data processing steps would be required to answer this seemingly simple question?

Following the rules of normalization, this traditional file design can be changed to a set of normalized tables that are much easier to query for answers to management questions, avoids setting an arbitrary limit on the number of attributes, and makes it easier to update data in the tables.

Exhibit 5.12
A View of the
Employee Table—
Pay Rate Not
Shown

Emp. #	Name	Job	Emp. Date	Dept. No.
4321	King	Welder	120389	30
4412	Arnold	Polisher	030191	30
2276	Samuels	Foreman	060779	30
1432	Fox	Mill Operator	102491	50
5005	Green	President	010179	00
2004	Long	Foreman	081281	40
3009	Carson	Supervisor	031279	30
3214	Brown	Painter	021489	20
6073	Wallinger	Foreman	031591	50
6523	Stone	Supervisor	020190	50

Exhibit 5.13
Sample Employee
Skills File

Employee ID
Employee Name
Department Number
Department Name
Department Manager
Skill ID #1
Skill #1 Description
Department ID where skill #1 was gained
Skill ID #2
Skill #2 Description
Department ID where skill #2 was gained
Skill ID #3
Skill #3 Description
Department ID where skill #3 was gained
Skill ID #4
Skill #4 Description
Department ID where skill #4 was gained
Skill ID #5
Skill #5 Description
Department ID where skill #5 was gained

Three Steps to Normalize Data

There are three steps to normalize data presented in a file. These steps are explained below with an example that converts the employee file in Exhibit 5.13 into a set of normalized tables.

Step one: Eliminate any repeating groups. A repeating group is a set of attributes that appears more than once. For this example, skill id, skill name, and department id where skill was gained is a repeating group. Exhibit 5.14 shows the file now divided into two tables to eliminate this repeating group.

Step 2: Eliminate redundant data (data that occur more than once). Exhibit 5.15 illustrates that the two tables from Exhibit 5.13 are now separated into three tables to eliminate redundant data.

Step 3: Eliminate attributes in a table that are not dependent on the key of that table. In the employee table, the department name and department manager are not dependent on the employee id. Thus a fourth table is formed as shown in Exhibit 5.16.

At this point, the tables are normalized so that the attributes in each table depend on the primary key.

Exhibit 5.14
Normalization Step
#1—Eliminate
Repeating Groups

Employee Table	Skill Table
Employee ID	Employee ID
Employee Name	Skill ID
Department ID	Skill Description
Department Name	Department ID where skill was gained
Department Manager	

Exhibit 5.15
Normalization Step
#2—Eliminate
Redundant Data

Employee Table	Employee Skill Table	Skill Table
Employee ID	Employee ID	Skill ID
Employee name	Skill ID	Skill description
Department ID	Department ID where skill was gained	
Department name		
Department manager		

■ OTHER TYPES OF DATA BASES

Object-Oriented Data Base

As powerful as the relational data base model is, a new data base structure is needed to handle the needs of such applications as expert systems, multimedia systems, computer aided systems engineering (CASE), and computer aided design (CAD). The data needed to support these applications are not simple business transactions such as sales invoices and payments to vendors, but complex data types such as text, image, sound, video, and graphics. These data types may vary substantially in type, length, content, and form. The object-oriented data base (OODB) is a solution to meet these needs. Indeed, object-oriented data base management systems (OODBMS) place no restrictions on the types or sizes of data elements that can be stored, and users are free to invent new data types of any complexity. In fact, OODBMS can manage any data that can be digitized, which makes them ideal for multimedia and other advanced applications.

An **object** consists of data values that describe the attributes of an entity and its relationships with other entities, plus the processes that can be performed upon the data. This property is called **encapsulation.** In addition, the object-oriented model supports **inheritance,** that is, new objects can be automatically created by replicating some or all of the characteristics of one or more other objects. Such capabilities allow designers to develop product designs, store them as objects in an OODB, and replicate and modify them to create new product designs.

Each object in the OODB is bound together with its own data and a set of instructions that describe the behavior and attributes of the object. Messages are used by one object to interact with another. For example, the object automobile in a data base of engineering drawings

Exhibit 5.16 Normalization Step #3—Eliminate Attributes Not Dependent on the Key

Employee Table	Employee Skill Table	Skill Table	Department Table
Employee ID	Employee ID	Skill ID	Department ID
Employee name	Skill ID	Skill description	Department name
Department ID	Department ID where skill was gained		Department manager

may have the attributes Model, Year, Color, and Engine. Stored with an engineering drawing of an automobile are the processes (programming instructions) required to display, rotate, expand, shrink, or explode the drawing on a screen.

Objects that have the same set of attributes and behaviors are grouped into a class. For example, automobile, truck, and jeep might be three classes of the object named vehicle in the engineering drawings data base. Furthermore, the attributes and processes of one object can be inherited by other objects in the same class. Thus, another automobile in the same class as the 4-door sedan may inherit its attributes and processes. This speeds application development time by reducing the amount of programming code that must be written, resulting in large libraries of objects that can be used over and over again. New applications can be assembled by putting off-the-shelf objects from these libraries together, just as a house can be built from its component parts.

Object-oriented data base technology has only recently been given widespread attention. Standards in the field are not firm, and because the technology is substantially different from other data base technology, there is a considerable learning curve for practitioners. While several commercial object-oriented data base management systems are available, many more are under development (Exhibit 5.17).

The use of object-oriented data bases to build traditional transaction processing and management reporting systems is likely to be limited in the near future. IT organizations are already struggling with a morass of different data bases, trying to integrate them and ensure their interoperability; they are hesitant to try yet another data base. Also the performance and reliability of OODBMS systems has not yet been determined, thus business is leery of deploying these systems in critical applications. With traditional data base management systems, the data are retrieved from the data base using a nonprocedural data base query language such as SQL and then are manipulated through routines written in a conventional programming language such as C or COBOL. The current lack of powerful, nonprocedural access for OODB

Exhibit 5.17
A Partial List of Object-Oriented Data Base Management Systems

Object-Oriented DBMS	Vendor	Application Program Interface
Objectivity/DB	Objectivity, Inc.	C++
Object/DB	Digital Equipment Corporation	C++
OpenODB	Hewlett Packard	C++
ObjectStore	Object Design, Inc.	C++
O2	O2 Technologies	C++
Versant ODBMS	Versant Object Technology Corp.	C++ and Smalltalk
GemStone	Servio Logic Corp.	Smalltalk
Ontos	Ontos Corp.	C++
Itasca	Itasca Systems, Inc.	Lisp
ObjectStore	Object Design	C++

will also slow their acceptance. The Object Management Group is a vendor consortium (including Digital Equipment Corporation, Hewlett Packard, IBM, and Object Design among others) trying to develop standards for object-oriented product development and to address these issues.

Text Management Data Base

Organizations are drowning in pools of electronic and paper documents. **Text management data bases** are the natural outgrowth of the use of computers to create and store documents electronically. On-line data base services are heavy users of text data base technology to store the full text of business and technical publications. Major corporations and government agencies have also developed large text data bases to contain both internally generated and external documents of all kinds.

A text management data base relies on an electronic document management system (**EDMS**) to help create, store, search, retrieve, modify, and assemble documents and other information stored as text data. The idea behind text retrieval is simple: You have a large collection of documents such as legal cases, medical journals, or newspaper articles. Most text retrieval products are based on indexing each word in a document or article. The real work of text management involves building these indexes when documents are first entered to the EDMS system. Once these indexes are built, users can easily search the text data base by telling the data base the words or phrases to locate. Exhibit 5.18 lists several EDMS Systems and Exhibit 5.19 shows some of the characteristics on which to evaluate the EDMS systems.

■ ADDITIONAL TECHNICAL TOPICS

The ERD Diagram

Management time is required to confirm the requirements for information presented by the ERD. Typically, business managers whose data are being modeled get involved in both creating the data model and reviewing it for correctness. Systems analysts trained in the techniques of data modeling interview the business managers to define the

Exhibit 5.18
A Partial List of
Text Management
(EDMS) Vendors

Alliance Technologies Inc.
BRS Software Products
Exoterica Corp.
Fulcrum Corp.
Knowledgeset Corp.
Open Text Corp.
Verity Inc.
Zylab (A Division of Information Dimensions, Inc.)

Exhibit 5.19
Characteristics
Important in
Evaluating an
EDMS

How fast does the product complete a search?
Can you search for closely related words?
Can you search for words in close proximity to one another?
Is there a way to integrate the text retrieval product into current applications?
What type of platform support does the vendor provide?
Is an interface to common commercial data bases available?

important entities and the relationships among the entities (these relationships are also called business rules since they are determined by business practices and processes). Rigorous conventions, standards, and guidelines are applied at all times, including concepts of data normalization that were covered earlier in this chapter.

One convention for drawing an ERD is described below; there are other ways to present the ERD model.

Entities are documented in an ERD as rectangles with each rectangle labeled with the name of the entity, usually a proper noun.

A **relationship** is an association that exists between two entities and is documented by drawing a line connecting the two entities. Each line is labeled with a verb. The number of times that one entity occurs in relation to another entity is referred to as its **connectivity,** of which there are three types: one-to-one, one-to-many, and many-to-many. To document the connectivity: connecting the two entities with a simple straight line indicates a **one-to-one** relationship, putting a crow's foot at one end of the line indicates a **one-to-many** relationship, and putting a crow's foot at each end of the line indicates a **many-to-many** relationship (Exhibit 5.20). The example in Exhibit 5.21 shows an employee with many skills belonging to one department, while the department can have many employees.

SQL as an Emerging Standard

SQL is a data base query and update language designed at IBM's San Jose, California, research labs by D. Chamberlin as part of a relational data base project known as Systems R. In the 1980s, IBM released two commercial relational data base systems that were based on the original efforts: SQL/DS for the IBM VM operating system and Database 2 for the IBM MVS operating system. SQL is used to define and manipulate data in relational form. It is both a data definition and a data manipulation language.

A dialect of SQL was adopted by the American National Standards Institute (ANSI) in 1986 and by the International Standards Organization (ISO) in 1987 as an official standard for relational data base systems. As a result, SQL is the preferred data manipulation language and data definition language for relational data base systems and is broadly used by many vendors, end users, and application developers.

Any SQL statement can be entered at a terminal or, alternatively, can be embedded in a program. Interactive SQL and embedded SQL

Exhibit 5.20
Representing the
Different Types of
Relationships in an
ERD

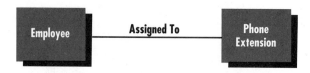

a. One-to-One Relationship

b. One-to-Many Relationship

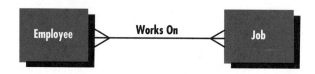

c. Many-to-Many Relationship

Exhibit 5.21
A Simple Entity
Relationship
Diagram (ERD)

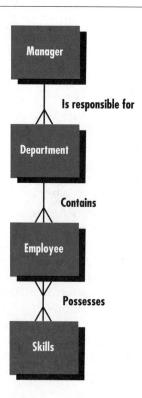

Exhibit 5.22
Basic SQL
Statements

SQL data definition statements are used to define and maintain data base objects (including data base tables) and to drop them when the entities are no longer needed.

CREATE TABLE PLANTS (COM_NAME CHAR 15, LAT_
NAME CHAR 20)
CREATE VIEW
CREATE INDEX

DROP TABLE PLANTS
DROP VIEW
DROP INDEX

ALTER TABLE
ALTER VIEW
ALTER INDEX

SQL data manipulation language statements are used to change the data in one of three ways: INSERT new rows of data (entities) into a table, UPDATE column values (attributes) in existing rows, and DELETE rows from tables.

INSERT INTO EMP VALUES (1234, 'DAVIS',
'SALESMAN', 7698, '14-FEB-1994' 1600, 500, 30)

UPDATE S SET Status = 'A' WHERE CITY = 'LONDON';
DELETE FROM EMP WHERE NAME IN ('LANE', 'SMITH')

SQL query language statements are used to query the data base or retrieve data, in any combination, expression, or order. Queries usually begin with the SQL-reserved word SELECT, followed by the data desired, and the table or views containing the source data, as in:

SELECT ENAME, MGR FROM EMP;

---

differ from each other in some aspects. For example, embedded SQL statements must be prefixed with EXEC SQL in order to distinguish them from the surrounding host language statements (Exhibit 5.22).

SQL is sometimes described as a nonprocedural language because users specify what data they want without specifying how to get it. The process of navigating around the physical data base to locate the data is performed automatically by the system, not manually by the user.

With SQL becoming an industry standard, programmers and data base administrators with knowledge of SQL are able to work in computing environments consisting of almost any computer hardware and DBMS. When moved from one division of a company to another or even to another company, programmers and data base administrators will need little additional technical training. Applications written using SQL can be run on different computer hardware with little or no changes.

SQL provides three data definition statements: create, alter, and drop to manage tables. The create table statement builds a new table with column names and data types specified by the user. The alter table statement allows the user to change an existing table (e.g., adding a new column). An existing table can be deleted at any time by means of the SQL drop table statement. Create view, alter view, and drop view statements have meanings similar to those explained above for table, as do create index, alter index, and drop index statements.

Exhibit 5.23
Results of Joining
the Employee and
Department Table

Emp. #	Name	Job	Emp. Date	Dept. No.	Dept. Name	Location
4321	King	Welder	120389	30	Welding	Harrison
4412	Arnold	Polisher	030191	30	Welding	Harrison
2276	Samuels	Foreman	060779	30	Welding	Harrison
1432	Fox	Mill Operator	102491	50	Machining	Harrison
5005	Green	President	010179	00	Accounting	Cincinnati
2004	Long	Foreman	081281	40	Assembly	Harrison
3009	Carson	Supervisor	031279	30	Welding	Harrison
3214	Brown	Painter	021489	60	Painting	Harrison
6073	Waller	Foreman	031591	50	Machining	Harrison
6523	Stone	Supervisor	020190	50	Machining	Harrison

```
SELECT EMP#, NAME, JOB, EMPDATE, DEPTNO, DEPTNAME, LOCATION
      FROM EMP, DEPT
      WHERE EMP. DEPTNO = DEPT. DEPTNO;
```

SQL provides four data manipulation statements: select, insert, update, and delete. The select statement is used to query or retrieve data. The result of the select operation is the creation of another table or relation. The insert statement is used to insert a row(s) into a table. The update statement is used to change a value(s) in a row(s) in a table. And the delete statement is used to remove a row(s) from a table.

A **join** is a special type of query in which data are combined from more than one table to form a new table. The ability to join two or more tables is one of the most powerful features of relational systems. The result is a table consisting of all rows appearing in either or both of the original relations. See Exhibit 5.23 as an example of a join of two tables—the employee (Exhibit 5.9) and department tables (Exhibit 5.10).

More on the Relational Data Model

Foreign Key

Foreign keys represent relationships between tables. A foreign key is an attribute (or set of attributes) whose values are derived from the primary key of another table. The existence of a foreign key implies that the table with the foreign key is related to the primary key in the table from which the foreign key is derived. For example, DEPTNO is the primary key for the department table. The DEPTNO attribute of the employee table is a foreign key referencing the department table. The foreign key DEPTNO of the employee table represents the relationship between employees and departments. The DEPTNO foreign key of the employee table allows one to determine that all department 00 employees work in the accounting department located in Cincinnati.

Referential Integrity

An integrity constraint is a rule that enforces a relationship within the data base. For example, one integrity constraint in our sample data base is that an employee in the employee table may not be assigned to a department that does not exist in the department table. Another example is that the manager number for an employee must be an employee number of another employee in the employee table. Such constraints help ensure the **referential integrity** of the data base—it ensures that relationships represented by primary keys and foreign keys are maintained. Referential integrity issues can also be raised if table entries are deleted. For example, suppose that department 20 is deleted from the department table. What happens to the rows in the employee table for those employees assigned to department 20? Referential integrity constraints would warn the user that deleting department 20 created a problem with the employee table.

Summary

Five key characteristics that determine the quality of data are accuracy, completeness, relevance, timeliness, and auditability.

Because information is derived from data, these same five characteristics apply to it.

Data critical to the success of an organization include data about its own internal operations, data that describe the business transactions that flow into the firm from external sources, and data that provide insight about the industry, market, and other elements of the environment in which the firm competes.

A corporate data base is a collection of computer accessible data that is carefully planned and managed to support the needs of multiple users.

The data hierarchy includes bits, character, data element, record, file, and data base.

A subject data base contains data about a subject of broad interest to many people throughout the company.

A functional data base serves the needs of a particular organizational unit.

In the traditional file-oriented approach to building information systems, the system and its associated files are designed to meet the specific needs of a single, particular business unit.

The traditional file-oriented approach suffers from many disadvantages, including data redundancy, program/data dependence, and lack of data integration.

In the data base management approach to building information systems, a common pool of data, the data base, is made available to many different systems. In addition, a data base management system provides the interface between the users and the actual data.

There are many advantages associated with the data base oriented approach: it enables sharing of integrated data, minimizes data redundancy, increases data integrity, improves programmer productivity, and improves data security.

Data management has as its goal to ensure that the data needed to solve business problems or exploit business opportunities are made available to the right people at the right time in the proper form to be of use.

Managers have a key role to play in the area of data management: they must recognize whether their needs are being met. If not, they must define their unmet needs and communicate them.

The components needed for effective data management include: data resource strategy, data resource plan, top management support, management involvement, data models, data standards, data dictionary, and data management specialists.

The data resource strategy establishes a basic position and provides a set of consistent principles to guide decision making in regard to data-related issues.

The data resource plan identifies the data most important to the enterprise and outlines projects necessary to develop a shared data resource of this data.

Corporate data standards are rules and practices used to ensure that data are understood and processed uniformly with predictable results.

The data administrator leads the process to develop a data resource strategy and data resource plan to make corporate data available to all users in a shared and controlled manner.

A data base administrator is a highly skilled and trained systems professional who works with end users and programmers in order to design, build, maintain, and manage the data base.

A relationship is an association that exists between two entities and may be a one-to-one, one-to-many, or many-to-many relationship.

With a relational data base system, data are perceived by the user as consisting of simple two-dimensional tables and the data base operators at the user's disposal are operators that generate new tables from old.

The primary key is an attribute (or set of attributes) that uniquely identifies one record from another.

Data views allow one to tailor the presentation of data to different types of users.

Data base management software includes the data definition language, data manipulation language, access method, and query language.

SQL is the standard data manipulation and definition language for relational data bases.

Object-oriented data base is an emerging technology capable of storing alphanumeric, text, image, sound, video, and graphics data.

An object consists of data values that describe the attributes of an entity and its relationships with other entities, plus the processes that can be performed upon the data.

A text management data base relies on an electronic document management system to help create, store, search, retrieve, modify, and assemble documents and other information stored as text data.

A Manager's Checklist

✔ Does your firm treat data as an important corporate asset?

✔ Has your firm established a data management function?

✔ Are there people in your firm who fill the role of data base administrator or data administrator?

✔ Do your information systems operate in a file-oriented environment or a data base oriented environment?

✔ Is your organization conducting any pilot projects to evaluate the use of object-oriented data base technology?

✔ Are you making use of text management data base systems?

Key Terms

access method	data base administrator
accuracy	data definition language
attributes	data dictionary
audit trail	data directory
auditability	data element
bits	data independence
byte	data integration
character	data integrity
column	data management
completeness	data manipulation language
connectivity	data redundancy
corporate data base	data resource plan
data administrator	data resource strategy
data base	data security

data standards
DBMS
EDMS
encapsulation
entity
entity relationship diagram
  (ERD)
file
file-oriented approach
foreign key
functional data base
hierarchy of data
index
inheritance
join
many-to-many
normalized data
object
object-oriented data base
one-to-many

one-to-one
primary key
program independence
programmer productivity
query language
record
relational data base model
relationship
relevance
referential integrity
row
schema
shared data resource
SQL
subject data base
subschema
table
text management data base
timeliness
view

Review Questions

1. What are five characteristics that define the quality of data?

2. Identify three sources of data critical to a business organization and explain how this data is organized into a data base.

3. Identify the three distinguishing characteristics of a relational data base.

4. What is the difference between a primary key and a foreign key?

5. Define the term normalized data and outline the three steps of the data normalization process.

6. State three advantages of building systems using relational data bases and normalized data.

7. Define the terms object and object-oriented data base. Name three potential applications for this technology.

8. What is a text management data base?

Discussion Questions

1. Discuss what it means to manage data as a resource of the company and tell why managers should be interested in good data management.

2. What role can business managers take to ensure good data management?

3. Must the quality of data always be high for the data to be useful?

4. Develop a simple ERD diagram for a student data base with at least four entities. Sketch the relationship among these entities. List at least three attributes for each entity.

5. How could you determine if a firm is gathering enough quality data from each of the three sources of data critical to its success?

6. What personal characteristics, education, skills, and experiences would you look for in someone to fill the role of data administrator?

Recommended Readings

1. Burgard, Mike. "Information Overload!" *UNIXWorld,* June 1993.

2. Codd, E. F. "A Relational Model of Data for Large Shared Data Banks." Communications of the ACM 13, No. 6, June 1970.

3. Date, C. J. *An Introduction to Database Systems: Volume I.* Reading, MA: Addison-Wesley, 1990.

4. Hansen, G. W. and Hansen, J. V. *Database Management and Design.* Englewood Cliffs, NJ: Prentice-Hall, 1992.

5. Khoshafian, Sertag and Abnous, Razmik. *Object Orientation: Concepts, Languages, Databases, and User Interfaces.* New York: John Wiley & Sons, Inc. 1990.

6. Taylor, David. *Object-Oriented Information Systems: Planning and Implementation.* New York: John Wiley & Sons, Inc. 1992.

A Manager's Dilemma

Case Study 5.1

Data Management versus Project Deadline

It is the end of the day, and suddenly two members of the IT organization come storming into your office, yelling at each other!

John, the Project Manager for the new General Ledger System, begins complaining bitterly that Andy, the Data Base Administrator assigned to his project, claims that the project failed to conform to established company standards for data management.

Andy interrupts John to insist that the next phase of the project be delayed until the team thoroughly documents all data entities and attributes associated with this project. Andy makes it clear that he feels this situation represents a test of the newly established IT policies for data management and that he, for one, is determined to hold the line.

John argues that this additional system documentation is not necessary. He and his team of five systems analysts and programmers have a combined total of thirty-two years' experience working projects in the company's finance and accounting areas. Besides, the project has been under way only two months and is already two weeks behind schedule. John reminds you that the new General Ledger System must be installed and operational by the end of the fiscal year, just six months away.

The one thing that Andy and John do agree on is that it will take one person two to four weeks to "capture" correct definitions for all the entities, and to enter these definitions and data relationships into the corporate data dictionary.

It is getting late and you are tired. You are listening to these two argue, and you know that they have come to you as the Corporate Data Administrator to make a decision. What will you say? How might this problem be avoided on future projects?

Case Study 5.2

Data Management Services for Midsize Banks

There is general confusion among midsize banks facing the challenge of using information systems. These banks have assets in the range of $300 million to $1 billion. They are in an awkward position: too big to run their businesses effectively on conventional midsize computers, but too small to be able to afford to develop specialized software, let alone the large-scale computers and information systems expertise necessary to run them.

Most midsize banks depend on service bureaus specializing in banking or on correspondent banks to support their data processing needs. Using this approach, the customer bank has computer terminals connected to the service bureau computer, and all data is transmitted to it for processing. The bank's data bases are stored on the service bureau's computer, and bank managers can request a limited number of standard reports to use for analyzing their business. But service bureau banking programs tend to be outdated and inflexible. Managers have to wait several months to get customized reports for revenue or productivity analyses, if they can get them at all.

Another problem with the service bureau approach is the lack of data integration. This limitation prevents a bank from determining, for example, which of its home mortgage customers also has an auto loan or savings account with the bank. This integration is crucial to relationship banking, the strategy of identifying key customers and selling them new bank products.

You are the Senior Vice-president of Information Services at a major data processing service bureau. You have decided to expand your services to better meet the needs of midsize banks. What unique services must you provide to midsize banks to appeal to them? How does the dilemma of midsize banks illustrate the need for data management? How would the service you propose address these issues?

Case Study 5.3

Data Model for Auto Rental Agency

Develop the high-level data model that would meet the total data needs of an auto rental agency. Identify five to nine entities of interest. Develop a one-sentence definition for each data entity. Draw a data model that shows the relationships between these entities. Identify three to six attributes of interest for each entity. Develop a one-sentence definition for each attribute.

Look at your model through the eyes of a Fleet Manager responsible for the care and maintenance of each automobile. Now look at your model through the eyes of the Sales Manager who is trying to develop a Frequent Renter Program. Review and revise your model as appropriate.

Case Study 5.4

Data Definitions

Interview four to six different individuals and document their definitions of these fundamental business terms: customer, supplier, and employee. Take each term and develop your own definition that you feel best captures the meaning of this term. This simple exercise should begin to give you an appreciation of why data definitions and data standards are key to creating a shared data resource that can be used by multiple people in different organizations.

Chapter 6

Transaction Processing and Management Reporting Systems

Learning Objectives

Upon completion of this chapter, you will be able to:

1. Define the term transaction processing system and give eight examples of such a system.

2. Name and briefly describe the five stages of processing data associated with a transaction processing system.

3. Discuss the difference between batch and interactive processing and provide some guidelines of when to use each.

4. Define the term management reporting system and describe three common types of reports produced by such systems.

5. Discuss the role of managers in ensuring that the transaction processing and management reporting systems are meeting the business needs of the firm.

Preview

Every successful organization must capture and process the detail data necessary to update records about the fundamental business operations of the firm. This is the role of the organization's many transaction processing systems. There is also a need to integrate data from many sources to provide data and information useful to support operations, management, and decision making in the organization. Management reporting systems address this need. Together, the transaction processing and management reporting systems are tools for managing data as a shared data resource—a collection of data that serves multiple business functions.

Issues

1. What role does the transaction processing system play in supporting the organization in order to meet business objectives?

2. How does the management reporting system interact with the transaction processing system, and what is its role in meeting the business objectives of the organization?

Trade-Offs

1. Which system is more important—the transaction processing system or the management reporting system?

2. Why shouldn't all transaction processing and management reporting systems be interactive?

A Manager Struggles with the Issues

As Assistant Controller, John's duties include responsibility for employee payroll. This was only the third month John had been in this position and for the second time, a problem arose with the Payroll System that kept it from running to completion. Computer programmers and other technical resources had been called in the middle of the night to come in and fix the problem. Fortunately, the problem was corrected and payroll checks were ready to distribute by 11 A.M., only an hour late (according to the union contract, the firm could be fined $100,000 if payroll checks were not distributed to employees by the end of the first shift at 3 P.M. In talking with the technical resources, the source of the problem turned out to be a change made to the payroll program that had not been thoroughly tested.

John was also disappointed to learn that a major systems and programming effort would be necessary before the special reports required to conform to the new state reporting regulations could be prepared. The technical people estimated that the changes would take three months, but John reckoned that with all the other problems with the Payroll System, it would take twice that time.

John wonders if the real problem is that the Payroll System is now over 15 years old and the people who originally built it are no longer with the firm. Is it time to think about replacing this system? Even if the system were replaced, how could John ensure that some future Assistant Controller would not face similar problems 15 years from now?

■ TRANSACTION PROCESSING SYSTEMS: THE BASIC FOUNDATION

Definition of a Transaction Processing System

A **transaction processing system** processes the detail data necessary to update records about the fundamental business operations of the organization. Every organization will have several dozen such systems: order entry, inventory control, payroll, accounts payable, accounts receivable, and general ledger, to name just a few. The input to these systems are data about or generated by basic business transactions such as orders, receipts, time cards, invoices, and checks. The result of processing business transaction data is that the records of the company are updated to reflect the status of the operation at the time of the last processed business transaction.

Every manufacturing company must perform marketing, finance, manufacturing, research and development, engineering, distribution, and personnel functions. Indeed, in many companies there are whole departments of dozens or even hundreds of people assigned responsibilities in these areas. Data and information are required to meet the objectives of each organizational unit. There is also a need for data and information to flow from one organizational unit to one or more other units. Transaction processing systems have been used successfully in many companies to support this need for capturing and sharing data. A high-level overview of several major transaction processing systems and their interfaces for a typical manufacturing company is shown in Exhibit 6.1.

Exhibit 6.1
Transaction Processing Systems Frequently Employed in a Manufacturing Company

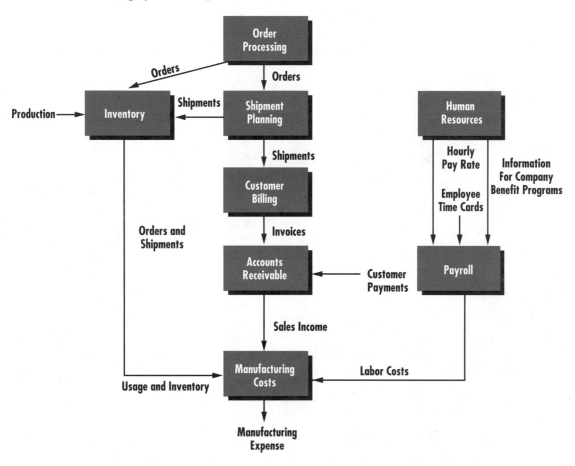

Why Business Managers Must Understand Transaction Processing Systems

Transaction processing systems are the backbone of any organization's information systems. They support the capture and processing of facts about the fundamental business operations of the organization—facts without which orders cannot be shipped, customers invoiced, and employees and vendors paid. Indeed, most organizations would grind to a screeching halt if their transaction processing systems failed to work. The loss of use of a transaction processing system for just a few hours can lead to losses of hundreds of thousands of dollars.

In many organizations today, these fundamental systems are batch processing systems built in the 1970s.

1. They operate inefficiently and unreliably—jeopardizing the smooth operation of business functions.

2. They are inflexible and difficult to modify to meet changing business needs.

3. They cannot provide rapid access to key information—information necessary to remain competitive in today's rapid-paced business environment, where a high level of customer service is mandatory for an organization to be successful.

Such systems no longer meet the challenges of the 1990s, and these antiquated systems are in the process of being upgraded and replaced by new transaction processing systems.

Business managers who manage the functions supported by these systems must judge if their information systems truly meet the needs of the business. They must recognize when it is time for a significant upgrade and be ready to lead the reengineering effort to ensure that the new system provides an improved and long-lasting solution. Increasingly, management will be held accountable for the effectiveness of transaction processing systems that support the fundamental business operations of the organization.

The Transaction Processing Cycle

Transaction processing systems capture and process data that describe fundamental business transactions. This data is used to update files and data bases of other transaction processing systems and to produce a variety of reports for use by people both within and outside the firm. The business transaction data go through a transaction processing cycle as shown in Exhibit 6.2.

Data Capture

The **data capture** process begins with the occurrence of a business event or transaction (e.g., taking a customer order, receiving a supplier's invoice, receiving a case of product from inventory) and results in the origination of data that are input to the transaction processing system. Data should be captured at the source where the event actually occurs, and it should be recorded accurately, in a timely fashion, with minimal manual effort, and in a form that can be directly input to the computer. Ideally, data should be captured in a form or medium that can be input directly to a system rather than keying the information from some type of document. This approach is called **source data automation.** An example of a source data automation device is scanning devices at the grocery checkout that read stock-keeping codes automatically. These devices are quicker and more accurate than having a cash register clerk enter codes manually.

Data Edit

An important step in processing transaction data is to edit the data for validity and completeness in order to detect any problems with the

Exhibit 6.2
The Transaction
Processing Cycle

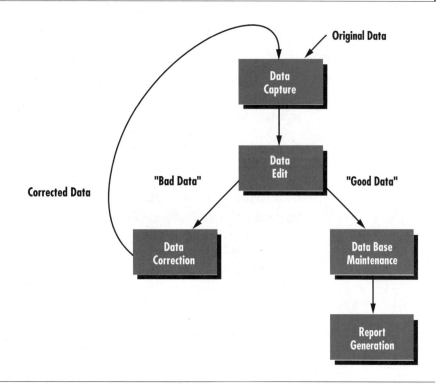

data. For example, quantity and cost data must be numeric and names must be alphabetic, otherwise the data is not valid. The codes associated with an individual transaction are edited against a master table of valid codes. If the code entered (or scanned) is not present in the master code table, the transaction is rejected. For example, a UPC code that is scanned must be in a master table of valid UPC codes.

Data Correction

It is not enough to reject invalid data. The system should present error messages that alert those responsible for the data edit function. These error messages must specify what problem is occurring, so that corrections can be made.

Data Base Maintenance

Data base maintenance involves updating files or data bases by adding new data, deleting data no longer needed, or changing old data to make it current. Adding a new employee to the employee data base, deleting an item no longer stocked from the inventory master table, and changing a customer's address are examples of data base maintenance and updating.

Report Generation

Transaction processing systems frequently produce several types of standard reports and other forms of output. These reports document and monitor the business transactions that occurred or were processed during a specific time period. Such reports provide an audit trail for transaction control purposes. These reports include:

Transaction Log The transaction log lists each output created as a result of the input to the system. For example, the payroll register is a transaction log that lists every paycheck printed on a specific payday by a payroll system.

Input and Error Listing This report lists each input transaction and any errors that result from editing the input or that result from processing the input data.

Accounting Summaries Accounting summaries document the financial impact of processing the transactions. For example, the result of processing a number of customer payments can be summarized by showing the amount of new credit extended, the amount of payment, and the current balance of accounts receivable.

Special Report Processing Users may request special reports using the operational data bases as their source.

Data Update Mode: Batch and Interactive

Batch Update

Some information systems are called **batch update** processing systems, meaning that business transactions are accumulated over a period of time and prepared for input to the computer for processing as a single unit or batch. The time period over which transactions are accumulated may be any length appropriate to meet the needs of the users of that system. For example, it may be important to process invoices and customer payments for the accounts receivable system on a daily basis. On the other hand, the payroll system may receive time cards and process them biweekly to create checks and update employee earnings records as well as to distribute labor costs. The essential characteristic of a batch update processing system is that there is some delay between the occurrence of an event and the eventual processing of the related transaction to update the organization's records.

Batch data processing was used almost exclusively when computers were first applied to business applications. This was the case partly because computers did not have the capability needed to support other forms of processing at an acceptable cost. Batch processing was also employed because it was the appropriate technology choice for the business functions that were undergoing conversion to computerized data processing.

Many of the early computer applications were accounting-oriented systems such as payroll, accounts receivable, and general ledger. These systems require considerable clerical effort to perform tedious calculations and update thousands of records of business transactions. By computerizing these jobs, management was able to reduce the number of clerical positions (or avoid hiring additional clerical people) and thus demonstrate real and tangible benefits that offset the cost of acquiring and maintaining computer hardware and software. Batch data processing was appropriate for these early computer applications and still is the best processing mode for many transaction processing systems.

Interactive Update

Interactive updating is a form of data processing in which the transaction data are processed immediately, without the delay of accumulating them into a batch. As soon as the required input is available, a computer program performs the necessary processing and updates the records affected by that single transaction. Consequently, at any time, the data in an interactive system always reflect the current status. One piece of input to the system is quickly followed by one piece of output.

Interactive updating is appropriate when the data are required to be current (up-to-the-minute or even up-to-the-second). Computers used to control manufacturing processes, reservation systems, and national defense systems are examples of interactive systems.

Batch versus Interactive Query

The manner in which a user may interact with a system to receive output is an important characteristic of management reporting systems. A user may request and receive data from a system in two basic ways: **batch** or **interactive.**

In batch mode, the user prepares a request and submits it to the computer, where it will run along with other batch jobs in the order in which it was submitted. If several batch jobs are ahead of it, it may take several minutes or even hours for the results to be returned to the user. The time from submission of a user request to receipt of the desired output is called the **turnaround time** of the batch system.

In an interactive system, a user's inquiry requires a quick response from the system. The user's inquiry will jump to the head of the service queue for immediate attention. The time from submission of the inquiry until receipt of the desired output is called the **response time** of an interactive system. The response time for a well-designed and efficiently operating interactive system is measured in a few seconds.

Exhibit 6.3 lists some variations of batch and interactive systems.

Why Not All Interactive Systems?

People generally would prefer receiving responses to their queries in a few seconds rather than waiting minutes or hours for a batch system turnaround. However, it does not make sense to have every system be interactive, for three basic reasons. First, interactive systems are more complex and take longer to develop than batch systems. A batch sys-

Exhibit 6.3
Variations of Batch
and Interactive
Systems

User Query Mode	Transaction Processing Mode	
	Batch	Interactive
Batch	Batch system	Interactive update with batch query process
Interactive	Batch update with interactive query	Interactive update with interactive query

tem can often be developed in far less time and at a lower cost. Second, interactive systems consume large amounts of computer resources. In order to provide fast response time to users, large amounts of computer memory, very fast processing capabilities, and special computer programs are required. Management must make a trade-off between the number of interactive systems to be run on the computer and the amount of money to be spent on computer resources. Third, as more and more interactive systems and users are added to a computer, the response time gets slower and slower. A typical curve for response time versus the number of users is shown in Exhibit 6.4. Once the number of users exceeds the **bend in the elbow** on the curve, all users expe-

Exhibit 6.4
Typical Response
Time versus
Number of Users
for an Interactive
System

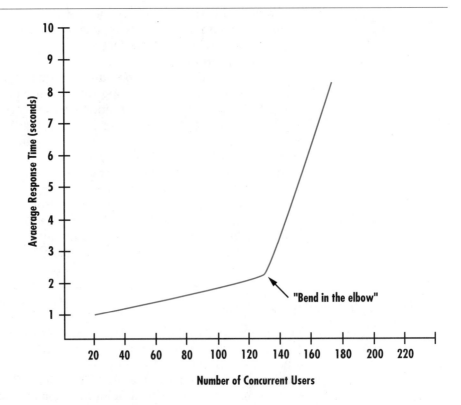

Real World Perspective

Interactive Reservation System of American Airlines

One of the earliest interactive transaction processing systems was American Airlines' SABRE system—an interactive reservation system. Prior to the system, reservation clerks never had an accurate count of how many passengers were booked on a flight. They had to rely on data that were several hours or even a day old. Typically, in the last day or two before a flight takes off, there is a flurry of activity, with some passengers canceling their reservations and others trying to book reservations. Without current seating information, booking space for flights was pretty much a gamble. Reservation clerks were pressured to try to fill the plane with passengers to maximize revenue, yet did not want to overbook the flight and upset passengers who thought they had reservations.

The SABRE system was developed in the early 1960s at a cost of over $250 million. With it, reservation clerks and travel agents can access up-to-the-minute data for use in booking seats. Each time a seat is sold, a transaction is generated to update the seating data for that flight. Reservation clerks and travel agents are provided with computer terminals that allow them to quickly access data in the system to find out the latest seating status. American Airlines has sold or rented its SABRE system to other airlines and travel agencies to handle their bookings. Over 65,000 terminals and printers are attached to the system, which handles over 10,000 daily fare changes for more than 600 different airlines around the world. In addition, thousands of users of software systems like Prodigy and CompuServe can access SABRE from their PCs and do everything a travel agent does except print their own ticket.

rience a dramatic slowdown in response time. At this point, either major increases in computer capacity are required or the number of simultaneous users must be limited. These three factors tend to limit the development of interactive computer applications to just those business processes that absolutely require interactive user response.

The Data Flow Diagram

Information systems can be difficult to understand because of the large number of procedures, forms, reports, files, people, and machines involved. Fortunately, some simple tools are available that eliminate the complexity. One such tool is the process model—a picture of the flow of data through a system and the processing performed on the data. Process models enable business managers to understand the essential inputs, outputs, processing, and relationships between processes. The process model, which depicts processes and how they interact or interface with one another, is much easier to understand than a written description of the system. The interactions between the processes are presented as data flows between processes, and so a process model is also frequently called a **data flow diagram (DFD).**

DFDs are quite easy to read and understand. There are two different sets of symbols in common use (Exhibit 6.5). Both sets of symbols are named after pairs of authors/consultants who helped define the structured analysis and design techniques of the 1970s: Gane-Sarson (Chris Gane and Trish Sarson) and Yourdon-DeMarco (Ed Yourdon and

Exhibit 6.5
Symbols Used in Developing a Data Flow Diagram

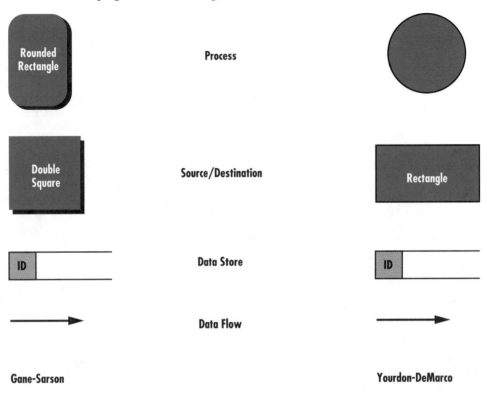

Gane-Sarson   Yourdon-DeMarco

Tom DeMarco). This text uses the Gane-Sarson symbols and discusses its components below.

Process

The Gane-Sarson DFD depicts a process, sometimes called activity, as a rounded rectangle. A process transforms inputs into outputs. Processes can represent activities performed by people, computers, or machines. The details of the processing—the logic or procedure—are not shown. This allows the viewer to see the big picture without getting lost in the details. A process is given a name that is a simple imperative statement consisting of an active verb and specific object (e.g., allocate stock to customer's order). A process must have at least one incoming data flow and at least one outgoing data flow.

Source/Destination

The square identifies sources and destinations. A source provides input to the system from outside the boundary of the system under study. A destination receives output from the system. Sources and destinations may include other organizations within the firm, organizations external to the firm, or other systems.

Data Store

Most systems also store data for later use. Data stores are depicted as narrow, open-ended boxes. Data stores include file cabinets, computer files, data bases, desk drawers, binders of data, and so on. Each data store is assigned a unique reference number. Data stores normally show data flows both entering and leaving (in other words, data must be created and used).

Data Flows

Finally, the arrows depict data flows. Data flows represent inputs or outputs such as reports, forms, documents, terminal displays, computer-to-computer transmissions, and so on. The data flow has a description of its contents written alongside it.

Common Transaction Processing Systems

Every organization that makes or sells goods or services must have an essential set of transaction processing systems. This set of systems includes: order processing, inventory, accounts receivable, accounts payable, payroll, general ledger, and human resources. These systems are briefly described below, and a DFD is presented for each of these systems.

Order Processing

The order processing system is critical to ensure that (1) customers' orders are filled in a timely manner; (2) sufficient finished product is available; and (3) because most customers buy on credit, customers are in good standing with the firm. Once an order is entered and accepted, the system prints an order confirmation for the customer and a packing slip that is used to select the ordered goods from a warehouse. If an order cannot be filled, a backorder is created—the order will be filled later when inventory is replenished. Exhibit 6.6 summarizes the primary input transactions and outputs of the order processing system.

Inventory

A manufacturing firm has several kinds of inventory, such as raw materials, work in process, finished goods, and maintenance parts. Thus several different inventory systems are needed, one for each type of inventory. Each system tracks the flow of specific items into and out of warehouses and plants. The systems may each need to keep track of hundreds of stockkeeping items, particularly for a large manufacturer of many different goods. However, it is not unusual for a small

Exhibit 6.6
Order Processing
System

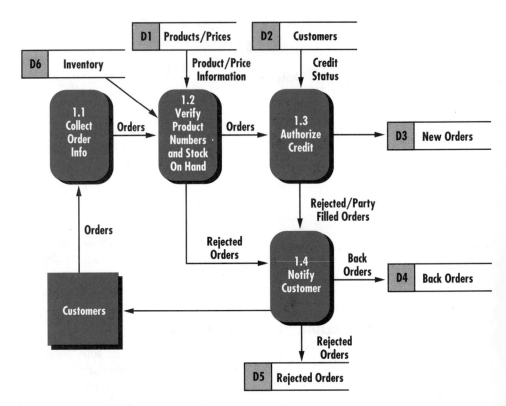

manufacturing firm to have well over $250,000 tied up in inventory. Exhibit 6.7 summarizes the primary input transactions and outputs of the inventory system.

Accounts Receivable

The accounts receivable system helps manage the cash flow of the company by keeping track of the money owed the company on charges for goods sold. When a customer purchases goods, the customer account is updated to reflect the charge. An invoice, bill, or statement reflecting the balance due is sent on a regular basis to active customers. Upon receipt of a payment, the amount due from that customer is reduced by the amount of the payment. The accounts receivable system is vital to managing the cash flow of the firm. One way in which this is done is through the identification of overdue accounts. Reports are generated that "age" accounts to identify customers whose accounts are overdue by more than 30, 60, or 90 days. Special action may be initiated to collect funds or reduce the customer's credit limit with the firm depending on the amount owed and degree of lateness. Exhibit 6.8 summarizes the primary input transactions and outputs of the accounts receivable system.

Exhibit 6.7
Inventory System

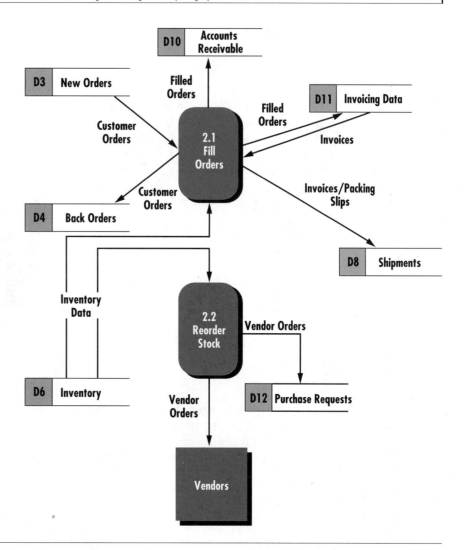

Accounts Payable

The accounts payable system is the mirror image of the accounts receivable system—it keeps track of the money owed by the company to its various creditors. When a purchase order requesting goods or services is created by an employee and sent to a supplier, a copy of the purchase order is sent to accounts payable. The accounts payable system creates a liability record for the cost of the goods. When goods are received from a supplier, they are checked and a receiving report is completed noting the date received, the quantity, and the condition of the goods. When an invoice is received from the supplier, it is matched to both the purchase order record and the receiving report. If this match is successful, a check for the amount owed is generated and sent to the supplier. Because creditors may give a discount for bills paid before the due date, the accounts payable system can be pro-

Exhibit 6.8
Accounts
Receivable System

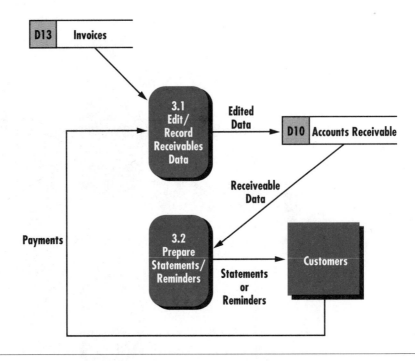

grammed to suspend payment until just before it is due. In this manner, the firm earns a discount for prompt payment and also earns interest on funds deposited in the bank. Exhibit 6.9 summarizes the primary input transactions and outputs of the accounts payable system.

Exhibit 6.9
Accounts Payable
System

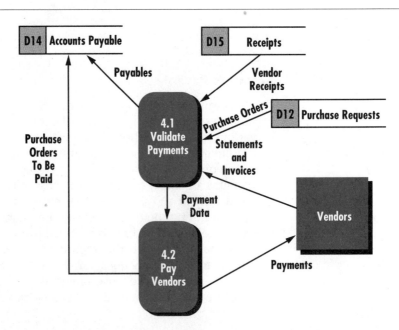

Payroll

The two primary outputs of the payroll system are the payroll check and stub, which are distributed to the employees, and the payroll register, which is a summary report of all payroll transactions. In addition, the payroll system prepares W-2 statements at the end of the year for tax purposes. In a manufacturing firm, hours worked and labor costs may be captured by job so this information can be passed to the manufacturing costs system. Exhibit 6.10 summarizes the primary input transactions and outputs of the payroll system.

General Ledger

Every monetary transaction that occurs within an organization must be properly recorded. Payment of a supplier's invoice, receipt of payment from a customer, or payment of an employee are examples of monetary transactions. The general ledger system keeps track of these transactions and provides the input necessary to produce the organization's financial statement. A financial statement includes the profit and loss statement and balance sheet. Exhibit 6.11 summarizes the primary input transactions and outputs of this system.

Human Resources

This system maintains information about employees needed for personnel planning, government reporting, and management of company

Exhibit 6.10 Payroll System

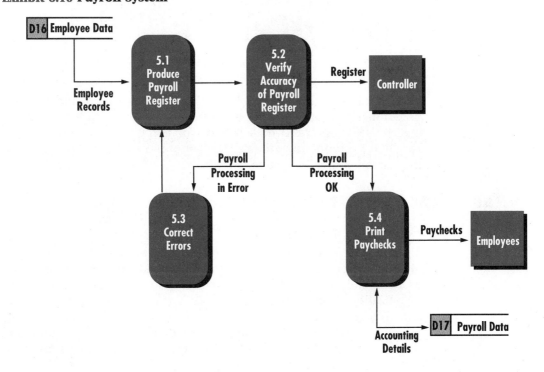

Exhibit 6.11
General Ledger
System

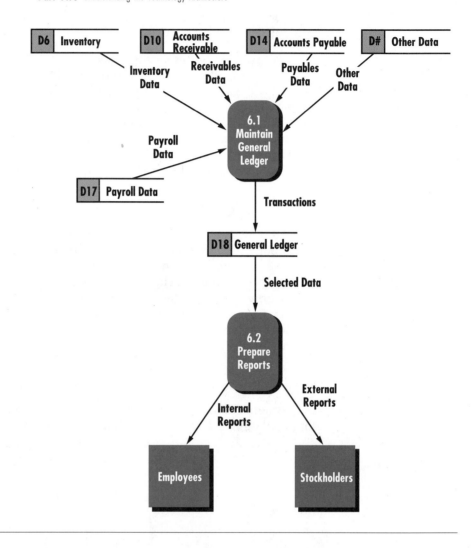

benefit programs. Employee information includes current and previous department, job title, rate of pay, performance ratings, job skills, training courses taken, and data needed for company benefit programs. Exhibit 6.12 summarizes the primary input transactions and outputs of the human resources system.

■ MANAGEMENT REPORTING SYSTEMS

Definition of a Management Reporting System

A **management reporting system (MRS)** is a computer system capable of integrating data from many sources to provide data and information useful to support operations, management, and decision making in an organization. The management reporting system is used to extract data, process it, and produce results meaningful to its users. This output may take many different forms: printed reports (detailed, summary, or exception reports), microfiche, microfilm, visual displays on video

Exhibit 6.12
Human Resources
System

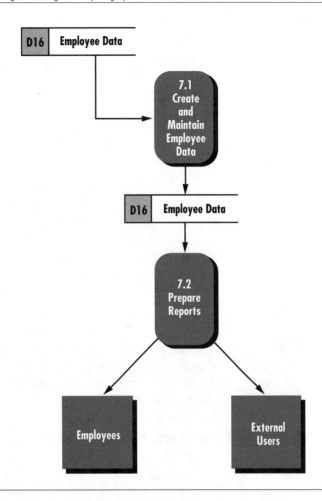

devices, and graphic output are five of the most common ways of presenting results. The MRS is used primarily to identify potential problems or areas of opportunity for improvement.

Much of the data for the MRS may be initially captured, stored, and processed to produce information by transaction processing systems. These data may be stored at the elemental level as raw transactions in large corporate data bases or files. Another approach is to summarize the data into information to reduce the volume of data that must be stored. This latter approach can lead to problems if there is a need to go back and reprocess the raw transactions to aggregate the data in some new way. Either way, the transaction processing systems feed data into the management reporting system.

Why Business Managers Must Understand Management Reporting Systems

An MRS integrates data from many sources to provide data and information useful to support operations, management, and decision making in an organization. These systems interface with the transaction processing systems of the organization to update data bases with data about the internal operations of the company, data that describe business transactions that flow into the firm, and data that can provide insights about the industry, market, and other elements of the environment.

The MRS can draw data from the data base and process it to provide management with information to identify opportunities for improvement or to help determine alternative courses of action. This data is critical to the success of the organization. Indeed, the ability of an organization to gather data, interpret it, and act on it quickly can distinguish the winners from the losers in a highly competitive marketplace.

From this brief discussion of the uses of an MRS, it is clear that a well-designed and well-managed data base represents an important asset of the organization. Indeed, many organizations consider their data bases to be a vital asset of the enterprise and manage them as such. The objective of this special management attention is to ensure that the data needed to solve business problems or exploit business opportunities are made available to the right people at the right time and in the proper form to be of use.

Business managers will be called on to obtain and sustain top management commitment to the concept of managing data as an important company asset. They will be involved in establishing the degree to which management and control of data should be centralized, and they will make decisions about how to use and manage data. They will also be involved in defining the subject data bases needed to support the fundamental operations of the company and in identifying the order in which these data bases need to be developed.

Common Kinds of Management Reports—Detail, Summary, Exception

Detail Report

The **detail report** has one line printed for each transaction processed or for each record in the database (Exhibit 6.13). Such a report is frequently used to verify that all transactions were entered and processed correctly. It is also the ultimate source of data to answer detailed questions and is an essential output from the transaction processing system.

Exhibit 6.13
Sample Detail
Report

			Daily Sales Detail Report			Prepared: 08/10/96
Order #	Customer ID	Salesperson ID	Planned Ship Date	Quantity	Item #	Amount
P12453	C89321	CAR	08/12/96	144	P1234	$3214
P12453	C89321	CAR	08/12/96	288	P3214	$5660
P12454	C03214	GWA	08/13/96	12	P4902	$1224
P12455	C52313	SAK	08/12/96	24	P4012	$2448
P12456	C34123	JMW	08/13/96	144	P3214	$ 720
....	....	....	....	....	....	....
....	....	....	....	....	....	....
....	....	....	....	....	....	....
....	....	....	....	....	....	....

Exhibit 6.14
Sample Summary
Report

Daily Sales by Salesperson Summary Report	
	Prepared: 08/10/96
Salesperson ID	**Amount**
CAR	$42,345
GWA	$38,950
SAK	$22,100
JWN	$12,350
....	....
....	....
....	....
....	....

Such a report, however, is often very long and is not a good source of high-level information for spotting trends or problems.

Summary Report

The **summary report** accumulates detailed data into a summarized format. It brings together one or more related transactions or records in the database and shows the total result (Exhibit 6.14). For example, individual sales transactions can be summarized to show one total by customer or by salesperson.

Exception Report

An **exception report** displays data only about exception conditions. Each line on this report is the result of some abnormal event. Thus the exception report is good for identifying opportunities for improvement, an essential role for effective managers. Its advantage is in reducing the amount of data that the manager receives by only presenting data about unusual situations. The report may present detailed or summary data. For example, a detailed exception report may show a line of information about each individual sales transaction that exceeds $10,000 (Exhibit 6.15). A summary exception report may produce a single line

Exhibit 6.15
Example Detailed
Exception Report

Daily Sales Exception Report—Orders Over $10,000						
						Prepared: 08/10/96
Order #	**Customer ID**	**Salesperson ID**	**Planned Ship Date**	**Quantity**	**Item #**	**Amount**
P21345	C89321	GWA	08/12/96	576	P1234	$12,856
P22153	C00453	CAR	08/12/96	288	P2314	$28,800
P23023	C32832	JWN	08/11/96	144	P2323	$14,400
....	....	....	....	....	....	....
....	....	....	....	....	....	....
....	....	....	....	....	....	....
....	....	....	....	....	....	....

Exhibit 6.16
Example Summary
Exception Report

Summary Exception Report—Salespeople 10% Under Quota		
Based on Sales Through April 1996		Prepared: 05/05/96
Salesperson ID	Quota	Actual Sales
JWN	$120,000	$74,500
SRA	$100,000	$54,250
....	....	....
....	....	....

of information for each salesperson who is more than 10 percent below their sales quota (Exhibit 6.16).

Triggering Management Reports—Periodic, Exception, On Demand

What causes a management report to be prepared? Usually some **triggering mechanism** causes the report to be printed or displayed. There are three common ways of triggering reports: a **periodic, exception,** or **on demand trigger.**

Periodic

Periodic reports are prepared on a regularly defined, predetermined schedule. For instance, input lists are printed nightly for batch processing jobs that run overnight, or the biweekly payroll system prints checks and a check register report each time the payroll system runs. Many accounting systems are triggered to prepare various accounting summaries after the books are closed for a particular month. The exact closing night may be predetermined to be the fifth working night of the month following the month being closed.

Exception

Exception reports are not prepared on any regularly scheduled basis but whenever certain conditions are met. For example, if the inventory level of a specific raw material used in manufacturing falls below the reorder point, a report displaying the current inventory level, reorder point, reorder quantity, average lead time, negotiated price per unit shipped, and preferred supplier for the item may be prepared.

On Demand

On demand reports are prepared whenever they are specifically requested by an end user. Requests may be several times a day for some period of time and then not again for a week or more. Exhibit 6.17 provides examples of the different types of reports and example triggers.

Exhibit 6.17
Examples of Different Types of Management Reports

Type Report	Timing or Trigger Periodic	Exception	On Demand
Detail	Daily Input List of All Sales	Individual Sales Over $10,000	Sales by Salesperson Sales by Customer
Summary	Daily Total Sales Monthly Total Sales	Salespeople Exceeding Quota	Total Sales by Salesperson Total Sales by Customer
Exception	Daily Error List		

Summary

A transaction processing system processes the detail data necessary to update records about the fundamental business operations of the company.

In many organizations today, the transaction processing systems are over fifteen years old and no longer meet the business challenges of the 1990s.

Business managers who manage the functions supported by transaction processing systems must judge if their information systems truly meet the needs of the business.

Business managers must recognize when it is time for a significant upgrade and be ready to lead the reengineering effort to ensure that the new system provides an improved and long-lasting solution.

Management must be held accountable for the effectiveness of transaction processing systems that support the fundamental business operations of the organization.

Business transaction data goes through a data processing cycle that includes the following steps: data capture, data edit, data control, data base maintenance, and document and report generation.

With batch processing systems, business transactions are accumulated over a period of time and prepared for input to the computer for processing as a single unit or batch. The time period over which transactions are accumulated may be any length appropriate to meet the needs of the users of that system.

Interactive updating is a form of data processing where the transaction data are processed immediately, without the delay of accumulating them into a batch.

In batch query mode, the user prepares a request and submits it to the computer, where it will run along with several other batch jobs in the order in which it was submitted. It may take several minutes or even hours to return the results to the user. The time from submission to receipt of output is called the turnaround time.

In an interactive query mode, the user's inquiry is immediately processed by the computer and the user receives a quick response from the system, typically measured in seconds (called the response time).

Not all systems need to be interactive update and/or interactive query. The manager must help decide when it is necessary to require interactive processing.

Nearly all manufacturing organizations have several transaction processing systems in common, including order processing, inventory, accounts receivable, accounts payable, payroll, general ledger, and human resources.

A management reporting system (MRS) is a computer system capable of integrating data from many sources to provide data and information useful to support operations, management, and decision making in an organization.

Much of the data for the MRS may be initially captured, stored, and processed to produce information by transaction processing systems.

MRSs interface with the transaction processing systems of the organization to update data bases with data about the internal operations of the company, data describing business transactions that flow into the firm, and data providing insights about the industry, market, and other elements of the environment.

There are three common types of management reports: the detail report, with one line printed for each transaction or database record processed; the summary report, which accumulates detailed data into a summarized format; and the exception report, in which each line on the report displays the result of some abnormal event.

Three triggering mechanisms cause a report to be printed: a periodic, exception, or demand trigger.

Manager's Checklist

✔ Can you identify the major transaction processing systems of your firm? How old are they and how well do they meet the needs of the business?

✔ Does your company employ source data automation techniques to capture basic business transactions?

✔ Do you receive any reports from a management reporting system? What sort of reports are they—detail, summary, exception reports? How well do they meet your needs?

Key Terms

batch query
batch update
bend in the elbow
data base maintenance

data capture
data correction
data edit
data flow diagram (DFD)

detail report	periodic trigger
exception report	report generation
exception trigger	response time
interactive query	source data automation
interactive update	summary report
management reporting system (MRS)	transaction processing system
	triggering mechanism
on demand trigger	turnaround time

Review Questions

1. Define the term transaction processing system and give eight examples of such a system.

2. Name and briefly describe the five stages of processing data associated with a transaction processing system.

3. What is the difference between interactive and batch update; interactive and batch query?

4. Define the term management reporting system and describe three common types of reports produced by such systems.

5. What is meant by a report trigger? What kinds of triggers are there?

Discussion Questions

1. Discuss the role of business managers in ensuring that their transaction processing systems are meeting the business needs of the firm.

2. Draw a high-level flowchart depicting the interactions among the transaction processing systems frequently employed in a manufacturing company.

3. What are some of the common limitations and inadequacies of basic transaction processing systems built in the 1970s and still in use?

4. Should all systems employ interactive update and interactive query? Why or why not?

5. Discuss the role of business managers in ensuring that their management reporting systems are meeting the business needs of the firm.

Recommended Readings

1. Gorry, G. Anthony and Michael Scott Morton. "A Framework for Management Information Systems." *Sloan Management Review* (Fall 1971).

2. Turban, Efraim. *Decision Support and Expert Systems, Management Support Systems.* 3rd Edition. New York: Macmillan, 1993.

3. Crane, Robert. "Accounting Systems." *Computerworld* 26 (February 24, 1992): 80ff.

4. Elliason, Alan L. *Online Business Computer Applications.* 3rd edition. New York: Macmillan, 1991.

5. Kumar, Vijay. "Current Trends in Transaction Processing Systems." *Journal of Systems Management* 41 (January 1990).

6. Leff, Avarham, and Carlton Pu. "A Classification of Transaction Processing Systems." *Computer* 24 (June 1991).

A Manager's Dilemma

Case Study 6.1

Breaking the Bottleneck

American Amalgamated is a one-hundred-year-old, $50 million company specializing in the manufacture of bolts, screws, and other fasteners. The company's fundamental transaction processing systems are relics originally created in the mid-1960s. Today these systems are patched and tattered from many program changes over the last thirty years.

There is a general awareness that management lacks timely data to make fundamental, day-to-day decisions. One bottleneck to providing managers with the data they need is the huge backlog of projects for the EDP Department. Any request for a special report is met with a chorus of groans from the programming staff, which is already busy adding more patches to existing systems.

A financial analyst reporting to you has recommended a solution to avoid the bottleneck of EDP: provide managers with interactive access to data files containing basic company transactions—orders, shipments, inventory, customer accounts, and so on. Through training on simple query languages, the financial analyst believes that managers will be able to create and format their own reports.

Do you think that this solution will get to the root of the problem? Could this solution introduce new problems? As the Comptroller of American Amalgamated, what would you recommend?

Case Study 6.2

Effective Management Reporting System Needed

For most of the 1980s, Bank of New England was a growing and highly profitable bank with assets increasing from $7 billion in 1985 to $31 billion in 1989. However, in 1989, the bank lost $1.1 billion, most of it due to credit losses in commercial real estate.

Since its troubles began, Bank of New England's credit department has been faced with making meticulous, monthly reports to the Office of Comptroller of the Currency. As a result of regulatory requirements and the lack of information systems to support the credit department, ad hoc systems were created to track the more than $2 billion in bad loans. Unfortunately, the development and actual use of these systems is very time-consuming, and the more time it takes to complete a report, the less time the credit department has to concentrate on the questionable loan itself.

What would you recommend to meet the requirement of monthly reports to the Office of Comptroller in a more time-efficient manner? What can be done to provide more useful, timely data for tracking potentially bad loans?

Case Study 6.3

Transaction Processing System Needed to Help Tupperware Process Orders

Tupperware is a $1 billion business based on selling high-quality, durable plastic food storage and serving containers through more than 350,000 independent dealers worldwide.

When demand for "hot" products skyrockets, orders often outstrip the individual capacity of the seventeen regional factories. In a business based on keeping dealers and salespeople armed with supply and enthusiasm, not being able to deliver any product is disastrous.

To avoid such problems, Tupperware wishes to implement a global order processing system to orchestrate its largely autonomous foreign units to manufacture for a global market.

List at least three basic requirements of an order processing system that must process orders on a global basis. Can you briefly describe how such a system might operate if a customer order from anywhere in the world may be filled from any factory in the world? Under what conditions would a customer order not be filled from the nearest factory?

Chapter 7

Decision Support and Expert Systems

Upon completion of this chapter, you will be able to:

1. Define the terms decision support system, executive information system, and expert system.

2. Outline the conditions under which the use of each of these systems is appropriate.

3. Specify the fundamental business benefits to be gained through each of these types of systems.

4. Discuss the role of the business manager in the development and use of these systems.

Preview

Decision support systems are being used increasingly by knowledge workers at all levels in the organization to aid them in their decision making activities. When provided with the appropriate data and used intelligently, these systems can greatly enhance the decision-making process. Group decision support systems can improve the decision making process of a group by speeding the process up, improving the quality of the decision, or increasing the acceptability of the decision. The executive information system and expert system are two variations of the decision support system.

Issues

1. What role should the management play in the design and implementation of decision support systems?

2. How much can use of a decision support system improve a decision?

Trade-Offs

1. How is a decision support system different from an expert system?

2. Under what conditions is use of an expert system appropriate? When is it inappropriate?

A Manager Struggles with the Issues

The company's purchasing department had been using computers for over fifteen years to handle the processing of requisitions, purchase orders, receipts, invoices, and other paperwork associated with the procurement of raw materials. This computerization process had proven very successful in reducing clerical staff and streamlining the purchasing process.

Now, members of both Information Technology and Purchasing were suggesting that some sort of system be developed to help make a fundamental purchase decision: from which vendors should the company buy and in what quantities. The decision is complex in that more than just minimizing cost needs to be considered. The members are concerned about buying too large a proportion of raw material from a single sup-

plier, since that company could be shut down by a strike or for some other reason. On the other hand, to help improve quality and service, they strongly desire to minimize the number of suppliers. The system would have to allow for significant human interaction and not just "grind through" the numbers to arrive at a solution.

A special project team has been formed to test the feasibility and usefulness of such a system without making a major commitment of resources. The two members of the team are Karen and John, who both joined the company about three years ago. Karen, with an MBA in quantitative analysis, is a member of the IT department. John is a buyer of plastic containers and corrugated boxes used to ship the finished product. How should these two proceed?

■ A FRAMEWORK FOR DECISION MAKING

Structured and Unstructured Problems

A **structured problem** is one that is routine and repetitive. For such a problem, it is likely that policy standards or guidelines already exist to help direct the decision maker. There may be a specified procedure that can be used to reach the correct decision. An **unstructured problem,** on the other hand, is one for which there is no defined solution process. The problem solution process must be developed using judgment, intuition, experience, rules of thumb, and any general guidelines that may apply.

Simon (reference 7) suggests a set of phases associated with decision making: (1) intelligence, (2) design, and (3) choice. The **intelligence phase** consists of discovering some problem or opportunity that needs to be addressed, after all, the decision maker must first be aware of a problem before a decision can be made. Also during this phase, data about the problem or opportunity are gathered that will help lead to a solution. During the **design phase,** the decision maker attempts to use the data and whatever other resources are available to develop a number of alternative solutions to the problem. In the **choice phase,** the decision maker selects one of the solutions to implement.

Gorry and Scott-Morton (reference 3) defined an unstructured problem as one in which all three phases of the decision process were unstructured. A structured problem is a problem in which all three phases are structured. A **semistructured problem** is one in which one or two phases are unstructured. Remembering what the terms struc-

Exhibit 7.1
A Definition of
Problem Types

Decision-Making Phases	Problem Type
All Structured	Structured
Some Structured/Some Unstuctured	Semistructured
All Unstructured	Unstructured

tured, unstructured, and semistructured mean will be useful in under-standing the topics in this chapter (Exhibit 7.1).

Types of Decisions a Manager Faces

Decision making is a constant and continuous management activity. Although managers perform many other activities, such as planning, organizing, communicating, and influencing others, it is the ability to make good, sound business decisions that distinguishes a strong manager from a weak one.

There are many different ways of looking at the decision-making process. One useful way is to think in terms of the type of decision to be made. Frequently, decisions are classified as operational, tactical, or strategic. Each type of decision has different characteristics and requires different types and sources of data (Exhibit 7.2).

Exhibit 7.2
A Hierarchy of
Decisions

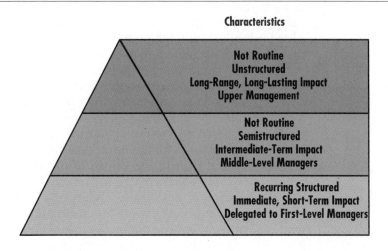

Characteristics

Not Routine
Unstructured
Long-Range, Long-Lasting Impact
Upper Management

Not Routine
Semistructured
Intermediate-Term Impact
Middle-Level Managers

Recurring Structured
Immediate, Short-Term Impact
Delegated to First-Level Managers

Operational Decisions

Operational decisions deal with the routine day-to-day operations of the organization. These are "bread-and-butter" activities that every organization must perform well in order to remain in business—order processing, inventory control, customer billing, production scheduling, and so on. The decisions associated with these activities are delegated to the lowest possible level of the organization, where they can be made quickly and most effectively. Decisions such as "Should we extend credit to this customer?" "How many tons of raw material should we order?" and "Is this customer eligible for our 2 percent discount?" are best handled by the clerical staff and first-line managers in charge of such operational activities.

Operational decisions tend to be recurring—the same question comes up again and again. As a result, the decision-making process becomes relatively routine and quite structured. The variables that should be considered in making the decision are identified, their values are known with a high degree of accuracy, and the relationship between variables and the decision is understood. For example, inventory-control clerks check inventory levels and reorder the previously set order amount for items that have fallen below the reorder point.

Executing operational decisions leads to the manager's desired results with a high degree of certainty. For example, once items are ordered to stock inventory, there is a high degree of certainty that inventory will be restocked.

Operational decisions tend to have an immediate but short-term impact on the firm. For example, should an inventory control clerk fail to reorder a high-turnover item, the item will soon be depleted. However, the firm can recover from the mistake and replenish the item within a short time with no long-lasting effect on profitability.

Tactical Decisions

Tactical decisions involve allocation and control of the firm's resources to meet the objectives that support the strategic goals of the business. These decisions are typically made by middle-level managers responsible for implementing the means for meeting the goals and objectives that upper management has established. Decisions such as "What credit limits should we set for each class of customer?" "Which supplier should be our primary source of raw materials?" and "Under what conditions is a customer eligible for a discount?" are examples of tactical decisions made by middle-level managers.

Tactical decisions are not as routine and structured as operational decisions. Many times all the important variables involved in a tactical decision are not known; the values of the variables identified as significant may not be known; and the relationship between the variables and the decision is not clearly understood. For example, selecting a low-cost supplier of raw materials can become a highly complex problem. A given supplier may offer the lowest delivered prices, but what if there is some unknown probability that a strike will occur at that supplier's plants and interrupt the flow of raw materials? Or what if this is a new supplier whose product quality, delivery reliability, and customer service are unknown? This lack of a clear relationship among all the variables leads to uncertainty—even if the course of action decided on by the manager is executed perfectly, will it obtain the desired result?

Tactical decisions have an intermediate impact on the firm. The impact may not be felt for a few weeks, but can affect operations for several weeks or longer. Although it may be very difficult to live with or reverse the impact of a poor tactical decision, one such bad decision will not destroy the firm.

Strategic Decisions

Strategic decisions include setting the goals of the company, defining the basic assumptions on which long-range planning should be based, and identifying the critical success factors of the firm. These decisions form the basis on which the firm will run and provide basic guidelines for others to follow in making tactical and operational decisions. "What strategy should we follow in competing against other firms—low-cost supplier or differentiation?" "Do we wish to compete in an entire market or in a subset or niche of the market?" "What is the proper balance between long-term sales growth and short-term profitability?" These are examples of strategic decisions.

Strategic decisions tend to be highly complex, unstructured, and nonrecurring. All the variables that need to be considered cannot be identified. Although values may be assigned to a few key variables that seem to influence the decision, there are many intangible, nonquantifiable factors that enter into the decision. Much of the information needed to reach the decision is about things external to the firm—information about competitors, suppliers, consumers, and the overall industry in which the firm competes. In many cases the information used to make the decision is based on rumors, feelings, and opinions. Due to the lack of precise data and clear cause-and-effect relationships, there is a high degree of uncertainty associated with the outcome of a strategic decision. These are tough decisions spiced with a high degree of risk that senior management must be prepared to make.

Strategic decisions have a long-range impact on the firm. It may take several months or even years to know the true effect of a strategic decision, and it is very difficult to reverse its impact. One or two incorrect strategic decisions in a single year can ruin a firm.

Exhibit 7.3 lists some characteristics of the data needed to make the three different kinds of decisions.

■ DECISION SUPPORT SYSTEMS

Definition of Decision Support System

A **decision support system (DSS)** is a computer-based information system used to help people reach decisions. A DSS can be applied to

Exhibit 7.3
Characteristics of
Data Needed to
Make Different
Kinds of Decisions

Characteristics	Operational	Tactical	Strategic
Can numeric values be assigned to almost all variables affecting the decision?	Yes	Most	No
Are most of the data needed about things internal to the organization?	Yes	Usually	No
Can most of the data be provided by sources internal to the firm?	Yes	Usually	No
Are most of the data needed about things that have already happened (i.e., historical data)?	Yes	No	No

support operational, tactical, or strategic decision making. A DSS can provide access to both corporate and externally generated data related to the problem being studied. The data can be input to a model that simulates the real world, displaying the results in a number of different ways including graphics (Exhibit 7.4). An ideal DSS requires minimal training for users.

A DSS is used to support decision making in a particular environment that includes the following conditions:

1. The problem is too complex to be solved manually—either there are too many data to be considered, the calculations are too involved, or both.

2. There is a need to conduct a sensitivity analysis to examine the impact of a change in the variables on the decision because the true value of many of the parameters is only known to be within some range.

3. There is a need for interaction between the decision maker and the system since intermediate results may influence the direction of the decision-making process—cutting off some alternatives and opening up others.

4. The decision maker using the system is comfortable with the use of quantitative methods to enhance decision making.

5. Ideally, the user has actually taken an active role in the development (or at least in the definition) of the system and clearly understands any assumptions or limitations associated with its use.

Exhibit 7.5 lists some areas in which to use DSS applications.

Managers who use a DSS feel they obtain the following benefits:

1. They are able to explore more options and bring more relevant data to bear on the problem. Thus they can make better decisions.

2. They are able to make a more factual and convincing recommendation.

Exhibit 7.4
Basic Components of a Decision Support System

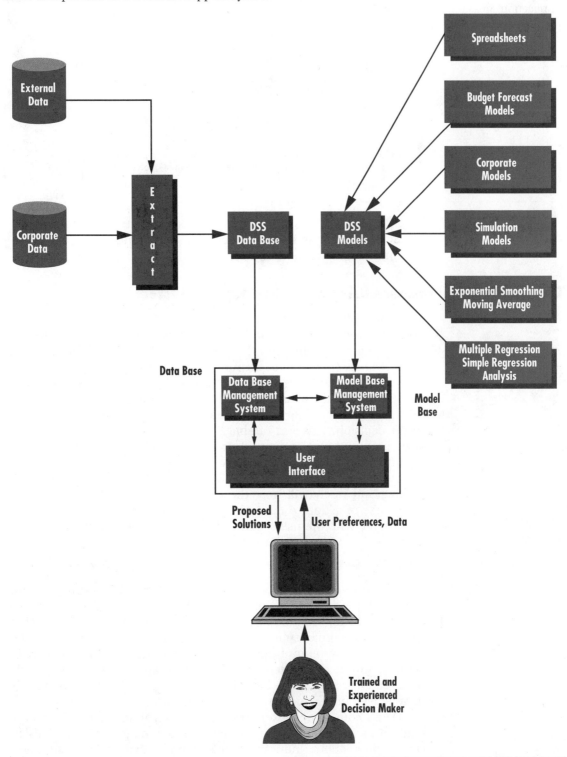

Exhibit 7.5
Frequent DSS
Application Areas

Area	Function
Financial planning	Budgeting, cash management Long-range planning Economic analysis, investment analysis Mergers, acquisitions
Marketing	Allocation of promotion budget to alternative programs Sales force deployment Price/volume/profit forecasting
Production planning	Inventory planning Quality management Production planning Capacity planning
Distribution	Plant and warehouse location selection Price/quantity discount analysis

3. They are able to reach decisions sooner and implement recommendations sooner.

Decision-Making Processes Using a Decision Support System

Decision makers must reach a mental state in which they are confident and prepared to take action. To reach this state, a DSS may be employed to gain insights into the problem and explore a number of options. DSS users want to examine and understand the relationships between input variables, output results, and problem constraints. Quite often some form of sensitivity analysis is conducted so that users build up their understanding of the problem and can identify the key factors in the decision. This sort of analysis is appropriate when dealing with structured and semistructured problems. Such analysis really cannot be applied to a totally unstructured problem.

Decision makers employ the DSS as a tool to help in the decision making, but rarely will treat the DSS as a crystal ball that tells them the course of action to take. The results of any analysis using the DSS must agree with the users' own intuitive feel for the problem.

Data Needed to Support the Decision-Making Process

A collection of data is needed to support most decision-making processes. These data are frequently drawn from the data bases created from processing the fundamental business transactions of the organization. For example, supporting decisions in the area of raw materials acquisition may require detailed transaction data about vendors, inventory, production schedules, lead times, and quality and quantity requirements. In order to integrate these data, it is imperative that the data be well understood by the designers of the DSS.

Data about things external to the organization are becoming recognized as increasingly important to the building of a DSS. This includes data about industry trends, competitive activity, suppliers, customers, and government regulations. Many computer-based public

Exhibit 7.6
Some of the
Available On-Line
Data Base Services

Data Base Service	Topics Covered	For More Information
Bibliographic Retrieval Services	Bibliography of business news	BRS Information Tech 1200 Route 7 Latham, NY 12110
CompuServe	Consumer and business services and electronic mail	CompuServe, Inc. 5000 Arlington Center Blvd. Columbus, OH 43220
DIALOG Information Services	Business, technical, and scientific news	DIALOG Information Services 3460 Hillview Ave. Palo Alto, CA 94304
The Source	Consumer services	Source Telecomputing 1616 Anderson Road McLean, VA 22102
Newsnet	Business and consumers	Newsnet, Inc. 945 Haverford Road Bryn Mawr, PA 19010
WESTLAW©	Legal, business, and News	West Publishing 620 Opperman Drive Eagan, MN 55123
BRKTHRU	Arts, humanities, medical, education, science, and technology	BRS Information Tech 1200 Route 7 Latham, NY 12110
Dow Jones/News Retrieval	Business, investments, stocks, and world news	Dow Jones/News Retrieval P.O. Box 300 Princeton, NJ 08540

data bases are readily accessible to provide vast amounts of data in these areas. So much data are available that the problem is in screening it to get only data that pertain to the decision at hand. A few of these public data bases are listed in Exhibit 7.6.

Data sources other than public data bases also exist. Company personnel can be trained to gather data about competitors using a variety of legal means: interviewing suppliers and customers of competitors; analyzing competitive products, promotion activity, and advertising copy; carefully reviewing annual stockholders' reports, government 10K reports, and credit reports; plus a host of other means. The organization that does not include these sources of data in its DSS may find itself at a distinct disadvantage to its competitors in the area of computer-assisted decision making.

A Trained and Experienced Decision Maker

A tool is only as effective as its user. The most elegantly designed DSS with a complete data base of facts is useless (or even harmful) in the hands of an unskilled user. The DSS will tend to amplify good judgment *or* naivete.

The user must understand the models available in the DSS—not just how to use them but also the basic assumptions on which they are based. For example, the use of a linear programming model on a problem whose variables violate the assumption of linearity will yield erroneous results for any unsuspecting decision maker. Likewise, the DSS user needs to understand the data used in the model. For example, many manufacturers ship finished products to an intermediate (broker or trade warehouse), who then sells the product to the end user. In order to analyze product movement, both shipment data (movement of product to the intermediate) and consumption data (movement of product from the intermediate to the end user) may be available for use. The DSS user must make the appropriate choice of data for the problem under study.

Exhibit 7.7 describes some of the commonly used models for forecasting. Exhibit 7.8 illustrates a number of the commonly used decision support system models.

Exhibit 7.7
A Glossary of Commonly Used Forecasting Terms

Budget Forecasting Model
A model generally used to consolidate budget information provided by separate departments using standard accounting practices. It may include capabilities to forecast cash flow, earnings per share, and other financial ratios resulting from performance according to budget.

Corporate Model
A mathematical representation or simulation of a company's accounting practices and financial policy guidelines. It is used to project financial results under a given set of assumptions and to evaluate the financial impact of alternative plans. Long-range forecasts are also calculated using such models.

Exponential Smoothing
A weighted, moving average method of forecasting in which past observations are geometrically discounted according to their age. The heaviest weight is assigned to the most recent data. The smoothing is called exponential because data points are weighted according to an exponential function of their age.

Forecast
The extrapolation of the past into the future. It is usually an objective computation involving data, as opposed to a prediction, which is a subjective estimate incorporating a manager's anticipation of changes and new influencing factors.

Macroeconomic Forecasting Model
A model or simulation that can be used to forecast gross national product (GNP), personal income, employment, price levels, and other indications of economic performance. The Wharton Model is an example.

Moving Average
A method of averaging out the roughness of random variation in a data series. A moving average uses only the most recent historical data in the series. The method gets its name from the way it slides along the data series, averaging each data point with its immediate predecessors.

Multiple Regression
A statistical technique for predicting the value of a dependent variable, which is assumed dependent upon one or more explanatory or independent variables.

Simple Regression Analysis
A statistical technique for predicting the value of one variable in terms of the given value of another variable.

Simulation
The technique of using representative or artificial operating and demand data to reproduce conditions that are likely to occur in the actual performance of a system. Most simulations are multiple-equation models that mimic some real-world situation.

Time Series
An ordered succession of numbers representing the values of a particular variable over a given period of time (e.g., monthly sales figures for 1994 through 1997).

Exhibit 7.8
Models Used as Building Blocks for Decision Support Systems

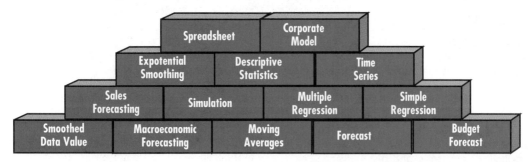

Why Business Managers Must Understand Decision-Support Systems

Decision making is a constant and continuous management activity. Although managers perform many other activities, such as planning, organizing, communicating, and influencing others, it is the ability to make good, sound business decisions that distinguishes a strong manager from a weak one. Decision support systems are being used increasingly by managers to address real business problems. No effective manager would ever rely solely on a DSS to actually make decisions, but when provided with appropriate data and used intelligently, these systems can greatly enhance the decision-making process.

As a potential tool in their arsenal of weapons, business managers need to understand the capabilities and limitations of such systems. Indeed, the manager with no access to an effective DSS is at a distinct disadvantage to peers within the organization and rivals within competing organizations.

■ GROUP DECISION SUPPORT

One definition of a work group is two or more people who work together to perform some task while acting as one unit. The formation of temporary work groups is becoming a common way to address special issues. Members of the work group may all be from the same department and report to the same manager or they may be from many different organizations. They may work at a single location or they may be scattered around the globe. They may gather to meet together at one time or they may never actually meet together as a group. Exhibit 7.9 illustrates four different work group situations. These situations depend on two variables: timing and geography. For example, when time

Real World Perspectives

Use of a DSS at Libbey-Owens-Ford

Libby-Owens-Ford (LOF) is an operating company of the Pilkington Group, which has over 400 subsidiary and related companies in the global glass market. LOF has 9,000 employees and annual sales of $900 million.

The feasibility of a formal production planning DSS was explored with the goal that the model would determine the optimum monthly levels of production, inventory, and distribution.

After nearly two years of effort, the DSS was brought to operational status. The final model involves over 100,000 decision variables. To run the DSS requires gathering data produced by many different information systems to provide market demand and sales data, freight rates, production rates and yields, manufacturing costs, inventory levels, and interplant rail schedules.

A production planner runs the DSS each month to develop production plans for each of the plants. These plans are transmitted to the production schedulers at the individual plants, who develop detailed daily schedules that reflect the monthly production plans developed by the system. The production planner spends one week per month updating the data base, running the model, analyzing the outputs, and releasing the plan to the production schedulers. The model is run 10 to 20 times each month to determine the production plan and address scenarios of interest.

The production planner through use of the DSS was able to suggest many changes in the manner in which customer orders are assigned to plants resulting in savings of over $700,000 per year. The production planner also was able to identify opportunities for greater use of interplant rail shipments that justified investment in rail car capacity and yielded annual savings in excess of $600,000. *SOURCE: Clarence H. Martin, Denver C. Dent, and James C. Eckart. "Integrated Production, Distribution, and Inventory Planning at Libbey-Owens-Ford." Interfaces 23, vol. 3, May–June 1993 (pp 68–78). Copyright 1993, The Operations Research Society of America and The Institute of Management Sciences, 290 Westminster St., Providence, RI 02903.* □

is a variable, the group can come together at the same time, or they may "meet" at different times through the exchange of documents, voice mail messages, e-mail notes, etc. When geography is a variable, the group can come together at the same place or meet electronically through the use of audio or teleconferencing or other means even though the members are in different physical locations.

There are many benefits to solving problems by working in groups; after all, the members of a group collectively have more knowledge than any one member. As a result, a group has the potential to be better at understanding a situation, identifying possible solutions, and evaluating the options to arrive at the best course of action. Not only can the quality of the decision be improved by working in a group, but the acceptance of the solution can be greatly increased. The active participation of members of the group in the decision-making process means that it is much less likely for them to resist the implementation

Exhibit 7.9
Four Possible Work Group Environments

Time	Geography
Same Time Same Place	Same Time Different Place
Different Time Same Place	Different Time Different Place

of the decision. In fact, because their ego is wrapped up in the decision, they are likely to be strongly committed to successful implementation.

There are also disadvantages to working in a group. Groups, while more thorough, usually take longer to reach a decision. Groups have a tendency to accept compromise solutions of relatively poor quality. There is also some pressure on the members of the group to conform with the others, thus there is a danger for **groupthink** in which all members seem to voice the same idea. If group dynamics are not managed carefully, a few members of the group can dominate the group and the majority of the group never gets an opportunity to express their ideas. The dominant members of the group are often surprised when the passive members of the group fail to support the group's recommendations. If these disadvantages are not overcome, an individual decision maker may be more effective than a work group.

In Chapter 8 we will discuss e-mail and various conferencing systems as examples of information technology that improve communication among people. Such information technology can aid the **group decision support (GDSS)** process. There are also specially designed GDSS software packages that help members of a group make decisions via a computer network, either a local area network or a wide area network, depending on the location of the members of the group.

Another approach to GDSS is the use of a high-tech **electronic meeting room.** Participants sit at a large U-shaped table where they can see one another; this arrangement helps increase openness and communications. Each participant has his or her own personal computer that is connected to all other participants via a local area network for the sharing of messages, graphics, and text. Special GDSS software is loaded on the personal computer for use by the participants. Individual ideas or group results can be displayed on a large-screen projection system connected to the local area network.

■ EXECUTIVE INFORMATION SYSTEM

The Role of Top Level Managers and Their Need for Information

Executives and senior managers, the top two levels of management in a corporation or division, are responsible for the planning, control, coordination, and operational activities of their organization to deliver business results. They manage people and other assets of the company to achieve these results. Their mode of operation is to delegate much of the detail work to subordinates—word processing is for secretaries and spreadsheets are for staff analysts to grapple with. Although they review budgets and plans and compare actual results to forecasts, they are not likely to manipulate the numbers themselves. Much of their time is spent monitoring the internal status of their organization to ensure that near-term (zero to twelve months) objectives will be met.

Top-level managers need data that will help them assess their organization's success and the performance of individuals critical to that success. They also need data to judge if the management team is taking action on what is vital to the organization's performance. To support long-term planning, executives are also keenly interested in data about the economic and competitive environment of the outside world. Historical data, forecasts, and data on trends are essential for this group of data users to be able to transform simple data into useful strategic information. The potential for **data overload** is extremely high. The data executives receive must be timely and pertinent to the decisions to be made.

Definition of an Executive Information System

An **executive information system** (**EIS**) accumulates data from a variety of internal and external sources and delivers timely and pertinent information to management. Although originally envisioned as a tool for the top two levels of management (hence the term *executive information system*), the use of EIS has penetrated down into the organization, many levels below the top executives. The system must be customized to meet the specific needs of managers whose needs and personal style may vary greatly. Indeed, the ability to integrate internal with external data and present this data in a form customized to meet the needs of the user is what distinguishes an EIS from a Management Reporting System (MRS) (see Chapter 6). The system must be able to extract, filter, and compress a broad range of internal and external data to present the information that the manager needs without creating a data overload situation. The system should highlight exceptions of interest to its user—variances from budgets, new trends, results outside control limits. It must also monitor and highlight critical success factors in an individual's area of responsibility.

The data that each manager may require can vary greatly even within the same organization. In general, what each will need is data that will help them to measure their organization's success, the performance of individuals critical to that success, and the external factors that have a bearing on its success. Exhibit 7.10 outlines the kinds of data that may be appropriate for many managers.

An EIS provides managers with an electronic window into the company's operations. The EIS accesses corporate data and provides timely, consistent, and relevant information that yields insights into how the business is running. By making such information easily available, the use of an EIS encourages managers to take a hands-on management approach.

Although an EIS can reduce the need for support staff who assemble and digest information for managers, the primary justification to invest in building one is not this potential cost savings. The EIS is justified by positioning it as a value-added tool providing new capability. It creates a new source of knowledge that helps the company enhance its performance and better serve its stockholders, employees, and customers.

An EIS can also be designed to enhance the planning process. Such a system taps into data bases of information about what is happening external to the firm. Access to such data enables managers to track trends and verify key planning assumptions. External data also provide

Exhibit 7.10
The Kinds of Data that Might Be Included in an EIS

Area	Historical	Current	Forecast
Overall performance			
Total sales	√	√	√
Total costs	√	√	√
Summarized financial data			
Sales by division, product, account, sales manager	√	√	√
Costs by category, plant, product	√	√	√
Cash flow		√	√
Key nonaccounting data			
Customer service/customer satisfaction indicators		√	√
Product quality		√	√
Promotion plans		√	√
External data			
Economic trends		√	√
Industry trends		√	√
Competitive activity		√	√
Consumer analysis		√	√
Project status			
Status of key projects (e.g., new product introductions, capacity expansion)		√	√
Personnel			
Performance data	√	√	√
Availability of key personnel		√	√

information about the firm's competitors, suppliers, customers, and the environment in which the firm operates. Such a system can become a catalyst that helps managers reevaluate the way the firm does business and even what business it is in.

Elements of a Successful Executive Information System

Standard Reports

The EIS must have the capability to navigate easily through large amounts of data to create standard reports. Each user of the EIS must be able to select a personal subset of these standard reports and focus the system according to individual responsibilities and interests. In addition to the ability to drill down to detail data, the standard reporting module should be able to present data in graphical form to show trends (e.g., monthly sales by district, weekly cost per unit of production by plant, and so on). These standard reports should include commentaries, text reports, numerical tables, and project status reports including Gantt or PERT charts.

Drill Down Capability

The ability to view high-level summary data and then to **drill down** through layers of data to view data in greater detail is one of the most useful features of an EIS. The EIS may be designed so that the manager

	Actual	Earnings by Quarter (Millions) Forecast	Variance
2nd Qtr. 1997	$12.6	$11.8	6.8%
1st Qtr. 1997	$10.8	$10.7	0.9%
4th Qtr. 1996	$14.3	$14.5	−1.4%
3rd Qtr. 1996	$12.8	$13.3	−3.8%
2nd Qtr. 1996	$10.4	$9.9	5.1%
1st Qtr. 1996	$9.9	$10.2	−2.9%

can simply move the cursor to a particular data aggregation and click the mouse to see the next level of detail beneath that currently displayed. Exhibits 7.11 a–d illustrate the use of the drill-down function for a consumer products firm with several product sectors, each of which contains one or more product categories with each product category made up of several individual products. A manager reviewing the business results for a quarter may see from high-level summary data that profits for the quarter exceeded the corporate forecast (Exhibit 7.11 a). Was it because sales were greater than expected or expenses less than expected or a combination of both? Thus drilling down to the layer below profits reveals sales and expense actuals versus forecasts (Exhibit 7.11 b). At this level it is determined that sales were up considerably over the forecast while expenses were roughly as expected. The manager would thus drill down another level of detail on sales to view sales by sector (Exhibit 7.11 c). Each sector varies some from the forecasted sales, but the health care sector exhibits the greatest variance. The manager may wish to drill down yet another level to view the product categories within the health care sector to determine that the toothpaste product category made the largest contribution to sales (Exhibit 7.11 d).

Short-Term Issues

The most critical business issues are almost always short-lived. Yet these are the very issues that consume the greatest part of a manager's time and energy. Most short-term issues command a high level of attention for a few months, get resolved, and then drop off the manager's list of interests. Critical issues tracking must allow users of the EIS to set and delete issues very quickly and without requiring the help of the

Qtr: 2nd Qtr. 1997	Sales and Expenses (Millions) Actual	Forecast	Variance
Gross Sales	$110.9	$108.3	2.4%
Expenses	$98.3	$96.5	1.9%
Profit	$12.6	$11.8	6.8%

Exhibit 7.11c
Third Layer of
Detail in Drill
Down

Qtr: 2nd Qtr. 1977	Sales by Sector (Millions) Actual	Forecast	Variance
Beauty Care	$34.5	$33.9	1.8%
Health Care	$30.0	$28.0	7.1%
Soap	$22.8	$23.0	−0.9%
Snacks	$12.1	$12.5	−3.2%
Electronics	$11.5	$10.9	5.5%
Total	$110.9	$108.3	2.4%

IT staff. The system must be able to integrate these short-lived issues with executive mail and other EIS applications, incorporate spreadsheets and documents created outside the EIS, and monitor important information such as due dates and changing priorities.

Exception Reporting

An EIS with exception reporting capabilities detects problems that the user might otherwise overlook. Exception reporting is a background process that continuously searches for numerical results that are out of line with expectations and brings those results, and only those results, to the manager's attention. The EIS should allow each individual user to determine the criteria for an exception report and should automatically produce a menu of identified exceptions.

Executive Brief

A manager should be able to select screens of data, text, or graphs and download them to a stand-alone workstation for later review or presentation at meetings. Managers must also have the ability to sequence these screens according to their own agenda or needs.

External Data

Most businesses have sources of specific industry data that are of critical competitive value to their operations. The EIS must be able to filter and

Exhibit 7.11d
Fourth Layer of
Detail in Drill
Down

Qtr: 2nd Qtr. 1997 Sector: Health Care	Sales by Product Category (Millions) Actual	Forecast	Variance
Toothpaste	$12.4	$10.5	18.1%
Mouthwash	$8.6	$8.8	−2.3%
Over the Counter Drugs	$5.8	$5.3	9.4%
Skin Care Products	$3.2	$3.4	−5.9%
Total	$30.0	$28.0	7.1%

integrate this key information with management reports, as well as to offer access to a broad range of economic data, stock prices, company-specific financial information, and a host of topical newsletters.

News

News delivered electronically should be more current and focused than news delivered through the print media. Through live connections to services such as the Dow Jones/News Retrieval Service and the McGraw-Hill News FM-band continuous transmission news service, the ideal EIS combines sophisticated news filtering capabilities with nearly instantaneous delivery of information.

Data Analysis

Data analysis should encompass a broad range of functionality, from a simple "pop-up calculator" to sophisticated modeling capabilities. The analytical tools for managers include ad hoc data base query, a full range of financial modeling and financial consolidation products, plus time series and regression analysis.

Exhibit 7.12
Elements of a Successful EIS

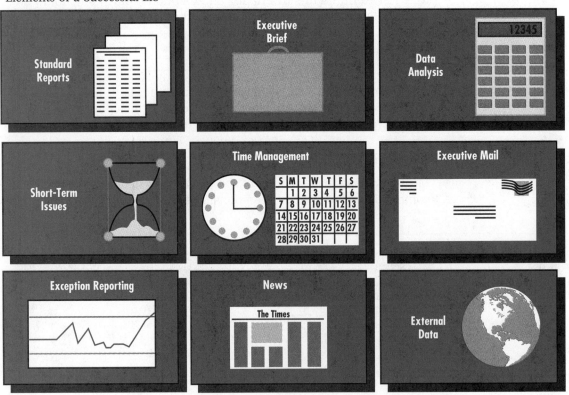

Executive Mail

An e-mail system that is part of an EIS should provide users with the ability to take any screen (including graphs and charts), annotate it (with a paste-on note), and mail it to any other manager with a minimum of keyboard interaction and complexity.

Time Management

Managers have many time-related commitments, meetings, and deadlines. The time management component of the EIS provides a calendar and suspense file for keeping track of important dates and times. In addition to keeping track of the manager's own personal schedule, it is important to know the availability of people with whom the manager may need to schedule a meeting: the manager's boss, subordinates, and key resources.

Data Retrieval

Managers should be able to access detailed operational data residing in corporate files and data bases as well as retrieve data from external data sources such as public data bases.

Issues Associated with an Executive Information System

The implications of trial usage of computers by executives extend far beyond the executive suite. When top management puts the seal of approval on personal computer usage, it suddenly becomes very important for middle managers to have personal computers on their desks. On the other hand, should top management be dissatisfied with their attempts to use the computer, there may be a slowdown in computer usage throughout the entire organization. Top management's frustration with computers was one of the main reasons for the reduced growth rate in personal computer sales in the late 1980s.

Another area of management concern associated with the growth in use of personal computers by executives is the potential for producing a number of financial models based on different assumptions. Of course, the results of the model can be no better than the data and the assumptions used. However, the potential of executives to implement plans based on the results of their analyses is tremendous.

The following benefits are frequently associated with using an EIS:

Benefits

■ It provides executives with key data and information in a summarized and custom-tailored form, thus reducing the amount of data they must review.

■ It eliminates communications bottlenecks between executives and staff personnel that can slow down the decision-making process.

■ It saves staff and executives' time.

■ It helps executives improve their understanding of the company and the environment in which it operates.

Some of the potential issues associated with using an EIS include the following:

Issues

■ The executives' success or lack of success with computers will have a major impact on the entire organization.

■ There is a potential to create a proliferation of financial models based on varying assumptions and data sources.

■ Line and staff subordinates are uncomfortable with executives' access to detailed operational data—especially if they do not have time to do their own analyses before the executives can access the data.

■ Using an EIS may not be compatible with the management style of many executives used to working through others.

Real World Perspective

Integrating Transaction Processing and EIS at Arby's

Bailey Co., one of the biggest franchisers of Arby's outlets with 61 restaurants in six states, decided that in a business characterized by fickle customers, margins of just 5%, and employee turnover as high as 300%, IT innovations are critical.

Its first IT project was Touch 2000, which allows customers to enter their orders directly into a point-of-sale system. Upon entry, an order is transmitted to the kitchen, cashier screens, and the store manager's workstation. The system helps minimize the problem of employee turnover, and customers seem to approve—the machine is never sullen or rude. In addition, the system offers suggestions for complementary menu items, handles orders in several languages, displays nutritional information, and automates coupon processing.

For Arby's managers, the system provides automated labor scheduling; sales-mix analysis; inventory control, which allows stores to reduce stock levels; and yield analysis, which compares actual materials usage to daily usage estimates.

A communications server in corporate headquarters collects data from all stores. That data is then stored on a minicomputer which handles general ledger, payroll, and other applications. It is also loaded onto a second personal computer, the primary file server for the executive information system.

The EIS is fully installed and used by all corporate managers. These managers can access sales information on a variety of levels. For example, if a manager wants to know how many orders for large fries were placed last month, he or she can make a simple query using a 486-based desktop PC via a Token Ring LAN. The numbers can be seen nationally, regionally, by state, or by store, and are automatically presented in chart form. Traveling district managers use notebook computers to query the system.

SOURCE: Linda Wilson. "Arby's IT: Rare and Well Done." InformationWeek. August 16, 1993. □

■ EXPERT SYSTEMS

Definition of an Expert System

An **expert system** is a variation of a decision support system that uses knowledge and inference procedures to solve problems that are difficult enough to require significant human expertise for their solution. An expert system is capable of recommending a decision and explaining the reasoning behind it. There are two kinds of expert systems: rule based and frame based. Only the rule based is discussed here, since it is the most widely used. Expert systems contain large stores of task-specific knowledge consisting of facts and heuristics. The facts represent a body of information that is widely shared and generally agreed upon by experts in the field. The **heuristics** are private rules of good judgment (rules of good guessing or plausible reasoning) that characterize expert-level decision making in the field. The performance level of an expert system is primarily a function of the size and quality of the knowledge base it possesses. This definition of an expert system was developed by Professor Edward Feigenbaum of Standard University, a leading researcher in expert systems.

Research into expert computer systems has been underway since the late 1950s. By the mid-1960s, researchers realized that computers could not be designed to think, but they could, if the information they contained was complete enough, be made to mimic human experts. As recently as 1980, expert systems research was still confined to a few research laboratories at MIT, Stanford, and Carnegie-Mellon. However, industry has awakened to the potential for expert systems. Today, most large corporations consider expert systems strategically valuable to their organizations.

Most early commercial expert systems were constructed as stand-alone consultation systems for advising the user in a very specific problem area. For example, an early successful expert system was the DENDRAL program developed at Stanford. This program was the result of a long-term collaboration between chemists and computer scientists automating the determination of molecular structure from empirical formulas and mass spectral data.

These early systems demonstrated the many potential benefits that accrue when expertise can be automated. However, these projects also required tremendous levels of effort. Building an expert system required years of work, special-purpose computing hardware, and highly trained personnel. Their cost was in the millions!

Components of an Expert System

An expert system consists of five basic components: (1) a **knowledge base** developed by capturing the knowledge of an expert; (2) an **inference engine,** which enables the system to simulate the problem-solving process of the human expert; (3) a **user interface** to provide facts about the problem to be solved; (4) an **explanation subsystem** to explain what rule it is considering and how the present question will provide data that will add support or help rule out that rule; and (5) a **knowledge acquisition subsystem,** which is the process used to study the expert's behavior, uncover the expert's underlying knowledge, and select and use a tool to build the expert system (Exhibit 7.13).

The key idea in building an expert system is that experts, be they human or machine, are often those who know more facts and heuristics about a domain than lesser problem solvers. The task of building a knowledge system, therefore, is predominantly one of teaching a system enough of these facts and heuristics to enable it to perform competently in a particular problem-solving context.

The knowledge base consists of a series of if/then rules concerning pertinent objects and events. The *if* part of the rule presents the solution and the *then* part is the response. An example if/then statement is, "If you want to reduce your weight, then reduce your calorie intake."

These if/then rules are known as the system's *heuristics.* The expert system must allow for the deletion of rules found to be no longer valid and the addition of new rules. Thus the knowledge base can be continually refined and the expert system continuously improved. Expert systems may have any number of rules, but the number is typically in the twenty to one thousand range. Most systems have well over one hundred rules.

Another form of entry to the knowledge base are examples. In place of if/then rules, these entries contain recorded examples, such as, "A basketball player shorter than 6'2"" and with a vertical jump less than

Exhibit 7.13
Components of an
Expert System

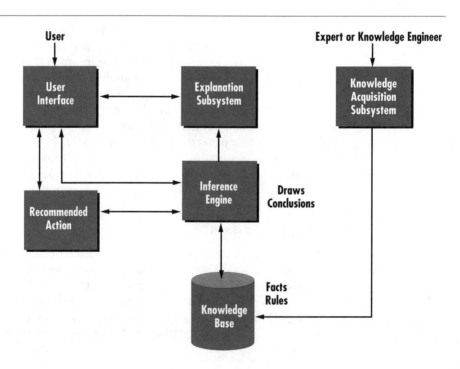

36" cannot play center." The knowledge base thus consists of a large number of if/then rules and examples.

But rules and examples are not enough. What makes an expert system an expert is the way rules are processed by the system and how they are acted on; this is done by the inference engine.

The inference engine is that part of an expert system that contains the inference and control strategies. It performs two major tasks. First, it examines existing facts and rules and adds new facts and rules when possible. Second, it decides in which order inferences are made. Based on the facts given to it by the user and reasoning rules, the inference engine derives conclusions that it attempts to verify by requesting additional facts from the user or by obtaining additional data from the data base. In doing so, the inference engine controls the consultation process with the user. Thus, an expert system is driven by the inference engine and the data entered during the consultation.

The two most common inference methods are **backward chaining** and **forward chaining.** Backward chaining starts with the *then* part of an if/then statement, and when this matches the same component in a problem, the system searches for appropriate *if* clauses. Forward chaining works in the reverse order.

Developing Expert Systems

Developing expert systems today is both complex and costly. In order to build an expert system, both the knowledge (facts) and logic of a human expert must be programmed into the system. As already discussed, these elements are referred to as the knowledge base and the inference engine. It is necessary for a **knowledge engineer** to interview the expert to capture and codify that expert's knowledge, which is of two types. The first type is the facts of the domain—widely shared and generally accepted knowledge that is written in books and journals. The second type is called **heuristic knowledge**—the knowledge of good practice and good judgment in a field that comes only from years of experience.

The logical thought processes (rules) used in problem solving are often difficult to identify and communicate to another individual. Even experts may not really understand how they arrive at a conclusion, since many of their tasks are performed unconsciously. A long period of thorough and exhaustive testing is required to ensure that the decisions made by the expert system correlate closely with the human expert's conclusions. Even once the system is certified and operating, continual quality checks and tracing are required to maintain and ensure the system's accuracy. The danger of an accuracy slip in the fields of nuclear power plant operation or medicine are clearly unacceptable!

Because of the time and effort involved in the task, an expert system is developed to address only a specific area of knowledge. This area of knowledge is called the **domain** and the human expert in it is called the **domain expert.** A careful evaluation of the domain of the expert system is needed to determine its stability and longevity, which

Real World Perspectives

Loan Probe

Each year auditors for commercial banks and thrift institutions must review loan loss reserves to determine whether sufficient funds have been set aside to cover the risk that some loans will become uncollectible. In the substantially changed and dynamic business environment of the 1990s, it has become much more difficult to assess the soundness of any given loan. The widespread severity of the savings and loan crisis is one indicator of this challenging audit environment.

Loan Probe was developed by KPMG Peat Marwick to help address this business challenge. KPMG was concerned not only with the increasing difficulty of auditing individual loans but also with the added challenge of training more than 2,500 bank auditors to perform effective loan evaluations and of ensuring consistently high quality in its audit work.

KPMG's approach to loan evaluation involves classification of a loan into one of four basic categories, each of which has specified loan loss reserve requirements:

LOAN CATEGORY	LOAN RESERVE AMOUNT
Special Mention	0–1%
Substandard	1–50%
Doubtful	>50%
Loss	100% minus collateral

There is a great deal of judgment involved in assigning a loan to a category (e.g., when does a Substandard loan become a Doubtful loan?) and in determining where in each category a given loan reserve requirement will fall (Substandard loans can range from 1 percent to 50 percent reserve requirements). These judgments are made by the loan auditor on the basis of an understanding of the company, industry, and individuals involved in the loan.

It usually requires two or three years of experience in the audit and banking practices at KPMG before an individual auditor is capable of handling most reserve calculations. Particularly difficult or risky cases are referred to more experienced auditors; in all cases the work of junior auditors is reviewed by partner-level managers who have ten or more years of relevant experience. In other words, the transfer of expertise is monitored by progressively more expensive talent.

Two very different types of data are used in evaluating a loan. First is a set of basic business judgments that assess the probable outlook for both the industry and the borrowing company's position in it. This assessment hinges on a combination of forecasts by industry experts (both inside and outside KPMG) and a set of projections based on local expertise. For example, a review of a loan to a Texas-based oil and gas company would include a forecast of the prospects for the global oil and gas industries, as well as a detailed assessment of the local Texas market for the company's products.

The second set of data affecting a loan audit is the financial calculations that identify current and future cash flows for the borrower to determine whether the loan can be serviced adequately.

Loan Probe is designed to categorize a loan and suggest the amount of loan loss reserves that should be set aside. The system calculates the suggested level of loan loss reserves for each individual loan in a portfolio and combines these assessments into an overall audit report.

The auditor interacts with the system by providing it with information on the company, the industry, and the specific loan being reviewed. The system relies on a financial model of the borrowing company's cash flows and a series of assessments about future prospects for the industry and the company. For example, Loan Probe makes three specific judgments:

1. The borrowing company's ability to liquidate the loan based on its current financial condition.
2. The borrower's projected ability to liquidate the loan based on future cash flows.
3. A rating of the borrower based on past loan repayment performance.

Loan Probe includes specialized knowledge for several dozen general industrial classifications and more than one hundred subspecialty industries, ranging from livestock pricing to Florida real estate valuation. Both general real

Continued

state loans and collateral loans can also be reviewed.

When the quality of the resulting audits is factored in, Loan Probe saves about thirty minutes per loan for a 33 percent productivity improvement.

The auditors who use Loan Probe seem to learn faster, because the system prints out a de-tailed report that identifies exactly how it reached each recommendation. The system essentially becomes a master tutor for junior auditors, since it describes for them how it reached its conclusions. SOURCE: John J. Sviokla, "Case Study: Loan Probe," Stage by Stage 9, no. 1 (January–February 1989), reprinted with permission from Nolan, Norton & Co., One Cranberry Hill, Lexington, MA 02173. □

should be weighed against its implementation cost. Many domains, such as the design of microcomputer chips, change quickly in their content and structure. Rapid changes in the knowledge or rules used to make decisions will quickly invalidate the system. On the other hand, the expert system should be built in a flexible manner so that new rules and knowledge can be added to the system—in effect, permitting the system to learn.

An expert system is designed to mimic the way in which an expert arrives at a decision. Conventional computer programs operate in a serial manner—one step at a time, one decision at a time. Interrelationships among variables are difficult to represent. Expert systems use symbolic relationships, making decisions based on consideration of many variables and their interrelationships. Thus, programming expert systems is different from programming conventional systems.

Special computer programming languages that make it easier to program logic relationships have been developed to implement expert systems. The most common of these are LISP and PROLOG. LISP is considered more precise and powerful.

LISP stands for List Processing Language and was developed in 1958, making FORTRAN the only older major language still in use. LISP is a very powerful language that is popular with programmers who build large and complex expert systems. LISP supports the creation and analysis of text information in addition to the usual arithmetic and logic operations supported by other languages.

PROLOG stands for PROgramming language for LOGic. It was developed in 1972. PROLOG is becoming increasingly accepted for developing expert systems. It contains direct mechanisms for implementing an inference engine. PROLOG implements a simplified version of predicate calculus and is thus considered a true logic language. Computation in PROLOG involves controlled logical deduction. One simply states certain facts, and then PROLOG can tell whether or not any specific conclusion can be deduced from these facts.

Rather than actually write the expert system using PROLOG or LISP, most expert systems today are developed using **expert system shells.** A shell is a tool that includes an easy-to-learn language to manage the rules that make up the knowledge base and an inference engine capable of reasoning with rule sets that the knowledge engineer builds. Use of a shell enables the developer to create an expert system much

Real World Perspective

Developing an Expert System at KPMG Peat Marwick

The Loan Probe Project began with a senior manager in charge of KPMG Peat Marwick's audit support and a consultant spending two days per week for over a year exploring how auditors evaluate loans. They talked to many different auditors (both experienced and inexperienced), examined hundreds of loan review packages, and began developing logic flow diagrams. As they worked, they spent much of their time with another partner with over seventeen years of auditing experience. In many respects, Loan Probe came to embody this partner's experiential knowledge of what constituted a good loan and what indicated a potentially troublesome loan.

When the team felt they had developed an adequate conceptual model of the loan review process, they took the model to a number of KPMG offices around the country for reviews, cri-

tiques, and modifications by other experienced auditors. Once the model had been essentially validated, it was then translated into software using an expert system shell—a packaged software product that embodied basic expert system logical structures and user interfaces.

The result of this effort was Loan Probe, an expert system with over five thousand rules that support the loan audit process. The total development and training costs for Loan Probe are estimated to be in the millions, but the potential gain of using Loan Probe is also in the millions. In 1987—the first year the system was actively used in the field—over one thousand KPMG auditors were trained to use Loan Probe in a series of two-day seminars. *SOURCE: John J. Sviokla, "Case Study: Loan Probe," Stage by Stage 9, no. 1 (1989), reprinted with permission from Nolan, Norton & Co., One Cranberry Hill, Lexington, MA 02173.* □

easier and faster than using PROLOG or LISP. Expert system shells vary widely in cost and capability but usually have such features as text editing, the ability to manipulate files, and an inference engine that runs the expert system. The developer must still provide the knowledge to the system.

Advantages and Disadvantages of Expert Systems

The use of a well-designed and effective expert system enables the novice to make good, consistent decisions—similar decisions to those made by an expert. Novices using such a system will apply the same logic as that of a leading expert in the field. With the system they will gain insights into the problem that they may never have discovered on their own. A novice can use the system to obtain advice quickly, leaving more time to plan the implementation of the decision before action must be taken.

Expert systems are best applied to problems that have a high degree of structure, i.e., ones that have a known process for solving the problem. Unfortunately, many important decisions in life and business are not structured. Furthermore, an expert system is not good at handling inconsistent or inconclusive data. Responses that conflict with previous responses or answers to questions like "sometimes" cannot be handled well. Approaches for addressing these problems will be covered in the next section.

When to Use an Expert System

The development of an expert system can require months for a knowledge engineer to capture the knowledge of an expert and codify it. This time is dear when one considers how valuable the time is of the expert. Thus the development of an expert system can be costly and time-consuming. Furthermore, if the knowledge base or solution process is changing due to rapid developments in the domain, the expert system can rapidly become obsolete. Thus expert systems are generally applied to narrowly defined, well-structured problems in which there is a stable body of knowledge and a high business payoff to overcome the cost of developing the system. It is essential that the knowledge of recognized experts, whose performance is substantially better than the average practitioner, be used in the development of an expert system. The best success comes when the task to which the expert system is applied is neither too easy nor too hard, requires symbolic reasoning and the use of heuristics, is narrow in scope, and is clearly defined. See Exhibit 7.14 for a partial list of expert system applications. Note the narrow, well-defined scope of these expert systems.

■ OTHER ARTIFICIAL INTELLIGENCE APPLICATIONS

Below is a brief discussion of three **artificial intelligence (AI)** applications that have a high potential to solve real business problems: neural networks, fuzzy logic, and virtual reality.

Exhibit 7.14
A Partial List of
Early Expert
Systems (1970s and
1980s)

Dendral	Infers the molecular structure of unknown compounds from mass spectral and nuclear response data.
Steamer	Instructs Navy personnel in the operation and maintenance of the propulsion plant for a 1078-class frigate.
Xsel	Reviews all orders for Digital Equipment Corporation (DEC) minicomputers for technical correctness and completeness.
Mycin	Aids physicians in diagnosing meningitis and other bacterial infections of the blood and prescribing treatment.
Drilling Advisor	Assists oil rig supervisors in resolving problems that arise in drilling for oil.
In Search	Provides users with a front-end to simplify use of the DIALOG on-line data bases.
Prospector	Provides consultation to geologists in the early stages of investigating a site for ore-grade deposits.
Puff	Helps interpret measurements from respiratory tests administered to patients in a pulmonary (lung) function laboratory.
Delta	Helps railroad maintenance personnel maintain General Electric diesel-electric locomotives.
Gensis	Helps design molecular genetics experiments and procedures.
Loan Adviser	Helps auditors review individual loans to assess if sufficient funds have been set aside to cover the risk that some loans will become uncollectible.

Neural Networks

Neural networks attempt to emulate the biological structure of the brain. A biological **neuron** consists of **axons, dendrites,** and **synapses.** Artificial neurons use wires to imitate the axons and dendrites and resistors containing weighted values as synapses. A neural network is composed of hundreds of interconnected processing elements that operate in parallel, shooting messages to each other at a rapid-fire pace.

The neural network can receive input and respond. This may look like a task that can be handled adequately by conventional means, but neural networks are computer programs with a difference. They have the capability of recognizing downgraded inputs. This gives the computer the capability, for the first time, of processing data that is either missing or incomplete. An example of this is handwriting recognition.

When the neural network is turned on, it searches laboriously for patterns on the input side that result in a particular output. Neural networks are data hungry: the more input they have, the more accurate they become. This, of course, makes perfect sense, as a neural network mimics the way the brain learns. When confronted with many examples leading to a particular output, our brains learn that this is the normal response to these inputs. Soon, the brain can anticipate the answer even though the inputs might be slightly irregular. Instead of programming the artificial neural network, the developer teaches it to solve problems. The neural network exhibits abilities for generalization, learning, abstraction, and even intuition. Thus neural networks offer a radically different approach to the processing of data and the solution of business problems.

A neural network is not programmed in the traditional sense, rather, it is trained by example. The training consists of many repetitions of inputs that express a variety of relationships. By progressively refining the weights of the simulated neurons the artificial neuron system discovers the relationships among the inputs. This discovery process constitutes learning.

The ability to learn based on adaptation is the major factor that distinguishes neural network systems from expert systems applications. Expert systems are programmed to make inferences based on data that describe the problem environment. Their major limitation is their inability to apply judgment and intuition. The neural network system, on the other hand, is able to adjust how it performs in response to the inputs it receives and to the desired outputs. Expert systems are being developed that incorporate neural networks, thus giving the system the combined ability to provide expert consultation and to improve its own expertise over time based on learning.

Neural networks are implemented in several ways. Some software packages that simulate the activity of a neural network with many processing elements are available. Specialized neural network coprocessor boards and chips for PCs that provide significantly greater processing power are also available. These chips are used in specific areas such as military weapons systems, image processing, and voice recognition. Most business applications depend on neural network packages primarily to accomplish applications ranging from credit risk assessment to check signature verification, investment forecasting, and manufacturing quality control.

Neural networks are quite good at recognition. They are currently used for both optical character recognition and speech recognition. As the technology matures, optical image recognition will also become possible. Optical image recognition is the ability of a computer to recognize, categorize, and index an image based on its content. For example, if a user scans a picture of an automobile, the optical image recognition system would not only recognize that the image is an automobile, but also what kind of automobile it is.

Fuzzy Logic Systems

Fuzzy logic systems apply the technique of inexact reasoning using the mathematical theory of fuzzy sets. This technique allows the computer to behave less precisely and logically than conventional computer programs. The philosophy behind this approach is that decision making isn't always a matter of black or white, true or false; it often involves grey areas and the term maybe.

Fuzzy logic is a method of reasoning that resembles human reasoning since it allows for approximate values and inferences (**fuzzy logic**) and incomplete and ambiguous data (**fuzzy data**). Thus fuzzy logic systems are able to process incomplete data and quickly provide approximate, but acceptable, solutions to problems that are difficult for other methods to solve. Indeed, fuzzy logic systems work best when the input is provided by sensors rather than humans because of the

Real World Perspective

Use of a Neural Net at Security Pacific Bank

Making the right decision on loan underwriting is a critical success factor for banks; in fact, if enough mistakes are made, the bank can suffer severe losses. Fortunately, enough statistics have been collected on the credit patterns of borrowers to make it possible to accurately predict the creditworthiness of most individuals. Most banks rely on the services of outside companies to perform this process known as credit scoring. Given the patterned nature of the input and the nature of the technology, Security Pacific Bank decided to replace these "score card" vendors with a loan underwriting artificial neural net system.

The loan underwriting system examines twenty-seven factors to arrive at one of two conclusions: strongly applicable to acceptance or strongly indicative of decline. If the loan is de-

clined, it is reviewed by a human underwriter who ultimately decides the financial fate of the borrower. All other loan requests are approved by the bank.

To train the neural net, Security Pacific provided more than 6,000 prior loan underwritings out of the 10,000 loans they had on file. Security Pacific found out what others before them had found out—a large percentage of the intended input is not appropriate to use as training data for a neural net due to corrupt or inconsistent data. Still, a training data base of 6,000 loans was considerable and provided the groundwork for what turned out to be a very successful loan underwriting system. *SOURCE: Robert McLeod, D. K. Malkotra, and Rashmi Malkotra. "Predicting Credit Risk: A Neural Network Approach." Journal of Retail Banking vol. 15, Fall 1993.* □

Exhibit 7.15
Partial Set of Fuzzy
Logic Rules for
Selecting a
Defensive Lineman

Potential value to team should be high

If height is too short,
  then value is somewhat decreased

If weight is too low,
  then value is somewhat decreased

If % body fat is too high
  then value is somewhat decreased

If speed for 40 yards is slow to very slow
  then value is greatly decreased

If weight bench pressed is good
  then value is generally increased

problem of linguistic vagueness and the difficulty of supplying action-able definitions.

Exhibit 7.15 shows a partial set of fuzzy rules for analyzing draft picks for a professional football team. Notice how it uses terminology that is deliberately imprecise, such as somewhat, good, and generally.

Japan leads in the practical use of fuzzy logic applications and has developed fuzzy logic microprocessor chips to control subway trains, elevators, automobiles, and the trading of shares on the Tokyo Stock Exchange. Increasingly, consumer products will feature fuzzy logic microprocessors to enhance their performance. We are already seeing this in auto-focus cameras, camcoders, air conditioners, and washing machines.

Virtual Reality

Virtual reality, also known as **artificial reality** and **cyberspace,** attempts to build more natural, realistic, and multisensory human/computer interfaces. Providing the participant with the ability to interact and move about rather than just watch makes virtual reality a truly revolutionary development and not just another form of computer simulation.

Virtual reality employs multisensory input-output devices such as a headset with video goggles and stereo earphones or a data glove and a jumpsuit with fiber optic sensors to track the user's body movements. The headset floods the eyes with three-dimensional images and the ears with stereophonic sound. It also tracks the eye and head movements so that the system always knows where the user is looking in the simulation. Data gloves and jumpsuits interpret hand and body movements and impart an impression of moving around in a virtual world. Objects can be moved or picked up, and the participant can travel about or walk from room to room. The multisensory devices enable the user to experience computer simulated "virtual worlds" three dimensionally through sight, sound, and touch, and thus, allow the user to interact with computer simulated objects and environments as if they actually exist.

Current applications of virtual reality include computer aided design (CAD), medical diagnostics and treatment, scientific experimentation in many physical and biological sciences, flight simulation for training pilots and astronauts, and 3-D video games. CAD is one of the more interesting virtual reality applications. Virtual reality enables architects and other designers to develop electronic 3-D models of buildings by entering the models themselves and examining, touching, and manipulating them from all angles. Scientists and engineers are using virtual reality to simulate everything from virtual weather patterns and virtual wind tunnels to virtual cities and virtual securities markets.

The use of virtual reality is limited only by our imagination and the cost of the technology. In the early 1990s, a basic virtual reality system consisting of a headset with goggles and headphones, a fiber optic data glove, a motion-sensing device, and a microcomputer workstation with 3-D modeling software cost about $50,000. To build a virtual reality world with less cumbersome devices, more realistic displays, and a more natural sense of motion, the cost climbs into hundreds of thousands of dollars. However, the cost of highly realistic multisensory virtual reality systems is expected to drop significantly in the future.

Real World Perspective

Virtual Reality Applications

Dartmouth Medical School

A surgeon, anxious about an upcoming procedure, takes advantage of virtual reality to prepare for an upcoming operation. Walking into the practice operating room, the surgeon sees an empty operating table. The surgeon dons strange-looking goggles and gloves covered with long, tentaclelike wires and thin joints. When wearing these devices, the surgeon suddenly "sees" a patient lying on the table. In the doctor's hand is a virtual scalpel, ready for use. The patient, who exists only in the memory banks of a computer, is amazingly lifelike. The doctor feels the resistance of the skin being cut and sees blood and tissue. As the doctor proceeds, the virtual patient's reactions to every step of the procedure can be observed. A few hours later, having practiced the surgery several times, the doctor is ready to perform actual surgery on the real patient.

University of North Carolina

At the University of North Carolina, virtual reality allows people to "walk through" the interior of buildings before they are built. Someone who dons a headset can, in effect, stroll through a building that exists only in the minds and blueprints of architects. Designs for buildings on the Chapel Hill campus were "walked through" and evaluated by architects and faculty before they were built.

Matushita Electric Works

Prospective kitchen buyers who visit the Matushita Electric Works of Osaka, Japan, can conduct a "walk through" of complete kitchens. They can walk around, open doors and cabinets, try out the stove and refrigerator, turn faucets on and off, and even change light fixtures according to their specific wishes.

City of Los Angeles

Urban planners in Los Angeles are creating virtual reality models of an 80-square block area of the city ravaged by civil violence. With virtual reality, users can "fly" over parts of the city for a bird's-eye view and make decisions to add or delete buildings or to change the locations of parks and trees.

■ DSS, EIS, AND MRS COMPARED

The DSS is significantly different from the MRS in both its use and its origin. An MRS provides management with corporate information in a predetermined, routinely reported format. The information available from the MRS is usually limited to the firm's operational data. Key information, significant trends, and relationships can easily be obscured by the detailed form of the generated reports. The MRS is most useful in helping management deal with structured problems associated with making routine operational decisions.

The MRS is developed by professional systems analysts and programmers. The analysts may spend weeks or even months defining the format and content of the management reports to be produced by the system. The programmers then spend perhaps as long or even longer carefully developing computer programs to produce the desired output. These programs tend to be inflexible, so it can be difficult to change the content or format of existing reports or to create new ones.

The DSS is developed to help managers deal with problems that are to some extent unstructured and nonroutine (e.g., strategic planning, evaluating investment opportunities, identifying key factors in a decision). External data (e.g., economic data, competitive activity, consumer trends) are often critical to these decisions, and in these cases the DSS must provide access to this kind of data. Although the DSS may be programmed to produce certain standard reports, it can also be programmed by the end user (the decision maker) to produce ad hoc reports. This capability is essential in enabling the users to deal effectively with the unstructured or semistructured problems they face. By creating ad hoc reports, users are able to analyze the data in any way that makes sense without being locked into the strict use of predefined reports.

An EIS helps executives in the top two levels of the organization improve their understanding of the company and the environment in which it operates. Each EIS is customized to extract, filter, and compress a broad range of internal and external data to present the information the executive needs without creating **data overload.** The EIS monitors and highlights the critical success factors in an individual executive's area of responsibility. Exhibit 7.16 compares the MRS, DSS, and EIS.

Summary

There are three phases in decision making: intelligence, design, and choice.

An unstructured problem is one in which all three phases of the decision process are unstructured. A semistructured problem has one or two unstructured phases and two or one structured phases. A structured problem is one in which all three phases are structured.

Decisions are frequently classified as operational, tactical, or strategic.

Exhibit 7.16
Comparison of DSS, EIS, and MRS

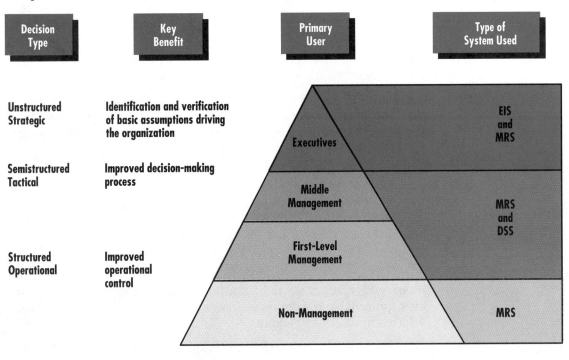

Decision Type	Key Benefit	Primary User	Type of System Used
Unstructured Strategic	Identification and verification of basic assumptions driving the organization	Executives	EIS and MRS
Semistructured Tactical	Improved decision-making process	Middle Management	MRS and DSS
		First-Level Management	
Structured Operational	Improved operational control	Non-Management	MRS

Operational decisions deal with the routine day-to-day activities of the organization. They are structured and recurring decisions with an immediate but short-term impact.

Tactical decisions involve allocation and control of the firm's resources to meet the objectives that support the strategic goals of the business. They are semistructured decisions with an intermediate impact on the firm that is not felt for a few weeks.

Strategic decisions include setting the goals of the company, defining the basic assumptions on which long-range planning should be based, and identifying the critical success factors of the firm. These decisions are unstructured and have a long-range impact on the firm.

A decision support system (DSS) is a comprehensive computer-based system used to help people reach decisions about semistructured problems.

A DSS enables managers to make better decisions, present a more factual and convincing recommendation, and reach decisions sooner.

The data needed to support a DSS are drawn from the data bases created from processing the fundamental business transactions of the organization. It may also include data about industry trends, competitive activity, suppliers, customers, and government regulations available in computer-based public data bases.

A DSS is only as effective as its user; a good DSS in the hands of an unskilled user can be harmful.

As a potential tool, business managers need to understand the capabilities and limitations of DSS.

A group decision support system (GDSS) is information technology that improves the decision-making process of a group by speeding the process up, improving the quality of the decision, or increasing the acceptability of the decision.

Another approach to GDSS is the use of a high-tech electronic meeting room where each participant has his or her own personal computer which is connected to a local area network for the sharing of messages, graphics, and text. Special GDSS software is loaded on the personal computer for use by the participants. Individual ideas or group results can be displayed on a large-screen projection system connected to the local area network.

An executive information system (EIS) accumulates data from a variety of internal and external sources and delivers timely and pertinent information to management.

The elements of a successful EIS include standard reports, short-term issues, exception reporting, executive brief, external data, news, data analysis, executive mail, time management, and data retrieval.

An expert system is a variation of a decision support system that uses knowledge and inference procedures to solve problems that are difficult enough to require significant human expertise for their solution.

An expert system consists of five basic components: a knowledge base, an inference engine, a user interface, an explanation subsystem, and a knowledge acquisition subsystem.

An expert's knowledge is of two types: facts of the domain and knowledge of good practice and good judgment (heuristic knowledge).

A neural network simulates a network of hundreds of parallel processing interconnected units, shooting messages at each other at a rapid fire pace. Such a network can receive input and respond.

A neural network has the ability to generalize, learn, and abstract. It can even exhibit intuition.

Expert systems will incorporate neural networks giving the system the combined ability to provide expert consultation and to improve its own expertise over time.

Fuzzy logic systems apply the technique of inexact reasoning using the mathematical theory of fuzzy sets. This allows the computer to behave less precisely and logically than the conventional computer.

Fuzzy logic systems are good at processing incomplete data and providing approximate, but acceptable solutions to problems that are difficult for other methods.

Virtual reality enables more realistic and multisensory human/computer interfaces.

A Manager's Checklist

✔ Can you classify the problems you deal with as structured, semi-structured, or unstructured?

✔ Does your company use any decision support, executive information, or expert systems to support decision making?

✔ Can you identify any opportunities to apply decision support, executive information, or expert systems in your organization?

Key Terms

artificial intelligence
artificial reality
axon
backward chaining
choice
cyberspace
data overload
decision-making support
decision support system
design
domain
domain expert
drill down
electronic meeting room
executive information system
expert system
expert system shell
explanation subsystem
forward chaining
fuzzy data
fuzzy logic

fuzzy logic system
group decision support
groupthink
heuristic knowledge
heuristics
inference engine
intelligence phase
knowledge acquisition
    subsystem
knowledge base
knowledge engineer
neural network
operational decision
semistructured problem
strategic decision
structured problem
tactical decision
unstructured problem
user interface
virtual reality

Review Questions

1. What are the differences between structured and unstructured problems; between operational, tactical, and strategic decisions?

2. Define the terms decision support system, executive information system, and expert system.

3. Identify three sources of data commonly used to feed a decision support system.

4. What are some of the advantages of group decision making? Some of the disadvantages?

5. How do the data needs of an executive vary from that of a middle-level manager? How are they similar?

6. Outline the conditions under which the use of a decision support system, executive information system, and expert system is appropriate.

7. What kinds of business benefits can be gained through the use of each of these types of systems?

8. Briefly explain how an artificial neural network works.

9. What is meant by fuzzy logic, fuzzy data?

Discussion Questions

1. Are the majority of the problems you deal with structured or unstructured in nature?

2. Can you identify a strategic decision that you have made in the past year?

3. Why might a manager decide to override the recommendations of a decision support system or expert system?

4. How would you distinguish a decision support system from an executive information system? From an expert system?

5. Discuss the role of the business manager in the development and use of these systems.

6. What are four key issues associated with the use of executive information systems?

7. Do you think that executive information systems should be restricted to use by executives?

8. How would you react if your doctor told you that an expert system was used to diagnose and recommend medication for a serious disease that you had contacted?

Recommended Readings

1. Coon, Dennis. *Introduction to Psychology, Exploration, and Application*, 5th edition. St. Paul, MN: West Publishing Company. 1989.

2. DeSanctis, G. and B. Gallupe. "Group Decision Support Systems: A New Frontier." *Management Science*, May 1987.

3. Gorry, G. M. and M. S. Scott-Morton. "A Framework for Management Information Systems." *Sloan Management Review*, Fall 1971.

4. Keyes, Jessica. *Infotrends: The Competitive Use of Information*. New York: McGraw-Hill, Inc. 1993.

5. McLeod, Robert, D. K. Malkotra, and Rashmi Malkotra. "Predicting Credit Risk: A Neural Network Approach." *Journal of Retail Banking* vol. 15, Fall 1993.

6. Olson, D. L. and J. F. Courtney, Jr. *Decision Support Models and Expert Systems*. New York: Macmillan, 1992.

7. Silver, Mark S. "Decisional Guidance for Computer-Based Decision Support." *MIS Quarterly* 15 (March 1991).

8. Simon, H. *The New Science of Management Decision.* Englewood Cliffs, NJ: Prentice-Hall, 1977.

9. Turbion, Eric. *Decision Support Systems,* 3rd edition. New York: Macmillan. 1993.

10. Turbin, Efraim. *Expert Systems and Applied Artificial Intelligence.* New York: Macmillan, 1992.

11. Watson, H. J., et al. (eds.) *Executive Support Systems.* New York: Wiley and Sons, 1992.

12. Wetherbe, James C. "Executive Information Requirements: Getting It Right." *MIS Quarterly* 15 (March 1991).

13. Zeidenberg, M. *Neural Computing in Artificial Intelligence.* Englewood Cliffs, NJ: Prentice-Hall, 1990.

A Manager's Dilemma

Case Study 7.1

Choices, Choices, Choices!

As the Head Buyer for a major supermarket chain, John is constantly being asked by manufacturers and distributors to stock their new products. Over fifty new items are being introduced each week. Many times these new products are launched with national advertising campaigns and special promotional allowances to both retailers, such as John's firm, and consumers. The store has only a limited amount of shelf and floor space to stock items. Thus, to add new products, the amount of shelf space allocated to existing products must be reduced, or items must be eliminated altogether.

John needs help in deciding which new items are worth stocking and which current items should be cut back or eliminated to make room for the new products. The firm's stores have been using scanner-based electronic checkouts, which have captured a wealth of data. John also has standard cost data for determining the cost of stocking an item depending on its size, weight, and other characteristics.

Is a DSS the solution to John's needs? How would you determine if a DSS could really help? What sort of data will be needed? What sort of models need to be developed? Should the manufacturers and distributors participate in the development of this DSS?

Case Study 7.2

Fashion Trends

Mantello, Inc. is a manufacturer of young women's sport and casual clothes with annual sales in excess of $250 million. Because the firm specializes in highly priced, highly fashionable clothes for women in the twenty to forty year age range, keeping up with the latest trends in what young women are thinking, doing, and wearing is critical.

A goal of the firm is to be a trendsetter and create whole new lines of clothes in anticipation of consumers' desires. While this is an extremely risky strategy, it has so far been highly profitable. As the Chief Executive Officer of the firm, Jill wonders if computers could be used to reduce the risk factors by confirming or denying the trends predicated by the firm's own market research group. If the number of unsuccessful lines could be reduced, Mantello, Inc. could easily double its profits!

Jill has been asked by the Vice-president of IT to invest $100,000 in the development of an EIS. The EIS would scan a tremendous number of magazines and newspapers, extract trend data, summarize, and report the results. Jill is uneasy with investing so much on an effort that she frankly is not optimistic about. Is there a way Jill can evaluate the feasibility of such a system at a lower cost? Do you think such a system could prove worthwhile?

Case Study 7.3

Developing an EIS at the Travelers

In the information-intensive business of insurance, the gap between transaction-based data and information that clearly relates to corporate objectives is felt acutely. The goal of the EIS developed at the Travelers was to create an easy-to-use system that would integrate and analyze company data and convert it into a business measuring and planning tool.

The EIS was developed by the Agency Marketing Group, the department responsible for products distributed through independent agents and serviced through field offices across the country. This organization has a clear need to accurately track performance and distribute information to management in a consistent, concise, and timely manner.

Prototyping was the method used to develop the EIS. The process involved a full partnership between the Agency Marketing Group organization and the technology experts. Business users stated what information they needed and asked the technology experts to produce it. Once the needs were established, continual communication between the partners gradually resulted in producing the final product.

Prototyping is an incremental process. The EIS was built gradually, and it was operable at each step along the way. This was advantageous in two ways. First, the system provided immediate payback; as soon as a computer program was complete, business users could use it. Second, actual use—as opposed to hypothetical demonstrations—produced better ideas for further development.

After some practical use, the business users could see where the system needed improving and could suggest logical additions to what the system was already producing. As they learned to use the system, they immediately applied their knowledge to enhance it. With this prototyping process, the development of the EIS will, in essence, never be finished, as new needs and new ideas will continue to be identified.

The primary need expressed was for integration. Management needed a system that would clarify relationships between such diverse factors as sales and claims for different products and regions, and that would compile the data so that overall performance could be understood. Prior to development of the EIS, each major product line had its own reporting system, which was, in turn, separated by such types of data as premiums, loss ratios, automation, and servicing performance. The goal, then, was to integrate the various types of data and to display them in a comprehensive manner.

To integrate information, consistency in definitions had to be established. Various definitions used by actuaries, underwriters, and sales personnel for a variety of products had to be developed so that valid comparisons could be established.

Questions

1. Is there a danger in following the prototyping approach as the development of the EIS will, in essence, never be finished, as new needs and new ideas will continue to be identified? How might this potential problem be managed?

2. How would you manage the use of the prototype system? Would you allow all one hundred home office vice-presidents, product managers, marketing managers, and the staff people who directly support the executive to evaluate and provide feedback on the prototype? Would you limit access to a small number of handpicked users who you know are supportive of the EIS concept? What are some of the pros and cons of each approach?

3. What sort of role might a data administrator and data base administrator have played in the development of this EIS?

Chapter 8

Office Automation

Upon completion of this chapter, you will be able to:

1. Explain why it is important to increase the productivity of knowledge workers.

2. Define the term office automation.

3. Briefly describe how electronic publishing systems work and the kinds of business benefits that they can provide.

4. Identify three forms of electronic communications systems. Briefly describe how they work and the kinds of business benefits that they can provide.

5. Identify three forms of electronic meetings. Briefly describe how they work and the kinds of business benefits that they can provide.

6. Identify two forms of imaging systems. Briefly describe how they work and the kinds of business benefits that they can provide.

7. State three reasons business managers need to understand and be involved in office automation efforts.

Preview

Office automation systems involve the planned integration of many new technologies with improved office processes to increase the productivity and effectiveness of all office workers, including managers, professionals, clerks, and secretaries. As such, office automation is essential in helping organizations manage the deluge of data and information. Managers who do not recognize the office automation revolution must become alert to its opportunities and risks. Not only does office automation affect the flow, processing, and dissemination of information; it also supports changes in the organization structure necessary to remain competitive.

Issues

1. What new problems can be introduced with the implementation of office automation technology?

2. What role can the business manager play in ensuring a high payoff from implementation of office automation technology?

3. How do managers decide who should get what components of office automation technology?

Trade-offs

1. Should the use of integrated software packages be encouraged or should users be told to select the best stand-alone package for the tasks they must perform?

2. There are several forms of electronic conferencing. When should each be used?

3. How much time should managers spend identifying and addressing their organization's office automation needs?

A Manager Struggles with the Issues

As the newly promoted manager of the western sales district in Seattle, Kristy often felt out of touch with the sales staff organization located in New York. It was bad enough that there was a three hour time difference, which narrowed the common working hours to only five hours per day less lunch hours. But to make matters worse, her job required her to be on the road roughly 50 percent of the time. As a result, when Kristy came back into the office, she frequently found a stack of messages from headquarters—many of them marked "Urgent" and several days old! Even when she was in her office, Kristy found it difficult to reach key people at headquarters. She was often caught up in a game of "telephone tag" and was forced to leave lengthy messages with secretaries who always seemed to jumble up facts and key dates. Kristy wondered if there weren't some means of keeping closer in touch with headquarters.

■ OFFICE AUTOMATION SYSTEMS

Office Productivity

Improving productivity helps reduce costs so that products and services remain competitive. In the past, management concentrated on achieving cost reductions by obtaining raw materials at low cost, reducing distribution expenses, improving production processes, and helping manufacturing employees become more efficient. But savings can come from anywhere in the company. The staff organizations that keep the company running smoothly but aren't actually making the end product have considerable potential for cost savings. Over half the workers in the United States today are **knowledge workers**—professionals, managers, executives, and clerical people whose jobs largely involve the processing or analysis of data. It is this group of workers that now needs productivity aids.

Definition of Office Automation

Office automation is the planned integration of new technology with improved office processes to increase the productivity and effectiveness of all knowledge workers, including managers, professionals, clerks, and secretaries. John Naisbitt writes in his best-seller *Megatrends,* "We are drowning in information but starved for knowledge and intelligence." Office automation is a tool that not only helps make knowledge out of data, but also helps move the knowledge from one person to another. Office automation systems create, process, store, retrieve, edit, and transmit text, graphics, images, voice, and other forms of communication among individuals, work groups, and organizations. Clearly then, office automation can greatly increase the productivity of knowledge workers.

Office automation is frequently associated with new technology such as image processing, electronic mail, video conferencing, and so on. But true productivity is never achieved by throwing high-tech aids at perceived problems in existing processes. Fundamental questions about the need to continue or restructure the basic business functions must be answered before sophisticated equipment is adopted. Chapter 10 discusses such business process reengineering ideas.

■ WORD PROCESSING/DESKTOP PUBLISHING

Word processing and **desktop publishing** systems help people capture their ideas in forms that are easily stored, updated, and transmitted. These systems are two types of office automation systems that are designed to transform ideas and data into useful forms that can be shared easily with others. They also boost productivity by reducing the time it takes to draft, proof, revise, copy, print, distribute, and file text material. Most importantly, these systems can be integrated into the creative process of the knowledge worker. Roughcut, initial ideas can be entered quickly and easily into the system, and this first cut can be easily modified after additional thinking and analysis.

Word processing and desktop publishing software have features that allow the user to enter, modify, format, and print text. The text entry operation has special features that reduce the author's effort. For example, when the computer determines that a word does not fit on the current line, it automatically moves it to the next line, a function called **word wrap.** The **centering function** allows the user to center a line of text merely by hitting a function key on the keyboard.

Word processing and desktop publishing software allow even the most novice typist to easily modify text and make attractive looking memos. The ease with which text is modified also boosts personal productivity.

Only the words to be changed are retyped, not entire pages, paragraphs, or sentences. Words, sentences, paragraphs, and even whole pages can be inserted, deleted, or rearranged, saving not only typing time, but also proofreading time—only new or retyped material must be proofread. Finally, when all revisions are complete and the text is approved, the final document can be printed rapidly at speeds in excess of ten pages/minute on a high-speed, high-quality laser printer.

Before a document is printed, the following items need to be set: the number of characters per inch, number of lines per page, vertical spacing (e.g., single or double spacing), left and right margins, and type of characters. The setting of these parameters is called **formatting the text.** Word processing and desktop publishing systems have features that make formatting a document, or changing the format of a document simple and quick.

All the capabilities of word processing make office secretaries and clerical people much more efficient. In addition, many managers and professionals have found that they can produce their own work more quickly using such systems. Engineers, attorneys, authors, consultants, and researchers use word processors to speed up and exercise greater control over the quality of their work.

Some word processing and desktop publishing software provide **image scanning** capabilities along with page composition functions to enable users to create documents that include several type fonts and sizes, graphics, and colors on each page. By combining graphics with proportionally spaced text, and then printing the results on a high-quality printer, users can create professional-looking documents ranging from in-house newsletters to magazines and textbooks at a fraction of the cost required for commercial typesetting.

The **page description language (PDL)** handles the combining of text and graphics into a final page format that fits the needs of the user. The most widely used PDL is Postscript from Adobe. Another useful element is clip art—previously created art images—that can be imported into a document.

To prepare a high quality document including both text and graphics, the user first prepares the text using a word processing program (Exhibit 8.1). A graphics package is then used to create any original graphics.

The user creates a **stylesheet** with the desktop publishing package. The stylesheet assigns fonts and type sizes to the various elements of the document, defines margins, and in general, specifies the format of the document.

The user then flows the text into columns on the page. Holes or frames for graphics are left in the text for drawings, photographs, or graphic images. The page composition functions automatically move excess text to another column or page and help size and place illustrations and headings. It is critical for this step that the system supports **WYSIWYG** (What You See Is What You Get), otherwise the user cannot see the appearance of a completed page and cannot adjust the positioning of various elements or decide on the size and style of fonts, the italics, boldfacing, headlines, and so on.

The user then inserts the graphic elements. These may be imported from an existing library of clip art or from an image scanner that is used for converting graphics, drawings, or photographs to graphic form.

When the pages look exactly the way the user desires, they are printed on a high-quality printer. Commercial typesetting equipment is capable of printing at 1,200 dots per inch (**dpi**). (For generally acceptable quality, the desktop publishing printer needs to print at least 300 dpi.) Once completed, the printed pages can be used as camera-ready copy for creating a plate that will be used in the printing process, or if only a few copies are needed, they can be printed on the high-quality printer.

■ ELECTRONIC COMMUNICATIONS SYSTEMS

Electronic Mail

Electronic mail or e-mail uses computer hardware and software to prepare, transmit, store, and retrieve messages (Exhibits 8.2a and b). In a

Exhibit 8.1
Steps in the
Desktop Publishing
Process

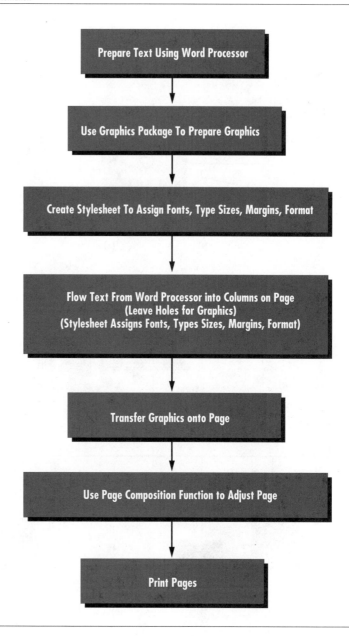

typical system, the message is prepared at a personal computer connected via a modem and telephone line to another computer that
serves as a host for the e-mail system. In preparing the message, text-
editing software, resident in either the host or the user's personal computer, can be used to create the text. The completed message is
transmitted to the host, and a copy of the message is placed in the
electronic in-box of each intended recipient. The electronic in-box is
actually space on a direct access storage device (DASD) that is assigned

Exhibit 8.2
E-mail Running on a Mainframe Computer

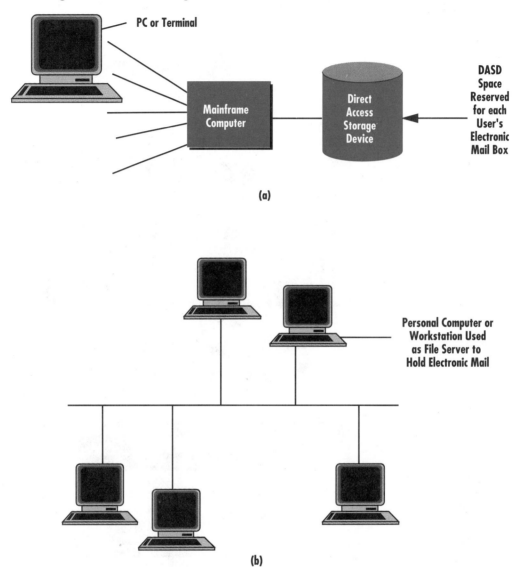

to each user of the system. The message can be retrieved when an intended recipient signs onto the e-mail system and requests any new messages, or the e-mail system may print or display messages on a regular and automatic basis, such as every four hours.

Most e-mail systems require that the user enter a log-on identification word and password before messages can be retrieved. This ensures privacy and security of messages. Mailing lists can be established to simplify addressing messages to groups of people with whom you communicate frequently (e.g., all the section level managers within a department, members of a project team, or employees at a certain location). Such a mailing list is often referred to as a conference and permits frequent and easy exchange of informal messages among all members of the conference. This form of system is called a **store-and-forward** system.

Many communications companies provide e-mail services, while some companies have developed their own private in-house e-mail systems. E-mail systems have a wide range of capabilities and services to which users may subscribe. Some systems allow users to create folders for storing messages related to the topic of that folder. Some systems support the creating, editing, and sending of graphics as well as text. Other systems provide bulletin board capabilities. Still others can automatically filter and sort incoming messages from on-line services such as the Dow Jones News/Retrieval Service and route them to appropriate user mailboxes and folders.

As discussed in Chapter 4, electronic mail is a key feature of the information highway. The ability to access a wide audience of people outside your firm is possible through use of the public e-mail systems associated with CompuServe, GEnie, Prodigy, and the Internet. Such systems enable worldwide communications.

E-Mail can greatly increase the efficiency of communications by reducing the interruptions from the telephone and unscheduled personal contacts. Furthermore, messages can be distributed to multiple recipients easily and quickly without the inconvenience and delay of scheduling meetings. Because past messages are saved in the computer, they can be reviewed if necessary. And because the messages are received in private at a time convenient to the user, the user has time to think before answering, and the responses are more likely to be clear and to the point. Opinions and feedback from remote experts and people who might be affected by a decision are easier to obtain with an e-mail system, thus improving the quality of the decision and the probability of its acceptance. For large organizations whose operations span the country or even the world, store-and-forward communications allow people to work around time zone changes, which otherwise greatly hinder the ability to communicate via phone or traditional means. Some users of e-mail estimate that they eliminate two hours of verbal communication for every hour of e-mail use.

Voice Mail

Various studies have shown that less than one-third of first-time phone calls are completed either because the number called is busy or the person called is away from the office. The caller must then redial later or leave a message for the person to return a call—one hopes at a time when the call initiator is in the office. This process of calling and leaving messages is referred to as telephone tag.

One solution to telephone tag is the popular answering machine—a simple recording device that provides callers with a short recorded announcement inviting them to leave their message at the beep.

Real World Perspective

Global E-Mail Strategy at Colgate-Palmolive

Over a five-year period, Colgate-Palmolive Co. linked dozens of incompatible e-mail systems at various locations around the world. Colgate wanted employees to be able to send messages and exchange files regardless of where they were or what personal computer or workstation they used. Colgate, like most multinationals, had literally dozens of incompatible e-mail systems that had sprung up over the years. None of these systems talked well to the others, and it was very difficult to send binary files, such as spreadsheets and other documents, between personal computers and the e-mail systems running on mainframe computers. Although it was new technology at the time, Colgate realized how employee productivity would increase if it had a corporate-wide messaging system.

The first step Colgate took was to call in General Electric Information Services Inc. (GEIS), a Value Added Network (VAN) provider, to unite Colgate's disparate mail environment. GEIS's e-mail service, Quik-Comm, provided the communications backbone to connect multiple Colgate sites around the world. Once Quik-Comm was in place, international communications problems were greatly reduced. Employees stopped playing telephone tag across the time zones and using inefficient fax services.

The next step was to move e-mail systems off the mainframes. Colgate realized the high costs associated with providing e-mail services on a mainframe; comparable or better service is achieved and costs lowered by providing e-mail using personal computers on a LAN. Because Colgate's 7,000-plus desktops include both IBM compatible personal computers and Macintoshes, Colgate's number one application rule was that software must run on both computers. The list of standard software includes Microsoft Word, Excel, Lotus cc:Mail, and Novell Netware. Colgate eagerly eliminated any quirky, proprietary, and "home-grown" applications that caused file or network compatibility problems. The company wanted all files, including spreadsheets or data base, to be sendable and readable by any other employee.

Now employees in 165 countries connect to the corporate network, easily exchanging e-mail and files without fear of incompatibilities. Budget coordinators around the world now send their corporate standard sales and cost spreadsheet to the New York headquarters for consolidation. The combination of a standard spreadsheet for reporting and the use of the electronic network has cut weeks of elapsed time and hundreds of hours of effort from the important task of reporting quarterly results. In similar fashion, budget forecasts are reported in standard spreadsheet fashion, enabling senior management to review the overall consolidated budget and to recommend necessary changes after seeing the total picture. Memos are sent quickly and cheaply to worldwide distribution lists thus speeding up communications and keeping everyone up to date with plans and results. *SOURCE:* Colgate Goes Global with Integrated E-mail Strategy. by Alice LaPlante at *InfoWorld*, February 8, 1993. ☐

Voice mail differs from an answering machine in that it supports the forwarding of voice messages to others. Voice mail is similar to text-oriented e-mail in that it can deliver the identical message to many different people or can be sent to a distant location overnight when telephone rates are lower. Voice mail is preferred over e-mail systems by many executives who prefer to talk and dial their own extensions, and who want to dictate reminders to themselves about future meetings or tasks. Exhibit 8.3 shows a typical voice-mail system. Exhibit 8.4 gives an example illustrating the time and dollar savings from using a voice-mail system. The actual amount of savings, of course, depends on a number of factors.

Exhibit 8.3
Typical Voice-Mail
System

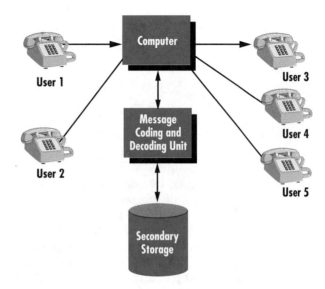

With voice mail, if the called party cannot be reached, the user simply dictates a message over the telephone. This spoken message is stored for later retrieval or forwarding to one or more recipients. In addition, store-and-forward voice-mail systems allow a user to simultaneously send, receive, redirect, and distribute voice messages to other voice-mail subscribers simply by means of a touch-tone telephone. The voice message may be set up for convenient delivery at a later time, either in the form of reconstituted speech or text. Thus, voice mail can eliminate many time-wasting telephone calls.

But voice mail is not for everyone. Adoption of voice mail may require a cultural change in the organization and will not happen overnight. Many people do not like voice mail because they want to talk to a real person and not a machine. These are the same people who hang up on answering machines. Other problems with voice-message systems include their relatively high cost, the need for substantial storage capacity, and the present lack of integration with other office auto-

Exhibit 8.4
A Typical Example
of the Savings
Potential with a
Voice-Mail System

Telephone Related Activity	Savings per User per Month	
	Minutes	**Dollars**
Reduce time spent placing calls by 2 minutes per day (Assume $80,000 per year professional)	44	$ 30
Reduce length of calls by 3 minutes per day	66	$ 45
Eliminate need for receptionist to cover phones (Assume one receptionist @ $30,000 for each 30 people)		$ 85
Total Savings	110	$160

mation systems. The requirement for a touch-tone phone is also a limitation in some areas of the world.

Facsimile (Fax)

A facsimile (fax) machine is a scanning device that permits the reproduction of an original document at remote locations. The fax machine can send copies of handwritten, graphic, and photographic materials. The availability of low-cost fax machines capable of transmitting at rates exceeding one page per minute has led to a tremendous increase in the use of this technology.

The sending of fax material begins with establishing a communications link between sending and receiving devices—a call is placed from the sending to the receiving device. This call can be placed manually or, in more sophisticated units, the fax machine can be programmed to "wake up" at a certain time and automatically place the call. Such a unit can operate unattended and make its calls at night when telephone rates are lowest. To achieve full benefit of automatic calling, the receiving device must have an automatic answering capability so that it too can operate unattended.

The next step is for a scanning device to read the material and convert the optical content of the original document into a form suitable for transmission. The image and nonimage (white spaces) are converted into analog signals on an analog machine or converted into compressed codes on a digital unit. The receiving device receives these signals and converts them into a copy of the original documents.

One of the features that distinguishes fax from other forms of electronic mail is that nonkeyboarded information, such as signatures, pictures, trademarks, charts, blueprints, and graphs, can be transmitted. Fax transmissions also cost less than express forms of mail and can be delivered in a matter of minutes. The relative quality of the received images depends on the quality of the fax equipment—anywhere from poor to excellent.

Fax communications with customers, suppliers, or even other locations of the same company is impossible unless the fax machines are compatible—they must use similar means for scanning a document, transmitting the scanned image, and printing the document. Fortunately, fax manufacturers recognized the need for compatibility and adopted standards to enable information to flow unhampered. Adherence to these standards ensures that one manufacturer's machines are compatible with another's. Thus a user can choose the appropriate fax machine to install based on costs and individual requirements rather than being limited to a single manufacturer and/or model.

The use of fax has become so common that personal computers frequently come with a fax board and a fax software package. This allows the personal computer user to transmit digital copies of text files to fax machines anywhere. Thus, fax machines can act as remote dial-up printers for personal computers.

Personal Digital Assistants (PDAs)

New types of portable personal computer hardware and software promise to extend the work environment to airports, hotels, and cars. Hewlett Packard, Apple, Motorola, IBM/Bell South, EO Inc., Sharp Electronics, Tandy, and Casio are investing millions of dollars to develop personal digital assistants (PDAs) (Exhibit 8.5). These are hand-held computers that keep track of names, addresses, phone numbers, appointments, to-do lists, and expenses. While some PDAs have their roots in calculators, others actually run DOS and provide palmtop versions of major desktop applications such as LOTUS 1-2-3 and LOTUS cc:Mail.

A key reason people use PDAs or notebook computers is to have access anytime, anywhere, to their homes, headquarters, mainframe computers, and LAN servers, and to on-line information services such as the Dow Jones News Retrieval. Users want to eliminate the difficulty of staying in touch with the home office. They need to be able to perform simple functions such as sending and receiving e-mail. Telecommunications vendors are scrambling to offer wireless communications services that meet these needs (see the section on wireless data communications, this chapter).

Some PDAs, which have built-in communications and organizer software, accept instructions handwritten with a special pen. PDA handwriting recognition technology can read the user's handwritten characters about 95 percent of the time. While that sounds good, it

Exhibit 8.5
Some of the
Capabilities of a
PDA

Text handling
   Ability to compose a short memo
   Support use of built-in or optional word processing package

Number handling
   Ability to create an expense report
   Support use of built-in or optional spreadsheet
   Ability to produce and display graphs

Graphic image handling
   Ability to draw freehand graph
   Ability to annotate graph

Scheduling
   Record appointments
   Remind user of appointments
   Alert user if conflicting appointments are scheduled
   Ability to search the schedule for appointments
   Able to reschedule appointments

Contact Management
   Able to record name, address, phone number, and notes
   Ability to search contact file by name, other info

Communications
   Able to send messages via fax or e-mail
   Able to retrieve information by connecting to an on-line service
   Able to send file from a PDA to a desktop system
   Able to send a message to a pager

actually means that, on average, one of every two phone numbers written on a PDA screen is misinterpreted by the software. Improvements can be expected in handwriting recognition technology.

Thus PDAs can replace a myriad of tools such as beepers, mobile phones, personal organizers, fax machines, and laptop computers.

Wireless Communications

Cellular phones (also called **mobile telephones**) are wireless phones that transmit and receive computer-controlled radio signals. Transmitting stations are placed strategically throughout a region, dividing the region into **cells.** Each cell is assigned a series of frequencies that are not available to adjacent cells (Exhibit 8.6). When a call is initiated, the local cell detects the request and assigns a transmitting channel and a different receiving frequency. The strength of the signal is monitored continuously by a computer system. When the signal strength begins to fade, the computer assumes that the caller is moving out of the cell and checks all the surrounding cells to determine which one is picking up the transmission. When signal strength reaches a predetermined level, the call is handed off to the next cell, and the telephone is instructed to transmit and receive on a different pair of frequencies. This transfer occurs so fast that it is often undetected by the user. Cellular units transmit to these stations, which in turn, connect the user to the regular phone system.

Another variation of **wireless communications** employs an infrastructure similar to the cellular telephone network. Specialized radio frequency (RF) modems connect the user's PDA, laptop, or palmtop computer via the serial port to the service provider's nearest radio transmission tower using radio frequency transmission. Users send and receive electronic mail, access host applications running at the corporate data center several states away, or access corporate LAN files through radio frequencies. This technology can be used for both short- and long-distance transmission.

Two-way, wide-area data communications are currently handled by two main wireless carriers (RAM Mobile Data—a joint venture of Ram Broadcasting and Bell South and Ardis—owned by IBM and Motorola) operating across the country (a third is the Cellular Digital Packet Data consortium, currently in development). Unfortunately, each has its own unique technical specifications and geographic coverage, and each uses different transmission equipment, switch gear, end-user radio modems, and protocols. None is interoperable with the others. An additional problem is the lack of a common e-mail directory standard and software to translate a user's e-mail address on the corporate e-mail system to an address on the wireless system and intelligent routing to move messages to the system to which the user is currently connected.

Motorola, Inc. laid the groundwork for a national wireless system to compete with cellular when it sold its specialized mobile radio (SMR) systems (used mostly for dispatching cabs and delivery vehicles) to

Nextel, Dial Page, and CenTell. These three SMR operators allied with Motorola have a unique opportunity to build a nationwide system that eventually will provide voice, data, paging, and dispatch services over the same network and a single phone.

Extending the reach of the corporate network to support an increasingly mobile workforce is full of problems such as immature tech-

Exhibit 8.6
Cellular Mobile Telephone System

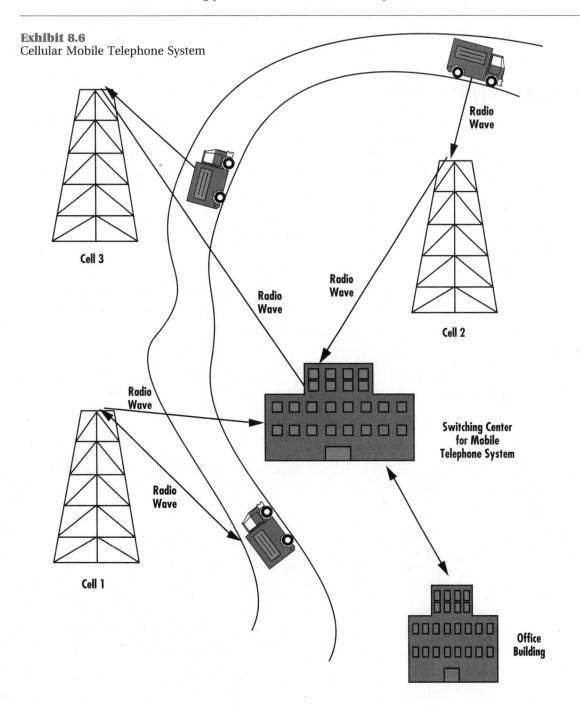

nology, lack of a nationwide wireless infrastructure, and spotty support. Nevertheless, many organizations are ready to take the plunge and are investing heavily to outfit their workers with the latest wireless has to offer. For example, American Express Corp. is testing a scheme to use Apple Newton's PDAs as the link between its 36 million cardholders and the retailers, restaurants, and other businesses that accept American Express cards. United Parcel Service and IBM have outfitted their field-workers with specialized computers that use built-in wireless modems and private radio communication networks.

■ TELECONFERENCING

Teleconferencing systems provide an alternative to in-person meetings. Not only are travel expenses reduced, but managerial effectiveness is increased through faster response to problems, access to more people, less duplication of effort by geographically dispersed sites, and reduced time when people are out of touch with one another. Teleconferencing involves the use of audio and video communications to allow meetings between participants scattered around the city, country, or globe, without the participants having to meet together physically.

Audio Conferencing

Audio conferencing is similar to a telephone call on a party line. Several people gather in a room with a special speaker and microphone device. Anyone in the room who speaks can be heard by all people involved in the audio conference. Experience shows that audio conferencing works best when the number of participants is less than seven, a copy of the agenda is sent to the participants in advance, and one person serves as a moderator to ensure that all people have an opportunity to participate and that the goals of the conference are achieved.

Video Conferencing

Video conferencing is a form of teleconferencing in which either full-motion or freeze-frame pictures are transmitted between two or more meeting sites. Full motion video communicates more clearly but requires more expensive transmission facilities than freeze-frame. With freeze-frame, still video snapshots are exchanged. Freeze-frame video has low operating costs because it uses conventional telephone lines to transmit the video images; any freeze-frame facility can be connected to any other facility through the public telephone network.

Full-motion video conferencing began in the television industry. Television programs originate from network studios and are distributed to local stations via satellite transmission. Programs are beamed via an uplink to a satellite and received at one or more local stations via a downlink. Network broadcasting involves sending signals that require a large amount of satellite transmission capacity and thus are very expensive.

The network broadcasting approach is too expensive for most business meetings. Instead, the signal is transmitted in a compressed digital format to reduce the amount of expensive satellite capacity required. The state of this technology continues to improve but currently exhibits some audio/visual synchronization problems that can be mildly distracting.

Three basic video conferencing options exist. One-way audio and one-way video sends signals from one location to multiple receiving sites and is similar to commercial TV. One-way video and two-way audio allows people at the receiving sites to engage in conversation with persons at the transmitting site while everyone views the same video signals. Two-way video and audio is the most expensive of the options but supports complete two-way visual and verbal communications.

Desktop Video Conferencing

The heart of any teleconferencing system is the coder-decoder units. Recent technology advances have enabled manufacturers to reduce the coder-decoder units from the size of a microwave oven to the size of a personal computer board. With reductions in size have come major reductions in cost. As a result, an individual personal computer can be integrated with a coder-decoder unit and a camera to support video-conferencing at the desktop level. Data, audio, and video signals are carried over a single wire using asynchronous transfer mode, fiber distributed data interchange, and fast Ethernet communications protocols.

Regardless of which form of teleconferencing is used, the quality of the audio portion of the conference must be very good. The acceptable range in video quality is much broader than audio. Slightly fuzzy pictures of participants or visual aids may detract from the overall effectiveness of the meeting, but if the words of the participants cannot be understood, the meeting is doomed for failure!

Exhibit 8.7 outlines some guidelines to use when considering which form of electronic meeting system meets your needs.

Electronic Calendaring

An **electronic calendaring** system involves the use of a shared data base to store and retrieve users' appointment calendars (Exhibit 8.8). Note that the equipment and communications arrangement is similar to that for e-mail or a LAN. In fact, it is quite common for e-mail systems and LAN operating systems to include an electronic calendar function.

The traditional phone call method for scheduling a meeting requires at least one telephone call to each participant to let him or her vote from a list of potential meeting times. It can take several hours or even a couple days to hear from everyone—remember about one third of calls are not completed since the called party is busy or out. Once everyone has been contacted to register their preferences, a time and date is set based on when the key "invitees" can attend. Then all the participants must be recontacted to let them know of the agreed to

Exhibit 8.7
Recommendations
on Use of Various
Forms of
Conferencing

Teleconferencing Method	When to Consider Using
Full motion video	Only if you can justify the high additional cost for full motion.
	The meeting requires full motion displays (e.g., to preview TV commercials or view some moving parts of an assembly).
Slow scan video	The main points of the meeting will be presented on overheads or flip charts.
Audio	Visuals are unimportant to get across the main points of the meeting.
Fax	The participants are widely dispersed geographically or are very difficult to convene.
	A dialogue spanning several days can be expected on the topic communicated in the facsimile.
	Graphics, images, as well as text, need to be communicated.
E-mail	The participants are widely dispersed geographically or are very difficult to convene.
	A dialogue spanning several days can be expected on the topic communicated in the facsimile.
	Text is the primary form of communications.

meeting time. Unfortunately, several hours or even days often elapse since the initial attempt to set the meeting. By now one or more key invitees may no longer be available. This necessitates a second round of calls. The time required to schedule a meeting for eight people in this manner can be hours.

Users of an electronic calendaring system can enter appointments, vacation days, holidays, regularly scheduled meetings, and "private time" (time the user does not wish to be interrupted). Users also enter updates to keep their appointment calendar current. They can review their own calendar and that of others as well. Since the calendars are kept on a shared data base, it is possible for any user to access any other user's appointment calendar. If a user wishes to schedule a meeting, he or she specifies who should attend and requests that the system

Real World Perspective

Use of Desktop Video Conferencing by Attorneys

The law firm of Lord Day and Lord, Barrett Smith in New York links lawyers with their clients via desktop video conferencing. Attorneys and clients can share text and images, including videotaped court testimony and legal documents, and discuss them while sitting at desktop workstation monitors.

A shared whiteboard enables users to display and mark up documents, drawings, video frames or images (such as photographic) evidence, or other case materials. Users can also select images of text from on-line litigation data bases and import them immediately into a conference. This approach saves the law firm money in travel time and expenses.

Exhibit 8.8
An Electronic
Calendaring System

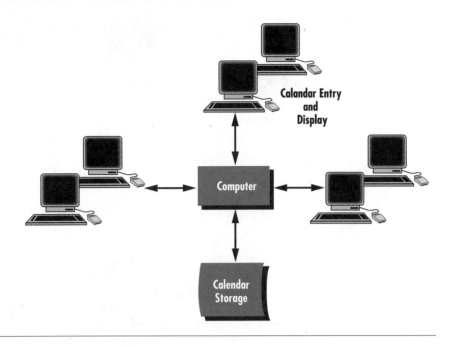

find the next time that all attendees are free to meet. Each individual's calendar is then updated to reflect the meeting time and date.

Many people refuse to participate in electronic calendaring systems by not entering their appointments or by not checking the calendar for meetings. They strongly believe that their time is their own to schedule and do not want to be automatically scheduled without direct personal contact with another person. Obviously, the effectiveness of an electronic calendaring system is diminished by each nonparticipant.

■ IMAGE PROCESSING SYSTEMS

Most of the information in today's office environment, whether in the form of text or graphics, is stored on paper. Not only do we receive and transmit information using paper, but most of the research information we gather (such as letters from customers and clippings from brochures) is usually stored on paper. While there is much talk about the paperless office of the future, the amount of information stored on paper continues to increase. It will be a long time before we become a paperless society. **Image processing** systems are one means of dealing with this increasing volume of paper documents.

Imaging allows users to scan, index, and archive text and graphics images electronically, leading to reduced clerical effort and the elimination of mountains of paperwork. These electronic images are accessible for search, retrieval, and display (Exhibits 8.9 and 8.10). The fact that imaging supports improved movement of and access to docu-

Exhibit 8.9
Major Processing
Steps for an
Imaging System

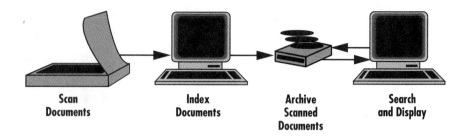

| Scan
Documents | Index
Documents | Archive
Scanned
Documents | Search
and Display |

ments is the principal reason for implementing imaging and workflow systems.

Imaging technology is used to support transaction processing applications that involve handling and expediting transactions such as claims, invoices, and purchase orders. It is also used in customer service applications for handling correspondence and field service support. Another common application is support of technical document control and editing. And, of course, imaging technology is used to archive large amounts of static information that requires occasional access.

Once seen as a stand-alone technology designed to reduce storage costs, imaging is now seen as a business solution that can lower costs, improve customer service, and increase efficiency. It's not enough to optically store the massive amounts of data that would otherwise be on paper. The real business payoff comes from finding ways to manage that data more effectively by merging it into normal business processes and into the flow of information around the office. Thus firms that are getting the greatest benefits from this technology have undergone some type of business process redesign that brings increased value beyond simply reducing storage costs.

An effective imaging system that is integrated into the work flow of the office can provide many benefits, including:

Exhibit 8.10
A Basic Imaging
System

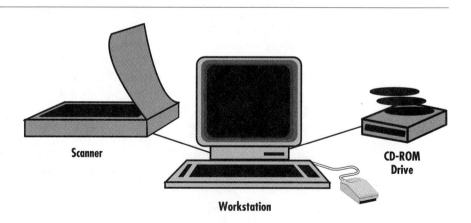

Scanner   CD-ROM
                                 Drive

Workstation

The storage of paper-based information is expensive, particularly if it is frequently accessed and needs to be located in the office. The savings from reduced office space and filing cabinets for storage can pay for some imaging systems in months.

Effective imaging systems greatly reduce the time required to retrieve and sort paper. This improves customer service and also reduces the number of people required for office operations.

The loss of information (either temporarily from misfiling or permanently through fire or theft) can be very costly to an organization. A well-designed imaging system greatly reduces the likelihood and severity of such a loss.

Two forms of imaging systems include the electronic document management system and multimedia systems. These are discussed below.

Real World Perspective

Image Processing Provides Benefits for Consolidated Freightways

Consolidated Freightways, Inc., of Menlo Park, California, is a major trucking firm that carries freight for hire throughout the United States. Consolidated uses image processing technology to reduce the cost of internal records management and restructure the internal flow of work.

The trucking industry is highly paper-intensive. Each shipment requires a bill of lading document (a legal description of the freight carried) and a delivery receipt (used to document that the shipment was delivered to its destination).

In the past, data from the bills of lading and delivery receipts were keyed into a data entry system for transmission to the firm's mainframe computer. The physical documents remained stored at the local Consolidated freight terminal handling the shipment. The Interstate Commerce Commission, which regulates trucking firms, requires shippers to keep such documents on file for three years. Thus Consolidated had nearly 150 million pieces of paper in storage at hundreds of local freight terminals throughout the United States. As a result, the firm spent half a million hours annually filing, retrieving, copying, and mailing the documents. In addition, bills of lading and delivery receipts are required by the Consolidated customer for billing purposes. Frequently, a Consolidated customer would request a copy of a document to complete their billing process. It generally took five to ten days for them to receive it.

Image processing dramatically cut the time spent collecting, filing, retrieving, copying, and mailing mountains of documents generated from the 75,000 shipments moved each day by Consolidated. Documents are now scanned daily at 48 freight processing locations. They are then immediately transmitted to the company's central image processing system in Portland, Oregon, over Consolidated's internal data communications network. Once the scanned documents arrive at the central site, customers can call in to an on-line system to request information about their shipments. They can also request images of key documents from their own computer terminals and direct that the images be sent to their computer terminals or fax machines. As a result, Consolidated's imaging system allows its customers to shrink their accounts receivable cycle by as much as eight days. SOURCE: Scott Wallace. "Imaging Can Be Everything." InformationWeek. June 24, 1991. □

Electronic Document Management

Most of the information flowing through offices today is still stored on paper. Over 90 percent of all information managed in a corporation is estimated to be in paper form with less than 10 percent stored in computer accessible form. The vast amount of information in the typical office environment is very difficult to organize and locate. Office workers frequently have to search numerous file drawers or cabinets (if the data is in paper form) or navigate several directories (if the information is in electronic format) to locate needed information. In fact, estimates have been made that office workers spend 15 to 30 percent of their time trying to locate information.

Electronic document management systems interface with other electronic communication systems such as word processing, desktop publishing, image processing, e-mail, voice mail, and electronic data interchange. Electronic document systems integrate output from all these systems to offer greater productivity, faster retrieval, improved work flow, lower costs, and a solution to the constant storage and retrieval problems created by paper documents.

Multimedia Systems

The combination of multimedia technology with traditional computer systems is an exciting new trend in information technology. Organizations worldwide are seeking new opportunities to leverage the millions of dollars they have invested in information technology by empowering customers to access corporate computers and data directly. **Multimedia systems** help users avoid the complexity of computers by presenting a user friendly front end that consists of touch-screen navigation and a rich interface that includes audio, images, graphics, motion video, animation, and text.

Multimedia technology is often packaged as a self-enclosed, walk-up **kiosk** that looks and acts like an automatic teller cash machine (ATM). Banks have long recognized the value of ATMs for providing service. Multimedia kiosks expand the ATM concept to meet customer service needs that are more complex than simply dispensing cash. Indeed, wherever organizations deliver routine information and services to customers, multimedia kiosks provide an opportunity to deliver excellent service at low cost. Retailers and manufacturers use multimedia kiosks to showcase products in retail locations with limited shelf space. Sports teams use kiosks to extend their ticketing systems directly to customers. Government agencies provide convenient kiosk access to employment services and other government functions.

Multimedia systems represent a whole new approach to combining computing and business that affects the way people communicate, work, and learn. Incorporating voice, data, and video with computing power helps transform business in three areas:

1. multimedia can provide an interactive front-end to existing information system applications and corporate data bases that make them easier to use and access;

2. multimedia enable new kinds of applications to be developed such as enhanced sales automation, just-in-time training, and desktop conferencing; and

3. multimedia can be the basis for business ventures that pioneer new markets based on delivery of interactive, multimedia information.

Entrepreneurs and innovators will use the power of multimedia to create new, and yet potentially vast, products and services that haven't yet been imagined.

■ OFFICE AUTOMATION ISSUES

The introduction of office automation technology into the workplace brings with it numerous issues involving the electronic supervision of workers, personal privacy, and the ethical use of information technology. **Electronic supervision** or **computer monitoring** involves using the computer to monitor the quantity and quality of work performed by employees using a terminal or PC. Secretaries and reservation agents are just two examples of people who rely heavily on office automation technology to complete their job. Software can measure the length of time it takes to handle a request, the number of keystrokes per second, and the number of errors made per work shift. These par-

Real World Perspective

Multimedia Applications

The Christian Science Publishing Society Monitor is a leader in developing a repository to hold all printed articles, news footage, color slides, videocassettes, and other media the publishing firm has stockpiled. The society is a Boston-based, nonprofit media operation that has published the Christian Science newspaper since 1909. Plans call for data and images to be accessible to more than 2,000 users in 36 bureaus over a corporate network.

Intel, the manufacturer of computer chips, is using multimedia to provide training for its employees on next-generation technology. Because work requirements change so rapidly in microprocessor manufacturing, Intel has built an easily updatable system of computer-based interactive work sessions. In one application, Intel has developed a training session on cleaning ion implanters, which are used in the manufacture of silicon wafers. Video chips embedded in training applications help show the worker exactly how to clean the latest implanters.

Federal Express has developed easy-to-use multimedia kiosks to streamline basic FedEx services for occasional customers. The kiosks offer step-by-step interactive entry, thus eliminating problems filling out what appears to be a fairly complex document. Each choice comes up on the screen, with a simple "yes" or "no" action or a request to key in some particular information. The process ensures that customers won't skip any essential steps. Customers can pay with a FedEx account number or a credit card. They can also use the kiosk to price their packages or check service availability at any zip code, and they can use the kiosk to track delivery of their packages. Such services are delivered through the kiosk's ability to connect with FedEx's host computers. The kiosks put FedEx computing power directly in the hands of customers.

ameters can be counted, charted, and analyzed to allow an employer to monitor an employee's work rate.

Employee organizations and unions believe that computer monitoring is a clear invasion of employee privacy. Unions representing office workers have filed grievances against it, and several unions and worker organizations are pressing for legislation prohibiting it. They believe that computer monitoring is an unfair way for management to determine productivity and pay. In addition, they believe that computer monitoring increases the stress level of workers, causing stress-related health problems. Management's point of view is that they can use computer monitoring as another supervisory tool; their intent is not to harass workers over minor details.

A growing concern is the use of the company's office automation systems for nonbusiness purposes, for example using e-mail to publicize a used car for sale or sending a fax inviting people to a social event. In some companies, such nonbusiness use of company resources is grounds for termination while in other companies, such use is accepted.

Another ethical question associated with office automation systems involves the viewing of others' electronic mail. Many people believe that viewing others' electronic mail should be regarded as unacceptable, similar to reading someone's U.S. mail. Others believe that an employee's supervisor should be allowed to view the employee's e-mail messages since the e-mail system is intended strictly for company business and should be used only on company time.

Some other issues concerning office automation systems are that e-mail and fax machines have sped up the office grapevine making it easy for rumors and gossip to travel at the speed of light. It also allows for flame mail—an electronic exchange of angry messages between people who send e-mail notes or leave voice mail messages that they later regret. And a special problem of e-mail is the office grammarian who offers on-line corrections of spellings and other errors. Such an individual upsets others and discourages the sending of informal notes for which e-mail is ideal. Still another problem is handling a situation by e-mail or voice mail when it should be done face-to-face. For example, a manager should never use e-mail or voice mail to reprimand a worker.

Managers must take steps to reduce the potential negative impact of the above-mentioned issues. One way is to document a code of ethics for use of office automation systems and to ensure that each user receives and reads it. Establishing a code of ethics clearly communicates how management intends these company resources to be used.

■ WHY MANAGERS MUST UNDERSTAND OFFICE AUTOMATION

In many organizations, the early office automation projects were directed at secretarial and clerical activities. An office automation application was implemented when the technology was cost justified and when a business unit understood the technology. Furthermore, these early applications were implemented in isolation—technology, vendor, and application design decisions were made in one business area with no understanding of what was being done in other areas. Thus pockets of office automation sprung up like isolated islands and resulted in the fragmentation of office automation applications. The limited and specialized functions performed by the many individual applications led to missed expectations between what the application delivered and what the business needs required. The diversity of vendors, equipment, and standards made it difficult, if not impossible, to share information across business units. Although there was no overall plan for the management and support of the office automation technology, business managers learned a lot from these initial applications:

■ Office automation hardware and software is expensive. It costs significantly more than the traditional equipment that it replaces.

■ Office automation needs to be thought out. One does not just put in new equipment without carefully considering the role of the work group using the equipment and the surrounding business processes.

■ Office automation changes people's work lives—for better or worse. In poor implementations, new roles are created with limited job responsibility, which leads to extreme job dissatisfaction. In good implementations, people's roles are expanded and job satisfaction increases.

■ The ease of use and lack of security of many office automation systems causes problems such as the inefficient and unauthorized use of e-mail, voice mail, and facsimile services.

These problems of office automation must be solved before knowledge workers can fully accept and cooperate with a technology that significantly changes their work roles, processes, and environment. Only then can the promise of increased productivity and job satisfaction be fulfilled.

Rethinking the Organization

Today the demands of increased competitiveness, expanding globalization and corporate downsizing are forcing a "reinvention" of the corporation. One form of this new corporation is the **horizontal organization** that eliminates both the traditional hierarchical reporting lines and the concept of functional or departmental boundaries (Exhibit 8.11). The horizontal organization (Exhibit 8.12) has a few senior executives in charge of traditional support functions such as finance and human resources. Everyone else works together in multidisciplinary teams that perform core processes, such as new product development or customer support. As a result, only three or four layers

Exhibit 8.11
The Traditional
Hierarchical
Organization

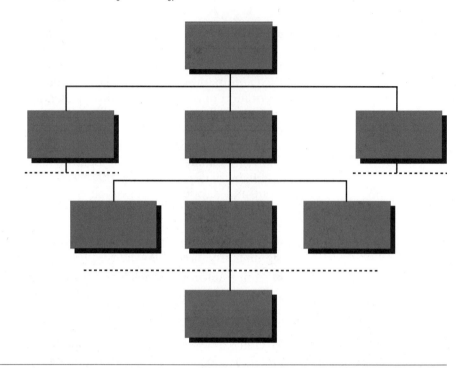

Exhibit 8.12
The Horizontal
Organization

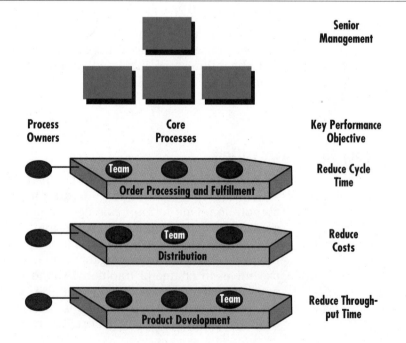

of management may exist between the chairman of the board and the people on a multidisciplinary team.

The key to this new organization is the formation of empowered business teams that have a high degree of autonomy. Members of this team must work in close concert with one another even though they may work at different physical locations, thus an excellent communication system is needed. In addition, the flattening of the organization increases the number of people who report to a manager. The number of direct reports is greatly increased, from three to five reports to ten or more. The senior manager can no longer have weekly one-on-one meetings with the direct reports; there simply is not enough time. Instead, other means of meeting and communicating must be developed. Office automation can help meet these needs and support the new competitive, global, horizontal organization.

The business manager must lead in the selection and implementation of the mix of office automation applications. These applications must be based on the characteristics of the organization; the nature of the industry; the activities of suppliers, customers, and competitors; personal preferences; and the resources available. Effective office automation requires that business processes be reengineered before specific office automation solutions are implemented. Some office automation applications may be implemented as alternatives to traditional communication methods. Other applications offer new opportunities to meet new challenges. Increasing the productivity of the knowledge workers is simply too critical to the firm's survival to be delegated to the technologists.

Summary

Over half the workers in the United States today are knowledge workers, and they are in need of productivity aids.

Office automation is the planned integration of new technology with improved office processes to increase productivity and effectiveness.

Fundamental questions about the need to continue or restructure basic business functions must be answered before adopting sophisticated office automation equipment.

Word processing and desktop publishing systems are two frequently employed systems that help people capture their ideas in forms that are easily stored, updated, and transmitted.

Word processing boosts productivity by reducing the time it takes to draft, proof, revise, copy, print, distribute, and file text material.

Desktop publishing systems combine word processing and image scanning capabilities along with page composition functions to allow users to create documents that include several type fonts and sizes, graphics, and colors on each page.

E-mail uses computer hardware and software to prepare, transmit, store, and retrieve messages.

E-mail systems have a wide range of capabilities and services to which the user may subscribe.

E-mail reduces interruptions, supports the broad sharing of information without requiring meetings, enables opinions and input from remote experts, and enables people to work around time zone changes.

Voice mail is similar to text-oriented mail in that it can deliver the same message to many different people or can be sent to a distant location overnight when the telephone rates are lower.

Facsimile is a copier device that permits reproduction of an original document at remote locations.

The availability of low-cost facsimile machines capable of transmitting at rates exceeding one page per minute has led to a tremendous increase in the use of this technology.

Electronic meeting systems provide an alternative to in-person meetings that reduce travel expenses, provide faster response to problems, increase access to people, reduce duplication of effort, and cut down on the time people are out of touch with one another.

Audio, video, and desktop conferencing are three forms of electronic meeting systems. It is essential that the audio portion of the conference is very good for an effective electronic meeting.

Most of the information in today's office environment, whether in the form of text or graphics, is stored on paper.

Imaging enables users to scan, index, and archive text and graphic images electronically. These images are then accessible for search, retrieval, and display.

The principal reason for implementing imaging and workflow systems is to support improved movement of and access to documents. Thus firms that get the greatest benefit from this technology must undergo a business process redesign that brings increased value beyond simply reducing paper storage costs.

Electronic document systems integrate output from other electronic communication systems, such as word processing, desktop publishing, image processing, e-mail, voice mail, and electronic data interchange, to offer greater productivity, faster retrieval, improved work flow, lower costs, and a solution to the constant storage and retrieval problems created by paper documents.

Multimedia systems help users avoid the complexity of computers by presenting a user friendly front end and a rich interface that includes audio, images, motion video, graphics, animation, and text.

Organizations worldwide are seeking new opportunities to leverage the millions of dollars they have invested in information technology by empowering customers to access corporate computers and data directly.

During the early stages of implementing office automation, pockets of this new technology sprung up like isolated islands resulting in the fragmentation of office automation applications.

Office automation hardware and software costs significantly more than the traditional equipment that it replaces.

Office automation needs to be thought out. One does not put in new equipment without carefully considering the role of the work group using the equipment and the surrounding business processes.

Office automation changes people's work lives—for better or worse.

The ease of use and lack of security of many office automation systems cause problems such as inefficient and unauthorized use of e-mail, voice mail, and facsimile services.

The business manager must lead in the selection and implementation of the mix of office automation applications. These must be chosen based on the characteristics of the organization; the nature of the industry; the activities of suppliers, customers, and competitors; personal preferences; and the resources available.

Exhibit 8.13 lists key office activities and indicates which of the office automation technologies discussed in this chapter support that activity.

Exhibit 8.13
An Office Automation Usage Matrix

Activity	Word Processing	Desktop Publishing	Electronic Mail	Voice Mail	Facsimile	Audio Conference	Video Conference	Desktop Conference	Electronic Calendaring	Electronic Document	Multimedia
Prepare Text Memo	√	√									
Send/Receive Text Memo			√		√						
Prepare Text/Graphics Memo		√									
Send/Receive Text/Graphics			√		√						
Send/Receive Voice Message				√		√					
Schedule Meeting									√		
Conduct Meeting						√	√	√			
Document Meeting Results	√	√	√								
Access Complex Application											√
Access Data Base											√
File/Retreive Text Memo										√	

A Manager's Checklist

✔ Do you know how many of your firm's employees can be classified as knowledge workers?

✔ Can you identify specific projects undertaken to improve the productivity of your firm's knowledge workers? Have these projects generally been successful in meeting their objectives?

✔ Is there a specific organization responsible for leading the development and implementation of office automation projects? What about for the ongoing support of office automation technology?

✔ Is office automation being implemented on a business unit by business unit basis resulting in "islands of office automation"?

Key Terms

audio conference
cells
cellular mobile telephone
centering function
computer monitoring
desktop publishing
desktop video conference
dpi
e-mail
e-mail conference
electronic calendaring
electronic document
   management
electronic in-box
electronic meeting
electronic publishing system
electronic supervision
facsimile
formatting of text
hierarchical organization
horizontal organization

image processing
image scanning
islands of office automation
knowledge worker
justification
kiosk
multimedia system
office automation
page description language
PDL
personal digital assistants
store-and-forward
stylesheet
teleconferencing
video conference
voice mail
wireless communications
word processing
word wrap
WYSIWYG

Review Questions

1. Define the term office automation.

2. Identify two forms of electronic publishing systems, briefly describe how they work, and describe the kinds of business benefits that they can provide.

3. Identify three forms of electronic communications systems, briefly describe how they work, and describe the kinds of business benefits that they can provide.

4. Identify three forms of electronic meetings, briefly describe how they work, and describe the kinds of business benefits that they can provide.

5. Identify two forms of imaging systems, briefly describe how they work, and describe the kinds of business benefits that they can provide.

6. State three reasons why business managers need to understand and be involved in office automation efforts.

Discussion Questions

1. Explain the need to increase the productivity of knowledge workers.

2. What is the difference between a word processing system and a desktop publishing system? When would you use one versus the other?

3. In what ways are voice mail and e-mail alike? How are they different? Are different people likely to use one versus the other?

4. Is it possible for an organization to achieve major increases in productivity simply through using the latest office automation technology?

5. What sort of role might a business manager take in leading an office automation effort?

Recommended Readings

1. Byrne, John A. "The Horizontal Corporation." *BusinessWeek*, Number 3351 (December 20, 1993).

2. Campbell, George and John Wallenbach. "Are Suites Worth It?" *PC World*, Vol. 12, No. 5 (May 1994).

3. Cullen, Scott W. "Multifunction Systems are New on the Scene." *The Office*, 113, No. 4 (April 1991).

4. English, David. "Getting Started with Desktop Publishing." *Compute*. Volume 15, No. 11, Issue 158 (November 1993).

5. English, David. "What Makes a Fast Forward Multimedia PC." *Compute*. Volume 15, No. 11, Issue 158 (November 1993).

6. Ferguson, Cortney S., Hugh J. Watson, and Robert Gatewood. "Strategic Planning for Office Automation." *Information & Management*, 21 (November 1991).

7. Fernberg, Patricia M. "Tailoring the Workstation to the Worker." *Modern Office Technology* 37 (June 1992).

8. Khoshafian, Sertag, Brad A. Baker, Razmik Abnous, and Kevin Shepherd. *Intelligent Offices*. New York: John Wiley & Sons, Inc., 1992.

9. Korzeinowski, Paul. " 'Paperless Office' Deluged with Paper." *Software Magazine*, 10, No. 2 (Feb. 1990).

10. Marshall, Patrick. "PDAs: Pocket Organizers with Power." *InfoWorld*. Vol. 16, Issue 16 (April 18, 1994).

11. Romei, Laura K. "Fax Integration: More Uses, Less Equipment." *Modern Office Technology* 37 (February 1992).

12. Sox, Charlene W. *Introduction to Office Automation*. Englewood Cliffs, NJ: Prentice-Hall, 1990.

13. Wallace, Scott. "Imaging Can Be Everything." *InformationWeek*. June 24, 1991.

14. White, Ron and Kyla Carson. "War of the Words." *PC Computing*, Vol. 6, No. 8 (August 1993).

15. Wolk, Sue. "Your Imaging Connection." *Modern Office Technology* 37 (June 1992).

A Manager's Dilemma

Case Study 8.1

Office Automation Decision Time

The financial analysis section, consisting of the controller, five analysts, twelve clerical assistants, and three secretaries, had been using the latest in office automation equipment on a trial basis for the past six months. This section had been selected to pilot the use of new office technology because of its responsibility for ensuring that the company uses its money wisely. It was felt this group would be a stiff, but fair and objective test group.

Now it was time for the controller to make a recommendation on the expansion of the technology to other parts of the company. Unfortunately, the right decision was unclear. Although almost everyone in the section felt the technology had helped them perform their jobs better, there was little hard data that could quantify the technology's value to the company. Using 20/20 hindsight, the controller wished the key evaluation criteria upon which to make the expansion decision had been better defined.

What evaluation criteria do you think are important? How could benefits be quantified? What could have been done to help prepare the financial analysis section to reach a good decision?

Case Study 8.2

Use of Integrated Packages

Integrated software packages have some disadvantages not apparent to the inexperienced personal computer user. Yes, it is nice to have just a single user interface to learn for multiple applications like word processing, spreadsheets, and data communications. And yes, the cost of the single integrated package is less than the sum of the individual packages needed to provide the same functions. However, the ease of use and range of features available in the applications included in the integrated package can be inferior to stand-alone single purpose software applications. For example, the spreadsheet package in the integrated software package may not be as easy to use, as powerful, or have as many functions as the best spreadsheet package available.

How would you evaluate whether or not it is appropriate to have people convert from multiple stand-alone single purpose software applications to integrated software packages? What are some of the costs and disadvantages of doing so? What are the advantages and savings associated with conversion to integrated packages? How can a choice be made?

Developing Information Systems

This section is based on the assumption that business managers can make the most informed decisions about the development and operation of information systems. The reason for this is simple: they know the most about the business and what is needed to be successful. Therefore, it is critical that managers become competent partners of the information technology organization in the evaluation of potential information technology projects and their development.

This section begins with a discussion of the information engineering methodology as a proven approach to the development of information systems. Chapter 10 presents an effective information technology planning process for expressing information systems needs and establishing the relative priority of projects. This chapter also addresses business area analysis and business process reengineering. Chapter 10 outlines an effective process for executing information systems projects.

Chapter 9

Information Engineering

Learning Objectives

Upon completion of this chapter, you will be able to:

1. Define the term system development methodology and identify the three components of a robust methodology.

2. Explain why strategies for achieving quality software are based on an accurate and complete definition of user requirements and the early detection and removal of defects.

3. Outline the four key features that distinguish the Information Engineering methodology from other system development methodologies.

4. State the objective of each stage of the Information Engineering methodology.

5. Define prototyping and discuss how this technique can be used to build high-quality systems.

6. Discuss the process for selecting a purchased software package.

7. Discuss the use of Computer Aided Systems Engineering (CASE) tools to improve the quality of information systems and increase productivity of systems analysts.

Preview

Developing information systems to meet business needs is a highly complex and difficult task. So much so that it is common for information system projects to overrun budgets and exceed scheduled completion dates. Worse yet, even when systems are finally completed, they often fail to meet the business needs they were designed to address. Indeed, some systems make the users' job more difficult to perform! Moreover, the demand for new information systems exceeds the capacity of most IT organizations to deliver them. As IT managers have become painfully aware of these problems, they have looked for ways to improve the situation. One strategy is to adopt a standard system development process, use CASE tools that support and enhance the process, and follow software quality control practices.

Issues

1. Why should management insist that system developers follow a standard system development methodology?

2. Should all projects follow the same system development approach?

3. What value can computer aided software engineering (CASE) tools add to the system development process?

4. What are efficient strategies for achieving quality software?

Trade-offs

1. Can you reduce the elapsed time of a project by not following a system development process?

2. How much should be invested in the acquisition of CASE tools and the training of people to use them?

3. How can project cost, schedule, quality, and system functionality be balanced to meet the needs of the business?

A Manager Struggles with the Issues

Kelly's head was throbbing as she left the meeting. This was the second time she had met with the project managers of key IT projects since taking over responsibility for Information Technology, along with her responsibilities for Market Research and Advertising. The goal of the meeting was simple: gain an understanding of the current status of key IT projects. Unfortunately, Kelly left these meetings more confused than when she went into them. The IT people seemed to talk in some foreign language. It was so bad, even the project managers couldn't seem to understand each other. Today, she had learned that one project was in the prefeasibility stage, another was starting preliminary analysis, and a third was doing scope definition—but that the three projects were all essentially at the same stage of early development. No wonder the meetings took so long when people used different phrases to say the same thing. Why couldn't these IT people develop some common terminology and a common approach toward working IT projects? Wouldn't there be many advantages to having people follow a standard work process?

■ SYSTEM DEVELOPMENT METHODOLOGY

Definition

A **methodology** is a collection of postulates, rules, and guidelines that provides a standard, proven process for the practitioner to follow. An example of a simple methodology is the set of directions posted at a self-service car wash. By following these directions (methodology), the user is assured of satisfactory results. However, if certain steps are omitted or done in the wrong sequence, the results may be very poor!

Step 1—Thoroughly rinse car with clear water.

Step 2—Soft spray with soapy water.

Step 3—Use foaming brush to remove dirt and/or mud.

Step 4—Apply wheel cleaner.

Step 5—Rinse car thoroughly.

If step 5 and 2 are reversed or either is omitted, the result is unsatisfactory.

A system development methodology is a standard, proven work process that enables system analysts, programmers, and end users to make controlled and orderly progress in developing information systems. It defines the activities in the system development process and the individual and group responsibilities for accomplishing these activities. It helps answer the basic software development questions of what shall we do next and for how long shall we do it? A methodology also recommends specific techniques for accomplishing the various activities. Most importantly, a methodology offers guidelines for managing the quality of the products (**deliverables**) produced during the various stages of the system development life cycle. A complete system development methodology begins with a stage that identifies potential

Exhibit 9.1
The Essential
Components of a
Methodology

Component	Explanation
Work Breakdown Structure	*What* to Do and *When* to Do It
Techniques	*How* to Do It
Quality Management	How to *Manage* the *Quality* of the Result

projects, addresses the support and maintenance of existing systems, and covers all activities in between.

Essential Components

A methodology can be viewed as consisting of three major components (Exhibit 9.1): a work breakdown structure that provides guidelines of what to do and when to do it, techniques on how to do what needs to be done, and advice on how to manage the quality of the results. These points are discussed below.

It is important to know that different authors, consultants, and organizations have developed various system development methodologies. The different methodologies require different work breakdown structures, employ different techniques, and have different strategies for managing the quality of results. Exhibit 9.2 lists a few system development methodologies in use.

Work Breakdown Structure

Developing an information system is not a simple process. It requires completing many activities that are complex in themselves, with many dependencies among the various activities. A methodology provides guidelines for what to do and when to do it by subdividing the development process into a series of smaller, related groups of activities called **stages.**

Each stage has a set of well-defined objectives. Completion of a stage requires the production of a set of major end products or deliv-

Exhibit 9.2
A List of Proprietary
System
Development
Methodologies

Methodology	Vendor
Information Engineering	James Martin Associates
Jackson System Development	Michael Jackson Systems, Ltd.
LSDM	Learmonth & Burchett Management Systems
Method/1	Arthur Andersen Consulting
Navigator	Ernst & Young
Prism	Hoskyns Group, Ltd.
Stradis	McDonnell Douglas
Yourdon	Yourdon, Inc.

Exhibit 9.3
Work Breakdown
Structure

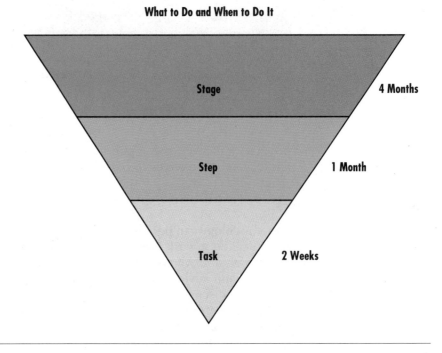

What to Do and When to Do It

Stage   4 Months

Step   1 Month

Task   2 Weeks

erables. Stages in turn are broken into **steps,** and steps are divided into **tasks.** A step is a significant development milestone at which progress against the system development plan can be measured. Each task leads to the creation of a specific system deliverable (e.g., a data flow diagram showing the business processes to be included in the scope of the project, a high-level data model showing the major data entities that the system must track, documentation of a system backup and recovery plan, etc.). This decomposition of a project into stages, steps, and tasks is called a **work breakdown structure** (Exhibit 9.3).

As a general rule of thumb, no stage should last for more than four months. Steps typically last no more than a month. Tasks last up to two weeks. The relative shortness of time ensures that project goals for each stage, step, and task are kept focused and well defined. It also ensures that progress (in terms of specific deliverables) can be measured frequently. Should a project's work breakdown structure be such that this rule of thumb is violated, the project is in danger of getting out of control.

The deliverables associated with a given stage provide the starting point for the next stage. In the next stage, the analyst expands the scope and depth of understanding of the new system to be constructed. Work done during each stage provides an opportunity to view the system in a different perspective.

An example of a work breakdown structure for the project definition stage is shown in Exhibit 9.4.

Exhibit 9.4
Typical Work
Breakdown
Structure

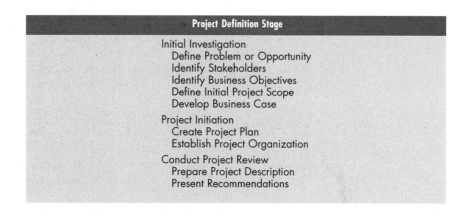

Project Definition Stage
Initial Investigation
Define Problem or Opportunity
Identify Stakeholders
Identify Business Objectives
Define Initial Project Scope
Develop Business Case
Project Initiation
Create Project Plan
Establish Project Organization
Conduct Project Review
Prepare Project Description
Present Recommendations

Techniques

A **technique** is a method or procedure for carrying out a mechanical operation or rendering an artistic work. System development techniques are rigorous procedures for creating system deliverables. They specify what inputs are required to begin a task, what outputs (the deliverables) will be produced, and they recommend a specific process to execute the task (Exhibit 9.5). For example, to complete the task of defining the scope of the system to be built, the technique of constructing a data flow diagram showing the business processes to be addressed by the system is recommended.

Many disciplines embrace standard techniques—accounting, medicine, and engineering, to name a few. The use of proven techniques turns the discipline into more of a science than an art and ensures a higher probability of success. It also allows practitioners to continually refine and improve techniques as the body of knowledge expands through experience. The techniques can be documented, allowing knowledge to pass from one practitioner to another.

Compare a group of civil engineers setting out to build a bridge to a group of system developers about to take on a major information systems project. While both groups have standard techniques and engineering principles to aid them in their effort, there are significant differences between the two groups.

First, the civil engineers can draw on thousands of years of accumulated knowledge and experience while software developers have a short 50 years of history of building computerized information systems.

Exhibit 9.5
Technique Defines
How to Execute a
Task

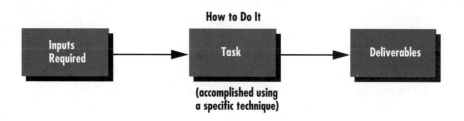

Second, there is universal acceptance among civil engineers that they must follow good engineering principles to be successful. On the other hand, most software developers view their work as more of an art than a science. They prefer to be highly creative and original in their approach rather than apply standard techniques.

Third, when the civil engineers complete the bridge, we expect that it will work correctly. We do not expect the bridge to collapse. On the other hand, we are not surprised if software has bugs. In fact, most software products carry a disclaimer of warranty (see the Real World Perspective, "Typical Software Product—Disclaimer of Warranty," for the actual wording of a disclaimer of warranty—the name of the company has been changed).

The differences between the two groups does not mean that software engineers are stupid or that they are doomed to failure on all their projects. It does mean that their results are not as predictable as the results of a civil engineering group. The software developers who ignore standard techniques will find it difficult to build on the learnings and experience of others. They are more likely to repeat mistakes common in the system development process, i.e., "those who fail to learn from history are doomed to repeat its mistakes." Their project is just as likely to be completed months early or months late. The project may come in over budget or under budget. The information system may meet the business needs for which it was developed and delight its end users or it may be viewed as a complete waste. The point is that when systems analysts and programmers have complete freedom to develop a system in any manner they please, the results are highly unpredictable.

Quality Management

Quality is the degree to which the attributes of a product or service enable it to meet the needs of its users. **Quality management** addresses how to define, measure, and refine the quality of the information system development process and the deliverables that result. Quality man-

Real World Perspective

Typical Software Product— Disclaimer of Warranty

The ABCXYZ* Company does not warrant that the ABCXYZ software in conjunction with any other hardware or software or services provided under this contract, addendum, or separate agreement, will operate to solve any general or specific customer problem, or meet any general or specific need.

The ABCXYZ Company shall not be liable to the customer for any liability, loss, or damage caused or alleged to be caused directly or indirectly, incidentally or consequently, by any of the software or services provided hereunder by an inadequacy thereof or deficiency or defect therein. In no event shall the ABCXYZ Company be liable for loss of profits, indirect, special, or consequential, or other damages arising out of any breach of this contract or obligations under this contract.

*The name of the company has been changed. □

agement's objective is to help system developers deliver high-quality systems—systems that indeed meet the needs of their users.

Some of the **quality attributes** of interest to the users of information systems are: correctness, reliability, robustness, maintainability, flexibility, availability, and efficiency, to name just a few. It is also likely that some of the attributes are more important than others, depending on the purpose of the information system and the needs of the end users. Efficiency, reliability, and correctness may be the most important quality factors for an interactive system used to process customer orders. Maintainability, flexibility, and portability (the ability to run on more than one vendor's hardware or operating system) may be the most important quality factors for a batch processing payroll system designed to have a long life. Thus the required quality characteristics for a successful project must be explicitly defined at the start of the project and all efforts should be directed at meeting those quality objectives. Exhibit 9.6 lists some quality attributes of frequent interest.

A **defect** is any error that, if not removed, would cause a system to fail to meet any of the quality attributes of interest to its users. The most obvious errors are ones that cause the system to fail to run to completion or that cause it to produce incorrect or incomplete results. Other kinds of defects are not as obvious, but are just as important. For instance, the system may not be able to perform certain functions that the user expected or the performance of certain functions may be awkward and inefficient for the users. The system frequently may be unavailable during times the end users expect to use it. The system may require more maintenance than expected, or it takes a lot of effort to locate and fix an error in the system.

Exhibit 9.6
Quality Attributes
of Frequent Interest

Availability	The percent of scheduled time the system is actually available for use.
Correctness	Extent to which a system meets its specifications and fulfills the objectives of its end users.
Efficiency	The amount of computing resources required by a system to perform a function.
Flexibility	The amount of effort required to modify the system.
Integrity	Extent to which access to software or data by unauthorized people can be controlled.
Interoperability	Effort required to link one system with another.
Maintainability	Effort required to locate and fix an error in the system.
Portability	Effort required to transfer a system from one hardware and/or software configuration to another.
Reliability	Extent to which a system can be expected to perform its intended function with the required precision.
Reusability	Extent to which portions of the system can be used in another system.
Testability	Effort required to test the system to ensure that it performs its intended function.

Many different researchers who have studied defects have determined that roughly two-thirds of system defects are the result of errors made in the early stages of an information system project (analysis and design) (Boehm, reference 1). Only one-third are the result of errors made in the later stage (construction).

An example of a defect made in the analysis stage of a payroll system is to incompletely state the process for determining overtime hours. The systems analyst may know that all hours over 40 hours in one week are counted as overtime hours. However, the systems analyst may fail to note that, for this particular company, all hours over eight hours in one day also count as overtime. This defect could be undetected until employee complaints and/or lawsuits over underpayment are filed with the controller.

An error detected in a later stage of the system development necessitates some level of rework for the preceding stages. For example, an error uncovered during system testing requires redoing portions of the analysis and design; changing the code of one or more programs; debugging, documenting and unit testing the changed program(s); modifying and correcting affected system documentation, (e.g., the User's Manual); and repeating portions of the system testing. Taking into account the amount of effort to perform this rework, it is easy to see that errors detected late in the life cycle are more difficult and costly to remove than errors detected earlier.

Studies at IBM, TRW, and GTE have shown very significant increases in the relative cost to remove defects (Boehm, reference 1). The results of these studies are summarized in Exhibit 9.7. Note that re-

Exhibit 9.7
The Relative Cost of Removing Software Defects

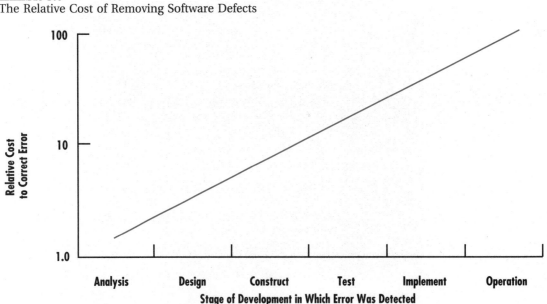

moving a defect found during the construction phase costs ten times more than if the defect had been detected and removed during the early steps of analysis. Also, removing a defect found in a system that is in operation will cost ten times more than if the defect were found and removed during system testing or a hundred times more than if the defect were detected and removed during analysis!

The results of these studies may be simplified as follows: The effort and cost associated with removing system defects increases dramatically as the project progresses from the early steps of analysis through the design stage into construction and finally into operation. Thus the primary goal of any software quality program must be the *early* detection and removal of defects.

Enlightened IT managers are beginning to realize that establishing effective processes to ensure that quality is built into systems adds little, if any, additional cost to the initial development of most systems. While additional effort is required to identify and remove defects early on in the project, this effort is much less extensive and costly than the effort required to identify and fix errors in a faulty system delivered to unhappy end users! Thus there may actually be a net reduction in effort when sound quality management practices are followed. Looking beyond the initial development phase, significant reductions in the cost and effort associated with system maintenance (including enhancements and fixes to the original system) are possible if the initial system is built to a high level of quality (Exhibit 9.8). Since most IT organizations spend more resources on system maintenance than on new system development, there is a strong incentive to deliver high-quality systems.

Exhibit 9.8
Cost to Build and
Maintain a Quality
System

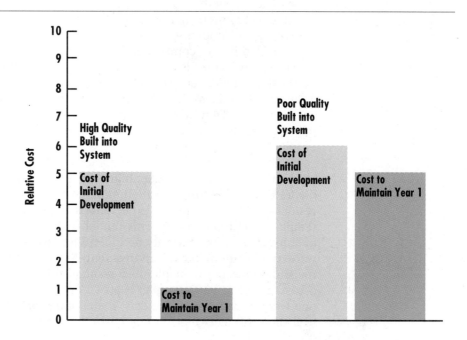

Real World Perspective

Bugs in Windows

Complaints about Unrecoverable Application Errors (UAE) in Windows have plagued Microsoft ever since the firm released the graphical user interface in 1990. Despite rave reviews overall (millions of users worldwide have purchased Windows), microcomputer managers, independent software vendors, and end users have complained about UAE messages that frequently come up while running Windows applications.

Paying the Price

The need for a major change in its computer systems drove Blue Cross and Blue Shield of Wisconsin to launch an ambitious information systems project. They needed an integrated computer system to handle business claims processing, enrollment processing, and cost containment. The project was completed on time,

but had one major problem: it didn't work correctly. At one point the system sent out hundreds of checks to a nonexistent town in Wisconsin. The company says $60 million in overpayments or duplicate checks were sent out in the system's first year. The debacle cost Blue Cross and Blue Shield 35,000 members.

Going from Bad to Worse

The Hamilton County Recorder's office signed a $900,000 contract to streamline office procedures with a new information system. The completed system turned a bad situation worse—backlogs in processing real estate titles grew from eight weeks to eighteen months! A group of lawyers and property owners, angry with the computer system, has vowed to file a costly taxpayer's suit.

Why Follow a Methodology

The demand for new systems far exceeds the capabilities of most information systems organizations to deliver them. Many systems being developed today are more complex than in the past. This results in information system organizations delivering systems much later than planned, and often in the systems not matching their users' needs. According to Coopers & Lybrand, 20 percent of all software projects are canceled before completion, 60 percent experience significant cost and schedule overruns, and 75 percent experience quality problems.

Business managers would like the development process to be more manageable and less dependent on the skills of individual analysts and programmers. They would like a well-defined, systematic process capable of delivering quality systems on time, every time. That is the goal of following a methodology.

Work done by the Software Engineering Institute at Carnegie Mellon Institute to develop a Capability Maturity Model for Software demonstrates how the use of a methodology can help ensure that project results closely meet users' expectations on timing, cost, and quality (Paulk, et al., reference 3). This model (Exhibit 9.9) defines five levels of software process maturity and identifies issues most critical to software quality and process improvement. As the maturity level increases, the difference between planned results and actual results decreases across projects. For example, if an IT organization operating at level one were to execute 50 projects, there would be a wide range in how well these projects met timing, cost, and quality expectations. Only a

Exhibit 9.9
The Five Steps of Software Process Maturity

Stages	Description
Initial	The software process is characterized as ad hoc, and occasionally even chaotic. Few processes are defined, and success depends on individual effort.
Repeatable	Basic project management processes are established to track cost, schedule, and functionality. The necessary process discipline is in place to repeat earlier successes on projects with similar applications.
Defined	The software process for both management and engineering activities are documented, standardized, and integrated into a standard software process for the organization. All projects use an approved, tailored version of the organization's standard software process for developing and maintaining software.
Managed	Detailed measures of the software process and product quality are collected. Both the software process and products are quantitatively understood and controlled.
Optimizing	Continuous process improvement is enabled by quantitative feedback from the process and from piloting innovative ideas and technologies.

very few would come close to meeting all three expectations. Most would miss one or more expectations by a considerable amount. However, if an IT organization operating at level five were to execute the same 50 projects, most projects would come very close to meeting all three expectations. Only a few would miss one or more expectations by very much. This is because a level five organization uses a carefully constructed software process (methodology) operating within known parameters, and the selection of the completion date is based on extensive historical data the organization possesses about their process and on their performance in applying it. Thus use of a methodology is one way to ensure predictable project results.

From the perspective of the IT organization, the use of a methodology provides a common, standard approach in which people can be trained to deliver high-quality systems. A methodology provides a standard set of terms to convey information about a project such as what stage it is in, what will occur during this stage, what deliverables need to be produced, and so on. This improves communication and reduces confusion and misunderstandings. The methodology provides time proven techniques and tools to produce the necessary deliverables. It also provides guidelines for checking the quality of these deliverables. In other words, the use of a methodology changes the system development effort from an art, which few may master, to a science that many can accomplish.

■ INFORMATION ENGINEERING

The term **information engineering** was first used in courses conducted at the IBM Systems Research Institute in the early 1970s. The original work on the subject, "Information Engineering," (reference 4) was coauthored by James Martin and Clive Finkelstein. Information engineering emerged as a systems development methodology in the 1980s. According to the Second Annual Report on CASE, published by CASE Research Corp., in Belvue, Washington, information engineering has become the leading system development methodology.

Key Features

Four key features clearly distinguish information engineering from other systems development methodologies. These features are summarized in Exhibit 9.10 and discussed below.

■ Information engineering applies the structure and discipline of engineering-like techniques, such as top down planning, data modeling, and process modeling, to the firm as a whole to develop information systems. This approach avoids the business-as-usual jumble of disjointed information systems that cannot work together (Exhibit 9.11). Indeed, information engineering provides a total framework for managing multiple concurrent or sequential projects while ensuring that the systems and their data bases fit together.

■ Information engineering provides a proven **process** and common terminology that allows business managers and IT professionals to communicate effectively and reach a consensus regarding strategic business plans and supporting systems plans. This ensures that information systems resources are spent developing the right systems at the right time. It avoids spending time and energy addressing low-priority business needs while more important needs go unmet.

■ Information engineering focuses on identifying and meeting business needs—not on defining system requirements. The delivery of such business-oriented systems ensures the effectiveness of the IT function. Business managers and systems analysts must form effective working partnerships to build effective systems. The active participation of business managers and end users throughout the information engineering process is required. Information engineering is not successful in organizations where

Exhibit 9.10
Key Features and
Benefits of
Information
Engineering

Feature	Benefit
Applies engineering-like techniques to the whole firm	Ensures systems and data bases fit together
Proven process for strategic business planning	Ensures right projects are worked
Focuses on identifying and meeting business needs	Ensures business needs are met
Uses data-driven development approach	Provides flexibility to support business changes

Exhibit 9.11
Information Engineering Work Breakdown Structure and Key Activities

Stage	Key Activities—Build System	Additional Activities—Install Package
Information Strategy Planning	Identify projects required to achieve vision Identify area of business for further study	
Business Area Analysis	Document fundamental business processes Assess need for business reengineering Define projects and data bases needed	Determine that package will meet needs
Design	Define users' business requirements Define how users will interact with system Develop details needed for programming	Develop an RFP Choose vendor and package Define necessary customization
Construction/Implementation	Build system to specification Test system components Test integrated system Prepare end users Conduct user acceptance test	
Maintenance	Make changes required for new environment Implement fixes	Add enhancements

business managers and end users are not involved in their information systems projects.

■ Information engineering is a **data-driven approach.** Thus systems analysts must focus on defining the data requirements of the system that they are building before defining the processes that will use the data. The data needed for strategic management of the firm are far more stable than the processes that gather and use it. When the data bases are built correctly, they will be flexible enough to support changes in business operations without major changes to the supporting systems.

Stages

The information engineering stages are briefly summarized here. They are discussed in more detail in Chapters 10 and 11.

Information Strategy Planning

Information engineering begins with the definition of a vision of the future for the firm. A plan is developed that specifies the sequence of related projects required to build the data bases and the information systems required to achieve this vision and meet the needs of the business. Areas of the business are selected to undergo analysis, the next stage of the information engineering process.

Business Area Analysis

In the **business area analysis** stage, key business elements within a defined business area are examined. The systems analysts use the analysis to create a basic system framework in preparation for stage three—

the detailed systems design. Business area analysis ensures that the information systems and data bases serving the business area integrate and work well together. The fundamental business processes supporting the area under study are also evaluated to see how well they meet the business needs. It is during this stage that the need for business process reengineering is considered.

It is also during the business area analysis stage that consideration is given to using a software package to automate the business processes rather than developing an original system. For many types of business needs, particularly in the financial and accounting areas, software packages that provide a large proportion of the functionality required by the users already exist. In general, the more common the business application, the more likely usable software is available. For instance, hundreds of software packages are available to perform payroll and accounts receivable functions. The software vendor usually bundles the application software with user documentation that explains how to get the system to do what the user wants it to do, system documentation that explains the technical workings of the application, user training in using the application to achieve desired results, and ongoing application support. This whole bundle is often called a software package.

Strategic planning and business area analysis create an information systems framework within which individual systems are designed and constructed so that they will work together. The plans and models in the framework are adjusted as systems are built or purchased and as business needs change.

Design

During the **design** stage, the project team, consisting of business managers, end users, systems analysts, and programmers, figures out exactly how the system will work and what the end users must do to use it. The team writes specifications that will be used later to construct the system. The design specifications document the precise form and content of the data base, screens, reports, programs, jobs, and other components of the system. Through years of experience, two powerful techniques for defining user needs have emerged: **joint application design** (JAD) and prototyping.

JAD involves structured group interviews of end users and managers from the various organizations that provide input to, use, or obtain output from the system. The interviews are led by a trained facilitator who possesses excellent leadership and communication skills. Because several people familiar with the same problems, issues, and opportunities are working together and building off one another's ideas, stronger, better system solutions are found.

A prototype technique is a trial or experimental version of the system. Its functionality closely matches the user requirements and business needs. As part of the prototype effort, proposed screen layouts and user dialogs are constructed. End users then use the prototype and provide feedback to the systems analysts and programmers. This feed-back is then used to refine the prototype so that it more closely matches the end user's needs.

If a software package is to be part of the solution, the package is selected and tested to determine whether it performs as expected. Any necessary changes to the software package (customization require-ments) are identified and included in the overall design. The first step in the software selection process is to define user requirements and perform an initial evaluation of vendors and packages. User require-ments are defined and communicated to vendors in a document called a Request for Proposal (RFP).

Once the design team has determined what needs to be con-structed, they estimate the resources and time required to build and fully implement a production version of the prototype. The team out-lines detailed strategies and plans for the construction stage of the proj-ect. This outline, along with the estimated benefits of the system, are used to provide a cost justification for the system. The team tries to determine if the expected benefits of the proposed system outweigh the costs of building it, operating it, maintaining it, and training people to use it.

Construction

During the **construction** stage, a working system is built according to the design specifications. In addition the organization is trained to use the system effectively. The systems analysts and programmers acquire and install any necessary computer hardware and equipment. They code, compile, debug, test, and integrate system components. They also may have to develop and test additional "one time only" programs to convert historical data into the format required for the new system. If a software package is installed, coding and testing is required for any changes to the package.

To prepare the organization to use the new system, the project team works on selling the system to the organization. The project team develops the required procedures, prepares system documentation, and trains end users and IT staff in the operation and maintenance of the system. They identify the positive, immediate, and certain **(PIC) benefits** that individuals will achieve through use of the new system. They also identify and overcome resistance to the new system. Often, conversion to a new system means changes in job roles, responsibili-ties, and how people are evaluated and rewarded. These changes must be identified and explained to those affected.

A critical aspect of the construction stage is the user acceptance test. During this test, the end users determine if the system indeed meets the business needs it was intended to address and if the system operates as expected. Obviously, failure of the user acceptance test is a serious setback for the project and means that major reworking or, perhaps, even abandoning the project is necessary.

Maintenance

System maintenance is defined as all changes made to a system after it has been installed as a working system. Each change that is made requires some level of repetition of the analysis, design, and construction life cycle. System maintenance can be broken into three types: (1) add enhancements to the product—improve the way the system operates or provide new capabilities, (2) make changes required to allow the system to run in a new environment (e.g., convert the system from running under one operating system to another), and (3) implement fixes to correct problems (bugs) in the system.

Real World Perspective

Strategic Planning and Business Area Analysis at Ryder

Ryder Systems, Inc., a $4 billion company with automotive, leasing, rental, and carrier divisions, faced shrinking markets, demanding customers, and aggressive competition. Senior management led a strategic planning study and identified three corporate goals for the firm: reduce costs, add true value to other Ryder services, and promote overall quality. The strategic planning process also confirmed that technology is a major factor in helping Ryder differentiate their service. All Ryder competitors have good trucks, keep them running well, and use good drivers; the distinguishing factor is technology and how it is employed to meet business needs.

During business area analysis, managers focused on identifying projects that would help achieve the corporate goals. These projects became the key strategic projects of the company. The strategic planning and business area analysis process eliminated working pet projects or projects that were not consistent with and supportive of corporate goals. The following projects were identified and were to be executed over a few years.

Ryder leases trucks, maintains vehicles owned by customers, and in some cases handles all the warehousing and distribution services for corporate customers such as Coca-Cola, Sears, and Xerox Corp. A logistics management system was needed to support this business aspect. Such a system would address fuel, drivers, insurance, and virtually everything but the product being delivered.

To bid on and win business, Ryder had to show not only a lower price but a higher level of efficiency than their competition. A system was needed to support the bidding process. This system needed built-in heuristics that allowed Ryder consultants to examine a customer's operations and find better ways to manage the fleet and distribute products. It would also analyze difficult distribution problems and create proposals to meet customer needs.

Keeping track of a fleet of 35,000 trucks and 5,000 dealers is difficult. A system was needed that would eliminate the paper pileups, resultant confusion, and needless expenses associated with maintaining a large fleet. The system would also track reservations and inventory, update rate information, and track sales.

Ryder managers also needed a yield management system that operated in a manner similar to the airlines' system for pricing seats. This system would help Ryder react to the competition and take advantage of price elasticity. It would also help Ryder balance their fleet by moving trucks from an area of surplus to one of scarcity.

The company also identified automation of its sales force as a strategic project. Ryder planned to equip its sales force with laptop personal computers to support analysis of customer needs and to develop more creative and competitive proposals.

Real World Perspective

System Maintenance Problems for the FAA

In January 1992, the General Accounting Office (GAO) reported that more than 1,700 of the nearly 4,000 software problems reported at air traffic control centers since 1987 were still unresolved. Of those, the Federal Aviation Agency

(FAA) estimated, nearly three-quarters of these problems could delay flights by impairing the air traffic controllers' ability to track aircraft. The GAO found the average FAA software bug remained uncorrected for 18 months.

■ ALTERNATIVE METHODOLOGIES

Over the years, a number of different system development methodologies have evolved. These methodologies include the waterfall approach, end user development, prototyping, and object oriented. Each of these approaches is briefly discussed below.

It is difficult for the nonpractitioner to appreciate why so many different methodologies exist. One reason for this variety is that **practitioners** frequently found fault with one approach and would modify it to create a new methodology. For instance, the waterfall approach is not used by those who have found the prototype approach superior. On the other hand the information engineering methodology tries to combine the best elements of both the waterfall approach and prototype approach. Such experimentation is to be expected in a discipline that is not yet 50 years old. Clearly, today much disagreement exists among practitioners as to which approach is best and if one approach should be used to the exclusion of all others. This disagreement is more evidence that system development is still evolving from an art to a science.

Another reason for the variety of system development methodologies is that certain methodologies are best suited for building certain kinds of systems under certain circumstances. For example, the waterfall methodology is excellent for building basic transaction processing systems whose requirements can be defined prior to writing code for the system. However, as firms began looking at purchasing software packages, new methodologies arose to fit these new situations.

Waterfall

The traditional or waterfall approach has been used for decades to develop bread-and-butter commercial business applications such as payroll, general ledger, accounts payable, accounts receivable, sales reporting, order processing, and inventory control. During the waterfall life cycle, the work to be done is divided into well-defined stages, and the work progress is managed and controlled by formal project management methods. The work progress is linear, meaning that once a stage is complete, work continues on to the next stage with no rework or iteration of the preceding stages (Exhibit 9.12). The waterfall meth-

Exhibit 9.12
Waterfall System Development Approach

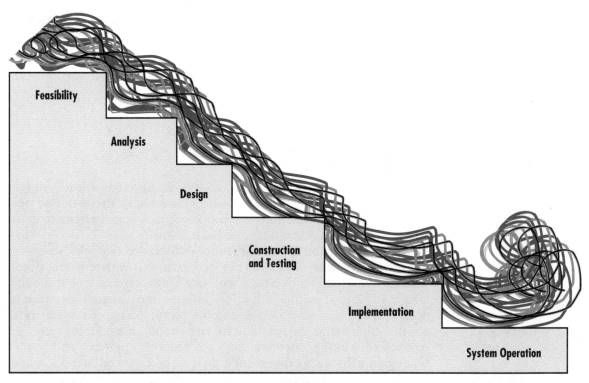

odology is most effective in the development of systems with requirements that are well understood and can be fully specified before any detail design or coding of programs begins. Note that this methodology assumes that the project has already been identified as worthy of addressing, thus the waterfall methodology does not include strategic planning in its scope. Because of this lack of a strategic planning step, organizations adopting the waterfall methodology need to implement a separate strategic planning process to identify and prioritize potential information systems projects.

Feasibility

Each project begins with an investigation of the problem or opportunity to determine if it is worth addressing. Business managers must determine the business benefits to be gained. The system developers then develop a rough estimate of the costs to implement a system to address the problem. Finally a decision is made based on this preliminary cost/benefit analysis as to whether the problem is worth addressing. If there is sufficient rationale to work the project, work continues into the next stage.

Analysis

Business managers and system developers work together to explicitly define what the system will do. The definition can be expressed in many different forms, from a simple list of business requirements to complex diagrams of required new business processes and data models. The estimate of benefits and costs associated with the project are then refined. Typically, several alternatives are evaluated. Often a much less expensive solution is developed. The alternative may not meet all the defined business requirements, but business managers often will sacrifice some requirements if a much lower cost solution can be delivered sooner. The "go/no go" decision is reviewed. Sometimes the project is canceled based on updated cost/benefit data. Assuming that the decision is to proceed, the system requirements are frozen—they cannot be changed without renegotiation of project cost and schedule.

Design

During the design stage the business managers and system developers define exactly how the system will work. Detailed technical specifications are written.

Construction and Testing

Programmers then use the technical specifications to write the programs for the new system. Each individual program is tested to ensure that it works as expected. Business managers may get involved in this stage when questions arise as to what the real business requirements are; such questions arise when the written system requirements and technical specifications are unclear or incomplete.

Implementation

During the implementation stage, conversion to the new system occurs. People are trained in their new roles, in the operation of new equipment, and on new procedures and the new software. A key factor in this stage is the user acceptance test. If the user acceptance test is not passed, full system operation is delayed until the system can pass the test.

System Operation

The system is operated to meet the business objectives for which it was developed.

System Maintenance and Enhancement

During the life of every system, changes that keep the system operating efficiently and effectively are needed. Often the reason for making changes to the system is that the business needs have changed. Business managers and system developers review these needed changes as yet another potential systems project, and the life cycle begins again with a feasibility study to determine the advisability of investing time and effort to implement these changes.

End User Development

Increasingly, end users have been taking a direct role in developing their own systems to serve their own area of business. Typically, these applications are small systems with no requirement to interface to other systems.

System development is just one of many responsibilities for end users, and a minor one at that. Thus end users do not need nor can they be expected to use the comprehensive system development methodology intended for full-time professional system developers. Instead, the information systems organization provides end users with help by identifying appropriate system building tools that can be easily used and by providing training in their use. Most information systems organizations also establish a central support group (e.g., an information center) to provide assistance and advice to end users. A typical end user development approach is outlined in Exhibit 9.13. More complete coverage of end user development is given in Chapter 13.

Prototyping

The **prototyping approach** to system development involves a highly iterative process of building, using, evaluating, and refining a system to improve mutual understanding of the system between the system developers and system users. This approach to defining system requirements is appropriate when users cannot prespecify exactly what they want the system to do. Prototyping may also be used to develop a working version of a key subsystem to support testing to see if stringent performance requirements (e.g., average response time of less than 2.5 seconds for all commonly performed transactions) can be met.

Prototyping is also effectively used to explore alternative user interfaces for a system, for example, exploring different input formats, screen displays, and report formats.

Practitioners have learned that the traditional waterfall approach and prototyping can be combined (Exhibit 9.14). The feasibility and analysis stages of the waterfall method can be used to define most of the requirements for the system and a prototype approach is then used

---

Exhibit 9.13
End User
Development
Process

Identify Need or Opportunity
Identify Appropriate End User Computing Tool
Develop Solution
Modify Solution
Formalize Solution

Exhibit 9.14
Prototyping Life Cycle

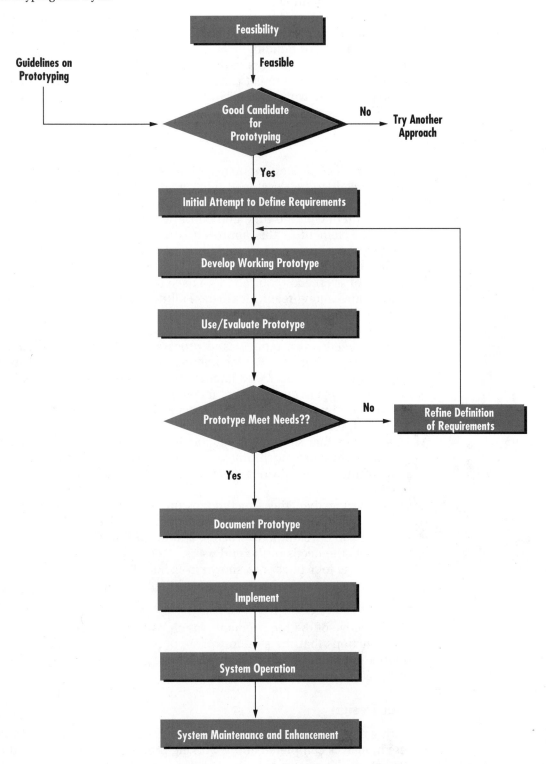

to refine user interface requirements and develop a working version of the system in minimal time.

It is more difficult to use formal project planning and control techniques with the prototyping approach because it is never known how many iterations of building, using, evaluating, and refining will be required. Business managers and system developers must use caution, however, as it is easy to get caught up in a vicious circle of build, use, evaluate, refine, without realizing the diminishing rate of return on subsequent changes.

RAD

Rapid Application Development (RAD) is used when an information system needs to be developed quickly and with fewer resources. It is based on a number of management techniques that have proven effective in reducing the time and effort needed to build systems.

A key element of this approach is working with a small team of end users, systems analysts, and programmers who are fully dedicated to the completion of the effort. Keeping the team small reduces the amount of overhead required to manage the team and improves communication among team members. Full dedication to the effort eliminates interruptions and distractions.

The team uses JAD sessions to involve end users in quickly defining business needs, data models, and process models of the desired system. These definitions are documented in Computer Aided Software Engineering tools (discussed later in this chapter) that are capable of automatically generating program code.

The team must work within a strict and very short time period (no more than three months) to develop a working version of the system. This ensures that something tangible is available for the end users to evaluate before too much time and effort is expended. If the early versions of the system do not meet the end users' needs, the system is modified.

Taken together, these techniques promote better communication between end users and system developers, involve end users in all stages of the development process, and ensure that the resulting system meets the needs of the end users.

RAD has four phases as shown in Exhibit 9.15.

Requirements Planning

The objective of the requirement planning phase is to define the business functions that the system will support, specify system scope, develop a preliminary cost/benefit analysis, and develop high-level data and process models.

User Design

During the user design phase, the detailed design of the data and process models is completed and a working prototype of the critical components of the system is built.

Exhibit 9.15
RAD Life Cycle

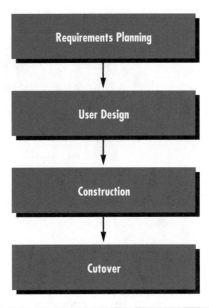

Construction

Skilled system developers build a portion of the system within a tight time constraint. The development team includes end users who help refine the requirements. The team also prepares for system cutover (next phase).

Cutover

The goal of the cutover phase is to convert to the new system. Activities include user training, data base conversion, and system cutover.

Object-Oriented Development

Object-oriented development is the hot new methodology of the mid-1990s. The object-oriented approach enables systems developers to create software that is readily comprehended and used by others. Unlike more traditional programming methods that are based on concepts such as data flow or mathematical logic, object-oriented development directly models the business process (Exhibit 9.16). Programs perform computations by passing messages between objects, which are computer analogs of entities in the real world.

An object consists of programming code that combines or encapsulates data and instructions about the operations to be performed on that data. The code describes all the significant attributes of the object and all the actions that the object may be called on to perform. When an operation involving the object is performed, a message is sent to the object. The message need only identify the operation to be performed—how it is to be performed is already embedded within the

Exhibit 9.16
Object-Oriented
Development

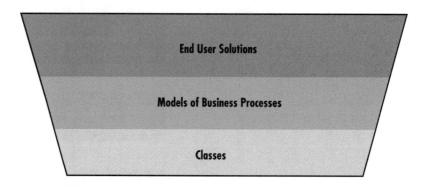

instructions (called methods) that are part of the object. For example, a class of objects is employees. Each object has data about the employee (e.g., social security number, name, department number, etc.), and there are operations that can be performed on the employee data (e.g., change salary, change department, add dependent, etc.).

Once an object has been created, it can be used to build similar objects that have the same behaviors and characteristics. Objects that are derived or related to one another are said to form a class. Each class contains specific instructions or methods that are unique to that class. Developers can create subclasses of objects that retain all the attributes of the parent class but have characteristics that are unique to that subclass. For example, the class employee may be broken into two subclasses: nonexempt (those who are paid hourly and are subject to hourly wage laws) and exempt (those who are paid on a monthly basis and are not subject to hourly wage laws). Subclasses can be further broken down into additional subclasses. For example, the subclass nonexempt could be broken into two sub-subclasses: full-time and part-time. In each instance, the subclass inherits all the capabilities of the classes above it. This method of passing traits down to subclasses is called **inheritance.**

Breaking down an application into entities and relationships that are meaningful to end users is a common technique in conventional software development methodologies. Unlike conventional development, however, object-oriented development preserves this same decomposition through the design and implementation phases. This makes the software intelligible to business managers who understand the business processes addressed. It also means that objects can be reused in developing new applications for the same business area. Being able to reuse a basic object and just add code for those characteristics that are specific to the new subclass saves much time and effort in the development and maintenance of systems.

Object-oriented development becomes even more efficient as the development organization builds libraries of reusable objects. With the libraries, updating code becomes much easier. If the original design of

Exhibit 9.17
Work Breakdown
Structure for
Object-Oriented
Development

Design Model of Business Activity
   Identify Potential Objects
   Identify Data
   Identify Operations to be Performed on Data
   Define Usage Scenarios

Construct Classes
   Check Libraries for Object Classes that Can Be Reused
   Modify Existing Object Classes to Create Useful New Subclasses
   Construct Required New Object Classes

Assemble Classes into Working Model
   Assemble Completed Classes
   Use Usage Scenarios to Test Assembly

Add Required Interfaces
   Develop End User Interfaces to System
   Develop Interfaces to Other Systems
   Test Interfaces

a parent class is modified, all members of the class automatically change to reflect the modification.

The differences between conventional and object-oriented development are significant. For those used to conventional system development, changing to the abstract approach of object-oriented development can be extremely difficult. There is at least a six-month learning curve before a developer can demonstrate any real expertise with the new object-oriented development approach.

Exhibit 9.17 shows how an object-oriented development approach would work in developing a new information system.

Design Model of Business Activity

The first step in developing a new information system is to design an object-based model that provides a simplified representation of the business process being supported. This step integrates the analysis and design phases of the traditional waterfall methodology. The team designing a new business process and the supporting computer systems must identify three things: the potential objects, the data, and the operations to be performed. The team must include people with first-hand knowledge of the business activity being modeled (i.e., business managers). The design team must also include software specialists who fully understand object technology. Once the business managers have worked up a basic model, the technical members of the team take over and drive the model down into a detail design. It is up to them to define the format of messages that objects send to each other, search for abstract classes that factor out common responsibilities, and develop the relationships in which a single class in the model can be subclassed to handle special cases.

A key part of the first step is to define usage scenarios that identify the various ways the work flows through the business model. These scenarios are used during structured walkthroughs in which members of the team play the roles of different objects. The corrections and improvements to the model that these walkthroughs produce allow most design defects to be eliminated before any code is written. At the end of this step the development team has a preliminary plan for the system that includes data models, preliminary object classes, and a high-level architecture specifying how the objects operate together.

Construct Classes

The second step in the process is to construct classes. Developers first check internal and external libraries for object classes that may be re-used. In some cases, existing classes can be modified to meet specialized needs. If the required modifications are unique to the current model, the existing class is used to create a new subclass to meet the specialized needs. If wholly new classes are required, the development team decides whether to build the new classes with internal resources, hire outside experts to create the new object classes, or purchase the new classes from object-development firms. Class construction includes comprehensive testing to ensure that every class is free of defects and fulfills all defined requirements. These test routines are stored with the class and rerun anytime the class is modified.

When a model is properly designed, all its classes are developed in isolation of each other. This means that a small design team, all of whom work independently, can generate the requirements for tens or hundreds of programmers. The class constructors must be good programmers, but they don't need to be experts in object technology. The class constructors are concerned primarily with coding individual functions and managing instance variables.

Assemble Classes into Working Model

The third step is to develop a working model. The completed classes are returned to the modeling team to assemble into a working model. The model is then tested to ensure that it works as expected. There is much communication between the modelers and class constructors as design errors, coding problems, and miscommunications are identified and corrected. The usage scenarios defined in the first step are used extensively for testing.

Add Required Interfaces

The final step in the process is to add required interfaces. The interfaces to be developed include screens, reports, graphical summaries, drill-down capabilities, and other useful functions. These activities can be carried out very efficiently with object-oriented interface development tools. Thus interface builders, like class constructors, need only minimal expertise in object-oriented technology. Their primary requirement is to be able to communicate well with managers and translate the manager's requests into simple, usable interfaces.

Real World Perspective

Object-Oriented Development at J. P. Morgan

The investment banking industry is highly competitive with new trading and financial products being introduced daily. The life span of these products is measured in weeks. The first two to three weeks after a product is introduced is usually its most profitable time period. In this pressure cooker environment, the time it takes to bring new products to market is a critical success factor.

As each new product is introduced, it requires some level of information system support to provide essential customer services and to generate reports to meet banking requirements. J. P. Morgan, the New York investment bank, was determined that the time to develop such supporting software would not slow down its introduction of new products. As a result, the firm is committed to converting to the object-oriented development approach to develop software. This change has enabled system developers to put new software together quickly using objects from software created to support previous products.

■ COMPUTER AIDED SYSTEMS ENGINEERING TOOLS

Definitions

Computer Aided Software Engineering (**CASE**) tools describe a wide range of tools that support the activities performed throughout the planning, analysis, design, construction, and maintenance system development life cycle (Exhibit 9.18). In this text, the term CASE tools excludes compilers, programming languages, and fourth-generation languages, but does include the following tools:

Strategic planning tools help management identify business needs by business area. These tools help the organization identify which projects are the most important to execute and in what sequences the various projects should be worked.

Upper CASE tools support the analysis and design stages. They provide graphics and text facilities to create and maintain data and modern analysis and design techniques. They help document system requirements, develop and maintain data and business process models, and create simulated interactive user dialogs. Some upper CASE tools have built-in rules or expert systems that provide error checking, consistency checking, analysis, and cross referencing, thus improving the quality of deliverables produced. For example, the CASE tool edits a data model and highlights any errors it detects. The use of upper CASE tools enforces a more careful definition of user requirements and fuller evaluation of options, resulting in improved quality of the results and increased productivity of the people (both IT and business managers) involved in the system development effort.

Lower CASE tools support the design and construction stages of the system development process. These tools automate the development of physical models that describe the system and its data base. Automatic code generators convert the results of the physical design into code (e.g., COBOL, code to define and generate interactive screens and user dialogs, and data base definition and manipulation code) for

Exhibit 9.18
CASE Tool Support for the System Development Process

Analysis			Design		Implementation				Operation	Maintenance Enhancement
Project Definition	Requirements Definition	Feasibility	Functional Design	Physical Design	Construct and Test	User Training	System Acceptance And Turnover	System Conversion		

Project Management

Upper CASE

Lower CASE

the target hardware and software environment. Again, the value of lower CASE tools is improved quality and productivity as the code that is generated is, ideally, free from any syntax errors and compiles error free the first time it is used.

Project management tools allow managers to estimate, schedule, track, and control the time and costs associated with a project. These tools help answer what-if questions based on various project, staffing, and schedule assumptions. The benefits of using project management tools are improved delivery of projects on time and on budget and better use of resources. These tools also include expert systems that help project managers review their approach to a project, assess and manage project risk, evaluate design and implementation options, and review the business case for executing the project. Thus there are fewer surprises with the project results.

A **repository,** also called a project dictionary and an **encyclopedia,** is where the information about the system being developed or modified is stored. The repository is actually a data base about an information system project. As such, it performs the functions of storing, organizing, updating, analyzing, and reporting all data and objects needed to create, enhance, or maintain an information system (Exhibit 9.19).

Data are collected and used to update the repository using the techniques associated with each activity of each step of the project. The steps include a definition of the business area processes and organization,

Exhibit 9.19
Repository

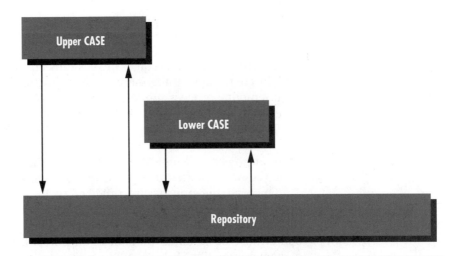

data and process models of the system, detailed definitions of each item, documentation of screens and reports, information about the methodology being used, project history, budgets, schedules, and so on.

The repository is the single, authoritative source of everything about a project. As such, it is a key asset to the project team. It is also invaluable when considering system changes associated with system maintenance. Each item in the repository is cross-referenced to all other components, such as programs, screens, files, and data bases. Thus it is possible to perform what is called **impact analysis:** If we change this object (e.g., length of a data item), what other objects (e.g., reports, screens, and programs) are affected?

Use of a repository helps achieve consistency among separate information system projects. The repository checks the accuracy, completeness, and consistency of the information it is given, with a precision far beyond that possible with manual techniques or text specifications.

The repository may run on a personal computer and store information about the objects associated with a single information system project. Other more powerful repository products are available that provide facilities for holding and managing the objects associated with many projects. Such large repositories must be stored on a computer that is easily accessible to all project teams.

Too often systems analysts and programmers reinvent the wheel. They unknowingly struggle to create a system or system component that has been created several times before. Major productivity gains result from employing reuseable designs, data models, or code. Reuseable objects can be cataloged in a repository so that they can be selected when needed and modified as required. Using a repository ensures information sharing that leads to tremendous improvements in software quality and productivity.

Use of CASE Tools

The various CASE tools may be used singly or may be combined to work together to increase quality and productivity during the building of information systems (exhibit 9.20).

During the analysis stage, the systems analyst uses an upper CASE tool to create and enter many objects into the repository (e.g., user requirements, process models, data models, report layouts, screen formats, data definitions, data editing rules, etc.).

During the design stage, the systems analyst uses a lower CASE tool to access the data in the repository and automatically generate a first-cut physical design of the system. The first-cut physical design is reviewed and updated using a lower CASE tool.

Once all the objects are finalized, a lower CASE tool is used to access the repository and generate program code and data base definition and manipulation code. Lower CASE tools currently generate somewhere between 25 percent to 99 percent of the code needed for a given application. It may still be necessary to write some of the code by hand or to modify the existing code. Provided that everything that preceded the code generation was done correctly, the information system should meet the needs of the users. The amount of effort required to test the system and be sure that it works as expected is greatly reduced.

A systems analyst using a CASE tool on an information systems project is similar to a manager using a word processor program to create a written recommendation. The word processor makes it easier to create and revise text. The built-in spell checker and grammar checker catch obvious errors. However, it is still possible to write a poor recommendation using a word processor program. So too is it possible to develop a poor system using CASE tools.

Exhibit 9.20
Advantages
Frequently
Associated with the
Use of CASE Tools

Leads to creation of high-quality, bug-free software

Reduces effort required to enhance and maintain systems

Reduces elapsed time and effort to develop systems

Helps enforce adherence to a standard system development methodology and recommended practices

Real World Perspective

Use of Information Engineering and CASE Tools at TWA

Trans World Airlines (TWA) instituted a frequent flier program in 1981. The original information system that supported the program was designed assuming 100,000 members. However, by 1987, TWA's program was so successful that over four million members were registered. A new frequent flier information system was required to handle the increased computing and reporting needs of the program.

Rather than just address the frequent flyer program in isolation, TWA followed the Information Engineering approach to define overall business needs. During the information strategy planning stage, the importance of a comprehensive customer data base became apparent. Such a data base was identified as the cornerstone, not just for the frequent flyer program, but for many other existing and proposed customer services.

The Information Engineering Facility (IEF) CASE tool from Texas Instruments was used to document both data and process models and system requirements. During the design and construction stages, the IEF was used to build the new frequent flyer system from the specifications defined in earlier stages.

Once the new frequent flyer system is successfully completed, TWA will develop the additional information systems defined in the planning and analysis stages. TWA will continue to use the Information Engineering methodology and IEF CASE tool in the design and construction of each new information system. Thus, the comprehensive customer data base that TWA saw as the cornerstone of its information systems strategic plan and that was begun with the frequent flyer system will be developed.

Summary

A system development methodology is a collection of postulates, rules, and guidelines that provides a standard, proven process for the planning, analysis, design, construction, and ongoing maintenance of information systems.

A complete system development methodology provides a work breakdown structure of what to do and when to do it, techniques for producing system deliverables, and guidelines to manage the quality of the results.

Allowing systems analysts and programmers complete freedom to develop a system leads to highly unpredictable results in terms of quality, cost, and schedule.

Quality is the degree to which the attributes of a product or service enable it to meet the needs of its users. The required quality characteristics vary from project to project and must be explicitly defined at the start of the project.

A defect is any error that, if not removed, would cause a system to fail to meet any of the quality objectives of interest to its users. Roughly two-thirds of system defects are the result of errors made in the early stages of an information system project.

The effort and cost associated with removing system defects increases dramatically as the project progresses from the early stages of planning and analysis into the later stages of construction and operation.

Information engineering is a system development methodology that divides the process of building a system into planning, analysis, design, and construction stages. It applies engineering-like techniques to the whole firm to develop information systems. It provides a proven process for strategic planning so that information system resources are spent working on the right projects at the right time. It focuses on identifying and meeting business needs—not on defining system requirements. It is a data-driven approach to developing information systems.

The use of a system development methodology helps management gain control over information system projects, allows system developers to deal with complex systems, helps the project team get off to a quick start, and avoids the mistakes of past projects.

System maintenance includes all changes made to a system after it has been installed and turned over to the end users as an operational system. Most IT organizations spend more resources on system maintenance than on new system development.

CASE tools support the activities performed during the planning, analysis, design, construction, implementation, and maintenance of systems. They include strategic planning tools; upper CASE tools to support analysis and design; lower CASE tools to support design, construction, and maintenance; project management tools; and a repository that stores information about the system.

In the hands of a well-trained systems analyst, a CASE tool can lead to the creation of high-quality software, reduce the effort and elapsed time to produce the system, and ensure adherence to a standard system development methodology and recommended practices.

The use of CASE tools does not guarantee quick, good results.

With object-oriented development, programs perform computations by passing messages between objects, which are computer analogs of entities in the real world.

An object consists of programming code that combines or encapsulates data and instructions about the operations to be performed on that data.

A Manager's Checklist

✔ Do you know if your IT organization follows a standard system development methodology? If so, is there any evidence that the methodology is helping to improve the quality of systems or productivity of system developers?

✔ Do you know if your IT organization is using CASE tools?

✔ Can you evaluate what stage in the capability maturity model your IT organization is at?

✔ Do you get involved in the IT projects in your area to ensure that the resulting system is one of high quality?

Key Terms

business area analysis
CASE
construction
data-driven approach
defect
deliverables
design
encyclopedia
high-quality system
impact analysis
information engineering
information strategy planning
inheritance
joint application design
lower CASE
methodology
object-oriented development
PIC benefits

practitioner
process
project management tools
prototyping
quality
quality attributes
quality management
repository
stage
steps
strategic planning tools
system acceptance test
system maintenance
tasks
techniques
upper CASE
work breakdown structure

Review Questions

1. Define the term system development methodology. Identify the three essential components of a robust methodology.

2. Define the terms software quality and software defect.

3. Why is it critical to identify and remove software defects as early as possible in the system development cycle?

4. Briefly discuss the role of the systems analyst in each of the stages of the information engineering approach.

5. Describe two techniques for defining the requirements of information system end users.

6. Define the term system maintenance. How much effort does the typical information systems organization put into system maintenance?

7. Define the term CASE.

8. Briefly describe the features of each type of CASE tool mentioned.

9. What are some of the potential benefits of using CASE?

Discussion Questions

1. Why are more and more organizations moving toward the use of a standard systems development methodology?

2. Why have different organizations adopted different system development methodologies?

3. Should information systems development be viewed as more of an art than a science? Why or why not?

4. Why don't all information systems projects have the same quality requirements?

5. How can the cost of a high-quality system actually be less than a low-quality system?

6. Do you think new systems analysts should be more involved in the planning and business analysis stages than is suggested in this chapter? Why or why not?

7. What advice can you offer to help sell the use of a new information system to its end users?

8. Should any information systems project be attempted without the use of a system development methodology and CASE tools?

9. Why is the repository such an important CASE tool?

10. If you were offered a position with a firm that did not employ a standard system development methodology and CASE tools, would you accept?

Recommended Readings

1. Boehm, Barry W. *Software Engineering Economics.* Englewood Cliffs, NJ: Prentice-Hall, 1981.

2. Jones, Capers. *Programming Productivity.* New York: McGraw-Hill, Inc., 1986.

3. Paulk, Mark C., Bill Curtis, Mary Beth Chrissis, and Charles V. Weber. "Capability Maturity Model for Software, Version 1.1." Pittsburg, PA: Software Engineering Institute, Carnegie Mellon University, February 1993.

4. Finkelstein, Clive and James Martin. *Information Engineering,* Volumes I and II. Lancashire, England: Savant Institute, 1981.

5. Martin, James. *Information Engineering, Book I, Introduction.* Englewood Cliffs, NJ: Prentice Hall, 1989.

6. Martin, James. *Information Engineering, Book II, Planning and Analysis.* Englewood Cliffs, NJ: Prentice Hall, 1989.

7. Martin, James. *Information Engineering, Book III, Design and Construction.* Englewood Cliffs, NJ: Prentice Hall, 1989.

8. Fairley, Richard E. *Software Engineering Concepts.* New York: McGraw-Hill, Inc., 1985.

9. King, David. *Current Practices in Software Development.* New York: Yourdon Press, 1984.

10. "Survey of MIS Quality." New York: John Diebold and Associates, 1988.

11. Layne, Richard, Bruce Caldwell, and Charles Pelton. "MIS Transformed." *InformationWEEK,* Issue 207 (Feb. 13, 1988).

12. *Handbook of Software Quality Assurance.* Eds. Gordon G. Schulmeyer and James I. McManus. New York: Van Nostrand Reinhold Company, 1987.

13. Perry, William E. *Quality Assurance for Information Systems: Methods, Tools, and Techniques.* Wellesley, MA: Q.E.D. Information Sciences, Inc., 1990.

14. Boehm, Barry W. "A Spiral Model of Software Development and Enhancement." *Computer* (May 1988).

15. Carlyle, Ralph Emmert. "Where Methodology Falls Short." *Datamation* (December 1, 1988).

16. Kerr, James M. "The Information Engineering Paradigm." *Journal of Systems Management* Vol. 42, No. 4, Issue No. 358 (April 1991).

17. Anonymous. "Product Review—Texas Instruments Information Engineering Facility—Part I." *CASE User* Vol. 1, No. 1 (July 1990).

18. Anonymous. "Product Review—Texas Instruments Information Engineering Facility—Part II." *CASE User* Vol. 1, No. 2 (Aug. 1990).

19. Hobler, William J. "Project Estimating with Information Engineering." *CASE User* Vol. 1, No. 3 (Sept. 1990).

20. Moblstrom, Dean. "Business-Driven Information Engineering." *CASE Trends* Vol. 3, No. 3 (May/June 1991).

A Manager's Dilemma

Poor Project Results

This was a disaster!! The new Order Entry System project team had just announced that the completion of the system was delayed—again. The project was originally scheduled to be completed in twelve months. However, two months prior to the original completion date, the project team announced a four-month delay. This announcement caught the Sales organization by surprise. They had already begun to close down some sales offices and transfer sales order entry clerks in anticipation of the new system. Now two months before the revised completion date, the project team announced another delay—three months this time!

Unfortunately, this is not the only project in trouble. The Finance organization is grumbling that the newly purchased General Ledger package does not meet the needs of the business. The new system is causing the staff to work overtime to complete their work.

As the recently appointed Manager of Application Development you are extremely concerned about these problems. Last month, as part of your initial orientation to these key projects, you asked the project managers of both efforts if they were using a system development methodology to help manage the projects. Both managers replied "yes," but now you wonder.

How would you proceed to verify if the project managers are using a system development methodology?

If there is a methodology in place, how will you determine if the project managers are really following it or if perhaps the methodology is faulty?

If neither manager is following a system development methodology, how would you motivate them to begin using one?

Could there be other causes for the delay in the Order Entry System and user dissatisfaction with the General Ledger System? How would you identify other possible causes?

Define a Methodology

Develop a methodology for a simple process with which you are familiar. Be sure to include a work breakdown structure, techniques, and quality management process. Share your methodology with someone and try to capture and incorporate his or her ideas for improvement.

Multiple Methodologies

The ATOZ Company's strategy for growth was to acquire other smaller companies. Each of these companies had system development staffs ranging from half a dozen to 50 or more people. As a result, there were pockets of system development people using various methodologies and CASE tools. A recent change in the information systems strategy called for central development of common corporate systems for the use of all organizational units. Will the existence of multiple methodologies and CASE tools help or hinder implementing this strategy? Why or why not?

Chapter 10

Information Technology Planning

Upon completion of this chapter, you will be able to:

1. Discuss the importance of IT strategic planning and the role of the business manager.

2. Outline a four-stage planning model and identify the goals and outputs of each stage.

3. Define the terms business process and business process reengineering.

4. State two criteria for evaluating if a business process should be reengineered.

5. Outline an effective process for identifying which of many potential IT projects should be worked.

Preview

It is more important to be effective and working on the right projects than it is to be efficient and working on the wrong projects. The key to being effective is management's involvement in developing a clear vision of where the firm is headed and supporting goals and strategies. With these firmly in mind, it is then possible to choose which of a multitude of potential information technology projects best supports the firm's goals and strategies and is "right to do." This chapter explains the need for an information technology strategic plan, outlines a process to develop such a plan, and provides guidelines useful for identifying project areas with high payoff potential. It also defines business process reengineering and how to determine if a business process needs to be reengineered.

Issues

1. Why is an IT plan needed?
2. What are the key elements of the IT plan?
3. How is a good IT plan developed?

Trade-offs

1. How long should be spent developing the IT plan versus executing it?
2. How do you identify which business areas require further analysis?
3. How bad must a business process be before it is a candidate for business reengineering?

A Manager Struggles with the Issues

A personal computer-based system that the bank would provide to key financial officers of its largest customers seemed like a good idea. Such a system would help to improve banking relationships with major clients. The system would allow the customers' chief financial officers or other authorized users to communicate with the bank's main computer to track, report, and analyze data concerning their company's funds. They would also be able to get the latest interest rates for various forms of corporate investments. The challenge was how to sell the idea to the bank's vice-president of operations.

Such a system presented several technical difficulties, not the least of which was concern over unauthorized access to data or, worse yet, compromise of the computer's security system. The system would be expensive to develop and operate, and unfortunately the system benefits were intangible. The hope was that the system would generate enough customer goodwill so that the bank would retain its key customers. The system even had the potential to lure major accounts away from the bank's competitors.

The costs and risks were high. The benefits were not clear. How could the concept be proven and sold to management? Was this project right to do?

■ THE INFORMATION TECHNOLOGY PLAN

Why Planning Is Critical to Success

> If we fail to plan, we plan to fail. *Anonymous*

Every organization faces hundreds of problems and opportunities for improvement. Because of scarce resources and finite organizational capacity to accommodate change, one of the major challenges facing managers is to decide which of several projects that address possible problems or opportunities should be initiated—a process called **strategic planning.** Indeed, one definition of strategic planning is that it is the process of deciding to which of several projects to assign resources. The importance of good planning cannot be overemphasized. Indeed, most managers agree that it is more important to be effective by working on the right things than to be efficient but working on the wrong things.

Elements of a Good Plan

For a manager to lead successfully, he or she must have a plan that includes a vision of where to go and some ideas on how to get there. Thus, effective leaders work with the members of their organization to develop an organizational plan to guide the efforts of the group. A good organizational plan (see Exhibit 10.1) includes the elements outlined below.

Vision

Vision is the view that top management has for the future of the company. The vision is generally expressed in terms of what the com-

Exhibit 10.1
Vision and Mission
for a Fortune 100
Company
*Source: Bristol-Myers
Squibb Company Annual
Report for 1989*

Vision
We are a company strongly oriented to research—to a search for breakthrough and innovative products. We are a company on the move—a company with the critical mass of financial strength, of scientific research, of marketing expertise, and of existing and future products to meet the global challenges we face and to assure us significant growth.

Mission
We are a company dedicated to enhancing life—from pharmaceuticals we will make and market, to the consumer, health care, and nutritional products we will continue to develop and sell.

Goals
- Achieve global preeminence in our pharmaceutical, consumer, medical device, and nutritional business.
- Firmly establish the company as one of the world's truly great research-based companies with a commitment to excellence in biomedical science that is recognized by the medical and scientific community around the world.

Objectives
- Achieve better than 15 percent annual compounded increase in per share earnings, along with continuing attention to margin improvement and increase or maintenance of market share.
- Achieve product leadership in our core businesses, both in the United States and in key foreign markets.

Strategies
- Coordinate sales and marketing activities and the scope and quality of the combined pharmaceutical research and development effort.
- Improve efficiency in the administrative and manufacturing areas of the company throughout the world to produce savings that will provide additional resources to invest in the company's future growth.

pany wants to become and wants to achieve. The vision for the company creates a model that represents what the organization will look like and what it will achieve in the future environment in which it will operate. Accomplishing management's vision depends on how well all the resources of the firm are developed and deployed toward achieving the vision.

Mission

Mission is the bottom-line purpose of the organization, in other words, why it exists. Organizational mission gives meaning and substance to the vision and provides legitimacy and purpose for the people who will have to accomplish the vision. Thus, an organization needs to set goals and objectives, establish a clear strategy, gain consensus and commitment, and successfully implement projects that help achieve the vision.

Goals

Goals are broad statements of the end results that the organization intends to achieve in fulfilling its mission.

Objectives

Objectives are specific and tangible measures of the results the organization wants to achieve.

Strategy

The **strategy** includes statements of how to reach the vision and achieve the organization's objectives. The strategy implemented by an organization is bounded by resource limitations and the perceptions, imagination, and boldness of its leadership. The difference between a successful and an unsuccessful strategy in any organization lies in how well it addresses the realities of its environment; how well it uses what it has to work with; and how well it compensates for its limitations. In a highly competitive situation, the latter may be the most important factor.

Consensus and Commitment

The leadership of the organization must agree and be dedicated to helping achieve the vision and mission.

Successful Implementation of Projects

Senior managers depend on project managers for the successful execution of specific projects to carry out the stated strategies and reach the desired objectives of the firm. Thus, project management is a form of delegation whereby senior managers delegate to project managers the authority and responsibility to initiate information systems projects to help support meeting the corporate vision.

The **organizational plan,** which outlines the vision, mission, goals, objectives, and strategies of the firm, becomes the primary input for the IT planning process. All elements of the IT plan flow from the organizational plan—the business processes that need improvement, the data and applications needed to support those business processes, the projects to be executed, and the resources and time required to complete those projects (Exhibit 10.2).

Business Processes

A **business process** is an activity or group of activities that is executed repeatedly. Using a process, we take input, add value to it, and provide value to an internal or external customer of that process. Within a process, we use an organization's resources (i.e., people, data, computer systems, equipment, etc.) to produce results. Examples include: the order processing process, the production planning process, and the new hire recruiting process. Key business processes required to achieve the business vision and mission need to be identified and prioritized. The relative importance of these business processes and the degree to

Exhibit 10.2
Elements of a Good
Plan

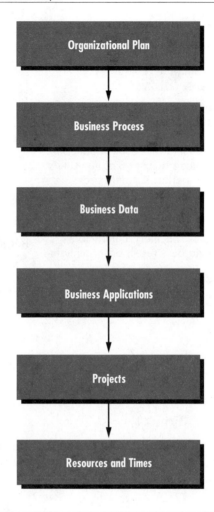

which they meet the business needs defines where to assign resources for further analysis. In some cases, a business process may need to be redefined or reengineered to better meet business needs prior to applying any information technology. The data flow diagram (Chapter 6) is often used to define and analyze business processes.

Business Data

Business data is the set of fundamental data needed to support the business processes. Data needs can be expressed in the form of a high-level logical data model that shows data entities (i.e., persons, places, or things) and the relationships among them.

Business Applications

Business applications are IT applications that support the business. An application is often some kind of information system, such as a

Real World Perspective

Integration of Information Technology and Corporate Strategy at Lithonia

Lithonia is the country's largest manufacturer of commercial lighting products, with 1993 sales of $608 million. Part of its success is due to Light Link, an IT application that puts a personal computer, software, and the ability to dial into Lithonia at each user's fingertips. Lithonia uses independent agents who act as intermediaries between the manufacturer and most customers. Light Link connects its warehouses and field sales teams with the agents, specifiers, contractors, and other people who buy, resell, or install lighting products.

It took seven years and $20 million to develop Light Link but when it was finally de-

ployed, agent response was immediate and positive. Using the system, independent lighting supply agents could now dial directly into Lithonia's computers for information on inventory, delivery dates, pricing, and other matters. The amount of time that agents spent on the phone with Lithonia representatives plunged, leaving them more time to sell.

This solution was possible because the company's senior vice-president of Information Technology and general manager of three of its product divisions understood all aspects of the lighting business. SOURCE: © 1991 by CMP Publications, Inc. 600 Community Drive, Manhasset, NY 11030. Reprinted from InformationWeek, January 17, 1992 with permission. □

new production planning system, that helps to support and automate a portion of the production planning process.

Project

A **project** is a set of activities that is designed to meet a specific objective. Quite often the project is to implement a specific data base or an information system.

Time and Resources

Each project requires time and resources to complete. Time is usually measured as elapsed time from project initiation—the number of weeks or months. **Resources** include people, time, and dollars to purchase necessary software and hardware.

A Four-Stage Planning Process

One approach to developing an IT plan is a four-stage process depicted in Exhibit 10.3 and discussed below.

Information Strategy Planning

An organization begins the information engineering process by developing an **information strategy plan.** There are two major steps to completing the plan. The first is determining the strategic opportunities, goals, critical success factors, and information needs of the different parts of the firm. The second step is creating an overview data model

Exhibit 10.3
A Four-Stage Planning Process

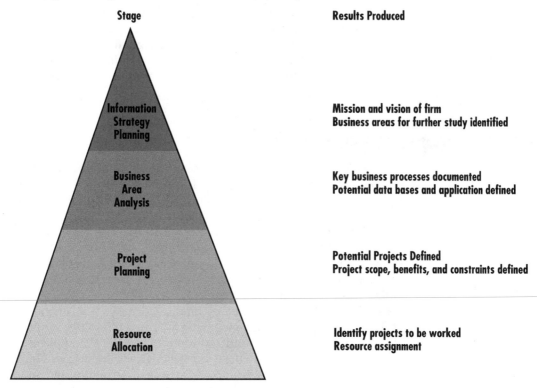

and process model of the firm and defining areas of the firm that would benefit from further business area analysis.

Business Area Analysis

The objective of the **business area analysis** stage is to determine what processes and data are necessary to enable the firm to achieve its vision and fulfill its mission. The goal here is to develop a model depicting how processes and data interrelate. The model should identify potential IT projects that meet key business needs.

Project Planning

The goal of **project planning** is to clearly define the scope, benefits, and constraints (e.g., total cost, elapsed time, etc.) associated with the potential projects identified during the business area analysis.

Resource Allocation

Based on the project planning data, management sets project priorities and begins to assign the appropriate resources to projects. Management's goal is to assign the right number of resources with the right kinds and levels of skills to complete the project within the constraints set during project planning. Often the project planning and resource allocation processes are iterative; if the resource allocation process determines that it is not possible to meet the original project constraints set during project planning, a project may get redefined so that it costs less, takes less time to complete, or can be assigned to people with a different level or set of skills.

■ A FRAMEWORK FOR PLANNING

Before discussing the four stages of planning, it is important to consider how management might view information technology and the planning process. Managers frequently use one of three models to place information technology in perspective.

The **Gibson/Nolan six-stage model** states that the relative level of spending on information technology within a single firm varies greatly over time. Senior managers have an opinion on which stage of IT evolution their organization is in. They look for projects and a level of IT spending consistent with that stage.

Porter's information technology hierarchy makes it clear that successful implementation of advanced information technology is possible only if a company has a sound foundation of basic IT applications. Managers hopefully have an appreciation for the IT hierarchy. They do not, for example, demand advanced executive information technology when the firm's basic transaction processing systems are old and fail to meet basic business needs.

The varying value model states that the value of information technology varies widely from industry to industry, firm to firm, and even department to department. Senior managers look for plans that are consistent with how management feels technology should be employed.

Gibson/Nolan Six-Stage Model

Gibson and Nolan (reference 5) offer a framework useful to managers for identifying issues associated with planning for IT growth. They discuss six stages of IT growth, each with its own distinct characteristics, opportunities, and problems. Their theory is based on the fact that for many firms and large organizations within a firm, the IT budget, when plotted over time from initial start-up to mature operation, resembles an S-shaped curve (Exhibit 10.4). The turnings of this curve correspond to major changes or stages in the way IT resources are managed. These six stages are:

1. **Initiation** The computer is placed in the organization.
2. **Contagion** A period of rapid and uncontrolled growth in the number and kinds of IT applications developed.

Exhibit 10.4
Six Stages of Information Technology Growth

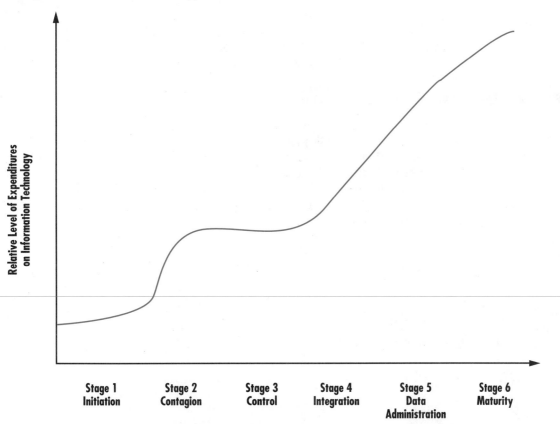

3. **Control** Top management gains control over IT resources by implementing formal control processes and standards that stifle almost all new information system projects.

4. **Integration** The use of information resources increases rapidly, providing new benefits and supporting the overall business strategy.

5. **Data Administration** Data are recognized as an important resource of the company. Efforts are made to manage data.

6. **Maturity** IT people and business managers are jointly held accountable for identifying and capitalizing on opportunities to use information technology.

The IT plan needs to be consistent with the organization's stage of IT growth. For example, if the organization is in the control stage, it will be difficult to sell any new project without strong economic justification. Thus, in such an organization, any project proposal must clearly define expected cost savings or increases in revenue if its proponents expect it to be adopted. On the other hand, projects that will help management gain control of computer usage and costs (e.g., a user charge-back system to recover costs of computer resources) stand a good chance of being accepted.

Porter's Information System Hierarchy

Porter (reference 10) emphasizes that successful implementation of information technology requires managing a sequence of systems, each of a higher order than the preceding one. **Porter's information system hierarchy** has eight levels of systems, arranged in order of their relative strategic importance to the organization (Exhibit 10.5).

Porter's fundamental premise is that lower-order systems must be in place before the next higher order can be successfully implemented. That is, management must build a proper foundation, then learn from and adapt lower-order systems before advancing to higher orders. A strategic higher-order system (e.g., an Executive Information System)

Exhibit 10.5
Porter's Information Technology Hierarchy

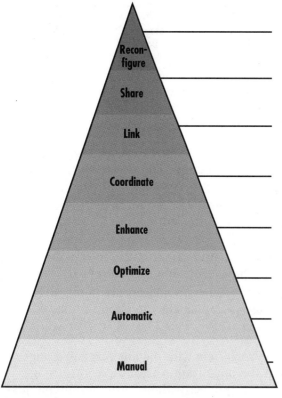

Recon-figure — This is the highest-order system. It requires a complete transformation of internal work processes or products and services (or both).

Share — Information technology that enhances economies of scope by sharing similar activities among different products.

Link — Information technology that creates connections between different corporate activities, such as sales with research and development or design with manufacturing. It can also involve establishing external linkages with customers and suppliers.

Coordinate — Information technology that can help to coordinate the activities with others in different parts of the organization, such as warehouses and factories.

Enhance — Information technology with substantial additional functionality above that provided by the traditional manual systems, such as CAD/CAM systems that enable flexible manufacturing or systems that provide order-tracking capability.

Optimize — Information technology that measures and controls many independent variables to optimize some result, such as cost or quality.

Automatic — Straightforward conversion of the traditional manual systems to computer-based systems that provide the same functionality.

Manual — Non-computer-based, traditional systems for accounting, order processing, inventory control, and so on.

cannot be implemented from scratch; it takes time and must evolve from lower-order systems (e.g., transaction processing systems). This is one reason why higher-order systems have the biggest and longest-lasting impact on competitive advantage. They are very hard to implement and take much time and effort for competitors to imitate.

However, the process of learning and evolving to higher-order systems can be accelerated by careful planning. Porter believes that rather than letting the system evolve by trial and error, management must pay careful attention to the architecture of its initial, lower-level systems to make sure that they can be built on. What managers must avoid is developing a patchwork of discrete systems to handle particular needs. They must be willing to invest in a higher-level infrastructure at the start. What may appear to be system overkill up front is actually necessary when building lower-level systems to assure the firm's ability to reach the more strategic higher-level capabilities. This means that traditional capital budgeting practices will not work. Managers with strategic vision must be willing to invest on faith. This is why the old platitude of strong senior management support holds especially true for the implementation of information technology that may eventually lead to competitive advantage.

A truly higher-order IT system crosses organizational as well as functional boundaries, notes Porter. Managers cannot think of marketing, production, or design as separate when informational linkages are prevalent. Similarly, distinctions between suppliers and buyers tend to disappear. Since these higher-order information systems change the way the business is carried out, they are truly strategic. However, Porter's information hierarchy demonstrates that we cannot ignore the importance of lower-order systems. Without their support, the strategic higher-order systems cannot be built or operate effectively.

The Varying Value of Information Technology

The value attached to information technology varies widely from industry to industry, company to company, and even organization to organization within the same firm. For some, IT is viewed as an opportunity to gain a strategic competitive advantage. Such firms look for ways to incorporate IT into the products and services that they provide their customers. Others view IT as just another tool to help improve organizational effectiveness and profitability. They expect IT to be applied in ways that help achieve the corporate mission and vision without necessarily providing a breakthrough in the fundamental products and services of the company. Still others view IT as merely an administrative convenience—it is a necessity in some areas of the firm, but by no means pervasive or strategic in nature.

None of these viewpoints is necessarily right or wrong. Individuals' viewpoints are based on their knowledge and experience with information technology. The key issue here is that senior management's view of IT will strongly influence the IT strategic planning process. Those involved in the planning process will be most successful in selling their plan if it is consistent with senior management's view of IT—a means to gain strategic competitive advantage, a tool to improve effectiveness and profitability, or an administrative convenience.

The Manager's Role in Planning

Today's organization must deal with tremendous changes to meet the goals of the enterprise.

- Globalization with increasing competition from all corners of the world
- The need for business reengineering
- A rapidly changing demographic profile of the work force
- The need to form more powerful alliances among suppliers and customers

Achieving corporate goals in the midst of all these changes requires the effective use of information technology. It is not enough to simply ensure that there is a strong connection between technology and strategy. Managers need to remove the barriers imposed by organizational structure and people's attitudes toward the use of new technology and toward change so that IT can become a catalyst for changes—changes that create totally new products and services for the organization.

Some companies have achieved remarkable results in reducing costs and improving the performance of their administrative and operational processes. Others have made only modest gains in selected areas of their operations. Unfortunately, far too many companies still fail to see the opportunities that technology can provide. To apply IT effectively, management must understand the technology and be able to visualize its application to solve business problems. Management must be willing to consider not just using IT to streamline the department or operation, but to change the fundamental work processes of the total organization and its relationship with customers and suppliers.

Management also has a key role to ensure that IT is viewed from the perspective of helping to achieve the organization's strategic business plan, rather than from merely a technical perspective (Exhibit 10.6).

Decisions on which IT projects are right to do were once made entirely by technologists. However, organizations now recognize that IT is a key tool in helping the firm achieve its strategic goals. Business managers must form an effective working partnership with information technologists to determine which opportunities and projects should be addressed for three good reasons. First, business managers are needed to develop an IT plan that is consistent with and supports the overall corporate strategy as revealed in the organizational plan. This ensures that the plan is relevant and worth executing. Second, business managers are needed to develop an IT plan that conforms to the stage of IT maturity within the firm. This ensures the feasibility of executing

Exhibit 10.6
The Manager's Role in Information Technology Planning

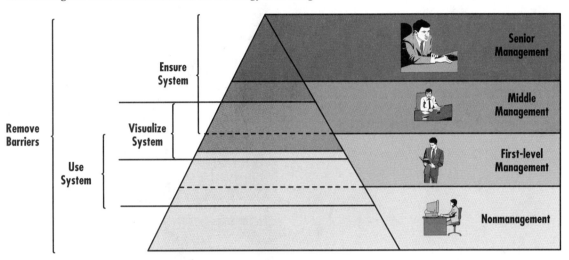

- **Visualize how information technology can be used to solve business problems.**

- **Remove barriers to the effective use of technology.**

- **Ensure that information technology is used to achieve the organization's strategic business plan.**

the plan. And, third, business managers are needed to develop an IT plan that matches management's view of the role of IT within the firm. This ensures the acceptance of the plan by senior management.

■ INFORMATION STRATEGY PLANNING

Information strategy planning focuses on the mission and vision of the firm and how information technology can be used to create new opportunities, address key problems, or achieve competitive advantage. During information strategy planning, areas in which to apply IT are identified for further analysis. Critical success factors of the firm are also identified. One approach for conducting this planning process is outlined in Exhibit 10.7 and described below.

Establish a Corporate Steering Committee

Many organizations establish a **corporate steering committee** to oversee the application of IT within the firm. The committee reviews proposals for new systems; identifies and helps prioritize business areas with high potential benefit from computerization; approves long-range plans, budgets, and staffing requests; and thereby steers the development of IT in a direction consistent with the corporation's overall business strategy.

Exhibit 10.7
An Effective
Information
Strategy Planning
Process

The ideal makeup of the committee includes managers from the major functional areas of the business (sales, finance, manufacturing, personnel). The level of management represented on the committee depends on the strategic relevance of IT. The more strategic the nature of the IT projects, the higher the level of management it is appropriate to have on the committee.

The corporate steering committee brings a broad perspective and many points of view on the decisions it must face. Many organizations realize that some representation by upper-level management is essential to ensure the IT planning contains strategic elements and does not focus too narrowly on the short term.

Two basic reasons dictate the need for a corporate steering committee. First, without upper-level management input, the IT organization will fall into a reactive role, merely responding to the expressed short-term needs of the operating level managers. As a result, the IT development effort will be directed at meeting daily operating needs, and few if any information resources will be left to deal with the unexpressed strategic needs of upper management—needs that in fact may hold the key to the future growth and prosperity of the organization, indeed to its very survival! Second, a bottom-up systems strategy is quite likely to be incompatible with the top-down strategic view of the business as seen by upper management. The IT organization and operating level managers may frequently find themselves at odds with upper management over the relative importance and justification for large, expensive systems needed to support business activities that may be undergoing fundamental strategic changes. Thus, systems and operating managers will find themselves spending extraordinary amounts of time trying to explain to management why something that appears obvious to them needs to be done. Upper management, on the other hand, may not recognize the degree to which systems and operating managers lack understanding of corporate strategy and may interpret their recommendations as unsound advice.

Initiate the Study

Strategic planning efforts are successful only if all the participants establish and agree on the scope, time frame, and expectations of what the study will produce. The goal of initiating the planning study is to work with those who have requested the study to establish these parameters.

Quite often, the need for a strategic plan will be identified at the senior management level. The results will also be presented to senior management for their action and approval. Clearly, with this level of attention, the results of the strategic planning study must be on target. Thus, it is wise to spend time with these managers to gain insights into their reasons for calling for a study: dissatisfaction with the current information technology's contribution to business objectives; a change in business objectives or a new business initiative that will require significant IT support; the timeliness of updating the previous plan (see Exhibit 10.7); or some other reason. The study must then be carefully planned to meet this need.

During these discussions, the leader of the strategic planning effort should also seek to establish the **scope** of the study. What extent of the enterprise should be studied? Should the current and potential impact of information technology be assessed for the entire firm, for one division, or for a group of related business processes (e.g., order processing)?

A key part of defining scope is to gain senior management agreement on the specific outputs or deliverables that will be produced from the study. If a successful study has been completed within your company, you may ask the managers to review and comment on those deliverables. What do they need to see that isn't in the example study? What don't they need that is in the example study? You may also prepare a specific list of deliverables to discuss with them.

The members of the study team must be identified and recruited to complete the study. Ideally, the study team members will collectively have expertise in the following areas:

■ A good grasp of the common issues and trends facing the industry in which you compete

■ A clear understanding of the business strategy and needs of the firm

■ A knowledge of how other companies in your industry are using or planning to use information technology and a vision of what information technology can do for your firm

■ A working knowledge of the people and processes of that portion of the organization included in the scope of the study

Since all this expertise is seldom found in one person, strategic planning teams frequently consist of two or more people.

If the organization has not participated in a successful IT strategic planning study, strong consideration should be given to engaging an experienced consultant who specializes in strategic planning for companies in your industry. Such a consultant may well cost in excess of $2,000 per day.

Frequently, a bottleneck is formed when trying to schedule time to meet with senior managers to complete study initiation activities, because these managers have extremely busy schedules. Thus, experience shows that a minimum of two weeks elapsed time is required to initialize the strategic planning study plus identify and recruit the members of the study team.

Define Industry and Technology Trends

Industry and technology trends are two important factors to consider in the business information planning process. Planners must try to forecast the impact of changes on the company so that the company's overall systems strategy takes into account forecasts of relevant trends. This approach will help minimize the impact of negative changes and capitalize on potential opportunities. It will also ensure that the company takes a proactive stand toward helping to make the future happen rather than just reacting to the winds of change.

Identification of industry trends should focus on gaining a better understanding of how changes in the business environment in which the company operates will influence the achievement of the **critical success factors** (activities crucial to a successful operation) or lead to the introduction of new critical success factors. Trends that are important to track include:

1. Changes in the services your customers expect to receive

2. Changes in the costs, sources, and availability of raw materials needed for production

3. Entry of new competitors

4. Changes in the size of the market for your products (perhaps through changes in demographics or areas of the country/world in which the products are sold)

Information about these kinds of trends can be gained through interviews with senior management of the company; discussions with customers, suppliers, and bankers; and from research services and institutions.

Information about technology trends should focus on how the technology can be better exploited to achieve results that have a high impact on the success of the firm. Trends that are important to watch include:

1. The continuing improvement in the cost/performance of computing devices (from microcomputer to supercomputer)

2. The increasing availability of ready-to-use software to meet a wide range of business needs

3. The improving ability of office automation to bring real increases in productivity to office workers

4. Expanding opportunities to employ telecommunications to link people, computers, and other devices for the sharing of information

5. The increasing ease and new ways by which end users can get data and information out of data bases

6. The growing use of artificial intelligence and expert systems

Identify Business Needs

During the business needs identification portion of the study, the planning team needs to obtain a clear picture of how well current information technology is being applied to meet current business needs. It then needs to identify and assess potential areas of future application of technology.

A key to the success of this part of the study is participation from the multiple organizations that have work processes under study or that may be affected by portions of the strategic plan. For example, if the plan is focused on the order-entry process, people involved in those functions that support or are affected by order processing ought to be included: order entry, shipping, inventory control, warehouse operations, billing, customer services, credit, and so on. Such participation will ensure that the processes are viewed with a cross-functional perspective, thus avoiding placing too much emphasis on meeting the needs of one group without sufficient consideration of the effect on others or without identification of their needs. The cross-functional approach also leads to defining stronger, better solutions by having several people familiar with the same problems, issues, and opportunities working together and building off one another's ideas.

A **structured group interview** session composed of users, managers, the strategic planning team, and an experienced session leader is an excellent way to define these needs. The session leader is a trained facilitator and possesses excellent meeting leadership and communication skills, but may not be experienced in the business area undergoing study.

Group interview sessions generally achieve better results if the session leader takes several different approaches to obtain the data needed to develop the strategic plan.

Identify the Underlying Business Processes

Following this approach, the group interview session leader helps the group to identify the business processes fundamental to the area of the business undergoing study. For example, in order processing, the fundamental business processes are order entry, shipping, inventory control, warehouse operations, billing, customer services, and credit approval.

The group develops a simple description of each process that identifies which decisions are made in which processes and, especially, how a decision made in one process affects other processes. The flow of material or data from one process to another is also identified.

Focus the Group on Current Problems

Under this approach, the group interview session leader helps the group to identify and discuss the problems associated with each process. Problems can be classified as serious or annoying to help focus the group's attention on the most pressing problems. It is helpful to probe to find the root cause of each serious problem by asking, "Why is this a serious problem, and what causes this to happen?" Then based on the identified root causes, people can be asked to identify creative ways of overcoming the serious problems.

Identify the Critical Success Factors

The critical success factors in any operation are those few essential activities that must go right if the operation is to be successful. If the results achieved in these activities are below par, then the results of the organization will also be substandard. The critical success factors are generally few (half a dozen or less). After all, not every activity is absolutely essential. Critical success factors will vary from industry to industry, but for a specific business activity (e.g., order entry) within a given industry, the critical success factors are likely to be very similar across all organizations in that industry.

The group interview facilitator can help the group to identify the critical success factors simply by defining the term (including a few examples) and asking people to identify them for the processes under study (Exhibit 10.8). As each critical success factor is uncovered, in-

Exhibit 10.8
Interview Questions
to Help Determine
the Critical Success
Factors of the
Organization

1. Can you briefly state the mission of the organization?
2. What goals have been set for the organization?
3. What are the key business activities that must be performed well to achieve each of these objectives?
4. What information is necessary to monitor the success of each key business activity?
5. Of all the information you receive to monitor each key business activity, which is the most important?
6. Is there any information that would be extremely useful but that you do not receive today?
7. Of all the information you receive that is not so useful, could any of it become more valuable if it were more accurate or timely, presented in a different form, or changed in some other way?

creased clarity and understanding can be gained by probing *why* people consider this to be a critical activity.

Once a particular activity is agreed to be critical, determine if management can quantify and report its value. The inability to measure and track a critical success factor is a red flag signaling the need for improved information technology.

In the area of order processing, some of the critical success factors might be: maximize the number of shipments received on time and without damage by the customer; provide accurate and timely customer billing; and minimize total inventory.

Evaluate the Overall Effectiveness

Effectiveness is a measure of how well an organization's products or services (or both) meet customer needs. For this particular perspective, it is essential to get meaningful and objective customer data. The data may be gathered in a variety of ways: via carefully designed question-

Real World Perspective

Critical Success Factors at Lend-Lease Trucks

Lend-Lease Trucks, Inc. is a $200 million national truck leasing company based in Minneapolis. Trucking is somewhat of a commodity business. Lend-Lease Trucks competes with the biggest trucking lessors in business: Ryder, Ruan, and Penske to name a few. For dedicated trucking services like moving and storage companies which frequently lease trucks, a truck is a truck, with a few minor exceptions.

Then how do trucking services like lend lease break the tie with other companies? The answer is servicing their customers' needs through flexible pricing, including special extras like diesel fuel which Lend-Lease sells at a discount to customers, and individualized contracts for mileage, usage, and maintenance. The ability to offer individualized extras and flexible billing to meet a company's particular needs is tantamount to success—the critical success factor. SOURCE: Elizabeth Child. "High-Speed Teams Get Lend-Lease Trucks Rolling." Journal of Systems Management January 1994. □

naires, through telephone surveys, by conducting specially designed group interview sessions with a number of customers, or through many other approaches. The data may be gathered directly by the organization or through employment of market research firms.

The term **customer** should be interpreted in the broadest, most general sense: anyone to whom you provide goods or services (or both). Thus for a staff organization within the firm, the customer may actually be employees or another organization within the firm. The Finance Department produces capital and profit forecasts for senior managers, budget summaries for department and section managers, and cost/benefit analyses for project managers. In this case, the customers of the Finance Department really are employees: senior managers, department and section managers, and project managers.

Prioritize Business Processes for Further Analysis

By this time, the strategic planning project team has learned a great deal about the various processes of the firm—which processes are key to meeting customer needs, which processes have serious problems and what they are, what are the critical success factors for each process, and how effective is each process. The focus of the study must now be narrowed and the key processes must be identified for further analysis.

An assumption can be made that the business processes most important to the customers are also the ones most critical to achieving the firm's vision and mission. If this is not the case, then something is wrong with the firm's overall business strategy. Accepting this assumption, a simple technique can be used to identify those business processes worthy of further analysis.

To use the technique, the team must carefully and objectively review the data about each process. The team must determine how important good performance is in each process in terms of meeting customers' needs. The measure might be made on a scale of 1 to 10, with 1 being not at all important and 10 being critical. Next, the team determines to what degree customer needs are NOT being met in each process. In other words, what is the degree of customer dissatisfaction? A 10 means that the customers are completely dissatisfied and a 1 means that customers are delighted with the firm's performance in this area. Then the team multiplies the importance rating by the customer dissatisfaction rating. The processes that are obvious candidates for further analysis are ones where the result is high relative to other areas. Exhibit 10.9 shows an example of this calculation performed for a hypothetical firm; processes have been sorted in priority from high to low.

Identify Business Areas for Further Analysis

Rather than study business processes in isolation, experience has shown that it makes sense to consider related business processes as a group. Related processes are ones in which a change in one business process

Exhibit 10.9
Example of the
Technique for
Identifying Business
Areas for Further
Analysis

Business Process	Importance	Dissatisfaction	Need to Improve
Enter and Control Customer Order	10	7	70
Ship Product	10	6	60
Control Product Inventory	6	8	48
Design Product	8	5	40
Market Product (Wholesale)	9	4	36
Advertise and Promote Product	7	3	21
Buy Finished Goods	3	5	15

may have an impact in another related one. Often these are processes where the output from one process becomes input to another.

The term business area means a set of related business processes that have much in common. One useful way to group processes into business areas is to create the "process involves data entity matrix" shown in Exhibit 10.10. The various business processes are rows in the matrix and the data entities are columns. A letter code is assigned to cells in the matrix to document that a process creates (C) the data entity or uses (U) the data entity. A business area is identified as a cluster of business processes that use and/or create the same set of data entities. The business areas in Exhibit 10.10 are shown blocked off in a rectangle with a dark boundary.

■ BUSINESS AREA ANALYSIS

In the business area analysis stage, the planning team determines what business processes and data are most critical for the firm to achieve its vision and fulfill its mission. The goal is not to design systems but to establish a framework that will ensure that separately designed systems will work together effectively. (Determining detailed procedures and defining system requirements are done in the design stage, not in the business area analysis stage.) The extent of the business covered and the depth of analysis should be such that the business area analysis for a given area is completed in three to six months.

Business area analysis is completely independent of the current information technology used to support a given area. This is because, regardless of the computer hardware or software used, the same data are still needed and the same basic business process is still performed even if wholesale changes are made in the information technology. Business area analysis is also independent of current information technology that may be utilized to automate all or a portion of the process under study. A given business area analysis project focuses exclusively on one area of the business at a time. However, it is possible that

Exhibit 10.10
The Process/Entity Matrix

Processes \ Data Entities	Objectives	Policies & Procedures	Organization Unit Desc	Product Forecasts	Bldg & Real Estate Reqt	Equipment Requirements	Organization Unit Budget	G/L Accounts Desc & Budget	Long Term Debt	Employee Requirements	Legal Requirements	Competitor	Marketplace	Product Description	Raw Material Description	Vendor Description	Buy Order	Product Warehouse Inventory	Shipment	Promotion	Customer Description	Customer Order	Seasonal Production Plan	Supplier Description	Purchase Order	Raw Material Inventory	Production Order	Equipment Description	Bldg & Real Estate Desc	Equipment Status	Accounts Receivable	Product Profitability	G/L Accounts Status	Accounts Payable	Employee Description	Employee Status
Establish Business Direction	C	C	C								U	U	U																			U	U			
Forecast Product Requirements	U			C														U					U													
Determine Facility & Eqt Reqts	U		U		C	C	U																					U	U	U						
Determine & Control Fin Reqts	U		U				C	C	C																					U						
Determine Personnel Reqts		U	U		U	U	U	U		C	U																									U
Comply With Legal Reqts		U						U			C			U																					U	U
Analyze Marketplace	U											C	C								U															
Design Product										U	U			C	C													U								
Buy Finished Goods			U											U	C	C														U						
Control Product Inventory														U		U	C	U								U										
Ship Product																		U	C			U														
Advertise & Promote Product													U	U					U	C													U			
Market Product (Wholesale)												U	U	U						U	C	U														
Enter & Control Customer Order														U				U	U	U	U	C									U					
Plan Seasonal Production			U											U									C				U	U							U	U
Purchase Raw Materials															U									U	C	C	U					U				
Control Raw Materials Inventory															U										U	C	U									
Schedule & Control Production														U	U								U			U	C	U		U					U	U
Acquire & Dispose Fac & Eqt					U	U																						C	C							
Maintain Equipment																					U							U		C						U
Manage Facilities																													U							
Manage Cash Receipts																			U	U											C					
Deter Product Profitability						U								U	U			U										U	U			C	U		U	U
Manage Accounts								U								U		U														U	C	U		U
Manage Cash Disbursements								U								U	U	U						U	U									C	U	U
Hire & Terminate Personnel	U	U			U					U	U																								C	U
Manage Personnel	U																																		U	C

multiple business area analysis projects are conducted concurrently to reduce the elapsed time required to study all key areas.

There are three models that have proven extremely worthwhile in studying business processes (keeping in mind the goal of providing a framework that will allow separately built systems to work together). These are the entity relationship diagram (Chapter 5), the data flow diagram (Chapter 6), and the process/entity matrix. This latter model, which shows how the processes and data within the business area interrelate, is critical in identifying potential IT projects to meet key business needs.

One approach for conducing a business area analysis is outlined in Exhibit 10.11 and described in the upcoming pages.

Exhibit 10.11
One Process for
Conducting
Business Area
Analysis

Document Data Entities and Relationships

An entity is a person, place, or thing of interest to the business. A typical business area may have several dozen entities that it must track in order to meet its objectives. However, the set of entity types important to a business area does not change much as time goes by—unless the firm moves into a fundamentally different type of business. Even if new information technology is applied or business processes are streamlined to improve efficiency, the underlying data required to support the business area remains constant. Thus starting the business area analysis with a definition of data entities and relationships provides a solid foundation upon which to build.

A data model that covers the scope of the business area undergoing analysis is built. While based on the high-level entity/relationship diagram built in the information strategy planning stage, this model is more narrow in scope (includes only data entities of interest to this business area) and more detailed than the earlier data model. The entity relationship diagram shows the data entities (persons, places, or things) and the relationships among those entities. Exhibit 10.12 outlines a process for creating an entity relationship model. Exhibit 10.13 illustrates an entity relationship model.

Exhibit 10.12
Process to Develop
an Entity
Relationship Model

Step 1 Identify the data entities that are important to this business area.

Step 2 Identify the relationships among each possible pair of data entities. There may be no relationship among some of the data entities; others will have a 1-to-1, 1-to-many, or many-to-many relationship.

Step 3 Identify the primary key for each data entity (the data attribute or attributes that uniquely identify that data entity from any other).

Step 4 Associate other data attributes with each data entity.

Step 5 Now that the data entities have been better defined, repeat steps 1 through 4 to refine the entity relationship diagram.

Document Fundamental Processes

A very wise person once said: "Don't change anything until you understand it." This saying is especially true for business processes. Lack of understanding can lead to making changes that only make a bad situation worse or result in less than optimal changes.

During the business area analysis stage, decisions to reengineer one or more of the current business processes will be made. Data flow diagrams enable business managers to understand the essential inputs, outputs, processing, and the relationships between processes. A data flow diagram is developed for each of the key processes identified for further analysis. Exhibit 10.14 outlines a process for creating a data flow diagram, while Exhibit 10.15 illustrates an example data flow diagram.

Exhibit 10.13
An Example Entity
Relationship

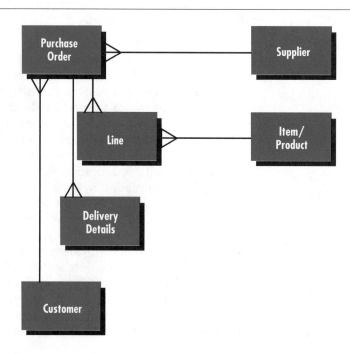

Exhibit 10.14
Process to Develop
a Data Flow
Diagram

Step 1 Break the process down into relatively elementary component operations. This is done by interviewing people who are involved in the process under study or simply through close observation. List major business occurrences or events within the system. Look for receipt of key input to the system, the production of important output by the system, and functions triggered based on timing.

Step 2 List the major data stores used in the process including computer files, data bases, manual files, file cabinets, etc.

Step 3 Draw a tentative data flow segment showing a major process and the data flow in and data flow out of this process. Draw additional data flow segments.

Step 4 Assemble the data flow segments into an initial, very rough data flow diagram. Some redrawing of some of the components may be necessary to improve the diagram's appearance.

Step 5 Identify the entities that are outside the scope of the business process to be analyzed (external entities). It is important to get agreement—what's in and what's out.

Step 6 Share this initial draft with several people to evaluate the diagram for completeness and consistency.

Identify any missing significant processes or data stores.

Make sure that each process receives some input and produces some output.

Each process should be given a name that includes a strong action verb and a specific subject (e.g., check customer credit).

Data sources should only connect to processes, not to other data sources or external entities.

The initial high-level data flow diagram should have four-to-eight processes and no more. If the number of processes exceeds eight, the diagram is too detailed.

Business process understanding begins with identifying the customers of the process, i.e., who receives the output from this process. A business process customer can be, in fact, very likely is, someone within the company. After the process customers are identified, the next step is to seek to understand their requirements, i.e., what do these customers need from the process and its output, what problems do they have with the current process, are there any measures of the quality and quantity of the output of the process.

Finally, the key decisions associated with the process must be identified. For each decision ask: "What is the best place for this decision to be made?" and "Who should be responsible for this decision?" The answers to these fundamental questions may indicate procedures that are quite different from the way the current process operates. Thus major changes in the business process, new IT applications, and organizational changes must be made.

Assess Need for Business Reengineering

Any process that operates at a high cost is a candidate for business process reengineering. Another symptom of a poor process is that it

Exhibit 10.15
An Example Data Flow Diagram

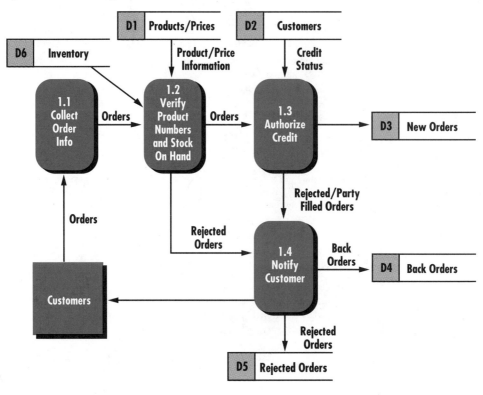

fails to meet the needs of its customers (for example, the results are often late, inaccurate, or incomplete). Exhibit 10.16 provides a simple test to determine if a business process needs to be reengineered.

Business reengineering involves radically changing the way work is done to completely eliminate non-value-added steps. A **non-value-added step** is one that does nothing for the customer of the business process. One way to identify non-added-value steps is to challenge each step in the process. Ask the people involved in the business process—"why do we perform this step?" Do not accept the initial answer, but keep asking why until a very solid reason for performing the step emerges. This may require four or five "whys." If the answer is "I don't know, we've always done it this way" or if it is not possible to develop a good reason for executing a step, the step is probably a non-value-added step. This can be confirmed by discussions with the customer of the business process. Should the business customer agree that the step does not add value, the step should be eliminated in the reengineering business process.

Relate Processes and Data Entities

The **process/entity matrix,** first created at the end of the information strategy stage (Exhibit 10.10), is updated for the business processes and

Exhibit 10.16
Quiz to Determine if a Process Should Be Reengineered

QUESTION	YES	NO
1. Are labor costs for this process high?		
2. Do customers complain that it takes too long?		
3. Is it extremely difficult to modify the process to meet changing business needs?		
4. Are system interface and liaison people required to enable customers to use the process?		
5. Is rework often required to correct errors?		
6. Are "expeditors" required to handle exceptions?		
7. Are there delays built into the process?		
8. Do people perform jobs with narrow responsibilities?		
9. Are there lots of "handoffs" from worker to worker?		
10. Are different people in different departments involved in the data entry/data capture step and the data processing and decision-making step?		

Add up the number of yes answers. If the result is greater than 6, the process is a good candidate for business reengineering.

data entities included in the business area undergoing study. At this stage, much more is known about the business area. It is very likely that new processes and data entities have been identified that were not recognized earlier. It is also possible that some processes have been combined into one or eliminated.

Define Potential Data Bases and IT Applications

The updated process/entity matrix makes it clear what data are needed to support the business area and its processes. Using this matrix, the project team can define potential data bases and IT applications to be built.

The sets of data entities that are common to several business processes represent an opportunity to build a data base. Such a data base can be **shared** across all the individual systems that are built to help automate the key business processes of a specific business area.

The project team can review the various processes to identify potential IT applications. These applications would involve either automating or reengineering and automating existing business processes.

■ RESOURCE ALLOCATION

The result of the information strategic planning and business area analysis is a collection of potential IT projects to which resources may be assigned. This collection of potential projects is often referred to as the **applications portfolio.** In most cases, the effort and resources needed to execute all these projects far exceed the available resources. Furthermore, if they were all implemented at the same time, the organization is not likely to have the capacity or the flexibility to adapt to the many changes in roles, responsibilities, business processes, procedures, equipment, and software that would result. So projects that represent the most worthwhile investments for the firm must somehow be selected from the applications portfolio. One approach is to categorize potential IT projects by the type of business benefit they are likely to provide, set an IT development strategy, and then choose projects consistent with that strategy.

Categorize Potential Projects

The objectives of each potential project should be reviewed to ensure that the project meets an important business need, is consistent with corporate strategy, and leads to the attainment of specific goals and objectives. A second check should be made to assess the degree of risk or uncertainty associated with each project. The risk assessment can be made on factors such as the following: (1) How well are the requirements of the system understood? (2) To what degree does the project require pioneering effort in technology that is new to the firm? (3) Is there a risk of severe business repercussions if the project is poorly implemented?

The fundamental reason for considering the project should be identified. Most IT projects fall into one of the following categories:

■ Implementation of this project will result in hard dollar savings to the company that can be quantified (e.g., reduce staff, cut operating costs, or increase sales).

■ Implementation of this project will result in soft dollar savings to the company, the magnitude of which will be difficult to measure (e.g., help managers make better decisions or improve control over the operations of the business).

■ Implementation of this project is required to meet a state or federal regulation (e.g., provide information on employment of the handicapped and minorities).

■ Implementation of this project is required to gain experience in the application of a new technology to business (e.g., evaluate the use of portable computers by salespeople to enhance customer presentations).

Set Strategy

At this point, evaluation of candidate projects from the portfolio are discussed with members of senior management or the corporate steering committee to arrive at agreement on which projects should be worked. Several possible overall strategies can be adopted. Some of the options include:

■ **Meet Immediate Needs** Allocate resources only to those projects that will clearly help meet critical business needs. This is a low-risk strategy that leads to the delivery of valuable systems to meet immediate needs. The emphasis on short-term results, however, may lead to overlooking strategic opportunities to significantly change the business over the long run.

■ **High Payoff** Allocate resources only to those projects that have an excellent cost/benefit ratio and thus a high payoff for the firm. Such a strategy neglects any pioneering efforts that may be necessary to better understand how technology may be applied in a new way or to a new area of the business.

■ **Low Risk** Allocate resources only to those projects that have a low level of risk. Although this approach minimizes any chance of failure, it is too conservative an approach for management to follow if it expects to really move the business forward.

The appropriate strategy may vary from organization to organization within the firm, depending on the stage of IT growth and management attitudes. However, the ideal overall strategy for the firm should include a mix of projects that meet critical business needs, provide a high payoff, and involve some pioneering to gain valuable experience.

■ PROJECT PLANNING

Project planning involves examining each project to be executed to set preliminary **project constraints** (project scope, degree of difficulty, expected cost range, desired completion date, etc.). Based on this examination, a plan of attack to complete the project successfully is developed (Exhibit 10.17). The project manager determines which of the many potential system development life cycles will be followed. As discussed in Chapter 9, this depends on the nature of the project. Once the life cycle is chosen, the tasks that need to be performed in each stage of the project are defined. The effort required to complete each task is estimated and checkpoints established to review project progress.

Project scope, cost, and completion date are variables that are a function of the number and the skill level of the people available to work the project. For example, a common situation is that insufficient people are available to complete the project by a desired date. In this case, some of the nonessential features planned for the full system may be eliminated in order to be able to deliver "something that works" by the deadline.

Summary

Strategic planning is the process of deciding to which of several projects to assign resources.

Exhibit 10.17
Sample Project
Description

Project Title
Upgrade the existing order-entry system

Project Scope
Identify improvements in the entire order-entry process from receipt of customer order through customer billing. Manual procedures, data processing hardware and software, order processing input and output forms, and internal controls are all to be reviewed and opportunities for improvement identified. Total replacement of the existing system may be appropriate.

Business Objectives

1. Reduce the order cycle time required to fill customer orders from eight days to five days.

2. Reduce customer billing errors from 7 percent to 1 percent or less.

3. Provide an efficient order-entry system that reduces the total order processing cost from $15 per order to less than $10 per order.

Business Justification

1. The objectives mentioned above must be met if the firm is to remain competitive. Market research surveys have shown that the firm's current poor level of customer service is the reason for our loss of market leadership over the last two years. Our market share has dropped from 21 percent to less than 16 percent, resulting in lost sales valued at over $2 million.

2. Improved efficiency in order processing will lead to a savings of $5 per order, or $100,000 per year.

3. More accurate billing will improve customer relations and lead to a reduction in the staff required for the accounts receivable business function.

Resources Required for Design Stage

1. User department staff time of twenty effort days valued at $8,000.

2. Systems and programming staff time of thirty effort days valued at $12,000.

A good organizational plan includes a vision, mission, goals, objectives, and strategy.

The organizational plan is the primary input for the IT planning process.

The IT plan includes the following elements: business processes, business data, business applications, projects, and resources and time.

A four-stage process to develop an IT plan includes information strategy planning, business area analysis, project planning, and resource allocation.

Information strategy planning determines the strategic opportunities, goals, critical success factors, and information needs of different parts of the firm. It also develops overview data and process models of the firm and identifies areas of the firm that would benefit from further analysis.

Business area analysis determines the processes and data required for the firm to achieve its vision and mission.

Project planning defines the scope, benefits, and constraints of individual potential projects.

Resource allocation involves determining which projects will be executed and what resources are required.

The Gibson/Nolan six-stage model explains that the relative level of spending on information technology within a single firm varies greatly over time.

Porter's information technology hierarchy makes it clear that successful implementation of advanced technology is possible only if there is a sound foundation of basic IT applications.

The varying value model reminds us that the value of IT varies widely from industry to industry, firm to firm, and even department to department.

The IT plan must be consistent with the overall corporate strategy as revealed in the organizational plan.

The IT plan must conform to the stage of maturity within the firm.

The IT plan must match management's view of the role of information technology.

One method to identify the business processes for further analysis is to multiply the importance rating by the customer dissatisfaction rating. The areas with the highest result are the ones needing the most attention.

The goal of business area analysis is to determine what business processes and data are most critical for the firm to achieve its vision and fulfill its mission.

Any business process that operates at a high cost or fails to meet the needs of its customers is a candidate for reengineering.

Business reengineering involves radically changing the way work is done to completely eliminate non-value-added steps.

Resource allocation involves identifying those projects to be executed and assigning people and dollars to them.

Project scope, cost, and completion date are variables that are a function of the number and skill level of the people available to work the project.

A Manager's Checklist

✔ Does your firm have a written vision and mission? What about your organization within the firm?

✔ Does a strategic plan exist for your firm? How about for the firm's use of information technology?

✔ Do the information technology projects that are executed relate well to the business objectives of the firm?

✔ Are any business processes being considered for reengineering? How was it determined which processes need reengineering?

✔ Are the projects that you are working on considered strategic?

Key Terms

applications portfolio
business applications
business area analysis
business data
business processes
contagion
control
corporate steering committee
critical success factor
customer
data administration
Gibson/Nolan six-stage model
goals
information strategy planning
initiation
integration
maturity

mission
non-value-added step
objectives
organizational plan
Porter's information system
   hierarchy
process/entity matrix
project
project constraints
project planning
resource allocation
resources
scope
strategic planning
strategy
structured group interview
vision

Review Questions

1. Why is an IT plan needed?

2. Give three reasons it is important for the business manager to be involved in the IT strategic planning process.

3. List and briefly describe the four key elements of the IT plan.

4. Outline a four-stage planning model and identify the goals and outputs of each stage.

5. Define the terms business process and business process reengineering.

6. State three criteria for evaluating if a business process should be reengineered.

7. What are the key elements of a business strategic plan?

Discussion Questions

1. You are in a firm where information technology is considered an administrative convenience. Is an information strategic plan needed? Why or why not?

2. Your firm has not updated its business plan in over three years. The IT manager has asked for your help in initiating a strategic planning process. What advice would you offer?

3. The CEO has requested you to start with the firm's recently completed business plan and to lead a group of senior and middle

managers to develop an IT plan in three months. She has asked you to tell her what you need in order to develop a good plan within this time limit. What would you say?

4. Your firm has no IT plan. However, it is clear that the customer order processing process is "broken" and fails to meet the customers' needs. Should you go ahead and begin business process reengineering in this area or wait until an IT plan has been developed?

Recommended Readings

1. Hammer, Michael. "Reengineering Work: Don't Automate, Obliterate." *Harvard Business Review* Vol. 90, No. 4 (July–August 1990).

2. Inglesby, Tom. "Reengineering the Business: The Time is Now." *Avalon Software White Paper* (October 1993).

3. Wetherbe, James C. "Reengineering the Business Process: Maximizing 'Value-Added' " from Systems Development." Index Summit Executive Forum (February 1991).

4. Diebold, John. "Charting a Future Course in Information Technology." *Journal of Business Strategy* 9 (May–June 1988).

5. Gibson, Cyrus and Richard L. Nolan. "Managing the Four Stages of EDP Growth." *Harvard Business Review* 52, no. 1 (January–February 1974).

6. Henderson, John C. and John G. Sifonis. "The Value of IS Planning: Understanding Consistency, Validity, and IS Markets." *MIS Quarterly* 12 (June 1988).

7. Johnston, H. Russell and Michael R. Vitale. "Creating Competitive Advantage with Interorganizational Information Systems." *MIS Quarterly* 12 (June 1988).

8. Kerr, Susan. "The New IS Force." *Datamation* 35 (1 August 1989).

9. Miron, Michael, John Cecil, Kevin Bradicich, and Gene Hall. "The Myths and Realities of Competitive Advantage." *Datamation* 34 (1 October 1988).

10. Porter, Michal E. "Reports." *Planning Review* (September/October 1988).

11. Rackoff, Nick, Charles Wiseman, and Walter Ullrich. "Information Systems for Competitive Advantage: Implementation of a Planning Process." *MIS Quarterly* (December 1985).

12. Martin, James. *Information Engineering, Book I Introduction.* Englewood Cliffs, NJ: Prentice-Hall Inc., 1989.

A Manager's Dilemma

Case Study 10.1

Information Technology Strategic Planning at Johnson's

Laurance T. Burden, forty-nine, took over as Senior Vice-president and the first CIO of S. C. Johnson & Son in November 1988. The establishment of the CIO position reflected the tenor of the times in the increasingly cost-conscious consumer goods industry. The demands of the competition forced the company to consider major changes in the way it conducted business, including reengineering key business processes. Information technology was chosen to become a driving force behind that renewal.

Prior to Burden's arrival, the IT chief wasn't even at the senior management level, and the IT function was a back-office support organization. A major study of the company by the New York consulting firm of Booz, Allen & Hamilton in 1988 told Johnson in no uncertain terms that if it wanted Raid, Brite, Pledge, Agree, Soft Sense, and its other market leaders to remain in their commanding positions, information technology must play a more active, even catalytic, role.

Specifically, the IT organization was asked to help break down the organizational walls that had isolated various divisions, from manufacturing, finance, and customer service to distribution, sales, and marketing. The chief stumbling block was a lack of teamwork. Customer service, both between divisions inside Johnson and the buyers of Johnson products, was to be the company watchword.

The old mass marketing rules that had driven consumer goods companies for so many years—where every customer received the same products, the same ads, and the same discounts—no longer applied. Johnson had to find a way to respond faster to segmented customer demands. All the on-going trends with distribution and sales required that Johnson become extremely proactive in serving its customers, yet Johnson was working in an environment where the trade knew more about what the clients needed than Johnson did.

The tool chosen to knock down those organizational walls was IT. Johnson's approach was to find a respected strategist like Burden, who could bring in a crack team to lead the change from the top down. In 1989, the die was cast when information technology was listed for the first time as one of the ten key corporate strategies to gain a competitive advantage.

As a privately held multinational company with thirteen thousand employees—three-quarters of whom work outside the United States—Johnson could take an approach that publicly held competitors would find difficult to match: investing for the next generation, not for the next quarter. For IT, this means long-term projects are less likely to be shot down because they don't yield short-term benefits. It is easier to mobilize long-term initiatives in a privately held company. Maximizing earnings per share is not always what is best for IT or for the company as a whole.

Burden spent much of his first year assembling a new IT management team, which included several new positions and new faces. With his new IT team in place, Burden then concentrated IT efforts on perfecting the interdivisional, cross-functional transaction processing system begun in July 1987. The system was scheduled to go into production by the end of the summer of 1990. A three-year program costing less than $5 million, Johnson's computer-integrated information customer service system (CICSS) was an IT solution to the corporation's call to improve customer service.

The focus on customer service was essential: consolidations had reduced the number of Johnson's wholesale customers from 600 to 250 in just three years. With more and more sales in the hands of fewer firms, the grocery and drug chains had even more leverage over suppliers like Johnson. For example, Super Valu, the second-largest wholesaler for supermarkets in the country, accounted for a full 10 percent of Johnson's volume. The role of the retailer had grown in importance; therefore, suppliers needed to focus more on how to serve retailers.

To a supplier like Johnson, a customer cutting back on inventory means reducing the lead time between order processing and delivery to stay competitive. With CICSS, the transaction processing that used to take fourteen working days now averaged around five. Without the system, that reduction in lead time would be impossible.

The pressure to cut the time lag between order processing and delivery was pushed to the breaking point in 1987 when Wal-Mart, the company's largest customer, went to electronic data interchange (EDI). Wal-Mart summarily announced that every paper order would have to be express mailed to Johnson—at Johnson's expense—if it didn't move to EDI. No faxes, no phone calls.

More pressure on the staff came from trying to keep track of increasingly complicated deals, preferred customers, and regional sales. Simple national marketing schemes—such as cutting $1 off the price of every case sold around the world for a month—were no longer the way to compete. Each region and each customer, depending on size, could be offered special incentives to buy.

By adding the flexibility to make better deals to the CICSS, the sales department reduced the amount of deductions it offered its customers from a high of $16 million to $4.5 million—a savings to the corporation of $11.5 million.

When information technology set out to alleviate the pressure on sales, the first steps focused on improving the customer service department. The focus quickly proved to be too narrow. In order to make a real dent in lagging customer service, each divisional head needed to know what the other was doing. The sales division, for example, needed to know the number of cases on hand in inventory. That information was locked up in the distribution division. The distribution division also needed to know the lead time in manufacturing new cases, information locked up in the manufacturing division. The promises to fill the daily orders that the various sales divisions fielded—some 150,000 per day—were based on paper printouts and educated guesses.

The idea at Johnson was to restructure the entire customer service process, not just streamline the operation of a division. The vice-presidents of sales, manufacturing, information technology, finance, and marketing formed a steering committee to track what happens to an order as it passes from organization to organization. By working with two other committees—one comprising work teams of IT personnel, the other a three-person liaison group linking both teams—the steering committee had the clout and the input from below to make major policy decisions.

Once they hammered out what amounted to a spaghetti chart of direct and dotted lines interconnecting twenty-five different operating systems and crisscrossing each division boundary several times, they decided a new division—customer service and logistics support, to be headed by the former Vice-president of Sales—made the most sense. Creating an entirely new division is a classic example of IT driving organizational change.

The CICSS can tell the user what is on an order in any one of the company's distribution centers around the country, as well as when those items are scheduled to ship. CICSS lets Johnson prioritize shipments and manage inventory effectively.

The key to Johnson's approach to CICSS was making sure business leaders with knowledge of where the industry was headed and with the power to make changes were involved in its planning. They managed to pull in senior executives in positioning the CICSS program as something bigger than IT—a whole new approach to meeting customer needs.

Burden believes IT people need to be just as creative and need to identify opportunities and serve up new projects just as much as the people in other departments who are running manufacturing or finance.

1. What were the key issues that led to the elevation of the role of the IT organization? Try to classify these issues as either business, organizational, or technical.

2. Given these key issues, do you feel that development of the CICSS was the most important effort for the IT organization to initiate? Can you suggest two or three other candidate projects?

3. What problems do you feel Burden may have faced in his first year with Johnson as he built his new management team, got on board with the CICSS project (already under way for sixteen months), and became the first IT manager involved in the company's strategic planning process?

4. Do you agree with the author's statement that it is easier to mobilize long-term initiatives in a privately held company?

SOURCE: © 1990 by CMP Publications, Inc., 600 Community Drive, Manhasset, NY 11030. Reprinted from *InformationWeek* with permission.

Case Study 10.2

The Integration of Information Technology and Strategic Planning at Sears

Sears, Roebuck & Company, now the second-largest U.S. retailer, is a family store for middle-class, home-owning Americans, with over 24 million credit card holders. When Sears was struggling to get out of a 1970s earnings nosedive, a strategic planning committee explored the possibility of diversification. After looking at a wide range of possible opportunities, Sears decided to expand into financial services. Underlying this strategic decision was the assumption that middle America was becoming more aware of savings and investment opportunities and that Sears could capture a sizable share of the business that had been conducted with traditional financial institutions in the past.

A task force, which was assembled at the corporate level and included members of the IT organization, explored possible opportunities and how to capitalize on them. The task force's objective was to develop a strategy to attract Sears' 36 million customers to its financial services.

In July 1982, Sears launched its campaign to become a major new force in the financial services industry: it opened the first branch outlets of the Sears Financial Network, a chain of "financial supermarkets" where shoppers could buy stocks, bonds, insurance, or houses, or open up IRAs. Although observers were skeptical of selling stocks and socks under one roof, the financial outlets proved highly successful and profitable. The trusted Sears name and the allure of one-stop shopping attracted new customers. Another plus for Sears customers was the fact that the financial outlets did not keep banker's hours—most Sears stores were open until 9:00 P.M. on weeknights, and all day Saturday and Sunday afternoons.

At any financial outlet, Sears customers can choose from a wide range of services. Shoppers can inquire about insurance coverage for their car, house, or family with Allstate Insurance (a longtime Sears subsidiary). Customers can also talk with Coldwell, Banker & Company (the largest independent real estate brokerage company in the United States, which Sears bought in 1981 as part of its master plan) for information about homes for sale. Clients can receive advice and invest in stocks, bonds, money market funds, and so on from Dean Witter Reynolds (a large brokerage firm, also acquired by Sears in 1981 as part of its master plan).

IT plays a key supporting role in the Sears Financial Network. Personal computers are used at the financial outlets to retrieve information stored in data bases, to compare investment options, and to calculate insurance premiums. Large mainframe computers are linked through communications to enable updating of corporate data bases with information from Sears outlets throughout the United States. Computer programs that can run on both personal computers and larger computers are used by Sears employees to help serve customers. Sears is also developing many information and transaction services for use by customers, including both an electronic payment system and a system that allows customers to enter their catalog orders directly into Sears computers.

In addition to providing support to the corporate strategy of expanding the Sears Financial Network and its services, IT constitutes a marketed product in its own right. Sears created a new corporate unit to leverage its huge data processing and data communications resources. Sears Communications, a Sears subsidiary, is a resale common carrier that sells the excess communications capacity on its network to other organizations.

It is now the 1990s, and Sears has lost its position as the nation's number-one retailer to Wal-Mart. Growth has been sluggish, and market share has decreased with net income declining. The formation of another strategic planning committee is being discussed. The CEO has asked you, senior Vice-president of Information Technology, to review the process followed last time and the results it produced.

Do you agree that there is value in reviewing the recommendations of the last strategic planning committee and the results it produced? What sort of lessons might be learned? How could such an analysis be conducted? Who should conduct this review? Neither you nor the current CEO participated in the last effort in the early 1980s.

Case Study 10.3

Developing the Ultimate Reservation System

American's Sabre and Covia's Apollo computerized reservation systems (CRS) are engaged in as hot a struggle as the airlines themselves. The business of United versus American as domestic carriers is no longer what the game is. The role of a global CRS is more than just a cost saver or a back-room operator—it is really the heart of the business.

In 1988, United sold half of Covia to a partnership of several other airlines. Allan Loren, previously president of Apple Computer's U.S. division, was hired as President and CEO of Covia. Loren believes that Covia still hasn't created the product that will truly differentiate Apollo in the minds of the travel agent or corporate buyer. His goal is to find an incentive for the travel agent or corporate user to want the Apollo system.

One idea is to create a new version of Apollo that will require considerably less training time. If end users could be trained in one day or less on site, that would create an immediate breakthrough. Cutting training time will have a big value for both large and small travel agencies. Small agencies won't have to send people out for long training periods, so their customer service won't suffer, and larger agencies won't have a big expense in training and retraining of new hires.

This upcoming product will be the key to the growth of Apollo and the carriers that own it. Covia wants to be not only the best in the business but also the biggest. Covia has the experience of having operated a CRS to service agents around the world—something Sabre has to figure out. From Loren's perspective, the future of the CRS is inexorably linked with that of the airline. There is no question that the carrier benefits from having a leading distribution network and the distributor benefits from having the leading carriers.

Imagine that you are the manager in charge of defining the new version of Apollo for Covia. How would you define what features the product must have to be truly superior to other CRS products? How would you create a CRS with more features but one that takes less time to learn? What complications are introduced if the CRS is to be used by agents around the world?

Case Study 10.4   # Ineffective Meetings

JoAnne has been IT Director for over three years and has sat in on the IT steering committee meetings since they began over seven months ago. Although at first she had high hopes that the meetings would finally give her an opportunity to share many of her excellent ideas with senior managers of the firm, she has become discouraged as the meetings have degenerated into gripe sessions. Each month a different manager complains loudly and bitterly about some system failure or pet project that is behind schedule. JoAnne feels the group has lost sight of their mission and wonders how to get the group to function effectively? What suggestions do you have?

Chapter 11

Design, Construction, and Maintenance

Upon completion of this chapter, you will be able to:

1. State the goal of the design and construction stages of an information systems project.

2. Discuss the key activities performed and the role of the business manager during each of the steps in the design and construction stages.

3. Discuss the JAD process and explain how it helps managers to define business needs clearly.

4. Define the term software maintenance and state five reasons why such a large amount of effort is expended against this activity.

5. Outline the project risks inherent in strategic information system projects.

6. Describe the 80/20 rule and how it can be applied to deliver effective results in minimum time and at low cost.

7. Discuss the problems associated with defining project feasibility too early.

Preview

The information engineering system development process is in broad use today. It is used both to develop new information systems and to purchase and install software packages. Organizations that follow this process are able to deliver information systems that closely match their user's needs in a shorter elapsed time and at lower cost than those who do not follow this process. The business manager has a critical role in the design and construction stages of this process.

Issues

1. What can business managers do to add real value to the information systems development process?

2. At what stage in its development should an information systems project be judged as "feasible," and what does that really mean?

3. What can systems users do to ensure that the system will really meet their needs prior to converting to the new system?

4. Why is so much effort spent on software maintenance? Is this level of effort appropriate?

Trade-offs

1. How much effort should business managers budget in support of an information systems project in their area of responsibility?

2. What trade-offs can be made to shorten the cost and the elapsed time to complete an information systems project?

3. What impact does designing a system with extremely thorough edits and controls have on the ease and speed of system operation?

4. What is the impact of reducing the level of effort spent on information system maintenance?

A Manager Struggles with the Issues

Management is extremely anxious to upgrade the old batch processing order-entry system to an on-line application. Because this is the organization's first on-line application, the IT organization recommended bringing in a new DBMS and upgrading to a larger mainframe computer to meet the need for fast transaction processing. The latest in CASE tools had been purchased for the project team members to help ensure rapid delivery of this critical system. And of course, consultants, lots of consultants—more than $25,000 per month in consulting fees! Yet in spite of all this, something was desperately wrong. Six months into the project there were no tangible signs of progress. Sure, the new mainframe was installed and running, but that was about the only thing that management could point to as real evidence of progress. The Manager of Customer Services, owner of the order-entry system, has put you on special assignment to help bring some order to the project and establish some means for tracking project progress.

■ THE INFORMATION ENGINEERING SYSTEM DEVELOPMENT LIFE CYCLE

What Is the Information Engineering System Development Life Cycle?

Following the information engineering system development life cycle (SDLC), the system development project is divided into well-defined stages, steps, and tasks, and the work progress is managed and controlled by formal project management methods. The user is involved in the production of deliverables during each step (Exhibit 11.1) and in the review and critique of these deliverables. At the end of each step, there is a formal review. If appropriate, the project steering team and users sign off that everything is OK to this point and authorize the project team to proceed on to the next step. Thus the work progress is very linear, so that once a step is done, work continues on to the next step with (ideally) no rework or iteration of preceding steps.

Even when restricting the discussion to the information engineering SDLC, different authors, consultants, and organizations have developed different solution approaches. These approaches, while similar, may recommend a different work breakdown structure, employ different techniques, have different strategies for managing the quality of results, and employ different tools. For example, this author recommends that project teams construct some sort of working prototype to confirm user requirements.

■ DESIGN

The design stage is divided into five steps discussed below.

Project Definition

The business purpose of the project definition phase is to obtain a clear definition of the problem or opportunity to be addressed. Unfortu-

Stage	Step	Task
Design	Project Definition	Define Problem and Its Causes Establish Project Constraints Identify Stakeholders Define Project Rationale Develop Plan for Next Steps
	Analysis	Study the Existing System Define Business Needs (JAD) Identify Alternatives Evaluate Alternatives Define Proposed Solution Identify Organizational Changes Update Project Plan and Business Case
	Functional Design	Define Functional Requirements Define Performance Requirements Define Internal Control Requirements Document System Acceptance Criteria Update Project Plan and Business Case
	Prototype	Build the Prototype Evaluate the Prototype
	Technical Design	Convert Logical Data Base Design to Physical Design Design Program Modules Conduct Design Review Develop Test Plans Create User Documentation Develop User Training Program Update Project Plan and Business Case
Construction	Code and Test Modules	Code Module Inspect Code Compile Module Test Module
	Testing	Integration Test System Test Acceptance Test
	Conversion	Deliver User Training Cutover
Maintenance		

nately, it is difficult to make a clear distinction between the results or goals we wish to achieve (the problem) and the various possible courses of action for getting those results (the solutions). Business managers constantly make the mistake of specifying the means of doing something rather than the result that is wanted. Thus, IT people are sent off to implement a solution without knowing the real problem that needs to be addressed. Developing a solution that really does not deliver the desired results can be wasted effort.

Define Problem and Its Causes

Recognizing the previously mentioned pitfalls of prescribing solutions without knowing the problem, an effective problem solver must shift

Exhibit 11.2
Questions to Define
the Problem or
Opportunity

Questions to Help Identify the Basic Problem
   What causes you to think that we have a problem?
   Could you describe what you feel is the basic problem?
   What sort of effects are generated by this problem?
   What factors or changes have caused this problem?

Questions to Help Obtain Further Clarification
   I'm not exactly clear on . . . . Could you explain more about . . .?
   What do you mean by . . .?
   Can you provide some examples?
   What else concerns you about . . .?
   What data do you have about . . .?
   Tell me more about . . . .

Questions to Identify Whose Problem It Is
   Who is having the problem?
   Who could take action to solve this problem?
   Who is interested in solving this problem?
   Who else needs to be involved in forming a solution, and how do they need to be involved?
   Is there anyone who wants to maintain the status quo? If so, why?

Questions to Assess the Importance of the Problem or Opportunity
   How significant is the problem?
   What are the best results we could expect from implementing a "perfect" solution?
   What's the worst thing that could happen if we did nothing?
   How soon is a solution needed? What is the penalty if this deadline is missed?

Questions to Help Plan the Next Steps
   I'm sure you've had some thoughts on . . . . What would you like to see happen?
   Based on your knowledge of the situation, what do you think is the best way to proceed?
   Is it expected that the current system (if it exists) will be the starting point for creating a new or revised system?

people's focus from prescribing solutions to identifying the basic problem or opportunity. It is then possible to begin a more rational problem-solving process, one based on all the data and objective analysis.

One way to identify the basic problem is for the problem solver to interview the people initiating the problem to obtain a clear, concise, written statement of the problem or opportunity that needs to be addressed. Exhibit 11.2 outlines some basic questions to help achieve this objective. The interview process should focus on understanding *why* something needs to be done rather than specifics on *what* needs to be done.

A good problem statement describes, in concise terms, the system, organization, product, or group having the problem and what exactly is wrong with it or them (Exhibit 11.3). The problem statement does *not* describe the solution to the problem.

Such an approach will help to clarify the opportunities, problems, or issues that require attention and perhaps some form of action. The problem solver must still be extremely wary, for most assuredly the initial statement of the problem or situation is not complete or is (unintentionally) misleading. Indeed, the basic assumption should be that the initial problem statement is either incomplete or incorrect.

The **fishbone diagram** (Exhibit 11.4) is another technique to help people define problems. The technique was developed by Dr. K.

Exhibit 11.3
Examples of Good
Problem Definition
Statements

> Problem 1
> The current level of accounts receivable overdue by more than ninety days is at an all-time high: 22 percent of average monthly sales.
>
> Problem 2
> Sales in four of our six sales districts have fallen below the sales forecast for each of the last three months.
>
> Problem 3
> The biweekly payroll system has failed to produce paychecks on time for the last two paydays.
>
> Problem 4
> Senior marketing managers are unable to evaluate the competition's reaction to our new product introductions.

Ishikasa of Japan. It shows the relationship between the problem and the factors that influence it. The problem is shown on the right side of the chart (the mouth of the fish), and the major factors are diagrammed on the left. Every problem most likely has major categories of factors and several minor factors related to each of the major factors. The detailed diagramming of a problem and all its factors takes on the shape of a fish skeleton; thus the name *fishbone diagram.*

The problem solver typically works with a small group of people (four to eight) who identified the problem, plus a few others who are

Exhibit 11.4
A Fishbone Diagram

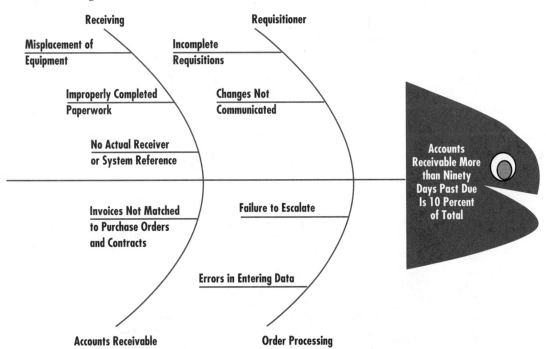

knowledgeable in the area to develop the fishbone diagram. The process of creating the fishbone diagram causes people to more clearly define the problem they need to address. Upon completion of this exercise, the group is usually in agreement on what is the problem they are facing and what are all its contributing factors. From here, work can proceed forward to resolve the problem. The fishbone diagram can also be used to define opportunities.

Establish Project Constraints

In addition to defining the fundamental problem to be addressed, it is also necessary to establish the constraints that must be met for any proposed solution to be acceptable. These constraints include the scope of the business to be addressed, key objectives to be met, and the constraints (e.g., cost and schedule) under which the project must proceed. The use of a group interview with key stakeholders, potential members of the project steering team, and system users is an effective way to gain agreement on scope. Key questions that can help define scope and **project constraints** include those listed in Exhibit 11.5.

At this early stage in the project, it is important to recognize that these constraints are really **soft constraints.** That is, management is usually still quite willing to explore trade-offs. They may be willing to consider a solution that is less expensive but addresses a narrower scope and is completed earlier than the original constraints. These trade-offs are made explicitly during the feasibility step later on during the analysis phase.

Identify Stakeholders

Stakeholders are people who have a stake in the success of the project. They are people who are or will be affected by the system and people who are needed to ensure its successful development, operation, or ongoing support. Stakeholders very importantly include those people

---

Exhibit 11.5
Questions to Define
Scope and Project
Constraints

What is the fundamental reason why management is calling for this study?
- Provide better control over operations?
- Reduce costs?
- Speed up the processing cycle of a given business function?

Which departments need to be included in this study?

- Who is the initial source of input data to feed this system?
- Who will use the results of this system and how?
- Who will be impacted by this system and how?

What budgetary and time limitations exist?

- Is there a specific event or date by which a solution is needed?
- How important is the solution of this problem to management?
- How many people should be put against solving this problem?

who are influential enough to kill the project. Stakeholders also include anyone who can exert enough influence on others to create an environment where successful implementation will be extremely difficult. The most important stakeholders include the **system sponsor, system owner, legitimizers,** and **opinion leaders** (Exhibit 11.6).

The sponsor justifies and pays for the expense and effort required to develop the information system. The sponsor verifies that the development of the system represents a sound use of company resources and sells senior management on the merits of the system. The project team must seek the approval of this individual for any proposed changes in system scope, project cost, or schedule. The sponsor grants the IT people access to the business organization and helps them to get started.

The system owner is the manager of the organization that will use the system to achieve the business benefits for which it was created. Throughout the project, the system owner ensures that the system being developed will indeed meet the needs of the business and that the owner's organization will be able to operate the system successfully. Once the system is complete, the system owner insists on an ongoing review of the system to ensure that it continues to meet the business needs for which it was designed.

The system sponsor and system owner are key and powerful players in the development of an information system. They must be identified early on in the project. Without clear identification of who will fill these vital roles, management should refuse to allocate resources to the project. Failure to identify a system sponsor and system owner is a red flag that cannot be ignored.

A legitimizer is a person who tends to protect the norms and values of the current system. Legitimizers may even have been involved in creating the current system. These people are experienced and highly competent in their job. They are viewed as experts by their fellow workers. The legitimizers are usually among the last group of people to support a change, but once their support is gained, the probability of

Exhibit 11.6
How to Establish
Strong Support for
a Project

1. Identify the sponsor and ensure that the sponsor not only understands the role but also agrees to fulfill the associated responsibilities.
2. Do not agree to a sponsor who is a member of the IT organization. If the project has a strong business benefit, a senior business manager should sponsor it.
3. Identify the system owner and ensure that the owner not only understands the role but also agrees to fulfill the associated responsibilities.
4. Do not agree to a system owner who is a member of the IT organization. If the project has a strong business benefit, a senior business manager should own the resultant system.
5. Identify all legitimizers and get them involved early on in the project. Seek their advice and counsel on how the existing system can be improved.
6. Identify opinion leaders and get them involved early on in the project. Share your ideas on how the existing system might be changed, and check their reaction.

successful implementation of any new system is greatly increased. The project team should identify the legitimizers and get them involved early on in the project, as well as ask for their advice and counsel on how the existing system could be improved.

Opinion leaders are people whom others watch to see their acceptance of new ideas and changes. These are creative people with a high degree of receptivity to change. Frequently, they are younger people who are recognized as up-and-comers. They may have little formal power in the organization. The project team should identify opinion leaders and get them involved early on in the project, as well as share ideas with them on how the existing system might be changed and check their reaction.

Define Project Rationale

A very preliminary business case is developed that outlines the areas of benefit and provides a rationale for continuation of the project. Because an organization always has more problems and opportunities than it can address with its limited resources, it is essential to ascertain if this effort is consistent with business strategy and to assess its relative priority against other projects. At this point, the project can be terminated or put on hold if it is deemed to be inconsistent with strategy or less important than other efforts that need staffing and resources.

Develop Plan for Next Steps

Finally, the stakeholders develop a plan for the next stage. The plan provides some idea of the level of resources and elapsed time required. The plan also clearly states the roles and responsibilities for key players that will be involved in the future work.

At this point in the project, it is a very serious mistake to develop an estimate of the project cost and completion date. Stakeholders should recognize all that has been done so far is to outline the project scope—the problem or area of opportunity to be explored. No real requirements for solution have been defined, nor has the nature of the solution been specified. Estimating cost and schedule should be strongly resisted until after completion of the analysis step.

The project definition step is typically a relatively short (no more than a couple of weeks) although extremely important step. Upon successful completion of this step, the problem to be addressed is clearly defined, the critical attributes of an acceptable solution are established, the key stakeholders to be involved in developing the solution are identified, a preliminary business case is developed, and a plan for the next steps in the rest of the project exists. Exhibit 11.7 summarizes the key deliverables produced and the responsibilities of the business manager during the project definition step.

The results of the project definition step are presented to the sponsor and system owner for their review and comment. They review the recommended actions presented by the project manager and make a

Exhibit 11.7
Work Breakdown Structure for the Project Definition Step

Stage of Information Engineering: Design Step: Project Definition		
Task	Deliverable	Key Management Responsibility
Define Problem and Its Causes	Problem Definition Statement Fishbone Diagram	Identify Basic Business Problem Provide Data about the Problem
Establish Project Constraints	Project Description	Define Scope of Business to be Addressed Identify Key Project Objectives Set Preliminary Cost and Schedule Limits
Identify Stakeholders	List of Stakeholders	Identify and Recruit Project Sponsor Identify and Recruit System Owner Identify Legitimizers Identify Opinion Leaders
Define Project Rationale	Statement of Project Benefits	Develop Rationale for Doing Project Ensure Project Is Consistent with Business Strategy Quantify Benefits Establish Relative Priority of Project
Develop Plan for Next Steps	Project Plan for Analysis Stage	Make Go/No-Go Decision to Proceed

go/no-go decision for the next step of the project: the analysis step of the design stage.

Analysis

During the analysis step two fundamental questions are asked: What will the system do? and, is the proposed system economically, technically, and operationally feasible? All analysis should be directed at answering these questions. These analysis tasks are summarized below.

Study the Existing System

To answer the first question, the project team studies the existing system, work processes, and business practices to gain a clear understanding of the strengths and limitations of the existing system. This knowledge forms the initial basis for a set of realistic requirements for the future system. Gaining a good understanding of the current system also provides an excellent starting point for developing a step-by-step plan to convert from the old system to the new one. Exhibit 11.8 summarizes the many areas of investigation needed for understanding the existing system.

There is yet another very compelling reason calling for a study of the current system. Such a study provides an excellent opportunity for the project team to establish rapport and a high level of credibility with the current system users. The users' acceptance of the team and their participation in the development of a solution are essential to the successful implementation and operation of any new system. Thus users

Exhibit 11.8
Areas of the
Existing System to
Be Investigated

Analyze Input Data and Methods
- Who prepares the input?
- How much effort is required?
- Are data prepared accurately and on time?
- What is the volume of input data?

Review Existing Methods and Procedures
- How are things done?
- Who does them?
- Are there unnecessary steps? Can tasks be streamlined?
- How many people are required?

Analyze System Output
- What are the most important outputs from the system?
- How often are they produced and who uses them?
- Do the outputs really meet the needs of the users?
- Does the cost of preparing and distributing the report exceed its value?

Review Internal Control
- Where are the critical points in the operation where some comparison, edit, or validation is performed?
- Does good documentation of the existing system exist?
- Do the users have a good understanding of the system and its procedures?
- Does the system operate predictably and reliably?

Review Data Files and Data Bases
- Who is responsible for maintaining them?
- Who accesses them, how often, and to do what?
- Are they kept up-to-date, accurate, and complete?
- How large are they?

must be given ample opportunity to air their feelings about the current system and ideas for improvement before moving to the next task. Furthermore, the more the users' ideas are incorporated into the new system, the more receptive the users are to changes necessary to implement it.

The best way to understand the current system is to observe the operation and to talk directly to the individuals who do the work. Selected members of the project team may begin their study of a given area or operation by discussing the activities of the organizational unit with the unit manager. The project team may then observe and speak with the workers to gain a greater understanding. Frequently the work gets done in ways that are different from the description given by the unit manager. Each interview should be friendly and informal. Notes should be taken as the interview progresses. It is a good idea to solicit the unit manager and workers for suggestions on how the current operation could be improved. These individuals are often the best source of new ideas. Further, because they have had an opportunity to participate in defining future changes, their acceptance of these changes later in the implementation process will be greatly improved.

Another source of information is the organization's documentation, often captured in Users' Manuals, Standards and Procedures Manuals, and technical documentation. These documents can be helpful in understanding current operations, however, conditions often change after documentation is printed.

Based on the interviews, observation, and review of documents, a rough, high-level data flow diagram of the operation can be drawn. This diagram then is used as a sort of road map. Members of the study team observe the operation a second time and modify the data flow diagram as required to reflect the way work is actually performed.

Occasionally, unit managers and their workers may be reluctant to schedule time to meet with the project team. The project sponsor can eliminate this problem by sending a memo to all managers with whom the project team must meet. The sponsor's memo must emphasize the importance of the project to the future success of the firm and request (politely) that all managers cooperate fully with the project team.

Upon completion of this task, the project team will know what problems exist in the current system and where the current system fails to meet existing business needs.

Define Business Needs

Future business needs need to be identified. The project team does not want to simply refine an existing system when major restructuring and reengineering are required.

With regard to defining future business needs, the project team can take the approach recommended in Chapter 10. At this time, a specific area of the business to be studied has been defined as a result of the project definition step. Thus the study can be more focused than during the development of a broad IT strategic plan covering many areas of the business. Briefly, the team would study underlying business processes, identify current problems, identify critical success factors, and evaluate overall effectiveness. Joint Application Development (JAD), is a powerful technique for defining business needs. End users and managers from the organizations that will provide input to, use, or obtain output from the system are brought together at one time. The JAD sessions are led by a trained facilitator who possesses excellent meeting leadership and communication skills. The JAD approach leads to defining stronger, better system solutions by having several people familiar with the same problems, issues, and opportunities working together and building off one another's ideas.

Considerable effort is required to execute a JAD session successfully. The JAD session is divided into three phases: prework, execution, and follow-up. Prework involves all preparation necessary to make the actual JAD session as successful as possible. Prework tasks include defining a clear goal for the session, identifying and recruiting the participants, establishing an agenda consistent with JAD principles and the goal of the session, and preparing the participants. Execution involves the actual running of the JAD session with users and others jointly developing key components of the system. Follow-up involves producing the formal JAD output and disseminating it for review and feedback from the participants and others. At the end of defining the business needs, the project team will know:

Where the current system fails to meet anticipated future business needs

What needs to be done to eliminate these shortcomings

Identify Alternatives

Everyone with any stake in the success of the system must work together during the analysis step to ensure that the system will do what is really needed and that a cost-effective alternative is chosen for implementation. The system analysts, system users, business managers, and the system owner must work together closely to assign priorities to system requirements and to identify and evaluate various systems alternatives.

Everyone involved in the system development process should recognize that the system requirements are rather flexible. The system requirements can be divided into categories, or rated as high-, medium-, and low-priority requirements. The high-priority requirements represent features that the system must have. The medium-priority requirements are important but not absolutely essential. The low-priority requirements are ones that would be nice. Using this priority assignment scheme, it is possible to identify a number of different system alternatives with varying costs, features, and benefits. Managers should look for an alternative that meets the minimum standard of satisfaction for the values and goals being sought instead of performing a painstaking analysis of every possible alternative. Thus managers tend to **satisfice**—that is, find an alternative that is good enough but not perfect. At least three alternatives should be identified and evaluated for possible implementation:

1. **The Do-Everything (Cadillac) Alternative** This alternative meets or exceeds all user requirements.

2. **The High-Cost with Lots of Features (Buick) Alternative** This alternative meets or exceeds all of the high-priority system requirements, meets or exceeds most of the medium-priority requirements, and even meets many low-priority requirements.

3. **The Low-Cost (Chevrolet) Alternative** This alternative doesn't have all the nice-to-have features (bells and whistles), but it provides the capabilities to get the essential job done. It meets or exceeds most, but perhaps not all, the high-priority requirements, a few of the medium-priority requirements, and almost none of the low-priority items.

Quite often, analysis of these three options reveals that nearly 80 percent of all the potential benefits associated with the system can be achieved through implementing the low-cost alternative for 20 percent of the expense associated with the high-cost alternative. Exhibit 11.9 provides an analysis of three alternatives.

Exhibit 11.9
Analysis of
Alternatives

User Needs	Alternatives		
	1	2	3
High-Priority Requirements			
Improve payment timeliness	Yes	Yes	Yes
Improve internal control	Yes	Yes	Yes
Minimize checking account balance	Yes	Yes	No
Medium-Priority Requirements			
Forecast cash flow for five days	Yes	Yes	Yes
Track vendors' level of business	Yes	Yes	No
Reduce manual check writing	Yes	Yes	No
Simplify reconciliation with bank	Yes	No	No
Low-Priority Requirements			
Write checks on multiple banks	Yes	No	No
Add check digit to vendor code	Yes	Yes	Yes
Produce check docket on microfiche	Yes	No	No
Estimated Development Cost	$250K	$150K	$50K
Annual Value of Tangible Benefits	$100K	$90K	$80K
Simple Payback Period—Years	2.5	1.7	0.6

Evaluate Alternatives

Each alternative should also be examined for technical, economic, and operational feasibility. The various alternatives must be weighed against one another to see which meets the needs of the business and is the most cost-effective proposal. To do nothing and keep the current system is always one alternative. In other words, sometimes the appropriate action is to maintain the status quo or perhaps make relatively minor changes to the way things are done currently without introducing a whole new system.

Technical feasibility is a measure of the degree of confidence the organization implementing the system has in the use of the technology (e.g., interactive decision support systems, large corporate data base, artificial intelligence). If there is strong doubt that the particular technology will work or that the vendor(s) involved in providing hardware or software are not viable, then the proposed solution may not be technically feasible.

Economic feasibility implies that the benefits associated with the system have been quantified and compared to all the costs associated with designing, implementing, operating, and enhancing and maintaining the system. Analysis of these benefits versus costs shows that a decision to implement the system is a sound economic decision with an acceptable rate of return on investment.

Operational feasibility means that the system is acceptable to the users and managers of the system. There are several questions to this aspect. Do users and managers agree with the new roles, responsibilities, business processes, and procedures associated with the new system? Do they feel that the system has been designed so that it supports them in the new roles? Are they confident that they can be trained to operate the system efficiently? Does the IT organization have the skilled personnel needed to develop, implement, operate, and support the system?

Define Proposed Solution

Producing level-1 and lower-level data flow diagrams of the alternative to be implemented is an excellent means of defining the proposed solution. The level-1 diagram shows the system boundaries, all data sources and recipients, the main system inputs and outputs, the primary system processes, and the usage of data between processes and data stores. Up to this point in the analysis, only the level-1 data flow diagram has been produced. It is now time to do a more thorough analysis and develop a separate data flow diagram for each of the half-dozen or so primary processes in the level-1 data flow diagram.

Identify Organizational Issues

Unfortunately, information technology is often introduced with little regard for the other elements of the total work system in which it is to be embedded—the business and the organization (Exhibit 11.10). The technology is chosen and optimized in isolation from any other part of the work system. Evaluation of the technology is an inward-looking process carried out by specialists and highly skilled technicians who feel that "outsiders," such as end users and their managers, have no part to play in implementing technology. Such an approach results in

Exhibit 11.10
The Major
Components of the
Work System

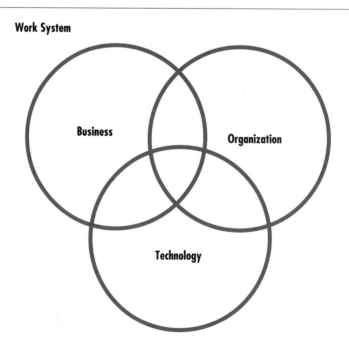

the use of technology in a way that disrupts the organization and does little to meet the needs of the business. Such applications of technology can only be classified as failures.

The project sponsor, system owner, and project team must identify all changes associated with implementing a proposed solution that affects the organization or its members. Examples include changes in the number or skills of people employed, changes in individuals' roles and responsibilities, or changes in the current business processes and practices. Exhibit 11.11 provides a set of questions useful in identifying organizational issues. The organizational units that are affected and how they are affected are also described. Some organizational units are only slightly affected. For others the change may be drastic—a department might be eliminated, for example.

The impact of information technology on employment is a major ethical issue with which business managers must struggle. While its introduction has created new jobs and increased productivity, IT has also led to a significant reduction in many types of job opportunities. For example, the use of Executive Information Systems has eliminated middle-level managers whose roles were to retrieve, report, and analyze data for senior managers. Furthermore, the jobs created by the application of IT often require different types of skills and education than the current set of employees possesses. Workers may become unemployed unless they can be retrained for new positions or new responsibilities. Thus business managers have to seriously review the impact of the proposed solution on the organization as a whole and on workers in particular.

It is wise to assign responsibility for bringing about the necessary organizational changes early in the project—long before system conversion. People with this responsibility must develop a plan for an orderly transition to the new organization. They need to identify specific actions required to accomplish the transition. The sequence and timing of these actions are also established so that they are consistent with the overall development and cutover schedule. Often specialists or human resource consultants are recruited to help make the organizational changes as smooth and successful as possible.

Exhibit 11.11
Questions to
Identify
Organizational
Issues

- How will people's jobs be affected?
  - Will there be changes in staffing levels?
  - Will there be a change in the content of people's jobs?
  - Will there be a change in the skill level required to perform jobs?
- What must we do to help people be successful in the future environment?
- How can we help people accept these changes?
- When is the best time to introduce this change?
- Will there be changes in organizational structure?
- Will we change business policies?
- Will we change business processes?

Update Project Plan and Business Case

Before finishing the analysis phase, the proposed system solution should be developed in sufficient detail to allow an accurate estimate of the cost to build and operate the system, as well as to estimate the value of the tangible benefits associated with the system.

At this point in the project, the use of an objective resource to help develop an estimate of the project costs and tangible benefits is strongly recommended. This resource can also help identify potential project risks. Many large organizations have financial analysts who study various project proposals (information systems, marketing initiatives, new plant and capacity projects, and so on). They see dozens of proposals a year and can provide an excellent objective perspective. They can also help to prepare the formal project proposal in business terms familiar to the project sponsor and system owner.

The results of the analysis phase are presented to the project sponsor and system owner for their review and comment. They listen to the recommended next steps presented by the project manager and make a go/no-go decision for the next phase. They may also recommend that a separate effort be initiated to capitalize on any opportunity to make a "quick hit" and implement any immediate ("aspirin") changes that seem appropriate.

Exhibit 11.12 summarizes the key deliverables and responsibilities during the analysis step of the design stage.

Exhibit 11.12
Work Breakdown Structure for the Analysis Step

Stage of Information Engineering: Design Step: Analysis		
Task	Deliverables	Key Management Responsibility
Study the Existing System	Data Flow Diagram—Current System ER Diagram—Current System	Communicate Information about the Current System: Work Processes and Business Practices
Define Business Needs	Specific Examples of Where/How Current System Fails to Meet Future Business Needs	Translate Vision of Future into Business Needs Identify Specific Shortcomings of the Current System
Identify Alternatives	Definition of at Least Three Options Low-, Medium-, and High-Cost Solution	Identify at Least Three Potential Solutions
Evaluate Alternatives	For Each Option Produce: Rough Cost/Benefit Analysis Estimate of Elapsed Time Required	Evaluate Pros and Cons of Each Alternative Determine Technical, Economic, and Operational Feasibility of Each Alternative
Define Proposed Solution	List of Pros and Cons	
Identify Organizational Changes	List of Organization Changes Individual Responsible for Successful Implementation of Changes	Identify All Changes Associated with Implementing Proposed Solution that Affect the Organization and Its Members
Update Project Plan and Business Case	Project Plan for Functional Design Step	Make Go/No-Go Decision to Proceed

Real World Perspective

Aspirin Solution for Accounts Payable Operation

The manager of accounts payable was alarmed that a large number of invoices were being paid too late to take advantage of the discount offered for prompt payment by vendors (e.g., 2 percent discount if paid within ten days, otherwise net within thirty days). A sample survey of vendor invoices and the checks associated with their payment revealed that over two hundred invoices per months were paid too late, losing about $20,000 per month in discounts. Armed with this information, the manager of accounts payable was able to convince the company comptroller to authorize accounts payable staff overtime and weekend operations, the "aspirin" solution—quick, cheap, and easy—but perhaps not long lasting. The additional cost of this overtime was about $6,000 per month, but it was estimated that the amount of discounts lost would be reduced to less than $9,000 per month, for a net savings of at least $5,000 per month. The comptroller insisted and the manager of accounts payable agreed that this should only be a temporary solution. The ideal solution was to upgrade or replace the existing accounts payable system so that all invoices were paid promptly with the existing number of employees (or preferably fewer) and with no overtime.

Functional Design

Following approval to proceed beyond the analysis step, the IT organization assigns technical people such as systems analysts, programmers, and equipment specialists to the project. These people focus on defining the technical requirements for computer programs and operations of the system. They select the best means of using existing computer hardware and software to build the system. If necessary, they evaluate the need for new computer hardware and software.

The managers in the end-user organization assign people to participate in the project to specify how the system will operate and to develop material needed to ensure that the system operates successfully—manual procedures, training, and operating manuals. The end-user organization is also responsible for making sure that the final system will operate reliably and dependably and will meet the needs of the organization. Thus, the end-user organization must have heavy and ongoing involvement in the design and implementation phases of the project.

The functional design step involves the creation of detailed models of the processes and the data required to support the new system. At this point, the system design is still independent of any specific hardware and software technology. Thus the functional design could potentially be implemented using IBM's DB2 data base management system running on a large IBM mainframe or the Oracle data base management system running on a DEC/VAX minicomputer.

Define Functional Requirements

The **functional requirements** task involves translating the business needs defined in the analysis step into information system requirements. One method to define system requirements is to work backward—by first defining what outputs the system must produce to meet the business needs, and then, given that the system must produce these outputs, determining what files and data bases already exist from which to draw the necessary information to produce those outputs. If the outputs cannot be entirely produced from existing files and data bases, the system developers should determine what specific pieces of data are missing. This data must be captured from input to the system. This approach is effective for defining requirements of management reporting systems.

An opposite approach might be taken if the system is primarily a transaction processing system. Under these circumstances, a more straightforward approach is appropriate. The system developers start by defining the types of transactions to be processed, determining which files and data bases need to be updated and maintained to process those transactions, and then defining the reports necessary to meet the needs of that particular business function.

Typically all the requirements of an information system are not equally important. Some requirements may be mandatory, implying that the system will not be acceptable unless these requirements are met in an agreed manner. Some requirements may be important, implying that these requirements, while significant, would not make the system unacceptable if they are absent. Some requirements may be desirable, implying that these requirements are less significant, which gives the system developer the opportunity to propose something that exceeds the basic requirements.

Exhibit 11.13 illustrates the various classifications of information system functional requirements.

Software requirements should be functional in nature—that is, they should describe what is required without implying how the system will meet its requirements. This provides maximum flexibility for the product designers.

Exhibit 11.13
Classifications of
Information System
Functional
Requirements

Value	Description
Mandatory	1. Generate checks for all invoices due for payment two days prior to due date. 2. Do not allow the payment amount to be changed after the invoice has been approved for payment.
Important	1. Produce a daily report forecasting the cash required to cover unpaid invoices that will come due on each of the next five work days. 2. Produce a monthly report that provides a summary of the level of year-to-date spending with each vendor. 3. Eliminate the need to produce checks manually.
Desirable	1. Be able to transmit check requests to multiple banks. 2. Add a seventh digit to the vendor code to serve as a check digit to eliminate miscoding. 3. Print a monthly check docket report on microfiche.

Real World Perspective

The "9-7-5" Rule of Mandatory Requirements

Jack M. Cooper was president and CEO of CSX Technology, the IT unit of CSX Corporation, a $7.7 billion holding company for rail transportation and energy businesses for the decade of the 1980s. While there, Cooper was famous for his "9-7-5" rule, which refers to knocking off 10 percent of the nonstrategic features of a system,

which can thus be considered frills. Doing so, he contends, can help information technology deliver the remaining 90 percent of the system features for approximately 70 percent of the estimated cost in about 50 percent of the elapsed time. SOURCE: Bruce Caldwell, "Seagram Chooses a Spirited CIO," InformationWeek 7 January 1991. □

Define Performance Requirements

In addition to defining the functional requirements, there is a need to define the system **performance requirements.** These requirements specify performance characteristics that the system must possess, such as the number of concurrent users the system must support, the size of files and tables, the number of transactions and tasks, and the amount of data to be processed within certain time periods for both normal and peak workload conditions. These requirements must be stated in specific, measurable terms such as: 95 percent of all customer inquiry transactions processed during normal workload conditions will be completed within three seconds, and no transaction will take longer than eight seconds.

The data and transaction volumes to be processed make up a key set of performance requirements to be defined. The system users help the system developers to estimate the number of occurrences associated with each entity and relationship. For example, in an order processing system, entities are likely to include customers, orders, line items, and so on. The minimum, maximum, and average number of occurrences are estimated, and a projection of potential growth levels is made (e.g., 1,200 orders per day with an average growth of 5 percent per year; or there is at least one line item, usually no more than twelve line items, and an average of three line items per order). This sort of information is critical during the technical design step to convert the logical data base design into a sound physical data base design.

The system users also help determine the volume of transactions that the system must handle. Again, it is useful to specify a minimum, maximum, and average number to enable an effective system design (e.g., an average of 1,200 new orders per eight-hour day with a maximum of 300 per hour occurring around 3:00 P.M. to 4:00 P.M. each day). The volume data is used to fine-tune the design to meet user response time goals.

It is also critical to define the need for **emergency alternate procedures** and backup equipment that will be invoked if the system cannot be executed in the normal fashion for some reason (e.g., because

Exhibit 11.14
Example of
Performance
Requirements

Value	Description
Mandatory	**1.** The system is up and fully functional 99.5 percent of the scheduled available time. **2.** Average user response time shall never exceed 3 seconds. **3.** All valid transactions are accurately and completely passed to the General Ledger System each night.
Important	**1.** The results of all overnight batch processing are available by 8 A.M. at least 95 percent of the time. **2.** The user's visual display device can "paint the screen" in 0.5 seconds or less.
Desirable	**1.** The results of any batch report request are available to the user within 2 hours. **2.** All microfiche output is available within 24 hours of request.

of fire or water damage to computer equipment or a power failure). Not every system requires emergency alternate procedures. Typically systems that control assets of the firm such as cash or inventory require some level of emergency alternate procedures. This includes systems such as accounts payable and accounts receivable, inventory control, and order processing. Most management reporting and decision support systems do not require emergency alternate procedures. While the inability to operate these systems may create a hardship and inconvenience, their loss for a day or even a week would not seriously impair the ability of the firm to continue operating.

Backup equipment and associated emergency alternate procedures may be extremely expensive. For example, it may be necessary to establish a duplicate data center complete with a functioning mainframe computer, operating system, peripheral devices, and backup operators. These potential costs need to be defined to assess the economic feasibility of the project before the project goes further. Exhibit 11.14 provides an example of performance requirements.

Define Internal Control Requirements

Internal control is the plan of the organization to safeguard its assets, check the accuracy of internal accounting data, promote operational efficiency, and encourage adherence to prescribed management practices. Internal control is a specific responsibility of the CEO, and it is delegated downward through the organization and consequently becomes a responsibility of all managers and employees. As organizations convert from old business processes to new or automated business processes, business managers must define the internal control requirements of the new system.

IT applications that affect the assets of the company (cash, inventory, equipment, etc.) or that encompass private or confidential information must be carefully designed with sound internal controls. There are three key areas of internal control with which management must be concerned: physical facility controls, procedural controls, and application system controls (Exhibit 11.15).

Physical facility controls protect the physical facilities and their contents from loss, destruction, and unauthorized access. Computer centers are frequently destroyed or temporarily incapacitated by accidents, natural disasters, sabotage, or vandalism. Data files on both disk and tape are subject to unauthorized access, industrial espionage, destruction, and theft. Therefore, physical safeguards and various control procedures are necessary to protect the hardware, software, and vital data resources of organizations using computers. This topic is covered more fully in Chapter 12.

Procedural controls include formalized standards, rules, procedures, and control disciplines that are essential to ensure that the organization's controls are properly executed and enforced. The most important procedural controls are separation of functions, written policies and procedures, and management supervision.

Separation of functions is a fundamental principle of internal control. This principle requires that job functions be designed to minimize the risk of errors or fraudulent manipulation of the organization's assets. Thus responsibilities for input, processing, output, and approval of transactions are usually divided among different people to restrict what each one can do. For example, in a well-designed system, the individuals who enter payee names and check requests do not have the authority to initiate payments or to sign checks. Business managers have the responsibility to define the job functions within the new system so that proper separation of functions is maintained.

Written policies and procedures establish formal standards for controlling information system operations. Before conversion to the new system, procedures must be formalized in writing and authorized by the appropriate level of management. Accountabilities and responsibilities under the new system must be clearly specified.

Supervision of personnel involved in control procedures ensures that the controls of an information system are implemented and work as intended.

Exhibit 11.15
Types of Internal
Control

Physical Facility Controls
    Hardware, Software Protection
    Data Protection
    Disaster Recovery

Procedural Controls
    Separation of Functions
    Written Policies and Procedures
    Management Supervision

Application System Controls
    Input Controls
    Processing Controls
    Output Controls

With supervision, weaknesses can be spotted, errors corrected, and deviations from the written policies and procedures identified. Without adequate supervision, even the most thorough set of controls may be bypassed or neglected. Supervisors' responsibilities under the new system must be clearly documented.

Application system controls are specific internal controls associated with an individual application such as the accounts payable or inventory control system. These controls include both computerized and manual procedures that encompass the input, process, and output functions.

Input controls address input authorization, data editing, and error handling. These controls are designed to ensure that all authorized transactions and only authorized transactions reach the computer; that each transaction is checked carefully for accuracy and completeness; and that a record is made of each transaction indicating whether it was valid or invalid and if invalid, why it was rejected from further processing.

Processing controls ensure that the data are complete and accurate through the processing cycle and that only valid transactions are used to update records of the company's operations.

Output controls ensure that the results of the processing cycle are accurate, complete, and correctly distributed. These controls are designed to ensure that each step in the processing cycle functioned correctly and to completion; that total and detail lines on all reports are correct and can be reconciled to the input data; that output totals agree with input and processing totals; and that all authorized users and only authorized users receive results from the system.

Business managers have the responsibility of defining these internal control requirements for application system control and ensuring that they are implemented in the final system.

Document System Acceptance Criteria

Acceptance criteria specify functional and performance tests that must be performed to enable the system owner and end users to determine whether or not to accept the system. They also define standards to be used to evaluate the acceptability of source code, system documentation, and user documentation. Thus, in addition to specific computer system tests to be conducted, acceptance criteria specify physical audits of source code, documents, and physical media.

Requirements must be verifiable from two points of view: it must be possible to verify that the information system requirements satisfy the customer's business needs, and it must be possible to verify that the subsequent work products satisfy the requirements.

Update Project Plan and Business Case

The estimate of the cost to build and operate the system is revised based on additional learnings to date. Likewise, the estimate of tangible benefits is also updated. The detailed work breakdown structure (Ex-

Exhibit 11.16
Work Breakdown Structure for the Functional Design Step

Stage of Information Engineering: Design Step: Functional Design		
Task	Deliverables	Key Management Responsibility
Define Functional Requirements	Information System Requirements	Translate Business Needs into System Requirements Identify Requirements as Mandatory, Important, or Desirable
Define Performance Requirements	System Performance Requirements	Translate Business Needs into System Performance Requirements Identify Requirements as Mandatory, Important, or Desirable Identify Need for Emergency Alternate Procedures in Event of Disaster
Define Internal Control Requirements	Internal Control Requirements	Translate Business Needs into Internal Control Requirements Identify Requirements as Mandatory, Important, or Desirable
Document Systems Acceptance Criteria	System Acceptance Test Plan	Document Tests to Be Performed to Determine if Users Should Accept the System
Update Project Plan and Business Case	Project Plan for Prototype and Technical Design Step	Make Go/No-Go Decision to Proceed

hibit 11.16) can be used to outline the tasks remaining to complete the project. The individuals assigned to those tasks can develop estimates of how long they will require to complete each task.

Prototype

It is common practice for an architect to build a scale model of a major project such as a large building, shopping mall, or bridge. This model is reviewed by all concerned parties to confirm key aspects of the project before actual work begins. As the model is reviewed, a number of suggestions for changes are likely to be made. Once the review is complete, work can begin on the real project with a high degree of confidence that the final product will closely match the users' needs.

A similar process is strongly recommended for information system developers. Some sort of working model of the system should be constructed to verify the accuracy and completeness of the system requirements. Such a working model is called a **prototype.**

A prototype puts something in front of the users that they can easily react to and then provide feedback to the information system developers. Thus building and then evaluating a prototype enhances the quality of communication among users and developers. Even a rudimentary prototype that works in a limited fashion demonstrates system features far better than volumes of documentation ever could. Users can better express and developers can better understand the specific functions that the information system can perform. For a highly complex system with requirements that might be easily misunderstood or not communicated, a prototype is an insurance policy against missing user requirements.

The focus in developing a prototype is gaining clarity on how the system must operate to meet user needs. It must be pointed out that the user seldom has a high degree of interest in specifying factors such as the data access security requirements, backup and recovery needs, and so on. Thus building and evaluating a prototype does help to define a large subset of user needs, but by no means does it define all system requirements.

User impatience may develop because considerable time is required to complete the final system once the prototyping process is finished. This is most likely to occur if the model developed during prototyping is not written in the intended production language (e.g., a fourth-generation language is used rather than COBOL) or because certain functions are not included in the prototype (e.g., editing of system input, generation of error messages, data access and control, or the data base update process). In these cases, *prior* to the start of prototyping, the system developers must establish expectations with the system users that considerable work may be required to convert the prototype to the final system. This may be true even though the users can see the system work by the end of the prototyping process. The users must understand that significant functionality must be added.

When not managed properly, prototyping may never end, since business needs are continually being refined. For this reason, users should understand in advance that the prototyping process will be taken to a specified level of functionality. Once the functions at that level are successfully demonstrated and accepted, the user is expected to give formal approval to build the final system based on the model.

Build the Prototype

At the prototype-building point in the functional design phase, a fairly complete set of user needs and information system requirements has been defined. These needs and requirements can be used by the system developers and users to quickly build an initial prototype.

The completeness of the prototype depends on the availability of prototyping tools and the nature of the system being built. The prototype can be as simple as putting together a series of mock-up screens drawn on paper and allowing the user to flip through the pages to simulate the on-line dialog required to perform different system functions. More powerful prototyping tools allow the system developer to build a more elaborate model that closely matches the functionality of the real system. A number of prototyping strategies are available, and an appropriate approach should be selected. The options include:

A **screen-only prototype** that simulates the interactive portion of the system. Such a prototype demonstrates only a very high level of functionality, such as the menu screens and several related screens and how the user will navigate through the screens to process different transactions. This sort of prototype is used to verify that the interactive dialog effectively meets the user's needs.

A **functional prototype** that simulates input data validation and updates of system data bases. Such a prototype performs edits on data entered into fields on the screens and displays appropriate error messages for each of the screens. The simulation may be made extremely realistic with built-in delays of varying lengths to simulate the expected response time for various transactions under different operating conditions (e.g., number of concurrent users). This sort of prototype is used to give the users a sense of what it will be like to operate the system.

A number of CASE tools and fourth-generation languages can be very effective in the process of prototyping. CASE tools that can be used to support the building of a prototype include screen painters, report generators, and code generators.

Screen Painters Screen painters write code to format or "paint" the screens with the desired content and format. The screen painter may interface to the data dictionary and retrieve information from the dictionary such as length of field or type of data to be entered (e.g., alphabetic or numeric).

Report Generators Report generators are similar to screen painters in that they create mock-up reports of the desired content and format. Screen painters are used for the interactive portions of the system, report generators for the batch portion. In addition, report generators can create totals, print edits, cause page breaks to happen, and sequence data in the proper order that it is to appear on the report.

Code Generators Code generators enable the analyst to generate modular units of source code from high-level specifications. The system can be generated and demonstrated, and then the specifications can be revised and the system regenerated and demonstrated again.

Evaluate the Prototype

Prototyping is, above all else, a highly interactive and iterative process. It requires the active involvement of both users and system developers. As they work together to build and evaluate the prototype, their creative thinking is stimulated. Development of a prototype helps generate many new ideas and insights into how the system could operate.

Once built, the prototype is given to the users for their evaluation. As the users work with the prototype, they are able to more fully identify and communicate their needs. The system developers then incorporate the necessary changes to refine the prototype. The refined prototype is given back to the users for further evaluation. Over time, the prototype evolves to the point that it very closely meets user needs. At this point, the prototype represents a clear definition of what the information system must do and how it must operate to meet the needs of the users.

Technical Design

During the technical design step, the specific information technology (computer hardware, operating system, data base management system, source code language, and so on) on which the system will be implemented is selected. The functional design is converted into a physical design that takes advantage of the specific capabilities of the selected hardware or software technology. It may be necessary to build a prototype of the system to ensure that the chosen technologies will meet performance and reliability constraints. For example, a prototype could be built to determine if the data base management system (e.g., Oracle, DB2, Sybase, and so on) and hardware platform (e.g., Tandem NonStop VLX, Hewlett Packard 9000-827, IBM 3090 model 400S, and so on) selected will meet user response time requirements for the size data base anticipated.

Convert Logical Data Base Design to Physical Design

The physical data base design process takes the ideal logical data base design and fine-tunes it for performance considerations (e.g., improved response time, reduced storage space, lower operating cost). This fine-tuning requires in-depth knowledge of the data base management software that will be used to implement the data base. As a result of the physical data base design, the logical data base design may be altered so that certain data entities are combined into one, summary totals are carried in the data records rather than calculated from elemental data, and some data elements may be repeated in more than one data entity (planned data redundancy).

Design Program Modules

At first glance, many systems appear to be quite complex. These systems seem complicated because they consist of many components and the relationships among the components are unclear. **Functional decomposition** is a systematic way of documenting system components and their relationships to reduce complexity. This process leads to simple systems whose individual components can be studied, implemented, fixed, and changed with little consideration of or effect on the other pieces of the system.

Functional decomposition starts with identifying the major functions performed by the system. Each of these major functions is then broken down (decomposed) into subordinate functions. The subordinate functions are broken down into sub-subordinate functions. The process continues in this hierarchical fashion until the system has been subdivided into elemental units called modules. A **module** is a basic system function that has a single, well-defined purpose (if it were a multipurpose function, it would not be elemental and could be further decomposed).

In a classic paper, Stevens, Myers, and Constantine (reference 8) outlined the basic principles for a design methodology called structured design. In a well-designed system, the modules are weakly coupled, which means they are independent of one another—a change in one does not affect any other. Also, each module should have strong cohesion, that is, it should perform a single, well-defined function. Following these two guidelines will help reduce system complexity and increase system flexibility to change. This results in systems that are easier to modify to meet changing business needs.

Some modules represent a function that is to be performed manually. Others represent a function that can be programmed to be performed by the computer. There are additional good design practices associated with the definition of computer program modules. These modules should be designed to have a single entry and a single exit point. A *single entry point* means that the execution of the module must always begin at the start of the module. A *single exit point* means the module always completes at the same point. These restrictions make it easier for the programmer to follow the program logic, since there is only one way to enter and exit each program.

Management should insist that such good design practices be followed in the development of information systems. That such principles are indeed being followed can be verified through management participation in the process of design review.

Conduct Design Review

The **design review** is a process to ensure that the final system is built with a high degree of quality and will indeed meet user needs. Members of the team who will implement the system and selected system users are given an opportunity to review the system design in detail. The design review will reveal problems, inaccuracies, ambiguities, and omissions in the system design *before* any program code is ever written.

The design review is not a onetime event at the end of the system design phase. Ideally, it is a philosophy of frequent review of pieces of the system design whenever a unit of documentation is ready for review. A design review could be held to review the source documents and procedures that will be used to capture the daily input to the system. Another design review could be held to review the system output from the daily system. Separate design reviews could be held to review the details of each program in the system. For a large system it would not be unreasonable to hold a dozen or more design reviews to go over major pieces of the system design. In Exhibit 11.17, some guidelines for an effective design review are given.

Exhibit 11.17
Guidelines for an
Effective Design
Review Process

- Conduct frequent design reviews whenever a significant piece of the design is ready to be reviewed.
- People included in the design review should be not only system analysts and programmers but also users. The number of people involved should be kept small (three to five) and should include those who will be responsible for implementing or using that piece of the design.
- The design review should last no more than one hour. If more time is required to complete the review, you are trying to review too large a piece of the design at one time.
- The reviewers should concentrate only on identifying what they feel may be an error, omission, or ambiguity in the design. This must be done constructively, with no attempt to criticize. For this reason, it is often best to include one's peers in the review and intentionally exclude project managers.
- The person responsible for the design must be cautioned not to become defensive or feel that his or her piece of design is under attack. Designers must try to accept the comments of their peers as constructive criticism meant to improve the overall quality of the entire project.
- The focus should be on identifying potential problem areas. Solutions should be worked outside the design review meeting with appropriate resources. This will help to ensure the meetings are brief and maximum time is spent on potential problem identification.
- A secretary should be appointed to take written notes that can be shared with the designer upon completion of the review.

Real World Perspective

GM's Principles for Systems Development Projects

The following ten principles must be adhered to before any systems development project is undertaken at GM:

1. Simplifying business practices through elimination and integration takes precedence over automation, whether developing new or enhancing existing information systems.

2. Business methods must be documented with process models and validated before being automated.

3. Corporate data standards must be followed so that data can be gathered and distilled into information that all can share.

4. Data will be entered only once.

5. Data will be accessible to all authorized users, while being safeguarded from unintentional or unauthorized alteration, destruction, and disclosure.

6. Priority will be given to developing and enhancing systems that contribute directly to corporate business strategies and effectiveness. Data

processing and communications efficiency should not be the prime determinant.

7. Common information systems will be deployed among all operating groups unless specific analysis establishes that they should be unique.

8. Before information systems are developed, a plan and a business case must first be prepared.

9. The architecture of the computing and communications infrastructure will be transparent to the information systems that rely on it.

10. GM users are responsible for the success of their information systems and accountable for the cost of information technology. That requires that the development of each data model, process model, and information system be led by a GM project manager (as opposed to an IT project manager). Once developed, each model and system should be operated and continuously improved under GM stewardship. *SOURCE: © 1991 by CMP Publications, Inc., 600 Community Drive, Manhasset, NY 11030. Reprinted from InformationWeek with permission.* □

Develop Test Plans

Two test plans need to be developed at this stage of the project. First, the test plan for **module testing** determines if the system correctly implements module requirements. The minimum criteria for this determination are: (1) compliance with technical design requirements; (2) assessment of timing, sizing, and accuracy; (3) performance at boundaries and interfaces and under stress and error conditions; and (4) measures of test coverage and software reliability and maintainability. The plan needs to include an approach to enable tracing of design requirements to test design cases, procedures, and execution results. Time should be allowed to document test results.

The second test plan is for **integration testing.** The integration test involves a planned and orderly progression of testing in which software elements, hardware elements, or both are combined and tested until the entire system has been integrated (Exhibit 11.18). It includes testing to determine if the system is in compliance with an increasingly larger set of functional requirements at each stage of integration.

Create User Documentation

A **user manual** conveys to the end user of a system the instructions for using the system to obtain the desired results such as: which func-

Exhibit 11.18
System Integration Testing

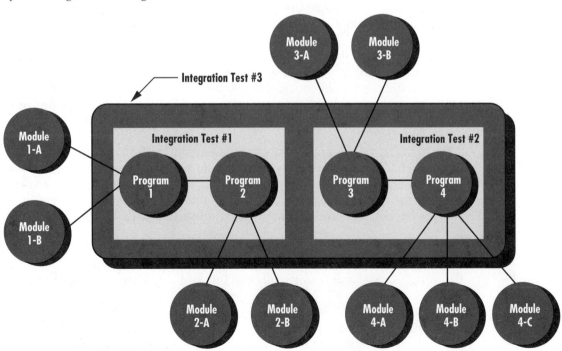

tion keys to hit to process a transaction, what to do to correct an input error, or how to request a specific report. While it may seem odd to worry about producing the user manual before any line of code has been written, this is indeed the time to spell out in detail exactly how the system will operate from the user's point of view. The creation of the user manual at this point in the system development process will force a very clear definition of how the system will work. The users can review the user manual to ensure that the functional requirements of the system will be met.

On some projects, a professional technical writer is assigned the task of writing a user manual. This usually leads to a very high-quality manual, but it can be expensive. On other projects, the IT professionals developing the system write the manual. After all, since they are the ones who built the system, they should be able to describe how it works. The problem with this reasoning is that the IT professional may describe the operation in a manner that is difficult for a noncomputer person to understand. A third choice for writing the user manual is to have the end users write their own manual. The advantage of this approach is that the users are sure that it is written with no technical jargon and in a manner that they can understand. The disadvantage of this approach is that it can be like pulling teeth to get the end users to write the manual.

Develop User Training Program

The types of training sessions required to introduce the new system need to be identified. For each training session, a determination must be made about the participants and their skill levels, session objectives, and the desired performance objectives upon completion of the training.

The training plan should outline training resource requirements, training budget, training locations, and the basic training schedule. The training schedule should be assessed to determine if it has an impact on the current implementation schedule. The schedule must allow time for the trainers themselves to be trained and become familiar with the system.

The training materials are developed depending on the training method selected (e.g., self-study, computer-assisted, videotape, classroom, and so on). The major products to be developed include the instructor's guide, the participants' guide, exercises, case studies, presentation materials, summaries, and user manuals.

Update Project Plan and Business Case

It is now possible, for really the first time, to have a full appreciation of all that will be required to build the system. Thus, a well-documented plan can be developed that describes the steps and schedule for system implementation. A PERT (Program Evaluation and Review Technique) or CPM (Critical Path Method) chart (Exhibit 11.19)

Exhibit 11.19
CPM Chart for System Implementation

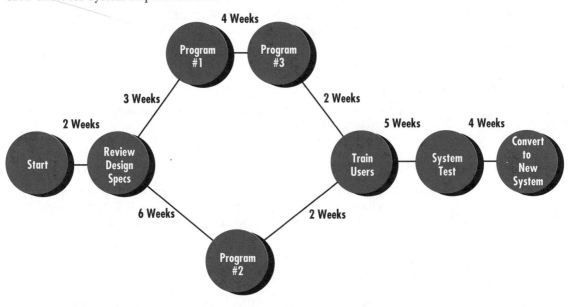

that provides a graphical representation of the sequence and dependency of these tasks is recommended. To build a PERT or CPM chart requires a good estimate of the effort required to complete each task, the resources assigned and their availability, and a knowledge of the dependency of one task on another.

Enough is now known about how the system will work that the costs (including possible emergency alternate procedures and backup equipment) and tangible benefits can be estimated more accurately. Management will also be interested in the estimate of the ongoing costs to operate and support the system.

Exhibit 11.20 suggests a number of questions for which the system sponsor and owner should get answers from the project team. If these

Exhibit 11.20
Questions to Ask
Before Project
Team Proceeds
with
Implementation

Has the need for emergency alternate procedures been decided?

Are system users confident that control over the operation has not been weakened?

Has a complete user manual been produced and carefully reviewed?

Have steps been taken to make the data input process as simple and accurate as possible?

Have project risks, costs, and benefits been reviewed by an objective financial analyst?

Has a detailed system implementation schedule been developed? Have the system users agreed that the schedule is workable?

Has a detailed acceptance test plan been documented, reviewed, and approved?

questions cannot yet be answered, it is an indication of incomplete planning for construction implementation. Serious consideration should be given to delaying the project until the plans are developed well enough to answer these questions.

■ CONSTRUCTION

The construction stage is divided into the following steps: code and test modules, testing, and conversion.

Code and Test Modules

This step involves the coding, compiling, inspecting, and testing of each module of each program that is required in the system. For even a medium-size system, this could very easily involve hundreds of modules.

Code Module

Coding a module involves writing detailed program statements according to the module specifications developed in the technical design step. Coding is tedious and requires great attention to detail. The programmer must follow the module design to code the program. The programmer must also be very precise in using the language. Each programming language has its own syntax, or coding rules, that must be followed or the program will fail to compile or operate as intended.

The best means of documenting a module is through the use of *comments* throughout the program. Comments are nonexecutable statements that describe the purpose of the module, highlight any assumptions about the data, and explain complex logic. A good rule of thumb is that 10 to 15 percent of the module statements should be comments. A program that is written in modular form following a structured design and that is well commented will be well documented and easy to maintain.

Inspect Code

Once the initial coding is complete, it should be inspected to ensure that the module is written in a manner easy for others to follow, that it is well documented, and that it is coded precisely to the system design. Such an inspection will remove faulty logic and ensure the module is written to conform to good programming standards and practices.

Compile Module

The module written by the programmer must be converted from source code (the language the programmer writes in, e.g., COBOL) into machine-executable instructions. This conversion process is performed by a special piece of software called a *compiler,* and the process is called *compiling the program.* The compiler reads and tries to interpret each line of code and convert it into the equivalent machine language instruction. The compiler produces an output listing of the source code and error messages that identify those lines of code that need to be corrected. It may be necessary to compile and correct the code several times before a clean compile (the compiler detects no errors in the source code) is obtained.

Test Module

Each module is tested following the test plan developed in the technical design step of the design phase of the project. Upon successful completion of these tests, the programmer should have a high degree of confidence that the module does conform to all module design specifications—it does what the technical designers said it should. During testing, problems arising from missed communications or errors in programming (or both) need to be corrected. Thus pieces of the module may need to be rewritten, recompiled, and retested.

Testing

The three levels of testing to be performed are: **integration test, system test,** and **acceptance test.**

Integration Test

The integration test involves a planned and orderly progression of testing in which software elements, hardware elements, or both are combined and tested until the entire system has been integrated.

System Test

System testing is the process of testing an integrated hardware and software system to verify that the system meets its specified requirements. The system test involves preparing realistic test data and processing the data all the way from start to finish through the system using the new hardware, software, and manual procedures. The results of this processing are then carefully checked to ensure the system is indeed operating according to the system design.

One way to perform system testing is through a process called *parallel operations.* This consists of providing the same input data to both the old and the new systems and then comparing the output reports, files, and other results. During parallel operations, many of the discrepancies that occur turn out to be undetected problems in the old system. However, it is very important that all differences between the results of the two systems be reconciled.

The system test should provide the system developers with a high degree of confidence that the system meets all system requirements.

At this point the system developers can turn over the system to end users for their acceptance test.

Acceptance Test

The acceptance test is a formal test to determine whether or not a system satisfies its acceptance criteria and whether or not a customer should accept the system. The purpose of the test is to eliminate unwelcome surprises after the system goes into production. Minor corrections may be made during acceptance testing to fine-tune system components that are just slightly off target, but acceptance testing should not be allowed to degenerate into a debugging process. Either the project was a success and the system meets user requirements and business needs, or it does not. The acceptance criteria and tests were defined in the functional design step of the analysis phase. No additional criteria should be introduced at this time.

Conversion

During the **conversion** step all the previous information engineering work is put into perspective. If the previous steps were well executed, conversion is relatively painless; the system will come up on time and perform as expected with users who are well trained and well prepared to make good use of it. If the previous work was not well performed then the conversion step is one of high drama, with long hours for everyone involved, and extreme tension among members of the project team, business managers, and end users.

Deliver User Training

For the system to become operational, a sufficient number of users must be trained in how to use the system. The hope is that the system users will have been substantially involved in developing the system. Their input should have been sought during the requirements definition phase, and the users should be able to see many of their ideas incorporated in the new system. Users should have participated in the design phase, figuring out just exactly how the system should work. They should also have been involved in design reviews of the various components of the system.

Thus many of the users will already have been exposed to the system in bits and pieces but may lack a total overall understanding of how the system will change their jobs and what they need to do to operate it. Other users may have had very little or no exposure to the system.

Training sessions for user personnel need to be carefully planned to meet the needs of each type of user—data-entry person, input-control supervisor, manager in charge of controlling the daily operation, manager in charge of the department in which the system is being installed, and so on. Each type of user has special training needs depending on how the user will interact with and use the system. In addition, all users should be given a good overview of the whole system so that they can appreciate how what they do (or fail to do) affects the other users of the system.

User training is absolutely essential to ensure that the users of the system fully understand and have the skills to operate the system in the manner intended. This level of understanding means the system is readily accepted by the users and that the system achieves the business needs for which it was implemented. It is a key step in the preparation for full installation of the new system.

The training must be timely so that users will begin to use the new system shortly after being trained. If there is too long a delay, users quickly forget what they learned. Users should strongly be considered to serve as trainers.

Cutover

System cutover includes all those activities that must be completed to successfully convert from the old system to the new one. The primary activities are *procedure conversion, file conversion,* and *system conversion.*

Procedure conversion involves completely documenting the operating procedures for the new system and training users to follow them. Operating procedures must be clearly spelled out with information on input, data files, methods, output, and internal control. These written operating procedures will need to be supplemented by oral communications during the training sessions.

File conversion involves converting data from one storage medium to another and may require that special programs be written to do this. These file conversion programs must be carefully tested, and the resulting new files must be manually reviewed for errors. It will not be possible to operate the new system until file conversion has taken place. This phase may be long and costly. Sufficient time and other resources should be built into the implementation schedule and budget.

The actual conversion to the new system can be accomplished using one of four basic approaches: (1) parallel conversion, (2) flash-cut conversion, (3) phased conversion, or (4) prototype conversion.

PARALLEL CONVERSION   The parallel conversion process involves running both the old and new systems side by side until all parties are convinced that the new system is performing satisfactorily. Use of the old system is then discontinued. Parallel conversion requires that input for both systems be prepared from source documents, entered into each system, input processed, output produced, output from both systems compared, and any differences reconciled. Many times the difference in output between the two systems will be due to bugs in the old system or changes in the definition of how the data are to be processed. There will also be times when the new system will be in error.

It should be clear from this discussion that considerable additional work is involved in a parallel conversion effort. Furthermore, as long as the old system is still there, some people may have an extremely difficult time letting go and fully converting to the new way of doing things.

FLASH-CUT CONVERSION   The flash-cut approach to system conversion involves terminating the use of the old system on one day and completely and totally converting to the new system on the next day. This approach can be extremely risky and requires a high degree of confidence in the system design and implementation team to build a system that will operate at an acceptable level right from the beginning. It has the advantage that the resources and length of time to perform system conversion are minimized (assuming there are not too many problems).

PHASED CONVERSION   The phased conversion approach is one in which the new system is gradually phased in and the old one phased out. This phase-in/phase-out process can be accomplished in many different ways. For example, with an accounts payable system, all new invoices from certain vendors may be processed and paid using the new system, while invoices for other vendors continue to be processed and paid using the old system.

The phased approach is similar to the parallel system conversion process, since the two systems must be operated simultaneously, resulting in increased effort to run both systems. Another problem is that the output of both systems must be combined to form a complete result. In the case of two accounts payable systems, the output files from both systems would have to be fed into the general ledger system to update all accounting records.

PROTOTYPE CONVERSION   The prototype conversion process involves converting to the new system in only a limited test environment. If the system operates successfully in the test environment, then its use is expanded. For example, a new marketing decision support system for a consumer products manufacturer may be initially operated for just one or a small number of the products that the firm manufactures. Often, in the test environment, minor problems are uncovered or enhancements are suggested. Appropriate changes can then be made prior to expanding the use of the system.

■ MAINTENANCE

Completed systems must be evaluated throughout their useful life. Some of the questions to be asked during the evaluation include: Is the system being used in the manner management intended? Does it continue to meet the needs of its users? Is there still a valid business reason for running it? Is it running as efficiently as it should? Is there an op-

Real World Perspective

System Conversion at Lend-Lease Trucks

Lend-Lease Trucks, Inc. is a $200 million national truck leasing company based in Minneapolis. In 1992, Lend-Lease found out that it had just six months to go off a mainframe system, install a new computer system customized for their business and convert all data—including thousands of contracts and vehicle records.

Lend-Lease had been spun off from their parent company, National Car Rental (NCR) a few years before and NCR had agreed to honor their information processing contract. However, NCR outsourced its processing including that for Lend-Lease to another company that charged $120,000 per month and was not interested in serving Lend-Lease beyond the next six months.

Though they were facing a very real deadline, Lend-Lease simply didn't want to transfer data to another system like the one they had. They wanted to install a new system that would meet their primary business goal: improved customer service. With the old system, there was little flexibility in the billing system, the information needed to run the business was inaccessible on a timely basis, and lack of data editing and processing integrity resulted in hundreds of erroneous bills that frustrated customers.

Ironically, Lend-Lease was able to turn the timing factor in their favor. There was no time for politicking, lengthy posturing nor changing minds. Lend-Lease virtually gave the project team a free hand so they could work efficiently.

After determining the requirements for the system, the project was broken into five tracks: technology, billing applications, financial applications, data conversion, and support services. Managers and operational users were assigned to the project. These were people who would be using the system once it was installed. They were creative thinkers with a clear idea of what was needed in the work environment and the information necessary to improve their job performance.

For each track, requirements were defined, process flow diagrams created, data models developed, and screen layouts designed. User documentation and processing specifications were developed simultaneously with these activities. Users sat down with the developers to jointly create the screens which would best help the users to do their daily work.

The system was implemented on time and operates at less than half the cost of the old system. It provides timely decision making information and accurate billing. *SOURCE: Elizabeth Child. "High-Speed Teams Get Lend-Lease Trucks Rolling."* Journal of Systems Management, *January 1994. Reprinted with permission of the Association for System Management.* □

portunity to enhance it to make it even more useful or efficient? Have there been significant changes in the way the business is conducted or changes in government regulations that necessitate changes in the system? Systems analysts, system users, system owners, and internal audit staff should be involved in a periodic review of each major system to answer these questions.

Management must know that it will be necessary to make many changes to most systems to extend their useful life or to keep them running efficiently. For most companies, system maintenance consumes a great amount of systems analysts' and programming time. Well-documented systems that contain well-designed programs are much easier to maintain. Management must insist on good documentation and ensure that good design and implementation practices are followed.

The monitor and support step is an ongoing continuous improvement stage during which corrections and enhancements are made to the system to allow it to more closely meet the needs of its users over time. Every business and organization changes and is affected by changes in the environment surrounding it. These changes frequently mean a change in the information systems that support the business. For example, changes in federal income tax rules may impose a requirement to change the payroll system's calculation of withholdings for employees. A sales restructure wherein two or more sales regions are combined into one will affect sales reporting and analysis systems.

Software maintenance is usually defined to include all changes made to a program or system after it has been installed. Software maintenance effort can be further broken down as follows:

60 percent to add enhancements to the product—to improve the way it operates or to provide new capabilities

20 percent for changes required to enable the product to run in a new environment (e.g., to convert the system from running under one operating system to another)

20 percent for fixes to correct problems

As can be seen from the previous figures, only about 20 percent of software maintenance is to correct poor work done during the initial building of the system. In most organizations, the majority of the maintenance done on systems is to add new capabilities to the systems or to enable them to run in a new environment (hardware or software). In these cases, maintenance should not be seen as a nonproductive effort but as a means for extending the investment already made in software so that it continues to be useful.

Roughly 16 percent of the total original development effort is required each year to maintain the system (Moad, reference 5). For example, a system that took six effort years to develop may require as much as one effort year of software maintenance per year! The typical life span for a software product is one to three years in development and five to fifteen years in use, during which time the system must be maintained.

Another perspective is that the total application development cost is at least $25 per line of code. Multiply this by the number of lines of code being maintained, and one obtains a rough estimate of the cost to replace the existing installed software base. For a large company, the installed software base can easily exceed 2 million lines of code; thus the replacement cost is well over $50 million!

Managers are just awakening to the enormous investment in software maintenance. They are alarmed by these statistics and the fact that good management tools for software maintenance are not available. Unfortunately, many organizations are still treating maintenance as a problem to be dealt with after the system is built, rather than planning to develop systems that can be easily maintained. Ned Chapin, lecturer on software maintenance, stated, "Historically, the builders of the program and systems have acted as though someone else—the user and maintainer—were going to pay the cost of use and maintenance.''

There are five basic reasons why so much effort is spent on fixing problems:

1. The need to extend the useful life of an existing system to meet new business needs or to operate in a new environment. Usually it is more effective to modify an existing system than to throw it out and start all over from scratch.

2. Systems are often installed prematurely without sufficient user acceptance testing to catch and eliminate errors before the system goes into production.

3. Poor communication between system developers and system users. Too often key user requirements are not defined clearly, or defined at all, and thus the final system falls far short of user expectations. An inordinate amount of effort is then expended in "software maintenance" to add expected functionality.

4. The system development methodology does not sufficiently stress the need to do certain things during system development to keep the software maintenance effort down.

5. Lack of documentation about the system—how it is to be operated and how it was constructed. Without such documentation it is difficult to make changes; it is like trying to remodel a house with no blueprint of the original construction.

Summary

The information engineering system development approach divides a project into several well-defined stages with a formal review process at the end of each stage.

The five steps of the design stage are project definition, analysis, functional design, prototype, and technical design.

During project definition, the business manager identifies the problem or opportunity to be addressed, provides a clear definition of the scope of what is to be studied, defines key stakeholders and their role in the project, assesses if the project is aligned with business strategy, and establishes the relative priority of the project.

During analysis, the business manager communicates information about the current system, provides a vision of the future and translates that vision into business needs, identifies and defines potential solutions, evaluates alternatives, selects the solution to be implemented, and assesses the technical, operational, and economic feasibility of the project.

During functional design, the business manager defines mandatory system requirements, clarifies the need for system controls and emergency alternative procedures, provides estimates of data and transaction volumes, documents system acceptance criteria, develops a detailed implementation plan, and revises estimates of system benefits and costs.

The building and evaluation of a prototype is strongly recommended to confirm that the system design, when implemented, will yield a system that operates reliably and dependably and meets the business needs.

The construction stage is divided into the code and test modules, testing, and conversion steps. During construction, the business manager reviews the results of system testing; plans, develops, and delivers user training; leads the system acceptance test process; and directs the conversion from the old system and business processes to the new.

During technical design, the specific information technology is selected and the functional design is converted into a physical design.

Once the system is completed, it is necessary to maintain and enhance the system throughout its useful life to ensure that it continues to meet the needs of the business.

Roughly 16 percent of the total original development effort is required for system maintenance and enhancement each year.

A Manager's Checklist

✔ Do you feel sufficiently involved in the development of systems in your area of responsibility?

✔ Is the information engineering system development approach being used on any projects for your organization?

✔ Do you have any rules of thumb to judge if the business managers and system users are sufficiently involved in the information systems projects for their organization?

✔ In your organization, can an information system project be stopped at the end of the analysis phase, or do all projects continue on into further design and construction?

✔ Can you identify those critical points in your operation where some form of internal control is necessary?

Key Terms

acceptance test	functional decomposition
conversion	functional prototype
design review	functional requirements
economic feasibility	integration test
emergency alternate	legitimizer
procedures	module
fishbone diagram	module testing

operational feasibility
opinion leader
performance requirements
project constraints
prototype
satisfice
screen-only prototype
soft constraints

software maintenance
stakeholders
system owner
system sponsor
system test
technical feasibility
user manual

**Review
Questions**

1. List the five major steps of the design stage and briefly describe the key responsibilities of the business manager in each phase.

2. What are the problems that can arise if insufficient time is allowed to define the real problem or opportunity to be addressed?

3. What does the term *stakeholder* mean? What kinds of stakeholders are there, and how can you identify them? Why should you identify them?

4. Why is it important to study the current system prior to identifying and recommending alternative solutions?

5. How can development of a prototype system prove valuable? What are some of the potential problems associated with including prototyping in the system development process?

6. System construction is often thought of as an activity for programmers. However, the system users have key activities for which they are responsible. What are these activities?

7. Define the term *software maintenance.* Why is so much effort spent on software maintenance?

**Discussion
Questions**

1. What would you do if you saw business managers in your organization refusing to get involved in information systems projects?

2. How could you recognize a project that is in trouble (over schedule, over budget, missing user requirements)? At what stage in the project can trouble first be identified?

3. What should members of the project team do if they think that the project constraints set by senior management are unrealistic?

4. Were there any techniques discussed in this chapter that you would consider using as tools to aid you in your role? If so, which ones? Give an example of where these techniques could be helpful.

5. Discuss: The conversion of a business process from a manual process to an automated process always decreases the level of control exerted by the managers in charge.

**Recommended
Readings**

1. Case, Albert F. "Structured Analysis and Design: The Evolution of a Methodology." *Journal of Systems Development* 7 (August 1987).

2. Gilb, Tom. *Principles of Software Engineering Management.* Reading, Mass.: Addison-Wesley, 1988.

3. Ishikawa, Kaoru. *What Is Quality Control, the Japanese Way.* Englewood Cliffs, NJ: Prentice-Hall, 1985.

4. Martin, Merle P. "The Human Connection in System Design: Human Factor Principles." *Journal of Systems Management* 38 (July 1987).

5. Moad, Jeff. "The Software Revolution." *Datamation* 36 (15 February 1990).

6. Potosnak, Kathleen. "Creating Software that People Can and Will Use." *IEEE Software* 4 (September 1987).

7. Seilheimer, Steven D. "The Importance of the Human Factor in an Information System Life Cycle." *Journal of Systems Management* 38 (July 1987).

8. Stevens, W., G. Meyers, and L. Constantine. "Structured Design." *IBM Systems Journal* 13, no. 2 (May 1974).

9. Teresko, John. "What MIS Should Be Telling You about CASE." *Industry Week* 239 (2 April 1990).

10. Martin, James. *Information Engineering, Book II Design and Construction.* Englewood Cliffs, NJ: Prentice-Hall, 1990.

A Manager's Dilemma

Case Study 11.1

A Taxing Problem

How could this have ever happened? There were pickets outside protesting over the many problems associated with the new property tax computer system! Some lawyers and property owners were so angry with the computer system that they filed a $50 million lawsuit against the City Council and the Department of Taxes!

It all started just over two years ago, when the City Council demanded that the whole system of assessing and collecting property taxes be improved. At that time, there was a nine-month delay from the time a property tax change (usually an increase) was approved by the voters and the time the rate changes were reflected in the property owner's tax bill. Also, because of the effort required, properties were only reevaluated every fourth year. The City Council believed the city was losing millions of dollars a year because of these delays in implementing tax changes. Thus a major information system development project was launched to eliminate the delays in implementing tax rate changes and to reduce the effort required to reevaluate property. This project was completed on time about twelve months ago.

During the past two years, two temporary tax levies expired, which should have led to a decrease of about $125 per year to the average home owner. However, the new tax system proved so difficult to use that Department of Taxes personnel were not able to update basic tax rate information. Nor were they able to update property records with the results of the latest reassessment completed twelve months ago. This reassessment indicated that property values, in general, should be reduced by 8 percent. Unfortunately, this information was leaked to the local newspapers.

Because of the inability to update the records in the new system, the Department of Taxes simply sent out a copy of the previous tax bill to all property owners. The taxpayers were incensed at receiving a tax bill that was, on the average, $200 more than current tax rates and property values could justify.

What led to such a mismatch between the system that was delivered and the system that was needed? What are some things that could have been done to identify that problems existed long before the system was completed?

Case Study 11.2

Evaluating Options

The new Credit and Accounts Receivable project team is completing the analysis phase of the project. They are equally divided between two possible options that seem to meet all user needs. Because you are the sponsor of the project, the project team is looking to you to help choose between the options. The table that follows summarizes some key facts about each option. Please answer the following questions:

1. What process would you follow to make this important decision?

2. Based on the following data, which option would you pick and why?

3. What steps would you take to reduce the project risk?

	OPTION #1	OPTION #2
Total Annual Tangible Benefits (Millions)	$1.5	$2.5
Total Development Cost (Millions)	$1.5	$3.0
Total Annual Operating Cost (Millions)	$0.5	$1.0
Time Required to Implement	9 months	18 months
Degree of Risk (Expressed in Probabilities)		
Benefits Will Be 50 Percent Less Than Expected	20%	35%
Cost Will Be 50 Percent Greater Than Expected	35%	20%
Organization Will Not Make Changes Necessary for System to Operate as Expected	20%	25%
Does System Meet All Mandatory User Requirements	Yes	Yes

Case Study 11.3

The IndoClean Company

The IndoClean Company is a distributor of industrial cleaning products in southwestern Ohio, northern Kentucky, and eastern Indiana. Its general office and main warehouse are located in northern Cincinnati. Additional warehouse space is rented in Ft. Thomas, Kentucky, and in Harrison, Ohio. The three warehouses form a sort of equilateral triangle, with each leg of the triangle extending about twenty-five miles.

As a distributor, IndoClean buys industrial cleaning products from major manufacturers such as Procter & Gamble, Lever Brothers, and others. These products are then warehoused and pulled from inventory to fill customer orders. Customers are primarily laundries, car washes, schools, and office buildings. Customers do not like to store large quantities of these cleaning products and thus order only a month's requirement at a time.

There is a family of products required to do an effective laundering job—detergent, brightener, bleach, soap, and softener. Thus, orders from a laundry customer will usually be for these five items at a time. Likewise, there is a family of products ordered at one time by car washes—body washer, wheel washer, tire and chrome cleaner, and wax. If IndoClean is out of stock on any one of the family of products, the customer will place the order with another distributor who can provide the entire set of products needed to do the job. As a result, IndoClean carries a heavy safety stock of all its products.

For any given item, IndoClean stocks the products of two or three different manufacturers. Many of the products are carried in more than one size—all the way from a five-pound bag to a fifty-five-pound drum. The combination of products, manufacturers, and sizes results in the need to track about four hundred stock-keeping units whose inventory levels must be controlled. IndoClean tries to maintain the appropriate inventory level of all four hundred stock-keeping units at each of the three warehouses through the use of a manual ledger card system. Operating this manual system requires only one clerk, since the inventory ledger cards are reviewed only every two weeks.

IndoClean's Controller is unsure about what steps should be taken to improve the manual accounts receivable operation. There seems to be no collection problem, because most of the customers pay before the sixty days allowed by the company. However, competitors of IndoClean have set their collection period at thirty days with no apparent customer ill will or collection problems. IndoClean's management has balked at this change because it would require hiring an additional clerk to do billing on a monthly basis instead of every two months as is the current practice.

The Controller has hired you as a consultant to answer the following questions:

1. Do you see any problems with our inventory control, accounts receivable, or billing operations? If so, what are they? What recommendations for improvement can you make that do not involve computerization?

2. Are there any areas of the business that could benefit from computerization? If so, which ones? How would they benefit? Is it possible to quantify these benefits?

3. Are the benefits of computerization sufficient to justify our getting our own computer? Does this mean we'll have to hire a programmer and a computer operator? Won't this be expensive? Nobody at IndoClean has any experience managing computer people—how will we know if they're doing a good job?

The following chart will help you answer IndoClean's questions.

IndoClean Company Summary for Last Year

Sales	$12 million; expected to increase 30% per year
Net Profit	$1 million; expected to increase 20% per year
Number of Employees	40
Number of Customer Accounts	1,800
Inventory	
Average value of inventory	$3.0 million
Number of stock-keeping units	400
Inventory carrying costs	33% of value of inventory
Lead time for stock replenishment	21 days
Accounts Receivable	
Aged trial balance prepared quarterly	
Terms of sale	Net 60 days
Accounts receivable balance	$3.0 million
Billing	
Average customer order	$1,000
Invoice mailed on average twelve days after delivery of order. Customer statement prepared every other month. Customers pay bills an average of fifty-five days after receipt.	
Invoices per month	1,000

Case Study 11.4

What's Wrong with Our System Development Process?

About two years ago, the firm implemented a standard system development process. All programmers, systems analysts, and project managers were trained in this process and expected to use it on all projects. It was thought that this would put an end to system development problems.

Unfortunately, everything was not OK. End users frequently complained that their projects were completed late, were over budget, and failed to meet the real business requirements. The Manager of Application Development has placed you on a three-month assignment to find out what's wrong and to make specific recommendations on how to fix it.

What sort of fact gathering needs to occur before you can make any recommendations? How would you proceed to get this data? What are some possible reasons for end-user unhappiness?

This section covers a wide range of topics with which business managers can expect to be involved. Business managers need to recognize that these issues exist and to help IT managers prepare to deal with them.

Chapter 12 presents an effective process for acquiring information technology resources including hardware, software, data, and resources. Chapter 13 discusses the important topic of end user computing. This chapter discusses what business managers can do to improve the effectiveness of their firm's end user computing and improve the waning relationship with the IT organization. Companies are becoming increasingly dependent upon the availability of information systems to support the day-to-day operations of the firm. At the same time, the risk of unauthorized access to information systems resources is becoming a topic of boardroom discussions. Chapter 14 addresses the important topics of computer security and disaster planning.

Chapter 12

Acquiring Information Technology Resources

Upon completion of this chapter, you will be able to:

1. Discuss the key role that business managers play in acquiring and installing cost-effective hardware and software.

2. State three guidelines to follow in negotiating a hardware or software contract.

3. Use the force-field analysis technique to prepare people to accept change.

4. Outline a four-step process to acquire data from external sources.

5. Identify three types of situations in which the use of an outside expert is appropriate.

6. List eight tips to ensure the effective use of consultants.

7. Define the term infrastructure plan, and explain how it is used to manage problems associated with a multivendor environment.

Preview

Successfully installing information technology requires that the proper organizational activities are chosen for automation, the technology is readily accepted by both management and clerical personnel, and it leads to real benefits to the organization. In addition, the hardware and software combination chosen must work reliably and cost effectively. This is a tough set of goals to reach! Only a careful and thorough approach ensures that these objectives are achieved.

Issues

1. What process should management follow to ensure the successful acquisition and installation of information technology?

2. How can management identify and quantify people's feelings for and against a change?

3. What is an RFP and how is it used?

4. How can managers improve their negotiating power in setting a final contract with the vendor?

5. When should management rely on the help of an outside consultant to address issues related to information technology?

Trade-offs

1. How much time should management devote to making sure the hardware and software selection process is a good one, versus the need to make a decision and get on with installing and using the information technology?

2. To what extent should employees' negative feelings toward information technology influence the decision to install it?

A Manager Struggles with the Issues

John was considering installing a computer system to manage the company's $20 million inventory, which was stored at four locations in the southwestern United States. He had held preliminary discussions with several computer vendors who could deliver a complete package (hardware, software, training, and support) that seemed to fill the bill. As a middle-level manager in charge of the company's finished product inventory, he had been delegated the authority to make the final decision. Having come up through the ranks, John was thoroughly familiar with inventory management and warehouse operations. He felt confident that he could select the best system to meet the company's needs. He wondered, though, if anyone else ought to be involved in the decision. He also worried about how the system would be accepted by the people who had to use it and what he could do to ensure its successful introduction.

■ THE HARDWARE AND SOFTWARE ACQUISITION PROCESS

The spending on information technology is being transferred outside the data processing department's budget. In many companies the purchase of personal computers, software, departmental systems, and other hardware and software for corporate end users appears on someone else's budget—not IT's. Diebold Group, a New York IT consulting and research firm, estimated that for every $100 in the IT budget spent on hardware, $60 was spent on hardware outside of IT. For every $100 spent on IT personnel, $40 went for people outside data processing who perform IT-like functions such as system development. International Data Corporation came up with similar numbers in a survey of 160 IT executives. The market research firm found out that end-user data processing spending constitutes 37 percent of total IT outlays.

The process of acquiring and installing the best possible hardware and software combination to meet a particular organization's needs can be complex and time-consuming. In order to make sure that proper organizational activities are chosen for automation, that the system is accepted by management and others who will use it, and that the hardware and software combination is as reliable and cost effective as possible, three steps must be carefully and thoroughly followed:

1. Acquire hardware and software to meet defined needs.
2. Install the hardware and software.
3. Evaluate the system, procedures, and personnel.

Exhibit 12.1 outlines these three steps, and the following sections discuss the activities involved in each of them.

Acquire Hardware and Software to Meet Defined Needs

There are two basic ways in which to approach the selection of hardware and software. The recommended way is to develop a **request for proposal (RFP)** in which management carefully defines the business

Exhibit 12.1
Steps in Acquiring
and Installing Cost-
effective Hardware
and Software

1. Acquire hardware and software to meet defined needs.
   Develop a request for proposal (RFP).
   Identify several qualified vendors.
   Submit RFP to qualified vendors.
   Evaluate vendor proposals.
   Select vendor.
   Negotiate the contract.
2. Install the hardware and software.
   Deal with people and organizational issues.
   Prepare the installation site.
   Prepare operating procedures.
   Select and train personnel.
   Convert files.
   Convert system.
3. Evaluate system, procedures, and personnel.

needs that must be met. The RFP is submitted to **qualified vendors,** who respond with a proposal to meet the specified needs. The RFP puts vendors into a directly competitive position so that they develop the most cost-effective solution to meet the real needs of the users. The drawback to this method is that the RFP can be difficult to prepare. Users frequently overlook key requirements, have difficulty in clearly stating their needs, or are unable to agree on the relative importance of desired system features. As a result, consultants are frequently employed to develop the RFP.

An alternative approach is to request that the vendors bring in their own systems personnel to define the needs of the business and to recommend appropriate solutions that involve their hardware and software. Generally, quite different solutions are recommended by the various vendors. Each vendor will propose a solution that takes advantage of the specific features of their hardware and software. In the end, the user must figuratively compare apples to oranges, making a final selection from among the various options very difficult. Furthermore, vendors may not gather all the pertinent facts in the available time, and thus their recommendations can be poor, causing impractical systems to be advocated. For these reasons, this latter approach should be avoided.

Develop a Request for Proposal

An RFP is a formal document that requests a vendor to propose a system solution to meet clearly defined business needs. It is important to give identical RFPs to all vendors concerned to avoid charges of unfairness. There are many ways to structure an RFP. The outline in Exhibit 12.2 is one suggested approach, and a sample RFP is presented at the end of this chapter.

Exhibit 12.2
Proposed Outline
for an RFP

Purpose of RFP
Company Background
Basic Requirements
Hardware Environment
Description of RFP Process

Section A—Current System Overview
Section B—System Requirements
Section C—Volume and Size Data
Section D—Required Contents of Vendor's Response to RFP

Identify Several Qualified Vendors

Datapro Research Corporation publishes annual reports evaluating data processing hardware and software from many vendors. *Computerworld, Datamation, PC Week, PC Computing,* and dozens of other business and computer magazines publish ratings or discussions about hardware and software. Reports and publications such as these are a good place to start identifying vendors you may wish to contact. Discussions with other organizations who have recently installed a similar computer system can add to or delete from your list. A review of vendors' annual reports or a recent Dun & Bradstreet report may eliminate financially weak vendors from the list. The list should include four to eight vendors who appear to be highly competent, well regarded, and financially stable. The vendors may include hardware manufacturers, software houses, or consulting firms who will acquire the appropriate hardware and software to meet your needs.

Submit RFP to Qualified Vendors

Bid invitations containing identical RFPs should be mailed to all competing vendors. Using a bid invitation and an RFP informs all vendors what requirements must be met, keeps the number of vendor questions manageable, and provides a fair basis for comparing all responses. Most likely, the vendors will need additional information and assistance as they progress in developing a response to your business needs. Keep an open mind to possible modifications to the specified requirements to take advantage of a particular vendor's special features. Such modifications can be beneficial and should not necessarily be discouraged. Vendors should even be encouraged to develop a creative solution to meet your needs.

Evaluate Vendor Proposals

The vendors should be given a reasonable amount of time to study the bid invitation and prepare their proposals. The time required may be one to three months. Request that the vendor submit several copies of the proposal followed by an oral presentation by the vendor's representative. At this presentation, the salesperson will stress the important

Exhibit 12.3
Example of
Vendor's Response
to Specific User
Needs

Feature	Importance	Availability		
		Now	Future	Not Likely
Letter-quality printed output	Mandatory	X		
Interfaces with DEC computer	Highly desirable		6/97	
Built-in redundant power source	Nice to have			X

points of the proposal and answer questions. After this process is followed for all vendors who replied to the bid invitation, the information in the various proposals must be carefully evaluated. Exhibit 12.3 shows a partial example of a vendor's response.

A quantitative method for choosing among the proposals is illustrated in Exhibit 12.4. The primary **criteria for evaluation** are identified and assigned a weighting factor. The most important criteria are assigned the heaviest weighting. Then each vendor's proposal is evaluated against each criterion and assigned a value. The total rating for each vendor is then determined by summing the individual values. The vendor with the highest total rating is the best-qualified vendor—ignoring costs.

Costs may be factored into the analysis in many ways. One way is to determine the proposal with the highest rate of return on investment based on estimated cost and savings data. Another way is to determine the most cost-effective proposal—that vendor with the lowest ratio of total cost to total rating. Management may then choose the best-qualified vendor, the vendor with the best rate of return, or the most cost-effective vendor. As shown in Exhibit 12.4, it is quite unlikely that the same vendor will be the highest rated in all three categories.

Vendors have a definite tendency to **overequip**—to present more equipment than what is really needed. After all, the job of the salesperson is to sell as much of the vendor's hardware and software as possible. Guard against this tendency by carefully reviewing the stated system requirements versus the vendor's proposal. Does the proposal meet too many of the nice-to-have features? How much could the cost be reduced if the system did not meet some of the lesser requirements? Which requirements add the most cost to the proposal? Those requirements that are not essential or cost effective should be dropped. One will usually find that a bare-bones system that does just what is absolutely required costs much less than the full-blown system with all the bells and whistles.

Select Vendor

Evaluating each vendor's proposal will reveal the more competitive vendors. A good practice is to analyze the three most competitive vendors. This subset of the initial vendors who you feel are most competitive are often referred to as "finalists." In the select vendor step the

Exhibit 12.4
Example of
Quantitative
Method of
Evaluating Vendor
Proposals for a
Hypothetical Order-
Entry Processing
System

Criteria for Evaluation	Importance of Criteria (weight)	Rankings Assigned to Each of Five Alternative Vendor Proposals (See Below)				
		1	2	3	4	5
1. Reduce internal order processing time to three days.	100	4	5	0	2	3
2. Reduce order processing cost to under $10/order.	70	5	4	3	0	2
3. Reduce percentage of orders incorrectly filled to under 1 percent.	70	3	2	4	1	5
4. System must be available at least 98 percent of regular work hours.	50	3	1	2	4	5
5. Quality of vendor training.	30	5	4	1	2	3
6. Quality of vendor support.	25	2	3	4	1	5
7. System capacity sufficient to handle 50 percent increase of order volume.	10	1	5	3	4	0
Vendor's total score (Sum of weight × ranking for all criteria)		1,320	1,215	750	595	1,255
Cost of alternative ($000's)		$320	$275	$145	$205	$400
Cost/score ($000's/ point)		.242	.226	.193	.344	.319
Projected rate of return		32%	38%	24%	12%	18%

Ranking
0 = Vendor cannot meet this requirement.
1 = Vendor barely meets this requirement, weakest vendor.
5 = Vendor far exceeds this requirement, strongest vendor.

Vendor 1 is the most qualified vendor with 1,320 total points.
Vendor 3 is the most cost effective with $.193 thousand dollars/point.
Vendor 2 has the best rate of return at 38 percent.

finalists are analyzed further to reach a decision. The time required to complete this step will depend on the thoroughness of the analysis and the number of finalists evaluated. These factors, in turn, depend on the closeness of the proposals and the amount of money involved. If one vendor seems clearly superior and the amount of money is relatively small, less analysis is required than if the proposals are very similar and the amount of money is very great.

Often, a carefully designed **benchmark test** will be run on the systems proposed by the different vendors to provide a basis for performance comparison. The benchmark test requires that each vendor's system try to accomplish the same set of results. The time and resources required to accomplish the specified results, as well as any other factors deemed important, are carefully measured as each vendor's system goes through the test. Thus the use of a benchmark test to select vendor hardware or software (or both) is similar to using the results of a one-hundred-yard dash to select sprinters for a track team.

The vendor's ability and willingness to provide the necessary sales and service support is an important factor. This should be confirmed with discussions with other users of the vendor's equipment. Exhibit 12.5 shows the potential steps involved in getting additional data on which to base the vendor selection. These steps are listed in order of increasing time and effort to complete them.

The next step is to gain more data about the finalists than was presented in the RFP. An effective way to accomplish this is to invite each of the finalists to send representatives to your firm to answer your questions on their proposal. Such a meeting provides an excellent opportunity to meet the local sales force and technical people who would be involved in the installation and support of the vendor's product. Be prepared for a strong "sales pitch" from each vendor. Keep the meeting on track by setting a definite schedule and carefully developing a set of questions in advance. In addition to vendor specific questions, ask each finalist for the names of three references, preferably ones similar to your own firm, (i.e., same industry, similar size in terms of sales and employees) who use the vendor's product in a manner similar to your intent.

Following each vendor's visit, call their references to gather additional data. (Exhibit 12.6 provides a sample set of vendor reference questions that will yield useful information.) After interviewing all references by phone, you may decide to visit one or more of the references to see their operation and to observe the use of the vendor's product firsthand.

If there is doubt that the vendors understand and/or can meet your requirements, plan to visit each finalist. Planning and executing these vendor visits requires a substantial amount of time for both your organization and the vendors'. In preparation for your visit, ask each vendor to create a demonstration version of their product that matches, as closely as possible, your own operation. Depending on the complexity of your operation, you may need to allow a couple weeks for each vendor to prepare such a demo. During the visit, try to assess the vendor's experience and level of understanding of your industry

Exhibit 12.5
Ways to Obtain More Data for the Vendor Selection Process (Listed in Order of Increasing Time and Effort for Completion)

Invite finalists to visit and answer questions on their proposal.

Conduct a phone interview with three references for each finalist.

Visit one or more reference sites.

Visit each finalist's site.

Evaluate the demonstration system that closely matches your operation.

Conduct a benchmark test of each finalist's system.

Exhibit 12.6
Questions for
Vendor References

Please tell me about your company's use of the vendor's product.

Why did you choose this vendor?

Who else did you consider? (Listen carefully for the names of your other finalists. If one is mentioned, ask why this vendor was not selected.)

Overall, are you satisfied with the vendor and the product?

What do you like least about the vendor and the product?

What enhancements to the product would you like to see made?

Are you satisfied with the vendor's support of the product?

If you were making this decision today, would you do anything differently?

Do you know of any company using this product who feels it has not met their needs?

Do you know of any company using ....? (Name the other contenders and their products. This will provide additional references, not handpicked by the vendor.)

and your firm's needs. Meet the technical support and training people to learn how they are staffed and prepared to meet the needs of customers. Bring up additional questions, issues, or concerns that may have been uncovered in talking with the references. Carefully view and evaluate the demonstration system built to match your business operations. Ideally, actual end users should be given an opportunity to try out the system. Their reaction to the system and its ease of use and response time, should be weighed heavily in the decision process.

Real World Perspective

Playing Hardball with Vendors

Allow at least three months in the installation schedule for resolving contract differences and negotiating.

Obtain the services of a qualified expert in the area of information systems acquisition—computer law, finance, and negotiations.

Request a copy of the vendor's standard contract as part of their response to your RFP. Review this contract closely with appropriate resources.

Do not proceed with serious negotiations until the person from the vendor's company with final authority to approve the contract has been identified and is present at the sessions.

Never agree to sign the standard contract.

Be willing to break off negotiations to make your point on an issue. Salespeople have defined sales and earnings goals; they are as eager to sell you the system, or more so, than you are to buy it.

Remember: If it is not written in the contract, it is not part of the deal. Get all oral representations written into the contract.

If the vendor claims you are getting their best price, request that a clause be added to the contract to the effect that the buyer is entitled to a rebate if at a later date it is found out that the system has been sold at a lower price to someone else.

Be wary of a package deal with everything you need at one low price. You may be buying something in the package you do not need.

Include penalty clauses for failure of the system to meet certain key requirements or for missed schedule dates.

Negotiate the Contract

In acquiring computer equipment, software, or services, one must remember that computer vendors negotiate contracts for their livelihood. Their marketing effort throughout the selection process is designed to make contract signing easy and seemingly a mere formality to be dispensed with quickly. *Warning:* Vendor contracts are not designed to protect the buyer or user. Many times the vendor's contract may carefully disclaim everything the vendor has said, shown, or written to you about how the proposed system will meet your needs. Careful analysis of a vendor's standard contract will usually reveal it to be an extremely one-sided, and therefore potentially dangerous, legal document. For example, there may be a provision that the vendor must be paid in full within thirty days of delivery of equipment. The wise buyer may want to stipulate that payment will be made within thirty days of the equipment being installed and operating to the buyer's satisfaction.

The typical buyer is at a distinct disadvantage when dealing with a vendor when it comes to negotiating the final contract. First, the user's infrequent acquisition of computer systems does not justify a full-time, in-house staff of experts in the fields of computer law, finance, and negotiation. Even the user's usual legal and financial resources from outside the company are likely to be unfamiliar with these specialized areas. The vendor, on the other hand, can draw on a small army of full-time staff trained and experienced in these areas. Second, the vendor has been down this path many times before. Vendors earn their living preparing marketing plans. These plans normally cover six months or longer, with every step planned to the last detail. These plans are based on the experience of dealing with dozens or even hundreds of customers on a regular basis. For the buyer, this may be a first-time (and last-time!) experience. The buyer is hopelessly outplanned and can be easily outmaneuvered. Failure to compensate for the vast disparity of planning, skills, experience, and resources between the buyer and the vendor will lull the buyer into a false sense of security.

The most important guideline to follow if this is your first computer system acquisition is to get qualified help. Obtain the services of a well-respected consultant who is an expert in the areas of computer law, finance, and negotiation to help finalize the deal. If you are a member of a large company, such a resource may exist within the purchasing, legal, finance, or IT departments. Someone in a small company may have to hire an outside resource.

A second guideline is to never agree to sign the vendor's standard contract. The standard contract has been carefully drawn up by the vendor's legal counsel—a full-time expert in computer contracts—to provide maximum protection to the vendor and with very little concern for the user's needs for protection. Obtain a copy of the vendor's standard contract early in the process of evaluating the finalists and go over it carefully with your resources. Be prepared to draw up several pages of addenda even if the vendor insists that the contract has been accepted virtually unchanged by dozens of customers.

Last but equally important, the process of contract negotiation can easily take three months or more. Build this elapsed time into your installation plans, and do not allow yourself to be rushed through negotiations in an effort to meet a deadline.

Install the Hardware and Software

Installation and conversion includes all the activities involved in successfully converting from the old system to the new one. These activities include dealing with any people and organizational issues, preparing the installation site, preparing operating procedures, selecting and training personnel, and performing file conversion and system conversion.

Deal with People and Organizational Issues

A frequently encountered stumbling block to the successful implementation of a new system is negative user reaction. Clerical staff may fear that their positions may be eliminated or their work altered in a way they do not like. Managers may see the introduction of computerized methods as a threat to their power and influence. Such fears can lead to resentment, lack of cooperation, or outright resistance. Any of these reactions can doom a system, no matter how carefully the rest of the project is planned.

It is imperative to understand people's feelings toward the new system to help them prepare for the changes to come. **Force-field analysis** is a useful tool for putting these feelings into perspective. Exhibit 12.7 is an example of force-field analysis of one clerical person's feelings upon first hearing that a computer was to be installed. The feelings

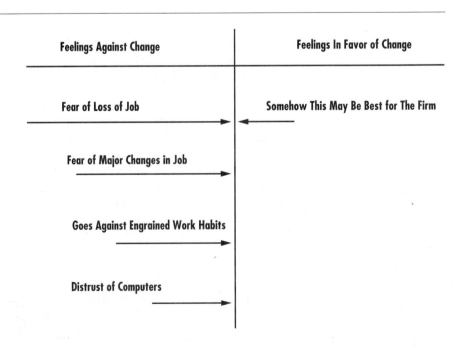

Exhibit 12.7
Force-field Analysis Showing Factors Influencing Clerical Worker's Feelings About the Implementation of New System— Before Preparation

Feelings Against Change	Feelings In Favor of Change
Fear of Loss of Job	Somehow This May Be Best for The Firm
Fear of Major Changes in Job	
Goes Against Engrained Work Habits	
Distrust of Computers	

listed on the left side are forces against the change to a new system. The length of each arrow represents the relative strength of that feeling, thus the longest arrow is the strongest force. The feelings listed on the right side are forces that support the change. The forces both for and against a specific change will vary from person to person as will the relative strength of each force. The force-field analysis in Exhibit 12.7 shows clearly that the individual has many strong feelings against change and will resist a change to the new system. These resisting forces are much stronger than the solitary positive feeling.

Negative feelings must be reduced or eliminated to help gain system acceptance. The fear of losing one's job can be eliminated by making it clear that the person will remain employed by the company. The fear of major changes in one's job can be reduced by allowing the person to participate in developing one's own new job description. If this is not possible, the person must be carefully informed of how the new job is to be performed. The positive impact of the change should be stressed. Some distrust of the computer can be dispelled by letting the person view a successful computer application and talk to some of the more enthusiastic users of the computer.

It is not enough to neutralize the negative feelings. Positive feelings must also be created to truly motivate the individual. The many tangible and intangible benefits for the organization as well as for the individual must be explained. In many computer installations, new positions are created that can lead to increased salaries and promotions. The system installation may also lead to job enrichment by enabling the individual to perform work in a new and more interesting way. Developing skills and knowledge in data processing can enhance career growth.

Exhibit 12.8 is an example of a force-field analysis of the clerical worker's feelings after an effective job of preparing the worker to accept the system. At this point, the staff should realize several things: (1) their role is essential to the success of the system, and therefore they are making an important contribution to the organization, (2) the devel-

Exhibit 12.8
Force-field Analysis Showing Factors Influencing Clerical Worker's Feelings About the Implementation of New System—After Preparation

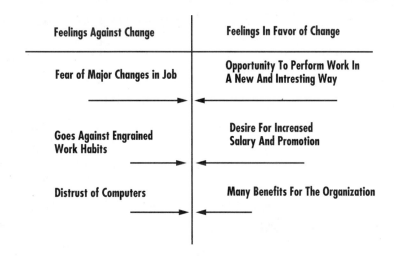

Exhibit 12.9
Force-field Analysis
Showing Factors
Influencing
Manager's Feelings
About
Implementation of
New System—
Before Preparation

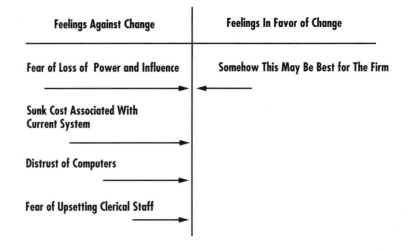

Feelings Against Change   **Feelings In Favor of Change**

Fear of Loss of Power and Influence   Somehow This May Be Best for The Firm

Sunk Cost Associated With
Current System

Distrust of Computers

Fear of Upsetting Clerical Staff

opment of skills and knowledge in data processing will enhance their career growth, and (3) each individual has an important responsibility to perform within certain deadlines and constraints to secure the potential benefits of data processing to both individuals and the organization. Exhibits 12.9 and 12.10 are before and after examples of force-field analyses of a manager of clerical personnel.

Prepare the Installation Site

Sufficient time and dollars must be allocated for **site preparation** in any major data processing installation. Site preparation requires establishing space where the proper environmental conditions can be maintained; ensuring ready access to sufficient electrical, telephone, and communications resources; and acquiring appropriate office space for

Exhibit 12.10
Force-field Analysis
Showing Factors
Influencing
Manager's Feelings
About
Implementation of
New System—
After Preparation

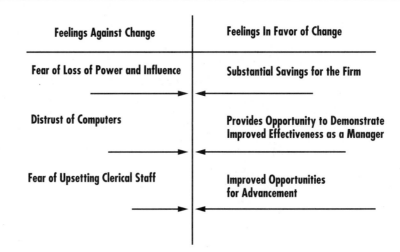

Feelings Against Change   **Feelings In Favor of Change**

Fear of Loss of Power and Influence   Substantial Savings for the Firm

Distrust of Computers   Provides Opportunity to Demonstrate
                                               Improved Effectiveness as a Manager

Fear of Upsetting Clerical Staff   Improved Opportunities
                                               for Advancement

users of the data processing workstations. Ideally these factors are discussed at length with the architects and the engineers as new office space is created or old office space is remodeled.

Maintaining proper environmental conditions means controlling temperature, humidity, dust, and electromagnetic interference. Temperatures outside the range of 65° to 75° or low humidity can damage equipment, especially the system's storage media. Electronic interference in power lines, either through conduction along wiring or by direct radiation, can cause equipment malfunction. Air conditioning, humidifiers, dehumidifiers, regular vacuuming to remove dust, and dedicated electrical lines may all be necessary to adequately control these environmental factors. Equipment must be selected with the size and shape of the area and number of occupants in mind. Data processing equipment may generate substantial heat on its own; this too must be considered. Good lighting that provides plenty of light without glare or reflection is also necessary.

The power requirements of each piece of equipment must be determined to ensure that sufficient wiring and electrical outlets are available in the space where the equipment is to be installed. Telephone outlets and access to any special cabling required to link the workstations to other devices also need to be considered. Placement of the outlets will depend on the location of furniture and equipment. Since these are likely to move frequently, placement should be planned to accommodate changes with relative ease. Be sure to generously overbuild the ability to meet power needs. It is not much more expensive to overbuild a power system than to put in the bare minimum initially; however, expanding a power system in the future could cost as much as the original installation.

Ergonomics is a body of knowledge, drawn principally from life sciences (psychology, physiology, anatomy) and engineering sciences (mechanics, physics, statistics), on the interaction between humans and their total task environment. The task environment includes not only tools, equipment, and layout, but also the temperature, lighting, sound levels, atmosphere, and air movement and social context of the task.

Studies by the National Institute of Occupational Safety and Health revealed that employees using video display devices appear to have more health complaints than those who don't. In particular, they complain of vision problems, backaches, neckaches, and similar muscle discomforts. Because of this, ergonomic design features are built into terminals and stressed as selling points by the manufacturers of office equipment. Lighting, the angle of the equipment to the user, and desk and chair height are critical factors in user comfort. The ergonomic features of a terminal should be carefully considered if the same user will be at the terminal more than one or two hours a day.

Human factors also need to be considered in design of the workplace to ensure comfort and eliminate stress and disturbances. All seats, desks, and lights should be easily adjustable. The work area should include plenty of space for printouts, manuals, and other documents. Background noise should be kept to ten to eighty decibels.

Office furnishings should be wisely selected for functionality, comfort, aesthetics, and economy. For example, data processing areas can be enhanced with attractive carpets, drapes, plants, and pictures that also help reduce the noise level. For personnel who will be performing data processing activities most of the time, ergonomic factors become increasingly important. The chair, workstation, keyboard, work surfaces, and storage areas should all be carefully designed and selected to make the most of user effectiveness by minimizing user fatigue, discomfort, and distraction from work.

Prepare Operating Procedures

Successful operation of an information system requires good operating procedures, which must be not only well defined but also designed so that the system operates in the manner intended. Furthermore, these procedures must be clearly communicated and understood by users and operators of the system. Several areas in which procedures must be defined are outlined in Exhibit 12.11.

Several guidelines should be followed in establishing procedures. Procedures must be simple and economical to use. They must also be fast and reliable. Because all things change with time, procedures must be flexible. Procedures should help managers accomplish business objectives; they shouldn't get in the way. And procedures must be acceptable to those who must follow them.

Select and Train Personnel

The people who will take charge of the operation of the equipment must be identified and trained. The number and types of people needed depend on several things: (1) how complex the equipment is

Exhibit 12.11
A Procedure Checklist to Help Make Sure that the System Operates as Management Intended

1. Safeguard against unauthorized access to confidential information and both intentional or accidental destruction of data.
2. Provide backup procedures so that a system failure cannot bring an essential activity of the business to a halt.
3. Ensure adequate system maintenance and service to minimize the possibility of lengthy periods of system unavailability, poor system quality, or unacceptable turnaround time.
4. Establish standard file-naming conventions so that information can be easily retrieved without danger of loss.
5. Establish appropriate work priority categories to enable operators to make decisions on which jobs should take precedence over others.
6. Train operators and users in the efficient and effective use of the system.
7. Provide for the backup of data used or created by the system.

to operate, (2) what specific duties the operators are to perform (e.g., change paper on the printer or load a new operating system), (3) the degree of support the operator is expected to provide if the system goes down, and (4) the level of system availability desired.

Often the vendor can train the system operators. The extent and quality of this training should be an important factor in vendor selection.

Convert Files

File conversion can involve converting manual files to computer-readable files or changing computer-readable files in one form to another form. The file conversion process can be long and tedious. Adequate time must be planned in the implementation schedule to complete the conversion process. Side benefits that can be gained during the conversion process are the correction of inaccurate data and the elimination of duplicate records or records that are no longer needed. However, these side benefits are gained only by spending even more effort and elapsed time against the file conversion process.

Convert System

At some point after the system has been thoroughly tested, all new transactions must be processed according to the new procedures and run on the new system. Many organizations elect to run a **parallel operation** for at least a short time. Under this form of operation, transactions are processed on both the old and new system. Any differences in results are noted, and the differences are carefully reconciled to understand why they occurred. Problems in the new system are noted and hopefully resolved. Once everyone is sufficiently confident in the new system, the operation is cut over from the old system to the new one, and the old system is no longer run.

Other approaches to system conversion are discussed in Chapter 11.

Evaluate Systems, Procedures, and Personnel

The operation of the entire data processing system, including procedures and personnel, needs to be evaluated on an ongoing basis to ensure that the system operates as management intended. In addition, it is useful to compare the cost of your computer system operation to that of another organization's. For example, you might compare what it costs your company to process a customer invoice with what it costs another company.

■ ACQUIRING DATA FROM EXTERNAL SOURCES

The Emergence of Data Vendors

Vast amounts of a wide variety of data are becoming available from **data vendors.** A data vendor is an organization that acquires data of interest to a number of individuals or organizations, adds value to the data, and then sells it. Dun & Bradstreet and its subsidiary, the A. C. Nielsen Company, are good examples of data vendors.

A. C. Nielsen has a number of data services it sells. Many of these services are based on scanner data obtained from supermarket check-outs. As each customer checks out, the universal product code (UPC) of each item is read by the scanner. The UPC identifies the brand, size, and other characteristics of the item, including the price and manu-facturer. These data are captured by individual stores in computer-readable form. Nielsen accumulates detailed data from over 1,600 stores throughout the United States, edits the data, aggregates the in-dividual stores' data to a higher level (perhaps to the supermarket chain or manufacturer level), and creates reports and computer tapes of these data, which it sells to its customers.

The scanner data provide detailed data about sales and pricing. Manufacturers of the items sold in the supermarket can use these data to see how their products sell compared to the competition and ex-amine the effect of price on sales. Supermarkets can compare their sales and pricing to other chains.

There are several other types of data available through other data vendors, as shown in Exhibit 12.12.

A recommended process to follow in acquiring data from data ven-dors is to follow an approach similar to that of acquiring IT hardware and software: (1) acquire data to meet defined needs, (2) deal with people and organizational needs, (3) install the data service, and (4) evaluate the data service.

Acquire the Data to Meet a Defined Need

People everywhere are suffering from data overload. They often have more data than they need to make decisions. What they need is a filter to capture the few really pertinent facts. Thus, data should not be ac-

Exhibit 12.12
A Subset of Data
Vendors Who
Provide Marketing
Data

Data Service	Vendor
Market measurement data	A. C. Nielsen SAMI
Television advertising	Broadcast advertisers reports A. C. Nielsen Leading national advertisers
Newspaper advertising	Majers Advertising checking bureau Keystrokes
Purchase patterns of consumers	Information Resources, Inc. A. C. Nielsen Burke
Demographic data	A. C. Nielsen U.S. government

quired from a data vendor just to provide more facts that may be interesting to know but just end up cluttering the decision-making process. Before buying additional data from a vendor, the following questions should be answered to ensure that the data will be used to meet a real business need:

1. Who needs these data?
2. What specific decisions will be made with these data?
3. Why can't existing sources of data support these decisions?
4. What advantages does this new source of data offer over our existing sources?
5. If we acquire this new source of data, can we eliminate any current data sources or data processing effort?

Deal with People and Organizational Needs

The main issues here are to (1) train people to understand the new data and use them effectively, and (2) prepare the organization to change current decision-making processes to incorporate the data. For example, prior to the advent of the Nielsen scanner data, marketing people obtained product movement and pricing data by taking a physical inventory of supermarkets or warehouses (or both). The manual effort involved in taking such an inventory dictated that only a few stores could be audited every four to eight weeks. The advent of scanner data made it possible to obtain product movement and pricing data on a regular weekly basis from over a thousand stores. Thus marketing managers had to learn how to effectively use the new data, which were much more complete, accurate, and timely than any they had used before. One change implemented was the increased use of graphics to plot weekly data over time to spot trends.

Install the Data Service

The process of installing a new data service may mean that new information technology must be constructed to receive the data from the vendor, edit the data, and convert the vendor codes to codes that are meaningful to your organization. For example, a thirteen-digit UPC must be converted to a brand, size, flavor/style code that your organization uses to identify its products. There will also be a need to develop manual procedures to handle the receipt and processing of data—particularly errors and exceptions.

Evaluate the Data Service

If possible, avoid any total commitment to a new data service until conducting at least a limited test by subscribing to the service for a short period of time and for a defined subset of the total data available. Does the data service meet your expectations of accuracy, timeliness, and, most important, usefulness? The data vendor should provide you with an opportunity to evaluate the service before finalizing any contract for obtaining the data on a regular and ongoing basis.

■ USING CONSULTANTS

As pointed out in the previous sections, **consultants** are often employed in the area of computer system acquisition to help develop the RFP or to negotiate the final contract with the vendor. In general, consultants are people who have an assured competence in a particular field or occupation who are called on to give expert or professional advice. Properly employed, they can provide valuable and worthwhile services. Unfortunately, many organizations frequently mismanage the use of these outside resources and end up with less than satisfactory results. The next three sections provide guidelines for deciding when using a consultant is appropriate, for selecting the right consultant, and for making sure you get good results from them.

When to Use a Consultant

There are three basic situations in which using an outside expert resource is appropriate: (1) to provide temporary staff to supplement the permanent employees, (2) to provide unique skills or knowledge to deal with a temporary problem or condition, or (3) to provide an objective outside expert opinion.

To Provide Temporary Staff

Most organizations at one time or another will find that they require more people or a different mix of people than they have available. This may happen for a host of reasons: an imposed budget restriction on the number of full-time employees, an inability to find people with the

---

Real World Perspective

Salomon Brothers Acquires Junk Bond Data Base

Drexel Burnham Lambert was a highly successful investment banking firm of the eighties that went into Chapter 11 in early 1990. Salomon Brothers acquired their high-yield junk bond data base and software with a bid of $2 million to become the winner in competitive bidding with fifteen other securities firms for this data and the hardware and software needed to access it.

The data base holds information on more than three thousand public and private high-yield securities. The three-gigabyte (3 billion bytes) data base includes securities profiles, data on who owns the securities, and pricing data that goes back five years.

The question is, What is the data really worth, and how long will it give Salomon a competitive edge? SOURCE: © 1990 by CMP Publications, Inc., 600 Community Drive, Manhasset, NY 11030. Reprinted from InformationWeek with permission. □

right mix of skills and experiences for a particular job, or the need to initiate a short-term project on a crash basis when other human resources are tied up. In situations such as these, an outside consulting firm may be able to provide skilled personnel to fill the gap.

The hourly rate for consultants may seem to be extremely high compared with the hourly rate for full-time employees. But one must consider the total cost of recruiting, relocating, training, and providing salary and benefits for a new permanent employee. Also, the trained consultant is ready to go now and does not require three months or longer of training to get started. (See Exhibit 12.13 for a listing of costs associated with hiring a new employee.)

To Provide Unique Skills

Using a consultant with special skills to meet a short-term need may be much more effective than developing an in-house expert to deal with the same problem. For example, to convert a software package from a computer language not used by anyone in the organization to a language that is commonly used is an ideal opportunity for employing a consultant with special skills—knowledge of both programming languages. In such a case, the cost to train a permanent employee and then to have this relative novice do the job would probably exceed the elapsed time and cost to hire an expert.

In general, it does not pay to develop in-house expertise to deal with onetime or short-lived problems. The manager who mistakenly deploys unqualified in-house resources to meet special onetime needs will experience one or more of the following negative results: (1) personnel time that could have been spent working productively on some other project will be lost; (2) employees may feel lost in an unfamiliar assignment, become disenchanted with the organization, and request a reassignment (putting the project even further behind), or, worse yet, resign; and (3) it may take several iterations to produce results that

Exhibit 12.13
Costs and Equivalent Hourly Rate Associated with a New Employee

Activity	Cost
1. Recruiting interviews (assume one out of four candidates is qualified and accepts offer, one day of time is invested in each candidate, and $625 in travel and other expenses for each candidate)	$ 4,000
2. Relocation of new employee	$ 5,000
3. Training (assume three months required and that costs for time of trainers, courses, and so on are valued at $10,000)	$20,000
4. First year's salary	$40,000
5. Value of first year's company benefits (assume 30 percent of starting salary for FICA and other company-paid benefits—insurance, vacation)	$12,000
Estimated company expense for new employee	$81,000
Hourly rate ($81,000/1920 hours/year) (assume eight hours/day for forty-eight weeks—four weeks off for vacation, holiday, and sickness)	$42/hour

match management's expectations due to lack of experience working in the new area.

To Provide an Objective Outside Expert Opinion

An outside independent consultant can often provide the necessary objectivity and expert opinion to help management make tough decisions—key decisions in an environment in which there may exist strong disagreement or uncertainty. The outside consultant is supposedly unaffected by internal company politics and can rise above such issues to help management recommend the course of action that yields the greatest benefit to the whole organization. However, the consultant has a strong instinct for survival, which can cause the consultant to side with the power forces in the organization. Unless carefully managed, the consultant may end up siding with the opinions of the most influential managers and incorporating minor suggestions that reflect some of the good ideas of others. The result can be that the consultant merely ends up telling management what they wanted to hear in the first place.

How to Select a Consultant

The correct approach in hiring a consultant is to hire a person and not the company. You should select your consultant as carefully as you would your own personal heart surgeon. Any evaluation must be done by carefully understanding the qualifications of the individual assigned to your project. Remember there are three types of consulting firms: (1) firms that deal in a wide range of specialties, (2) smaller, more specialized firms that only address a narrow range of problems, and (3) individual consultants. In working with the smaller organizations, you stand the best chance of getting to influence the selection of the actual individual who will work on your project, or "engagement," as the consulting firms refer to it.

One must be especially careful in working with a large firm. You will likely be drawn to that firm based on its reputation and assume that whoever is assigned to work on your problem will possess all the good attributes you associate with that firm. This is not necessarily so. You must also recognize that it is not the various customer reps, partners, and managers who impressed you with their credentials that will do the consulting. In most cases, the person assigned to your project will be whoever is available, including the recent new hire.

Exhibit 12.14 briefly describes what to look for when choosing an individual consultant.

How to Make Sure You Get Your Money's Worth

Once you've decided to hire a consultant, precisely define the problem to be addressed. Make sure you can provide the consultant with pertinent background information and can identify where and how to get

Exhibit 12.14
Some Approaches
to Selecting the
Individual
Consultant

- Carefully review the consultant's resumé.
- Has the consultant worked with other clients on similar problems? Ask for references and check them.
- Try to understand the type of working relationship the consultant establishes with clients:
    Do they run a collaborative process?
    Are they good listeners?
    Are they enthusiastic?
    Do they keep the client well informed—no surprises!
- Do they really know their field and keep current in it?
- Try to arrange for the consultant to meet with other members of your staff so they can evaluate the consultant's interpersonal skills and ability to develop a good working relationship.

the facts to perform the analysis. Indicate specific people on your staff who should be involved. This preparatory work will not only save you time and money by reducing the effort of the consultant, but can also help ensure that the consultant gets off to a good start.

In defining the work the consultant is to perform, it is to your advantage to segment the project or subdivide a major project into two or more smaller efforts. For example, you need the analysis of an information system to be followed up with the development of an RFP for a hardware system on which the system will be run. This effort should be segmented into at least two projects: (1) perform the analysis and (2) develop the RFP for the hardware system. If a consultant agrees to perform the initial analysis, inform the consultant that there may be no further work on the project for the consultant's firm. On occasion, consulting firms will perform the analysis with such complexity as to preclude other firms from being involved in the development of the RFP.

Develop your own written contract for the engagement (see Exhibit 12.15). Never accept the standard contract of consultants. If they wrote it, it will be to their advantage, not yours. Everything in such a standard contract is negotiable. Be sure it covers everything you want, strike out sections you don't like, and be sure that protective clauses protect you

Exhibit 12.15
Points to be
Included in a
Written Contract
with a Consultant

Specify what deliverables constitute acceptable completion of the assignment.

Define a time schedule for completing each deliverable.

Obtain an estimated cost for every deliverable.

Specify certain daily sums to be deducted from the amount owed if the consultant fails to meet certain time performance limitations.

Specify that you have the right to terminate at will without prior written notice.

Require written status reports or meetings on a regular, specified basis.

Clearly identify the responsibilities of both the client and the consultant.

Exhibit 12.16
An Approach to the
Effective Use of
Consultants

Define scope of study carefully.

Divide study into project segments.

Plan project segments in detail.

Listen to your own employees.

Verify that project requires a consultant.

Select consultant carefully.

Define your own staff's time requirements.

Contract for deliverables and schedules.

as well as them. Never rely on an oral representation, since the actual written agreement will contain a clause barring such representations from being presented as evidence in the event of any disagreement.

As a last step before hiring a consultant, listen to your own people. Do they have a clear and well thought out solution to the problem? Have you just been turning a deaf ear to their suggestions? Take the time to seek their advice, and see if they agree with the idea of bringing in an outside consultant. Be prepared to deal with some resistance if they feel threatened. But if you hear that they have a good approach to solving the problem, you may not need to hire the consultant.

Exhibit 12.16 summarizes the approach to ensure effective use of a consultant on your project.

■ MANAGING THE MULTIVENDOR ENVIRONMENT

A modern business organization has many diverse IT needs. Microcomputers are needed to support end-user computing, minicomputers to serve as departmental computing platforms, and mainframe computers to provide large central computing capacity. Local area, campus, and wide area communications networks and accompanying additional software and hardware devices are needed to link all the computers together. Each piece of computing hardware may come with many peripheral devices such as data storage devices, printers, plotters, and a wide range of input devices. Operating systems, utility programs, application packages, and other software are needed to make the hardware useful. It is no wonder that today most companies exist in a **multivendor environment** with dozens of different vendors providing solutions to various needs.

While a multivendor environment is almost inevitable, it is not always well managed. Indeed, there are several recurring problems associated with such a situation.

First, when a problem arises, vendors have been known to point fingers at one another rather than cooperate to isolate and solve the problem. Often there is a problem communicating data from one vendor's hardware device on a network to another vendor's hardware device. In such a situation, it can be extremely difficult to isolate where the problem may lie and to resolve it.

Second, it takes substantial effort to support each vendor—to work with vendors to ensure that they provide good service after the sale, update new releases of hardware or software (or both), train and support users, and so on. As a rough rule-of-thumb, you can estimate that it takes the part-time effort of two or three people to support each vendor, or a minimum of $100,000 per year in people costs.

Third, the multivendor environment complicates the trend toward networking and electronic data interchange. Managers wish to minimize the expense of linking and integrating hardware and software into a network. However, the use of a gateway (a combination of hardware and software that permits networks using different communications protocols to talk with one another) must be employed in the multivendor environment. This adds yet another vendor and set of hardware and software into the current solution mix.

Increasingly, organizations are developing an infrastructure plan to provide guidelines on implementing hardware, systems software, and communication networks. Exhibit 12.17 shows an example infrastructure plan for a company using IBM platforms. The "Today" column indicates what the company is currently using, and the "Future" column indicates where the company wants to be. This plan may look three to five years into the future, but typically has some very specific short-term targets as well. A key element of the **infrastructure plan** is the movement toward adopting and using industry standards for communications, making a determined effort to migrate to industry standard hardware and software, and reducing the number of vendors with which organizations must deal. The term **industry standard** here means standard for the industry in which the organization is a member. Thus a consumer goods firm adopts and uses standards that apply to consumer goods companies.

This strategy provides many benefits. Adoption of industry communications standards ensures that an organization will be able to

---

Exhibit 12.17
Example of Establishment of Standards for IBM Platforms

Type	Where Used	IBM Standard Computing Platforms Today		Future	
		Operating system	Hardware	Operating system	Hardware
Microcomputer	Workstation	MS-DOS System 7	IBM PS/2 MAC	OS/2	IBM Compatibles
Minicomputer	Small mainframe	MPE System 3X OS/400	HP3000 IBM System 3X IBM AS/400	OS/400	IBM AS/400
Mainframe	General computing	DOS/VSE	IBM 43XX	MVS	IBM3XXX

meet customer and supplier expectations. For example, the hundreds of suppliers to the major U.S. automobile manufacturers are expected to comply with electronic data interchange standards for exchanging information on orders and invoices. Failure to comply may well mean loss of significant business.

Once a hardware or software product achieves industry standard status, other vendors begin to create hardware or software (or both) that is compatible with that standard. Thus, the use of industry standard products ensures that the hardware and software selected are at least adequate and will continue to be improved and supported for years to come.

The use of industry standards makes it easier to find people who are trained and have experience with the particular standard products of that industry. This makes it easier to hire experienced employees and find consultants familiar with the hardware and software that you are using. It also means that your own people can become expert in using standard products and don't have to relearn a whole new set of products each time they are promoted or change jobs within the firm.

Summary

Successful installation of a new information system requires that the proper organizational activities are chosen for automation, the system is readily accepted by management and clerical personnel, and the system leads to real benefits to the organization.

The RFP is a formal document that requests vendors to propose a system solution to meet a set of clearly defined business needs.

The typical business manager is at a distinct disadvantage when negotiating with a vendor. Thus, using a trained and experienced resource is highly recommended.

A frequently encountered stumbling block to the successful implementation of a new system is negative user reaction. Such feelings should be identified and reduced or eliminated.

Consultants are often employed in the area of computer system acquisition to help develop the RFP or to negotiate the final contract with the vendor.

Consultants are also used to provide temporary staff to supplement permanent employees or to provide an objective outside expert opinion.

Care must be taken in selecting the right consultant and managing the consultant to get good results.

An infrastructure plan provides guidelines on implementing hardware, systems software, and communications networks. The infrastructure plan should recommend using industry standards for communications, hardware, and software, and reducing the number of vendors.

A Manager's Checklist

✔ Do you know what percentage of total company spending on information resources appears in your budget?

✔ Do you develop an RFP to define business needs before making a major acquisition?

✔ Do you attempt to develop a competitive bidding situation on major purchases?

✔ Are steps taken to improve the users' reception of new information technology?

✔ Are human factors sufficiently considered in workplace design?

✔ Does your organization use consultants appropriately?

✔ Does your organization have an infrastructure plan?

Key Terms

bid invitations
consultant
criteria for evaluation
data vendors
ergonomics
file conversion
force-field analysis
industry standard

infrastructure plan
multivendor environment
overequip
parallel operation
qualified vendors
request for proposal (RFP)
site preparation

Review Questions

1. Briefly outline an effective process for the acquisition and installation of an information system.

2. Why is the typical business manager at a distinct disadvantage when it comes to negotiating the final contract with a hardware or software vendor? What can the manager do to improve the odds?

3. Why is it so important to address the people and organizational issues associated with conversion to an information system? What are some of these issues likely to be?

4. What is ergonomics? When should ergonomic considerations be included in system installation plans?

5. Identify three basic situations in which using an outside consultant may be appropriate.

6. What are some of the problems associated with a multivendor environment?

Discussion Questions

1. You have decided to follow the formal RFP process to select a software vendor. After sending out the RFP, you receive calls from several vendors commenting that it will be time-consuming to respond formally to your RFP. They wish to schedule an appointment

to demonstrate their product rather than complete your RFP. How do you respond?

2. A major new system is scheduled to be installed that will have a dramatic impact on the jobs of over thirty clerical and five managerial people. Discuss how you might ease the way for them to accept this major change.

3. As a middle-level manager responsible for completion of the analysis step of a project to implement a new finished product inventory control system, senior management has asked your opinion about hiring a consulting firm to complete the project. Their goal is to free you up to return to your regular responsibilities as Plant Warehouse Manager. How might you respond to this recommendation?

4. Discuss: Regardless of cost, the ergonomics of the workplace and the workstation must always be of the highest quality.

5. You are a member of the board of a large, not-for-profit hospital. A recommendation has just been made to the board to hire a national consulting firm to identify recommendations for improvements at the hospital. The engagement will involve the use of three consultants over the next nine months at an estimated cost of $500,000. What questions might you ask to determine if the recommendation should be approved?

6. Discuss: How can the development of an infrastructure plan help manage the multivendor environment?

Recommended Readings

1. Archer, Norman P. "End User Software Selection." *Journal of Systems Management* 39 (July 1988).

2. Bienkowski, Danek. "Selecting and Implementing Project Management Software." *Journal of Information Systems Management* 5 (Fall 1988).

3. Rockart, J. "Chief Executives Define Their Own Data Needs." *Harvard Business Review* 57, no. 2 (March–April 1979).

4. Carlson, Kyla K. "War of the Words—Is It Time to Change Your Word Processor?" *PC Computing* vol. 6, no. 8 (August 1993).

5. Bates, Cindy. "Super Printers." *PC Computing* vol. 6, no. 8 (August 1993).

6. Amirrezvani, Anita. "Reliability and Service—Help Is On The Way . . . But When?" *PC World* vol. 12, no. 6 (June 1994).

A Manager's Dilemma

Selecting a Software Package for the Sports Authority

The Sport's Authority is based in Ft. Lauderdale, Florida, with additional stores in Miami and Tampa. Annual sales for 1988 were $15 million. Each store is roughly forty thousand square feet and sells sporting equipment, clothing, and shoes. The time at which the events in this case study are taking place is prior to opening the first store in November 1987.

The Director of Information Technology is reviewing the process that her staff had followed to select the chain's IT system.

"We made a strategic decision to select the IBM System 38 as the primary hardware for running all the chain's IT systems. After all, how can the firm lose by going with IBM? Besides, the IBM System 38 is a tried and proven hardware platform. There is a good buyer's market for the IBM System 38, and there are a large number of people with the experience to operate the hardware available. In addition, a large selection of retail chain software is available from a wide variety of vendors for the IBM System 38.

"What is wanted is a system that will allow management of merchandise in the most efficient way possible and, at the same time, that will help keep down some of the overhead such as accounts payable and merchandising assistance. In the event that these needs cannot be met with software for the System 38, the hardware decision will be rethought.

"The base package we selected is called the Integrated Retail Information System, or IRIS. It was developed by Lawson/SMS, the retail division of Lawson Associates based in Sarasota, Florida. The package includes inventory management, purchase order management, receiving and store transfers, price management, management inquiry and reports, physical inventory processing, data base, integration to financial software, and an interface to point-of-sale software.

"A key distinguishing feature of IRIS is the way it supports tracking merchandise. Softlines (apparel, clothing, and shoes) can be tracked by style, color, and size. This makes it possible to track how our size six pink Reeboks are selling or just check on how Reeboks in general are doing. Hardlines (equipment) can be tracked by stockkeeping unit (sku) just as we wish. Basically we have one sku for Ewing basketballs, one for Dr. J. basketballs, and so on. This gives our buyers all the information they need without giving them more information than they need.

"Three competing packages were examined, but they only supported soft-line merchandise. Tracking of hardline merchandise with these packages would have been extremely difficult.

"Another disadvantage of the competing packages is that they are distribution center or warehouse oriented. This is incompatible with

441

the Sport's Authority pattern of direct shipments. As you well know, we receive all merchandise directly from our vendors with inventory updated at the receiving dock. With the IRIS system, the receiving crew keys in data as they receive each shipment (e.g., received ten Ewing basketballs). This then sets up a payable for us to pay the vendor, and it also adds ten to the on-hand inventory.

"The screens to support the receiving operation are easy to use. There are help screens to guide users if they need help.

"The vendor is very willing to make any necessary modifications to the package."

Do you believe that all the key facts to make a decision on this hardware and software package have been presented? If so, would you agree with the recommendation of the IT Director? If not, what additional facts do you feel are important?

SOURCE: "The Sport's Authority Scores with 'Ideal' MIS Systems," Chain Store Age Executive 61, no. 1 (January 1989). Reprinted with permission. Copyright Lebhar Friedman, January 1989, 425 Park Ave., New York, NY 10022.

Case Study 12.2

Too Good a Deal to Pass Up

You are the Manager of Customer Service and are attending a national conference for business managers in your industry. The conference includes a large exposition of software packages to meet the needs of companies in your industry. A vendor salesperson has just offered you a substantial discount on a complete hardware and software system for on-line order processing for your $15-million-a-year company. You have seen other order-entry systems at this conference, and this package does seem to best meet your company's needs. The only catch is, to receive the discount you must sign their contract before the conference is over in three days. At the discounted price of $150,000, the package is over $50,000 less expensive than the next lowest cost package. What would you do?

Case Study 12.3

Time for a Change

The Acme, Acme, and Keller Manufacturing Company specializes in the design and manufacture of containers for carrying all kinds of hazardous materials and toxic waste. The company was formed just three years ago but has already become a highly profitable organization. Sales growth has far exceeded the owners' most optimistic goals. Annual sales this year will exceed $10 million and could easily hit $25 million next year.

With all the rapid growth, little time has been spent on looking at how to run the company more efficiently. The focus has been on getting new customers. Now, though, the company is starting to pay the price for all this rapid growth. Company sales and accounting records are total chaos. The part-time accountant hired to handle federal, state, and local taxes is threatening to quit. Customers are constantly complaining about incorrect invoices. The company's cash flow is being choked by the slow manual process used to prepare customer invoices weeks after the customers receive their shipments. On three occasions in the past year, payroll checks to employees had to be delayed until the payroll clerk was able to complete the manual preparation of the checks.

It is clear that some major improvements in internal procedures are required to help the company keep growing. Unfortunately, the three partners cannot agree on the approach to take to solve the problem. One partner wants to hire her son, a recent graduate with a degree in finance from a large midwestern university, to take charge of all administrative operations. Another partner wants to hire a consultant to come in and study the situation and make appropriate recommendations. The third partner insists that all they need to do is buy a computer and convert all the manual procedures to computerized operations.

What are the pros and cons of each of the proposed solutions? Which approach would you recommend? If you were one of the partners, what would you do to ensure that this approach to solving the problem is successful?

Case Study 12.4

Opportunity Knocks

Acme, Acme, and Keller couldn't believe their good fortune! Their major competitor is on the brink of bankruptcy. Acme, Acme, and Keller has been offered an opportunity to acquire all their competitor's computer hardware and software at a savings of tens of thousands of dollars below the normal dealer price. Since it is clear that a computer will eventually be needed, the partners are in agreement to purchase the computer hardware and software. They have come to you, the company Controller, to see if the company can afford $100,000 to complete the transaction. What would you recommend?

■ APPENDIX: EXAMPLE RFP

This appendix presents an example RFP to serve as a model for managers involved in the selection of software packages. The information presented is outlined below.

Recommended Outline for an RFP

Purpose of RFP
Company Background
Basic Requirements
Hardware Environment
Description of RFP Process

Section A—Current System Overview
Section B—System Requirements
Section C—Volume and Size Data
Section D—Required Contents of Vendor's Response to RFP

Request for Proposal ABCD Company Basic Accounting Systems

Purpose of RFP

The purpose of this Request for Proposal (RFP) is to invite vendors to submit proposals for the supply, installation, and maintenance of an integrated order processing, billing, accounts receivable, accounts payable, and general ledger software package for three subsidiaries of the ABCD Company's Far East region. The three subsidiaries are located in Tokyo, Japan; Hong Kong; and Manila, Philippines.

Our intent is to purchase one integrated software package solution from one vendor that will be identical in each country. This consistency of applications is expected to improve our ability to share data and expertise across country borders and to permit a region-wide view of our business.

In responding to the RFP, vendors should feel free to bid their software products, customization capabilities, and related support services that will most effectively meet the requirements as described in the RFP.

The vendor is responsible for the supply and installation of the software. This includes any customization that is agreed to by both parties and the necessary integration of all software and hardware components. This RFP is concerned with the procurement of all goods and services necessary for the fulfillment of our requirements comprising but not limited to:

Configuration, procurement, delivery, installation, customization, testing, and maintenance of all system modules

Necessary implementation assistance including, but not limited to, user education, operator training, manuals, documentation, and guidance during initial production running of the system

A definition of the ongoing support relationship, including responsibilities of both parties, and problem escalation procedures

Company Background

The ABCD's Far East region is composed of two divisions. The region headquarters is in Tokyo, Japan. Each subsidiary operates as a decentralized business with their own manufacturing capability.

There are two divisions with seven product categories: Paper Products Division (including plates, cups, and napkins; sanitary napkins; and disposable diapers) and Personal Care Product Division (includes oral care, hair care, facial care, and foot care). Additional divisions (Food Products and Health Products) are likely in the next twelve to eighteen months. Currently we have 45 brands and handle 358 products (stockkeeping units).

Basic system needs are in the area of order processing, billing, accounts receivable, accounts payable, and general ledger. Each subsidiary has developed systems in-house using RPG or COBOL languages and running on an IBM System 36. However, each subsidiary is planning to install an IBM AS/400 machine within the next three to six months.

Basic Requirements

The system should have the ability to communicate with suppliers and customers through standard EDI transactions and route intracompany invoices from one subsidiary to another.

The software vendor must have adequate support and training capabilities within the Far East region.

The system should have adequate backup and journaling capability to enable rapid recovery with reentry of data kept to an absolute minimum.

The system must provide acceptable security measures to prevent unauthorized access to sensitive data.

The system must run in the AS/400 environment.

Hardware Environment

Although all the subsidiaries plan to install an IBM AS/400 Model B45, we will require vendor assistance in calculating capacity requirements for short- and long-term operations. At a minimum, each system will require the capacity to process all applications and maintain at least one year of history on-line. Additional information on processing volume is presented in section C.

User access is by IBM 3477 display stations or IBM PS/2 class personal computers using 5250 emulation and PC support.

Description of RFP Process

Please designate one primary and one alternate RFP representative for your company. All responses and inquiries to this RFP should be directed to:

Mrs. Geraldine Rockford
The ABCD Company
29 Cove Rd.
Malibu, CA 99091

Phone: 213-555-2368
Fax: 213-555-7860

All requirements, system design, documentation, and information obtained by the vendor in connection with this RFP are the property of the ABCD Company and as such must be treated as confidential and not used for any purpose other than replying to this RFP and for fulfillment of any other subsequent contract, if awarded.

All information obtained by the ABCD Company from vendors, in connection with this RFP, will be treated as confidential, except where such information is freely offered by the vendor and is considered public domain.

Neither the lowest-priced nor any proposal shall necessarily be accepted. Note, however, that we present this RFP with the intent of accepting one proposal unless all proposals are considered unacceptable.

There will be no payment to vendors for work related to the material supplied in the preparation and presentation of the RFP response.

Event	Date
Release of RFP	October 1, 199x
Deadline for vendor proposals	November 3, 199x
Vendor presentations	November 3–November 14, 199x
Selection of "finalists"	November 21, 199x
Benchmark tests for "finalists"	November 24–December 16, 199x
Announcement of winning vendor	December 23, 199x

Written replies to this RFP should use the format described in section D.

Vendors are invited to personally follow up on their written proposals with a presentation in our offices in Tokyo, Japan. Vendors will schedule a one- or two-day presentation for the time period November 3 to November 14. This meeting will provide Far East systems and end-user personnel with an opportunity to meet directly with vendor representatives. An IBM AS/400 Model B45 will be available for system demonstrations during the vendor presentations. Vendor software may be loaded using the machine's standard magnetic tape drive.

Those vendors who most closely meet the system requirements will be asked to perform a benchmark test on the IBM AS/400 Model B45 in Tokyo, Japan, during the period November 24 to December 16. The benchmark will simulate the processing of two days' worth of business and the production of all required outputs.

A Selection Committee comprising systems and end users will either select a vendor or determine that none of the current vendors meets our requirements sufficiently.

The Selection Committee will select the vendor who can meet the specified technical requirements of this RFP at the best overall effective cost while providing adequate support.

The successful vendor will be informed by phone and confirmation sent by letter. Unsuccessful vendors will be informed in a similar manner.

Section A—Current System Overview

This section contains a description of systems and business processes as they operate today. (For brevity, only the accounts receivable system and business processes are described. An actual RFP would address all areas including order processing, shipping, billing, accounts payable, and general ledger.)

Basic Information

There are three different payment types: cash in advance (cash), cash in advance (check), and credit. The sales representatives collect payments from the customer and can bring the check, money order, or cash to the office personally, or mail it. Customers can also mail their payments directly to the General Office.

When the customer payment arrives at the ABCD Company, the amount, date, and invoice number are entered into the system. The system applies the payment to that invoice. If the invoice number is not available, the system distributes (using first in, first out) the payment among the pending balances. The Credit Department can make further changes to redistribute the amount paid.

The transactions that affect the balance of a customer are:

credit transactions	debit transactions
net payment	debit note
gross payment	returned check
credit note	debit voucher
partial cancellation	shipment
complete cancellation	late discount
issue discount	demurrage

All customers have a customer number for the order-shipping-billing system. When the Sales Department has a new customer, the Credit Department is advised and assigns a customer number and an accounts receivable number.

The credit limit is set by the Credit Department and established in U.S. dollars. There is a 2 percent discount for payment in ten days with balance due in thirty days. Discount terms are effective from the point in time when the final invoice is printed at the warehouse, not when the order is delivered. This is a problem area with many of our customers.

Accounts Receivable Process

A file with all the final invoices of the day is produced by the order-shipping-billing system. This file is processed by the accounts receivable system along with several other transactions (payment received, checks received, debit note, and so on). The customer balance is updated when an invoice is produced by the order-shipping-billing system. For the checks received, the check voucher is entered into the system for control purposes. Once all the daily transactions are entered into the system, a validation run is made and an input and error report is produced. The Credit Department works with this report to correct all error messages, verifying valid dates to confirm discounts. After this review, the Credit Department enters into the system all the needed corrections, and the validation is performed again. This step is repeated until an error-free report is obtained. Transactions are then manually posted to the customer accounts.

Other reports produced by the system include:

Aging Report Shows the unpaid and difference invoice balances, dividing the balances according to the age of the order (0–10 days, 11–29 days, 30–59 days, 60–89 days, and over 90 days)

Letters for Customers Produced as a reminder to make prompt payment with the due balance

Credit and Debit Notes Produced to notify customers of the credits and/ or debits posted to their accounts

Section B—System Requirements

General Requirements

This section provides general requirements that apply to all modules of the integrated order, shipping, billing, accounts receivable, accounts payable, and general ledger software package.

Data Fields The proposed system must be able to accommodate large dollar amounts—at least thirteen integer positions plus two positions for decimals.

Consolidation The system must be able to consolidate all financial information across all categories and all subsidiaries.

Language All end-user portions of the system, such as user manuals, help screens, error messages, and reports, must be available in English.

Security It will be necessary to restrict access to the system according to the functions performed by each user (e.g., order-entry clerk cannot access accounts receivable data). A log must be kept of the use of the system, invalid access trials, terminals used, log-on IDs not used in a specified period, and so on.

Currencies The system must be able to show reports in a multiple currency environment as requested. Exchange rates will be easy to update, and a history of exchange rates will be maintained.

Backup and Recovery The system must have the capability to make selective backups of all data and files according to user requirements. A transaction logging capability is required that will allow recovery of data bases up to the point of failure.

Electronic Data Interchange The system must offer strong EDI capabilities for customers to receive orders and send status of orders; with suppliers to place an order, update the status of an order, and update inventories; and with banks to post payments, report checks paid to customers, and make automatic reconciliations.

Specific Accounts Receivable Requirements

Critical Requirements The system must be fully integrated with the billing software module and general ledger software module.
The system must share the same customer master file with the order-entry system.
The system must provide on-line information about customers' balances.
The system must validate all input data on-line, before posting occurs.
The system must be able to apply payments to several invoices and to make partial payments to invoices.

Important Requirements The system must produce aging reports.
The system must automatically prepare letters, credit notes, and debit notes.
The system must be able to provide information about accounts one week before the due date to speed collections.

Section C—Volume and Size Data

The following data is provided about the volume and size of the business operations.

	Japan	Hong Kong	Philippines
Total Sales (U.S. Millions of Dollars)	$150	$100	$75
Number of Accounts	3,000	2,500	1,000
Orders/Day	200	175	150
Shipments/Day	185	125	105
Supplier Invoices/Day	155	105	100
Customer Checks/Day	155	135	95
Number of Clerks—Currently			
Order Processing	5	4	3
Billing	3	3	3
Accounts receivable	4	3	3
Accounts payable	4	4	3
General ledger	3	3	3

Section D—Required Contents of Vendor's Response to RFP

This section is intended to structure your response so that each vendor provides information in a comparable form. This will greatly simplify the comparison process. Failure to conform to this structure will put your response at a disadvantage.

Form of Response

We require that your response be in the following format.

Responses should follow the document structure of section B (e.g., use the same part, section, item, construction, and identification and present them in the same sequence).

Requirement number, "available" or "not available," followed by a brief explanation or description and cost or "included" if included at no additional cost.

Make responses brief and supply the information directly rather than provide references to appendices, technical manuals, or other sources. Cost figures should be your best estimate of total customization costs to design and implement the requirements in a quality manner.

Submission Instructions

Two copies of each written proposal should be sent to the ABCD Company contact. Any additional documentation you wish to send should be packaged separately.

Vendor responses must be received no later than 5:00 P.M. on November 3, 199x. Responses received after this date may be disqualified.

Chapter 13

End-User Computing

Learning Objectives

Upon completion of this chapter, you will be able to:

1. Identify two key shortcomings of the traditional systems development process that led to an increase in end-user computing.

2. Define the term end-user computing and name six classes of end-user computing.

3. Identify two major classes of end user computing tools and describe their capabilities and limitations.

4. Describe a scenario for when it is appropriate and when it is not appropriate to use end-user programming.

5. Describe the role filled by an information center.

6. Briefly describe four strategies for supporting end-user computing and identify eight areas where strategies are needed.

Preview

The increasing demands of managers for quick answers and the rapid pace of business change has pitched traditional computer programming into a crisis. Information technology has become indispensable, but a long applications backlog is common, and major systems that do not meet user needs are frequently delivered. The availability of useful software packages and increasingly more powerful microcomputers, combined with new end-user-oriented programming tools, have given rise to end-user computing. Applications created by end users can be good or bad, sensible or incomprehensible. Rather than waging battle, IT and business managers can work together to provide an environment that encourages and ensures effective end-user computing.

Issues

1. What are the limitations of the traditional approach to information system development, and why can it lead to end-user dissatisfaction?

2. How can IT and business managers create a healthy environment for end-user computing?

3. What are effective strategies for supporting end-user computing?

Trade-offs

1. When are IT professionals needed to develop an information system, and when are they not?

2. How much of IT resources should be allocated to support end-user computing?

3. What strategies are appropriate to manage end-user computing in your organization?

A Manager Struggles with the Issues

Kim just didn't understand it. She had been hired as a brand manager for a large consumer goods company. She was expected to develop a marketing strategy including advertising, copy, new product introductions, promotions, and pricing. Why should she have to attend a two-day class on end-user computing? Computing—that was the domain of the bits and bytes people, not future executives. In her last job, she had all the programming support she needed. And actually she had needed very little, thank you very much. Getting things from the computer just took too long and seldom seemed worth the effort. If she needed some numbers quickly, Kim would just have some of her brand assistants stay late to crank them out.

■ LIMITATIONS OF TRADITIONAL SYSTEM DEVELOPMENT

Even the most successful IT organizations are unable to keep up with the explosive demand for their services as awareness and acceptance of information as a resource spreads. It is not uncommon for there to be a backlog of defined and explicitly expressed user requests for systems work in excess of a year (Exhibit 13.1).

In addition to the large backlog, the systems that are delivered often fail to meet the needs of the user. The primary cause of this prob-

Exhibit 13.1
The Applications Backlog

Visible
Backlog
Approved but
not yet started

Invisible Backlog
Identified but not
yet approved

Source: Munro, Malcom, and Sid L. Huff. "Managing End-User Computing." Journal of Systems Management *39 (December 1988).*

Exhibit 13.2
Missed User Expectations

**What users thought
they wanted**

**What users said
they wanted**

**What the systems
analysts designed**

**What the users
received**

**What the users
really needed**

lem is miscommunication—the basic inability of people to express their needs to one another. Miscommunication happens every day in the exchange of even simple ideas among people of similar backgrounds, training, beliefs, and interests (Exhibit 13.2). Is it any wonder that it happens during a large and complex information project developed in a multicultural environment with computer-oriented specialists working with business managers?

■ WHAT IS END-USER COMPUTING?

Definition of End-User Computing

In many organizations, a growing number of end users are becoming able to run and/or develop information systems with little or no assistance from the IT organization. Any situation in which workers use or control computer-based equipment is called **end-user computing.** End users may have access to department or company-wide systems and programs, including those developed by outside vendors and those developed in-house.

Categories of End-User Computing

The following summary of six end-user types is based on a classic paper published in 1983 (Rockart and Flannery).

Nonprogramming End Users

Nonprogramming end users have little or no computer skills and only use software that has been developed by others. They run menu-driven applications that require no computer or programming skills. They rely entirely on others for technical help when needed. Without further training or experience, they are not capable of developing their own applications.

Command-Level Users

Command-level users operate software packages and applications written by others. They are also capable of using fourth-generation languages to create simple query routines to access data bases and produce their own ad hoc reports. They have some basic computer and programming troubleshooting skills and are capable of solving some kinds of problems.

End-User Programmers

End-user programmers not only can use prewritten programs and packages and fourth-generation languages but also can write their own programs. They are computer literate and can create programs, simple systems (a collection of programs integrated to accomplish a goal), and reports for others in the previous two categories.

Functional Support Personnel

Functional support personnel are assigned to the organization's functional business units and not the IT organization. They have a high level of skill and understanding of computers and end-user computing tools and processes. They are capable of performing problem solving to correct most problems. Their role is to provide a high level of support for end users in their organization.

End-User Computing Support Personnel

End-user computing support personnel are IT specialists assigned to the IT organization. They support end users in the development and operation of end-user developed systems.

DP Programmers

DP programmers are IT professionals who are assigned to the IT organization and who are dedicated to providing support for end users through the development of larger, more complex systems. They often perform their services for a contract fee.

This classification makes it clear that there is no one typical end user. There are instead many different types, each with their own needs.

Exhibit 13.3
The Six Classes of End-User Computing

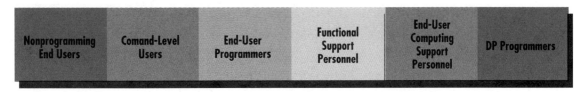

| Nonprogramming End Users | Comand-Level Users | End-User Programmers | Functional Support Personnel | End-User Computing Support Personnel | DP Programmers |

End Users Considered to be Doing End-User Programming

Source: John F. Rockart and Lauren S. Flannery, "The Management of End-User Computing," Communications of the ACM *26 (October 1983). Copyright 1983, Association for Computing Machinery, Inc.*

The three classes of end users who are considered to be doing end-user computing are the command-level users, end-user programmers, and functional support personnel (see Exhibit 13.3).

■ END-USER COMPUTING TOOLS

There are two major classes of end-user computing tools: **application packages** and **fourth-generation languages.** The use of these tools and the kinds of tools within these classes vary by type of end user, as shown in Exhibit 13.4 and as discussed next.

Application Packages

Application packages are prewritten software packages that are marketed commercially. They are available to support common business functions such as payroll, accounts payable, accounts receivable, a wide range of human resource-related functions, production scheduling, inventory control, and so on. Many of the packages allow for some customization through specification of key parameters (e.g., an accounts receivable package would allow the end user to specify the discount terms allowed customers for prompt payment, such as 2 percent—10, net 30).

Although application packages for complex business operations require installation by information systems professionals, computer vendors are increasingly enlisting the help of corporate end users in defining product development and marketing strategies. Dialogs between vendors and end users usually take place during trade shows and user group meetings. It has also become a common practice for IT managers to bring along users to product demonstrations. Some vendors' marketing orientation focuses on the end user as an individual who is becoming more influential and powerful in defining the course of desktop computing. Other companies may see the balance of power

Exhibit 13.4
Use of Tools to Support End-User Computing

	Nonprogramming	Command Level	End-User Programmers
Characteristics	Little or no computer skills Rely on others for troubleshooting	Capable of using fourth-generation languages and personal computer software to create reports and graphs and perform analysis Able to do some troubleshooting	Capable of developing their own complete systems Fully capable of doing their own troubleshooting
Tools Used	Vendor and/or in-house developed applications that are menu driven or require simple "fill in the blanks"	Fourth-generation languages including query languages, report generators, graphics languages, statistical analysis, and spreadsheets	Fourth-generation languages Application generators
Typical Usage	Data entry to complete transaction processing	Develop program to extract selected data from a data base and format it into a report	Develop small system to extract selected data from a mainframe data base and download it into a personal computer spreadsheet for further analysis
Specific Examples of Tools Used	Application packages from software vendors Applications developed internally by others	Query Languages/ Report Generators ■ Datatrieve ■ RPG III Graphics Languages ■ Harvard Graphics ■ Tell-A-Graf	Statistical Analysis ■ SAS ■ Express Financial Modeling/Spreadsheets ■ Lotus 1-2-3 ■ Excel Natural Languages ■ Intellect ■ Natural	Command Level Tools ■ Focus ■ Oracle ■ IFPS PLUS

in corporate computing remaining on the side of the IT organization but recognize that both IT and end users will have to work together.

Fourth-Generation Programming Languages

Nigel Reade first coined the term *fourth-generation language* in an article in *Datamation* in 1979. Since Reade identified the fourth-generation language, many people have tried to define it. In 1982, James Martin, a widely read author and world-renowned consultant, provided his often-repeated version: "A high-level language that provides an integrated syntax with data definition, data maintenance, and data analysis yielding productivity gains of 10:1 over COBOL" (Martin, 1982). Such languages allow end users to develop their own computer programs and even to link together a series of programs into a full-scale system. These languages may run on micro, mini, or mainframe computer platforms. Indeed, many of them run on all three. Using James Martin's broad definition, there are actually many classes of fourth-generation languages including: **query language/report writers, graphics languages, statistical analysis packages,** and **decision support/financial modeling tools** (Exhibit 13.5). These variations of fourth-generation languages are described next.

Query Language/Report Writers

Query language/report writers are capable of supporting ad hoc requests for data. They can search a data base or file, using simple or complex selection criteria to retrieve data relating to multiple records. They may support data base and file maintenance (add, delete, change records) as well. Query languages usually allow for on-line user access and response. Report writers allow the user to create batch reports.

The use of a natural language interface is increasing for both query languages and report writers. Such an interface accepts instructions without regard to format or syntax in the natural language of the end users, within certain syntax and vocabulary restrictions. These natural languages interpret many common words, but other words peculiar to a specific application, company, or user must be added to its lexicon, or dictionary of words, so that they can be interpreted by the natural language. Use of a natural language allows end users to express their information needs in their plain, everyday speaking language. (See Chapter 3 for further discussion of the use of natural languages to simplify access to computer data bases.)

Exhibit 13.5
Fourth-Generation
Languages

Category/Product	Vendor
Query Language/Report Writers	
Datatrieve	DEC
RPG III	IBM
Intellect	Artificial Intelligence
Natural Language	Natural Language, Inc.
QBE	IBM
QMF	IBM
SQL/DS	IBM
Graphics Language	
Harvard Graphics	Software Publishing Company
Tell-A-Graf	Isso
Business Graphics	Business Professional Graphics
Statistical Analysis	
Express	Management Decision Systems
SAS	SAS, Inc.
Decision Support/Financial Modeling	
LOTUS 1-2-3	Lotus Development
Excel	Microsoft
Products with Modules that Address More than One of the Above Categories	
FOCUS	Information Builders, Inc.
System W	Comshare, Inc.
IFPS PLUS	Execucom System Corp.

Graphics Languages

Often information is more easily understood when presented graphically. It is easy for interrelationships between data items to be obscured among rows, columns, pages, and totals of a tabular report. Graphics languages add a powerful visual dimension to reporting, reducing large volumes of information into easily understood graphs and charts. They retrieve data from files or data bases and display them in graphics format. End users can ask for data and specify how they are to be charted. Some graphics languages can perform arithmetic (e.g., profit = sales − expenses) and logical operations (e.g., plot only data values that lie outside a certain range).

Managers typically spend 60 percent of their time in meetings either receiving or making presentations. Including graphics in these presentations can speed up and enhance the communication of information. Graphics also add a high degree of professionalism that counts for a lot with both other managers within the organization and customers, vendors, and others from the outside. According to a Wharton School of Business study, a speaker presenting information supported by overhead graphics is perceived as better prepared, more professional, and more persuasive than a speaker who uses no overheads. Furthermore, group decisions are reached faster and meetings are shorter when graphics are used.

For a number of years, the business manager's lack of understanding of computers and their capabilities eliminated any potential use of computer graphics. But now software designed for personal computers and nonprogrammers has begun to overcome this natural resistance to try something new. Most personal computer business graphics software packages are carefully designed for easy use even by non-computer-oriented people. Typically they feature menu-driven formats with computer-generated promptings that guide users as they go along. Managers, professionals, and others can generate bar, cluster, pie, or line charts simply and easily in very little time. In addition to producing graphic output, the user can add text information to label or explain the chart and select from a rainbow of colors and shading options.

Statistical Analysis Packages

Simple functions such as averages, minimums, maximums, counts, and percentages are included as options with a statistical analysis package. More complex functions such as calculation of mean and standard deviation of a set of data, determination of correlation coefficients, cross tabulations, exponential smoothing and forecasting, time series analysis, and other analyses are available in more powerful statistical analysis packages. To perform a statistical analysis, the user selects an operation from a menu of available options and responds to prompts for the necessary parameters. Part of the input required is to specify what set of data is to be analyzed (e.g., perform a linear regression analysis between price and market share data points for the time period July 1, 1996, to January 1, 1997).

Real World Perspective

Using Computer Graphics at PepsiCo

PepsiCo uses computer graphics technology to speed up and improve managerial decision making. The consumer products giant invested $250,000 in decision support graphics hardware and software. How has this investment in technology been received? In the first year of use, managers created over eighty thousand charts and slides using this equipment—twenty times more than the year before!

An early payback on the investment in computer graphics came when product managers were faced with a tough decision over the introduction of Slice, a new lemon-lime soft drink. Pepsi had to find bottlers to sign up and compete with 7-Up and Bubble-Up, the two brands that dominated the lemon-lime soda market across two-thirds of the nation. Tens of millions of dollars and several managers' careers were on the line.

The Pepsi brand managers resorted to computer graphics. The computer was able to extract numbers from a corporate data base that identified bottlers making lemon-lime soda for the competition and bottlers free to support Slice with bottling capacity and advertising dollars. Instead of the usual computer printout that would require wading through reams of paper, a vivid color-coded map was produced that clearly revealed the level and location of competitive activity. The map revealed that Texas, an area considered essential for Slice's success, was wide open. Slice quickly hit Texas supermarkets with national roll-out planned for eight to ten months later.

Decision Support/Financial Modeling Tools

Decision support and financial modeling tools allow construction of complex business models. They are commonly used to support people involved in preparing financial statements such as balance sheets, income and expense records, or financial models for projected capital needs, budget forecasts, and pro forma income statements. Electronic spreadsheets such as Lotus 1-2-3 or EXCEL are the most commonly used sets of these tools. Other tools include decision support system generators such as IFPS PLUS, which provides a complete environment for analysis including embedded spreadsheet, graphics, and reporting tools as well as built-in what-if and explanation capabilities.

When Should a Manager Use a Spreadsheet?

There are several factors that a manager should consider in deciding to use a spreadsheet. First, what is the quality of the available information? It is pointless to apply a spreadsheet if the source data are highly questionable. After all, the spreadsheet will perform flawless math calculations, but what good is that if the input values are incorrect? Second, what is the cost of building the spreadsheet model and performing the analysis versus the cost of making a wrong decision? It makes no sense to develop and run a model at a cost of $5,000 if the cost of a wrong decision is only $1,000. Third, and most important, is the nature of the problem itself. Some problems are just not quantitative, and using a model is totally inappropriate. Decisions that involve questions of moral values, company goals, and judgments about humans are essentially qualitative and should not be modeled. In

Exhibit 13.6
Keys to a Successful
Spreadsheet
Presentation

1. Know what your audience is looking for. Do they want the numbers shown horizontally or vertically? Do they want the "bottom line" shown first, or do they want it to be last? Do they use other reports similar to this one, and if so, how are these reports laid out?

2. Keep the analysis simple! Impress people with the quality of the analysis and not with the quantity of numbers involved.

3. Make sure that your assumptions are clear and well defined. Be prepared to discuss and defend if necessary any of the assumptions used in the analysis. Anyone sophisticated enough to understand a spreadsheet is going to want to probe the assumptions that led to the conclusion.

4. Can the results be presented graphically? After all, one picture is worth a thousand words.

5. Preview the presentation for a small portion of the intended audience to get their reactions and suggestions for improvement before sharing the results with the entire group.

short, if the problem is quantitative, good data are available, and the cost of a wrong decision is high, then using a spreadsheet is probably appropriate.

Exhibit 13.6 summarizes the keys to a successful spreadsheet presentation.

Characteristics of a Fourth-Generation Language

Nonprocedural Language

If you were to write detailed directions explaining how to get to your home (without drawing a map) for a friend, you would be using a

Real World Perspective

Use of Personal Computers at Procter & Gamble

Procter & Gamble (P&G) is a large, multi-national, multidivisional consumer goods company with sales of over $40 billion in 1994. Major product divisions include Bar Soap and Household Cleaning, Beauty Care, Packaged Soap and Detergents, Health and Personal Care, Food and Beverage, and Paper. These divisions subscribe to Information Resources Inc. (IRI) scanner data to track the performance of P&G and competitors' products. These data are obtained from scanner-based checkouts throughout the United States on a weekly basis and collected by IRI to be shared with IRI data subscribers. The data provide an estimate of product consumption and price by geographic region of the United States. The scanner-based data are augmented

with additional data that indicate relative levels of sales merchandising—percentge of stores that feature, display, and/or sell a given product.

At P&G, market share (percentage of total consumer consumption of a given category of products) is monitored very closely. A 1 percent change in the large markets in which P&G competes can mean tens of millions of dollars in sales revenue. Brand assistants in the advertising department of many of the divisions use personal computers to extract IRI scanner data from computer data bases and perform a market share analysis. The analysis might include having the computer plot market share over a several week period and then analyzing the causal data (price, percentage of stores that feature, display, or sell) to determine why share went up or down.

procedural language process. You would be extremely careful not to leave out any detail or your friend might get lost. If, on the other hand, you were simply to give your friend your street address, you would be using a **nonprocedural language** process. You would not need to worry that you might have left out a turn or forgotten to mention an important landmark.

PL/1, COBOL, and FORTRAN are **procedural languages,** which means that the programmer must specify to the computer in exacting, step-by-step detail how it is to do something. All procedures and all calculations must be carefully thought out, designed, and coded so that no small step is overlooked. If there are any mistakes, the program either will fail to compile and thus be unable to execute or, perhaps even worse, will run but give incorrect results.

A nonprocedural programming language allows the user to merely state what is to be done without specifying how. Key words such as LIST, TITLE, PLOT, and TOTAL can be used to define an entire procedure that the computer is to perform. When a program is written using a nonprocedural language, the detail format of an output report need not be coded. The use of the verb PRINT produces a report in a reasonable format based on what is to be printed or displayed. The user can learn to override the defaults, but for most nonprofessional programmers, this is not necessary and is counterproductive to getting maximum results from minimum effort.

Easy to Learn

An essential characteristic of fourth-generation languages is that they can be learned quite easily even by people not trained in computer technology. Fourth-generation languages use English-like commands and key words, not computerese. The syntax, or combination of key words, verbs, and their objects, is also English-like and designed to be logical, easy to learn, and easy to remember. A nonprogrammer can begin writing simple programs with just a few hours of training.

Highly Productive

The use of fourth-generation programming languages reduces the amount of code to be written. For example, the following two-line FOCUS program could not be written in less than twenty lines of COBOL, PL/1 or FORTRAN code—a ten-to-one productivity improvement!

- TABLE FILE PRODUCT
- LIST PROD—TYPE AND AMOUNT BY AREA BY MONTH

These two lines of code are an entire FOCUS program to prepare a summary report of sales by month and by district. It is left to the FOCUS software to decide how to format the list, when to skip pages, how to number the pages, and how to sort the data into the proper sequence. Without a fourth-generation language, all these details must

Exhibit 13.7
Typical Increase in Productivity through Use of Fourth-Generation Language

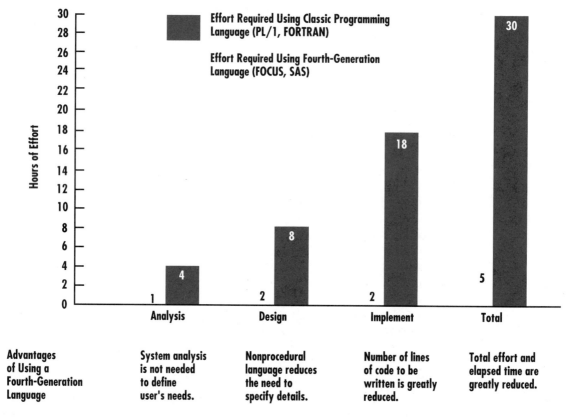

| Advantages of Using a Fourth-Generation Language | System analysis is not needed to define user's needs. | Nonprocedural language reduces the need to specify details. | Number of lines of code to be written is greatly reduced. | Total effort and elapsed time are greatly reduced. |

be figured out by the program designer. Clearly then, programming effort *and* systems design effort are reduced.

A third area of productivity improvement is in the system analysis phase. The traditional approach calls for a systems analyst to interview the user to determine what the system is to do and to document this in a set of detailed system specifications. As already discussed, this process can become long and drawn out and still result in an inaccurate definition of what the system is to do. Fourth-generation languages allow users to directly translate their requirements into a program without using an intermediary. The potential for miscommunication and the need for a lengthy document defining system requirements are eliminated (Exhibit 13.7).

When End-User Programming Is Appropriate and When It Is Not

Although fourth-generation programming languages allow end users to develop their own programs and simple systems, this approach should

Real World Perspective

Report Generation Using FOCUS—A Popular Fourth-Generation Language

The sales manager has requested a summary report of sales by month and by district for January through June. Assume that a file named SALES exists and that it contains invoice data for the past year. DOLLARS is the invoice amount of the sale. MONTH is the month in which the sale was made. DISTRICT is the eight-character code that identifies the district. This report could be generated with the following simple FOCUS commands.

TABLE is a FOCUS key word used to request a tabular report. SUM is a FOCUS verb that means total the values of a data field. The word BY signals FOCUS to put the lines of the report in order by the field whose name follows. ACROSS tells FOCUS to spread the columns of the report by the field whose name follows. The request can be made in free form so the lines of code may begin and end in any column and there may be one or more (your choice) spaces between words. Results of this request would look something like this:

TABLE FILE SALES

SUM DOLLARS

BY DISTRICT

ACROSS MONTH FROM 1 TO 6

District	Month					
	1	2	3	4	5	6
Chicago	9347.98	7890.65	8789.90	6254.87	5564.39	8326.54
Decatur	0.00	0.00	0.00	0.00	4532.89	7658.65
Moline	3456.98	2876.56	4894.97	3438.89	2543.66	664.21
St Louis	9876.45	4567.76	3456.87	3645.98	5678.32	3478.23

not always be followed. Certain kinds of programs and systems can be developed effectively this way but others cannot (Exhibit 13.8).

Applications that require complex processing, the matching of multiple files and data bases, or the processing of an extremely high volume of transactions are generally not considered good candidates for development by end users using fourth-generation languages. Such applications, if not developed by professional programmers, may require substantial amounts of computer resources and may run for long periods of time. However, short of these restrictions, there is a wide range of applications that can be developed by end users.

Traditional corporate production systems such as payroll, general ledger, accounts payable, and inventory control are examples of systems that the end user should not be involved in programming. Development of these types of systems is best left to the professional systems analysts and programmers. The design of these systems requires great attention to detail, careful consideration of system and data backup issues, and implementation of security safeguards. These issues require much more in-depth systems training than is appropriate for a nonprogrammer.

On the other hand, once these corporate production systems and their associated data base(s) are built, the end user may wish to query the data base, extract data for analysis, and create ad hoc reports. The use of fourth-generation languages by the end user to fulfill these requests is a sound strategy and can provide tenfold increases in productivity over traditional approaches.

Exhibit 13.8
When Programmers
Are Needed and
When They Are Not

System Development Can Be Done by End Users If:

1. The user has a need for ad hoc reports—one type of report today, some other report tomorrow.

2. The program logic, calculations, or report formats will be changed frequently.

3. The program will extract data from an already existing data base that is well defined and well managed.

4. The user program will not update or change any values in the data base.

System Development Should Not Be Done by End Users If:

1. The system is critical to the operation of the business and will need to be repaired within hours if it fails.

2. The data base for the system must be defined and constructed from several different sources.

3. Input to the system will be used to update corporate data bases.

4. The data base will be extremely large (more than 250,000 records).

5. Users will want the system to be highly tuned to achieve the minimum response time.

■ INFORMATION CENTERS

The **information center** concept began in IBM Canada in the late 1970s. Its objective is to help end users become comfortable with information processing so that they can use it in their day-to-day operations for increased efficiency and enhanced decision-making ability. The key strategy necessary to accomplish this goal is to promote, support, and encourage end-user application development. A side benefit of this approach is that by increasing end users' ability to develop their own solutions, the IT department has more time to address the more complex applications that are beyond the capabilities of end users.

The information center must be staffed by people with good IT skills, but it is even more important that they have an excellent appreciation for applying information processing to solve basic business problems. They need to be able to talk to business managers and office workers in business terms, not computerese. The information center consultants need excellent interpersonal skills, including the ability to help and teach others in a manner that will encourage users to return when they need more help. Above all, the consultants cannot treat users as if they were a burden to be disposed of as quickly as possible.

The information center resources help end users to develop their own applications. This can be done effectively with a minimum of direct user-to-consultant contact by using self-paced computer-assisted instructions. The other aspect of training is much more difficult—teaching the user to distinguish potentially good computer applications from bad ones. The best teacher here is user experience.

Exhibit 13.9 summarizes the activities of an information center.

Exhibit 13.9
Activities
Frequently
Performed by an
Information Center

Troubleshooting
Isolate and correct system problems.
Restore a system file, program, or data after a system failure.

Maintenance
Help ensure that users' hardware is in working order.
Provide maintenance service to repair or replace problems.

Consulting
Provide advice on selecting appropriate tools.
Help users debug their programs.
Ensure users back up their disks to avoid future trouble.
Serve as a clearinghouse to share tips and ideas.

Training
Develop plans to meet anticipated future user needs.
Provide training to help end users be efficient and effective.
Provide users with access to reference material.

Support Access to Data Bases
Make sure end users are aware of data sources of potential value.
Help users gain authorization to access data bases.
Help download data from mainframe to microcomputer.

Hardware and Software Acquisition
Assist in analyzing needs and recommend hardware and software appropriate
to the user.
Help users prepare necessary justification and paperwork.
Assist with installation of hardware and software.

Research
Investigate new products and services for possible use.

Real World Perspective

Using an Information Center at United Technologies

The Essex group of United Technologies is a major manufacturer of wire and cable. Like many other companies, it found the demand for information was constantly increasing. Unfortunately, the backlog for traditional system development was also growing. So United Technologies opened an information center to enable employees to meet their own departmental and individual information processing needs. The information center was not designed to replace traditional systems development, but rather to complement it by providing more users access to corporate computing facilities and data.

Two service consultants operate the walk-in facility throughout the workday. The consultants conduct required introductory classes for center users and specialized courses in various fourth-generation programming languages. Users develop their own programs for financial analysis, modeling, numerical analysis, and reporting. The consultants also assist users in designing initial applications and applying the tools.

Within the first year, over five hundred users were trained, with over thirty new users scheduled for training each month.

■ THE EVOLVING IT–END-USER RELATIONSHIP

The nature of the IT–end-user relationship is undergoing continual evolution. In the early days of data processing (prior to the mid-seventies), for most firms, all computing was directly controlled through the IT organization. There were enormous barriers, both technical and administrative, that made end-user computing impossible.

As users became increasingly aware of how they could use the computer, and as end-user computing capabilities became available (mid-seventies to late eighties), many IT organizations were slow to change. Most IT managers had limited contact with end users. Many realized that they were not supporting end users as well as they could but did not know or did not want to do much to improve the relationship. Many IT managers conceded that their jobs were stressful because of their position between end users and top management. The growing number of microcomputer users in the face of static training and support resources in most organizations compounded the problem. As a result, end-user computing went underground with business managers circumventing the procedures and controls established to maintain IT control over all computing. Advanced microcomputer users took on more of the work that was once considered the responsibility of IT. End users found ways to support one another by drawing on the expertise of the more computer-literate workers within their department.

Today most organizations are moving toward an environment where IT is a service organization that actively promotes and supports end-user computing. Enlightened IT professionals and end users are building better working relationships. From the end users' perspective, there is a need for effective end-user computing so that creative end users with the knowledge of both business and technology can address a variety of business concerns. End-user computing is seen as one means to provide management with better information that allows them to act more responsively. From the professionals' side, IT can empower end users to take advantage of the technology without being too dependent on IT. The trend has changed from "us versus them" to "all of us working together."

■ STRATEGIES FOR SUPPORTING END-USER COMPUTING

Today's IT and business managers are caught in the middle of the end-user computing revolution. Many lack a specific strategy and instead see end-user computing as just another isolated problem or solution (depending on their point of view) in their plans to achieve business goals. However, those managers who ignore end-user computing do so at their own risk. Consider the following points.

End-user computing hardware is becoming more powerful and less expensive, so that it is now possible to put more than 20 MIPS (millions of instructions per second) microcomputers on the desks of all office workers. Each such microcomputer has the raw processing power equivalent to the large mainframes that corporations used to do all the firm's data processing in the early 1980s! Such computing capacity makes it very reasonable to consider moving information processing from large, central computers to mini or microcomputers dispersed throughout the firm. This process is called **downsizing** (Chapter 2).

End-user computing can shift tasks and responsibilities back and forth between the IT organization and business functions. Who will be responsible for the development of programs and their support, providing end-user consulting and support, making hardware and software acquisition decisions? These are just some of the issues that arise with end-user computing.

Clearly, these issues are too important to ignore. At some point, end-user computing will become so large in cost or so pervasive in application (or both) that it will require thoughtful attention.

Munro and Huff (1988) examined management actions to cope with end-user computing and identified two primary forces that are active: *acceleration* and *control*. Depending on the level of acceleration and control, organizations operate under one of four alternative strategies (Exhibit 13.10):

> The *laissez-faire strategy*, where there is limited interest in end-user computing and so little effort need be expended to control it.
>
> The *containment strategy*, where end-user computing is developed slowly and carefully within defined constraints and boundaries, which are usually established and monitored by the IT organization.
>
> The *expansionist strategy*, where an organization decides to provide lots of resources to support end-user computing and implement it with limited or no controls.
>
> The *controlled growth strategy*, where end-user computing is supported and encouraged so as to stimulate fast growth but with appropriate control.

Munro and Huff found that most organizations either first accelerated at high speed with little or no control and then implemented strong controls or vice versa. Most organizations eventually end up in the center of the grid with acceleration and control roughly in balance.

Exhibit 13.10
Strategies for End-User Computing

| Expansionist | Controlled Growth |
| Laissez-faire | Containment |

Real World Perspective

End-User Computing at 3M

3M expects that the use of microcomputers by its employees to share information will help foster innovation. Data on such topics as marketing, product development, and competition and cost are shared by the firm's ten thousand micro-computer users in forty U.S. divisions. Each division is a separate entity that is responsible for the development of its own products; product de-velopment information is available to all employ-ees through the use of microcomputers. The open channel communications of the corporation are designed to encourage a synergistic project ap-proach within the divisions. IT and information center groups meet with representatives from end-user groups in information exchange meet-ings to determine IT needs in conjunction with user needs.

Staffing

Various surveys on microcomputer support show that there are typi-cally ten to twenty support personnel for every one thousand installed microcomputers. Sites with fewer than thirty microcomputers tend to rely more on part-time staffing for microcomputer support than do sites with higher numbers of installed microcomputers.

Standards for Software Development

The enforcement of in-house software development tracking and ac-companying standards facilitates software quality. End-user developed applications are organizational systems that are usually crucial to the business of the company. Unfortunately, the experiences of many end-user organizations starting to use fourth-generation languages to de-velop applications closely parallel the experience of the IT organization when developing its initial computer applications for the organization. Some of these problems are listed next.

Lack of an Effective System Development Process

Lack of an effective system development process leads to developing applications that fail to meet user requirements. End users (like many IT professionals) are quick to develop programs without fully under-standing the root of the problem or the needs that must be addressed. As a result, the initial attempt at meeting a business need through an end-user-developed application may have to be scrapped and the pro-cess restarted. IT and business system developers need to work jointly to document a standard system development process and procedures that lead to efficient development of quality applications.

Application Duplication

Application duplication occurs when one user or group develops an application very similar to one developed elsewhere. Without good communications among developers, duplication of effort is very likely to occur. Establish both informal and formal means for end users to exchange ideas and programs such as monthly meetings or an end-user newsletter.

Inadequate Testing of End-User Applications

Inadequate testing of end-user applications may result in erroneous output. These incorrect results may go undetected and be used as input for decision making or be shared with others both inside and outside the firm. Establish a quality assurance program with a key element being independent testing—testing of an end-user-developed application by someone other than who developed the application.

Poor or Nonexistent Program Documentation

The real value of documentation is not so much for the person who develops the application, but for the person who inherits it. This person may have to use or modify the application without access to the original developer. There is a higher risk that this "second end user" may abandon the application if it is poorly documented. IT and business managers need to develop reasonable documentation standards and insist that business managers require the development of adequate documentation.

Development of Applications that Are Difficult to Enhance

Changes in the needs of the business often dictate corresponding changes in the applications developed to support the business. Inexperienced programmers tend to write programs in a manner that is easiest for them as the original developer. They may take shortcuts and approaches that make it nearly impossible for someone to follow their logic and make changes to the application. Training courses need to emphasize the need to develop programs that are easy to enhance and maintain. Programming guidelines or "best practices" can be developed that will encourage good programming by end users.

Insufficiently Integrated Systems

Insufficiently integrated systems require the reentry of critical data by the end users. Frequently end-user-developed systems are not integrated with other organizational systems that produce results that serve as input to the end user's system. Data that is copied from reports and reentered is prone to error. These situations need to be identified and a quality check performed on the data entry. Better yet, the need to reenter the data can be eliminated by providing an interface between the two systems.

Data Management

There is a high risk that files or data bases will proliferate and lead to the existence of very similar yet different sources of data (see Chapter 5). For example, consider a shipment data base maintained on the mainframe computer. This data base is the company's official source of information about product shipments to customers. Managers in sales, advertising, finance, and manufacturing will want to access these data and analyze them for many different purposes. Suppose each manager accesses the data base just once a day to extract that day's recorded shipments and then uses that information to update a month-to-date file on the manager's personal computer. Not only does this represent inefficiency and duplication of effort, it can also lead to differences between the numbers used in analyses performed on the personal computer and the official sales figures of the company, as illustrated by the following two equations:

$$\text{Raw sales} = \text{quantity shipped as recorded daily.}$$

$$\text{Official sales} = \text{raw sales} - \text{customer returns} \pm \text{corrections to}$$
$$\text{order data-entry errors.}$$

Thus there can be a significant difference between raw sales figures and official sales figures. Unfortunately, customer returns and data-entry errors are difficult to identify and process. Corrections for these problems are frequently made at the end of the month rather than on a daily basis. These corrections are not likely to be captured and applied correctly by the personal computer users.

Control over updating (add, delete, change) a mainframe computer data base with transactions from personal computer users needs to be very tight. There is a distinct possibility that more than one user may have created updates for the same data base record. After the contents of a personal computer data base are sent back to the mainframe computer, the mainframe data base management system needs to ensure that the user is authorized to update the records and fields involved, edit each transaction for invalid, incorrect, or unauthorized changes, and guard against multiple updates to the same records or fields (or both).

One approach to ensuring data integrity is to make it clear that the data base on the mainframe computer is the authoritative source of information and is considered correct because it includes more edits and controls. If a difference arises between reports produced from a personal computer file and the mainframe data base, it is the personal computer user's responsibility to locate and clear the discrepancy. Another approach, although perhaps not as practical, is to insist that end users not create any data base or file on their personal computers for use outside their own departments.

A well-designed and managed data base provides a rock solid foundation on which user applications can be built. The data base provides an accurate, consistent, complete, up-to-date common source of data that can be shared by multiple users to meet different needs.

Using a common source of data reduces the potential for different users to obtain different results even though they process data in the same fashion.

When users access different sources of data for analysis, the likelihood of obtaining different results is very high. For example, suppose that two different users are tracking sales volume. One user accesses a daily shipment file and accumulates total volume. The second user waits until the end of the month and accesses a monthly shipment file to determine total volume. It is quite likely the two users may obtain significantly different totals. The monthly shipment file may include adjustments for customer returns and exclude shipments to company-owned warehouses to balance stock positions. Thus both users may write their own programs and be willing to swear their results are correct while the other's results must be incorrect!

The existence of a predefined data base structure also improves the productivity of user application development. The creator of the application does not need to design the data or their structure but merely uses what already exists. The user can access a data base dictionary to obtain an accurate description of the data. Report headings and titles for fields to be placed in column headings of reports may also be stored in the data dictionary.

Many IT organizations provide a quality assurance function to ensure that end-user-developed programs and their associated documentation (e.g., user manual) meet corporate standards. This function helps to improve the return on investment in end-user programming by enabling others to use and support the programs, besides the person who wrote them.

Personal Computer Acquisition

According to most estimates, at least 3 million personal computers will be acquired for use in the office each year. Chaos will result if potential users are left entirely on their own to select whatever personal computer they feel best meets their needs. This approach can easily lead to half a dozen or more different brands of personal computers that are incompatible with one another and the mainframe computer. Such a potpourri of devices leads to extremely high support costs. It is also likely that users will become increasingly disenchanted with their personal computers once they advance beyond the initial application for which they were acquired and it becomes apparent that lack of support and compatibility is a severe handicap.

Most organizations have instituted guidelines and procurement policies to squelch uncontrolled and unauthorized acquisition of personal computers. These policies need to cover three specific points:

1. Justification Potential users of personal computers should be asked to justify their acquisition. One approach is through cost/

benefit analysis, with users explaining how the job is currently done and all related costs versus how the job would be done using a personal computer. Any tangible benefits (e.g., staff time savings) or intangible benefits (e.g., higher quality) should be clearly identified.

2. Vendor Selection Guidelines One approach is to limit the number of brands of personal computers to only two or three. This automatically reduces the opportunity for creating problems due to multiple incompatible devices. It also eases the support burden by reducing the number of different devices that must be learned by both the support organization and the users. Thus, as users move from one job to the next, they likely will not have to learn how to operate an entirely new personal computer in addition to the other training they need to master the new job. Exhibit 13.11 illustrates some alternatives for setting computer acquisition guidelines.

3. Establish a Control Point for Their Acquisition In many cases, the proper organization to perform this function is the purchasing department. Purchasing is trained in how to get the best value for the dollars spent, how to evaluate one vendor versus another, and how to negotiate volume discount contracts for the entire organization.

Training

A recent survey of the five hundred-member Corporate Advisory Panel found that corporate and institutional microcomputer management personnel spend 23 percent of their time on system installation, maintenance, and repair. Formal classroom end-user training takes up 9 percent of the support staff.

There is a growing need for more effective training to support end-user computing. The need is made more acute by the rapid growth in

Exhibit 13.11
Alternatives for
Setting Computer
Acquisition
Guidelines

Let Users Make Their Own Choices	Set a Corporate Standard
Advantages	
1. Ensures that individual user needs are met provided they make good choices.	1. Minimizes the effort to select a personal computer.
2. Reduces potential conflict between IT group and users.	2. Reduces the effort to train and support users.
	3. Enables negotiation of large volume discounts.
	4. Simplifies maintenance.
Disadvantages	
1. It takes a lot of effort and time for an individual to justify anything other than the corporate standard.	1. Almost impossible to enforce.

Real World Perspective

Setting Computer Acquisition Guidelines at KPMG Peat Marwick

KPMG Peat Marwick, an international accounting firm, established not one but many acceptable personal computers for use within the firm. After extensive evaluation, it became clear that no one personal computer best met the diverse needs of the firm.

The auditing department wanted a vendor with a solid reputation that was a recognized leader in the technology. The personal computer had to be portable, easy to use, and cost effective. Their choice was the Apple Macintosh.

The tax department went through a similar decision process but with different selection criteria. They decided the IBM PC best met their needs.

The consulting department felt a standard should not be enforced because of the individual nature of the consultant's work. As a result, these managers use Gavilans, IBM PCs, Apples, or whatever system they feel best meets their needs.

Thus, KPMG Peat Marwick has established some fairly broad but widely accepted standards for the user of personal computers.

the power and complexity of microcomputer applications, a phenomenon that has resulted in technology outpacing training. This situation presents both a challenge and an opportunity. The challenge is coming up with more responsive training programs that focus on the use of microcomputers in solving business problems and in promoting good information management practices among users. The opportunity lies in utilizing training to gain influence and support, and to direct the course of end-user computing.

The IT organization is seen as more responsive when it can strengthen end-user self-sufficiency to reduce the demand made by users for IT support. One way to achieve this is to educate the end users following a training program that addresses the four key elements outlined next.

First, problem-solving skills that employees can apply to real business problems should be taught. Too often, programs to train employees as end users of computer software teach only the mechanics of using the software but not the problem-solving skills needed to apply them. Training in Lotus 1-2-3, for example, teaches keystrokes necessary to enter and manipulate data and perhaps the concepts underlying the spreadsheet, but not analytic or modeling skills. Managers and employees may be frustrated with the results of computer training because they expect it to also improve problem solving and prepare the end user for most sophisticated analytic tasks.

Second, end-user training should include some troubleshooting methods (program debugging, file backup and recovery, and so on) to reduce user anxiety, promote self-sufficiency, and ease some of the demand on IT staff. Troubleshooting guidelines must attract user attention and should be given to each user department. Telephone support staff could also reinforce the idea by asking if users have referred to their troubleshooting guidelines; if the support staff continues to get problems that are addressed in the guidelines, that is a sign that the guidelines are not working.

–   Third, functional support personnel should be developed so that IT can focus on supporting these specialists, who, in turn, support the end users in their organization. These people are assigned to the organization's functional business units and not the IT organization. They have a high level of skill and understanding of computers and end-user computing tools and processes. They are capable of performing problem solving to correct most problems. Their role is to provide a high level of support for end users in their organization. They can be trained to be trainers to reduce end-user training expenses.

–   Fourth, a process for end-user application development must be taught so that users can analyze business problems from a computer perspective and assess alternative solutions. Training end users in some of the broader principles behind information systems development can prevent major problems, especially as more end users develop increasingly complex applications. Without the proper systems perspective, end users are prone to inadequately analyze the consequences of a specific application decision. Systems perspective training should concentrate on analyzing problems, gauging the appropriateness of a computer-based or some other solution, estimating the scope of the development effort, evaluating alternative solutions, and testing and validating applications.

Funding

End-user computer costs typically make up roughly 30 to 50 percent of the corporate IT budget. Training and maintenance costs for microcomputers are budgeted centrally and then billed back to the individual departments in most organizations. Some provide for microcomputer training on a corporate level, but most charge all or part back to the individual departments requiring training. The same results are found for repair and maintenance costs.

Charge-back, the process of billing end users or their departments for PC support, training, or other services, also has a dark side. Charge-back can emphasize the overhead expense of an internal microcomputer staff and can also make end users feel that unnecessary control is being exerted over them. This may stifle the innovative use of microcomputers and may cause skimping on development projects.

Installation, Maintenance, and Repair

As already mentioned, corporate and institutional microcomputer management personnel spend 23 percent of their time on system installation, maintenance, and repair. These are tasks that end users have no desire to tackle. Indeed, the prospect of installing one's computer hardware and loading on the software can be quite overwhelming for the uninitiated. Furthermore, there are good reasons to establish set guidelines for software installation that will ensure more efficient use of hardware resources and simplify maintenance work. It is easier to ensure that these guidelines will be followed if only a limited number of trained people do the installations.

While the IT staff typically retains much of the responsibility for these activities, increasingly the actual work is contracted out to service organizations.

Security

Most companies today take strong precautions to safeguard sensitive data stored on their mainframe computer. Such data might include employee salary data, customer lists, new product rollout plans, financial data, and so on. Personal computers are capable of accessing the mainframe and quickly reproducing data onto floppy disks with the risk of critical data being widely disseminated with no control.

Data kept on the personal computer also require protection. It is quite possible that the three to six months' worth of data or models stored on floppy disks or hard disk is worth much more than the computer. Imagine the consequences if someone inadvertently or otherwise erased all the spreadsheet models developed in the past six months! Or imagine if someone were to reformat the hard disk on which accounts receivable, payroll, or inventory data bases were stored!

Data security is an important concern for management that must be resolved before the broad introduction of personal computers throughout the company. Data security must be dealt with on two levels: (1) control of access to the mainframe and (2) control of access to the personal computer.

The owner of the mainframe data base may limit the personal computer users' access to information by defining files, records, or fields that may not be accessed. Access can even be restricted by requiring users to enter a password to obtain data from the data base. These security and privacy restrictions are provided by the data base management system that resides on the mainframe computer.

Most mainframe computers also have access-control software (e.g., IBM's Resource Access Control Facility) that requires users to enter a password and log-on identification to use the computer. Files and data sets can also be password protected to limit their access to only users authorized by the owner of the data.

Proper use of this mainframe software ensures control over who is downloading data from the mainframe to the personal computer so that no sensitive data are released unknowingly.

Personal computer solutions to data security are available that are similar to those employed on the mainframe. Users can limit the use of their personal computer through software that requires the entry of a password to access data. Hardware enhancements, such as a lock that requires a special key, make the personal computer physically secure from unauthorized use.

Exhibit 13.12 summarizes the various strategies for effective support of end user computing.

Exhibit 13.12
Summary of Strategies for Effective Management of End-User Computing

Strategy Area	Potential Problem	Recommendation
Staffing	End users do not receive necessary support	Plan on thirteen support workers to one thousand users
Software development	Applications fail to meet user requirements	Define standard system development process
	Duplicated development effort	Conduct monthly user meetings Publish newsletter
	Applications produce incorrect results Lack of documentation makes use impossible Applications difficult to change	Conduct independent testing Define documentation guidelines Insist guidelines are followed Address need for flexibility in training Define best practices that ensure flexibility
Data management	Redundant and duplicate files and data bases are inefficient and can lead to inconsistent analyses	Define the authoritative source of data for various types of analyses
Hardware	End users purchase nonstandard equipment	Establish hardware standards
Training	Ineffective use of human and computing resources	Teach problem-solving skills Teach troubleshooting methods Develop functional support personnel Teach application development process
Funding	End users spend resources ineffectively	Charge back costs to end users
Install, maintain	Installation can be difficult for end users	Establish installation guidelines Employ service organization
Data security	Threats to data security and integrity	Establish owner of mainframe data bases Limit access to authorized users Require log-on IDs and passwords Install keylocks on personal computers

Summary

Even the most successful IT organizations have a large applications development backlog and fail to deliver systems that meet users' needs.

Any situation in which workers use or control computer-based equipment can be called end-user computing.

There is a wide range in types of end users.

The two basic types of end-user computing tools include application packages and fourth-generation languages.

Fourth-generation programming languages are nonprocedural in nature, easy to learn, and highly productive.

The use of fourth-generation programming languages by end users should not include building applications such as corporate production systems or those that require complex processing, matching of multiple files and data bases, or processing an extremely high volume of transactions.

The use of information centers is an effective strategy to promote, support, and encourage end-user application development.

Most firms today are moving toward an improved working partnership between the IT organization and other organizations within the firm.

IT and business managers need to establish a strategy on end-user computing because it is too important to ignore.

An effective strategy for end-user computing needs to address the following areas: staffing, standards for software development, hardware, training, funding, and technical support.

A Manager's Checklist

✔ Is end-user computing encouraged in your organization? If so, how? Should even more be done to encourage its use?

✔ Are IT and business managers working in partnership to support end-user computing, or are they working at odds?

✔ Is there evidence of successful end-user computing in your firm?

✔ How would you describe the IT-user relationship in your firm? Do others agree?

Key Terms

application duplication
application packages
applications backlog
charge-back
decision support/financial
  modeling tool
downsizing

end-user computing
fourth-generation languages
graphics language
information center
nonprocedural language
query language/report writer
statistical analysis packages

Review Questions

1. Define the term *end-user computing*.

2. Identify and briefly describe the various classifications of end users.

3. What are the characteristics of a fourth-generation language?

4. What is an information center, and what is its role in supporting end-user computing?

5. What are the key issues associated with application development by end users?

6. How does data management apply to end-user computing?

7. What are the key elements of an effective training program for end-user computing?

Discussion Questions

1. You have been asked to work with the IT organization to establish a strategy to provide strong support for end-user computing. What would be the key elements of your strategy?

2. You are an IT manager who is determined to keep total and absolute control over all computing and to squash any signs of end-user computing in your firm. What sort of policies would you implement? What actions might you take? Can you think of any reason for an IT manager to act in this way?

3. What guidelines would you offer for deciding when and to what extent the IT organization needs to be involved in creating an end-user-developed application?

4. How can you ensure that people involved in end-user computing will safeguard sensitive data? If you cannot guarantee this, should end-user computing be held back?

5. Do you think that all end-user computing expenses should be charged back directly to the end user? Why or why not?

Recommended Readings

1. Alavi, Maryam, R. Ryan Nelson, and Ira R. Weiss. "Strategies for End-User Computing: An Integrative Framework." *Journal of Management Information Systems* 4 (Winter 1987–88).

2. Carr, Houston H. "Information Centers: The IBM Model Versus Practice." *MIS Quarterly* 11 (September 1987).

3. Frank, Jonathan. "Quality Control of Personal Computing." *Journal of Systems Management* 39 (December 1988).

4. Leitheiser, Robert L., and James C. Wetherbe. "Service Support Levels: An Organized Approach to End-User Computing." *MIS Quarterly* 10 (December 1986).

5. Munro, Malcom, and Sid L. Huff. "Managing End-User Computing." *Journal of Systems Management* 39 (December 1988).

6. Rivard, Suzanne, and Sid. L. Huff. "Factors of Success for End-User Computing." *Communications of the ACM* (May 1988).

7. Soat, John, and Mike Filton. "The Desktop Agenda." *Information Week* (4 January 1993).

8. Tate, Paul. "Helping the Help Desk." *Information Week* (27 July 1992).

A Manager's Dilemma

Starting End-User Computing

The company Controller has just placed on your desk a recommendation to purchase a minicomputer and a fourth-generation software package at a cost of $70,000 plus $15,000 per year for maintenance. The Controller plans to install the system as a departmental computer for the company's two dozen financial analysts and accountants to access financial data and create ad hoc reports. The necessary data would be downloaded on a daily basis from the corporate financial data base.

While the Controller presents a convincing case to justify the expense, as the company's Budget Analyst, you feel uneasy for two reasons: (1) up to now, the IT Department has done all program development, and (2) all programs and data reside strictly on the company's single mainframe computer.

What steps should be taken to ensure that the recommendation is sound and well thought out?

Assuming you agreed with the recommendation, what steps would you take to ensure the success of the project?

Choosing a Fourth-Generation Language

You have had an uneasy feeling ever since the study began, and now your suspicions are confirmed. The IT Department and the Distribution Department cannot agree on which fourth-generation language is appropriate for members of the Distribution Department to use. After three months of study, they have polarized into two groups: the IT Department prefers LOBO because it runs efficiently with minimal use of computer resources; the Distribution Department agrees that LOBO is more efficient, but strongly prefers FOXY because it is much easier to learn and use. How would you resolve this difference of opinion?

The Tower of Babel

This is the third proposal to introduce a fourth-generation programming language in the past eighth months! The first proposal had been approved quickly. The IT Department and the Finance Department seemed so convinced it was right to begin letting financial analysts write their own programs. The second request raised a few eyebrows when Engineering said they need a different fourth-generation language. But it too was approved. Now a third fourth-generation language has been proposed—just because Production Planning and Inventory Control people need improved forecasting capabilities!

Each language costs about $30,000 plus another $9,000 per year for maintenance. Also, people have to be trained in their use. The IT Department has dedicated a person to help train and support users. On top of all the expense, it seems that the many different programming languages are creating a situation in which one department's programs and data bases cannot be used by another department. As a member of the IT steering committee responsible for approving the proposal, what would you recommend?

Case Study 13.4

Getting End-User Computing onto Solid Ground

You have drawn a six-month special assignment to review the state of end-user computing in your company and to make specific recommendations for improvement. You know from firsthand experience that there are many problems in this area.

You need to gain the end users' perspective on how well their needs are being met. You also think it is important to understand the IT Department's perspective on end-user computing. As a result of your recommendations, you hope to form a stronger alliance between end users and the IT Department.

How would you proceed? Who would you involve in order to achieve a better working relationship between end users and the IT Department? Do you think most of your time will be spent gathering facts or making recommendations? Why?

Chapter 14

Computer Security and Disaster Planning

Learning Objectives

Upon completion of this chapter, you will be able to:

1. Define the term computer crime and give six examples of computer crime.

2. Discuss management's role in safeguarding against computer crime.

3. Apply the concept of reasonable assurance and risk management to identify the importance of security measures and allocate resources to obtain the desired level of security.

4. Discuss management's role in protecting the firm from a disruption in the event of a disaster.

5. Outline seven key areas that need to be addressed in a disaster recovery plan.

6. Identify four options for alternate data processing sites in the event of a disaster and discuss their pros and cons.

Preview

The risk of computer crime or computer abuse of the individual's right to privacy is increasing rapidly. In addition, companies that depend heavily on the availability of data processing services to continue day-to-day operations are increasingly vulnerable to even a short interruption in computer services. Top management recognizes these potentially serious problems and looks for reasonable assurances to safeguard against such risks.

Issues

1. What is the concept of reasonable assurance, and what is its impact on the implementation of IT safeguards?

2. What steps can business managers take to improve the computer security of an organization?

3. What are the key elements of a business resumption plan?

4. How can you evaluate the security and backup procedures for an organization's computer data and systems?

Trade-offs

1. How much effort should be spent on developing a disaster recovery plan versus effort spent on avoiding a disaster?

2. How much computer security is enough?

3. Is computer security a responsibility of the company's computer experts or of general management?

A Manager Struggles with the Issues

Tammy has just joined Acme Manufacturing, a small custom manufacturer of plastic and glass bottles. Her major in college was accounting with a minor in information processing. Tammy was assigned to Acme's newly established internal auditing department. Her responsibilities include reviewing information technology to ensure that appropriate internal controls are included.

She wonders just how to go about establishing the sorts of controls that are appropriate and what to do when she finds systems that do not have appropriate internal controls. She does not want to become known as a "policewoman." She wonders if the current system development process could be modified to more explicitly address the need for good internal controls.

■ COMPUTER CRIME

Computer crime is a serious management problem. The U.S. Department of Justice defines **computer crime** as any illegal act for which knowledge of computer technology is essential for its perpetration, investigation, or prosecution. Under this broad definition, there are several forms of computer crime: (1) the altering of data stored on or destined for a computer data base, (2) the destruction or manipulation of computer programs, (3) the illegal copying of computer software, (4) the theft of computer time for personal use, (5) the accessing of personal or confidential data for unauthorized purposes, and (6) the theft of money by altering computer records (Exhibit 14.1).

Although no valid and accurate measure of the magnitude of computer crime exists, it is estimated that the loss may well be in excess of $3 billion per year. A study by the Future Computing research firm estimates that fully one-half of all copies of popular personal computer software are pirated, with a resulting loss in revenues to the software vendors of $2 billion to $3 billion per year.

The risk of computer crime is rapidly increasing as a result of (1) the growth in computer use within business organizations, (2) the increasing number of employees who are computer competent and who have access to personal computers or computer terminals, and (3) the ability to access remote computers through both public and private data networks. There are also unique problems in conducting investigations of computer-related crimes. Few companies report ille-

Exhibit 14.1
The Top Security
Problems

Rank	Security Problems
#1	Unauthorized computer access
#2	Tapping data communications
#3	Physical access to telecommunications network
#4	Tapping voice and fax networks
#5	Remote access to PBX
#6	Voice mail fraud

Source: Mary Thyfault, Stephanie Stahl, and Joseph C. Panettieri. "Weak Links." InformationWeek, *August 10, 1992. Copyright © 1992 by CMP Publications, Inc., 600 Community Drive, Manhasset, NY 11030. Reprinted from* InformationWeek *with permission.*

gal activity for fear of public discredit or notoriety. Business managers are often unable even to detect that a crime has been committed. Evidence that a crime has been committed (e.g., unauthorized access to a system) can be easily destroyed, so it is difficult to prove illegal activity. Prosecution is severely hampered by a lack of state and federal statutes that apply to the area of computer crime.

The Federal Bureau of Investigation estimates that 1 percent of all computer crime is detected and approximately 7 percent of detected crimes are reported to the police. Moreover, in those cases prosecuted, only 3 percent result in a jail sentence for the accused. Thus, only about one in twenty-two thousand computer criminals will end up in jail!

Management's Increasing Responsibility for Computer Security

The role of the computer is changing, not only within the company, agency, or institution but also with respect to other computers linked to it via a network. Computers in today's organizations are being accessed at a growing rate—both internally by employees at all levels and externally by customers, suppliers, and joint venture partners. Technology to interconnect systems is being used to gain improved service and productivity. For example, financial institutions have developed cash management systems that allow their corporate customers not only to monitor their account balances on a daily basis but also to initiate electronic transfers of funds.

Many manufacturing companies are using electronic document interchange (EDI) to eliminate paper purchase orders, invoices, and change orders, thereby achieving savings in personnel and inventory costs and providing more timely service. EDI is based on a widely accepted set of international standards and enables federal agencies and private organizations to exchange business data and documents electronically. Using EDI to become more efficient means an ever-increasing flow of data. These instances of interenterprise data exchange illustrate the need for interoperability of the security mechanisms to maintain the necessary controls in this paperless environment. Unguarded, this flow of data is vulnerable to spies, vandals, and **hackers** (those who seek to gain unauthorized access to protected data or software). Even though the data is not secret, so much information will eventually be exchanged that a competitor or enemy government could learn much by sorting through it.

The increasing role of the computer is shifting responsibility for the most basic of computer security issues from the systems analyst and programmer to the business manager. Those issues are deciding what level of security is enough and how to achieve that level. Traditionally these questions have been the domain of IT people, and the response has been to require log-on IDs and passwords to access the mainframe computer. But in a world where sales of communications and networking products far outstrip any other kind of peripheral and over 50 percent of all microcomputers are expected to be connected via networks, those safeguards are no longer enough.

Profile of a Computer Criminal

If the FBI were to produce a composite portrait of the typical computer criminal, the picture that would emerge would show a young, talented employee working in a position of trust in a company. The median age of those who commit computer-related crimes is only twenty-five. In most cases they are employees who think of themselves as modern-day Robin Hoods and consider the illegal activity to be a game or a challenging intellectual exercise. In general, these employees commit the illegal activity while at work. Usually they work alone and enlist the aid of an accomplice only when they run up against the limits of their technical ability to gain further access to the computer system (Exhibit 14.2).

Despite all the publicity and handwringing over hacker penetration of computer systems, only 3 percent of security breaches are perpetrated by outsiders, according to a survey by R. J. Milford Associates of Mission Viejo, California. By contrast, 13 percent are committed by dishonest employees and 6 percent by disgruntled employees. Perhaps more alarming, 65 percent are caused by mistake. The greatest threats to computer security come from internal rather than outside sources. Yet, by and large, companies have only paid lip service to the situation.

Infamous Computer Crimes

An operations manager at Wells Fargo bank produced bogus deposits in an account at one branch using the bank's computerized interbranch account settlement process to withdraw funds to cover the deposit from a different branch. New fraudulent credits were created to cover the withdrawal to keep the computer from uncovering the imbalance. This rollover process continued for two years before being discovered, with an estimated loss to the bank of over $20 million.

The officers of the Equity Funding insurance holding company used computers to create phony insurance policies that were then sold to reinsurers. It was finally discovered that over $140 million of the company's assets were fictitious, with more than $25 million in falsified insurance policies.

A computer consultant to Security Pacific Bank tricked an employee into revealing the electronic funds transfer code. He later called

Exhibit 14.2
Spectrum of
Computer
Criminals

Type of Criminal	Purpose
Hacker	Attempts to trespass for achievement
Prankster	Attempts to trespass to defy authority
Amateur	Steals computer time for personal use
Pro	Makes a living from computer crime
Spy	Commits computer crime to gain an advantage
Terrorist	Commits computer crime to advocate extreme position

and, posing as a bank branch manager, used the code to transfer over $10 million to a Swiss account.

The Association of Data Processing Service Organizations (ADAPSO) announced a lawsuit filed jointly with MicroPro (a personal computer software vendor) against the Wilson Jones Company and their parent company, American Brands. The suit charged Wilson Jones with distributing pirated copies of WordStar and other MicroPro software. It asked for $225,000 for breach of license, plus profits from bogus copies, damages, penalties, and legal fees.

Internal Control

Internal control encompasses the design of organizational structure, procedures, and policies concerned with decision processes and the means by which management directs an organization to meet its legal and ethical responsibilities to its owners, employees, suppliers, customers, and society in general. Internal control is the plan of the organization to safeguard its assets, check the accuracy of its internal accounting data, promote operational efficiency, and encourage adherence to prescribed management policies. Internal control is a specific responsibility of the CEO, and it is delegated downward through the organization and consequently becomes a responsibility of all managers and employees. Fortunately, a number of principles exist that can help guide managers responsible for implementing good systems of internal control and combating computer crime.

■ PROVIDING FOR REASONABLE ASSURANCE AGAINST COMPUTER CRIME

The Concept of Reasonable Assurance

The concept of **reasonable assurance** recognizes that managers must use their judgment to ensure that the cost of a control does not exceed the benefit to be obtained by its implementation or the possible risk involved. The omission of any generally accepted control, however, should be thoroughly studied, documented, and properly authorized. For example, if it costs $10,000 per year to implement controls to eliminate the risk of loss of $1,000 per year, management would apply the principle of reasonable assurance and elect not to implement the controls.

The following sections provide some guidelines for providing reasonable assurance against computer crime.

The Foreign Corrupt Practices Act became codified in 1977 in the wake of a number of scandals in the public and private sectors. The thrust of the act was to make bribes to foreign officials by U.S. companies a criminal offense. The act requires that a company's internal controls be sufficient to provide reasonable assurance that four specific objectives are met:

1. All transactions must be authorized (e.g., ensure that only certain people can enter data to the computer system).

2. All transactions must be recorded (e.g., ensure that a record is created for all data submitted to the computer).

3. Control access to data (e.g., control physical access to computer equipment and data).

4. Ensure the auditability of data (e.g., ensure that the information being produced is correct and verifiable).

The Securities and Exchange Commission is the body that enforces the act and requires documentation of the company's system of internal controls to achieve these objectives.

Business managers must retain primary responsibility for controlling the business functions they assign to process on a computer. Managers must ensure that they have the same or an improved level of control over these functions as they would if they were performed manually. For example, the manager of accounts payable must be held accountable for the controls built into the new computerized system and cannot abdicate that responsibility to the systems staff that designs and implements the new system.

The system designer is responsible for pointing out and reviewing all exposures to risk with the business manager. The system designer must ensure that the manager's control of the business function is not compromised when converting to a new system. The system designer must review any potential exposure to risk with the manager, recommend alternatives to reduce the risk, and implement appropriate solutions. For example, if the accounts payable clerk can enter a change to the amount to be paid to the supplier, this potential risk should be pointed out to the manager of accounts payable, and either the system should be changed to prohibit this ability or a procedure should be designed to detect whenever the amount to be paid is changed.

Instructions and documentation sufficient to provide a complete and thorough understanding of computer systems and of the associated procedures for using and controlling the systems should be maintained. Such documentation not only will be required by company auditors to ensure conformance with the Foreign Corrupt Practices Act, but also will prove invaluable for managers and users of the system to verify that the system is performing correctly and that everything is under control.

Incompatible functions for internal control purposes are those that place people in a position to both perpetrate and conceal errors or irregularities in the normal course of their duties. Anyone who records transactions or has access to assets is in a position to perpetrate errors or irregularities. Consequently, internal control must eliminate the opportunity for concealment. For example, anyone who records disbursements could omit the recording of a check, either intentionally or by mistake. If the same person reconciles the bank statement, the failure to record the check could be concealed through an improper reconciliation. This example illustrates the principle that procedures designed to detect errors and irregularities should be performed by people other than those who are in a position to perpetrate them.

A Model for Risk Management

A useful approach to dealing with security issues is the concept of **risk management.** The organization identifies the importance of security to the firm and then allocates the resources to obtain the desired level of security. However, no amount of resources can guarantee a perfect security system. Thus, managers must learn to deal with uncertainty and to manage the risk of a security breach versus the cost of preventing one. The following list outlines one effective way to manage security risks, and Exhibit 14.3 graphically represents this process.

1. Determine the relative importance of security to the firm through interviews with top management.

2. Identify specific areas in which security is a concern.

3. Prioritize these areas of threats and concentrate on the high-threat–high-potential-loss areas.

4. Evaluate the current system of internal control in these high-threat–high-potential-loss areas.

5. Identify and evaluate potential improvements in security to reduce the level of threat. (Apply the principle of reasonable assurance and compare the cost of additional controls versus the value of the potential loss without the additional controls.)

6. Recommend the appropriate improvements (in some cases, no improvement may be required).

7. Obtain management approval to make necessary changes.

8. Implement necessary changes.

9. Periodically review the security procedures to ensure that they are being followed and are still effective.

Data and Systems Security

Computer data and systems can represent a valuable asset of the company. Computer-related white-collar crime involving the manipulation of systems and data has received considerable publicity. Destruction or theft of data by a disgruntled employee is not uncommon. Computer equipment and software can be designed to provide a relatively high degree of security. Two basic areas of security need to be addressed: **access security** and **communications security.**

Access Security

Only authorized people should be able to gain access to computer input and output devices. Computer and data-entry devices may be kept

Exhibit 14.3
A Model for
Security Risk
Management

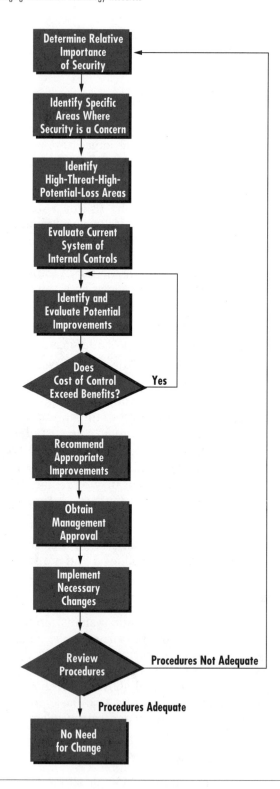

Real World Perspective

ACF2: A Software Package for Data Security

ACF2 is a software product designed to improve the security of the IBM MVS operating systems. ACF2 was designed so that all data are protected by default. No one except the designated owner can access a data set until the owner or the ACF2 security manager enters an access rule into ACF2 that specifies to whom and under what circumstances access approval will be given. Each user's authority to access the operating system, the user-defined addressable resources, and the data sets are established at job initiation or at log-on during password verification. The owner of the data set can request a report detailing all unauthorized attempts at accessing each and every data set owned.

in controlled access rooms that require a key, a magnetic card, or knowledge of a combination to gain access. Furthermore, the different classes of authorized users should be limited in what they may do. For example, the payroll data-entry clerk should not have access to an accounts payable file.

Many software packages are available to help manage user access to software and data residing on a computer. With such a package, each user is given a password that allows, within the operating system of the computer, access to certain types of functions. The passwords verify that the individuals are who they purport to be. Once users are authenticated, their authority to perform specific activities is validated on the basis of who they are rather than what they know. For passwords to be effective, they must be changed periodically.

Communications Security

Communications security must deal with two types of unauthorized tapping of a communications line: (1) passive listening to information and messages sent over the line and (2) tapping a communications line to modify the transmission. **Data encryption,** or **cryptography,** is a coding technique that safeguards the security of transmitted information. With data encryption, each character of data sent is replaced with other coded characters. The substitution algorithm is determined by the sender according to a selected key. The data encryption technique keeps the data secure even when the unauthorized interceptor has complete knowledge of the encryption algorithm but doesn't have the key.

A good encryption system forces unauthorized listeners to spend great effort to decipher a message. The National Bureau of Standards adopted IBM's data encryption model, called DES, as the nation's official data encryption standard (Exhibit 14.4). DES is a single-chip device that receives a 64-bit unencrypted input called **plaintext** and produces a 64-bit encrypted output called **ciphertext.** The DES procedure generates billions of different permutations for each 64-bit input. The only practical way to decipher the output is to know the key used to scramble the data. When the ciphertext is run backward

Exhibit 14.4
The National Bureau of Standards Data Encryption Standard

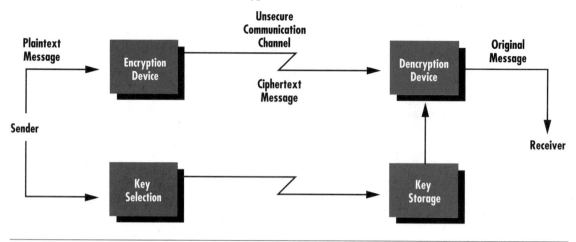

through the algorithm, **cleartext** results. In this way, the original message is recovered after the ciphertext has been transmitted to the receiving party. To exchange an encrypted message successfully, the sender and the receiver must use the same key. However, the key must remain unknown to outsiders to prevent their translating the message in ciphertext into cleartext.

See Exhibit 14.5 for a summary of what security measures need to protect.

Commonly Used Penetration Methods

Piggybacking is a method of gaining entry to controlled access areas. One such method is that an unauthorized person with an armful of

Exhibit 14.5
What Security
Measures Need to
Protect

Information

Awaiting input to or pickup from computers

Stored or being processed inside computers, office automation equipment (e.g., word processors), and personal computers

Transmitted on communications lines going to or coming from computers

Stored on portable media such as diskettes, tapes, and cassettes

Computer Hardware

Large mainframe computers in corporate data centers

Minicomputers in office or plant locations

Office automation equipment

Terminals, printers, and displays

Communications facilities supporting computers

Storage devices like diskettes, tapes, or cassettes

Real World Perspective

Data Security Officer

Some organizations have established the role of Data Security Officer (DSO) to ensure a safe environment for the processing, storage, and transmission of data. The DSO must be willing to call management's attention to current weaknesses and problems. In many cases, management will find this information unnerving. All too often, problems are ignored rather than dealt with. The DSO must be tactful but persistent in seeing that problems are corrected.

The DSO uncovers problems or opportunities for improvement by thorough, ongoing testing of security controls, systems, and procedures to ensure they are working properly. Attempts to penetrate security are made. Procedures are tested to see if they can be circumvented. Variations from the norm must be reported, as must the procedures that work correctly.

In some organizations where security is an important concern, the DSO role is filled on a permanent full-time basis. Other organizations may assign the DSO role on a temporary part-time basis. Yet a third approach is to hire a consultant who specializes in security to conduct an audit on a regular basis.

computer printouts and tape reels stands by the locked door. When an authorized person arrives and opens the door, the piggybacker goes in after the authorized person. Turnstiles, mantraps (a double-doored closet through which only one person can move at a time), TV camera monitoring, or a stationed guard are the usual methods for preventing piggybacking.

Impersonation is the process of one person assuming the identity of another. Physical access to computer equipment requires positive identification of an authorized user. Verification of an individual is based on some combination of something the user knows (e.g., a password), something the user has (fingerprints), or something the user possesses (a key). Someone with the correct combination of identification characteristics can impersonate someone else.

Data diddling involves changing data during or prior to computer processing. For example, a data-entry clerk could modify the amount to be paid or the payee on an invoice. Control totals and check registers are means of safeguarding against this method.

Superzapping is the use of a special program (superzap) that provides overriding or universal access to correct operating system malfunctions. The superzap program is a master key to the computer and can provide access to information by someone who is not authorized. Management must closely guard superzap programs.

The *salami technique* involves the theft of small amounts of assets from a large number of sources. For example, the rounded pennies from calculation of daily interest may be diverted from a large number of savings accounts into one account.

Logic bomb is computer logic hidden inside a program that executes only at a specified time to perform an unauthorized procedure. For example, an employee could trigger the erasure of the entire personnel file if the employee's name were ever removed.

Exhibit 14.6
Top Ten Security
Solutions

*Source: Mary Thyfault,
Stephanie Stahl, and
Joseph C. Panettieri.
"Weak Links."*
InformationWeek, *August
10, 1992. Copyright ©
1992 by CMP
Publications, Inc., 600
Community Drive,
Manhasset, NY 11030.
Reprinted from*
InformationWeek *with
permission.*

Rank	Solution
#1	Computer network passwords
#2	Computer network audit trail
#3	Limit physical access to telecom gear
#4	Telecommunications security training
#5	Dial-back protection on computer network
#6	Data Encryption
#7	Secure encryption keys
#8	Fax encryption
#9	Private-line encryption
#10	Remote encryption gear

Wiretapping is the interception of signals by unauthorized individuals. The equipment needed to set up a wiretap on an unprotected data communications channel is readily available at local electronics stores.

Ten security solutions are listed in Exhibit 14.6.

Computer Viruses

Our society as a whole has only recently become aware of the threat of **computer viruses,** largely as a result of a 1988 incident where a Cornell University student planted a virus and brought more than six thousand computers hooked up to the worldwide ARPAnet (also called DARPAnet and INTERnet) network to a grinding halt. ARPA stands for the Defense Department's Advance Research Projects Agency. ARPAnet interconnects computer centers at dozens of government locations and

Real World Perspective

Federal Reserve Systems' Fedwire

The Federal Reserve System is the nation's central bank and consists of a seven-member board of governors in Washington, D.C., plus a nationwide network of twelve Federal Reserve banks and twenty-five branches. The network handles over thirty thousand messages per day with a cash value greater than $400 billion, or an average of about $13 million per message!

Up until 1984, the Fedwire had a star configuration with all traffic relayed through four Control Data Corporation Cyber 1000 computers located deep inside Mount Pony in Culpeper, Virginia. The new network design, FRCS-80 (Federal Communications System for the 1980s), is designed as a mesh network with each Federal Reserve bank linked to two others. The change

was made to make penetration of the network more difficult and to make it possible for the network to continue operating even if a problem arose at Culpeper.

Officials acknowledge that no security system is perfect and that each year, about a half-dozen security exceptions are found. Each exception is examined to determine the cause, and appropriate follow-up action is taken to keep it from happening again. There are two types of security concerns with a network such as the FRCS-80: that someone will gain unauthorized access to confidential data and that someone will initiate a fraudulent cash exchange. In both cases, the most vulnerable point in the network is the people operating it.

universities with contracts for ARPA research projects. This incident proved once and for all that viruses are more than just annoying to the computer user. They can be extremely harmful, so much so that many would consider them criminal.

The ARPAnet incident, however, is only the most well-known incident. The Computer Virus Industry Association receives an average of fifteen to twenty reports a day. Dozens of strains of computer viruses have been identified (e.g., Disk Killer destroys all data on the disk drives of the personal computer and then displays the message I WISH YOU LUCK). *Business Week* estimated in August 1988 that up to that time, there may have been as many as 250,000 virus incidents. While we are most familiar with the ARPAnet virus, there have been attacks at tens of thousands of large and small corporations and at U.S. government locations including NASA, SDI, the Environment Protection Agency, and even the U.S. House of Representatives. Fortune 100 companies have dozens of virus incidents each month.

The FBI defines a computer virus as any computer program that is not readily discernible to the user and which has the capacity to infect other computer systems by re-creating itself unpredictably or causing some other specific action under predetermined circumstances. Another unique characteristic of the virus is its ability to remain dormant in a computer for some time without doing specific damage. A virus can hide in a computer system until a certain date or until a certain number of files have been collected before doing any damage.

Contrary to popular opinion, a virus is usually placed in a system by a person who has authorized access, not by a hacker who has broken into the system. Viruses are often transmitted to unsuspecting users when logging onto a network to receive electronic messages or retrieve public access programs. They can also be picked up from reading infected diskettes or other storage media used to hold programs or data (or both). With today's technology, viruses can originate in an office, an academic institution, or in a home personal computer almost anywhere in the world. Also the virus threat is not limited to personal computers, although personal computers continue to be the preferred target.

Computer viruses differ in their effects, depending on the intent (and sometimes the competence) of the designer. They may or may not cause damage or disrupt computer services. They can range from being nearly harmless to being devastating, causing complete shutdowns of the systems and the massive destruction of data. Cleaning up the aftermath can easily cost tens of thousands of dollars.

Viruses can also harm a company indirectly. Suppose a bank is hit with a computer virus. Even if the virus does no actual damage, its existence may reflect poorly on the bank's security. Knowledge of such a breach of security could lead worried depositors to close their accounts and do business elsewhere. This is one reason why so many firms are afraid to admit to being hit by a virus.

Viruses are often difficult to trace and are frequently not discovered until it is too late to prevent the intended harm. Investigation may be complicated by the many permutations that viruses can undergo and by the widespread geographic areas involved. As already discussed, owners of the affected systems are sometimes more concerned with downplaying the attack and repairing the damage than with prosecuting the offender. And because a particular virus may cause only a small amount of damage to many different users, no single user may consider the event significant enough to report.

Security experts have found that the motives of those who create viruses include intellectual curiosity, desire for publicity or notoriety, deliberate denial of service, and industrial or other sabotage of computer systems and data bases. Virus creators range from young students, who fail to consider the consequences of creating and transmitting a virus, to disgruntled employees and others who clearly intend to commit a malicious act.

Real World Perspective

The Robert Morris Case

In November 1988, Robert Morris, a Cornell University graduate student and son of one of the country's leading experts in computer security, planted a worm in the ARPA network. Morris achieved national notoriety when a program he had designed to take advantage of several security flaws in the Unix operating system worked better than he had intended—it slowed or completely stopped computer operations at university and government locations on some six thousand computers hooked up to ARPAnet.

While Morris was not "hacking" in the usual sense—that is, attempting to break into specific computers to steal specific information—his actions raised the fears of many corporate computer security experts. The Information Systems Security Association immediately contacted the United States attorney general, asking that the case be prosecuted to the fullest extent of the law.

However, the Morris case fell into the pattern of light sentences for computer criminals. U.S. district judge Howard Munson said he could find no analogies to other crimes to guide him in his deliberations, and added that he had received many letters about the case. Morris was sentenced in May 1990 to three years of probation, four hundred hours of community service, and a

$10,000 fine. Surprisingly, the sentence did not prohibit Morris from participating in the computer industry.

The Computer Fraud and Abuse Act was applied in the Robert Morris case. It is primarily designed to protect our nation's government owned or operated computers. Private companies or individuals are not protected by this law unless:

More than $1,000 worth of damage has been caused, and the damage is intentional.

Companies in the private sector are using their computers on a government project.

A financial institution is affected, and the perpetrator of the virus acquires information from the institution.

Despite new and rewritten laws that address specific aspects of computer crime, such cases are likely to remain difficult to prosecute. Often corporations don't want to report them for fear of bad publicity. And the difficulty in assigning a dollar value to the damage done has a great impact on sentencing. In the Morris case, estimates of the cost of coping with the ARPAnet worm ran from a few thousand dollars to $90 million. And law enforcement bodies still give computer crime low priority.

Software Piracy

Have you ever purchased software from a vendor and then made several illegal copies for your boss, subordinates, or co-workers? Have you ever transferred copyrighted software via electronic bulletin boards? If you answered yes to either of the previous questions, you are practicing **software piracy** and thus are putting your company in jeopardy of costly fines, added expenses, and potential lawsuits.

Large and small software companies lose over $2 billion annually because of software piracy. As a result, companies are starting to fight back by way of the Software Publishers Association (SPA). This group represents nearly five hundred personal computer software publishers. The association is currently sending letters to chief executive officers of corporations who are believed to have illegal copies of software within their company. The SPA conducts an audit on those companies to identify any illegal software that has not been legitimately purchased from the software company. If the company is guilty of software piracy, the penalty may include fines as high as $500,000. In addition, the company must purchase legal copies of all pirated software.

Five Practical Steps to Ensure Computer Security

If the ARPAnet case is an indication of how the legal system will deal with creators of computer viruses, then companies cannot depend on the law to deter such activities. The security of computer systems must be currently viewed as beyond the scope of law enforcement. Thus information and business managers must build and operate secure computer systems. If hardware or software (or both) is purchased from a vendor, managers must ensure that security is a critical component of the system.

Business managers and computer users must continue to be aware of the importance of computer security. They must understand the

Real World Perspective

Software Publishers Association Catches Pirate

The Software Publishers Association is a Washington-based lobby group representing more than five hundred companies in the PC software industry. The SPA announced in May 1991 that it had won a $350,000 settlement against Parametrix Corporation, which had been charged with illegal copying. The suit was brought in February 1990, when the SPA and federal marshalls raided the firm.

According to Parametrix, the firm had been moving toward internal control of software copying but didn't get legal fast enough. In fact, Parametrix believed that as of 1 March 1990, there was no more illegal software in the building.

Parametrix was happy with the settlement because the eventual cost of the damages from the lawsuit would have been much more than the settlement.

importance of protecting the information that resides on their computers. Demonstrating good computer security practices and procedures is essential to protecting against data loss and destruction.

Computer security must clearly be addressed as a top priority whenever networks link various computers and companies together. A vulnerability on one system may lead to compromise on all other systems connected to the network.

Steps that managers can take to reduce their vulnerability to computer viruses include the following:

■ Install anti-virus software.

■ Test sample diskettes from each mass shipment.

■ Prohibit the sharing of software or diskettes.

■ Check periodically for unexpected changes in program size and other signs of viruses.

Steps that managers can take to reduce software piracy include the following:

■ Verify the authenticity and integrity of software before using it.

■ Purchase enough copies of software from vendors to meet demand and to make illegal copying less tempting.

Protecting Your Personal Computer

The new personal computers bring with them some new security features and some new security concerns. These machines come equipped with two password facilities. The first is a power-on password, which is invoked when the computer is turned on. The second is a keyboard password, which can be invoked when away from your desk for an extended period. Both of these facilities *seem* to provide good security. However, since both can be easily bypassed, they may not prevent a knowledgeable person from accessing your computer.

There are also access control packages (menu managers) with password protection, which may give you a false sense of security. BEWARE! These packages are invoked by a boot-up batch file and can be bypassed by pressing CTRL-BREAK during execution of the batch file routine or by booting from a DOS diskette.

PC security software is available (e.g., SecretDisk II) that enables you to protect sensitive information without putting your entire PC under lock and key. Such software conceals your private files on a logical disk drive where all data and programs are encrypted and password protected. Only your password can unlock and decrypt your information.

For those who prefer hardware controls, there is also a keylock for the personal computer that will lock out both the keyboard and the mouse. Disk drives equipped with individual locks are also available.

PC users must also protect against the outright theft of the entire machine itself! Experts estimate that more than ten thousand laptop computers are stolen each year.

■ DISASTER PLANNING

While disasters are generally unpredictable, for the unprepared company hit by one, the results are generally predictable. Interruptions in business operations, loss of revenue, decreased quality of service, and high costs for providing limited interim service affect the company's stockholders, employees, and customers. In addition to the catastrophic impact on the company, senior management may also suffer personally. Legal action can be taken if it can be proven that management was negligent by not providing for the security and continued operation of the company through good contingency planning.

In spite of these high stakes, less than half of roughly 250,000 U.S. data processing sites have an adequate disaster plan. Only slightly more than 1 percent of these sites subscribe to commercial facilities that could provide alternate processing site services in the event of a major disaster. A study conducted by the New York research firm of Find/SVP, surveyed 450 executives at Fortune 1000 firms. It found that unplanned systems downtime occurs nine times a year on average, that systems stay down an average of four hours, and that customer dissatisfaction and lost productivity are the two most negative effects of the crashes. Based on this study, it is projected that computer service interruptions cost U.S. businesses over $4 billion a year and result in more than 37 million hours in lost worker productivity.

Fortunately, managers are beginning to realize the potential impact a computer disaster could bring their company. As a result, those companies that depend heavily on the availability of data processing services to continue day-to-day operations are establishing a disaster recovery plan.

Since the exact nature of a disaster cannot be predicted, management cannot plan for a specific disaster. However, **contingency plans** can be prepared, not only for the generic disaster but also for any probable scenario. Such a plan outlines what is to be done in the event that a fire, flood, power failure, terrorist activity, or some other occurrence renders the existing business and/or computer facilities unusable. Such a plan reduces the number of snap judgment decisions that must be made at a time when people are under intense pressure to restore company operations. A good disaster recovery plan facilitates the smooth and rapid restoration of critical business operations. Exhibit 14.7 summarizes several major disasters.

Scope of Contingency Plan

The scope of the contingency plan must address the following areas:

■ Identification of key personnel to be contacted in the event of an emergency. Such a list includes employees, senior officers of the company, vendor contacts, key suppliers and customers, and contacts at organizations that can provide aid, such as local fire and police departments.

Exhibit 14.7
The Ten Worst U.S. Information Technology Disasters

Source: Joseph C. Panettieri. "Survival of the Fittest." InformationWeek, *January 10, 1994.*

Rank	Description	Date	Data Centers Hit
#1	Nationwide Internet virus	May 1988	500+
#2	Chicago flood	April 1992	400
#3	New York power outage	August 1990	320
#4	Chicago/Hinsdale fire	May 1988	175
#5	Hurrican Andrew	Sept 1992	150
#6	Nationwide Pakistani virus	May 1988	90+
#7	San Francisco earthquake	Oct 1989	90
#8	Seattle power outage	August 1988	75
#9	Chicago flood	August 1987	64
#10	East coast blizzard	March 1993	50
#10	Los Angeles riot	April/May 1992	50

■ An outline of disaster recovery guidelines that spell out the role that each of the previously mentioned key people must take in the event of a disaster.

■ A step-by-step guide of what actions must be taken to communicate the problem to the necessary people and to restore operations to an agreed-to level sufficient to support critical business operations. A well-designed set of procedures can help bring a little order to chaos.

■ Procedures to retrieve backup files and update them to current status. Most companies make multiple files of critical data and store one or more copies off-site, away from the data center.

■ Procedures to establish an adequate hardware, electric utility, and telecommunications environment to provide the agreed-to level of support for critical operations. Some companies make arrangements with other companies to share similar computer equipment in the event of a disaster. Others actually acquire duplicate hardware and build a backup data center.

■ Procedures to establish an appropriate software environment for backup operations. A current copy of the operating system as well as the application software must be available in the event the original is unusable.

■ Procedures to restore operations or transfer them to an alternate site in the event of a disaster in the system user area. It is entirely possible that a fire or other problem may affect the user work area without causing any damage to the data center. Managers recognize that if the data center is inoperable, the corporation as a whole is at risk. However, it is essential to recognize that if any of the corporate operations outside the data center are damaged, the disruption can be just as great!

Management should work with users of each critical system to ensure that there is a good disaster recovery plan. The first step in setting up a disaster recovery plan (see Exhibit 14.8) is to perform a thorough

Exhibit 14.8
Developing a
Disaster Recovery
Plan

1. Perform a risk assessment.
2. Recommend and implement safeguards.
3. Develop a priority list of computer applications.
4. Define disaster recovery plans for high-priority systems.
5. Practice the emergency alternate procedures.

risk assessment using the nine-step model used for security analysis, which was shown in Exhibit 14.3. This frequently involves sending both IT and non-IT people to data processing locations to identify threats to each individual environment—for example, a location particularly vulnerable to power brownouts.

After the initial survey, the team then analyzes the possibility of a loss caused by the identified threat. The principle of reasonable assurance should be used to recommend those safeguards that are cost effective to implement.

A priority list of the computer applications should also be developed. Many companies identify three classes of systems: (1) those that must be restored immediately and whose continued operation are absolutely essential for the day-to-day operation of the company (e.g., accounts receivable), (2) those that must eventually be restored—say, within a week or so of a disaster, and (3) those that may be deferred indefinitely without a major impact on the organization (see Exhibit 14.9).

Exhibit 14.9
A Sample Priority
List of Computer
Applications

Highest-Priority Computer Applications
Those applications that affect the cash flow or manage the assets of the company. The company may be in serious trouble and unable to function if these are lost even for just part of a day.

- Order entry
- Accounts receivable
- Customer billing
- Inventory control
- Payroll

Medium-Priority Computer Applications
These applications are important to the company but do not need to be restored immediately. The company can continue to run for a few days without the information or results produced by these applications.

- Capital forecast
- Budget reporting
- Sales analysis reporting

Lower-Priority Computer Applications
Although these applications benefit the company and are used to help control or manage the business, they are not essential to its operation or survival. The company can continue operating indefinitely without them.

- Personnel department productivity reports
- Office space planning

All this planning for a potential computer disaster is of little value if the plan does not really work or if people do not understand it. It is critical that at least once a year the plan is put to the test in a simulated computer disaster and that people are forced to follow the emergency alternate procedures.

Uninterruptible Power Source

Large computer systems require uninterrupted and controlled power supplies. Plugging such systems directly into electrical lines causes major problems. If the power is lost, even momentarily, the data and programs stored in semi-conductor primary storage are lost. Power spikes (increases in current voltage, often caused by thunderstorms) can heavily damage a computer system.

Most data centers have some sort of uninterruptible power system (**UPS**). But unless it is complete with long-running diesel generators, the UPS provides power for only five to fifteen minutes. This is time enough to bring everything down in a controlled shutdown so that data and programs are not lost. Fortunately, most power outages last less than three hours. It is possible, however, that a corporation could be faced with a major long-term power outage as the result of an earthquake, tornado, or other natural disaster. A standard UPS would be of little value at that point, even though the corporation was untouched in the disaster.

Many organizations install their own power supply systems to ensure a dependable and ''clean'' source of electrical power free of spikes. Such a system consists of batteries and backup generators. The batteries are continuously charged by the incoming public electrical service, and the computer draws its power from the batteries. A surge suppressor at the utility service entrance is recommended to protect the computer equipment, the UPS itself, and the electronic components in the data center air-conditioning equipment. The computer is thus insulated from the electrical service lines and power spikes are prevented. If there is a power outage, the batteries will be sufficient for a short duration. The backup diesel generator provides electricity over an extended period of time during longer-lasting power outages.

Large industrial batteries used to back up computer systems in the event of a power failure pose a risk. The problem occurs when acid eats away the unit's electrical connections. The degree of corrosion may be invisible to the eye. But when the current stored within the power cell is tapped during a power outage, even minor damage permits heat to rapidly build up and cause an explosion. Large chunks of metal can fly across the room, injuring employees and damaging equipment. The only way to guard against this problem is to test battery resistance levels on an ongoing basis, something that 75 percent of data centers using batteries for emergency backup fail to do, which places both their employees and their computers in danger.

Telecommunications

The potential consequences of a public telephone network failure are on the minds of every corporate IT director in the United States today—and with good reason. Dozens of random network outages caused by line breaks or hardware or software failures occur across the country on a weekly basis, most of them going unnoticed and unreported except by the company that is directly affected.

The bigger the disaster, the more public notice it gains. A fire in a Hinsdale, Illinois, telephone company office wiped out use of 118,000 long-distance lines, 36,000 digital private lines, and 35,000 local analog lines; the cost in network downtime for affected companies ran into millions.

For their part in attempting to avoid a major problem, the major communication carriers (AT&T, MCI, and Sprint) are building light-wave systems that form a nationwide grid with many alternative paths for route diversity. They are installing better switching mechanisms that enable most network failures to be bypassed within milliseconds without any significant service interruption to users. They are also upgrading their long-distance network with fault-tolerant computers. For individual business organizations, network redundancy is also the strategy. Dial-up backup circuits are installed for critical information paths. Alternate routing schemes are devised, and care is taken to divide up critical circuits among the major communications carriers to minimize the effects of any one network failure.

Even with diversity, self-healing networks, and other safety measures, there is really no such thing as a risk-free networking environment. Realistically, no company can be entirely protected against every possible network failure.

Real World Perspective

UPS Helps Manufacturer

For one family-owned company in Oklahoma's infamous "Tornado Alley," expecting the worst from the weather is just business as usual. Even when the area is not breeding tornados, violent seasonal storms are common.

Kim-Ray Corp of Oklahoma City makes pressure valves for the oil-drilling industry. They really rely on UPS during the storm season. Before UPS was installed, every time there was a flicker of lightening, they could count on something going down. In fact, several years ago, Kim-Ray's shop floor was taken out not once but four times in rapid succession during a particularly nasty storm spell. Each time it took about four hours to get going again.

The company initially installed an on-line UPS system to protect its data collection system. Subsequently, after payroll, accounting, invoicing, and manufacturing applications were developed on a mid-range computer, a larger UPS was installed to protect it as well. If the computer goes down, all work stops. Now when storm clouds gather in Tornado Alley, lightening poses no threat to Kim-Ray Operations. SOURCE: "When Nature Calls," in "The Critical Power Protection Match-Up, Information vs. Infrastructure." InformationWeek, September 28, 1992. □

Real World Perspective
Alternate Strategies on Disaster Planning

Chemical Bank of New York processes business transactions worth an estimated $160 billion per day—a sum large enough to disrupt the national economy if a significant interruption in its telecommunications capability ever occurred. Management's assessment of the bank's vulnerability showed that in the case of a long-distance network failure, not all of its critical systems would be affected. In addition to its voice network, Chemical Bank has twenty thousand on-line terminals, widely dispersed throughout the United States. With even a serious network problem, not all these terminals would be immediately affected, especially if local telephone company facilities were available. For its national data

network, Chemical has built a dedicated broadband system with complete backup facilities, using combinations of AT&T, MCI, and Sprint long-distance carriers for protection against the failure of one of them.

On the other hand, Corning is an example of a company that is reluctant to invest in the expense of an elaborate alternative routing or contingency plan in case of a national telephone network failure. This is primarily because Corning's main business with its customers is not as information intensive as a bank or financial service. Corning is not a high-transaction-volume company that can be disrupted by a few minutes of downtime.

Business and IT managers need to raise senior management's consciousness to the need for hybrid (i.e., public and private) network architectures, as well as use of multiple common carriers. If communications is strategic to the organization, the company needs to retain private networks for critical applications and divert overflow traffic to public networks.

Alternate Data Processing Site

In the event that a disaster destroys the data center, data processing capability to support critical business operations must be reestablished at a backup site. There are essentially four backup site strategies, which are illustrated in Exhibit 14.10.

One strategy adopted by some companies is to enter into a **reciprocal agreement** with another company. Following this approach, companies with similar hardware configurations agree with one another to permit short-term sharing of the unaffected data center until the company experiencing the disaster is up and running again. Contingency planning thus becomes a cooperative effort between the two companies. The primary advantage of this strategy is that it is inexpensive. However, such an approach may only serve to provide a false sense of security. If a disaster occurs at one company, both companies are forced to reduce their level of data processing services to support only those operations critical to the business. Even support of just the critical operations for the two companies may require more capacity than the single company's data center can provide. Thus the operation of both companies can become tenuous. Worse yet, the disaster could be widespread and affect both companies (e.g., a flood or earthquake), leaving both companies with no data processing capability.

Exhibit 14.10
Options for Alternate Data Processing Sites

Company A
Data Center Fully
Operational

Company B
Data Center Fully
Operational

Option 1

Company A
Data Center Fully
Operational

Cold Site

Option 2

Company A
Data Center Fully
Operational

Hot Site
Data Center Fully
Operational,
Provided By Disaster
Recovery Service

Option 3

Company A
Data Center #1 Fully
Operational

Company A
Data Center #2 Fully
Operational

Option 4

Another approach is to arrange for a **cold site,** or a facility to house a mainframe computer system including environmental control, electrical service, and telecommunications facilities. The company may contract with a disaster recovery service to provide a cold site in case of a disaster, or may rent, lease, or purchase suitable space. In the event of a disaster, the affected company must provide its own hardware. Thus after a disaster, a company must obtain and install an entire computer system. This strategy places extremely high pressure on quick installation of an operating data center. It may be appropriate if the company can afford to be down for several days.

A strategy taken by companies that must be assured of rapid recovery in the event of a disaster is the **hot site** arrangement. The hot site contains a complete data center including a working mainframe computer system compatible with the one it is backing up. The company may decide to contract with a disaster recovery service to provide a hot site in case of disaster. This strategy can be very expensive, but minimizes downtime and enables the company to be up and running in a matter of a few hours. In forming a contract with the disaster recovery service, the company needs to be aware that the same disaster might affect several companies with contracts for emergency use of the same hot site.

A lower-cost variation of the hot site strategy can be used by companies with more than one data center. In the event of a disaster, one

Exhibit 14.11
The Most Common
Causes of
Computer
Downtime

*Source: George Vorsheim,
"Computer Fires Cause
Most Downtime,"* ISP
News, *March–April 1990,
published by
Environment/One,
Schenectady, New York
12309.*

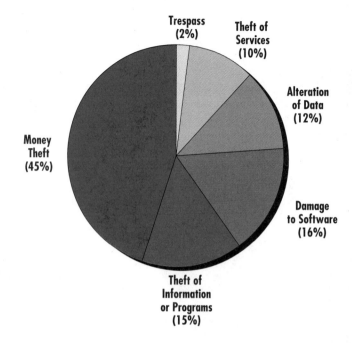

of the data centers backs up the other. In the event of a disaster, non-critical operations are suspended and the second data center provides support for all of the company's essential applications.

Fire Control

Fire is the most likely physical threat to a computer facility (Exhibit 14.11). The best fire control is to store backup copies of data and programs at another location and to arrange for emergency use of alternative computer hardware. In addition, many computer centers use a fire suppression gas known as *halon.* (Water can destroy the computer's sensitive electronic equipment.) The halon is released by fire and smoke detection systems and is effective in extinguishing fires. The primary disadvantage of halon is cost. If the gas is accidentally released, a firm may have to pay several thousand dollars to replace it. Less expensive gases exist but are impractical because they are poisonous; halon is not.

Real World Perspectives

Diaster Hits Financial Center

On Monday, 13 August 1990, disaster hit. A blaze roared through a lower Manhattan electrical substation, reducing it to molten slag. By week's end, New York's financial center was reeling from the resulting blackout as loss of business, due in large part to the shutdown of computer and phone systems, mounted into the hundreds of millions of dollars.

IT managers for a dozen major banks declared disasters, and more than three hundred Manhattan-based businesses went on the alert. The extent of damage to corporate IT operations appeared to exceed even the harm caused by the 1989 earthquake in San Francisco. As late as Thursday, some five thousand homes and offices, including more than fifty financial institutions, remained without power. Chief among those was the Federal Reserve Bank of New York, whose electronic funds transfer services, collectively known as Fedwire, were unable to open.

Fedwire, the main electronic payments system in the country, connects Federal Reserve banks, the Treasury Department, and other federal agencies with roughly eight thousand depository institutions. The New York Fed uses the system to clear some $900 billion on an average day.

By midday Thursday, Fedwire service had been restored, but not until the Fed had shifted its settlement operations to a hot site in Pearl River, New York. The system had been operating on emergency power since the fire broke out, but problems with one of the backup generators forced Fedwire off-line and caused the Fed to move its operations.

Other firms that were hard hit were Citibank N.A., Prudential-Bache Securities, Credit Lyonnaise, and Manufacturers Hanover Trust Company. All of these firms experienced problems with their emergency backup generators and were forced to shift their computer operations to alternate sites.

Disaster Planning Pays Off at Banker's Trust

A series of brief power failures that disrupted computer operations at Banker's Trust Company jolted the firm's upper management. Although the outages were minor, bank executives realized that even a slightly longer occurrence at the wrong time could cost the bank millions. They decided that disaster avoidance can be viewed as another way of making money—by not losing it.

After the outages, a senior-level committee was quickly established to look at potential sources of system failure. Nearly $10 million was spent to shore up key support systems on which IT depends. The program includes extensive emergency training for bank employees, including staging mock blackouts at the bank's data centers twice a year.

When a fire in an electrical substation knocked out service to lower Manhattan in August 1990, emergency systems at Bankers Trust Company kicked in so swiftly that the bank hardly missed a beat.

Financial Services Firms Band Together for Disaster Recovery

Several financial services firms have banded together to spur development of a joint disaster recovery facility with full trading capabilities. For these technology-heavy companies that means no more scrambling during phone or power outages.

The project began in 1990 when 14 New York-based firms, Dean Witter, and Morgan Stanley Group Inc. kicked in $5,000 apiece to sponsor a study. Interviews were held with more than 300 of these firms' employees including head traders, Chief Information Officers, and telecommunications directors. After reviewing these results, the group put out a joint Request for Proposal to meet their combined needs. Contingency Trading Facility Inc. was the winner and agreed to provide backup services for a one-time membership fee of $5,000 and a $10,000 emergency declaration charge for each disaster.
SOURCE: "Hot Site Hot Issue for Trading Firms." Mary E. Thyfault with Diane Medina. InformationWeek, January 27, 1992. Copyright © 1992 by CMP Publications, Inc., 600 Community Drive, Manhasset, NY 11030. Reprinted from InformationWeek with permission. □

Continued

IT Audit Checklist

Access Control to the Computer Center

1. Is the location readily identifiable as a computer center?
2. Is there a secure means to control access to the computer center?
3. Must visitors request an appointment in advance?
4. Is the movement of visitors restricted or controlled?
5. Do employees challenge unfamiliar visitors?

Access Control to the Communications Center

1. Are areas that provide electronic communications for the computer center adequately protected with safeguards equivalent to those for the operations area?
2. Is there adequate air conditioning for the communications center equipment and personnel?
3. Is there good electrical power with battery backup and devices to protect against power spikes or brownouts?
4. Are there locks on all phone company connection rooms?
5. Are there alarms in major connection rooms?
6. Are there multiple routing paths for critical communication lines?
7. Are the identity and authorization of employees of the phone company verified?

Access Control to Computing Resources

1. Are vital software and documentation kept in a safe and secure location?
2. Are copies of vital software and documentation stored in a backup location in case a disaster (fire, earthquake) destroys the data center?
3. Is access to essential software and documentation restricted to a need-to-know basis?
4. Are changes to software documented as to who made them and when they were made, for trace purposes?

5. Are security software utilities and access codes used? Are they periodically validated?
6. Are passwords required to identify terminal users?
7. Are users required to change their passwords frequently?
8. Does the operating system have built-in protection to prevent bypassing other security software?
9. Does the security software provide multiple-level access control to files and data bases?
10. Are programming changes documented and controlled?

Fire Protection

1. Are fire resistant materials used for partitions, walls, doors, and furnishings?
2. Are heat or smoke detection devices installed?
3. Do these devices automatically turn off air conditioning?
4. Are required paper supplies and other combustible materials stored away from the computer area?
5. Is smoking restricted?
6. Do the fire extinguishers use carbon dioxide, a halogenated agent, or water?
7. Are personnel trained in firefighting?
8. Are fire drills conducted regularly?
9. Are emergency power switches (including air conditioning) located at the exits?
10. Are there heavy-duty fire dampers in all air ducts?
11. Does insurance cover losses due to fire, water, or smoke damage?

Protection against Flooding or Water Damage

1. Is the computer room located below the water grade?
2. Do overhead steam or water pipes exist?
3. Is the computer equipment water cooled?
4. Is there good drainage under the raised floor of the computer room, on the floors above, or adjacent areas?

Continued

5. Are plastic covers readily available to protect equipment from water leakage?
6. Are there anti-backup drains in the floor?
7. Does insurance cover flood and water damage?

Electric Power

1. Is the data center located where the power supply is considered to be reliable?
2. In the event of a power outage, how long would it take to have power restored to the area?
3. Are there surges in electric power due to nearby heavy equipment or for other reasons?
4. Is there a need for power protection against surges or brownouts?
5. Is there a need for battery backup?

Air Conditioning

1. Does the data center have its own dedicated air-conditioning system?
2. Are backup air-conditioning facilities available?
3. Does the emergency power-off switch include air conditioning?
4. Can temperature and humidity be regulated and monitored even when the computer room is unattended?

Personnel Considerations

1. Is a background check performed on job applicants before hiring (including fingerprinting)?
2. Are employee background checks updated after employment?
3. Is there a manager in charge of computer security with clear and well-defined responsibilities?
4. Are there policies and procedures that relate to computer security and computer backup?
5. Are operations personnel well trained, and do they understand security policies and procedures?
6. Do operations personnel consider security an important part of their jobs?
7. Is there a list of authorized vendor service personnel?
8. Is positive identification required before vendor service personnel are admitted to the data center?

9. Are vendor service personnel supervised while in the data center?
10. Is a record kept of all visitors who enter the data center?
11. Are vendor employee background checks required? Are they verified?
12. Are nonexempt employees supervised by an exempt employee during each shift?
13. Are terminated or reassigned personnel required to return all keys, materials, access badges, and the like that were assigned to them?
14. When an employee is terminated or re-assigned, are passwords, procedures, and locks changed to deny access to that employee?

Business Resumption Planning

1. Has a formal, written disaster recovery plan been approved?
2. Is there a specific manager in charge of disaster recovery planning, and does that person have clear and well-understood responsibilities?
3. Have the various application systems been classified as to relative priority in the event of limited computer resources?
4. Have users of the various application systems developed emergency alternate procedures? Are these procedures tested in a realistic manner at least once a year?
5. Is there a backup data center or alternate computer included in the disaster recovery plan? Has there ever been a test to run critical applications at the backup data center?
6. Are extra copies made of critical files, data sets, and data bases—both master files and transaction files? Are these extra copies stored at a location other than the primary data center?
7. Are extra copies made of program source code, program load modules, and program documentation? Are these stored at a location other than the primary data center?
8. Are there copies of the current operating system and other systems software necessary to create the proper operating environment at the backup data center? Are these stored at a location other than the primary data center?
9. Are there recovery procedures for computer operator errors that may inadvertently destroy valuable data or programs?
10. Is there at least an annual simulation of a complete loss of the data center and a thorough testing of the entire disaster recovery plan?

Summary

Computer crime is a serious management problem. Only one percent of all computer crimes are detected, and only seven percent of these detected crimes are reported to the police.

Managers employ the concept of reasonable assurance to ensure that the cost of a control does not exceed the benefit to be obtained by its implementation. Possible risk must also be evaluated.

Business managers must retain primary responsibility for controlling the business functions they assign to process on a computer.

The system designer is responsible for pointing out and reviewing all exposures to risk with the business manager.

An organization can use risk management to identify the importance of security to the firm and then allocate the resources to obtain the desired level of security.

Those companies that depend heavily on the availability of data processing services to continue day-to-day operations are establishing disaster recovery plans. Such plans need to be well documented and tested periodically.

This chapter includes a useful IT audit checklist that can be used to assess the adequacy of a data center's security and disaster recovery plan.

A Manager's Checklist

✔ Does your firm have a disaster recovery plan? Is it tested periodically?

✔ Is computer crime treated as a serious issue in your firm?

✔ Are business managers held responsible for controlling the business functions they assign for processing on the computer?

✔ Are system designers encouraged to point out and review all exposures to risk with the business manager?

Key Terms

access security	hacker
ciphertext	hot site
cleartext	internal control
cold site	plain text
communications security	reasonable assurance
computer crime	reciprocal agreement
computer virus	risk management
contingency plan	software piracy
cryptography	UPS
data encryption	

Review Questions

1. What is the concept of reasonable assurance?

2. How can the segregation of business functions lead to improved internal control?

3. Outline specific actions you can take to protect your personal computer and the data on it.

4. What steps can a business manager take to improve the computer security of an organization?

5. What are the key elements of a disaster recovery plan?

6. What options exist for providing an alternate data processing site?

Discussion Questions

1. How much computer security is enough?

2. How much effort should be spent in developing a disaster recovery plan versus effort spent in trying to avoid a disaster?

3. Given that most computer crime is perpetrated by insiders, do you believe that companies should implement tougher screening of prospective employees and weed out those who appear to be security risks? If so, how might they do this?

Recommended Readings

1. Coleman, Randall M. "Six Steps to Contingency Planning." *ISP News* (March–April 1990).

2. Fletcher, Sue. "Prevention Is Better than Cure." *Public Finance and Accountancy* (2 February 1990).

3. Miles, J. B. "Network at Risk." *InformationWeek* (23 July 1990).

4. Weyhausen, Catherine. "The Key to Disaster Recovery." *ISP News* (March–April 1990).

5. Vorsheim, George. "Computer Fires Cause the Most Downtime." *IPS News* (March–April 1990).

6. Klein, Paula. "The More Things Change . . . Client/Server Raises Demand for UPS Systems, Hot Sites." *InformationWeek* (16 August 1993).

7. Levi, Philip. "Your PCs Are More Vulnerable Than You Think." *Chief Information Officer Journal* (March–April 1993).

A Manager's Dilemma

An Intentional Security Leak?

It has been three months since you left your old firm to come to one of its major competitors. You received a promotion and a 20 percent salary increase and have no regrets, even though it seems you are working harder than ever before. It's after 6:00 P.M., and you are about to leave for the day. Just for kicks, you dial the phone number to gain access to the computer at your old firm. Your hands tremble just a little as you enter your old log-on ID and password. To your utter amazement, the computer responds to your codes and grants you access to the on-line budget and marketing information system! You can't believe it!

The budget and marketing data base contains secret data about the firm's plans for future product research and development, plus details of future product promotions including budget amounts and timing. Gaining access to this data will allow you to know in advance every new market initiative your former company plans to make and will allow your new firm to beat them to the punch!

You proceed to request information for the next quarter's marketing plan and print it off. You then log off the computer, stuff the printouts in your briefcase, and go home for the night.

That night you find it difficult to sleep because you are so excited! You wonder if you should share your findings with other members of your staff and work together on a strategy to thwart each new initiative of your former employee. Or perhaps you should just keep the data to yourself and then look like a genius as you are able to call each move of the competition. As you are dozing off, a disturbing thought enters your mind: What if you were intentionally granted access to the data base and the data you captured were phony plans to trick you into making the wrong moves at the wrong time?

If this were you, what would you do?

Catching Software Pirates

Imagine that you are the chief investigator for the Software Publishers Association, a Washington-based lobby group representing more than seven hundred companies in the PC software industry. As chief auditor, your staff investigates companies to find evidence of illegal software copying.

If found guilty, the company may pay fines in excess of $100,000. In addition, the firm must purchase legal copies of all pirated software. Usually, suits are settled out of court for less than $300,000.

Identify at least three good sources for tips on firms that may be copying software illegally.

What evidence of proof of purchase would you expect a firm to be able to provide?

What safeguards and policies would you expect to see in firms to discourage their employees from copying software?

Case Study 14.3 — Where's the Disaster Recovery Plan?

As the recently hired director of IT, you are alarmed at the total lack of disaster recovery planning. There is no backup computing facility, almost no insurance other than fire protection, and users have defined only manual emergency alternate procedures that have never been tested. Such lack of planning is an embarrassment for a major insurance company with annual sales in excess of $500 million!

You were hired specifically to streamline office procedures and paperwork by applying computer-based technology. Management expects major reductions in the number of clerical staff as a result of your work. You are now faced with a dilemma—how to tell management of the sad state of affairs and convince them of the urgency for strong immediate action even though it may delay the projects needed to make the company more profitable.

How can you convince management to defer some of their pet projects and turn their attention to the need for a disaster plan? Or, is it possible to address disaster planning simultaneously with the development of major new systems?

Case Study 14.4 — Applying the IT Audit Checklist

Get permission from a data center manager to conduct an interview and to inspect the data center facilities using the audit checklist presented at the end of this chapter. What are your findings? What recommendations would you make based on these findings?

GLOSSARY

acceptance test   A test conducted to demonstrate to the system owner and users that the system delivered supports all functional requirements and adheres to quality and performance objectives.

access method   A data base management system uses an access method to handle the details of physical access to data that might be physically disaggregated and stored on multiple storage devices. The access method retrieves and aggregates the data into the simple, logical format needed by an application program.

access security   Ensures that only authorized people can gain access to computer input/output devices.

accountability   A system characteristic that permits the identification of those persons responsible for its performance.

accounts payable system   A system that provides control over payments to suppliers, issues checks to those suppliers, and provides information for effective cash management.

accounts receivable system   A system that is used for billing customers, maintaining records of amounts due from customers, and providing data for effective credit management.

accuracy   A qualitative assessment of freedom from error.

active data dictionary   One closely integrated with a data base management system so that it can enforce the same definition of data in all executable programs that reference the data base management system.

ad hoc request   A request for information that has not been previously specified.

ADA   A multipurpose, procedure-oriented language developed by the U.S. Department of Defense.

address   A particular portion of storage or some other data source or destination.

algorithm   A rule or procedure for solving a problem.

alpha test   The in-house testing of a software product by the vendor prior to its release for beta testing.

alphanumeric   A character set that contains letters, digits, punctuation, and special symbols (related to alpha and numeric).

analog   Pertaining to data consisting of continuously variable physical quantities.

analog computer   A computer that processes analog data.

analysis graphics   Graphics that help users to analyze and understand detailed statistical data by representing them in charts and graphs.

analyst   A person who defines problems and develops algorithms and procedures for solutions to problems.

ANSI   American National Standards Institute. Develops and maintains standards on many aspects of information system technology.

APL   A Programming Language. A programming language with an unusual syntax and character set, primarily designed for mathematical applications, particularly those involving numeric or literal arrays.

application   A problem or task to which the computer can be applied.

application backlog   Information systems projects approved but not yet started.

application development group   The information system group responsible for developing new business applications to meet business needs.

application generator   A programming tool that allows programmers to specify what processing tasks are to be performed; the tool then generates the programs to perform those tasks.

application programmer   A programmer who writes or maintains (or both writes and maintains) application programs.

application prototyping   A system development approach in which system developers and users form a working model of an application system that meets the current best definition of user needs. As user needs become more completely defined through use of the prototype system, the system is modified.

applications portfolio   The collection of potential information systems that an organization may elect to implement.

applications software   Computer program instructions that enable a computer to perform a specific operation or business function, such as prepare the company payroll or track account receivables.

architecture A model that captures the needs and wants of a customer within the constraints of a set of established standards, or the infrastructure. It usually integrates principles and standards in a new and useful way.

archival storage Data storage not under the direct control of the computer on which backup information and records not frequently needed are kept.

artificial intelligence A broad area of computer science that explores how computers can be used to perform tasks requiring the human characteristics of intelligence, intuition, and imagination.

ASCII American Standard Code for Information Interchange. A 7-bit binary code with an additional eighth bit for parity checking.

assemble To translate a program expressed in an assembly language into a machine language equivalent.

assembly language A low-level symbolic language whose statements may be instructions or declarations. The instructions usually have a one-to-one correspondence with machine instructions.

asymmetric multiprocessing A computer architecture in which the computer has more than one CPU and each processor handles a different task, such as general processing or input/output operations.

asynchronous transmission A data transmission method in which each byte of data is transmitted separately.

attenuation The law of nature that a signal attenuates (grows weaker) as it travels farther from its source.

attribute A particular characteristic of interest about an entity.

audio teleconferencing A form of telephone communications that involves the use of a special speaker and microphone system to enable everyone in a room who speaks to be heard by all people involved in the audio conference, including people who may be in a distant conference room.

audit trail A history of some aspect of the firm's activity that enables past activity to be reconstructed.

auditability The capability to reconstruct processing steps and trace information back to its origins.

backbone LAN A local area network that serves a fairly large geographical area, such as a campus or group of buildings. It may connect two or more local area networks. The backbone local area network may have hundreds or even thousands of nodes and may provide service to people in multiple departments or buildings.

backup Pertaining to equipment, procedures, or data bases that can be used to restart the system in the event of a failure.

backward chaining A form of inference used in an expert system that starts with the *then* part of an if/then statement; when this part matches the same component in a problem, the system searches for the appropriate *if* clauses.

baseband LAN A local area network that uses transmission media over which all communications take place on the same channel.

BASIC Beginners All-purpose Symbolic Instructional Code. A high-level programming language with a small number of statements and a simple syntax; it is widely used in writing interactive applications for microcomputers.

batch An accumulation of data to be processed.

batch query A request for data that is handled in a batch data processing mode with a number of requests accumulated and handled as a set of requests.

batch total The sum resulting from the addition of a specific numeric field from each record in a batch of records; used for control and checking purposes.

batch update processing system A business system for which transactions are accumulated over a period of time and prepared for input to the computer as a single unit or batch. Thus, for such a system, there is a delay between the occurrence of an event and the eventual processing of the related transaction to update the organization's records.

baud A unit of signaling speed equal to the number of discrete conditions or signal events per second.

benchmark program A sample program that is representative of at least part of the buyer's primary computer workload and that is executed on various computer configurations to provide information useful in making a computer acquisition decision.

benchmark test A test for comparing the performance of several computer hardware systems while running the same software or comparing the performance of several programs that are run on the same computer.

beta test The testing of a software product in a live environment prior to its release to the public.

bid invitation A letter sent to qualified vendors to request a formal proposal to a business need.

bill of material The list of parts and subassemblies, along with their quantities, that go into the production of a finished good.

binary A condition that has two possible values.

bit Data that is to be processed or stored in a computer is represented as binary numbers (0 or 1) called bits.

bit mapped A system in which each possible dot of a video display is controlled by a single bit of memory.

bootstrap   A program used to start (or boot) the computer, usually by clearing the primary memory, setting up various devices, and loading the operating system from secondary storage or read-only memory.

bottleneck   A slowdown in one part of the system that can cause the entire system to operate below capacity.

boundary   The area that separates one system from another.

BPI   Bits per inch. A measure of the data-recording density on secondary storage.

BPS   Bits per second. The number of bits that can be transmitted per second over a communications channel.

breakeven analysis   An evaluation technique that calculates the time required for total project tangible benefits to equal total project costs.

bridge   A protocol-independent hardware device that permits data communications between devices on separate networks.

broadband LAN   A local area network that uses transmission media that carry data over multiple channels.

bubble memory   A memory device that uses no power. It uses a thin magnetic recording film that looks like bubbles.

budget forecasting model   A model used to consolidate budget information provided by separate departments using standard accounting practices. It may include capabilities to forecast cash flow, earnings per share, and other financial ratios resulting from performance according to budget.

bug   A logic or syntax error in a program, a logic error in the design of a computer system, or a hardware fault.

bundling   The selling of hardware and software together as a package.

bus   A pathway or channel for moving data and instructions between hardware devices.

bus local area network   A computer network that permits the connection of terminals, peripheral devices, and microcomputers along an open-ended central cable.

business area analysis   A stage of the information engineering process which involves examination of key business elements within a defined business area.

business graphics   Pictorial representation of business data.

business information planning   A structured approach for getting system planners more closely involved with business managers and upper-level management to identify overall information and system needs.

business reengineering   The fundamental analysis and design of everything associated with a business area to achieve dramatic performance improvement and the management of associated business changes.

byte   A binary character string operated upon as a unit and usually shorter than a computer word.

C   A microcomputer and computer programming language that supports structured programming. It can perform many tasks that would normally require the use of assembly language.

CAD   Computer-Aided Design or Computer-Assisted Design. The term covers a wide range of systems that function as tools to expedite the design of mechanical or electronic devices (or both).

CAI   Computer-Aided Instruction. Use of the computer as an aid in the educational process. The application usually involves a dialog between the student and a computer program that presents information to the student and asks questions to reinforce learning. The application informs the student as mistakes are made.

CAM   Computer-Aided Manufacturing. The use of computers in the manufacturing process.

capacity planning   The process by which MIS planners determine the amount of hardware resources required to meet anticipated demands.

cartridge   For tape: one of the ways recording tape is packaged. For disks: cartridges are plastic shells that hold removable hard disks.

CASE   Computer-Aided Software Engineering. Tools that enhance and enforce the use of system development methodology through automation of specific techniques or generation of code (or both).

cash flow analysis   A process that produces a report reflecting the money entering and leaving the firm during a specific time period such as a year.

cash flow model   A mathematical model that is used to conduct cash flow analysis.

cassette   A package for magnetic tape similar in appearance to a standard audio cassette, but filled with tape optimized for digital recording.

cathode ray tube   An electronic vacuum tube, such as a TV picture tube, in which a beam of electrons can be moved to draw lines or to form characters or symbols on its luminescent screen.

cell   In a spreadsheet, a cell is the intersection of a row and a column.

central file server (program)   Program that controls the access to files by individual workstations in a LAN.

central processing unit (CPU)   A highly complex, extensive set of electronic circuitry that executes stored program instructions in a computer. The CPU consists of a control unit, the arithmetic and logic unit, and registers.

centralization The creation of a single functional unit with responsibility for providing information processing services to all operating units in the organization.

chain A series of records linked together so that a record that is referred by another record contains an embedded pointer that points to yet a third record.

channel A device that connects the processing unit and main storage with the I/O control units.

channel capacity The number of bits per second that can be transmitted over a communications channel.

character A unit of alphanumeric data.

checkpoint and restart A procedure whereby program processing reverts back to the previous checkpoint for resumption of processing that has been interrupted by some type of failure. The storage and register contents that were saved are reloaded, and transactions from that point are reprocessed.

chief executive officer (CEO) The person who is the top-ranked manager of a firm. The CEO is usually the chairperson of the board of directors or the president.

chief financial officer (CFO) The top-ranked financial executive in a firm, usually the vice-president of finance.

chief information officer (CIO) The person in charge of the firm's information resources, who participates with the other executives in mapping out the corporate strategy.

chip An integrated circuit on a piece of semiconductive material.

CIM Computer-Integrated Manufacturing. An architecture that integrates several technologies through information system technology. Computer integration links production control functions with handling systems, purchasing, distribution, and finance, as well as with such technology manufacturing systems as in-line process control, contamination control, electronics assembly and testing, yield measurement and management, and CAD/CAM.

ciphertext A 64-bit encrypted output from the National Bureau of Standards data encryption model.

CISC An acronym for complex instruction set computer, a design for the CPU of a computer based on the use of many predefined, elementary circuits and logical operations that the processor performs when it executes an instruction.

classify The identification of a data item with a certain category. For instance, a sales transaction can be classified as credit or cash.

client server A computer architecture in which computers called clients use messages to request services of the many computers called servers in the network.

clone   A hardware device or a software package that emulates a product with an established reputation and market presence.

closed system   A system that does not interface with its environment.

CMOS   Memory that requires little power; the acronym stands for complementary metal oxide semiconductor.

coaxial cable   A shielded wire that is used as a medium to transmit data between computers and between computers and peripheral devices.

COBOL   COmmon Business-Oriented Language. A mainframe computer language that is available on microcomputers.

CODASYL   Conference on Data Systems Languages.

Code   (1) A set of rules that maps the elements of one set—the coded set—onto the elements of another set—the code element set. (2) Loosely, one or more computer programs, or part of a computer program.

coding   The process of developing the programming language source code for a computer program, usually done by carefully following written program specifications.

cold site   A backup computing facility that contains everything necessary to resume processing in the event of a disaster, except the computer.

common carrier   A company such as AT&T, MCI, or GTE, which furnishes communications facilities for a fee.

communications   Any process that permits data to pass from a sender to one or more receivers.

communications channel   The medium over which a message is carried.

communications protocol   A set of rules governing the flow of data through a communications system.

communications security   Seeks to eliminate passive listening to information and messages sent over the line and tapping transmission of a communications line to modify the transmission.

compatibility   The ability of one computer or hardware component to work with another computer or hardware component.

competitive advantage   A term used to describe a company's leveraging of computer and information technologies to gain an advantage over its competitors.

competitive intelligence   Knowledge about what competing firms are doing or planning to do.

compile   To translate a computer program expressed in a high-level language into a program expressed in an intermediate language, assembly language, or machine language.

compiler　Utility software used to convert source code written in a programming language into an executable load module that can be executed by the computer.

computer architecture　The overall way in which the primary components of the computer are arranged and the way they function together.

computer crime　A crime committed through the use of software or data residing on a computer.

computer fraud　Illegal use of computer facilities to misappropriate corporate resources. This includes unauthorized changes to both software and hardware systems.

computer literacy　Knowledge of how the computer works, its limitations, and its capabilities.

computer network　An integration of computer systems, workstations, and communications links.

computer virus　Any computer program that is not readily discernible to the user and which has the capacity to infect other computer systems by recreating itself unpredictably or causing some other specific action under predetermined circumstances.

confidentiality　Limits on the use and dissemination of information collected from individuals.

consultant　An information systems expert who provides advice or help (or both).

contention　A line control procedure in which each workstation contends with other workstations for service by sending requests for service to the host processor.

contingency plan　A plan that details what to do in the event of a disaster or severe disruption of normal operations.

control　The process of comparing actual results to planned results.

control total　A sum resulting from the addition of a specified field from each record in a group of records; used in checking machine, program, and data reliability.

conventions　The standard, accepted abbreviations and symbols and their meanings for users of information systems technology.

conversion　The process of changing from one method of data processing to another.

copy-protected　Copy-protected tapes or disks have been recorded in such a way that prevents the data on them from being copied, although they can be read and used.

corporate model　A mathematical representation or simulation of a company's accounting practices and financial policy guidelines. It is also used to project financial results under a given set of assumptions and to evaluate the financial impact of alternative plans. Long-range forecasts are also calculated using such models.

cost benefit analysis   The activity of comparing anticipated costs of a computer application with its anticipated benefits.

coupled processor   A computer architecture in which the computer has more than one complete CPU which allows it to perform multiprocessing, that is, execute more than one instruction at the same time.

CPM   Critical Path Method. A network modeling technique that enables project managers to see the relationships among the various activities involved in a project and to select the approach that optimizes the use of resources while meeting project deadlines.

crewing analysis   Determining the number of people and the required skills needed to complete a set of manual tasks.

criteria for evaluation   Requirements used to compare one vendor's proposal with another's.

critical success factors   The few essential activities that must go right if the business unit is to be successful.

CRT   See cathode ray tube.

cryptography   A communications crime-prevention technology that uses methods of data encryption and decryption to scramble messages sent over communications links.

CSMA/CD   Carrier Sense Multiple Access/Collision Detection. A communications protocol that operates like a party line.

cursor   A symbol on the computer monitor that indicates where text will be typed. The cursor is often a line or a box and may be steady or blinking.

cyberphobia   The irrational fear of and aversion to computers.

cyberspace   Another word for virtual reality, a computer environment which employs multisensory input-output devices to enable the user to experience computer simulated virtual worlds three dimensionally through sight, sound, and touch.

DASD   Direct Access Storage Device. A storage device capable of using direct access to obtain records.

data   Raw facts that have been collected, organized, and stored.

data administrator   A person with the responsibility to ensure that the corporation's data is available to all users in a shared and controlled manner.

data base   A well-defined collection of computer-accessible data that provides a common source of data for people in many different organizations.

data base administrator   A highly skilled and trained information systems professional who works with end users and programmers in order to design, build, maintain, and manage the data base.

data base design   (1) The tasks associated with the development of the design of data bases, such as data modeling, collecting end-user views, normalization, conversion of logical data model to physical data model, and so on. (2) The deliverable resulting from the logical or physical data base design stages, such as the entity-relationship models, normalized data base, physical data base tables, and so on.

data base directory   A tool that identifies where data may be found.

data base machine   A computer dedicated entirely to the use of a data base management system.

data base management system   Software that provides an interface between computer applications and a set of coordinated and integrated physical files contained in the data base.

data center consolidation   Reduction of the number of data center locations to produce cost savings, improve management control, and standardize applications and technology, or as a result of merging with another company.

data channel   A small special-purpose computer that manages the communications between input/output devices and the CPU of the computer.

data communications system   The collection of hardware and software that enables the transmission of data over a communications channel.

data cube   A multidimensional representation of key business variables such as time, geography, and data type.

data definition   The process of creating a schema or model that identifies and describes the data entities, their attributes, and their relationships.

data definition language   A computer language used to describe the way that data is actually stored and to relate the physical storage of the data to the logical structure of the data.

data dictionary   A tool that helps list and describe the data entities and attributes.

data element   One or more characters of data that represent a single fact such as part number, amount owed, or street address.

data encryption   A coding technique that can be used to safeguard the security of transmitted information. With data encryption, each character of data sent is replaced with other coded characters.

data entry   The process of entering data into a computer system for processing or storage.

data flow diagram   A picture that shows the source, processing, and destination of key pieces of data in a system.

data independence   A lack of dependence between the physical structure of data storage and the structure of application programs.

data integrity   The accuracy, completeness, and timeliness of the data.

data management   Includes a number of related activities directed at managing data as a resource.

data manipulation language   A computer language that supports the access, retrieval, and use of data in a data base.

data model   A model that communicates information about entities (things), attributes (characteristics), and their relationships.

data overload   A condition where management is overwhelmed by the sheer volume of data reaching them.

data redundancy   The situation in which identical data exists in two or more locations.

data resource plan   Identifies the data most important to the enterprise and outlines projects necessary to develop shared data resources of this data.

data resource strategy   Establishes a basic position and provides a consistent set of principles to guide decision making in regard to data-related issues.

data store   A place for storing data between two or more processes.

data switch   A device similar to a telephone exchange, which can establish a data communications link between any of the devices connected to it.

data vendor   An organization that acquires data of interest to a number of individuals or organizations adds value to the data and then sells it.

debug   To eliminate bugs in a program or system.

decentralization   Creation of a functional unit within each operating unit with responsibility for servicing the information processing needs within that unit.

decision support system   A comprehensive computer-based system used to help people reach decisions about semistructured problems.

decoder   Any device that converts a received signal into a form useful to the receiver.

deliverable   A tangible output of the system development process; for example, a data flow diagram of the existing system or a data model of the required system.

Delphi method An approach to gathering opinions that involves successive responses from a panel. For each round, the panel leader provides feedback from the previous round, which serves to bring the divergent views together. This iterative process continues until the divergent viewpoints converge.

demand trigger A triggering mechanism that causes a report to be printed or displayed.

departmental computing The use of minicomputers to support the computing needs of large departments or business units within a company.

design review A process to ensure that the final system is built with a high degree of quality and will meet user needs. It involves providing an opportunity for members of the team that will implement the system and selected system users to review the system design in detail.

desktop publishing Computer-aided publishing that uses data processing equipment small enough to fit on a desktop or table and is suitable for an end user.

digitize To translate an image, voice, or other analog signal into a digital form computers can recognize.

DIP switches A collection of small switches on a *Dual In-line Package* used to select options on circuit boards without having to modify the hardware.

direct access The facility to obtain data from a storage device or to enter data into a storage device in such a way that the process depends only on the location of those data and not on a reference to data previously accessed.

direct access storage device A storage device capable of using direct access to obtain records.

direct conversion A method of converting to a new information system, such that the old system is discontinued one workday and the new system is started the next day.

directory A table of identifiers and references to the corresponding items of data.

disaster plan A formal plan that outlines in detail the actions to be taken in the event that the organization's computing resources are damaged, destroyed, or otherwise rendered inoperable.

disk drive A magnetic storage device that records data on flat rotating disks.

diskette A thin, flexible disk for secondary random access data storage.

distributed data base A data base that resides on two or more computers at the same time. The data base is either replicated at multiple locations or is partitioned into subsets with various subsets in different locations.

distributed data processing   A computer system in which one or more of the following functions are distributed: (1) information processing, (2) network processing, or (3) data base storage.

documentation   Narrative supplied with a system to help the user operate the system and to help system support people maintain and support the system.

domain   The field of knowledge covered by an expert or an expert system.

dot pitch   A measure of quality of a monitor, it is the distance between one phosphor dot on the screen and the next nearest dot of the same color.

downloading   The process of taking information from a mainframe computer and transmitting it to a personal computer.

downsizing   Moving computer applications off the mainframe and onto smaller, less expensive platforms such as workstations or midrange computers.

downtime   The time during which a computer system is not available.

DRAM   An acronym for dynamic random access memory, a computer memory chip that uses one transistor and a tiny storage device to store one bit of data. The chip must be energized hundreds of times per second to continue to hold the bit of data.

drill down   A term usually associated with the use of executive information systems whereby the user is able to retrieve successively more detailed information.

duplex   Pertaining to communications in which data can be sent and received at the same time.

EBCDIC   Extended Binary Coded Decimal Interchange Code. The standard code developed and used by IBM for its mainframe computers. It is a binary code made up of 8 bits.

echo check   A check to determine the correctness of the transmission of data in which the received data are returned to the source for comparison with the originally transmitted data.

econometric model   A large-scale mathematical model that is used to forecast the activity of the nation's economy.

economic feasibility   The degree to which the benefits of the system outweigh all costs associated with the development and operation of the system.

EDI   See electronic data interchange.

edit   To examine data for error conditions.

editor   A program through which text can be entered into the computer memory, displayed on the screen, and manipulated as the user chooses. An editor is an aid for writing a program. It is also the central component of a word processor.

electronic bulletin board   A use of electronic mail whereby the same message is sent to all users of the system. It is a way of broadcasting information on a wide scale.

electronic data interchange (EDI)   The design of computer-based systems to facilitate the flow of data from one firm to another, such as electronic transmission of purchase orders and invoices.

electronic funds transfer   A computer-based system allowing electronic transfer of money from one account to another.

electronic mail   Any communications service that permits the transmission and storage of messages by electronic means.

electronic publishing system   A computer based to system that aids in the drafting, proofing, revising, copying, printing, distributing, and filing of text material.

emergency alternate procedures   A plan that specifies the actions to be taken in the event of a disaster that renders all or part of the information system inoperable.

encoder   Any device that converts the original message into a form that can be transmitted.

encryption   The act of converting programs or data into a secret code or cipher.

end user   The individual providing input to the computer or using computer output.

end-user data base management system   A data base management system capable of being used by nonprogrammers to obtain data necessary to create ad hoc reports.

end-user computing   Any situation in which workers use or control computer-based equipment.

engineering/scientific graphics   Includes CAD (computer-aided design), CAM (computer-aided manufacturing), and CADD (computer-aided design and drafting).

enterprise data model   A clear and simple definition of the business entities (things) of importance to the firm, the attributes that describe them, and the relationships or business rules that tie one entity to another.

entity   A basic item about which it is necessary to keep data.

entropy   The tendency of a system to move toward disorder, complete lack of useful function, and death.

EPROM   Erasable Programmable Read Only Memory chips. This type of chip makes it easy for individuals to produce custom programs.

ergonomics   The science of designing computer hardware and software to make them more easy and comfortable to use.

error handling   Procedures for detecting errors in input data and for ensuring that those errors are corrected before the data are processed.

ethics   A set of ground rules governing how people behave.

example-based system   A form of expert system in which the human knowledge is represented as a number of recorded examples.

exception report   A report generated only if an activity or system gets out of control and requires attention.

exception trigger   A condition which when met causes an exception report to be printed or displayed.

executive information system   A decision support system customized to meet the needs of management. Such a system can extract, filter, and compress a wide range of internal and external data to present information to the manager without creating a data overload situation.

expansion board   A printed circuit board that accommodates extra components for the purpose of expanding the capabilities of a computer.

expert system   A computer system that uses knowledge and inference procedures to solve problems that are difficult enough to require significant human expertise for their solution.

exponential smoothing   A weighted, moving average method of forecasting in which past observations are geometrically discounted according to their age. The heaviest weight is assigned to the most recent data. The smoothing is called exponential because data points are weighted according to an exponential function of their age.

extract   To select and remove from a set of items those that meet some criteria; for example, to obtain specific records from a file.

facilities management vendor   A firm that specializes in managing, staffing, and operating computer installations for its customers.

facsimile   A communications device that can be used to send copies of handwritten, typewritten, graphic, and photographic material to distant locations.

factory local area network   A local area network within a factory that connects workstations, minicomputers, programmable controllers, robots, and many other devices.

feasibility study   A study to determine the economic, technical, and operational feasibility of a proposed information system.

feedback   Information about the outputs or process of the system is fed back as an input to the system, perhaps leading to changes in the transformation process or future outputs (or both).

fiber optics   The use of laser technology to produce an intense narrow beam of light that can be modulated or changed in frequency to convey a prodigious amount of data.

field engineer   The person who maintains the information systems hardware. Usually the field engineer is an employee of the firm that manufactured the equipment.

file   A collection of similar records.

file management program   Program designed to store, update, and retrieve data. These programs are limited to managing data on a single file at a time.

file server   The computer that controls the storage and retrieval of files from a common disk when a number of computers are connected together to form a system.

file transfer program   Software that will move data from a mainframe computer to a personal computer and reformat the data into a form suitable for use on the personal computer.

final form text   Text stored in electronic form so that it can be printed or displayed but not modified.

fine-tuning   Removing bottlenecks and reallocating work among system resources in order to obtain maximum output from the given resources.

firmware   Hard-wired logic for performing certain computer functions; built into a particular computer or hardware device often in the form of ROM (read-only memory) or PROM (programmable read-only memory).

fishbone diagram   A technique used to show the relationship between the problem and the factors that influence the problem.

fixed disk   A disk that is permanently mounted in its disk drive, or the disk and drive combination.

flash-cut   An approach to system conversion that involves terminating the use of the old system one day and completely and totally converting to the new system the next day.

flat file   A file containing only fixed-length records of equal length.

flat screen display   A small, lightweight, low-power monitor used in portable computers. Their displays use gas plasma or liquid crystal technology, and can be color or monochrome.

floppy disk   A data storage medium (typically 3½-inch, 5¼-inch, or 8-inch in diameter) made of polyester film covered with a magnetic coating.

footprint   The amount of space taken on a desk by the worker's personal computer or workstation.

force-field analysis   A technique that helps clarify people's feelings toward a new system and helps prepare them for the changes to come.

forecast   The extrapolation of the past into the future. It is usually an objective computation involving data, as opposed to a prediction, which is a subjective estimate incorporating a manager's anticipation of changes and new influencing factors.

format   (1) Defines how data is stored on the storage medium. It also defines how characters are placed on a piece of paper and how the characters are displayed on the screen. (2) An instruction used to tell the microcomputer to prepare a diskette or disk for use. Magnetic marks are made on the media to identify tracks and sectors where the data is to be stored.

FORTRAN   FORmula TRANslator. A mainframe computer language now available on microcomputers. Used in engineering and scientific applications.

forward chaining   A form of inference used in an expert system that starts with the *if* part of an if/then statement; when this part matches the same component in a problem, the system searches for the appropriate *then* clauses.

fourth-generation language   A language that allows you to develop a program by describing to the computer what you want to do rather than programming it in a how-to, step-by-step fashion.

freeware   Public domain software that is available to the public at no cost.

front-end processor   A special-purpose computer for handling the data communications tasks in support of a mainframe computer.

full-duplex   A communications channel over which both communications partners can send and receive at the same time.

function key   A key that sends special instructions to the microcomputer. In some programs the user may define the instructions sent by the function keys.

functional area   An organizational unit or business corresponding to its major duty or activity, such as engineering or finance.

functional decomposition   A process for documenting system components and their relationships to reduce system complexity. The process involves continually subdividing the system into components until elemental single-purpose system modules have been defined.

functional prototype   A prototype system able to simulate data validation and updates of system data bases.

functional requirements   Requirements that define the specific functions to be performed by the system—inputs and transactions to be processed, outputs and reports to be produced.

fuzzy data   Data that is incomplete or ambiguous.

fuzzy logic   A method of reasoning that resembles human reasoning since it allows for approximate values and inferences and incomplete and ambiguous data.

Gantt chart   A graph in which activities are plotted as bars on a time scale.

gateway   Software that permits computers of different design architectures to communicate with one another.

generations   A means of referencing items with respect to time and ancestry such that an item without antecedents is designated the first generation, and subsequent derivations are designated as the nth generation, where n-1 is the number of derivations from the original.

gigabyte   One billion bytes of storage.

goal   Broad statements of the end results that the organization intends to achieve to fulfill its mission.

goal-seeking   A process where the system components work together to achieve a common goal.

grandfather-father-son   A means of providing backup for files; results in the current version having two generations of backup.

graphics   The making of charts and pictures.

groupthink   A situation that can arise in group decision making where all members of the group seem to voice the same idea.

GUI   An acronym for graphical user interface, an interface for computer users that employs the use of a mouse to point and click on icons to send commands to the computer.

hacker   An individual who uses personal knowledge and means to gain unauthorized access to protected data or software.

half-duplex   A communications channel over which one partner can send and the other receive at any given time.

handshaking   The process of establishing a communications link between the source and destination.

hard copy   A readable printed copy of computer output.

hard disk drive   Data storage device that may be fixed or removable for storing data or programs.

hard error   An error in disk data that persists when the disk is reread.

hardware   The physical devices that make up a computer system.

hashing   A method of direct access in which the address is calculated from the key data element.

header   (1) The top part of a report, including the column headings. (2) In a file, the first record that contains descriptive information concerning the file.

hex   Short for hexadecimal. A hex file is a file stored using numbers based on sixteen.

holistic view   A view that deals with the whole of the problem rather than simply understanding its individual parts. This approach would consider the technological, business, and organizational issues associated with making a change to a system.

host computer   The primary or controlling computer in a multiple computer operations or data communications network.

hot site   A backup computing facility containing everything needed to provide the organization with substitute information processing in the event of an emergency.

hierarchical data base schema   A data base schema in which all data relationships follow a parent-child relationship; each parent record may have one or more dependent records or children, but each child can have but one parent.

hierarchical network   A distributed system design where a superior/subordinate relationship exists among distributed computer installations.

high-level language   A computer language such as COBOL, FORTRAN, or PL/1 whose key words resemble English.

human factors   The positive and negative behavioral implications of introducing information systems technology into the workplace.

human resources information systems   The functional information system that meets the needs of the organization's managers for personnel information.

icon   Pictographs that are used in place of words or phrases on screen displays.

if-then-else   A programming construct in which either one of two possible outcomes of action is taken, depending on whether a certain logical condition is true or false.

impact printer   A printer in which printing is the result of mechanical impact.

implementation   The phase of system development that involves construction, testing, user training, and installation.

index   A mechanism by which a program orders the records in a file.

index-sequential access method   A direct access data storage scheme that uses an index to locate and access data stored on a direct access storage device.

inference engine   The part of an expert system that contains the inference and control strategies. It examines existing facts and rules and adds new facts and rules when possible. It also decides in which order inferences are made.

information   Data that has been collected and processed into a meaningful form.

information center   A facility in which computing resources and consultants are made available to end users to enable them to build their own computer applications.

information engineering   A systems development methodology that emerged in the 1980s that employs engineering-like techniques, provides a proven process and common terms for system development, focuses on identifying and meeting business needs, and emphasizes understanding the data requirements of the system.

information float   The time to communicate information.

information society   Refers to our current society where most of us work with information rather than produce goods.

information system   A special class of system whose components are people, procedures, and equipment that work interdependently under some means of control to process data and provide information to users.

information systems hierarchy   Eight layers of systems, each of a higher order than the preceding one, such that the lower-order system must be in place before the next higher order can be successfully implemented.

information systems technology   A wide range of technologies that are based on applications of the integrated circuit.

infrastructure   The hardware, systems software, and communications networks of an organization.

in-house development   The process by which an organization produces its own application program instead of purchasing a software package or having someone else build it on contract.

ink jet printer   A printer that uses jets of ink to produce characters.

input   Data to be processed by the computer.

input controls   Controls ensuring that all input data are authorized, accurate, and properly converted to machine-readable form.

input/output devices   Devices used to communicate with the computer to get data and instructions in and out.

inquiry   A request for data or information.

instruction   A programming language statement that specifies a particular computer operation be performed.

instruction set   Instructions built into the computer. The instruction set is contained in the microprocessor.

integrated circuit   A device containing miniature electronic circuits that have been deposited photochemically on a chip of silicon material.

integrated data   Data of different kinds and from different sources that can be related because they have common keys.

integrated file transfer program   Software that runs on both a mainframe and a personal computer. Allows the personal computer user to extract data from a data base on the mainframe and convert it into a usable form on the personal computer.

integrated package   A software package that typically includes the functions of electronic spreadsheet, word processing, data base management, and communications.

integration test   A planned and orderly progression of testing in which software elements, hardware elements, or both are combined and tested until the entire system has been tested.

interactive query   A request for data handled in an interactive data processing mode where the individual request is processed immediately upon receipt.

interactive update   A form of data processing in which the transaction data are processed immediately without the delay of accumulating them into a batch.

interface   A point of communication between two or more processes, persons, or other physical entities.

internal control   Encompasses the design of organizational structure, procedures, and policies concerned with decision processes and the means by which management directs an organization to meet its legal and ethical responsibilities to its owners, employees, suppliers, customers, and society in general. It is the plan of the organization to safeguard its assets, check the accuracy of internal accounting data, promote operational efficiency, and encourage adherence to prescribed management policies.

international data transfer   The movement of data across national boundaries through data communication networks.

interrupt   A signal to the CPU that some event has happened—for example, a channel interrupt signals the start or completion of an input/output operation.

I/O   Input/output.

ISO   The International Standards Organization.

JAD   Joint Application Development. An interactive group session approach to define system scope, requirements, and/or system design.

JCL   Job Control Language. A problem-oriented language designed to identify the computer job and describe its requirements to the operating system.

job   A collection of related application programs such as the payroll job or the end-of-month accounting job.

job queue   A line of jobs awaiting their turn for execution within the computer.

just-in-time (JIT)   An approach to production control that emphasizes very small lot sizes and the use of a physical signal, called *kaban,* to signal the movement of materials from one production step to another.

key   The data element or set of data elements associated with a record that uniquely identify that record from any other record in the file or data base.

keyword   In a programming language, a special word that tells the computer which operations to perform (e.g., READ, WRITE).

kilobyte   1,024 bytes (2 to the 10th power).

knowledge   The assignment of meaning to information by a human being.

knowledge acquisition   The identification of the thought processes applied by an expert in solving a problem. Once acquired, the thought processes are incorporated in the knowledge base of an expert system.

knowledge base   The collection of human learning stored in an expert system, often represented by a series of if/then rules concerning pertinent objects and events.

knowledge engineer   One who interviews an expert to capture and codify the expert's knowledge.

knowledge engineering   The branch of computer science that pertains to the design and development of expert systems.

knowledge workers   Professionals, managers, executives, and clerical people whose job largely involves the processing or analysis of data.

LAN   See local area network.

LAN operating system   An operating system that manages the operation of the LAN including controlling access to files, interactions among the various devices on the LAN, and provides security.

LAN topology   The relative physical and logical arrangement of stations in the network.

language   A unified, related set of commands or instructions that the computer can accept.

laser disks   A media for storing large quantities of text, audio, and video information based on laser technology.

laser printer   Printer that uses laser technology to produce high-quality output at high speed.

LCD   Liquid Crystal Display microcomputer output device.

leading edge   The forefront of computer technology.

leased line   A permanent or semipermanent communications channel leased through a common carrier.

leasing   A contract arrangement that binds the user of a system to rent it over a relatively long period of time. Leasing typically costs less than a rental arrangement.

left justify   Line up characters such that the first nonblank character in each line is on the left margin.

legitimizer   A person who tends to protect the norms and values of the current system. The legitimizer may even have been involved in creating the current system.

leveled data flow diagram   A hierarchically partitioned data flow diagram. Each level describes in more detail the data flows shown in the level above it. Increased partitioning at lower levels keeps the diagram at a manageable size.

lexicon   The dictionary of words that can be interpreted by a particular natural language.

library   A repository for demountable recorded media, such as magnetic disk packs, tapes, and cassettes.

linear bus   A LAN in which the devices are arranged along a single length of cable that can be extended at one of the ends.

link testing   Testing the back-to-back running of a series of modules or programs so that the output from one is used as input to the next.

linkage editor   Utility software that can combine the object modules of several programs to create a load module—a ready-to-execute version of the program.

load   To transfer programs or data from secondary to primary storage.

local area network (LAN)   A private network that supports the sharing of data and resources over intraoffice, intrabuilding, or intrafacility communications facilities.

local data   Data that are used only in one computer of a distributed data processing environment.

logical model   A system model that emphasizes what is to be done rather than who or what does it.

logical view   Representation of data in a data base in a format that is meaningful to the application programmer and end user.

LOGO   A microcomputer educational language that uses graphics for programming.

logoff   The procedure by which a user ends a terminal session.

logon   The procedure by which a user begins a terminal session, usually involving entry of a logon ID and password.

low-level language   A computer language near machine language.

lower CASE tool   A software tool that automates some of the activities associated with the physical design, construction, and testing and implementation of an information system.

machine cycle   The time it takes to retrieve, interpret, and execute a program instruction.

machine language   The programming language in which a computer executes all programs, without regard to the language of the original code.

macro   Custom routines that substitute a few keystrokes for many. They may be created by the user and saved on disk as routines that are recalled with a few keystrokes when needed in spreadsheets or similar programs.

macro instruction   A set of program instructions that may be invoked simply by a one-line reference to the set.

macroeconomic forecasting model   A model or simulation that can be used to forecast gross national product (GNP), personal income, employment, price levels, and other indications of economic performance. The Wharton model is an example.

magnetic disk   A flat, circular plate with a magnetizable surface layer on one or both sides on which data can be stored.

magnetic tape A tape with a magnetizable surface layer on which data can be stored by magnetic recording.

mainframe A large computing system.

maintainability The ease with which maintenance of a functional unit can be performed in accordance with defined standards.

maintenance The ongoing process by which information systems and software are updated and enhanced to keep up with changing requirements.

management reporting system A system capable of integrating data from many sources to generate reports in a predetermined, routinely reported format that provide information useful to management.

man-machine boundary The line of demarcation between manual operations and computerized functions.

manufacturing automation protocol (MAP) A standard for factory LAN's initially promoted by General Motors.

mass storage Storage device having a very large storage capacity, measured in gigabytes.

master file A file that is used as the primary source of data in a given job and that is relatively permanent, even though its contents may change.

matrix printer A printer in which each character is represented by a pattern of dots.

megabyte One million bytes (actually 2 to the 20th power, or 1,048,576).

menu A list of possible actions displayed on a screen and from which the user may select.

message The data that passes during communications from a sender to one or more receivers.

microcode Predefined, elementary circuits and logical operations that the computer processor performs when it executes an instruction.

microcomputer Includes a microprocessor, electronic circuitry for handling input/output signals from peripheral devices, and memory chips mounted on a single circuit board called a motherboard.

microprocessor A microchip with all the elements necessary for it to function as the central processing unit of a computer.

microprogramming A technique of placing programs in hardware devices.

microsecond One-millionth of a second.

microwave transmission The transmission of signals at the high end of the radio spectrum—3 gigahertz to 30 gigahertz.

midrange computer Formerly called the minicomputer, this class of computer covers a broad range of capability between the mainframe and the microcomputer.

milestone A significant point on the way to completion of a project.

MIPS Millions of instructions per second.

mission statement A brief, simple statement of the basic objectives of the organization or business unit.

model A representation of a real world situation that allows management to simulate what will happen under different conditions.

modem A hardware component of a communications system that converts data from a binary form to an analog form and vice versa.

modular software Programs built from individual modules that can be put together to form a system. The user has the option of purchasing only those modules desired.

module An elemental unit of a system with a single, well-defined purpose.

module testing Testing to determine if the system correctly implements module requirements.

Monochrome monitor A monitor that displays characters that are green, amber, or black and white.

Moore's Law Gordon Moore, chairman of the board of Intel, hypothesized that the transistor densities on a single chip will double every 18 months.

motherboard A printed circuit board or card containing the microprocessor, computer memory, and selected controller circuits to direct the signals that are received from external connectors.

moving average A method of averaging out the roughness of random variation in a data series. A moving average uses only the most recent historical data in the series. The method gets its name from the way it slides along the data series, averaging each data point with its immediate predecessors.

MRP Manufacturing Resource Planning System. A software system that integrates all of the resources involved in the material flow through a manufacturing firm. The MRP-II system includes portions of the output subsystems of the manufacturing information system and interfaces with other subsystems.

MS/DOS Microsoft Disk Operating System. Personal computer disk operating system used on the IBM PC and look-alike family of microcomputers.

multimedia A computer capable of displaying data and information in multiple forms—alphanumeric, text, image, sound, video, and graphics data.

multiple regression A statistical technique predicting the value of a dependent variable, which is assumed dependent upon one or more explanatory or independent variables.

multiplexer A piece of telecommunications equipment that combines several independent channels of data onto a single high-speed data circuit.

multiprocessing system A computer system with more than one central processing unit.

multiprogramming The ability of the CPU to execute two or more tasks from different applications concurrently.

multitasking The ability of the computer to perform more than one task at a time.

multivendor environment An environment common to many organizations where many different vendors provide solutions to various needs.

nanosecond One-billionth of a second.

natural language The ordinary spoken language that one uses in everyday conversation.

navigational data base management systems Any data base management system in which all data relationships must be predefined by the data base designer.

net present value Represents the net amount by which project returns exceed project investments, after allowing for the cost of capital and the passage of time.

network In data communications, a configuration in which two or more terminal or processor installations are connected.

network control The means by which nodes attached to a local area network gain access to and share the transmission media.

network data base schema A data base schema that supports the representation of a many-to-many relationship.

neural network An approach to the processing of data that emulates the biological structure of the brain by use of a network of hundreds of parallel processing interconnected units that shoot messages at each other rapidly.

node Either a user or a server on a local area network.

noise Unwanted signals that interfere with communications.

nonprocedural language A programming language that does not require the programmer to outline step-by-step what the computer must do. A nonprocedural language allows the user to specify what must be done without specifying how.

nonrecurring costs The initial costs of a computer system that are not expected to arise in years subsequent to the initial installation.

nonvolatile storage Primary or secondary storage that does not lose the data stored in it when the electrical power is interrupted.

normalized relation A data relationship is normalized if the data elements for each record in the table depend on the key, the whole key, and nothing else but the key of that record.

object Self contained items that combine data and processes that cooperate by passing strictly defined messages to one another to form working programs.

object oriented database A database capable of managing any data that can be digitized including: alphanumeric, text, image, sound, video, and graphics data.

object oriented programming A form of programming that enables programmers to build programs based on objects that combine both data and processes.

object program A machine-level program that results from the compilation of a source program.

objective A specific description of where the organization wants to go and how soon it will get there.

office automation The planned integration of many new technologies with improved office processes to increase the productivity and effectiveness of all office workers.

off-line Data or devices that are not under the direct control of the computer. Usually a person must place an off-line reel of tape on a tape drive before the computer can access data stored on it.

off the shelf software Commercially developed application programs that can be purchased by users to meet their needs.

open system A system that can exchange information, energy, or material with its environment.

open system architecture One in which software can be easily run on hardware from different vendors, and hardware from different vendors can be linked together in a multivendor telecommunications network.

operating system System software that manages the many tasks that are going on concurrently within the computer. It also provides an interface between the computer hardware, software, and system users.

operational decisions Decisions that deal with the routine, day-to-day operations of the organization.

operational feasibility   The ability to run a computer system on a regular and reliable basis that will consistently meet the system user time constraints.

operations group   Organization that runs and supports the computer hardware and software systems and telecommunications networks that support the business.

opinion leaders   People whom others watch to see their acceptance of new ideas and changes.

optical laser disk   A read-only secondary medium that uses laser technology.

optical scanner   A scanner that uses light for examining patterns.

order processing system   A system that takes customer orders, initiates shipping requests, keeps track of back orders, and produces various sales analysis reports.

OSI Reference Model   The Open Systems Interconnection Reference Model is a seven-layer model for defining the capabilities and services needed for network communications.

output   Results of processing the input data.

output controls   Controls that help assure the accuracy of computer results and proper distribution of output.

outsourcing   The hiring of an outside vendor to perform nonessential activities of the firm.

overlapped processing   A form of processing in which the CPU and data channel operate in a parallel fashion with both input/output and computations going on at the same time.

packaged software   Software that is generalized and packaged to be used, with very little or no modification, in a variety of environments.

palette   The overall selection of colors or shades available in a graphics display system.

parallel conversion   A system conversion process that involves running both the old and new system side-by-side until all parties are convinced that the new system is performing satisfactorily.

parallel port   A connection through which data are transmitted 8 bits at a time (in parallel). Generally used with printers.

parallel transmission   A form of data transmission where several bits are transmitted at the same time over parallel communication paths.

parameter   A factor that has a variable value.

parity bit   An additional bit added to a string of bits for error checking and detection.

partitioning   Decomposing a data flow diagram into smaller, more detailed diagrams.

Pascal   A simple and structured programming language for general use.

password   A word or phrase known only to an individual. When entered, it identifies the user to the system and permits the user to gain access to those files and services for which the user is authorized.

patch   To modify a program in a rough or expedient way.

payback period   The length of time until project tangible benefits equal total project costs.

PBX   Private Branch Exchange. A switchboard in an organization's location where all its telephone lines terminate.

pen based system   A computer that accepts input data and instructions handwritten by the user.

performance monitor   System management software that captures and summarizes data about the utilization of key computer resources to predict system performance, perform capacity planning, establish production schedules, and plan for hardware/software acquisitions.

performance requirements   Specified performance characteristics that the system must possess, such as the number of concurrent users the system must support, the size of files and tables, the number of transactions, tasks, and the amount of data to be processed, with certain time periods for both normal and peak workload conditions.

performance tuning   Modifying the application design, data base design, or possibly the hardware to improve the performance characteristics of a system.

peripheral equipment   A functional unit that provides services external to a processing unit.

PERT   Program Evaluation and Review Technique. A scheduling method using networks consisting of activities that consume resources and take time and events that mark the beginning and end of the activities.

phased conversion   A system conversion process in which the new system is gradually phased in and the old one phased out.

physical data base design   The process of refining the ''ideal'' logical data base design for improved performance in the real world.

picosecond   One-trillionth of a second.

pilot conversion   A method of converting to a new system in which the new system is introduced in some selected departments. If it functions satisfactorily, then it is extended to the whole organization.

pixel   A dot on the microcomputer screen used to create numbers, graphics, and other characters.

PL/1   A multipurpose, procedure-oriented language.

plug-compatible   A hardware unit produced by one manufacturer that can directly replace units produced by another manufacturer.

point-of-sale data entry   Immediate entry of sales transactions to the computer through a cash register that is connected to the computer.

polling   A line control procedure in which each workstation is polled in rotation to determine whether a message is ready to be sent.

port   An input/output connection for interfacing peripherals and computers.

portability   The ability to move software from one computer to another and still have it run.

post-implementation review   A critical examination of an information system after it has been put into production. The examination may focus on the system itself, the process used to develop the system, or both.

precision   The number of digits allowed to express a number.

presentation graphics   High-resolution, multicolor graphic art images suitable for producing slides and overheads to be shared with an audience.

primary key   The field(s) or attribute(s) in a record that uniquely identifies that record from all other records.

primary storage   The storage within the central processing unit of the computer that stores programs while they are running, the data programs access, and the operating system.

print spooler   A program that sets aside part of the RAM or disk to receive text to be sent to the printer.

private line   A dedicated communications channel between any two points in a computer network.

procedure-oriented language   A high-level language whose general purpose instruction set can be used to model scientific and business-oriented problems.

process   A systematic sequence of operations to produce a specified result.

process control   Automatic control of a process in which a computer is used for the regulation of usually continuous operations or processes.

professional programmer class DBMS   A data base management system used by professional programmers (not end users) to support large transaction processing systems and large data bases. The system must perform in a very reliable and efficient manner.

program   Computer instructions structured and ordered in a manner that, when executed, causes a computer to perform a particular function. Also the act of producing computer software.

program and data independence   A situation in which there is a separation of the physical workings of the data base management system and the physical storage of the data from the logical functions that the programmer needs to perform.

program specs   The detail specifications that describe the input, processing, and output of a computer program. These are used to develop the programming source code of the program.

programmable decision   A decision that is made within the guidelines of established policy.

programmer   One who writes programs.

programmer/analyst   A position title of one who performs both the programming and systems analysis functions.

programming language   A set of commands or instructions with which people can communicate instructions to the computer.

project constraints   Criteria that must be met for any proposed solution to be acceptable, such as the scope of the business to be addressed, key objectives to be met, cost, and schedule.

project manager   The person responsible for organizing the efforts of a project team.

PROM   Programmable Read Only Memory. A read-only memory into which data or programs can be written by an external programming device.

proprietary   That which is owned exclusively by an individual or corporation, such as a patent or copyright.

protocol   A set of codes to be transmitted and received in the proper sequence to guarantee that the desired terminals and computers are linked together and can send intelligible messages back and forth.

prototype   A trial or experimental version of an application.

prototype conversion   A system conversion process that involves converting to the new system in only a limited test environment. If the system performs well in this test environment, then its use is expanded.

prototyping   An iterative process for problem solving that involves defining the users' needs, developing a prototype solution, using the prototype, and modifying it based on user feedback.

pseudocode   Nonexecutable program code used as an aid to develop and document structured programs.

qualified vendor   Vendors that have proven to be highly competent, well regarded, and financially stable.

query   A request for information.

query language   A high-level computer language used to retrieve specific information from a data base.

RAID   An acronym for redundant arrays of independent disk, an option to the traditional magnetic disk packs in which the disks are configured to work in parallel, reading or writing data simultaneously to provide highly reliable data backup and recovery features.

RAM   Random Access Memory. Memory used for data and program storage by the user. The user can read and write in RAM.

random   Something that occurs in no particular order.

random access   Synonym for direct access.

real-time system   A system in which the transactions are processed immediately and the records affected by that transaction are also updated immediately.

reasonable assurance   Managers must use their judgment to ensure that the cost of a control does not exceed the benefit to be obtained by its implementation or the possible risk involved.

reasonableness check   A program control that monitors the value of input data to ensure that it is within proper limits.

reciprocal agreement   An agreement among two or more firms to share similar computer equipment in the event of a disaster at one firm.

record   A group of related data elements.

recurring costs   The costs expected to continually arise throughout the life of the information system installation.

reengineering   See business reengineering.

register   A storage device having a specified storage capacity, such as a bit, byte, or computer word, and usually intended for a special purpose.

relational data base schema   A data base schema in which relationships are represented in normalized tables.

relevance   The usefulness of data for decision-making purposes.

reliability A quality held by that which is dependable and can be trusted.

remote job entry Submission of a job to the computer via an input unit that has access to a computer through a communications link.

request for proposal (RFP) A document that specifies the requirements for equipment and software to be purchased.

resolution The sharpness of the image produced by a monitor.

response time The time from submission of a user inquiry to an interactive system until receipt of the desired output.

reusable code Modules of programming code that can be called and used as needed.

reverse video Characters on a video display terminal presented as black on a light background; used for highlighting.

revisable form text Text stored in electronic form so that its content and format can be modified by each person to whom it is distributed or by whom it is obtained from a library.

RGB A monitor capable of displaying characters in red, green, and blue.

right justify To line up characters such that the last nonblank character in each line is on the right margin.

ring network A communications network in which devices in the network are linked together in a circular pattern.

RISC An acronym for reduced instruction set architecture, a computer design that employs minimal built-in microcode so that the CPU can execute instructions faster and is easier and cheaper to build than the traditional CISC CPU.

risk analysis In project management, determining the many possible things that can go wrong with the project and developing action plans to minimize these risks.

risk management In computer security, determining the possible threats to the security of a system and the undesirable events that can result and developing action plans or backups that are cost-effective.

robot A reprogrammable, multifunctional manipulator designed to move material, parts, tools, or specialized devices through variable programmed motions for the performance of a variety of tasks.

ROM Read-Only Memory. Memory that the user can only read from, not write to.

rounding The process of replacing a number with the closest possible number, after dropping some of its decimal digits.

router Devices that support internetwork communications at the network level of the OSI model. Routers determine the preferred paths to a final destination depending on the needs of the network and its users.

RS-232C port A personal computer input/output port through which data are transmitted and received serially, one bit at a time. It can be used in modems, printers, or other serial devices.

rule The most commonly used method of representing knowledge to an expert system. A rule consists of a condition and an action.

rule-based system A form of expert system in which the human knowledge is captured in a series of if/then rules concerning pertinent objects and events.

runaway project One that greatly exceeds budget—perhaps by millions of dollars—and is months, sometimes years, behind schedule.

scan To read sequentially, item by item.

schema The logical view of a data base that describes the data elements and their relationships.

scratch To erase data on a disk or tape or delete their identification so that they can be used for another purpose.

screen-only prototype A prototype that can simulate only the interactive portion of a system.

scroll Text is moved up and down to display text that cannot be shown on the monitor at one time.

secondary key A key that is not a primary key, but for which an index is maintained; it can identify more than one record.

secondary storage devices Devices such as magnetic tape, magnetic disks, and diskettes used to store data and program instructions external to the main memory of the computer.

sector A division of a track on a disk.

security monitor System management software that monitors and controls access to the computer system.

self-documenting A characteristic of a computer language whose statements are easy enough to understand that English descriptions of the program steps are not necessary.

semiconductor A solid crystalline substance, such as silicon, that has a conductivity greater than good insulators but less than good conductors such as metals.

semistructured problem A problem in which one or two of the phases associated with decision making (intelligence, design, choice) are unstructured.

sequential search   A search of a file that starts at the beginning and examines each record in turn to find a particular record.

serial transmission   A form of communications where data is sent one bit at a time.

server   A device on a LAN that shares its resources with the user of the LAN.

service bureau   A company that provides computer services on an as-needed basis and charges for the service based on an hourly rate.

shared data   The use of the same data by multiple people in different organization units or business functions.

shareware   Relatively inexpensive software that is produced by individuals or very small firms and distributed on the honor system through electronic bulletin boards.

shielding   Putting a protective coating around twisted pair to make the medium less vulnerable to electrical noise.

simple regression analysis   A statistical technique for predicting the value of one variable in terms of the given value of another variable.

simulate   To build a model or imitation of something that occurs in the real world, such as a business process, the economy, or an automobile.

smart card   A card or badge with an embedded microprocessor.

SNA   System Network Architecture. A data communications system used to connect various IBM devices.

soft constraint   Project constraints that have some degree of flexibility; the schedule can slip somewhat if the cost can be substantially reduced.

soft error   An error in reading data from the disk that does not occur if those same data are read again.

software   Programs or instructions that tell the computer what to do.

software application   A computer program that does meaningful work for an end user.

software engineering   The application of scientific principles to the development of information systems.

software maintenance   All changes made to a program or system after it has been installed.

software piracy   Providing or acquiring software that has not been legitimately purchased from the software company.

software portability　The capability to run computer software on multiple manufacturers' hardware.

sort　To segregate items into groups according to the specified criteria.

sort key　A key used as a basis for determining the sequence of items in a set.

source code　A program written in a higher-level language than machine language. It is called source code because it is the starting point, or source, in the compilation process to produce object code.

source data automation　Capturing data at their source and sending the data directly to the computer.

source document　The original document from which data are entered.

source language　A language from which statements must be translated before they can be understood.

spooling　The process by which output or input is loaded temporarily to secondary storage. It is then output or input as appropriate devices become available.

spreadsheet　A method for organizing, calculating, and presenting financial, statistical, and other data for managerial decision making.

SQL　A data base query and update language adopted by the American National Standards Institute and the International Standards Organization as an official standard for relational data base systems.

SRAM　An acronym for static random access memory, memory chips that employ transistors that do not require constant energizing to hold data.

stakeholders　People who have a stake in the success of the project, including people who are or will be affected by the system and people needed to ensure its successful development, operation, or ongoing support. Stakeholders importantly include those people who are influential enough to kill the project. Stakeholders also include people who can exert enough influence on others to create an environment where successful implementation will be extremely difficult.

standard　An acknowledged guideline or norm against which performance is measured.

star network　A communications network with a central host computer or communications controller through which other devices in the network must route their messages.

steering committee　A committee that oversees the application of information systems technology within the firm.

store-and-forward system　A message system where messages can be stored until the intended recipients request their messages.

stored program concept   The idea of reading program instructions into the memory of the computer for execution. This allows programs to be written and stored on a secondary storage device and then read into main memory when executing the program is desired.

stakeholders   People who have a stake in the success of a project, they are people who are or will be affected by the system and people who are needed to ensure its successful development, operation, or ongoing support.

strategic alliance   A partnership between suppliers and customers to enable them to work more closely than ever before considered.

strategic business initiative   A project or activity that supports or leads to meeting a strategic business objective.

strategic business unit   A self-contained organizational subunit with major responsibility for an important business activity.

strategic competitive advantage   The ability to achieve and maintain above-average profitability over the long run.

strategic decision   A decision made by senior management that has a long-lasting and powerful effect on the organization.

strategy   Statements of how the organization is going to reach its vision or achieve its objectives.

structured analysis   A systems analysis methodology used in systems development.

structured English   A tool for describing program logic in English-like terminology. It uses the vocabulary of English combined with the logical constructs of a programming language to make the logic understandable to humans.

structured group interview   A process for defining business needs that involves users and managers from multiple organizations. The session leader is a trained facilitator and possesses excellent meeting leadership and communications skills.

structured problem   A problem that is routine and repetitive in nature; it has a specified procedure to follow to reach the correct decision.

structured walkthrough   A system design review process to ensure that the final system is built with a high degree of quality and will meet the users' needs.

subroutine   A sequence of program instructions that are called and executed as needed. A subroutine may be used in one or more computer programs and at one or more points in a computer program.

subschema   The logical view of the part of a data base that is of interest to a particular business application.

subsystem   A secondary or subordinate system, usually capable of operating independently of a controlling system.

symbolic language   A programming language that expresses addresses and operation codes of instructions in symbols convenient to humans rather than machine language.

synchronous transmission   A data transmission method in which a long stream of bytes is transmitted without interruption. This method is economical for complex, high-speed data communications equipment that handles large amounts of data.

synergy   A situation where the components of a system work together in a way so that the integrated action of the separate components has a greater effect than the sum of the individual components operating independently.

syntax   The manner in which data or instructions must be organized and presented to the computer to be understood and acted upon.

system   A collection of people, machines, and methods organized to meet a specific objective.

system boundary   Systems have a boundary that separates them from their environment.

system design   The second phase of information systems development wherein a set of technical specifications is developed that forms a detailed plan for implementing the system.

system development methodology   Written standardized procedures that depict the activities in the system development process and define the individual and group responsibilities.

system documentation   The documentation of the system that provides an overview of the features and functionality of the system.

system implementation   The process of converting the system design into a complete and tested system that is fully operational and that can be used by system users to meet their needs.

system integrators   Firms that work with their customers to provide complete system solutions. They provide hardware, software, and project accountability.

system life cycle   The stages through which an information system evolves.

system maintenance   The process of correcting errors discovered in the system or changing the system to meet new requirements or to operate in a new environment.

system map   A pictorial representation of how the components of a system fit together to accomplish their objective.

system owner   The manager of the organization that will use the system to achieve the business benefits for which it was created.

system programmer   A programmer who plans, generates, maintains, extends, and controls the use of an operating system with the aim of improving the overall productivity of an installation.

system scope   The boundary of the system to be studied.

system software   A set of programs that control the use of hardware and software resources. These programs allocate system resources to application programs, based on their needs and priorities.

system sponsor   The person who verifies that the development of the system represents a sound use of company resources and sells senior management on the merits of the system.

system test   The process of testing an integrated hardware and software system to verify that the system meets its specified requirements.

system users   The people who will use the system to achieve business benefits.

systemic   Of or affecting the entire system.

systems analysis   Study of an activity to determine what must be accomplished and how to accomplish it.

systems analyst   A person whose responsibility is to analyze, design, and develop information systems.

systems approach   An approach to problem solving, comprising systems philosophy, systems analysis, and systems management.

systems management   An approach to address the business, technological, and organizational issues associated with making a change to a system.

systems philosophy   An overall model for thinking about things as systems.

table   An array of data, each item of which may be unambiguously identified by means of one or more arguments.

tactical decisions   Decisions that involve allocation and control of the firm's resources to meet the objectives that support the strategic goals of the business.

task   The basic unit of work in a work breakdown structure. Completion of a task leads to creation of a system deliverable.

technical feasibility   The ability of the system to meet the stated user requirements through the use of the chosen technology.

technology architecture   The technology architecture provides a framework for using information systems technology in the firm and ensuring that systems and data can be shared across organizational units. It includes an infrastructure plan, data management plan, applications, system development methodology, and CASE.

technology development   An organization responsible for finding matches between unmet business needs and new information systems technologies.

technology transfer   The application of existing technology to a current problem or situation.

telecommunication access method   The method by which traffic on a network is controlled.

telecommunications   Communication between remote devices.

telecommuting   "Commuting" via a communications link between home and office.

terminal   Any device capable of sending and receiving data over a communications channel.

terminal emulation   One computer terminal simulating the communications protocol used by another form of computer terminal.

test data   Data used to test new systems for errors. This test data is comprehensive enough to cover all possible types of valid and invalid inputs so that program performance can be checked under all conditions.

text conferencing   A computer-based system to prepare, transmit, store, and retrieve informal messages.

text editor   A program that makes possible creating, changing, storage, and retrieval of text in the file.

text file   A computer file that contains words and characters. Such files are commonly created in word processing.

third-generation language   A programming language such as FORTRAN, COBOL, PL/1, Pascal, or BASIC that requires you to instruct the computer in a procedural or step-by-step fashion.

third party   A company other than the user or the computer hardware system manufacturer.

throughput   A measure of the amount of work performed by a computer system over a given period of time.

time series   An ordered succession of numbers representing the values of a particular variable over a given period of time (e.g., monthly sales figures for 1992 through 1996).

timeliness   The speed with which data are provided to the user for decision making.

timesharing   A situation where more than one terminal may be connected to and operated at one time on the same computer.

toggle   The action of pressing a single key on a keyboard to switch between two or more modes of operation, such as insert and replace.

token passing   A network control scheme that permits a node to transmit only when it possesses a token, or special bit sequence circulating on the network.

top-down design   An approach to system and program design that begins at the highest level of generalization; design strategies are then developed at successive levels of decreasing generalization until the detailed specifications are achieved.

topology   The manner in which devices in a LAN are physically arranged relative to one another.

trace   A record of the sequence of execution of a computer program.

track   An invisible magnetic circle written on a diskette or disk for use as a guide for where data can be written or read.

transaction   A business event such as a sale to a customer.

transaction file   A file containing records of data activity (transactions) used to update a data base or master file.

transaction processing system   A system that captures the detail data necessary to update existing records whenever stored data about the fundamental business operations of the organization must be changed.

translation   The generation of object code from source code.

transmission media   The media over which communications signals are carried.

transparent   A reference to a procedure or activity that occurs automatically and does not have to be considered in the use or design of a program or information system.

Trojan Horse   A public domain program with inviting functional capabilities that, when downloaded from a bulletin board system and executed, does irreparable damage to the disk files of an unknowing victim.

trunk   A communications line between a PBX and the public telephone network's end office.

turnaround document   A document that can be sent out to users and can also be read by the computer when it is returned.

turnaround time   The time from submission of a user request to a batch processing system to receipt of the desired output.

turnkey system vendor   A vendor that provides both the computer hardware and software to meet a user's computing needs. In theory, all the user has to do is turn the key.

tuple   A group of related fields (a row) in a relational data base.

twisted pair   Twisted pairs of copper wire or common telephone wire used as a transmission medium.

uninterruptible power source (UPS)   A buffer between an external power source and a computer system that supplies clean and continuous power.

unit testing   A phase of computer program testing in which the programs that make up an information system are tested individually.

UNIX   An operating system, originally developed by AT&T Bell Labs, able to run on many different models of computers from various manufacturers.

unstructured problem   A problem for which there is no defined solution process; thus, a solution must be developed using judgment, intuition, experience, rules of thumb, and any general guidelines that may apply.

UPC   Universal Product Code. A bar-coded symbol printed on the package of a consumer product. The UPC is read by an optical reader or by an optical scanner and is used to identify and price the product.

update   To modify a file or data base with add, delete, or change transactions.

upload   To transfer a file from your computer or terminal to another computer.

upper CASE tool   A software tool that is intended to support the phases of the system life cycle leading up to the physical design and programming activities.

UPS   See uninterruptible power source.

user acceptance testing   That stage of system testing where the system is presented for the scrutiny of the users and user managers whose departments will ultimately use the system.

user-friendly   A computer system that is simple for even nonsystems people to learn to use.

user interface   The connection between the users of the system and the system.

user liaison   A person who serves as the technical interface between the users of a system and the developers or maintainers (or both) of the system.

user manual   Documentation that conveys to the end user of a system the instructions for using the system to obtain the desired results.

user views   Physical outputs from a system such as reports, screens on a video display device, checks, error listings, and so on.

utilities   Programs that support the operation of the operating system by adding capabilities.

validation   The checking of data for correctness, or compliance with applicable standards, rules, and conventions.

value-added chain   A series of interdependent activities that bring a product or a service to the customer.

VAN   Value-Added Network. A specialized common carrier that adds value over and above the standard services of a common carrier.

variable   A parameter that may take on various values.

VDT   Video Display Terminal. A terminal on which printed and graphic information is displayed on a TV-like monitor and data is entered on a typewriter-like keyboard.

vendor   A supplier.

vendor support   Services provided by the seller of a hardware or software system. These typically include training, repair and maintenance, installation, testing, consulting, and backup arrangements.

verifiability   The ability to confirm the accuracy of data. Accuracy can be confirmed by comparing with other data of known accuracy or by tracing back to the original source.

very local area network   A local area network that serves people in a very compact geographic area, such as a single office.

video disk   A secondary storage medium that permits storage and direct access to video or pictorial information.

video teleconferencing   A form of electronic conferencing in which either full-motion or freeze-frame pictures are transmitted between two or more meeting sites.

videotext   The merging of text and graphics in an interactive communications-based information network.

virtual machine   The processing capabilities of one computer system created through software and hardware in a different computer system.

virtual memory   A special memory management technique that, in effect, makes more memory available than the amount of main memory that actually exists on the system.

virtual reality   Also known as artificial reality and cyberspace, a computer environment which employs multisensory input-output devices to enable the user to experience computer simulated virtual worlds three dimensionally through sight, sound, and touch.

virus   A program that is written with malicious intent and loaded to the computer system of an unsuspecting victim. Ultimately the program destroys or introduces errors in programs and data bases.

vision   The view that top management has for the future of the company. It is generally expressed in terms of what the company wants to become and wants to achieve.

vision system   A system that can simulate the function of the human eye.

visual language   A programming language that uses the object orientation of object orientation programming languages to enable software developers to create working applications by connecting various objects and drawing, pointing, and clicking on objects instead of writing code.

VLIW   Very Long Instruction Word. A microprocessor design based on development of a software compiler that interprets program instructions only once, off-line, thus providing the chip ample time to execute instructions.

VLSI   Very Large Scale Integration. The production of computer chips with hundreds of thousands or even millions of components on each chip.

voice data entry device   A device that permits voice input to a computer system (also called a voice recognition device).

voice mail   A voice message store-and-forward system that allows the user to send, receive, redirect, and distribute voice messages.

voice recognition system   A computer that can analyze and classify speech patterns and convert them into digital codes.

voice response unit   A device that enables output from a computer system in the form of user-recorded words, phrases, music, alarms, or anything that might be recorded on tape.

volatile storage   A storage device whose contents are lost when the power is interrupted.

Von Neumann architecture computer   A computer with a single powerful processor that performs its work sequentially, a single task at a time, and whose program instructions are read into the memory of the computer.

walkthrough   A step-by-step review of the documentation or other work produced by a systems analyst or programmer.

WAN   Wide Area Network. A network that connects computers, terminals, and devices over distances greater than a single cluster of buildings, involving distances of many miles rather than feet.

Wariner-Orr diagram   A systems analysis and design technique for documenting a system using a hierarchical arrangement of brackets.

window   A rectangular section on a display screen that is dedicated to a specific activity or application.

Windows   Personal computer software from Microsoft that provides multiple function capability and allows users to transfer data and text between applications.

wireless   Any one of a number of electronic transmission options that does not require wires or cables to connect sender and receiver.

word processing system   A computer system that enables its users to enter, display, store, and process text. These systems typically include powerful editing and text-formatting capabilities.

word size   Microcomputers commonly process 16 or 32 bits at a time. A 16-bit microcomputer may process two 8-bit bytes (characters) at one time. The overall speed of a microcomputer is a function of the number of bits per word or word size.

work breakdown structure   The decomposition of a project into stages, steps and tasks.

workstation   A powerful personal computer system that supports the tasks of an individual such as an engineer, architect, or stockbroker.

worm   A program that erases data or programs (or both) from a computer system's memory, usually with malicious intent.

WORM   Write Once, Read Many. An optical laser disk that can be read many times after data are written to it, but the data cannot be changed or erased.

write protection notch   On a $5^{1}/_{4}$-inch diskette, the write protection notch is covered to prevent writing to the diskette. On an 8-inch diskette, the notch is uncovered.

X.25   A standard communications protocol for networks that use packet switching.

X.75   A standard communications protocol for networks that involve international interconnections.

zoom   A software command that expands a window to fill the entire screen.

INDEX